Health Economics and Policy

Selected Writings by Victor Fuchs

VICTOR R. FUCHS

Stanford

Health Economics and Policy

Selected Writings by Victor Fuchs

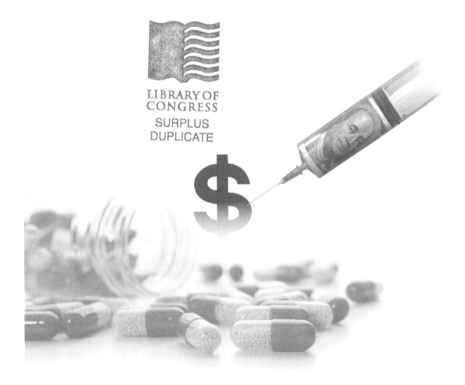

LIBRARY OF
CONGRESS
SURPLUS
DUPLICATE

W World Scientific

NEW JERSEY · LONDON · SINGAPORE · BEIJING · SHANGHAI · HONG KONG · TAIPEI · CHENNAI · TOKYO

Published by

World Scientific Publishing Co. Pte. Ltd.

5 Toh Tuck Link, Singapore 596224

USA office: 27 Warren Street, Suite 401-402, Hackensack, NJ 07601

UK office: 57 Shelton Street, Covent Garden, London WC2H 9HE

Library of Congress Cataloging-in-Publication Data

Names: Fuchs, Victor R., author.

Title: Health economics and policy : selected writings by Victor Fuchs / by Victor R. Fuchs.

Description: New Jersey : World Scientific, [2018] |
    Includes bibliographical references and index.

Identifiers: LCCN 2017051203 | ISBN 9789813232860 (hardcover)

Subjects: | MESH: Economics, Medical | Health Policy | United States | Collected Works

Classification: LCC RA410.A1 | NLM W 7 | DDC 338.4/73621--dc23

LC record available at https://lccn.loc.gov/2017051203

British Library Cataloguing-in-Publication Data

A catalogue record for this book is available from the British Library.

For any available supplementary material, please visit
http://www.worldscientific.com/worldscibooks/10.1142/10786#t=suppl

Desk Editor: Alisha Nguyen

Typeset by Stallion Press
Email: enquiries@stallionpress.com

Printed in Singapore

Praise from Experts

"Victor Fuchs' insights, captured in articles written over his long career, have brilliantly informed and enlivened the debate over the failures and successes of our health care system, while constantly pointing the way to better, and more equitable care and outcomes for all Americans."

Leonard Schaeffer
Professor USC Health Policy
Founder and First CEO, Wellpoint

"This collection of Victor Fuchs seminal writings highlights not only his knowledge and incisive thinking about important health policy issues over five decades, but his unparalled wisdom. A gem of a collection."

Stephen M. Shortell
Professor of Health Policy and Management Emeritus
Dean Emeritus, School of Public Health, UC-Berkeley

"Fuchs' intellectual vision was trans-disciplinary before the term was first uttered. He taught us that nearly all health care problems benefit from the perspective of economics, but none can be resolved from that perspective alone."

Kenneth Warner
Professor Emeritus and Dean Emeritus
University of Michigan School of Public Health

"Victor Fuchs is known as the Dean of Health Economics — and these seminal papers show exactly why."

Atul Gawande, M. D.
Professor of Surgery, Harvard Medical School

To my children, their spouses, their children,
their spouses, and their children.

Other Health-Related Books by Victor Fuchs

Author

The Service Economy (1968)
Who Shall Live? Health, Economics and Social Choice (1974), *2nd Expanded Edition* (2011)
How We Live (1983)
The Health Economy (1986)
The Future of Health Policy (1993)

Editor

Production and Productivity in the Service Industries (1969)
Economic Aspects of Health (1982)
Individual and Social Responsibility: Childcare, Education, Medical Care, and Long-Term Care in the United States (1996)

Contents

Foreword

Sir Angus Deaton, Ph.D.

Dwight D. Eisenhower Professor of Economics and International Affairs, Emeritus, Princeton University
2015 Nobel Prize Laureate in Economics

Victor Fuchs has been writing about health economics for more than half a century and the papers in this admirable collection span the whole period. Included are several of my favorite pieces, long known and a pleasure to read again, as well as several gems that I had missed. All the papers represent what Fuchs calls the economic perspective on health, of which Fuchs has long been the master. They go beyond any narrow conception of health, addressing questions in philosophy, medicine, demography, population health, individual health, public policy, insurance, and the industrial organization of healthcare. Health is the leading example of a topic that cannot be adequately addressed from any single discipline; economists must talk to (and listen to) physicians, and vice versa. Policy requires both; as Fuchs notes, "The economic perspective alone is rarely sufficient for good policymaking, but it is usually necessary. To neglect it, to assume that resources are unlimited or that human behavior is insensitive to changes in incentives and constraints, is often an invitation to disaster." These words should be engraved on the walls of Congress.

Much of health economics focuses on the market for healthcare, on the organization of the healthcare industry, and on how healthcare should best be delivered. The market for healthcare is not like the market for onions, or even for automobiles, and its peculiarities call for major revisions of the standard economic model. Lives are at risk, insurance — or the lack of it — is important, and there is pervasive uncertainty about the course of disease and the effects that treatment will bring, about which patients know much less than their physicians. No developed country has a healthcare system that operates without substantial government involvement in financing or delivery, though the US has much less than most. The US also spends much more on healthcare than do other similar countries, so that the design of the system is a perennial and always controversial topic in politics.

Fuchs is an indispensable guide to this territory which he explores in Parts 3, 4, and 5, not only in the US, but also in comparisons with other countries, frequently addressing the question of why healthcare in the US is organized so differently. Fuchs does not endorse the simplistic but often heard position that we can look to other countries as laboratories to find out what works, and then adopt the best arrangements here. Americans are different from the British or the French. They are less egalitarian, more heterogeneous and much less trusting of government, so they are less likely to accept government restrictions on healthcare. The ideal healthcare system in America may be very different from the ideal healthcare system in Germany or Switzerland.

Even so, Fuchs notes that our different tastes — if that is what they are — have become exorbitantly expensive; we spend 18 percent of our (larger) GDP compared with around 12 percent in other (less well-off) countries, or something in the order of a trillion dollars a year. We get nothing, or perhaps even less than nothing, for the trillion dollars, at least in terms of health, though the expenditures do yield handsome livings for many of those in the industry. Life expectancy in the US is lower than in similarly rich countries; for white non-Hispanics, it was lower in 2014 than in 2013, and for the whole population, was lower in 2015 than in 2014. As I write, millions of Americans are addicted to legally prescribed opioids, and more people are dying of overdoses from these drugs than died at the height of the AIDS epidemic.

In recent years, and in several of the papers here, Fuchs has come to argue that it is time to give government a much larger role in the provision and financing of healthcare. And of course, he does not stop there, but develops a detailed plan that would make things much better, a plan that is laid out in Part 5.

Fuchs knows better than anyone that change is difficult; indeed, one of the reasons that reform is so hard is not a lack of plans, but the number of players who can veto change, and who have effectively done so in the past. To get those players on board, there is the risk that reform will be excessively tailored to the interests of the providers of healthcare, not its users, making the new system more

expensive than the old. Fuchs has long noted that many people who are insured
by their employers believe that their healthcare comes for free, not out of their
wages. So that even though American middle-class workers are paying dearly for
an exorbitantly expensive healthcare system, which is a major causal factor in the
stagnation of their earnings, they do not see the connection, and are resistant to
the change that would benefit them so much. All of this, and more, is developed
in the essays here, which are an essential background to anyone who wants to
understand the mess we are in and what might be done about it.

When I first came to think about health, it was because I was interested in
wellbeing, and because health is so central to leading a good life or indeed any
sort of life at all. Many of the papers in this book are not about healthcare at all,
but about health, and about the non-medical causes of health. Once again, this is
fertile territory for the economic perspective, and especially for Fuchs, who talks
to both economists and physicians. Economists have too often taken the view that
health comes from healthcare, though they recognize the importance of smoking,
while the medical and epidemiological literature, perhaps paradoxically, gives
little weight to healthcare, attributing health to socio-economic status, whose very
definition has been something of a mystery to economists. Fuchs fully accepts
the importance of social determinants of health, but insists that we ask the right
questions, and think about what is going on: is it income, is it poverty, is it
education, or something else? Socioeconomic status is not a concept that is useful
for policy.

In a beautiful paper on education written 35 years ago, Chapter 2.2 in this
collection, Fuchs and Farrell note that while those with a college degree are less
likely to smoke, the college-bound were also less likely to smoke; it is not the
college education that leads to better health behaviors, but the kind of person you
are. Forward-thinking people are more likely to go to college and are less likely
to smoke. Whether education improves health, and how, remains a central topic
in health, and much recent research — for example looking at episodes where
school-leaving ages were increased so that a group of people were forced to accept
more education — has confirmed Fuchs' skepticism. But the topic is far from
settled, as is the related question of the respective roles of income and education.
As in other areas of health, this is an area where Fuchs has been asking the right
questions and setting the agenda long before the rest of us caught up.

This collection represents an extraordinary intellectual achievement, and
should be a handbook for anyone thinking about health and health policy. Fuchs is
a fine writer with a knack for the right words or the right metaphor that reaches out
to the wide audience that is essential on these issues. For example, philosophers
have argued for many years about the value of life at different ages. Is it better to

save the life of a child, who has many years ahead that could be lost, the life of an active person in midlife, whose interests and pursuits benefit many today, or an elder, who is a repository of accumulated wisdom. Fuchs captures the essence in the unforgettable suggestion that we judge a life's value by the number of people who come to the funeral, small for the young — who barely exist except to their parents — and the very old — who have outlived all of their friends, but high for those cut down in midlife, whose activities are entwined with the lives of others.

In the last paper here, he muses on writing and provides a better summary of his work than I can, "Good writing is partly a matter of character: be honest with your readers and respect their needs and abilities." Every one of these essays documents Fuchs' success in meeting this standard.

Foreword

Victor J. Dzau, M.D.

President, National Academy of Medicine
Chancellor Emeritus, Duke University

Victor Fuchs, who has been called the "dean" of American health economists, is one of the world's most influential figures in health, medicine, and policy. His prolific contributions to health economics have spanned five decades — indeed, he helped to pioneer the field. Today, there are dedicated journals, conferences, academic programs, and thousands of professionals and practitioners of health economics across the globe. However, this was not always the case. The study of health and health care as an important field in economics emerged only in the last 20 years, as countries witnessed major expansion and reorganization of health systems and rapid increases in spending. Victor Fuchs was truly ahead of his time: he began studying the field over 50 years ago. His work helped revolutionize the way we think about health and charted a course for the emerging field.

Fuchs stands alongside Kenneth Arrow and Michael Grossman as a visionary scholar who brought health economics into the mainstream. However, he stands apart in his ability to make the field accessible and applicable, greatly magnifying the impact of his work. Therefore, it is fitting that this collection of his writings bridges the fields of health economics *and* the corresponding policy implications.

Fuchs' immense influence beyond the field of health economics is due in part to his appreciation of the need to understand health care institutions and the culture of medicine in order to make useful contributions to public policy. He has never hesitated to discuss his ideas with physicians — and he is uniquely skilled at making economic concepts readily accessible to non-economists, a fact I can attest to firsthand. I first met Fuchs in the 1990s, when I was Chair of Medicine at Stanford University. At the time, my focus was on clinical practice and research, but Fuchs opened my eyes to the centrality of economics in health. The lessons he imparted were tremendously influential to me in my later role as head of Duke University Health System. And his wisdom remains with me now as president of the National Academy of Medicine (NAM), an independent, nonpartisan, nongovernmental organization that provides evidence-based advice on science, health, and medicine to the nation and the world. I am proud to note that Fuchs numbers among the NAM's distinguished membership.

The NAM, formerly known as the Institute of Medicine (IOM), and the broader National Academies organization in which it operates, has since 1970 informed policy on everything from improving the quality of health care and reducing medical errors to ensuring that our military and veterans get the care they need — from financing graduate medical education to identifying priorities for health reform. It is hard to imagine discussing any of these issues without including the perspective of health economists.

The need for an economic lens on health policy — and for Fuchs' insight in particular — has never been greater than it is now, seven years after the passage of the Affordable Care Act, as the new presidential administration weighs next steps for health reform.

Although the writings that follow were published over the course of 50 years, they could not be more relevant to the current debate.

It is clear that health reform is sorely needed. Health care spending is at an unsustainable high: in 2015, spending grew by 5.8 percent, totaling $3.2 trillion or close to 18 percent of United States GDP. It has been estimated by the IOM that approximately 30 percent of that spending can be attributed wasteful or excess costs, including costs associated with unnecessary services, inefficiently delivered services, excess administrative costs, prices that are too high, missed prevention opportunities, and fraud. Furthermore, although the US spends more on health care than any other developed nation, our health outcomes lag far behind those of other developed nations across a number of indicators.

It is unfortunate that much of the recent political debate has cast health reform as a contentious partisan issue centered around insurance coverage. What we need instead is an open and substantive conversation about fundamental priorities for improving health outcomes and reducing cost. Lasting health reform will only succeed if it rests upon the essential economic principles that govern effective health systems.

Fuchs' work has influenced the thinking of policy makers, health professionals, and laypersons alike. His insights provide a framework for understanding the behavior of health care markets, particularly the forces driving costs, as well as the broader factors shaping the direction of health reform. His important and extensive writings could be considered the single most authoritative guidebook on health economics.

Indeed, the first edition of his now-classic 1974 book, *Who Shall Live?* is one of the earliest and most widely accepted introductory texts to health economics. In this volume, Fuchs applied fundamental economic concepts to health — notably, the need to allocate scarce resources and the necessity of choice at the individual and societal level. He also identified the three major challenges facing the US health system: "high and rapidly rising costs, inequality and difficulties of access, and large disparities in health levels within the United States and between the United States and other countries." The insight and perspicuity of Fuchs' analysis is striking: in the 43 years since the publication of this book, we have seen wide-ranging and transformative changes in health and medicine, yet these same challenges remain.

The pieces in this remarkable collection capture the essential economic principles laid out by Fuchs early in his career, while also addressing major changes in health, medicine, and policy over the past 50 years. His contributions to the field are deep and wide-ranging. Below are only a few highlights that I find especially compelling.

One of Fuchs' major contributions to the field, and perhaps the best testament to his thoughtfulness and foresight, is his focus on the economics of health, not just health care. Early on, he realized that nonmedical factors play an important role in shaping health; he showed that additional spending on medical services has a limited effect on health outcomes. To many individuals well versed in health and health policy, these concepts may not seem revolutionary. But when Fuchs first wrote about them, they were revolutionary indeed. It is easy to forget that the social determinants of health have only recently gained widespread recognition. It is telling that in the 1960s health economics was often called "medical economics." Fuchs' writings, reprinted in Part 2 of this volume, underscore the importance of socioeconomic factors to health, particularly poverty and education, and show how much further we have to go in terms of understanding and intervention. His call for researchers to study the interactions between genetic factors and social determinants is likely to gain even more validation in light of the growing momentum behind precision medicine.

With health care spending accounting for one-fifth of the US economy, it is no surprise that rising costs are the topic of considerable discussion and debate. Fuchs has written extensively about factors that influence health expenditures, such as trends in physician supply, health insurance, the structure of health systems, and the rise of medical innovations — topics addressed in Parts 3–6 of this book.

Fuchs' writings about the impact of the supply of physicians on health care utilization and expenditure in Part 3 are particularly notable and have obvious implications for health policy and the practice of medicine. His widely-cited 1978 paper, "The Supply of Surgeons and the Demand for Operations," suggests that surgeons drive increased utilization and expenditures. Although some may disagree with his conclusions about physician-induced demand, there is no doubt that we must pay more attention to the size and distribution of the US health workforce, with an emphasis on primary care as the cornerstone of a strong health system.

Also of particular interest is Fuchs' work at the intersection of economics and social attitudes and values. His research, captured in Part 5, helps to explain why the US stands apart from other high-income democracies in its lack of support for government-led health insurance. He notes that a major obstacle is the lack of support for both redistribution of wealth and government economic intervention — both necessary precursors to national health insurance. In Part 7, he puts forward policy recommendations for comprehensive reform of the US health system based on not only his deep understanding of fundamental economic principles but also his knowledge of US medical institutions and American values. Although his proposed reforms may seem unattainable, there is reason to remain optimistic — the enactment of sweeping health reform would not be the first time America has witnessed once-unthinkable social progress.

Towering figures such as Victor Fuchs, whose steadfast commitment to improving the US health system through fundamental reforms and the courage to speak truth to power, provide a beacon as we navigate the critical next stage of health reform.

Part 1

Health Economics

Introduction

Fifty years ago health economics was a minor sub-specialty in economics with little attention from academics or the general public. Now it is a large field with thousands of professionals around the world. It is a rare week in the United States that does not feature at least one major health economics story: sky-high drug prices, contested merger proposals, rising insurance premiums, a surge in suicides, or other health issues. It is the responsibility of health economists to provide understanding of the complex interactions of patients, physicians, drug companies, hospitals, insurance companies, and other stakeholders in the more than three trillion dollar a year U.S. health economy. Some health economists teach in economics departments, others in schools of business, public health, medicine, or public policy. Some are researchers in industry, government, or non-profit institutes.

Part 1 is intended for highly disparate audiences: economists (articles 1.1 and 1.4), readers who have no familiarity with economics (1.2 and 1.3), and the op-ed for all readers with an interest in health policy. The first paper is my 1989 response to the editors of *The New Palgrave Dictionary of Economics* (almost 2,000 entries) to provide the entry on health economics. I chose to emphasize empirical studies of health and medical care that draw on concepts from finance and insurance, industrial organization, labor economics, and public finance. The fourth paper, an invited lecture to the International Health Economics Association World Congress in 1999, documents the wide variety of journals other than economics — health services research, health policy, medical — that publish research by health economists. The audience for health economics research includes not only other economists, but also public health officials, health care administrators and planners, physicians, and other health care professionals.

The second and third paper and the op-ed explain basic economic concepts such as demand and supply, the margin, elasticity, and monopoly that economists use to study behavior in health care markets. All three pieces overlap, contain some duplication, and differ in complexity. All are useful for thinking about efficiency in the production of health care and equity in its distribution. The simplest is the lecture to philosophers. Many health policy problems arise because health and health care differ from most other goods and services. All three pieces illustrate how economics can help inform policies concerning health and health care, but they also show its limitations. As in every field, policy choices in health depend on values as well as understanding of causal relations, but the valuation of life is more complex than the valuation of a pound of butter or other goods and services that are bought and sold in markets. Health is produced by individuals and families as well as market supplied medical care; thus concepts such as household production and the allocation of time within households play an important role in health economics. More than most of my colleagues, I like to emphasize the importance of applying economic concepts to the study of *health* as well as *medical care*. When I came into the field in the 1960s, it was often referred to as "medical economics." That is no longer true, but the majority of research still focuses on health care, not health.

I also want to emphasize the importance of health economists becoming familiar with health care institutions and technology if they wish to make useful contributions to public or clinical policy. Economic theory tells us that when France changed the financing of national health insurance from a payroll tax to a compulsory contribution on payroll at the same rate, it was really no change at all. French health experts, however, were delighted with the change because the tax was paid to the Minister of Finance, while the contribution would be paid to the Minister of Social Insurance, a much more reliable friend of health insurance.

A subject of continuing interest to economists is the welfare effect of health insurance, especially the effects of moral hazard and adverse selection. The research is of high quality, but I think a more important research question is why the U.S. approach to health insurance–employment based plans, Medicaid, Medicare, and insurance exchanges differs so much from the national health insurance plans of most OECD countries. The consequences of that difference for the cost and quality of care also deserve careful study.

Recent trends in the consolidation of health care organizations into larger units though mergers and acquisitions have been a subject of considerable interest to health economists. This consolidation could be of benefit to society if it leads to greater efficiency in the production of care, but consolidation may also give more monopoly power to the larger organization and result in higher prices to patients. Several government agencies will typically review proposed consolidation when an already large organization is involved. Analysis of the public welfare benefits or harm of the merging entities requires attention to many factors. Some health care organizations such as Kaiser Permanente in California are fully integrated, providing insurance, hospital, physician, and other services under a single contract at lower cost than traditional forms of organization. But the Kaiser type of organization has not spread widely. Contrast that with food retailing, for example, where a low cost entry such as Walmart became nationwide and the largest food retailer in the country in a relatively short time. Economists and other social scientists are far from a full understanding of the forces that determine the structure and behavior of the U.S. health care industry.

Some health economists pursue traditional labor subjects such as the level of wages and wage differentials in health care occupations. The so-called "nurse shortage," much discussed when I entered the field and ever since, is not a mystery to economists but appears to be to everyone else. Many hospitals say they have unfilled nursing positions which they cannot fill because of the "shortage." If they raised the wage, the shortage would disappear. But because the hospital has some monopsony power (it doesn't face a completely elastic supply of nurses), it is financially better off living with the shortage than raising the wage, which it would also have to pay to nurses already employed. Another subject of interest is the effect of licensure laws and professional certification for an increasing number of health care occupations. Many health economists with a labor economics background also lead the way in the study of the demand for health and the household production of health, including studies of the role of education and other social determinants.

Because U.S. health care now consume almost 18 percent of GDP and more than half is funded by government through direct expenditures or forgiveness of taxes, health economics attracts attention from economists who specialize in public finance. As Alice Rivlin (1931–) famously said, "Long-run fiscal policy is health policy." Given the importance of health care expenditures for federal budget deficits and the national debt, even macro-economists are switching some of their research activity to health.

A health economics sub-specialty that I think should get more attention is the economics of innovation. Over time, changes in medical science and technology are major sources of longer life expectancy and other measures of better health. Unfortunately, these changes are also usually a principal reasons for increases in health care costs. Because almost 80 percent of an increase in U.S. life expectancy is now realized after age 65, the effect on national production of increased life expectancy is minimal, but the need to fund health care and other expenses of the elderly is great. A shift in emphasis from innovations that increase life expectancy to those that improve the quality of life would probably be desirable. Also needed is a shift to value-conscious innovation instead of the "progress at any price" attitude that has dominated biomedical innovation. The U.S. economy cannot continue to cope with increases in health care costs fueled in large part by innovations produced in an environment that ignores cost. Health economics offers many opportunities to contribute to social welfare through analyses of patent laws, the competitive structure of health care industries, the legislation that governs the FDA, and the purchasing policies of Federal health insurance as they influence a shift toward more value-conscious health care innovation.

1.1

Health Economics

Health economics is an applied field in which empirical research predominates. It draws its theoretical inspiration principally from four traditional areas of economics: finance and insurance, industrial organization, labour, and public finance. Some of the most useful work employs only elementary economic concepts but requires detailed knowledge of health technology and institutions. Policy-oriented research plays a major role, and many important policy-relevant articles are published in journals read by physicians and others with direct involvement in health (e.g. Enthoven, 1978).

The systematic application of economic concepts and methods to the health field is relatively recent. In a comprehensive bibliography of health economics based on English language sources through 1974,[3] fewer than 10 percent of the entries are dated prior to 1963. In that year a seminal article by Arrow (1963) discussed many of the central theoretical problems, and a few years later a major monograph based on modern econometric methods appeared.[9]

The literature prior to 1963, thoroughly reviewed by Klarman (1965), was primarily institutional and descriptive. Significant contributions include discussions of US medical care institutions,[4,15,41] mental illness,[8] public health,[44] and the British National Health Service.[23] The first US conference on health

Originally published in John Eatwell, Murray Milgate, and Peter Newman (eds.) (1989), *The New Palgrave: Social Economics*, pp. 119–129. New York, NY: Macmillan Reference Books. Copyright by Macmillan Reference Books.

economics was held in 1962,[26] the first international conference in 1973,[32] and the first widely adopted textbook did not appear until 1979.[10]

The field divides naturally into two distinct, albeit related, subjects: the economics of health *per se*, and the economics of medical care. The latter has received much more attention from economists than the former, but it is useful to consider health first because the demand for medical care is, in part, derived from the demand for health, and because many of the theoretical and empirical problems in the economics of medical care arise because of difficulties in measuring, valuing, and analysing health.

Health: Concepts, Measures, and Valuation

Health is multidimensional. With the exception of the dichotomy between life and death, there is no completely objective, invariant ordering across individuals or populations with respect to health. Health can be defined according to criteria such as life expectancy, capacity for work, need for medical care, or ability to perform a variety of personal and social functions. Economists' attempts to measure and analyse differences in health across individuals and populations have typically focused on mortality (especially age-specific and age-adjusted death rates), morbidity (as evidenced by symptoms or diagnosed illnesses), or self-evaluations of health status. There have also been several attempts to take account simultaneously of mortality, morbidity, and health-related limitations by weighting years of life according to illness and disability.

Despite claims that health is more important than any other goal and that human life is priceless, economists note that individuals make tradeoffs between health and other goals and that the valuation of health (including life itself) is necessary for the rational allocation of scarce resources. The two leading approaches to the valuation of human life are 'discounted future earnings' and 'willingness to pay'. Rice (1966) estimated the costs of various illnesses as the sum of direct expenditures for medical care, the foregone earnings attributable to morbidity, plus the cost of premature death, which is assumed to be equal to the present value of future earnings. Willingness to pay is usually defined as the amount of money an individual would require (pay) in exchange for an increase (decrease) in the risk of death. This approach is preferred on theoretical grounds,[18,25,38] but difficult to estimate empirically. Two oft-quoted studies that infer the value of life from risk-related wage differentials differ five-fold in their estimates.[42,43]

The Determinants and Consequences of Variations in Health

Health is sometimes modelled as a dependent and sometimes as an independent variable, although frequently causality runs in both directions. Health has been studied as a function of medical care, income, education, age, sex, race, marital status, environmental pollution, and personal behaviours such as cigarette smoking, diet, and exercise. Grossman (1972) developed a model of the *demand* for health — both as a consumption commodity that enters directly into utility and as an investment commodity that contributes to the production of other goods and services. In his model, variables such as age and schooling affect the optimal level of health by changing its shadow price. Most studies that make health the dependent variable take a *production function* approach[2] with health depending on income, medical care, education, and other inputs.

There is a strong positive correlation between income and health among less developed countries, but, *ceteris paribus*, the relationship tends to disappear at higher levels of income. This may reflect a high income elasticity of demand for other goods and services that adversely affect health, or may result from stress or other harmful side effects of earning more money. Also, as the average level of income rises, those diseases that stem from poverty tend to disappear and those that are not related to income form an increasing share of the burden of illness.

Advances in medical care such as the introduction of antibiotics have had significant effects on mortality and morbidity, but holding constant the state of medical science, the marginal effect of an increase in the quantity of medical care on health appears to be small in developed countries. Elimination of financial barriers to care, as in the British National Health Service, has not been accompanied by a reduction in the traditional mortality differentials across social classes. In all countries health is strongly correlated with years of schooling, but the explanation is not firmly established. Education may increase the efficiency with which individuals produce health. Alternatively, some third variable, such as time preference, may simultaneously affect schooling and health.[7] Marital status and health are strongly correlated (more so for men than for women), but the causality probably runs both ways. Other interesting correlations include those between wife's education and husband's health, and between parents' education and children's health.

Health has frequently been used as an independent variable to explain labour force participation, particularly at older ages. Not only do retired persons frequently cite poor health as the reason for retirement, but current workers who report a health limitation are more likely to withdraw from work in subsequent years. Health status has also been used to explain wages, productivity, school performance, fertility, and the demand for medical care. The results are often sensitive to the particular measure of health that is used, but the direction of effect generally confirms *a priori* predictions.

Health as a Commodity

Health is both an intermediate commodity that affects production and a final commodity that affects utility directly. When health is included in the utility function several questions arise. Do standard theories regarding risk aversion and time discounting with respect to income apply equally to health? How is the marginal utility of income affected by changes in health levels? Both income and health are, in part, exogenously determined by initial endowments, and these endowments are likely to be positively correlated. The endogenous aspects of income and health are subject to many forces, some that may produce positive correlation and some the reverse. Although utility is a function of health, there can be a considerable difference between maximizing health (as measured, say, by life expectancy) and maximizing utility. The value of a given reduction in the probability of death (as evidenced by willingness to pay) is higher when the probability is high than when it is low. Thus programmes to treat the seriously ill at high cost per death averted are often preferred to preventive programmes that avert deaths at lower costs.

Many health problems have a significant genetic component, while others are attributable to unfavourable experiences during the foetal period, at delivery, or in childhood. The resulting heterogeneity among individuals poses a variety of problems for analysis and policy. Unobserved heterogeneity can bias inferences about the effects of health interventions, especially in studies based on non-experimental data.[35] For instance, if people born with weak hearts are less inclined to exercise vigorously, the true effect of exercise on heart disease may be less than that inferred from observational studies. When heterogeneity is observable, the problem becomes primarily one of incorporating both efficiency and distributional considerations into policy analysis. Whose health should be considered in setting standards for air pollution or occupational safety? Under what circumstances should persons in poor health be required to pay actuarially fair health-insurance premiums?

The externalities associated with health have attracted considerable discussion. Analysis of the benefits of vaccination or the costs of pollution is fairly straightforward, but other externalities are less conventional. Individuals may derive utility from knowing that the poor sick among them are receiving medical care. They could attempt to achieve this through voluntary philanthropy, but the amount purchased is likely to be less than socially optimal because each individual's contribution would maximize private utility, ignoring the effects on others.[30] These health-centred philanthropic externalities are sometimes invoked to explain the widespread subsidization of medical care for the poor through national health insurance or other institutional arrangements in preference to general income redistribution.

Medical Care

Medical care accounts for more than 10 percent of gross national product in the United States and approximately that much in several other developed countries. By contrast, restraints on input prices and quantities result in about a 6 percent share in the United Kingdom. The effect on health of such wide variation in medical care expenditures is not clear. Governments in all countries play a large role as regulators, subsidizers, direct buyers, or producers of medical care. Economists have paid considerable attention to the reasons for and consequences of these governmental interventions. One useful way of categorizing economic research on medical care is to relate it to the older, better established areas of specialization that furnish most of the concepts used in health economics. Some studies, to be sure, draw their inspiration from and enrich more than one area.

Finance and Insurance

Risk aversion and uncertainty about future health create a demand for health insurance.[1,33] Once insurance is in place, moral hazard leads to over-utilization of medical care.[29] These two observations have generated a huge amount of research on the role of health insurance in health services.[36] The effect of insurance on the demand for care is better understood than is the demand for insurance itself. The usual risk aversion story, for example, cannot explain why many people purchase policies that cover the first dollar of expenditure but have a ceiling beyond which expenditures are not covered.

Asymmetry in information about potential demand for medical care creates another analytical and policy problem for insurance markets. When the consumer knows a great deal more about his health status and preferences than does the insurance company, adverse selection can lead to a breakdown in the free market in insurance. Group insurance is a typical solution, with participation achieved by compulsion, direct subsidies, or indirect subsidies via the tax system. Compulsory health insurance is also advocated to deal with the free rider problem. The possibility of free riders implies that even countries without explicit national insurance have public or private programmes that provide some kind of implicit universal coverage.

Many research methods, including a large-scale prospective controlled experiment[27] have been used to study the effect of insurance on the demand for care. As a result, few empirical propositions in economics have been as well established as the downward slope of the demand curve for medical care. Nevertheless, precise estimates of price elasticity (net of insurance) are difficult to obtain, in part because the features of some insurance policies — deductibles, varying coinsurance rates, and limits on indemnity payments — imply that the consumer faces a variable price under uncertainty.[19]

One solution to the risk aversion/moral hazard dilemma is for insurance to be provided in the form of contingent claims. For each identifiable condition the insured would be covered for care up to the point where the marginal benefit equals the marginal cost. Consumers, when well, may prefer that type of contract, but once sick they will want any care that has positive marginal benefit. Furthermore, the physician may want to provide care up to the point where marginal benefit is zero. The insurer's task is to enforce the tighter standard on the patient and the physician. This will often require some deception or nonprice rationing which patients can try to offset by strategic behaviour. The resulting loss of trust and less than candid exchange of information between patient and physician can adversely affect the production of care.

Industrial Organization

Probably the largest range of problems and the largest volume of research in health economics falls in the area of industrial organization. There are many different, though related, industries to study: for example, physicians' services, hospitals, drugs, nursing homes, dental care. The topics covered range from licensure and regulation[31] to price discrimination[20] and nonprice rationing[11] to technological innovation and diffusion.[37] Organization in the narrow sense of the term is of considerable interest because of the admixture of public, private nonprofit, and for-profit hospitals, and because the modes of physician practice range from solo fee-for-service to huge groups of salaried physicians. Behaviour inside the organization is particularly important in analysing nonprofit hospitals (the dominant form of organization in the United States) because the trustees, the administrator, the attending physicians, and the house staff all have considerable power and frequently have different objectives.

Medical care is, in many respects, the quintessential service industry. First, it is extremely difficult to measure output. As a result, standard economic accounts show little or no gain in productivity over time despite large expenditures for research and development and rapid technological change. Second, the consumer frequently plays a major role in the production process. This means not only that the value of the patient's time is part of the cost of care, but that the patient's knowledge, skill, and motivation, and the level of trust between patient and physician can affect the outcome of the care process. Third, the physician often knows a great deal more than the patient does about the patient's need for various types of care. This asymmetry of information has been used to explain the unwillingness of most societies to rely solely on competitive market forces to insure appropriate behaviour by physicians. Fourth, because output cannot be stored and short-run supply is relatively inelastic, productivity is sensitive to changes in demand. The stochastic nature of the demand for hospital care results in excess capacity and the problem is exacerbated by systematic variation in demand according to day of week and month of year.

Despite the difficulty of measuring output, numerous estimates of hospital short-run and long-run cost functions have been made.[22] In the short run, marginal cost is below average cost in most hospitals. Long-run average cost tends to fall with increasing size until about 200 beds and then tends to be constant with a possible rise after a size of about 500 beds. Most researchers have defined output as a day of care or as a hospital admission. Standardization for patient mix can only be done incompletely, and failure to measure the effects of care on health is a serious limitation. To be sure, changes in health are only one aspect of output. A consideration fraction of resources in hospitals and nursing homes is devoted to *caring* for people who are in pain or who are disabled, regardless of whether their health status is (or even can be) improved. Also, a significant fraction of physicians' time is devoted to providing information and validation independently of any intended or actual effect on health status.

The problem of measuring output also increases the difficulty of analysing the demand for care. Additional complications result from the possibility that physicians may shift the patient's demand.[6,40] Some economists concede that physicians have the power to shift demand, but believe that it is sufficiently and uniformly exploited so that further shifting can be ignored. Others argue that the amount of shifting varies with exogenous changes in the physician/population ratio. This follows from a model in which physicians maximize utility as a function of income, leisure, and 'correct practice'. The empirical evidence is consistent with this model,[14] but it is consistent with other explanations as well.

Perhaps less controversial is the proposition that physicians can and do change their patients' demand for hospital care. One example of this is in the United States is the lower hospital utilization by patients enrolled in prepaid group practice plans such as Kaiser Permanente.[24] Patients pay a single annual premium for total care regardless of the quantity of services used; physicians typically receive a salary or a share of the net income after the hospital and other costs have been paid. An even more spectacular change in hospital utilization emerged when Medicare (the US publicly funded insurance for the elderly) changed from retrospective cost-reimbursement to prospective payment per admission in a particular diagnosis-related group. In just two years the average length of stay of patients 65 years of age and older in short-term general hospitals fell 12 percent without any change in conventional demand variables.

The demand for care usually increases as health worsens, but not always. For instance, an elderly person who is in good general health may demand a variety of surgical interventions for specific problems such as hip replacement or lens implantation; a person of the same age who is in bad health may not.

Problems in measuring output imply problems in measuring price. An alternative approach to the estimation of price change is to measure change in the total cost of treating a defined illness or medical condition. A price index calculated by this method was found to rise more rapidly than the conventional medical care price index,[39] possibly as a result of unmeasured changes in output. Technological advances may have increased the cost of care by making it possible for the physician to do more things for the patient.

Economic research on drugs falls into two main categories that reflect differing policy concerns in the United States before and after the 1962 Kefauver-Harris Amendments to the Pure Food and Drug Act. Prior to the amendments, attention was focused on price fixing, price discrimination (manufacturers' prices vary in several ways, depending upon the type of customer), and on alleged socially wasteful expenditures for product differentiation. Since 1962 economic research has shifted to the volume and character of innovation. A decrease in the flow of new drugs has been attributed to the increased cost of satisfying regulatory requirements.[16] Despite the questions raised by economists regarding the net benefit of tighter controls, other countries have tended to follow the policy direction set by the United States in 1962.

In recent years in the United States and many other countries, the major health policy questions have revolved around efforts to contain the cost of care. Most economists have argued for greater reliance on market mechanisms and less on regulation,[46] but an intricate web of social, political, and economic considerations seems to preclude a pure laissez-faire approach to health.[13]

Labour Economics

Much of the research on the economics of *health* comes out of labour economics, especially the human capital branch. Concerning medical care, labour economists have been primarily interested in the demand and supply of various health occupations. Numerous studies of the earnings of physicians have mostly confirmed the results of a pioneering study[12] that physicians, on average, realize an excellent return on their investment in medical education. Research on choice of speciality and location, however, does not support any simple model of physicians as income maximizers. Some specialities appear to have more intrinsic appeal than others, and the wide geographical variation in the physician/population ratio in the United States is not primarily the result of variation in fees or income. Changes in physician distribution by speciality or location, however, do conform closely to predictions based on standard utility maximization.[28]

Research on nurses in the United States has focused heavily on an alleged persistent 'shortage'. One explanation is that the principal employers of nurses — hospitals — have monopsony power.[45] Faced with rising supply curves, hospitals equate the marginal cost of nurses with their marginal revenue product and set the wage on the supply curve. The 'shortage' simply reflects the fact that the hospital administrator would like to hire more nurses at the going wage, but has no incentive to raise the wage.

Public Finance

Ever since Bismarck introduced compulsory health insurance to Germany in 1883, the financing of health care has been of increasing concern to governments and to economists who specialize in public finance. Even in the United States, the last major holdout against national health insurance, government pays directly for about 42 percent of all health-care expenditures, and pays indirectly for an appreciable additional share through tax exemptions and allowances. Numerous reasons have been offered as to why governments pay for health care, but each has its shortcomings.

All explanations that are health related (e.g., 'health is a right', 'the government has an obligation to reduce or eliminate class differentials in mortality') are suspect because in Bismarck's time there was virtually no connection between medical care and health, and even today the connection at the margin is highly circumscribed. The explanation that medical care is a 'merit' good seems circular. Governments are said to subsidize 'merit' goods, but the only way to identify them is by the presence of government subsidies. The standard externality-public good explanation applies to the prevention and treatment of communicable diseases, but this accounts for only a small fraction of health care. Subsidies in other industries such as agriculture or the merchant marine can frequently be explained by pressure from producers, but government subsidies for health care have usually been opposed by the producers of care.

Subsidies for health care are frequently defended on the grounds that it is unfair to allow the distribution of health care to be determined by the distribution of income. Many economists counter by saying it would be more efficient to redistribute income and then let the poor decide how much of the increase they want to devote to health care and how much to other goods and services. The crux of the problem seems to be that the amount of redistribution that society wants to make to an individual may depend on the individual's need for care. The greater the need, the greater society's willingness to redistribute. It may be more efficient to combine the determination of need with the redistribution via the delivery of care than to separate the functions.

One special problem arises in this field from the proposition that in order to reduce inequality, governments should limit the amount of care that individuals can obtain. This view is virtually inescapable once a government is committed to equality in health care and constrained to keep the health budget within limits set by general budgetary considerations. No country can afford to provide health care for all its citizens up to the point where the marginal benefit is zero.

Economists spend a great deal of time deploring the fact that no country shows much interest in evaluating the outcome of medical care. It might be more fruitful to try to explain why this is so. No doubt part of the answer is that evaluation is very difficult, but part may be related to the symbolic and political role that medical care plays in modern society. When governments, insurance companies, or employers promise to finance all necessary and appropriate care, they typically have to introduce implicit constraints to keep from going bankrupt. A thorough evaluation would make these constraints explicit and could create a great deal of dissatisfaction.

Future Research

Because health economics is predominantly applied and policy-oriented, future research will undoubtedly be influenced by the changing nature of health problems and by developments in medical science. Thus, it is reasonable to expect to see more attention to the health problems of the elderly — chronic illness and the need for long-term care. Among the non-elderly, health problems stemming from substance abuse are large and growing in importance. The new understanding of the role of genetic factors in disease creates dramatic opportunities for screening and intervention, but these opportunities will pose problems of enormous complexity for analysis and policy. The gap between what is technically possible and what is economically feasible will probably widen; thus, the demand for guidance concerning the efficiency and equity implications of alternative health policies is likely to grow. Further development of health economics as an established field of inquiry will help to meet that demand.

References

1. Arrow, K. J. (1963). "Uncertainly and the Welfare Economics of Medical Care." *American Economic Review* **53**(5): 941–973.
2. Auster, R., Leveson, I. and Sarachek, D. (1969). "The Production of Health, an Exploratory Study." *Journal of Human Resources* **4**(Fail): 412–436.
3. Culyer, A. J., Wiseman, J. and Walker, A. (1977). *An Annotated Bibliography of Health Economics*. St. Martin's Press: London, Martin Robertison: New York.
4. Davis, M. M. and Rorem, C. R. (1932). *The Crisis in Hospital Finance*. University of Chicago Press: Chicago.
5. Enthoven, A. E. (1978). "Consumer-Choice Health Plan." *New England Journal of Medicine* **298**, 23 March and 30 March.
6. Evans, R. G. (1974). "Supplier-Induced Demand: Some Empirical Evidence and Implications." In *The Economics of Health and Medical Care*, ed. M. Perlman, Macmillan: London.
7. Farrell, P. and Fuchs, V. R. (1982). "Schooling and Health: The Cigarette Connection." *Journal of Health Economics* **1**(3): 217–230.
8. Fein, R. (1958). *Economics of Mental Illness*. Basic Books: New York.
9. Feldstein, M. S. (1967). *Economic Analysis for Health Service Efficiency*. North-Holland: Amsterdam.
10. Feldstein, P. (1983). *Health Care Economics* 2nd edn. John Wiley & Sons: New York.
11. Friedman, B. (1978). "On the Rationing of Health Services and Resource Availability." *Journal of Human Resources* **13**(Supplement): 57–75.
12. Friedman, M. and Kuznets, S. (1945). *Income from Independent Professional Practice*. General Series No. 45, National Bureau of Economic Research: New York.
13. Fuchs, V. R. (1974). *Who Shall Live? Health, Economics, and Social Choice*. Basic Books: New York.
14. Fuchs, V. R. (1978). "The Supply of Surgeons and the Demand for Operations." *Journal of Human Resources* **13**(Supplement): 35–56.
15. Ginzberg, E. (1954). "What Every Economist Should Know About Health and Medicine." *American Economic Review* **44**(1): 104–119.

16. Grabowski, H. G., Vernon, J. M., and Thomas, L. G. (1978). "Estimating the Effects of Regulation on Innovation: An International Comparative Analysis of the Pharmaceutical Industry." *Journal of Law and Economics* **21**(1): 133–163.

17. Grossman, M. (1972). *The Demand for Health: A Theoretical and Empirical Investigation.* National Bureau of Economic Research: New York.

18. Jones-Lee, M. (1974). "The Value of Changes in the Probability of Death or Injury." *Journal of Political Economy* **82**(4): 835–849.

19. Keeler, E. B., Newhouse, J. P. *et al.* (1977). "Deductibles and Demand: A Theory of the Consumer Facing a Variable Price Schedule Under Uncertainty." *Econometrica* **45**(3): 641–655.

20. Kessel, R. A. (1958). "Price Discrimination in Medicine." *Journal of Law and Economics* **1**(2): 20–53.

21. Klarman, H. E. (1965). *The Economics of Health.* Columbia University Press: New York.

22. Lave, J. R. and Lave, L. B. (1970). "Hospital Cost Functions: Estimating Cost Functions for Multi-product Firms." *American Economic Review* **60**(3): 379–395.

23. Lees, D. S. (1961). *Health Through Choice.* Hobart Paper No. 14, Institute of Economic Affairs: London.

24. Luft, H. S. (1981). *Health Maintenance Organizations: Dimensions of Performance.* John Wiley & Sons: New York.

25. Mishan, E. J. (1971). "Evaluation of Life and Limb: A Theoretical Approach." *Journal of Political Economy* **79**(4): 687–705.

26. Mushkin, S. J. (ed.) (1964). *The Economics of Health and Medical Care.* University of Michigan Press: Ann Arbor.

27. Newhouse, J. P., Manning, W. G., Morris, C. N., Orr, L. L., Duan, N., Keeler, E. B., Leibowitz, A., Marquis, K. H., Marquis, M. S., Phelps, C. E. and Brook, R. H. (1981). "Some Interim Results from a Controlled Trial of Cost Sharing in Health Insurance." *New England Journal of Medicine* **305**: 1501–1507.

28. Newhouse, J. P., Williams, A. P., Bennet, B. W. and Schwartz, W. B. (1982). "Does the Geographical Distribution of Physicians Reflect Market Failure?" *Bell Journal of Economics* **13**(2): 493–505.

29. Pauly, M. V. (1968). "The Economics of Moral Hazard: Comment." *American Economic Review* **58**(3): 531–536.

30. Pauly, M. V. (1971). *Medical Care at Public Expense. A Study in Applied Welfare Economics.* Praeger: New York.

31. Peltzman, S. (1973). "An Evaluation of Consumer Protection Legislation: The 1962 Drug Amendments." *Journal of Political Economy* **81**(5): 1049–1091.

32. Perlman, M. (ed.) (1974). *The Economics of Health and Medical Care.* Macmillan: London.

33. Phelps, C. (1973). *The Demand for Health Insurance: A Theoretical and Empirical Investigation.* The Rand Corporation: Santa Monica, No. R-1054–OEO.

34. Rice, D. P. (1966). *Estimating the Cost of Illness.* USDHEW, Public Health Service Publication: Washington, DC, pp. 947–956.

35. Rosenzweig, M. R. and Schultz, T. P. (1982). "The Behavior of Mothers as Inputs to Child Health: The Determinants of Birth Weight, Gestation, and Rate of Fetal

Growth." In *Economic Aspects of Health*, ed. V. R. Fuchs. University of Chicago Press: Chicago.

36. Rosett, R. N. (ed.) (1976). *The Role of Health Insurance in the Health Services Sector.* National Bureau of Economic Research: New York.

37. Russell, L. B. (1979). *Technology in Hospitals.* Brookings: Washington, DC.

38. Schelling, T. C. (1968). "The Life you Save May Be Your Own." In *Problems in Public Expenditure Analysis*, ed. S. B. Chase. Brookings: Washington, DC.

39. Scitovsky, A. A. (1967). "Changes in the Costs of Treatment of Selected Illnesses, 1951–65." *American Economic Review* **57**(4): 1182–1195.

40. Sloan, F. and Feldman, R. (1978). "Competition Among Physicians." In *Competition in the Health Care Sector: Past, Present, and Future*, ed. W. Greenberg. Federal Trade Commission: Washington, DC.

41. Somers, H. M. and Somers, A. R. (1961). *Doctors, Patients, and Health Insurance.* Brookings: Washington, DC.

42. Thaler, R. and Rosen, S. (1976). "The Value of Saving a Life: Evidence from the Labor Market." In *Household Production and Consumption*, ed. N. E. Terleckyj. National Bureau of Economic Research: New York.

43. Viscusi, K. W. (1978). "Labour Market Valuations of Life and Limb: Empirical Evidence and Policy Implications." *Public Policy* **26**(3): 359–386.

44. Weisbrod, B. A. (1961). *Economics of Public Health.* University of Pennsylvania Press: Philadelphia.

45. Yett, D. E. (1975). *An Economic Analysis of the Nurse Shortage.* Heath: Lexington, Mass.

46. Zeckhauser, R. and Zook, C. (1981). "Failures to Control Heallh Costs: Departures from First Principles." In *A New Approach to the Economics of Health Care*, ed. Mancur Olson, American Enterprise Institute for Public Policy Research: Washington, DC.

1.2

Health Care and the United States Economic System: An Essay in Abnormal Physiology

Health care affects and is affected by the economic system in so many ways as to preclude any attempt at complete enumeration or description. The objective of this paper is more modest. I shall assume that the reader is reasonably familiar with health care, its institutions, technology and personnel, but is less familiar with an "economic system" that is used by economists to describe and analyze economic behavior. Therefore, major emphasis will be given to indicating the place of health care in this system and showing how related economic concepts can contribute to an understanding of problems of health care in the United States. I shall also attempt to indicate some of the limitations of economics in dealing with such a complex area of human activity and concern.

Introduction

Definitions

Health care can be defined as those activities that are undertaken with the objective of restoring, preserving or enhancing the physical and mental well-being of people. These activities may be aimed at the relief of pain, the removal of disabilities, the restoration of functions, the prevention of illness and accidents or the postponement of death. Some health care is produced within the "household;"

Originally published in *Milbank Memorial Fund Quarterly*, 50(2, Part 1):211–237, April 1972. Copyright by Milbank Memorial Fund.

e.g., the triage, first-aid and nursing services rendered to children by parents. Some is bought and sold in the "market"; e.g., physicians' services, hospital services. Most health care is applied to identifiable individuals but some may be aimed at a population, e.g., fluoridation of a water supply.

The *economic system* consists of the network of institutions, laws and rules created by society to answer the universal economic questions: (a) What goods and services shall be produced? (b) How shall they be produced? and (c) For whom shall they be produced?[1] Every society needs an economic system because *resources* (natural, human and manmade) are scarce relative to human wants. The resources have alternative uses and there is a multiplicity of competing wants. Thus, decisions must be made regarding the use of these resources in production and the distribution of the resulting output among the members of society.

Two fallacies

Before turning to several important issues concerning health care in relation to the economic system it will be useful to dispose of two fallacies that have frequently obstructed clear thinking in this area.

1. Resources are no longer scarce. Some people seem to be so inspired, terrified or confused by automation and other technologic advances as to proclaim the end of scarcity. A decade ago it was not unusual to find writers prophesying that in ten years no one would have to work because machines would turn out all the goods and services needed. The falsity of such predictions becomes more apparent each year. That inefficiency and waste exist in the economy cannot be denied. That some resources are underutilized is clear every time the unemployment figures are announced. That the resources devoted to war could be used to satisfy other wants is self-evident. But the fundamental fact remains that even if all these imperfections were eliminated total output would still fall far short of the amount people would like to have. Resources would still be scarce in the sense that choices would have to be made. An economic system would still be needed. Not only is this true now, but it will continue to be true in the foreseeable future. Some advances in technology make it possible to carry out current activities with fewer resources (e.g., automated laboratories) , but others open up new demands (e.g., for renal dialysis or organ transplants) that put further strains on resources. Moreover, time, the ultimate scarce resource, becomes more valuable the more productive we become.[2,3]

2. Health is the most important goal. Some of those in the health field recognize that we cannot satisfy all wants, but they seem to believe that health is more important than all other goals and therefore questions of scarcity and

allocation are not applicable in this area. It requires only a casual study of human behavior to reveal the fallacy of this position. Every day in manifold ways people make choices that affect health and it is clear that they frequently place a higher value on satisfying other wants; e.g., smoking, overeating, careless driving, failure to take medicine.

Criteria for an economic system in relation to health care

What is it that we want the economic system to do with respect to health care? Given the scarcity of resources and the existence of competing goals we want a system that will result in:

1. An optimum amount of resources devoted to health care;
2. These resources being combined in an optimal way;
3. An optimal distribution of health care;
4. An optimal allocation of resources between current provision of health care and investment for future health care through research, education and so forth.

The general rule for reaching such optima is "equality at the margin." For instance, the first criterion would be met if the last dollar's worth of resources devoted to health care increased human satisfaction by exactly the same amount as the last dollar's worth devoted to other goals.

The contrast between this view of a social optimum and the notion of "optimal care" as used in the health field can be appreciated with the aid of Figure 1. The relation between health and health care inputs can usually be described by a curve that may rise at an increasing rate at first, but then rises at a decreasing rate and eventually levels off or declines.[a] "Optimal care" in medicine would usually be defined as the point where no further increment in health is possible; i.e., point A.[b] The social optimum, however, requires that inputs of resources not exceed the point where the value of an additional increment to health is exactly equal to the cost of the inputs required to obtain that increment (point B). It should be noted that point C, where the *ratio* of benefits to costs is at a maximum, is not the optimal point because additional inputs still add more to benefits than to costs. One of the problems with current health care policy is that it frequently fluctuates between

---

[a]Health might be measured by life expectancy, absence of disabilities, speed of recovery after surgery and so forth. Health care inputs might refer to the size of a health care program, or the total amount of care given to a particular patient or a particular aspect of care such as number of tests or number of days in the hospital.

[b]This assumes that some input — e.g., the state of technology — is fixed at any given point in time.

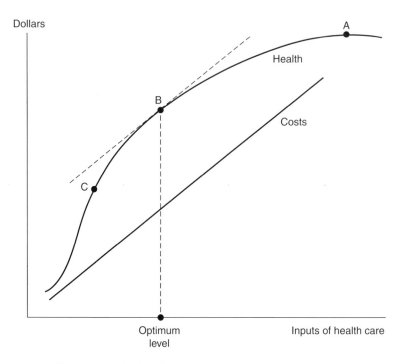

Fig. 1.   Determination of Optimum Level of Health Care Utilization.

trying to drive utilization to A, and then, in frenzied attempts to contain costs, cuts back some programs to point C or below.

Types of economic systems

Economists have identified three "pure types" of economic systems — traditional, centrally directed and market price. Every actual economy is a blend of types, but their relative importance can and does vary greatly. Most primitive and feudal societies rely heavily upon a traditional system; the process of decision-making is embedded in the total culture — its customs, traditions and religious rituals. In some ancient empires (Egypt, Babylonia) central direction played a major role. The basic decisions were made by one man or a small group of men who controlled the power apparatus of the society and were in a position to enforce their decisions concerning the allocation of resources and the distribution of output. This system has also been dominant in the Soviet Union since 1928 and in many other countries since World War II. The United States, Canada and most countries of Western Europe have relied heavily on a market system for the past century or two. Thus a discussion of health care and the United States economy requires a close look at the working of a market system. An additional reason for concentrating on this third type is for its normative value. Under certain specified conditions the results produced by the theoretical market system set a standard against which the performance of any real economy can be evaluated.[c]

The elementary model

The elementary model of a market system consists of a collection of decision-making units called *households* and another collection called *firms.* The households own all the productive resources in the society. They make these resources available to firms who transform them into goods and services, which are then distributed back to the households. The flow of resources and of goods and services is facilitated by a counterflow of money (see Figure 2).[d] This is called

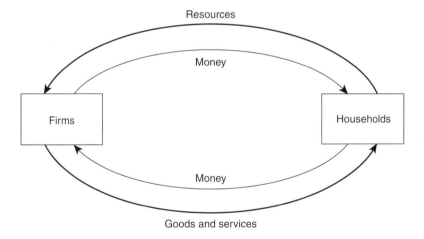

Fig. 2.   Elementary Model of a Market System.

---

[c]This point is well recognized in the theoretical literature on socialist planning (cf., Lange, O., On the Economic Theory of Socialism, in Lippincott, B. E. (Editor), *On the economic theory of socialism,* Minneapolis, University of Minnesota Press, 1956) and in the attempts of the Soviet government and other East European governments to make greater use of the market mechanism.

[d]The flow of resources (and the reciprocal flow of goods and services) in the United States is currently at a rate of approximately one trillion dollars per annum. About seven percent of these resources flow to "firms" producing health care. Fifteen years ago only about 4.5 percent of such smaller resource flow went in that direction. The resource flow, measured in dollars, depends upon the quantities of various resources and their prices. Over long periods of time prices of equivalent resources usually change at about the same rate in all sectors of the economy. Thus the increased share in dollar terms reflects a substantial increase in the share of real resources as well. This large shift of resources over a relatively short period of time is the most important element in the present "health care crisis."

a market system because the exchanges of resources and of goods and services for money take place in markets where *prices* and *quantities* are determined. These prices are the signals or controls that trigger changes in behavior as required by changes in technology or preferences. The market system is sometimes referred to as the "price" system.

In the markets for resources the households are the *suppliers* and the firms provide the *demand.* In the markets for goods and services the firms are the suppliers and the households are the source of demand. In each market the interaction between demand and supply determines the quantities and prices of the various resources and goods and services (see Figure 3).

The income of each household depends upon the quantity and quality of resources available to it (including time) and their prices; the amount of income determines its share of the total flow of goods and services. The household is assumed to spend its income (and time) in such a way as to maximize *utility* (i.e., satisfaction). It does this by following the principle of "equality at the margin;" i.e., it adjusts its purchases so that marginal utility (the satisfaction added by the last unit purchased) of each commodity is proportional to its price.

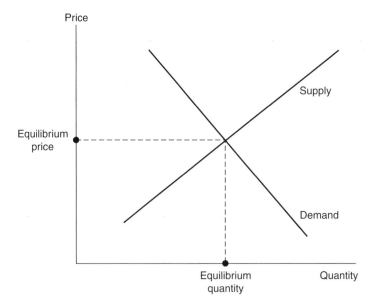

Fig. 3.   A Typical Market.

It is assumed that firms attempt to maximize *profits* (the difference between what they must pay the households for the use of resources and what they get from them for the goods and services they produce). To maximize profits they too must follow the equality at the margin rule, adjusting their use of different types of resources so that the marginal products (the addition to output obtained from one additional unit of input) are proportional to price.

If the markets are perfectly competitive and if certain other conditions are met, it can be shown that a market system produces an optimum allocation of resources, given the distribution of resources among households and given their "tastes" or preferences. The United States economy departs in many respects from the abstract perfectly competitive market system; this is particularly noticeable in the health care sector. The main body of this paper is devoted to a discussion of these departures and the problems they pose for health care policy.

Imperfectly Competitive Markets

The essence of a competitive market is (1) that there are many well-informed buyers and sellers no one of whom is large enough to influence price; (2) that the buyers and sellers act independently (i.e., no collusion); and (3) that there is free entry for other buyers and sellers not currently in the market. Most health care markets depart substantially from competitive conditions, sometimes inevitably, and sometimes as the result of deliberate public or private policy. A discussion of some of the principal problems follows.

Fewness of sellers

In most towns and even moderate size cities the market is too small to support enough hospitals or enough practitioners in each speciality to fulfill the requirements of a workably competitive market. For instance, most students of hospital costs believe there are significant economies of scale in general hospitals up to a size of 200 or 300 beds, and some believe that economies are to be realized in even larger hospitals. Assuming a ratio of four beds per 1,000 population, a city of 60,000 could support just one 240 bed hospital. Thus, it would be extremely uneconomical to require numerous competitive hospitals except in large, densely populated markets. These constraints are even more significant when specialty care is considered. It is doubtful that even a population of one million would justify enough independent maternity, open heart surgery and transplant services and the like to approximate competitive conditions.[e]

In such a condition of "natural monopoly" the traditional United States response has been to introduce public utility regulation (e.g., electricity, telephone, transportation). The results, however, have not always been satisfactory, partly because the regulators often tend to serve the regulated rather than the public and partly because it is inherently difficult to set standards of performance without competitive yardsticks. Many other countries rely on government ownership and control, but the United States experience with government hospitals has not, on balance, been favorable. Another possible solution is the development of what J. K. Galbraith has termed "countervailing power" and what the economics textbooks describe as bilateral monopoly. If, for instance, in a one-hospital town all the consumers were organized into a single body for purposes of bargaining with the hospital, at least some of the disadvantages of monopoly would be lessened.

The typical "solution" in the hospital field has been to emphasize the "nonprofit" character of the hospitals and to assume that therefore the hospital will not abuse its monopoly power. Two criticisms of this "solution" are (a) the absence of a profit incentive may lead to waste, inefficiency and unnecessary duplication, and (2) the hospitals may be run for the benefit of the physicians.[4]

Cooperation (collusion) among sellers

Even when numerous sellers of the same health service are in the same market there may be significant advantages to society if they do not maintain a completely arms-length competitive posture vis-á-vis one another. The free exchange of information, cooperative efforts to meet crisis situations and reciprocal backup arrangements may help to reduce costs and increase patient satisfaction. Unfortunately, the intimacy and trust developed through such activities may spill over in less desirable directions such as price fixing, exclusion of would-be rivals and other restrictions on competition. For 200 years economists have been impressed with the wisdom of Adam Smith's observation that "people of the same trade seldom meet together, even for merriment and diversion, but the conversation ends in a conspiracy against the public, or in some contrivance to raise prices."

---

[e]The fact that these services proliferate contrary to what economies of scale would indicate is the result of other problems such as the absence of appropriate incentives and constraints for physicians and hospital administrators.

Pathologists have been found guilty of price-fixing, and price discrimination by physicians is not uncommon. The latter practice, which physicians view benevolently as a way of reducing inequality of access to medical care, is viewed by some economists as evidence of the use of monopoly power to maximize profits.[5]

Restrictions on entry

Probably the most obvious and most deliberate interference with competition in the market for physicians' services is the barrier to entry imposed by compulsory licensure. The case for licensure presumably rests on the proposition that the consumer is a poor judge of the quality of medical care and therefore needs guidance concerning the qualifications of those proposing to sell such care. Assuming this to be true the need for guidance could be met by voluntary *certification,* rather than compulsory licensure. Indeed, the need could probably be better met through certification because there could be several grades or categories and periodic recertification would be more practicable (and less threatening) than periodic relicensure. Under a certification system patients would be free to choose the level of expertise that they wanted, including uncertified practitioners.

The principal objections that could be raised against such a system are that some patients might receive bad treatment at the hands of uncertified practitioners, and that it might result in an expansion of unnecessary care. The obvious advantages of such a system are greater availability of care and lower prices. For certain health care needs, practitioners with lesser qualifications than present physicians have would clearly be adequate. The existing system results in some persons receiving no care, or being treated by persons without any medical training (e.g., family members, neighbors, friends).

Another example of entry restrictions is the system of limiting hospital privileges to certain physicians. This has been justified in terms of the desire to insure quality of care (in the institution) and as a way of obtaining free services from the physicians. However, it can also be viewed in an economic context as a way of limiting competition.

In general, the codes of professional ethics that physicians have evolved undoubtedly serve many useful social purposes. But it is well to recall Kenneth Arrow's observation that "codes of professional ethics, which arise out of the principal-agent relation and afford protection to the principals, can serve also as a cloak for monopoly by the agents."[6]

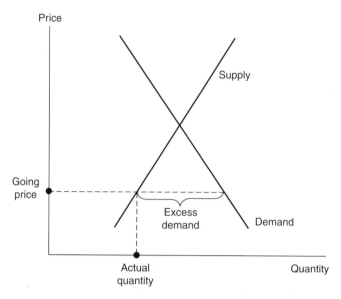

Fig. 4.   Excess Demand.

Disequilibrium

One disturbing characteristic of some health care markets is the failure of price to reach an equilibrium level (the level where the quantity demanded and the quantity supplied are equal). For instance, the market for house calls seems to be characterized by excess demand (see Figure 4). The "going price," about $20 per visit, is not high enough to bring supply and demand into balance. The quantity (number of house calls) that patients are willing and able to pay for at that price is much greater than the quantity physicians are willing to supply. Some observers, notably Martin Feldstein,[7] believe that the market for physicians' services in general is characterized by excess demand.

The market for general surgery, however, can best be described as an example of excess supply (see Figure 5).[8] At the going price for most general surgical procedures, $300 for a herniorrhaphy, the quantity that surgeons are willing and able to do is much greater than the quantity demanded. A condition of excess supply is also probably present for many types of specialty surgery (ophthalmology, gynecology).

The persistence of a disequilibrium price is a clear indication that the market departs substantially from the competitive norm. In the case of excess demand, physicians are apparently reluctant to let the price of house calls rise to their equilibrium level; they introduce a form of rationing instead. This may

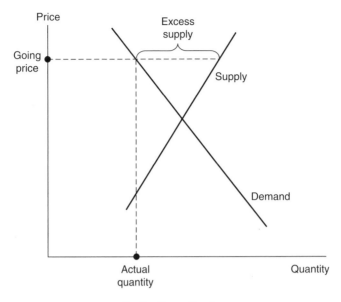

Fig. 5.   Excess Supply.

yield certain psychic satisfactions in lieu of the higher income that is clearly possible. In the excess supply example, the price fails to fall either because the individual surgeon does not think it would be to his advantage to cut price or because surgeons have collectively reached this decision. A contributing factor is the option that most surgeons have of using their nonsurgical time for general practice or other income-producing activities.

The alleged shortage of nurses indicates another potentially troublesome health care market. If what is meant by "shortage" is that it would be nice to have more nurses, no analytical problem arises and the point is trivial. In that sense there is a shortage of every type of good or service. If, however, the allegation refers to a shortage in the sense shown in Figure 4 (i.e., an excess demand for nurses), the failure of nurses' salaries to rise to their equilibrium level must be explained. Some investigators[9,10] claim that it is monopsonistic behavior on the part of hospitals that keeps nurses' salaries from rising to the point where supply and demand would be equal.

Costs of information

The elementary competitive model assumes that all information relevant to decision-making is known by the households and firms — prices, production possibilities, utility to be derived from different commodities. In the real world, of course, such information may be difficult or even impossible to obtain. High information costs are characteristic of many health care markets; frequently the only way a person can know whether he needs to see a physician is to see a physician. The incorporation of information costs into economic analysis is relatively recent,[11] and the theory is far from complete. Many health care markets function poorly because of imperfect information but there is considerable disagreement as to how to make them function better. One point might have general validity. Where the costs of information are increased as a result of public or private policy, reversal of that policy would probably be desirable. For instance, restrictions on the right of physicians to advertise and on the right of pharmacies to advertise prices of prescription drugs ought to be reexamined in the light of the consumer's need to know more about physicians and drugs to make intelligent choices. A study of variations in restrictions on advertising by optometrists and opticians found that prices were substantially lower in states that permitted advertising.[12]

Externalities

An externality exists when the actions taken by an individual household or firm will impose costs or confer benefits on other households or firms, and where no feasible way exists of arranging direct compensation for these costs or benefits. The presence of externalities indicates that the individual household or firm, in attempting to maximize its own utility or profit, will not make socially optimal decisions.[f] A classic example of an externality is the costs of air pollution imposed on others by the smoke emanating from a factory. Another classic example is the benefit to society that results when an individual decides to be vaccinated or treated for a communicable disease.

One way to deal with externalities is for the state to prohibit or require certain actions. Another is to attempt to modify the prices facing individual firms or households (through taxes or subsidies) so that the price properly reflects the social costs or benefits. In principle, use of the price mechanism will permit a much closer approximation to a social optimum, but practical difficulties may preclude the price approach in some situations.

Externalities are very important to health care in the broadest sense of the term. Consider, for instance, the effects of automobiles on health. The decisions

---

[f]The firm or household will presumably equate *its* marginal cost and *its* marginal benefit. The social optimum requires taking into account the costs or benefits imposed on others.

of individual households involving the purchase and use of an automobile, the speed and manner of driving, the amount of maintenance and repair and even the choice of gasoline have potentially important implications for the health of others, but these implications are not reflected in the prices facing the household. Similar problems arise in connection with many other consumption or production activities that create environmental health hazards.

In seeking to reduce such hazards a few central points should be kept in mind. First, costs (resources used or wants unsatisfied) are usually associated with the reduction of hazards, and these costs frequently increase at an accelerating rate, the greater the reduction desired. It follows, therefore, that the social goal should rarely be the complete elimination of the hazard, but rather its reduction to the point where the value of a further reduction is less than the cost of achieving it. A major problem for health care policy is to identify these externalities, estimate their effects and impose appropriate taxes or subsidies so that individual households and firms, in seeking to maximize their own utility or profits, will make socially appropriate decisions.

Medical research is a good example of an activity with large external benefits, and, therefore, in the absence of specific public policy, too little will be undertaken. One solution is to permit the discoverer of new knowledge to appropriate the benefits (e.g., through patent protection), but with regard to much health research this solution will frequently not be feasible or acceptable. The alternative is for the government to subsidize research. It has done this to a considerable degree; the question is how much health research is socially desirable? The answer, in principle, is the same as for any other decision regarding the use of scarce resources — the optimum level of research is reached when the incremental value of the prospective benefits is equal to the incremental cost. The more basic the research the more likely it is to give rise to external benefits, but the more difficult it is to estimate their value or incidence.

In contrast to environmental programs and medical research, medical care today frequently does not involve significant external benefits. For instance, the benefits of most surgery accrue primarily to the patient and his family. This is equally true for treatment of most major diseases such as heart disease and cancer.[g] The best known examples of externalities arising from medical care involve the prevention of and treatment for communicable diseases. Another

---

[g]When medical care keeps an employed head of family alive and well, a type of external benefit is created because society does not have to provide for his or her dependents. Much medical care, however, goes to the young or the aged or to keeping people alive but not well enough to work so it is doubtful if on balance a positive externality exists in this sense.

potentially important source of externalities is the treatment of mental illness, but lack of knowledge concerning causes or cures makes it difficult to reach firm policy conclusions in this area.

One important application of the externality idea is with respect to the problem of inequality of access to care. A frequent criticism of the market system is that it results in an unequal and "unfair" distribution of income.[h] Households that are poorly endowed with resources will earn relatively little and will command only a small share of the nation's output.

Many people would like to see a reduction of inequality, either in general or with respect to a particular commodity (medical care). To the extent that they are prepared to back their demand for less inequality through voluntary redistribution (philanthropy), no modification of the elementary model is required. We simply note that some households derive utility from giving money to others or from knowing that other households are receiving medical care. They are, therefore, willing to devote a part of their income (or part of their time) for that purpose. The purchase of a good or service for someone else is no different analytically from the purchase of a good or service for one's own household.

The externality problem arises because a philanthropic act by one household confers benefits on all other households that derive utility from observing a decrease in inequality. If each potential philanthropist considers only the psychic benefits *he* derives from reducing inequality, the total volume of philanthropy will be less than warranted by the collective desires of the group.[i]

One solution is compulsory redistribution. Society, working through government, may decide that the distribution of income resulting from the market system is inequitable or otherwise unsatisfactory and may seek to change it through taxation. This requires only a slight modification of the elementary model. The simplest way to do this is to take money away from some households and give it to others. Each household is then free to allocate its income as it pleases.

For any given amount of redistribution the utility of households is presumably maximized by a general tax on the income of some households and grants of income to others rather than by taxing particular forms of spending or by subsidizing particular types of consumption. Mathematical proofs of this proposition are available and its plausibility is obvious. If a household is offered

---

[h]What would constitute a "fair" distribution of income has never been satisfactorily answered by economists or anyone else. One feature of the market system that makes it attractive to some is that a household's share of goods and services will be roughly proportional to its contribution to total output as evaluated by all households collectively.

[i]Note the analogy with the individual household's decision regarding vaccination.

a choice of either $100 or $100 worth of health care, it will prefer the former because it can use the additional income to buy more health care (if that is what it wants), but usually utility will be maximized by increasing consumption of many other commodities as well. Similarly, if a household is offered a choice between giving up $100 and giving up $100 worth of health care, its utility will be diminished less by the general tax on income.

Despite the obvious logic of the foregoing many nonpoor seem more inclined toward a reduction in inequality in the consumption of particular commodities (medical care is a conspicuous example) than toward a general redistribution of income.[13] Two reasons may explain this behavior. First, the non-poor may believe that significant externalities are associated with medical care (in addition to the psychic benefits of observing a reduction in inequality) that are not associated with other commodities. The earlier discussion indicated some grounds for skepticism concerning this belief.[j] A second reason may be that the nonpoor think they know better what will maximize the utility of the poor than do the poor themselves.

A special aspect of the problem arises when the emphasis is put on reducing inequality of access to medical care *per se* rather than raising the consumption of medical care by the poor. This goal may require rationing the amount available to the nonpoor as well as subsidizing the poor. One economist has argued that the British approach to health care through a national health service can best be understood in these terms.[14]

Compulsory insurance

At the extreme, the demand for reductions in inequality takes the form of an assertion that "health care is a right;" that if someone needs health care society has an obligation to provide it. To the extent that society honors that obligation, the incentive for households to provide for their own health care (as through voluntary insurance) is diminished. Those without insurance and especially those individuals who prior to their illness could have afforded the normal premium, become, in effect, "freeloaders" on the rest of society.

If this behavior is widespread, the only solutions are to make insurance compulsory or to modify the ethical imperative. Thus far the United States has opted for a little of each. Insurance is virtually compulsory for many through their employment contract; on the other hand, free care is made less attractive by means tests, long waiting lines, unpleasant surroundings and similar inconveniences.

---

[j] However, where medical care for the poor is tied to using them for teaching and research purposes, significant externalities are probably present.

Another argument advanced in favor of compulsory insurance is that it overcomes the problem of adverse selection. If insurance is completely voluntary it may be impractical to adjust each household's premium to its expected utilization. To the extent that uniform premiums are charged, however, households with lower than average expected utilization have an incentive to drop out and this process can continue until the plan collapses.

It seems likely that the United States will move further in the direction of compulsory insurance, but this development is likely to create new problems even as it solves others. It increases the incentive to reduce health care in the home and throws more of the burden on collectively provided care. If the money price of market-provided care goes to zero, people will tend to use more than the amount they would like to use if they were free to shift resources to satisfy other wants.

Some Limitations of the Model

The "taste" for health

It is becoming increasingly evident that many health problems are related to individual behavior. In the absence of dramatic breakthroughs in medical science the greatest potential for improving health is through changes in what people do and do not do to and for themselves. Household decisions concerning diet, exercise, smoking, drinking, work and recreation are of critical importance.

It is useful to distinguish between two different classes of decisions. The first consists of those that affect health, but without the decision maker's awareness of these effects. In such instances, public policies are needed to increase information. The question of how much of this activity can be justified can be answered (in principle) along the familiar lines of weighing incremental costs and benefits.

A more difficult problem is posed by those decisions that are made with full information available, and that, according to economists, reflect the household's "tastes." Tastes is a catchall term given by economists to the underlying preference patterns that determine demand at any given structure of income and prices. The overeater, the heavy smoker, the steady drinker are all presumably maximizing their utility, given their tastes. They may be knowingly shortening their lives. Should it be an object of public policy to try to change their tastes — to try to increase people's tastes for health? Economics can provide very little guidance in this area because economists have no way, even in principle, of saying what has happened to utility once tastes have changed. Economists are not, of course, alone in this dilemma. None of the other social sciences has a well-developed theory of preference formation or the capacity to make judgments about the relative merits of different social goals.

The issues involved are extremely complex. Tastes are not acquired at birth or formed in a vacuum. It seems that economists should make an effort to determine how the working of the economic system itself influences tastes. They should study the impact of advertising and other sales efforts on demand, and try to determine whether taxation or subsidies of such efforts and counter efforts are justified. Tastes are also undoubtedly influenced by the information and entertainment media, by the schools, by religious institutions and by other organizations that are either tax supported, subsidized through tax exemptions or regulated by government to some degree.

Another way of thinking about this problem has been proposed by Gary Becker and Robert Michael.[k] In their approach, all households have the same basic wants or "tastes." They try to satisfy these basic wants by producing "commodities" with the aid of purchased goods and services plus inputs of their own time. Households differ greatly in their ability to produce different "commodities" and these differences explain much of the observed differences in purchases of goods and services in the market.

This approach has been developed and applied to health by Michael Grossman.[15] In his model it is the household, not the physician or the hospital, that produces health. Health care and other goods and services (food, shelter) are used in the production of health and some goods (e.g., cigarettes) may have negative effects.

If one pursues this approach, it could be a legitimate aim of public policy to help households become more efficient producers of health.[16] The chief ways of doing this would be through health education and by providing more information about the health care that is purchased in the market. It is of some interest to note that the United States government currently assumes more responsibility for informing consumers about the quality of steaks they buy than about the quality of hospitals or physicians they use.

Behavior within households and firms

A significant shortcoming of the elementary model in analyzing health care is its treatment of the firm and the household as the basic elements of analysis. In recent

---

[k]But there would be no a priori case for favoring health over other commodities. The choice should depend upon relative costs and benefits.

years some economists have directed their attention to decision-making within the firm[17–19] and within the household.[2,20]

Attention to decision-making and allocation within the firm is particularly important if we are to try to understand one of the major institutions in health care, the nonprofit, voluntary hospital. It is relatively easy to identify several significant interest groups within the hospital — the board of directors, the management, the full-time medical staff, the attending staff — but it is more difficult to weigh their impact to formulate a predictive theory of hospital behavior. When the goals of the various interest groups are similar, the simple theory of the profit-maximizing firm may be adequate, but when they conflict, (e.g., the selection of cases for admission) such a theory is obviously incomplete.

Decision-making and allocation within the household also pose problems that have special relevance to health care. The quantity and quality of health care provided to children by parents differ greatly among households, even among households with equal incomes. The ability of parents to "produce" health for themselves and for their children seems to vary considerably. Society feels an obligation to protect the health rights of minors, but has found this difficult to do. The health care provided elderly parents by their children also varies greatly. The decline of family ties tends to shift some production of health care from households to firms, and part of the observed rising cost of health care in recent decades is undoubtedly attributable to such a shift; e.g., the growth of nursing homes.

Implications for Technologic Change

This paper has discussed health care in relation to the economic system. The conference, however, is primarily concerned with technologic change, so it is appropriate to conclude with an attempt to relate the preceding discussion to technology.

Certainly the most important point to be made is that the basic economic principles concerning resource allocation and utility maximization apply in a world of technologic change as well as in a static one. Neither blanket endorsement nor condemnation of technology is rational; every change in technology involves costs and benefits and wise social policy depends upon an accurate assessment of their relative magnitudes.

There is a widespread belief that the health care sector harbors many wonderful technologic changes that have not been diffused widely and rapidly enough. An opposing view has been advanced by Richard Nelson of Yale, one of the nation's leading students of the economics of technologic change. He has written, "In both defense and health there has been a lot of R and D, and technical change has been extremely rapid; but it also has been extremely expensive and poorly screened ... In health one has the strong impression that one of the reasons for rising health costs has been the proclivity of doctors and hospitals to adopt almost any plausible new thing — drugs, surgical methods, equipment — that increases capability in any dimension (and some for which even that isn't clear) without regard to cost."[21]

Nelson's view has considerable validity. The tendency toward rapid and indiscriminate adoption of innovations in the medical care field can be attributed in part to efforts of suppliers of the innovation, especially drug companies. Possibly the most important reason is the technologic imperative that influences medical choices.[22] This is instilled in physicians by their training, and reinforced by present systems of financing health care. It produces the attitude that if something can be done it should be done. Most medical decision-makers, be they physicians or hospital administrators, are not trained to weigh marginal benefits against marginal costs. Moreover, present methods of third party payment and provider reimbursement do not give them any inducement to acquire that ability. To be sure, patient pressure and the ethical imperative to do everything possible for the patient make this a complex problem. But a more rational approach could result in saving more lives and providing greater overall patient satisfaction.

Another popular misconception is that any change in health care technology that reduces labor requirements must be desirable. No such a priori assumption is warranted. A change in technology that is capital saving and labor intensive may be more valuable than the reverse, and a change that permits the substitution of two relatively unskilled workers for one highly skilled one may be more valuable than either.

The nature of technologic change can have profound effects on resource requirements, and some attention should be paid to this matter in granting funds for research and development. In choosing between two projects, for instance, it is not sufficient to consider only the importance of the problem and the probability of success. The granting agency should also consider what resources will be required to implement the solution if the project is successful.'[23] Some technologic advances, such as the antibiotic drugs, greatly reduced the demand for physicians' services. Others, such as organ transplants, greatly increased demand.[24]

Traditional societies resist or inhibit technologic change. Society probably errs in the opposite direction. We seem to be fascinated by technology and often look to it to solve problems when less expensive solutions lie elsewhere. This may be particularly true of health care. It is to be hoped that this conference, with its emphasis on technology, will not serve to divert attention from other fundamental questions concerning the organization and financing of health care and personal responsibility for health.

Consider the problem of hospital costs. Hundreds of millions are being spent to make hospitals more efficient through new technology, but the return is likely to be small compared to the savings possible now with existing technology through reductions in utilization. Most informed observers believe that on any given day approximately 20 percent of the patients in the average general hospital do not need to be there. Research probably will prove this to be a conservative estimate because it still assumes customary medical interventions, conventional lengths of stay and so forth.

What, for instance, is the appropriate length of stay after hernia surgery? A British team, in a carefully controlled study, showed that patients discharged one day after surgery did as well as those discharged after six days. Another British team compared surgical repair of varicose veins with injection compression sclerotherapy. The former method involves expensive hospitalization; the latter is done on an outpatient basis at minimum cost. Outcomes seem to be similar, (except that surgical patients lost four times as many days from work) and patients seem to prefer the injection/compression technique.[25]

No reasonable person would want to inhibit the development of new technologies or their application to health problems. But everyone concerned with American health care should realize that the most pressing problems are not centered around technology and their solutions will probably be found in other directions. As this paper has suggested, we need to make health care markets work better; we need to quantify and control the externalities that affect health; and we need to recognize the importance of individual behavior and personal responsibility for health. Substantial alterations in organization, financing and education are required to achieve these objectives.

These are the realities. Tomorrow's technology may help to bring about these changes, but let us not underestimate what is possible today if we have the will to do it. Let us not oversell technology. Let us not divert attention and misdirect energies that could be devoted to the complex task of creating a more equitable, more effective and more efficient health care system.

References

1. Samuelson, P. (XXX). *Economics.* McGraw-Hill Book Company: New York.
2. Becker, G. S. (1965). "A Theory of the Allocation of Time." *Economic Journal* **75**: 493–517.

3. Linder, S. B. (1970). *The Harried Leisure Class*. Columbia University Press: New York.

4. Pauly, M. V. and Redisch, M. (1969). *The Not-for-Profit Hospital as a Physicians' Cooperative*. Northwestern University, mimeographed.

5. Kessel, R. A. (1958). "Price Discrimination in Medicine." *Journal of Law and Economics* **1**: 20–53.

6. Arrow, K. J. (1969). "The Organization of Economic Activity: Issues Pertinent to the Choice of Market vs. Non-Market Allocations." In *The Analysis and Evaluation of Public Expenditures: The p.p.b. System,* Subcommittee on Economy in Government of the Joint Economic Committee, 91st Congress of the United States, First Session, Vol. 1, p. 62.

7. Feldstein, M. S. (1970). "The Rising Price of Physicians' Services." *The Review of Economics and Statistics* **52**: 121–133.

8. Hughes, E. F. X., Fuchs, V. R., Jacoby, J. and Lewit, E. (1972). "Surgical Work Loads in a Community Practice." *Surgery* **71**: 315–327.

9. Altman, S. H. (1970). "The Structure of Nursing Education and Its Impact on Supply," In *Empirical Studies in Health Economics,* ed. H. E. Klarman. The Johns Hopkins Press: Baltimore.

10. Yett, D. E. (1970). "The Chronic Shortage of Nurses: A Public Policy Dilemma." In *Empirical Studies in Health Economics*, ed. H. E. Klarman. The Johns Hopkins Press: Baltimore.

11. For a pioneering article see Stigler, G. (1961). "The Economics of Information." *Journal of Political Economy* **69**: 213–225.

12. Benham, L. (1971). *The Effect of Advertising on Prices*. Graduate School of Business, Chicago, mimeographed.

13. Pauly, M. V. (1971). *Medical Care at Public Expense: A Study in Applied Welfare Economics*. Praeger Publishers, Inc.: New York.

14. Lindsay, C. M. (1969). "Medical Care and the Economics of Sharing." *Economica,* **36**.

15. Becker, G. S. and Michael, R. T. (1970). *On the Theory of Consumer Demand*, mimeographed.

16. Grossman, M. (in press) *The Demand for Health: A Theoretical and Empirical Investigation*. National Bureau of Economic Research: New York.

17. Cyert, R. M. and March, J. G. (1964). "The Behavioral Theory of the Firm: A Behavioral Science-Economics Amalgam." In *New Perspectives in Organization Research*, ed. W. W. Cooper. John Wiley & Sons, Inc.: New York.

18. Simon, H. A. (1962). "New Developments in the Theory of the Firm." *American Economic Review* **52**: 1–15.

19. Williamson, O. E. (1970). *Corporate Control and Business Behavior*. Prentice-Hall, Inc.: Engle-wood Cliffs, New Jersey.

20. Gronau, R. (1971). "The Intrafamily Allocation of Time: The Value of the House wives' Time." Paper presented at the *National Bureau of Economic Research Conference on Research in Income and Wealth*.

21. Nelson, R. R. (1972). "Issues and Suggestions for the Study of Industrial Organizations in a Regime of Rapid Technical Change." In *Policy Issues and Research*

Opportunities in Industrial Organization, ed. V. R. Fuchs. National Bureau of Economic Research: New York.

22. Fuchs, V. R. (1968). "The Growing Demand for Medical Care." *New England Journal of Medicine* **279**(4): 190–195.

23. Weisbrod, B. A. (1971). "Costs and Benefits of Medical Research: A Case Study of Poliomyelitis." *Journal of Political Economy* **79**: 527–544.

24. Fuchs, V. R. and Kramer, M. J. (1971). "The Market for Physicians' Services in the United States." 1948–1968.

25. Ford, G. R. (1971). "Innovations in Care: Treatment of Hernia and Varicose Veins." In *Portfolio for Health*, ed. G. McLachlan. Oxford University Press: London, for Nuffield Provincial Hospitals Trust.

1.3

What Every Philosopher Should Know About Health Economics

The Great Health Care Debate of 1994 was like the uses of this world to Hamlet —
"weary, stale, flat, and unprofitable." Why did so much effort by so many produce so little
understanding and no reform? The finger of blame has pointed in many directions: "the
Clinton Plan was unworkable"; "the plan was poorly explained to the public"; "the political
strategy was misconceived"; "special interests triumphed over the general interest." Each
of these explanations has some merit, but I believe the fundamental reason has been
the unwillingness of policy makers and the public to make the difficult choices that are
inevitable if the U.S. is to improve its approach to health care. What are the difficulties?

If You Don't Know Where You're Going, Any Road Will Get You There

Part of the problem is that we have not decided what it is we want our health
care system to do. There are several possible goals or criteria for assessing the
performance of a health care system. Health economics suggests three dimensions
of "output": technological, public health, and access to service. In addition, each

Originally published in *Proceedings of the American Philosophical Society*, 140(2):185–194, 1996.
Copyright by American Philosophical Society.

of these must be considered from the perspectives of distributional equity and efficiency in the use of scarce resources.

Until now the U.S. system has emphasized pushing the technological frontier; we have the most advanced medical technologies in the greatest abundance. The U.S. is where the world's ambitious young physicians go for advanced training, and where the super-rich from Third World countries go when they want high-tech medical care. In this sense the U.S. has the best health care system in the world. But another way of judging the merits of a system is by the health of the population. This could be based on simple measures such as life expectancy or on more complex ones that take into account quality of life, as indicated by the absence of morbidity or disability.

From this perspective the U.S. ranks below average among economically developed countries, according to most measures. Physicians may argue that poor health levels in the United States are the result of social and cultural factors, and there is much truth in this argument. But if improvement in health is an important goal, and if physicians concede that they are not effective in modifying diet, exercise, drinking, and smoking, and that they are incapable of changing the physical and psychosocial environments that affect health, some reallocation of resources to research and services that have more impact on health may be in order.

Health *care* has always meant more than improving health outcomes. Particularly important are the caring function (sympathy and reassurance) and the validation function (provision of professional certification of health status). Until this century, the service, caring, and validation offered by health professionals were undoubtedly more valuable than their therapeutic interventions. Even today many health problems are either self-limiting or incurable, but people who are sick or in pain want access to physicians, nurses, and other health professionals. Thus, an important criterion for evaluating a health care system is the availability of services. Is it easy to get to see a physician? Or to reach one by telephone? How long does a bedridden hospital patient lie in urine before someone responds to a call? Do health aides regularly visit the homebound elderly? Are dying patients treated with compassion?

Each of the three dimensions of technology, public health, and service can be looked at from the perspective of distributional equity. All else held constant, many people believe that a more equal system is a better and more just system. Indeed, they might even be willing to sacrifice a little from one of the other goals in order to achieve more equality. Consider, for instance, a country that has an average life expectancy of seventy-six years, but that also has great inequality. Some of its citizens die in childhood or as young adults while others live past ninety years of age. Given any reasonable assumption about risk aversion, most people would prefer to be born into a country in which everyone lives to age seventy-five. Similar arguments can be made about the distribution of technology or of service.

Efficiency in the use of scarce resources is another criterion that can be applied to technology, public health, and the provision of services. At any given time, resources used for health care are not available for education, housing, automobiles, and the thousands of other goods and services that people want. Much of the criticism of the U.S. health care system arises because Americans spend 40 percent more than Canadians for health care, and the excess over European countries is even greater. In England, high-tech medicine is severely rationed, but the level of public health is about the same as in the U.S., and per capita spending for health care is less than half the American average. Without some consensus regarding the goals of our health care system it is unrealistic to expect any agreement about the means of achieving them.

There Are Two Necessary and Sufficient Conditions for Universal Coverage

Why are thirty-five million to forty million Americans without health insurance? There are only two logical explanations. First, most of them are too poor or too sick to afford the premiums. A family with an annual income of $15,000 or $20,000 per year is too affluent to qualify for Medicaid but can hardly afford to pay directly $5,000 for health insurance or to forego that amount in wages by seeking employment-based insurance. Even a middle income family with serious health problems cannot afford the very high premiums that would be actuarially appropriate, given their expected utilization of care.

Second, there are those who can afford to pay but are unwilling to do so. To achieve universal coverage there must be subsidization for the first group and compulsion for the second. No nation achieves universal coverage without subsidization and compulsion. Both elements are essential. Subsidies without compulsion will not work; indeed, they could make matters worse since the healthy flee from the subsidized common pool, only to return when they expect to use a great deal of care. Compulsion without subsidies would be a cruel hoax for the millions of poor and sick who cannot afford health insurance.

There are two principal ways to achieve universal coverage: an explicit tax earmarked for health care with implicit subsidies for the poor and sick, or mandates (an implicit tax) with explicit subsidies based on individual or family income. The U.S. could have universal coverage next year if the public (and the policy makers) were prepared to bite the bullet of subsidization and compulsion. Last year's policy debacle reflected, in part, the unwillingness of the administration and Congress to mount a meaningful, informative debate on this issue.

Cost-containment: "No Pain, No Gain"

There is widespread belief in the U.S. that expenditures for health care are too high and growing too rapidly. The basic facts are clear. In 1994 Americans spent about $3,600 per person for health care, for a total bill of close to one trillion dollars. By comparison, spending for education from kindergarten through graduate school was less than half as large, and defense expenditures were even smaller, about $280 billion. Over the last forty years health care expenditures have grown 3 percent per annum faster than expenditures for all other goods and services. If health spending continues to outpace the rest of the economy at that rate by 2030, the health sector will consume almost one-third of the Gross Domestic Product.

Why should the health sector's share of the GDP be a cause for concern? Every country must spend 100 percent of its GDP on something. If the U.S. spends a larger share on health care, Japan may spend a larger share on food, Canada on housing, and so on. There are, however, three good reasons for concern about costs. First, there is a presumption (well supported by economic theory and empirical research) that many of the health services currently utilized do not provide benefits to patients that are commensurate with their cost to society. Second, there is a growing body of evidence that suggests that the U.S. health care system uses more resources than necessary to produce the services it currently provides. The waste of resources occurs principally in two areas. First, compared with health care in other countries, the American system requires much more administration (including marketing, billing, and collection).[3] Second, there is considerable excess capacity of facilities, equipment, and specialized personnel.[2] In many American cities there are excess supplies of hospital beds, high-tech equipment, and certain procedure-oriented specialists; charges and fees remain high, however, and the excess capacity has persisted for decades. For example, in 1990 there were 113 California hospitals that offered open-heart surgery, but more than half of these units performed fewer than two hundred procedures per year, a level that experts believe is the minimum necessary for efficient, high-quality care. Another example: the lithotripter (a machine used to dissolve kidney stones) in the Wellesley Hospital in Toronto serves about fifty patients per week. The proliferation of lithotripters in California hospitals is so great that many have fewer than five cases per week.

The least important but still valid reason for cost containment is to eliminate abnormally high returns to some producers of health care goods and services. The drug industry, for instance, consistently earns a rate of return that is far above the average for other manufacturing industries. Also, American physicians enjoy higher earnings (relative to the average employed person) than do physicians in most other industrialized countries.

What can be done to contain health care spending? Expenditures are identically equal to the product of three terms: the quantity of services, the ratio of the quantity of resources to the quantity of services (the inverse of productivity), and the prices of the resources; i.e.,

$$EXP \equiv Q_{services} \cdot \frac{Q_{resources}}{Q_{services}} \cdot P_{resources}.$$

Thus, there are only three possible routes to lower costs: reduce services, produce the services with fewer resources, or cut the prices paid to the resources. Each route involves pain for someone.

Consider, for instance, a cutback in services. If the costs of the services to be eliminated are greater than their benefits, there is a gain to society as a whole. But services are not provided to society as a whole; they are received by particular individuals and groups. More than a third of all health care is provided to Americans aged sixty-five or over; any attempt to reduce this care would be vigorously resisted by the American Association of Retired Persons. The Children's Defense Fund would protest cutbacks in services to children; the veterans' organizations want more, not fewer, services for veterans, and so on. Advocacy groups concerned with specific diseases such as cancer or diabetes would surely oppose any reduction in services to the patients that they represent. Reductions in services are also usually opposed by those who provide them. Radiologists are not likely to recommend fewer radiological services, and transplant surgeons typically do not welcome measures to reduce the number of transplantations.

Improvements in efficiency, like reductions in services, also impose burdens on particular individuals and groups. Every dollar spent on administration is a dollar of income to someone; it should, therefore, come as no surprise that where one stands on "administrative waste" depends on where one sits. Elimination of excess capacity would undoubtedly inconvenience some patients, either because they would have to wait for procedures or they would have to travel a greater distance to obtain them. The pain experienced by physicians and drug companies when their income and profits are reduced is so obvious as to require no elaboration. Such reductions may also have negative effects on some patients through changes in the behavior of physicians, or in the research activities of the drug companies. In brief, the iron law of cost containment is "no pain, no gain."

The Fundamental Problem of Health Economics

The fundamental problem of health economics arises from a conflict between *risk aversion* and *moral hazard*. The utilization of medical care is highly concentrated and often difficult to predict for individuals. In any one year, 5 percent of the population accounts for more than 50 percent of all expenditures.[1] To avoid the risk of large medical bills, most people prefer payment of a known insurance premium. But when they are insured, people tend to use more medical care than when they are not. This is termed "moral hazard." The nature of the problem can be seen in Figure 1. The quantity of medical care (i.e., number of physician visits, hospital days, operations, prescriptions, and so on) is measured along the horizontal axis. The vertical axis is calibrated in terms of dollars. The marginal (incremental) benefit of additional units of care declines as the quantity of care increases. (The linear function is a simplifying assumption which does not change the nature of the argument.) Also, for simplicity, the marginal cost of each additional unit of care is assumed to remain constant.

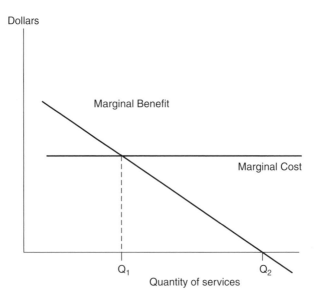

Fig. 1.   The Fundamental Problem of Health Economics.

What is the optimal amount of care? For a patient without insurance, the optimal amount is the level at which the marginal cost and the marginal benefit are equal, i.e., Q_1. If a patient were uncertain about the marginal benefit, a conscientious physician acting as a perfect agent of the patient would also recommend Q_1. From a social point of view Q_1 is also the optimal amount of care because of the equality between marginal cost and marginal benefit. Any smaller quantity of care would result in a marginal benefit greater than the marginal cost, and any amount greater than Q_1 would have the reverse effect.

Because people are typically risk-averse, they seek health insurance. But with full insurance, the marginal cost of care to a patient is zero, i.e., the horizontal axis. In that case the patient would want care up to the point where the marginal benefit is zero, i.e., Q_2. A conscientious physician, acting as a perfect agent of an insured patient, would also recommend Q_2, which is the technological optimum. The social optimum, however, is still at Q_1, where the marginal cost to society is equal to the marginal benefit.

Any care to the right of Q_2 has a negative marginal benefit, i.e., it does more harm than good; it is "unnecessary." Care between Q_1 and Q_2 is not "unnecessary," although the fact that the cost exceeds the benefit makes it socially undesirable. This is the fundamental problem; insured patients want Q_2, and their physicians would like to provide Q_2, but the extra cost is excessive, relative to the benefit. Every health plan, private or national, faces this problem, and no perfect solution for it has yet been found.

The Second Fundamental Problem of Health Economics

The conflict between risk-aversion and moral-hazard would pose a major problem even if everyone with the same medical condition had the same marginal benefit for any given amount of care, as depicted in Figure 1. But the problem is exacerbated when the marginal benefit differs among individuals, as shown in Figure 2. Differences in marginal benefit for a given medical condition arise for several reasons, the most important of which is differences in income. Individuals with higher income will usually place a higher value on care (i.e., have higher marginal benefits) than those with lower income. This is true for every level of care up to the point where the marginal benefit for all becomes zero. This amount (Q_2) is defined by the technology and is the same for all individuals. With this scenario we can see there is an additional conflict between pressure for equality of care across individuals as opposed to allowing freedom of choice and achieving closer correspondence between marginal cost and marginal benefit for each individual.

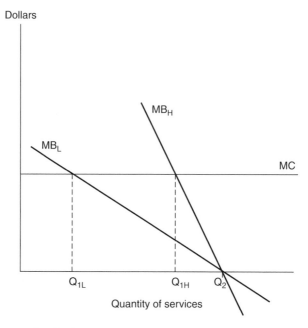

Fig. 2.   The Second Fundamental Problem of Health Economics.

We Must Learn to Cope With an Aging Society

At the beginning of this century there were ten children (under age eighteen) in the United States for every person age sixty-five or older. By 1960 the ratio had fallen to four to one; by 1990 it was two to one; and the ratio continues to fall. This demographic revolution has major implications for politics, economics, and social dynamics. The implications for health care are particularly striking because the elderly now consume almost 40 percent of all health care in the United States, and the proportion grows every year. In principle, the amount of health care that the elderly can consume is limited only by the imagination and ingenuity of scientists, physicians, drug companies, and other producers of health care goods and services. Beyond some age, which varies from person to person, almost every part of the body can benefit from repair or replacement. Rehabilitation therapy and assistance with daily living for the frail or disabled elderly create two other potentially huge sources of demand. What kind of health policy will keep insured elderly from demanding and receiving all of the care that might do them some good without regard to cost?

Currently there is considerable discussion and debate over the right to death with dignity. The goal is to give terminally ill patients or their families the right to refuse certain kinds of treatment that will prolong their dying. Some states are moving further; they propose to give terminally ill patients the right to request physician assistance in ending their lives. As financial and ethical pressures mount, we probably will see the right to death with dignity transformed into an expectation and eventually into an obligation. This development will create enormous stresses for patients and their families, health professionals, and government.

The nation must confront the question of not only how much health care to provide the elderly, but also what kind of care. Americans who turn sixty-five in 1995 can expect to receive, on average, about $200,000 worth of health care before they die. This estimate assumes no further inflation in health care prices and no further advances in technology; the actual figure will probably be larger. Much of this money will go for high-tech, high-cost interventions. Between one-fourth and one-third of the total will be spent in the last year of life. At the same time many of the sick elderly will suffer from a lack of low-tech, "high-touch" services such as visiting nurses and nurses' aides and will experience hardships with respect to housing, transportation, shopping, and social services. If the elderly, at age sixty-five, could choose the pattern of spending that they prefer, many might opt for a mix very different from the one they will actually receive. They might prefer more focus on the quality of life, even at the expense of a small decrease in average life expectancy.

In conclusion, neither the policy makers in Washington nor the public have been willing to make the difficult choices that are inevitable if the U.S. is to improve its approach to health care. These include establishing priorities for the health care system, accepting the necessity of subsidization and compulsion if we wish to achieve universal coverage, recognizing that containment of expenditures must impose burdens on patients and providers, coping with an aging society, and balancing the competing demands of efficiency, justice, freedom, and security.

References

1. Berk, M. L. and Monheit, A. C. (1992). "The Concentration of Health Expenditures: An Update." *Health Affairs* **11**(1): 145–149.
2. Fuchs, V. R. and Hahn, J. S. (1990). "How Does Canada Do It? A Comparison of Expenditures for Physicians' Services in the United States and Canada." *New England Journal of Medicine* **323**(13): 884–890; and Redelmeier, D. A. and Fuchs, V. R. (1993).

"Hospital Expenditures in the United States and Canada." *New England Journal of Medicine* **328**(11): 772–778.

3. Woolhandler, S. and Himmelstein, D. U. (1991). "The Deteriorating Administrative Efficiency of the U.S. Health Care System." *New England Journal of Medicine* **324**: 1253–1258; U.S. General Accounting Office (1991). *Canadian Health Insurance: Lessons for the United States.* U.S. Government Printing Office: Washington, DC, GAO/HRD-91-90.

1.4

The Future of Health Economics

This paper discusses health economics as a behavioral science and as input into health policy and health services research. I illustrate the dual role with data on publications and citations of two leading health economics journals and three leading American health economists. Five important and relatively new topics in economics are commended to health economists who focus on economics as a behavioral science. This is followed by suggestions for health economists in their role of providing input to health policy and health services research. I discuss the strengths and weaknesses of economics, the role of values, and the potential for interdisciplinary and multidisciplinary research. The fourth section presents reasons why I believe the strong demand for health economics will continue, and the paper concludes with a sermon addressed primarily to recent entrants to the field.

keywords: Health economics; Behavioral science; Health policy; Health services research.

The future of health economics depends heavily on how well health economists carry out two distinct albeit related missions: (a) enhancing understanding of economic behavior and (b) providing valuable input into health policy and health services research. This paper examines both roles and suggests ways to make them more fruitful in the years ahead.

Originally published in *Journal of Health Economics*, 19:141–157, 2000. Copyright by Elsevier Science B.V.

Although the focus is on the future, it is useful to note the tremendous expansion of the field in the past 35 years. In the US, the number of PhDs awarded annually in health economics has increased more than 12-fold since 1965. Health economists now hold regular faculty appointments in many leading economics departments as well as in schools of business, public policy, medicine, and public health. They also serve in important positions in government agencies that make health-related decisions. This expansion has been worldwide. The iHEA World Conference in Rotterdam in June 1999 attracted over 800 participants from 55 countries; just one-fourth came from the United States. The principal reasons for this rapid growth, I believe, have been intellectual advances, greater availability of data, and, probably most importantly, ever-increasing health care expenditures.[9]

There has also been a vast expansion of health economics as input into health policy and health services research. This expansion did not come easily at first. For example, my appointments to the President's Committee on Mental Retardation and the US Health Services Research Study Section in the mid-1960s were greeted with surprise and suspicion by many physicians, sociologists, psychologists, and other traditional participants in those domains. By the mid-1980s, however, US health economists were playing a dominant role in health policy and health services research because they were particularly well-equipped to help with the difficult choices facing public and private decision makers. To be sure, pockets of strong resistance to the application of economics to health problems remain. As I shall note later, some of that resistance is justified.

The Two Hats of Health Economics

The great British scientist, Lord Kelvin, said "When we cannot measure, our knowledge is meager and imperfect."[a] In order to throw some quantitative light on the "two hats" of health economics, I have categorized data on citations and publications by five types of journals: (1) economics (excluding health); (2) other disciplines (excluding economics and health); (3) health economics; (4) health policy and health services research; and (5) medical.[b] Table 1 shows the relative frequency of citations *in* the two leading health economics journals in 1996[c]

---

[a]Upon hearing this the American economic theorist, Jacob Viner, is supposed to have snorted "Even when we can measure, our knowledge is meager and imperfect."

[b]The sources, *Journal Citation Reports* and *Social SciSearch*® *at LANL*, include papers and citations from 1973 to 1999. There are approximately 1700 journals covered; they are predominantly but not exclusively English language publications.

[c]This year was chosen because the data were available to me in electronic form.

Table 1. Distribution of Citations *in Journal of Health Economics* and *Health Economics* in 1996, by Type of Journal.

Type of journal	Percent of citations[a]	
	JHE	HE
Economics (except health)	42	24
Other disciplines (not economics or health)	16	11
Health economics	16	16
Health policy and health services research	16	23
Medical	10	26
	100	100

[a]Journals with only one citation in JHE or HE were not included in the distributions.
Source: Journal Citation Reports, 1996, Social Science ed.

Table 2. Distribution of Citations *to Journal of Health Economics* and *Health Economics* in 1996, by Type of Journal.

Type of journal	Percent of citations[a]	
	JHE	HE
Economics (except health)	20	0
Other disciplines (not economics or health)	7	0
Health economics	30	31
Health policy and health services research	37	34
Medical	7	36
	100[b]	100[b]

[a]Journals with only one citation in JHE or HE were not included in the distributions.
[b]Totals may not equal 100 because of rounding.
Source: Journal Citation Reports, 1996, Social Science ed.

by type of journal. We see that 42% of the citations in the *Journal of Health Economics* were to economics journals (excluding health economics), while the papers in *Health Economics* drew less heavily on economics with only 24% of citations coming from that field. By contrast, *Health Economics* papers drew more heavily on health policy, health services research, and medical journals. The citations[d] *to* the *Journal of Health Economics* and *Health Economics* (Table 2) also reveal significant differences between the two journals. In 1996, there were no citations to *Health Economics* in either economics journals or journals of other

---

[d]The citations appeared in 1996, but could have referred to any publications in *JHE* and *HE* between 1973 and 1996.

disciplines such as statistics, demography, or operations research; by contrast, more than one-fourth of the citations to the *Journal of Health Economics* were in journals with no direct connection to the health field. Medical journals accounted for more than one-third of the citations to *Health Economics*, but only 7% of the citations to the *Journal of Health Economics*.

Tables 3 and 4 also illustrate the "two hat" nature of health economics by showing the distributions of papers and citations to papers of three leading American health economists whom I identified by conducting an informal survey

Table 3.   Distribution of Papers[a] of Three Leading American Health Economists[b] by Type of Journal.

| | Economist (percent of papers) | | |
Type of journal	A	B	C
Economics (except health)	51	30	18
Other disciplines (not economics or health)	13	4	6
Health economics	15	14	10
Health policy and health services research	13	41	36
Medical	8	10	30
	100	100[c]	100

[a]Published after 1972.
[b]PhD received after 1965.
[c]Totals may not always equal 100 because of rounding.
Source: Social SciSearch® at LANL, version 1.0 (Stanford University Libraries).

Table 4.   Distribution of Citations to Papers[a,b] of Three Leading American Health Economists[c] by Type of Journal in Which Citation Appeared.

| | Economist (percent of papers) | | |
Type of journal	A	B	C
Economics (except health)	30	27	16
Other disciplines (not economics or health)	23	21	9
Health economics	16	12	16
Health policy and health services research	14	29	41
Medical	18	12	18
	100[d]	100[d]	100

[a]First-authored papers only.
[b]Published after 1972.
[c]PhD received after 1965.
[d]Totals may not always equal 100 because of rounding.
Source: Social SciSearch® at LANL, version 1.0 (Stanford University Libraries).

of knowledgeable experts. The survey asked each respondent to name four or five health economists whose work has had the "most impact," with the respondents free to define impact as they wished. According to the replies, the economists represented in the tables are arguably *the* three leading American health economists of their generation, but given the informality of the survey and the subjective nature of the responses, I only claim that they are certainly *among* the leading scholars in the field. It is also worth noting that I chose only economists who received their PhDs after 1965 and who have made their reputations entirely, or almost entirely, in health economics.

All three scholars have published from 10% to 15% of their papers in health economics journals *per se*. But otherwise, the distributions of their papers vary enormously, with Economist A publishing almost two-thirds in economics and other nonhealth disciplines and C publishing only one-fourth in those two types of journals. By contrast, C published two-thirds in health policy, health services research, and medical journals compared to A's one-fifth in those three types of journals. Economist B's distribution of papers is intermediate between A and C. Not surprisingly, the same qualitative differences emerge in Table 4 for the distribution of citations[e] to the papers of the three economists, but the differences are not as great as in Table 3. One possible explanation for the greater differences in Table 3 is that the results include *all* papers, whereas the distribution of citations in Table 4 is based on first-authored papers only. Also, because citations to an author's work tend to be concentrated on a relatively small number of papers, it would not be surprising if the pattern of citations differed substantially from the pattern of publications.

The comparisons between the journals or among the health economists are not intended to suggest that one pattern of publication or citation is "better" than another. In my view, both "hats" are important. Health economists should strive for and respect high quality research whether it advances economics in general or contributes more directly to health policy and medical care.

Health Economics as Behavioral Science

As the data in first section suggest, some health economists stay closer to economics as a behavioral science while others give more emphasis to health policy and health services research. Moreover, the same scholar may develop a diversified research portfolio that shifts in emphasis from time to time. For those whose research bent lies in the direction of economics as behavioral science, I

---

[e]The citations appeared in 1990–1999 covering first-authored papers published from 1973 to 1999.

would like to suggest five areas where I believe health economists can make a significant contribution: endogenous technology and preferences, social norms, principal-agent problems, behavioral economics, and measurement and analysis of quality of life.[f]

Endogenous technology and preferences

Traditionally, standard economic models focus on the normative and positive aspects of maximization, taking technology and preferences as given. The assumption of exogenous technology and preferences may be reasonable for a good deal of economic analysis, but there is increasing awareness that for some problems the assumption is not warranted. Fifty years ago, Jacob Schmookler began an ambitious program of empirical research on the question of technology. He concluded that "technological change... is usually not apart from the normal processes of production and consumption, but a part of them" (Samuelson, 1948, p. 207). Recently, economists interested in economic growth have been emphasizing endogenous technology, but there has been only a little effort to apply this concept to medical care. It should not be difficult to show that the character, shape, and pace of medical innovations are influenced by market forces as well as by exogenous scientific discoveries.

Systematic research on the (partial) endogeneity of preferences is more recent,[16] but is already evident in the work of numerous economists spanning the ideological and methodological spectrums.[3,5] Attempts to uncover the endogenous aspects of technology and preferences in health and medical care could be extremely fruitful; the empirical results generated by health economists could enrich the mainstream literature.

Social (including professional) norms

The endogeneity of preferences is closely related to an exciting and relatively new area of economic research, the role of social norms in economic behavior. There is increasing awareness that social norms can affect consumer demand, labor force participation, employer–employee relations, and many other kinds of economic interactions (see Akerlof and Yellen, 1990). According to Assar Lindbeck, social norms in Sweden in the second half of the twentieth century were strongly influenced by the economic policies of the welfare state.[17,18] Sociologists and anthropologists have long recognized that social norms affect attitudes toward

---

[f]This list is not meant to be exhaustive. These five areas look particularly promising to me.

health and the use of medical care. Health economists could profitably incorporate this perspective into their analyses.

Professional norms are an aspect of social norms that are particularly important in health care. They can play a key role in ameliorating many imperfections in medical markets, as Arrow (1963) noted, but this theme has not been adequately developed in the health economics literature. Moreover, many policy analysts mistakenly ignore such norms in their preoccupation with debating the merits of competition vs. government regulation. Given the complex and dynamic nature of medical technology and the highly personal and emotionally charged character of many medical encounters, neither competition nor regulation, alone or in combination, can provide an adequate basis for the social control of medical care.[12] I believe professional norms are a critical third element.

Principal–agent problem

Unlike the relatively unexplored role of social norms, the principal–agent problem occupies a well-established niche in economic theory[15,21] and has been fruitfully applied to problems ranging from executive compensation to economic development. The physician–patient relationship appears to epitomize the principal–agent problem and warrants intensive study by economists.[20] More recently another form of the principal–agent problem has emerged in health care, namely the relation between physicians and their managed care organizations. Research on physicians as agents of their patients and their organizations would nicely complement research on professional norms.

Behavioral economics

The pioneering work in behavioral economics was done mostly by psychologists, especially Daniel Kahneman and Amos Tversky.[14,29] Economist Richard Thaler also deserves credit for forcing economists to confront behaviors that are not adequately encompassed in standard models.[27,28] This literature emphasizes the importance of relative rather than absolute levels of outcomes, a disproportional aversion to losses compared with desire for gains, the roles of fairness, reciprocal altruism and revenge, systematic biases in judgment, and the importance of framing. An excellent review of this literature was recently published by Rabin (1998). I do not believe that behavioral economics will replace standard models for most problems, but there are some areas where new insights could substantially increase understanding. Health and medical care appear to be prime candidates for benefitting from attention to behavioral economics because uncertainty is rampant, stakes are often high, and trade-offs are often difficult.

Quality of life: Measurement and analysis

The fifth and final item on my list of promising areas for future work is the measurement and analysis of quality of life. This is not a subject, however, where mainstream economics has a great deal already "on the shelf." On the contrary, health economists who work on quality of life issues are probably ahead of their mainstream colleagues.[7] The challenge to health economists is to use their results to give substance to the vast but mostly amorphous literature on utility.

Economics as Input to Health Policy and Health Services Research

Economics is a necessary input to good health policy (macro or micro), but to be most effective it usually must be supplemented by insights from other disciplines and by explicit attention to values.

Strengths of economics

The greatest strengths of economics and economists are a framework of systematic theory, an array of concepts and questions that are particularly relevant to the choices facing policy makers, and skill in drawing inferences from imperfect data. Because health economists often take standard economic theory for granted (like being able to walk or talk), it is easy to underestimate the advantage this framework offers economics over the other social and behavioral sciences. When economists encounter a new problem, one with which they have had no previous experience, they immediately have a way to begin thinking about it long before data collection begins. Scholars in the other "policy sciences" do not.[g] They typically require some detailed knowledge of the particular problem before they can begin to think productively about it. Economists' framework of systematic theory facilitates the transfer of knowledge drawn from other fields of study to the health field.

Health economists have also inherited from economics a set of concepts and questions that have proven to be particularly relevant to the policy problems

---

[g] I base this in part on having spent two years as a Fellow at the Center for Advanced Study in the Behavioral Sciences, where I interacted regularly with some of the nation's leading psychologists, sociologists, political scientists, and anthropologists.

that have emerged in health during the past three decades. Scarcity, substitution, incentives, marginal analysis, and the like were "just what the doctor ordered," although in many cases the "patient" found the medicine bitter and failed to follow the prescribed advice.

Another strength of economists is skill at drawing inferences from imperfect data. Indeed, a standard joke among sociologists is that "there are no data so bad that an economist won't use them." To some extent that's true. Economists take pride in the fact that they can frequently massage poor quality data so as to draw some reasonable inferences from them. But such statistical legerdemain has a downside; many economists neglect the important task of trying to get better data. Even if the conclusions don't change, results based on better data will command more respect in policy circles, and that alone can justify the effort.

Weaknesses of economics

Economists have many strengths, but scholars in the other behavioral sciences are better at some aspects of research. For instance, psychologists have been successfully carrying out controlled experiments for generations. In recent years a few economists[13] have been developing *experimental* economics and this approach bears watching to see if any new important findings emerge. *Survey research* is another approach where health economists could learn from others, especially sociologists and political scientists who have extensive experience at designing and administering surveys, choosing samples, and the like. Sometimes health economists could profitably incorporate survey research in their efforts to contribute to health policy.

Also, many economists do not pay enough attention to institutions. Institutions *matter,* and sometimes they matter a great deal, particularly in health care. I'll illustrate this by considering two alternative methods for financing a national health plan. One way is with a payroll tax of 7% earmarked for health care. The second approach is a mandatory contribution of 7% of payroll earmarked for health care. Most economists would see little difference between those two approaches. Many would say that they are identical.[h] But in the real world they could be very different. Why? Because the first plan would probably be administered by the Ministry of Finance (the Department of Treasury in the US), while the second plan would be administered by the Ministry of Social Insurance or its equivalent (the Department of Health and Human Services in the US). Depending on the country, people might have very different judgments

---

[h] And might be little non-economists who fail to see the equivalence.

about whether their health insurance plan should be administered by the finance department or by the social insurance department. Overseas, I've met people who say, "In my country I wouldn't trust the finance ministry as far as I could throw them. I want that money to go into social insurance." In the United States, many people would have more confidence in the Treasury than in Health and Human Services. Moreover, even within the same country different individuals and different interest groups would probably differ in their preferences.

Institutions matter in part because history matters. Consider, for example, health insurance in Canada and in the US. It is not possible to understand why these two countries have such sharply divergent approaches without familiarity with their histories.[19] Moreover, language matters. Health economists need look no farther than the phrase "employer-provided health insurance" to see how language can mislead the public and distort policy discussions. Economists have been very good at showing the world the importance of economic incentives, even in health. But we err if we think that *only* incentives matter. To be more useful in the arena of health policy and health services research, economists need to pay more attention to institutions, history, and language.[23]

Interdisciplinary and multidisciplinary research

The preceding discussion of the strengths and weaknesses of economics suggests that health policy and health services research require inputs from many disciplines, i.e., interdisciplinary or multidisciplinary research. The former is very difficult to execute but the latter is quite feasible, and often very necessary. To understand why interdisciplinary research is so difficult, we must ask what it is that distinguishes one discipline from another. Most important, in my view, are the *concepts* that the discipline uses. To appreciate this point, I suggest that you try the following experiment. Ask a few leading economists of your acquaintance to write down the 10 to 20 most important concepts in economics. Then ask a few leading psychologists, sociologists, and political scientists to do the same thing. You will find that there is almost no overlap in the lists of concepts. The concepts that we think are important do not appear on their lists, and vice-versa. This discordance makes true interdisciplinary research — a blending and fusion of concepts — unlikely.

The next most distinguishing feature of a discipline is the *questions* it seeks to answer. Again, ask representatives from the different behavioral sciences "What are the most important, the most central, the most enduring questions in your field?" and wide differences in the answers will be apparent across the disciplines. There may be a little more overlap of questions than concepts, but basically the different disciplines have different interests. The philosopher Haack (1998, p. 59) points out that disciplines are like maps; different maps answer different questions. Suppose you are planning a trip to Northern California. You would almost surely want a map that showed the roads and highways, cities and towns, the locations of airports, and so on. But you might also be interested in hiking and camping and fishing, so you would also want another map — a topographical map which shows altitudes, the location of lakes, rivers, and campgrounds. It is also possible that you would want to consult a meteorological map to learn about expected temperatures and precipitation, and one can imagine still other maps (e.g., one showing places of historical and cultural interest). One map is no "better" than another; they simply serve different purposes. The same is true of disciplines. They attempt to answer different questions, all of which may be relevant to a policy decision.

In addition to differences in concepts and questions, the disciplines also differ in their methods. To oversimplify, economists are good at building models, at econometrics, and at teasing inferences from "natural experiments." Psychologists are masters of the controlled experiment, while sociologists and political scientists have expertise in survey research. Interdisciplinary research in the behavioral sciences thus far has largely taken the form of borrowing methods. One of my colleagues in political science, for example, tells his graduate students, "We have some good questions, but if you want to learn how to answer them, go take the econometrics sequence." Many sociologists have begun to import econometric methods. Some economists have made considerable investments in survey research and others have been conducting controlled experiments. The exchange of methods is no doubt useful, but so long as the disciplines employ distinct concepts and address different questions, true interdisciplinary research will remain elusive.

Multidisciplinary research, on the other hand, is very feasible and often necessary. It involves policy analysts drawing on the results of studies from several disciplines and integrating these results. This approach will usually provide more understanding and contribute to better decisions than would be possible through reliance on a single discipline.

The role of values

Finally, I come to the role of values, and offer two cautionary comments. First, when doing research, be aware of your values and guard against allowing them to bias your research. Values can shape framing of the problem, choice of data, and judgment concerning the reliability of the results. A good scholar will try as much as possible to keep his or her values from influencing the research. Second, when making policy recommendations, be as explicit as possible about the respective roles of your *analysis* and your *values* in those recommendations. Economists are naive if they expect that good economic research with strong results will translate immediately into policy. Policy depends on analysis *and* on values; sensitivity to that interaction will make economists more useful contributors to health policy.

Will the Bull Market in Health Economics Continue?

Health economics has enjoyed several decades of remarkable growth, but will this bull market continue? Several trends suggest to me that it *will*, at least for the next decade or two.

Factors fueling the demand for health economics

First, there will be a growing gap between what medicine *can* do and what it is *economically feasible* to do. Because technological change is, in part, endogenous, the gap is not likely to widen indefinitely, but there will be a lag between the constraints imposed by financial limits and their effect on the flow of medical advances. The outpouring of expensive new drugs and procedures that are already in the R&D pipeline will make the necessity for choice starker and more urgent. Decision makers at all levels will inevitably look to economics, the discipline that emphasizes trade-offs and provides a rigorous way of thinking about them.

Second, aging populations will put more pressure on health care resources. In the United States, people over 65 consume three to four times as much medical care per capita as people under 65, and those 85 and over consume three times as much as those 65 to 69. Given the trends in medical technology and demography, the problem of financing health care for the elderly will soon equal and then surpass the problem of financing retirement.[10]

Third, the recent large increase in resources devoted to technology assessment, outcomes research, and evidence-based medicine centers will create a much richer database. These better data will make economic analyses more reliable and more widely accepted.

Finally, I believe that the current anti-egalitarian trends evident in most modern societies will also increase the demand for health economics. Although the dominant trend in what is loosely called the "West" over the last several hundred years has been egalitarian, I believe that the last 20 years have been marked by a halt and even a reversal of the trend toward greater economic equality. In his classic textbook, *Economics,* Samuelson[24] noted that every society faces three basic economic questions: What?, How? and For Whom? In a completely egalitarian health care system, the "What?" and "How?" questions require economic analysis, but the "For Whom?" question is irrelevant. If the health care system is *not* egalitarian, however, distributive questions are also important for both analysis and policy. Economics cannot offer definitive solutions to questions of distribution, but economists can help analyze the causes and the consequences of changes in distribution.

Reasons for anti-egalitarian trend

Anti-egalitarian policies are fueled by several forces that apply to the economy as a whole: the growth of international business competition, an increasing awareness of some negative consequences of the welfare state, the collapse of socialist economies in Eastern Europe, and the absence of major wars. Several other reasons are specific to health care. First, there is a growing awareness that socioeconomic differentials in health status are not primarily related to access to medical care. One of the major arguments advanced in support of national health insurance plans was that they would eliminate or at least substantially reduce the strong association between socioeconomic status and health. Many decades of experience, however, have demonstrated the inability of egalitarian plans to achieve these objectives.[8] It is still possible to argue in favor of equal access to health care on other grounds, but it is not possible to contend that equal access to health care equalizes health outcomes.

Second, many of the medical innovations that have appeared in recent years are addressed primarily to improving the *quality* of life, not to *extending* life.[i] The original rationale for equal access to medical care was that everyone ought to have an equal chance to live, regardless of economic position. But as the emphasis shifts from extending life to improving its quality, it is questionable whether medical care will get the egalitarian priority that it now gets under the old rationale of extending life. If society wants to improve the quality of life for the poor, there are many other areas requiring attention, including education, housing, transportation, and public safety.

The third reason is a growing awareness of the *probabilistic* nature of medical services. Whether one considers preventive, diagnostic, therapeutic, or rehabilitative interventions, there is rarely certainty regarding outcomes. In an influential pioneering book, Cochrane[6] wrote, "All medical care that's effective

---

[i]Examples include drugs to treat baldness and erectile dysfunction.

should be free to all." No country can come close to following that precept today. There are literally thousands of medical interventions that have *some* effectiveness; i.e., that have some probability of doing some good for some patients. The probability ranges from very low to very high, depending on the intervention and the patient. In such a world, questions of access become much more complicated for analysis and policy. Most people will find the case for equal access to interventions with a high probability of success more compelling than for interventions with low probability. To be sure, probability of success is not the only relevant criterion; the magnitude of the effect of a successful intervention on well-being is also important. In addition, decision makers need to consider the possibility of heterogeneity in patient preferences with regard to extension of life, restoration of function, relief of symptoms, and side effects of the intervention. Thus, questions about where to draw the line, and whether the same line should or could apply to all, will challenge analysts and policy makers for the foreseeable future.

Concluding Homilies

I conclude this essay on the future of health economics by offering five homilies distilled from almost a half century of teaching and research.

Remember your roots

Most of the readers of this essay were economists before they were health economists. Much of your intellectual strength and ability to do good work in the health field comes from your training in economics. If you maintain those ties and keep up with the major advances in economics, you will be able to sustain your effectiveness over a long career. If you simply live off your accumulated capital, you will eventually run dry. Moreover, at least some health economists should try to nourish their economic roots by feeding back their theoretical or empirical results into the economics mainstream.

Learn a great deal about health care technology and institutions

A solid working knowledge of economics is necessary, but rarely sufficient to be an effective health economist. When I asked a representative sample of leading American theorists to answer some basic questions regarding health economics, their replies, on average, were only slightly better than could be obtained by tossing a coin.[9,j] Any economist who is serious about health economics must learn a great deal about health care technology and institutions.

Work hard and, more importantly, work smart

"Keep up with economics." "Learn more about health." How can one person do all that and still complete some research? Working hard is an obvious, but probably superfluous, answer. It is difficult to get through graduate school without learning how to work hard. Working smart is different. In my experience you don't learn how to work smart in graduate school. Almost the reverse is true. You're expected to learn everything, to master a huge array of theoretical results and techniques, with little regard for their validity or relevance.[k] Working smart is just the opposite. It requires the ability to discriminate, to choose what to learn, from a torrent of new work. Economic theory is very important, but much new work at any given time is faddish and self-referential, the intellectual equivalent of flexing one's muscles on the beach.[l] A similar story can be told about medical research. Tens of thousands of medical articles are published every year; many of them contradict some previously published article. Working smart means learning how to identify what is important and relevant. No health economist can stay on top of two entire literatures. Cultivate the ability to be selective in the seminars and conferences you attend, selective in the review articles that you read, selective in the experts you consult. The goal is to capture *most* of what is valuable and relevant in new mainstream economics and in medicine.

Don't try to be a scholar and a player at the same time

A player is someone who is actively participating in a partisan, political process. A scholar is trying to enhance understanding, without fear or favor. Both roles are important for society, and the same person can fill both at different times,[m] but it is not possible to be an effective player and a first-rate scholar simultaneously. Successful players and scholars have some characteristics in common,[n] but the two roles also require different skills and virtues. The most

---

[j]Practicing physicians (who presumably have little or no training in economics) did equally poorly on the same questions.

[k]A leading economics professor told me that he felt obliged to teach graduate students a currently "hot" theory even if he believed it was wrong because the students would be expected to know the theory when they entered the job market.

[l]See Blinder (1999) for a similar view.

[m]Many good scholars have gone on to become effective players. It is rare for someone to be a player for an extended period and then produce high quality scholarship.

important quality for a player is loyalty to the team, and especially to the captain of the team. An economist-player who cannot put aside reservations, qualifications, and questions about the team's policy will soon be marginalized as a player. Another important attribute is speed. The economist-player who can devise a new policy initiative overnight or who can identify the weaknesses in the other side's proposals even as they are being made will often carry the day. Finally, a player must be tough, must have sharp elbows. Toughness is needed to win intra-team squabbles and to withstand the slings and arrows of the other side. Loyalty, speed, and toughness are not necessarily incompatible with the role of a scholar, but great scholarship usually requires a different set of virtues.

Cultivate the scholarly virtues

Excellence in research requires many virtues, but three are preeminent. The first is honesty, in two senses. A scholar must be self-consciously honest in carrying out research. This means confronting the limitations and qualifications of one's own data and methods. In addition, a scholar must strive for honesty in reporting the results of research. A second virtue is courage, again in two senses. Scholars should not be timid about the choice of problems or the method(s) of attack. "Faint heart never won fair lady" — or produced great research. Once the research is complete, courage is required to present and defend the results, especially when they challenge current opinion. The third scholarly virtue is patience, and again it is needed in two senses. A few great scientific advances come quickly, but most are the result of years and often decades of intense and persistent work. Beware the temptation to become a member of the "paper-of-the-month" club. If you have chosen a worthy problem, devote whatever time is required to get it right, be it a semester or a decade. And finally, have patience in waiting for acceptance of your results. The economics literature is studded with examples of major articles that were rejected when first submitted.[26] Even when a significant result is published, the world often will not immediately snap to attention and salute you. But if your work is valid and relevant, and if you are patient, people will eventually take notice and your efforts will bear fruit.

In my experience, health economics can be intellectually stimulating, socially useful, and personally rewarding. It has been a privilege and a pleasure to work in the field. To this possibly biased observer, the future of health economics looks extremely bright.

---

[n] e.g., intelligence, creativity, stamina, and the ability to communicate effectively.

References

1. Akerloff, G. A. and Yellen, J. L. (1990). "The Fair Wage-Effort Hypothesis and Unemployment." *Quarterly Journal of Economics* **105**: 255–283.
2. Arrow, K. (1963). "Uncertainty and the Welfare Economics of Medical Care." *American Economic Review* **53**: 941–973.
3. Becker, G. S. and Mulligan, C. B. (1997). "The Endogenous Determination of Time Preference." *Quarterly Journal of Economics* **112**: 729–758.
4. Blinder, A. S. (1999). *Economics Becomes a Science — Or Does It?* Princeton University mimeo.
5. Bowles, S. (1998). "Endogenous Preferences: The Cultural Consequences of Markets and Other Economic Institutions." *Journal of Economic Literature* **36**: 75–111.
6. Cochrane, A. L. (1972). "*Effectiveness and Efficiency: Random Reflections on Health Services.*" Nuffield Provincial Hospitals Trust: London.
7. Dolan, P. (1999). "The Measurement of Health-Related Quality of Life for Use in Resource Allocation Decisions in Health Care." In *Handbook of Health Economics* eds. Newhouse, J. P. and Culyer, A. J. Elsevier: North Holland, Amsterdam.
8. Fuchs, V. (1991). "National Health Insurance Revisited." *Health Affairs* **Winter**: 7–17.
9. Fuchs, V. (1996). "Economics, Values, and Health Care Reform." *The American Economic Review* **86**: 1–24.
10. Fuchs, V. (1998) "Provide, Provide: The Economics of Aging". In Medicare Reform: Issues and Answers, Saving, T. R. and Rattenmaier, A., eds. University of Chicago Press: Chicago.
11. Haack, S. (1998). "Between the Scylla of Scientism and the Charybdis of Apriorism." In The Philosophy of Sir Peter Strawson (Library of Living Philosophers), ed. Hahn, L. Open Court: LaSalle, IL.
12. Iglehart, J. K. (1998). "Physicians as Agents of Social Control: The Thoughts of Victor Fuchs." *Health Affairs* **17**: 90–96.
13. Kagel, J. H. and Roth, A. E. (eds.) (1995). *The Handbook of Experimental Economics* Princeton University Press: Princeton, NJ.
14. Kahneman, D. and Tversky, A. (1979). "Prospect Theory: An Analysis of Decision Under Risk." *Econometrica* **47**: 263–291.
15. Krebs, D. (1990). *A Course in Economic Theory*, Chap. 16. Princeton University Press: Princeton.
16. Lindbeck, A. (1995). "Welfare State Disincentives with Endogenous Habits and Norms." *Scandinavian Journal of Economics* **47**: 457–494.
17. Lindbeck, A. (1997). "The Swedish Experiment." *Journal of Economic Literature* **35**: 1273–1319.
18. Lindbeck, A., Nyberg, S. and Weibull, J. W. (1999). "Social Norms and Economic Incentives in the Welfare State." *Quarterly Journal of Economics* **114**: 1–35.
19. Lipset, S. M. (1990). *Continental Divide*. Routledge. New York.
20. McGuire, T. G. (1999). "Physician Agency". In *Handbook of Health Economics*, Newhouse, J. P. and Culyer, A. J. eds. Elsevier: North Holland, Athsterdam.
21. Pratt, J. W. and Zeckhauser, R. J. (eds.) (1985). *Principals and Agents*. Harvard Business School Press: Boston.

22. Rabin, M. (1998). "Psychology and Economics." *Journal of Economic Literature* **36**: 11–46.

23. Romer, P. M. (1996). "Preferences, Promises, and the Politics of Entitlement." In Individual and Social Responsibility: Child Care, Education, Medical Care, and Long-Term Care in America, ed. Fuchs, V. R. University of Chicago Press: Chicago.

24. Samuelson, P. (1948). *Economics*. McGraw-Hill: New York.

25. Schmookler, J. (1966). *Invention and Economic Growth*. Harvard University Press: Cambridge, MA.

26. Shepherd, G. and Gans, J. S. (1994). "How are the Mighty Fallen: Rejected Classic Articles by Leading Economists." *Journal of Economic Literature* **8**(Winter): 65–179.

27. Thaler, R. H. (1991a). *The Winner's Curse*. Free Press: New York.

28. Thaler, R. H. (1991b). *Quasi-Rational Economics*. Russell Sage Foundation: New York.

29. Tversky, A. and Kahneman, D. (1991). "Loss Aversion in Riskless Choice: A Reference-Dependent Model." *Quarterly Journal of Economics* **106**: 1039–1061.

Op-Ed

Major Concepts of Health Care Economics

This article applies major economic concepts, such as supply, demand, monopoly, monopsony, adverse selection, and moral hazard, to central features of U.S. health care. These illustrations help explain some of the principal problems of health policy-high cost and the uninsured — and why solutions are difficult to obtain.

Health care should be viewed from many perspectives: biological, ethical, political, and economic. The economic perspective is distinct primarily in the concepts that it uses.[1,2] This article applies several major economic concepts to important features of U.S. health care to help noneconomists increase their understanding of current problems of health policy.

The discipline of economics focuses primarily on the operation of a "market-price" economy, so named because the interaction of supply and demand determines the prices (and quantities) of inputs and outputs in markets. Prices serve as signals that influence the behavior of suppliers and demanders. In his seminal book The *Wealth of Nations,* Adam Smith analyzed how such an economy works and argued that this system is the best route to economic success and

Originally published in *Annals of Internal Medicine*, 162:380–383, 2015. Copyright by American College of Physicians.

personal freedom. In his day (1776), most major markets like those for wheat and bread were relatively simple. Today, the markets in some industries are exceedingly complex, and perhaps none more so than in health care.

A primary focus of health care economics is to identify what determines quantity, price, and expenditures (the product of quantity and price). A related goal is to determine whether the quantity, price, or both substantially differ from what would prevail if the industry produced the socially most appropriate amount of care at as low a total cost to society as possible. In calculating social costs and benefits, economists include externalities that arise when producers or consumers make choices that do not consider the effects on others, such as the external costs of pollution or the external benefits of vaccination.

For the economist, the optimum circumstance is when the marginal benefit and marginal cost of health care are equal — any greater amount would use resources that could be more beneficial elsewhere. However, this is difficult to assess. There is not 1 market for health care but many thousands, differentiated by such factors as disease, technology, location, and physician and patient characteristics. In thinking about cost, economists include "opportunity cost," which could be forgone earnings, as an important part of the expense of medical education and training.

Supply

Because supply and demand determine quantity and price, it is useful to identify important special features that affect health care supply and demand in the United States. The prices of many inputs to health care, such as brand-name prescription drugs and specialist fees, are higher in the United States than in peer countries.[3,4] Higher prices for drugs, devices, and equipment (or, more specifically, lower prices in other countries) are primarily the result of central buying in those countries. In economic terms, the quasi-monopoly power that drug manufacturers achieve through patents and marketing is offset in other countries by the monopsony power of governments that typically pay for approximately 75% of care.

The U.S. government pays for approximately 50% of care but is restrained from negotiating with suppliers for lower prices by legislation and industry lobbying. Physician specialists in the United States sustain higher fees through various organizational devices, including consolidation of practices and professional control of entry, lack of transparency of fees, and the difficulty that patients have in determining the need for and quality of care. Other countries negotiate fees with physicians and control access to specialists to keep expenditures down.

Higher output prices (for procedures, visits, and tests) reflect higher input prices but are also of concern because they vary greatly in what seems to be the same market. They differ among providers in the same market and patients of the same provider.[5] The ability to price-discriminate, that is, to charge different patients different prices for the same service, is prima facie evidence of some monopoly power. Sellers increase profits by setting prices high for buyers who do not have good alternatives and lower for those who do. Mergers and acquisitions have often been a route to greater market control by hospitals. Vertical integration, the merging of hospital and physician groups into a single entity, has also been questioned by antitrust regulators but may cause substantial gains in production efficiency that more than offset any potential increase in monopoly power. Indeed, some of the most efficient care in the country is delivered by organizations that have integrated hospitals, physicians, and insurance.[6]

Determining the most efficient size of an organization to deliver care because of economies of scale is one of the most difficult factors in economic analyses of health care. That a 100-bed hospital is likely to have lower costs than one with 50 beds for similar care is axiomatic because the larger hospital can spread the overhead costs of some central services, such as pharmacy, laboratory, and radiography, over more patients. For care that requires expensive technology and specialized personnel, the economies of scale may justify a much larger hospital. However, greater size often brings greater power to extract a monopoly price from buyers, and in some large hospitals, diseconomies of scale set in as result of difficulties of communication and coordination and escalating costs of administration. That some hospitals can specialize in 1 kind of care, such as cardiac surgery, to achieve optimal scale and efficiency further complicates the policy problem. Such specialization shifts the burden and cost to general hospitals that must be able to care for all kinds of patients. A hospital's costs increase when it must care for a wide variety of health problems, each with its own optimal scale.

A considerable amount of care in the United States is probably produced at an inefficient scale, particularly if one considers the related problem of failure to use the most efficient combination of inputs. The possibility of substitution among inputs to produce a given output at a lower cost is emphasized by economists but much less so by physicians and others trained in the application of a specialized technology. For the economist, technology influences but does not determine the "best" combination of inputs. The lowest cost for a given quality-adjusted output depends on relative prices of alternative inputs as well as their contribution to production. For example, access to primary care is often discussed in medicine, and some see the only solution as training more primary care physicians. Others recommend more use of nurse practitioners and physician assistants. Still others say that the cost of nurse practitioners has increased so much relative to that of primary care physicians that they are no longer a cost-effective substitute. Dr. Tim Garson has gone 1 step further in substitutions of inputs by training and employing low-cost "grand-aides" who, supervised by nurse practitioners, provide first-line primary care in the home, especially for elderly patients with multiple chronic problems. In pilot tests in 2 pediatric Medicaid settings, Garson reported a large decrease in total cost by reducing clinic and emergency department visits.[7]

Output prices are higher in the United States than in other countries partly because of its more complex system of financing and paying for care.[8] Hundreds of insurance companies try to sell their services to millions of employers and persons at substantial administrative expense. Physicians and hospitals incur huge costs in billing many public and private third-party payers and individual patients. These costs all go into the output prices that determine expenditures for any given quantity of care.

Probably the most important difference in supply between the United States and peer countries is the mix of services offered.[9] In the United States, a higher proportion of physician visits are to specialists or sub-specialists. This circumstance would probably result in higher expenditures even if specialist fees were not higher because of greater use of expensive diagnostic and therapeutic interventions.

A related characteristic of supply in the United States that sets it apart from other countries is greater standby capacity. For example, on a per capita basis, persons in the United States receive 2.5 times as many magnetic resonance imaging scans as citizens of the average Organisation for Economic Co-operation and Development country, but the United States has approximately 4 times as many magnetic resonance imaging machines. Using the ratio of scans to machines in the other countries as a standard, this fact implies a standby capacity in the United States of more than one fourth of these machines. As a result, scans are usually available more quickly and in a more convenient location in the United States than in other countries. The cost of the extra machines, however, adds to expenditures. Lastly, the supply of health care in the United States is more expensive because it includes more privacy, space, and other amenities in hospitals and clinics.

Demand

For most persons, the demand for health care is uncertain and utilization is highly concentrated. Although one half of the population has no contact with the health care industry in any given year, approximately 5% are said to account for 50% of expenditures. Because most persons are risk-averse, a person's uncertainty about demand for health care becomes a demand for health insurance. Another factor also motivates insurance demand: Most persons of moderate or low income prefer to pay for major expenditures (for example, automobiles, refrigerators, and televisions) on a regular monthly basis rather than on a cash basis when they arise.

Health care is often a "big-ticket" item, and health insurance surely is. The annual premium for a family policy currently exceeds $15,000 and often surpasses $20,000. Regular periodic payment, sometimes called "prepayment" in the insurance industry, is particularly useful to many persons when it is automatically deducted from implicit wages and is not available for other spending. The demand for employment-based insurance in the United States is also stimulated by the tax law, which treats the employer's contribution to the premium as tax-free to the employee, although virtually all economists believe that it is simply another form of compensation similar to wages.

A person's demand for health care in the presence of insurance is greater than what it would be without insurance because it lowers the price to the patient.[10] This effect is labeled "moral hazard." It contributes to higher health care expenditures because it increases the demand for care for any given health status. It may also increase demand by biasing persons against behaviors that protect and enhance health.

Attempts to tinker with the terms of insurance through deductibles and copays are partial offsets to moral hazard, but a 20% copay for a $500 procedure just increases the price to $100. Large deductibles with full insurance above a certain level restrain utilization less than advocates claim because patients can accelerate or delay many interventions to take place in the year when the deductible will be met; therefore, the patient faces no cost. Insurance, moreover, cannot be a good explanation for higher expenditures in the United States than in other countries because those countries have more widespread insurance coverage but lower expenditures. Constraints on input prices, a different mix of services, and lower administrative costs in those countries better explain their lower expenditures.

Because patients with pain or other symptoms often do not know the cause of their problem or the interventions necessary to diagnose and treat it, they are susceptible to supplier-induced demand.[11] In a fee-for-service payment system, some health care organizations and individual physicians order diagnostic and therapeutic interventions of doubtful value to increase revenue. This situation can be rationalized by the fact that the insured patient may pay nothing and the intervention may help in defending a malpractice suit. When a particular intervention is widespread in a community, it becomes the standard of care and individual physicians may be loathe not to recommend it regardless of its lack of effectiveness. Changes in methods of reimbursement, such as a shift to capitation payment, could eliminate supplier-induced demand but may induce undertreatment.

One of the biggest potential problems facing voluntary systems of health insurance is the likelihood of adverse selection. Patients typically know more about their potential utilization of care than insurance companies. A premium based on the company's knowledge will be too low to cover the costs of care for high users and will result in a loss. It will be too high for those who expect to be low utilizers and may result in loss of customers. Economics usually concludes that choice is good and more choice is better than less, but this is questionable in the case of health insurance. Some companies will insure only groups of persons to protect against adverse selection of individuals. The mandate for coverage included in the Patient Protection and Affordable Care Act is another effort to solve this problem.

The demand for most goods and services in the United States depends primarily on the willingness and ability of persons or their families to pay, but health care is different because government subsidizes demand by paying for part or all of some patients' care. Sometimes, as with Medicaid, the subsidy is conditional on having a low income. In other cases, as in Medicare, the subsidy is universal, although the government has recently levied a partially offsetting charge on Medicare beneficiaries with incomes above a certain level. Income-tested insurance (for example, Medicaid) helps the poor get care but can induce evasion and avoidance of reported income more than a universal benefit does.

Conclusion

This brief survey of major economic concepts applied to important features of health care in the United States sheds light on the principal policy problems: high cost and the uninsured. In the United States, health care expenditures comprise more than 17% of the gross domestic product compared with 11% in other high-income democracies. The gross domestic product in the United States was approximately $17 trillion in 2014. Thus, the 6-percentage-point difference is $1 trillion. Other countries realize lower costs through a more activist role for government to reduce prices of inputs, simplify the financing and payment of care, and effect a change in output composition to a less-expensive mix. In the United States, despite high expenditures millions of persons remain uninsured even after implementation of the Affordable Care Act. To achieve universal coverage requires subsidies for the poor and the sick and compulsory participation by the entire population.

The Affordable Care Act has introduced substantial changes in health insurance markets but has not made major changes in financing, organization, or delivery of care. Such reform is unlikely for 2 reasons. First, large-scale change in health care would undoubtedly leave some persons worse off even if most persons would benefit. In the Declaration of Independence, Thomas Jefferson noted the reluctance of people to trade known present problems for uncertain future benefits. Two centuries later, in their Nobel Prize-winning "Prospect Theory: An Analysis of Decision Under Risk," Daniel Kahneman and Amos Tversky argued that most persons give greater weight to a possible loss than to a possible gain of equal magnitude.[12] Moreover, for some persons and groups, the potential losses from health care reform are large and predictable. These potential losers are sufficiently well-financed to be able to use the complex political system in the United States to block major changes. Only a severe political, financial, or medical crisis might make current political calculations and alignments irrelevant and large-scale reform possible.

References

1. Culyer, A. J. (2005). *The Dictionary of Health Economics*, Edward Elgar: Northampton, MA.
2. Eatwell, J., Milgate, M., and Newman, P. (eds.) (1987). *The New Palgrave: A Dictionary of Economics*, 1st edn. Macmillan: London.
3. Cohen, J., Malins, A. and Shahpurwala, Z. (2013). "Compared to US Practice, Evidence-based Reviews in Europe Appear to Lead to Lower Prices for Some Drugs." *Health Affairs (Millwood)* **32**: 762–770.
4. Laugesen, M. J. and Glied, S. A. (2011). "Higher Fees Paid to US Physicians Drive Higher Spending for Physician Services Compared to Other Countries." *Health Affairs (Millwood)* **30**: 1647–1656.
5. White, C., Reschovsky J. D. and Bond A. M. (2014). "Understanding Differences Between High- and Low-Price Hospitals: Implications for Efforts to Rein in Costs." *Health Affairs (Millwood)* **33**: 324–331.
6. Cutler, D. M., McClellan M. and Newhouse J. P. (2000). "How Does Managed Care Do It?" *The RAND Journal of Economics* **31**: 526–548.
7. Garson, A Jr, Green, D. M., Rodriguez, L., Beech, R. and Nye, C. (2012). "A New Corps of Trained Grand-Aides has the Potential to Extend Reach of Primary Care Workforce and Save Money." *Health Affairs (Millwood)* **31**: 1016–1021.
8. Cutler, D. M. and Ly, D. P. (2011). "The (Paper) Work of Medicine: Understanding International Medical Costs." *Journal of Economics Perspectives* **25**: 3–25.

9. Fuchs, V. R. (2013). "How and Why US Health Care Differs from that in Other OECD Countries." *The Journal of American Medical Association* **309**: 33–34.

10. Newhouse, J. P. (1982). "A Summary of the Rand Health Insurance Study." *Annals of the New York Academy of Sciences* **387**: 111–114.

11. Fuchs, V. R. (1978). "The Supply of Surgeons and the Demand for Operations." *Journal of Human Resources* **13**(Suppl): 35–56.

12. Kahneman, D. and Tversky, A. (1979). "Prospect Theory: An Analysis of Decision Under Risk." *Econometrica* **47**: 263–292.

Part 2

Who Shall Live?

Introduction

Wealth and health are the cornerstones of a good life. Yes, there are other things that matter as Saadi, the medieval Persian poet, reminds us,

"If of thy mortal goods thou art bereft,

And from thy slender store

Two loaves of bread alone to thee are left,

Sell one, and with the dole,

Buy hyacinths to feed thy soul."

Most people, however, place a high value on health, especially when dealing with its opposite.

Measurement of the health of an individual or of a population is difficult, partly because health is multi-dimensional. Pain, loss of function, disability are all negatives on the health scale, but valuation is usually partly subjective. The most widely recognized measure is the difference between life and death. Life expectancy at birth (measured by the mean age of death of a cohort) is often used as a measure of the health a population, and variation in age of death of individuals within a cohort provides a measure of the inequality of health.

The most important questions about life expectancy for economists are what determines it for populations, what determines variation in age of death of individuals within a population, and how to value life. There is also growing interest in measuring "quality of life," motivated in part by the observation that medicine is gaining the ability to delay death, often at great cost, without restoring the patient to anything like a full life.

In discussions of the determinants of health, poverty often gets major attention. The first paper in Part 2 was written for a conference on poverty and health organized by Eli Ginzberg (1911–2002) and David E. Rogers (1926–1994), two of my early mentors in health. Ginzberg was one of the last of the "institutionalist" economists, having studied with Wesley Clair Mitchell at Columbia. Ginzberg had a long career as a professor in Columbia's Graduate School of Business, specializing in "manpower" and health issues. He was a prolific author and an advisor to many U.S. presidents. I met Eli at Columbia, and we became life long friends. David Rogers was one of the most brilliant medical students and physicians of his generation. He was appointed chair of medicine at Vanderbilt at age 33, then dean of Johns Hopkins School of Medicine and Medical Director of Johns Hopkins Hospital, and then the first president of the Robert Wood Johnson Foundation in 1972. His sister and my brother were married in 1950, and I tried to answer his questions about economics while he tutored me about what medicine could and could not do. He kept me from the fate of many medical students who are taught things that are wrong or incomplete.

The relationship between poverty and health and the role of sanitation and nutrition as prime reasons for that relationship had been well-established. In my paper, I suggested some auxiliary questions that might lead to a deeper understanding of the relationship. Definition of the "poor" was a long-standing interest of mine because the prevalent view in the U.S. centered on not having enough income to acquire a "fixed" basket of *necessities*. History showed that periodically the fixed basket had to be expanded; income growth and technologic change created necessities for one generation that had not existed or been luxuries for an earlier one. If an absolute unchanged standard is problematic, so is a purely relative approach such as defining the poor as the bottom 15% or 20% of the income distribution. In that formulation, the percent in poverty could never change. In 1965 I suggested a combination of relative and absolute standard — those with incomes less than half of the median income adjusted for household size and composition. Under this standard the percent poor would change if there was a change in the distribution of income at the lower end. By this measure, the poor were about 20% of the U.S. population in the 1960s and close to 20% in the most recent statistics. Below one half of the median has been adopted as the poverty standard in most OECD countries but not in the U.S., which still uses a fixed standard based on a slightly modified basket of commodities chosen decades ago.

What explains the correlation between poverty and health? Part of the answer probably involves causality running from health to poverty. But even if we concentrate on causality running from poverty to health, there are usually many confounding variables such as education, family structure, or racism that preclude determining a simple effect of income.

If low income is the cause of poor health, how does additional income lead to better health? Access to medical care? Better nutrition? Less stress? Better housing? Or other pathways? "All of the above" does not help guide policy unless the recommendation is to provide more cash to the poor and let them decide what they most want. Some economists favor that approach, but many professionals who work with the poor favor food stamps, subsidized housing, and free medical care. Numerous other questions about the relationship between poverty and health and about providing medical care to the poor (insurance vs. direct services) are discussed in the paper.

In studies of the determinants of health, years of schooling often is the strongest correlate. Cigarette smoking is also frequently identified as a major cause of mortality, and in recent times there is usually a strong negative correlation between cigarette smoking and years of schooling. The second paper in Part 2 describes a test of whether additional schooling explains differences in the probability of smoking. For a sample of young males whose smoking history, schooling, and other variables were obtained in a survey, a regression of the probability of smoking at age 24 on years of schooling resulted in a sharp downward slope, thus supporting the conventional wisdom that the probability declines with additional schooling. However, when the probability of smoking at age 17 was regressed on the years of schooling the subjects would complete at age 24, the result was the same sharp downward slope. It was to the left of the one at age 24 but similar in size of effect. This result calls into question that the additional schooling was the cause of the change in the probability of smoking.

The third paper reviews the many social determinants of health, noting observations that tended to support the relationship and reasons to have some doubt. In the 1970s, I was a strong proponent of the idea that social determinants played a major role in human health. As Rene Dubos wrote in *The Dreams of Reason: Science and Utopias* (1961), "...each civilization creates its own diseases." Throughout most of human history, most humans had difficulty getting enough to eat. Today, in the United States, obesity is a major health problem.

Over time the importance of social determinants has gained wider acceptance within the medical community; meanwhile I was having concerns about the details. My 2004 paper reflects these concerns. First, we are far from understanding the mechanisms that result in a causal correlation between individual social determinants and health. This is most notable for the black-white difference in neo-natal mortality, where the negative correlation with income and education is very strong. The black-white ratio of education and of income is higher than it was 60 years ago, but the black-white neo-natality ratio has remained double. For life expectancy in general, years of schooling is usually the strongest correlate. Individuals with master degrees will, on average, have longer lives than those with bachelor degrees. But what role does education play? Is the differential larger for those with a masters in biology or computer science than those who studied art history or French literature? We don't know. Or consider the fact that the relation between life expectancy and income shows diminishing returns as income increases, but the relation between life expectancy and years of schooling does not. An increase of one year at the graduate level has as large an effect as one more year in high school or elementary school. Why? The paper raises other anomalies. It closes by urging researchers to look more carefully at interactions between genes and social determinants. For example, exposure to stress and the probability of depression apparently varies depending upon the presence or absence of a single gene.

The op-ed on social determinants, written at the end of 2016, continues the discussion of the questions raised in the paper. It supports the importance of social determinants but urges care in the way relationships are described. The context is often crucial for determining the relative importance of different determinants. The second op-ed on black gains in life expectancy provides interesting insights into the media and politics. Prior to writing this piece I had read and heard numerous stories about the failure of blacks to make progress, and these stories were sometimes backed by data on racial differences in education and income. Candidate Trump blamed Clinton and the Democrats for this failure of blacks. But a gain of six years in life expectancy for blacks over a period when whites gained only three years seemed to me to have relevance to the discussion. The reaction to my piece was curious in two respects. First, most people I had contact with found the story to be surprising. This was true for Stanford physicians, who said it did not match their experience and perhaps my data were not reliable. (I was using data from the Center for Disease Control, Vital Statistics series, by far, the most reliable mortality statistics.) Second, there was *no reaction* from the media, or either the Republican or Democratic campaigns, or anyone else. Over several decades I have published scores of op-eds in *JAMA* and *NEJM*, and other journals, and after each, there is usually a flurry of emails and phone calls asking for more details or for explanations and discussion of the results. In this case, nothing. Both the Left and the Right apparently decided that this story of black progress did not fit in with the arguments they were making. It also must have been true for the media which was mostly committed to one side or the other. Such substantial progress by blacks in such an important area as life expectancy was news, but apparently not news that anyone wanted to spread.

2.1

Poverty and Health: Asking the Right Questions

Gertrude Stein, confidante of the leading writers, artists, and intellectuals of her time, lay dying. Her closest friend and lifetime companion, Alice B. Toklas, leaned forward and said, "Gertrude, what's the answer?" Gertrude looked up and with her last breath said, "Alice, what's the question?"

We have been brought together in this conference to discuss "medical care and the health of the poor." But what is the question? Or, more appropriately, what are the questions? Opinions will no doubt differ, and some may wonder why the issue is raised at all. At most conferences participants arrive prepared with a ready supply of answers. They seek to advance this or that position or program, and, like a popular TV game show, the only questions that matter are those for which answers are already in hand.

But this is a different game. I must ask your indulgence while I engage in what some may regard as an "academic exercise." After all, of what possible use is an economist if not to discuss whether something that works in practice also works

Originally published in David E. Rogers and Eli Ginzberg (eds.) (1993), *Medical Care and the Health of the Poor*, pp. 9–20, Cornell University Medical College, Eighth Conference on Health Policy. Boulder, CO: Westview Press. Reprinted in *The American Economist*, 36(2):12–18, Fall 1992. Copyright by Westview Press.

in theory? But, what if we observe something that doesn't work in practice — such as health care for the poor? The purpose of this paper is to raise theoretical questions about poverty and health in order to elicit answers that might improve public policy.

Who Are the Poor?

A logical place to begin is by asking what we mean by poverty; that is, who are the poor? This question has a long history within economics, and even from the perspective of that single discipline gives rise to considerable controversy over definition and measurement. The question becomes even more important, however, when poverty is discussed in relation to health. As an economic concept, there is general agreement that poverty refers to some measure of income (or wealth) which indicates "inadequate" command over material resources. At health conferences, however, the concept often gets transformed into an amorphous set of "socioeconomic conditions," or an ill-defined "culture of poverty."

Let us try to avoid such confusion. This is not to deny that people can be "poor" in ways other than economic. They can be "spiritually impoverished," "morally bankrupt," in "poor health," and so on. But, to the extent possible, let us strive for clarity. If we mean low income, let's say low income. If we mean education, let's say education. And if we mean alcoholism, cigarette smoking, crime, drug abuse, fragmented families, hazardous occupations, sexual promiscuity, slum housing, social alienation, or unhealthy diets, let's say so explicitly. If we constantly redefine poverty to include anything and everything that contributes to poor health, we will make little progress either in theory or practice.

Even when poverty is defined in terms of income, there are numerous questions such as adjustment for size and composition of household, but we can leave them to the specialists.[1] There is one conceptual issue, however, which is so important as to require explicit discussion. Should poverty be defined according to some fixed standard (absolute income), or by position in the income distribution (relative income)? In my judgment, we need to combine both approaches. If we cling only to a fixed standard, economic growth gradually raises almost everyone out of poverty so defined, but the problems we usually associate with poverty persist. So-called "subsistence" budgets are adjusted to new social norms. On the other hand, to define poverty in terms of the bottom 10 or 20 percent of the income distribution does not help us get to the heart of the problem either. In a society with little inequality of income, being at the lower end need not have the same negative implications as when the distribution is very unequal.

People usually think of themselves as poor (and are regarded as poor) when their command over material resources is much less than others. Poverty, as an economic concept, is largely a matter of economic distance. Thus, in 1965, I proposed a poverty threshold of one-half of median income.[2] The choice of one-half was somewhat arbitrary, but the basic idea would not change if a level of four-tenths or six-tenths were chosen instead. There is considerable resistance to such a definition because a reduction in poverty so defined requires a change in the distribution of income — always a difficult task for political economy. But I believe it is the only realistic way to think about poverty. In this respect, as in so many others, Adam Smith had a clear view of the matter over 200 years ago. He wrote, "By necessaries I understand not only the commodities which are indispensably necessary for the support of life but whatever the custom of the country renders it indecent for creditable people even of the lowest order to be without."[3]

What Is the Relation Between Poverty and Health?

Once we have identified the poor, the next question concerns their health relative to the rest of the population. We know in general the answer to this question — on average those with low income have worse health. There are, however, several aspects of the question that deserve further exploration. How does the relation vary with different measures of health, such as morbidity, disability, or mortality? Is the relation different for different diseases? Is it different at different stages of the life cycle? Is the relation stronger in some countries than in others? If any of these questions are answered in the affirmative (and they surely will be), the next step would be to seek to determine the reasons for the variation. Such inquiries could provide valuable inputs into the next stage of analysis when we seek to make inferences about causality.

Is Low Income the Cause of Poor Health?

Many writers simply assert that poverty is the cause of poor health, without rigorous testing. In England, social class is often used as a proxy for poverty, but this is problematic, as illustrated in Table 1. There is a large differential in mortality between the lowest and the highest class and a large differential in income as well, but more detailed inspection reveals a complex pattern. Class II

Table 1.   Indexes of Mortality and Income in England
and Wales by Social Class, 1971 (Class I = 100)

	Age-adjusted mortality, men 15–64 years of age	Gross weekly income
I. Professional	100	100
II. Managerial	105	77
III. Skilled	136	58
IV. Semi-skilled	148	51
V. Unskilled	179	50

Source: Adapted from Wilkinson, pp. 2 and 11. Richard
G. Wilkinson, "Socioeconomic Differences in Mortality:
Interpreting the Data on Their Size and Trends," in
Richard G. Wilkinson, ed., *Class and Health: Research
and Longitudinal Data* (London and New York: Tavi-
stock Publications, 1986).

has only 5 percent greater mortality than class I, even though income is 23 percent
lower. In contrast, the differential in mortality between classes IV and V is 21
percent, but the income difference is only 2 percent. It may be tempting to explain
these data by asserting that the relationship between income and mortality is
nonlinear. Thus, at low levels of income, i.e., classes IV and V, even a small
increase in income has a strong effect on mortality, while at high levels, i.e.,
classes I and II, the effect is very weak. This explanation won't wash, however,
once we note that the mortality differentials between classes I and V were no
smaller in 1971 than in 1951. During those two decades real earnings rose by
more than 50 percent for all classes; thus if nonlinearity is the explanation for the
pattern shown in Table 1, there should have been an appreciable narrowing in the
class mortality differentials between 1951 and 1971. No such decrease occurred.
Furthermore, there was no decrease between 1971 and 1981 despite additional
increases in real income.

England is not alone in experiencing persistence of class (occupation)
differentials in mortality in the face of rising real income and universal coverage
for medical care. In Scandinavia, the age-standardized mortality ratio for male
hotel, restaurant, and food service workers is double that of teachers and technical
workers.[4] A Swedish study of age-standardized death rates among employed
men ages 45–64 found substantial differences across occupations in 1966–1970
and slightly greater differentials in 1976–1980.[5] In Sweden, there is growing
recognition that these differentials cannot be explained by differential access to
health care. Johan Callthorp, M.D., writes, "There is no systematic evidence
that the health care system is inequitable in the sense that those in greater

need get less care or that there are barriers towards the lower socioeconomic groups."[6]

What Explains the Correlation Between Poverty and Health?

The fact that variables A and B are correlated does not, of course, prove that A is the cause of B. Two other possibilities must be considered. First, the causality may run in the opposite direction; B may be the cause of A. The possibility that health affects social class has been explored extensively by British writers.[7] Almost all agree that there is some "selective mobility," but no consensus has emerged regarding its importance. R. G. Wilkinson concludes that "its contribution to observed class differences in health is probably always small."[8] But Roy Carr-Hill writes "There is an effect which should not be ignored: the size of the effect could be substantial, but it cannot be estimated properly without a lifelong longitudinal study."[9]

Attention must also be paid to the other logical possibility, namely that there are one or more "third variables" that are the cause both of low income and poor health. These variables could include genetic endowment as well as numerous socioeconomic factors. Among the latter, most U.S. studies have focused on schooling. There is a vast literature that explores the relation between health and education.[10] To be sure, income and education are correlated, but the correlation is not so high as to preclude attempting to sort out their separate relationships with health. In the United States, the coefficient of correlation between education and income within age-sex-race groups never reaches as much as .50 and is typically around .40. When health is regressed on both income and schooling, the latter variable always dominates the former. Indeed, in some studies, income is negatively related to health, once years of schooling is controlled for.[11]

Why Is There Such a Strong Correlation Between Schooling and Health?

One possible answer, of course, is that schooling is the cause of good health. That is, at any given level of income, those with more education know how to use medical care more effectively, choose better diets and other health behaviors, and so on. This line of reasoning has been developed most fully by Michael Grossman.[12] But again, as a matter of logic, we must consider two other possibilities. Good health may lead to more schooling, or, there may be "third variables" that affect both schooling and health. Among the "third variables," my favorite candidates are time preference[13] and self-efficacy.[14]

Time preference is an economic concept that refers to the rate at which people discount the future relative to the present. Individuals with high rates of time preference will tend to invest less in the future: on average they will have less education, lower income, and worse health. A perfect capital market would enable those with low rates of time discount to provide funds to those with high rates until their rates were equal at the margin, but the real world bears little resemblance to this theoretical model. For one thing, low income individuals who want to borrow a great deal cannot provide effective collateral. Also, many choices about health do not involve money; thus there is no effective market in which individuals with different rates of time preference can make trades.

Self-efficacy is a psychological term that describes people's beliefs in their capability to exercise control over their own behavior and their environment. Differences among individuals in self-efficacy are probably correlated across several domains, such as health and education, thus helping to explain the close relationship between these variables.

How Does Low Income Affect Health?

Let us return to the line of inquiry that has poverty as a cause of poor health. Within that framework the central question concerns the mechanism through which low income translates into bad health. To what extent does the health of the poor suffer because they have inadequate access to medical care? To what extent is their poor health the result of deficiencies in other health-producing goods and services such as good food, good housing, or a safe environment? If poor health is attributable to inadequate medical care, are the barriers faced by the poor simply a matter of purchasing power, or are there other impediments?

What Are the Most Important Health Problems Facing the Poor?

In addressing this question it is important to distinguish between relative risk and absolute risk, a distinction that is often obscured in the media and even in policy discussions. For example, infant mortality may be twice as high among the poor as the non-poor (a relative risk of 2 to 1), while the differential in mortality from heart disease may be only 50 percent (relative risk 1.5 to 1). The absolute level of risk of infant mortality, however, may be very low relative to heart disease mortality; thus, the poor might benefit more from efforts devoted to heart disease rather than to infant mortality.

To illustrate this point, consider the tremendous attention given by the media (and many health policy experts) to black-white differences in infant mortality and the relative neglect of other black-white health differentials. It is true that the black infant death rate is double the white rate, while the difference in overall life expectancy is only 9 percent (75.9 years versus 69.7 years in the United States in 1989). But if the black infant mortality rate were reduced to the white level (and all other age-specific rates remained unchanged), black life expectancy would only rise by six-tenths of a year. Over 90 percent of the black-white difference in life expectancy would remain. Isn't there a danger that undue emphasis on attention-grabbing headlines results in a misallocation of health care resources from the perspective of those whose health problems are being addressed?

Which Health Problems of the Poor Are Most Amenable to Solution?

In order to make rational allocations of resources to alleviate the health problems of the poor it is necessary but not sufficient to know the relative importance of the problems. It is also necessary to know how readily the problems can be solved or alleviated. Unfortunately, the bulk of health policy research dwells on documenting the problems of the poor, while neglecting the more difficult task of assessing the efficacy of alternative interventions. Policymakers and the public need to know both the costs and the benefits of such alternatives. For example, treatment for infectious diseases may be very efficacious, while treatment for cancer may not be. Some prevention programs such as immunizations may provide a great deal of benefit for little cost, but others, such as mass screening of cholesterol levels, may use a vast amount of resources for limited benefits.

Are There Reasons for Providing Medical Care to the Poor Other than Improving Health Outcomes?

Suppose the contribution of medical care to health at the margin is quite small. Is that sufficient reason to ignore the provision of care to the poor? Not necessarily. In his critique of the Oregon plan for rationing medical care to the poor, Bruce Vladeck writes, "We expect the health system to take care of sick people whether or not they are going to get better."[15]

Medical care may be valued by the poor (as it is by the nonpoor) for the caring and validation services that it provides. If this is the case, serious questions arise concerning the *kind* of care provided to the poor. In particular, is "high-tech" overemphasized at the expense of simpler, more valuable services? The fact that medical care has value apart from improving health outcomes provides no grounds for rejecting a cost-benefit approach to resource allocation. But it does highlight the need to incorporate the value of all services in such analyses.

What Policy Instruments Are Available to Help the Poor?

A sociologist tried to explain poverty to a colleague in economics. "You know, the poor are different from you and me." "Yes," replied the economist, "they have less money." This apocryphal exchange highlights a continuing controversy over the best way to help the poor with respect to health or anything else. If more resources are to be allocated to the poor, is it better to provide cash and allow the poor to decide how to spend it, or should the transfers be tied to particular goods and services? The arguments for tied transfers usually derive from a paternalistic assumption that the poor, left to their own devices, will not spend the money "wisely," i.e., they will buy cake when those making the transfers think they should buy bread. A more sophisticated version of this argument invokes "externalities." It may be the case that forcing the poor to spend their additional resources on immunizations rather than alcohol helps the nonpoor because the former creates positive externalities, while the latter creates negative ones for other explanations by economic theorists for tied transfers, see.[16] But the same is true of expenditures by the nonpoor.

Paternalism aside, there is the practical question of whether tied transfers can alter consumption patterns. If a family that previously spent $250 per month on food receives $100 worth of food stamps, there is no reason to expect their spending on food to rise to $350. Indeed, food expenditures are not likely to increase by any more than if they were given $100 in cash. The relative price of food, at the margin, is no different after the transfer than before. The only way to assure a disproportionate increase in food consumption would be to provide food stamps greater in amount than what the family would voluntarily spend on food, given its income plus the cash value of the food stamps.

In devising programs for the poor, physicians usually advocate more medical care, educators more schooling, the construction industry more housing, and so on. But what area(s) would the poor give highest priority? This question may be beyond the scope of this conference, but it cries out for attention from policy analysts in some setting.

In choosing between in-kind and cash programs, policymakers should also consider the pecuniary effects of alternative transfers to the poor.[17] One result of Medicare and Medicaid, for example, was higher incomes for physicians — surely not a goal of the Great Society. These programs also led to an increase in the price of medical care for the general public, including many low income persons who did not qualify for Medicaid. If, instead of Medicare and Medicaid, the government had transferred to the elderly and the poor an equivalent amount of cash, some of it would have been used for medical care, but much of it would have been used for other goods and services, including food, clothing, consumer durables, and the like. The income and price effects would probably have been very different from those of Medicare and Medicaid, and possibly more egalitarian.

Why Are Americans Less Willing than Others to Subsidize Medical Care for the Poor?

The health policy literature abounds with papers that describe and decry the difficulty faced by poor Americans in obtaining health care. But these papers are typically silent as to why the United States is the only major industrialized country that does not have national health insurance. In 1976, I proposed several answers to this question: distrust of government, the heterogeneity of the population, the weakness of "noblesse oblige," and a robust voluntary sector.[18] In a recent paper I reappraise these explanations in the light of subsequent political, social, and economic developments.[19] 1 have a healthy respect for my opinion, but it would be useful to hear other views on this question.

What Is the Most Efficient Way to Provide Medical Care for the Poor?

The debate on this issue is clear cut. On the one hand are those who want to provide the poor with health insurance and leave it to them to obtain the care they need. The contrary view advocates special programs directly aimed at providing care for the poor. Inasmuch as both approaches have been tried in the United States and abroad, it should be possible to make some judgments about their relative costs and benefits.

Is it acceptable to provide highly cost-effective care for the poor although the care is different from that available to the nonpoor? A good example is prenatal care and delivery of babies. The Maternity Center Association can provide high quality midwifery service in their childbearing center for less than half of what Medicaid pays for in-hospital normal childbirth.[20] At present, some poor women get the high-cost care and some get little or no care.

The question of efficient provision of care to the poor is complicated by the fact that there may be gross inefficiencies in care provided to the nonpoor — overtesting, inappropriate surgery, and so on. Should programs for the poor aim at reproducing these misallocations of resources?

What Is "Two-tier" Medical Care?

Discussions of medical care for the poor frequently invoke the phrase "two-tier" medicine. For strict egalitarians this is a deplorable concept. But others have argued that an explicit two-tier system would serve the American poor better than does the present jumble of services that range from no care (e.g., prenatal) to the most sophisticated (e.g., neonatal intensive). In thinking about this issue it may be useful to notice that two-tier systems can vary greatly, as shown in Figure 1. In both systems, the people in the first tier receive more and better service than those in the second. But in version A most of the population is in the first tier and only the poor are in tier two. In version B the proportions are reversed; most of the population is in the second tier and only the affluent and/or well-connected are in tier one.

Version A provides a "safety net"; version B provides an "escape valve." Most Americans tend to associate two-tier medicine with version A; most other countries have opted for version B. Several interesting questions may be posed about these alternative approaches. Do the two versions have different consequences for cost, access, and quality? For example, consider cost.

Suppose expenditures *per capita* in tier 1 are identical in the two systems and the same is true for tier 2 except that in each country they are 50 percent less than

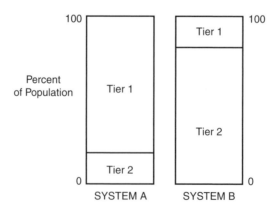

Fig. 1.   Two Versions of "Two-tier" Medical Care.

tier 1. Suppose that in system A 80 percent of the population are in tier 1 and 20 percent in tier 2, and that the proportions are reversed in system B. In that case, the average expenditure per person in system A will be 50 percent greater than in system B.

What are the political, social, and economic factors that lead a country to adopt one version or the other? It would seem that individuals who were certain that they would be in tier 2 under either system would prefer B. Similarly, individuals who were certain that they would be in tier 1 under either system might also prefer B. Supporters of A are likely to be individuals who think they would be in tier 1 under A, but in tier 2 under B. Many Americans probably fit that category.

What Is Basic Medical Care?

A frequent conclusion of health policy discussions in the United States is that everyone should have access to "basic" medical care. Many observers believe that the nonpoor would be more willing to subsidize a "basic" package than they would complete equality of care. Problems arise, however, in trying to define the contents of that package. Moreover, no matter how it is defined at any point in time, no one should imagine that the contents can remain fixed over time. In a world of changing technology and rising real income, a fixed approach to basic care will prove no more satisfactory than will a fixed poverty standard based on some notion of subsistence. The basic care package will constantly have to change in order to include "whatever the custom of the country renders it indecent for creditable people, even of the lowest order, to be without."

Summary

In summary, there are numerous questions about poverty and health that need to be addressed, both at this conference and subsequently. Many of them concern the relation between poverty and health: its extent, pattern, and explanations. Other questions revolve around possible confounding variables such as education, which is correlated with income and health. Still other questions focus on medical care: its efficacy in improving health, its value to the poor, the best way to provide it. In pursuing these questions we need to find a middle road between a mindless optimism that ignores reality and a constricting pessimism that denies the possibility of creating a more efficient and more just society.

References

1. Palmer, J. L., Smeeding, T. and Jenks, C. (1988). "The Uses and Limits of Income Comparisons." In J. L. Palmer, T. Smeeding, and B. B. Torrey. (eds.), *The Vulnerable*, Urban Institute Press: Washington, DC, pp. 9–27.
2. Fuchs, V. R. (1965). "Toward a Theory of Poverty." In *The Concept of Poverty, Task Force on Economic Growth and Opportunity, First Report*. Chamber of Commerce of the United States: Washington, DC, pp. 71–91.
3. Smith, A. (1937). *The Wealth of Nations*. Random House: New York, Modern Library edition, p. 821.
4. Andersen, O. (1991). "Occupational Impacts on Mortality Declines in the Nordic Countries." In *Future Demographic Trends in Europe and North America*, ed. W. Lutz. Academic Press: New York, p. 46.
5. Callthorp, J. (1989). "The 'Swedish Model' Under Pressure — How to Maintain Equity and Develop Quality?." *Quality Assurance in Health Care* 1(1): 11–22.
6. Callthorp, "The 'Swedish Model'." *op. cit.*
7. Fox, A. J. (1984). *Social Class and Occupational Mobility Shortly Before Men Become Fathers*, OPCS Series LS No. 2, HMSO: London. Stern, J. (1983). "Social Mobility and the Interpretation of Social Class Mortality Differentials." *J. Social Policy* 12: 27–49; Wadsworth, M. E. J. (1986). "Serious Illness in Childhood and Its Association with Later life Achievement." In *Class and Health: Research and Longitudinal Data*, ed. R. G. Wilkinson. Tavistock Publications: London and New York.
8. Wilkinson, R. G. (1986). "Socioeconomic Differences in Mortality: Interpreting the Data on Their Size and Trends." In *Class and Health: Research and Longitudinal Data*, ed. R. G. Wilkinson. Tavistock Publications: London and New York, p. 10.
9. Carr-Hill, R. (1987). "The Inequalities in Health Debate: A Critical Review of the Issues." *Journal of Social Policy* 16: 509–542.
10. Berger, M. C. and Paul Leigh, J. (1989). "Schooling, Self-Selection, and Health." *Journal of Human Resources* 24: 435–455; Farrell, P. and Fuchs, V. R. (1982). "Schooling and Health: The Cigarette Connection." *Journal of Health Economics* 1: 217–230; Grossman, M. (1976). "The Correlation between Health and Schooling." In *Household Production and Consumption*, ed. N. E. Terleckyj. Columbia University Press: New York (for NBER); Kenkel, D. S. (1991). "Health Behavior, Health Knowledge, and Schooling." *Journal of Political Economy* 99: 287–304.
11. Auster, R. Leveson, I. and Sarachek, D. (1969). "The Production of Health, an Exploratory Study." *Journal of Human Resources* 4: 412–436.
12. Grossman, M. "The Correlation between Health and Schooling." *op. cit.*
13. Fuchs, V. R. (1982). "Time Preference and Health: An Exploratory Study." In *Economic Aspects of Health*, ed. V. R. Fuchs. (University of Chicago Press: Chicago, pp. 93–120.
14. Bandura, A. (1991). "Self-Efficacy Mechanism in Physiological Activation and Health-Promoting Behavior." In *Neural Biology of Learning, Emotion and Affect*, ed. J. Madden IV. Raven Press Ltd.: New york, pp. 229–269.

15. Vladeck, B. C. (1991). "Unhealthy Rations". *The American Prospect* (NJ, Princeton) **Summer**: 102.

16. Bruce, N. and Waldman, M. (1991). "Transfers in Kind: Why They Can Be Efficient and Nonpaternalistic." *American Economic Review* **81**: 1345–1351.

17. Coate, S., Johnson, S. and Zeckhauser, R. (1992). *Robin-Hooding Rents: Exploiting the Pecuniary Effects of In-Kind Programs.* Harvard University, mimeographed.

18. Fuchs, V. R. (1976). "From Bismarck to Woodcock: The 'Irrational' Pursuit of National Health Insurance". *Journal of Law and Economics* **19**: 347–359.

19. Fuchs, V. R. (1991). "National Health Insurance Revisited". *Health Affairs* **10**: 1–11.

20. Personal Communication from Ruth Watson Lubic (1991).

2.2

Schooling and Health:
The Cigarette Connection

Schooling is significantly correlated with health status, but is the relationship causal? This paper tests the hypothesis that schooling causes differences in an important health-affecting behavior: cigarette smoking. The most striking result is that for persons with 12 to 18 years of completed schooling, the strong negative relation between schooling and smoking observed at age 24 is accounted for by differences in smoking behavior at age 17, when all subjects were still in the same grade. Causality from schooling to smoking, and by implication from schooling to health, is rejected in favor of a 'third variable' hypothesis.

Introduction

One of the strongest generalizations to emerge from empirical research on health in the United States is a positive correlation between years of schooling and health status. At one time this relationship was viewed as a 'class' or 'socioeconomic status' effect and was thought to be significantly influenced by a positive relation between schooling and income and a positive effect of income on health.[1] Numerous studies by economists during the past decade, however, have revealed a large, statistically significant relationship between health and years of schooling after controlling for differences in income.[a]

The central question now is: Is increased schooling a causal factor for better health — or are both schooling and health differences manifestations of some other underlying 'third variable'?

Originally published in *Journal of Health Economics*, 1(3):217–230, 1982. Copyright by North-Holland. Written with Phillip Farrell.
[a]For example, see Ref. 1, 8, 16, 18.

In a detailed exploration of the subject[10] hypothesized that additional years of schooling make an individual a more efficient producer of his own health. Schooling could increase knowledge about health effects of behavior and medical care options, change preferences, or train a person to better process and act upon information. Or perhaps schooling increases the individual's ability to develop strategies of self-control.[19] On the other hand, the schooling-health correlation may result from the action of some underlying differences among individuals that affect both schooling and health behaviors, such as family socialization, mental ability, or internal rate of time preference.

One attempt to test for schooling effects in the use of, and outcomes from, in-hospital surgical operations had essentially negative results.[7] Years of schooling was not systematically related to the stage of the disease at the time of surgery, qualifications of the surgeon, length of hospital stay, or even outcome of the surgery (controlling for the initially better general health of those with more schooling).

This paper examines the possibility that schooling affects health through an effect on cigarette smoking — an important determinant of health status. It is well known that cigarette smoking and years of schooling are negatively correlated, at least at high-school levels or above. In a 1975 national probability survey the proportion of high-school graduates who smoked was more than 50% higher than that of college graduates (DHEW, 1976). A negative relation between smoking and health is also well established. Among males with life insurance the gross difference in life expectancy at age 35 between non-smokers and those who smoke a pack a day is approximately six years.[12] Even within a relatively homogeneous population such as regular participants in the Kaiser-Permanente Multiphasic Health checkups, the age-sex-race-adjusted death rate for cigarette smokers is double that of non-smokers.[5]

Our research strategy is to examine the smoking behavior of different cohorts of men and women before and after they have completed their formal schooling. If additional years of schooling have an effect, it will show up in a change in behavior.

We first describe the source and nature of our sample of retrospective smoking histories, define the variables, and explain the method of analysis. We also examine the possibility of a bias towards under-reporting of smoking behaviors in the survey and present evidence that such bias is insignificant.

Next, we present and interpret the results of the data analysis. Our principal finding is that the amount of formal schooling a person will eventually achieve predicts his smoking behavior *before* the schooling is actually realized and that realizing the additional years of schooling has no marginal effect on smoking behavior. We reject the hypothesis that schooling differences are causal to smoking differences in favor of the existence of one or more underlying third variables that are determinants of both schooling and smoking behaviors.

Our second finding is that the strong negative correlation between schooling and smoking developed only after the spread of information that smoking was a serious health hazard. This implies that the mechanism behind the schooling–smoking relation may also give rise to the schooling-health relationship.

In the final section of the paper we speculate on the nature of the 'third variable' behind the schooling–smoking correlation and present some evidence that casts doubt on either the social class or mental ability hypothesis.

Data and Methods

The sample

The data used in this paper are drawn from 2,504 personal interviews conducted in the fall of 1979 by the Stanford Heart Disease Prevention Program (SHDPP) among residents aged 12 to 75 years in randomly selected households in four small California cities: Modesto, Monterey, Salinas, and San Luis Obispo. All cities are located in predominantly agricultural areas; their populations range between 30,000 and 130,000 (in 1975). The interviews were taken as part of a health education experiment designed to test the effectiveness of techniques for altering smoking, exercise, and dietary behaviors in order to reduce risk of heart disease.[14]

The relations between schooling and health and schooling and smoking status in this sample are similar to those reported in national surveys. Health status as measured by days of normal activity limited by illness, health care utilization, and personal satisfaction with health show systematic improvement with increased schooling. The proportion smoking cigarettes on a daily basis declines with years of schooling (except at the very lowest levels of schooling). Men are more likely to smoke than women, and the proportion smoking is higher at age 24 than at age 17.

For the regression analyses that follow, a subset of 1,183 survey respondents was selected consisting of white, non-Hispanic men and women who were not students at the time of the survey, had completed 12 to 18 years of schooling, and who were at least 24 years old; 45% were men and 55% women. Non-whites and Hispanics (about 17% of the survey respondents) were excluded because the sample size was inadequate to explore interactions among ethnicity, schooling, and smoking. Persons still in school or under age 24 were excluded in order to focus on those who have had ample opportunity to reveal their decisions about schooling and initiation of smoking. Over 90% of the ever regular smokers in the SHDPP survey began smoking by age 24. Using a higher cut-off age (to capture a higher percentage of all possible smokers) would remove from the study too many of the younger cohorts who have been most exposed to information about the health consequences of smoking.

To test the hypothesis of a causal relationship between schooling and smoking, we observe the smoking behavior of our sample of individuals at age 17, when they all have approximately the same amount of schooling, and at age 24, when they have completed differing amounts of schooling. Assuming uninterrupted attendance in school from age 6 onward, those with more than 18 years of schooling were excluded so that everyone in our sample (including those just age 24 in 1979) could be observed after the completion of schooling. Persons with less than 12 years of schooling were excluded so that the entire sample would still be in school at age 17. This lower schooling limit was selected as a compromise between including persons with a wide range of schooling achievement and observing them all while still in school at an age when a significant proportion of all eventual smokers had already begun to smoke.

With this sample we can study the effects of additional years of schooling (beyond 12) on smoking behavior; we cannot explicitly investigate the effects of differences in the quality or type of schooling, although the effects should be similar since differences in quality of schooling are a particular dimension of quantity of education, ceteris paribus.

The variables

Respondents to the SHDPP 1979 survey were asked if they had ever smoked cigarettes on a daily basis. Those who responded affirmatively are classified as 'ever regular smokers'. Ever regular smokers were also asked at what age they began smoking and whether they had smoked in the past week. Those who had smoked in the past week are considered current regular smokers; those who had not are considered former regular smokers. Former regular smokers were asked how long ago they quit. The answers to these questions were used to construct retrospective histories of smoking status.[b]

---

[b]Spells of non-smoking by ever regular smokers were ignored, since their duration and timing were not recorded in the survey. For our purposes the error thus introduced in determination of smoking status at 17 or 24 is negligible.

Education was recorded in the SHDPP 1979 survey as number of years of formal schooling completed. Education was tried in the analyses in both continuous and categorical forms with similar results. Family background characteristics such as cultural traditions (including religion), income, and whether the parents smoked are possibly important influences on whether a person begins to smoke. Unfortunately, the only such background characteristic included in the 1979 SHDPP survey was father's years of completed schooling.[c] The absence of other background variables may be less of a problem in this relatively homogeneous sample than in a national sample.

Cohorts were defined according to historical periods of possibly different smoking behavior. The critical years were believed to be entry into World War II (1942), the first appearance in the popular press of articles linking smoking to lung cancer[d] (c. 1953), and the publication of the first Surgeon General's Report on Smoking and Health (DHEW, 1964). Survey respondents were assigned to the cohort that included the calendar year when they were 17 years of age. The four cohorts defined by these three important years were roughly equal in size in these data.

Possible bias in variables

Potential systematic bias in the measurement of smoking status is an important concern, especially if bias is correlated with education. The most obvious potential source of bias when using survey results is the possibility that respondents lie about their smoking status or history in order to avoid perceived social stigma or disapproval. Fortunately, the SHDPP survey tested for the presence of two smoking by-products: carbon monoxide in expired air samples and thiocyanate in blood samples. These tests establish the veracity of self-reported current smoking behavior and, by extension, previous smoking behavior (since the motivation to lie — social stigma — would be less strong for previous smoking than for current smoking). All of the female self-reported non-smokers (including former smokers) and 97.5% of the male ones had levels of smoking by-products well below 'threshold levels' used to classify typical smokers (8 ppm CO and 100 micromoles/liter thiocyanate[22]). For self-reported non-smokers, mean levels of these by-products (and thus the probability of lying) decreased with increased

---

[c] Approximately 17 percent of the white survey respondents did not give father's schooling; the median years of completed father's schooling for their ten-year age cohort was assigned. Regressions were also tried excluding those missing father's years of completed schooling. Results were the same as the full sample with median values assigned to missing observations.

[d] For example, Ref. 4, 13, 15, 17.

years of schooling, though only the differences in CO levels were statistically significant.[e] If present at all, systematic bias due to 'lying' is thus very minor and works in the direction of reducing, not increasing, the observed strength of the schooling–smoking relation.

Another potential source of bias is differential survivorship of smokers and non-smokers. The direction and size of bias depends upon the absolute difference in mortality, the true proportion who were smokers at different levels of schooling, and possible effects on death rates of interactions between smoking and education. We have attempted to estimate the potential bias assuming mortality rates for smokers that were double those of non-smokers, and concluded that even for our oldest cohort the effect is small unless the interaction between smoking and education was very large.[f] Most important of all, considering the purposes of this

---

[e] In our subset of whites aged 24–75, the mean levels of expired air CO (ppm) and blood thiocyanate (micro-moles/liter) for self-reported smokers and non-smokers varied by years of schooling as follows (standard errors of the means in parentheses):

	Smokers		Non-smokers	
	Men	Women	Men	Women
CO				
12 years schooling	28.7	25.6	6.26	4.08
	(1.95)	(1.86)	(0.62)	(0.12)
16+ years schooling	26.0	17.9	4.79	3.80
	(2.24)	(2.02)	(0.24)	(0.12)
Thiocyanate				
12 years schooling	154.1	166.3	65.6	48.9
	(6.26)	(5.68)	(4.04)	(1.57)
16+ years schooling	155.1	135.2	62.3	49.3
	(8.83)	(11.32)	(2.57)	(1.73)

[f] To estimate the maximum survivorship bias, use our cohort of 17-year-olds in 1921–41 (born 1904–24). Assume all were born in 1915 and experienced the age-specific death rates of successive decennial cross-sections (e.g., the number surviving to 1920 estimated from death rates for 0- to 5-year-olds observed in 1920, etc.). Further assume that at every age after 25, persons smoking by age 25 experience an age-specific mortality rate twice that of those who were not smoking by age 25 (this surely overstates differential mortality because of later starting and stopping behavior). Finally, assume that the ratio of survival rates of smokers and non-smokers in this cohort to the year 1979 (defined as variable C) is independent of years of schooling. Using U.S. Life Tables for decennial years and apportioning deaths between initial smokers and non-smokers according to the observed proportions of smokers at age 24 in this cohort and the 2 to 1 mortality rate assumption, C is calculated at 0.81 for white men and 0.87 for white women.

Let T_a be the true proportion of smokers at age a and O_a be the observed proportion from a survey of cohort survivors. Then

$$T_a = O_a/(C + O_a - C O_a).$$

paper, the effect on the comparison between the schooling–smoking relation at ages 17 and 24 is negligible.

The model

Our analysis aims to test two questions: whether the schooling–smoking relation developed as a result of the spread of information about adverse health effects of smoking (i.e., whether it is health-motivated); and whether the relation is only observable after schooling differences are realized (i.e., whether schooling differences are causal to smoking differences). Our model must therefore permit estimation of the schooling–smoking relation separately by cohort and at ages before and after the schooling is actually realized. The model must also take into account the fact that the observation of individual smoking behavior is dichotomous, not continuous. It is also desirable to control for other influences in the decision to smoke. Clearly, men and women have been influenced by different societal attitudes and expectations towards smoking in the last half-century.[11] Our model will therefore estimate the smoking-schooling relation separately by sex. The only other background control variable available in this sample is father's education, which will be included in the model.

To meet these needs, we divide the sample into subsets defined by sex and cohort, and then estimate[g] the parameters of the logistic function

$$P_a = 1/(1 + e^{-\beta X}),$$

where P_a is the probability of smoking at age a (17 or 24), X is the vector of independent variables consisting of intercept, own years of schooling completed and father's years of schooling completed, and β is the vector of estimated

---

Using the predicted probabilities of smoking at ages 17 and 24 for specific sex/cohort/schooling cells that we obtain from estimating our regression model (see table 2) as the 'observed' proportions, the 'true' proportions, adjusted for effects of differential survivorship, can be calculated from the formula above. For men, T_{17} ranges from 14% to 16% higher than O_{17} for years of schooling from 12 to 18; T_{24} ranges from 6% to 9% higher than O_{24}. For women, T_{17} is 11% higher than O_{17} for all schooling categories; T_{24} varies from 8% to 9% higher than O_{24}. These are the maximum effects of survivorship bias, which diminishes rapidly for the younger cohorts. The bias in the coefficient of schooling can be approximated by considering the change in slope (between 'observed' and 'true' proportions) of a straight line drawn between the smoking probabilities for the 12th and 18th graders. For men, the true slope is 10% higher than the observed slope at age 17, and 6% lower at age 24. For women, the true slope is 13% higher than the observed slope at age 17, and 4% higher at age 24. Differences of this size are practically and statistically insignificant, considering the very small schooling coefficients estimated for this cohort.

[g]Estimation was done by the method of maximum likelihood using the iterative procedure *LOGIST* of the Statistical Analysis System, version 79.5, on an IBM 370/3081 processor.

parameters. Observed proportions of smokers correspond closely to proportions predicted by these regressions, indicating the appropriateness of this functional form.

Results

Table 1 reports the results of maximum-likelihood logit regressions in which the probability of smoking is a function of years of own schooling and years of father's schooling, separately estimated by sex and cohort. Identical regressions were estimated for the probability of smoking at age 17 and age 24 with schooling measured in both cases as the number of years the individual would eventually complete (by 1979). This specification permits a test of whether the schooling–smoking relation observed in this sample was established before or after the additional years of schooling were obtained. The schooling coefficients by cohort allow a test of whether the effect was associated with the news of adverse health effects from smoking.

The most striking result is the absence of any significant increase in the size of the schooling coefficient between the ages of 17 and 24.[h] The negative relation

---

[h]To specify an exact test for the significance of the differences in the schooling coefficients between the two ages, one would need a model that accounted for the paired nature of the observations and the correlations of the error terms from the two age regressions. A conservative test of the hypothesis of no difference is possible by simply pooling the observations at ages 17 and 24 and then re-estimating the regressions by cohort and sex with interaction terms for the age of the observation. The standard error of the interaction (difference) coefficient for schooling will be biased downward. A difference which is not significant in this test will thus not be significant with correctly estimated unbiased standard errors. In this simple test, the significance level (two-tailed) for a difference in the schooling coefficient by age is greater than 0.2 for all sex/cohort regressions.

The finding of no change in the schooling coefficients between the two ages in the logistic model means that realizing additional years of schooling results in no change in the relative odds of smoking as a function of eventual schooling. This is not the same as asserting that realizing additional schooling will give no change in the relative proportions of smokers as a function of eventual schooling. But the logistic model is clearly the more appropriate one. To illustrate, use as an example two groups of men from our 1953–63 cohort: those who eventually complete 18 years of schooling, and those who eventually complete only 12 years of schooling. Using the predicted probabilities of smoking from table 2 (which correspond closely to the observed proportions of smokers), we see that the relative odds of smoking for the eventual 18th graders versus the eventual 12th graders at age 17 are:

$$(0.08/0.92)/(0.62/0.38) = 0.053.$$

The relative odds of smoking for the two groups at age 24, after they have differentiated on the schooling dimension, equals 0.051. These relative odds at the two ages are nearly identical. However, the relative proportions of smokers for eventual 18th graders versus eventual 12th graders rises from 0.129 to 0.25 between the ages of 17 and 24. These relative proportions are clearly different. But how could one expect them to be the same? The proportion of smokers at those two ages is affected by

between completed schooling and smoking is generally as strong at age 17 as at age 24 for all cohorts; for women, the relationship is even stronger at age 17 than at age 24 for the two most recent cohorts. At age 17, however, the individuals were all still in the same school grade (approximately). The relative differences in the probability of smoking that are observed at age 24 between persons with differing years of schooling are already present at age 17, before the schooling is obtained. The additional schooling cannot be the cause of the differential smoking behavior, since the realization of the schooling does not have any marginal effect on the size of the schooling coefficient.

The second important result is that the differences in smoking by years of schooling appear to be motivated, at least in part, by health concerns. This can be seen in the variation in the schooling coefficients by cohort, which shows how the schooling–smoking relation has changed over time. This variation is important because before 1953 there was little public discussion linking cigarettes to bad health, and before 1964 there was little explicit public anti-smoking policy.

The regression results in table 1 show that schooling has a sharply different relation to smoking in the periods before and after health consequences of smoking became a major public concern, rather than a gradually changing relation over time. Though all but one are negative, the schooling coefficients for the two pre-1953 cohorts for all sex/age smoking combinations are small; none are significantly different from zero ($p > 0.10$ for all). On the other hand, all the post-1953 cohort coefficients are strongly negative and significantly different from zero (at $p < 0.01$), except for the 1953-63 cohort for women, where the coefficient at age 17 is less significant (different from zero at $p < 0.05$) and the coefficient at age 24 is still quite small and insignificant.

The only significant differences in schooling coefficients among cohorts are between the pre-1953 and post-1953 cohorts, not within either of these two groupings ($p > 0.10$ for all within-group tests). For men at both ages, post-1953 cohort coefficients are significantly different from the pre-1953 cohort coefficients (at $p < 0.05$). For women, the only strongly significant difference ($p < 0.05$) is between the 1964–72 cohort and the pre-1953 cohorts at age 17. The results for women show a weaker relation between the schooling coefficient and the spread of information about health effects of smoking than do the results for men. The 'pure

---

other factors besides eventual schooling (not least of which is simply the passage from adolescence to adulthood with greater income and freedom). Thus, it is not surprising to see a 260% increase in the proportion smoking for the group of eventual 18th graders between ages 17 and 24 (of whom only 8 percent were smoking at 17), but such a percentage increase between ages 17 and 24 in proportion smoking would have been mathematically impossible for the group of eventual 12th graders, of whom 62 percent were already smoking at age 17.

Table 1. Maximum-Likelihood Logit Regression Results for Probability of Smoking at Age 17 and Age 24, by Sex and Age Cohort.[a] White Men and Women Aged 24 to 75 Years, With 12 to 18 Years of Completed Schooling. Asymptotic Standard Errors of Coefficients in Parentheses.

Variable	Men				Women			
	1921–41	1942–52	1953–63	1964–72	1921–41	1942–52	1953–63	1964–72
Smoking at age 17								
Years of schooling	−0.098	−0.141	−0.487[c]	−0.317[c]	0.026	−0.130	−0.305[b]	−0.454
	(0.123)	(0.110)	(0.131)	(0.100)	(0.127)	(0.152)	(0.136)	(0.122)
Father's years of schooling	−0.065	0.115	0.033	−0.083	0.012	0.059	0.122	−0.040
	(0.057)	(0.068)	(0.066)	(0.051)	(0.074)	(0.073)	(0.068)	(0.057)
Intercept	0.851	0.217	5.984[c]	4.614[c]	−2.664	−0.736	1.407	5.556[c]
	(1.618)	(1.528)	(1.728)	(1.362)	(1.690)	(1.947)	(1.630)	(1.546)
N	130	98	120	178	189	130	143	195
$\bar{P}$	0.262	0.327	0.375	0.287	0.101	0.131	0.210	0.246
Smoking at age 24								
Years of schooling	−0.078	−0.154	−0.490[c]	−0.352[c]	−0.108	−0.160	−0.098	−0.305[c]
	(0.104)	(0.101)	(0.125)	(0.090)	(0.084)	(0.100)	(0.091)	(0.094)
Father's years of schooling	−0.012	0.103	0.090	−0.092	0.098[b]	0.021	−0.020	0.004
	(0.049)	(0.066)	(0.063)	(0.049)	(0.049)	(0.051)	(0.051)	(0.049)
Intercept	1.766	1.349	6.541[c]	6.065[c]	−0.011	1.589	1.521	3.706[c]
	(1.366)	(1.444)	(1.681)	(1.290)	(1.087)	(1.307)	(1.193)	(1.209)
N	130	98	120	178	189	130	143	195
$\bar{P}$	0.646	0.520	0.617	0.455	0.365	0.408	0.483	0.379

[a]Cohort defined by calendar year when respondent became 17 years old.
[b]Significant at $p < 0.05$.
[c]Significant at $p < 0.01$.

schooling' correlation for women may be contaminated more than for men by correlations between schooling and social class and social class and propensity to smoke.[11]

The coefficients for father's schooling by cohort in table 1 are small and all but one are statistically insignificant. Nor do we find any systematic pattern of variation in the coefficients by cohort. Even if own schooling is left out of the regression or father's schooling is restricted to have the same coefficient across all cohorts, the father's schooling coefficient remains weak. Father's schooling may perform poorly in these regressions because of correlation with several potentially conflicting influences on smoking, such as social class, own education, and family income.

The intercept coefficients in table 1 show the partial effect of cohort, holding the effect of interactions between schooling and cohort at zero. To obtain the mean effect of cohort holding schooling constant at some nonzero level, one must sum the simple intercept coefficient and the effect of the schooling coefficient evaluated at the specified level of schooling. We evaluated the inter-cohort effects with schooling held constant at the mean value of the whole sample (rather than zero) to judge the overall time trend in smoking behavior for the average person.

At mean schooling levels the partial effect of cohort for men is increased smoking in successively younger cohorts up to the 1953–63 cohort for both ages (except for a dip at age 24 in the 1942–52 cohort), followed by a sharp decline in smoking in the 1964–72 cohort. For women, smoking increases in successive cohorts right through the 1964–72 cohort at age 17; at age 24, smoking increases through the 1953–63 cohort and then drops sharply in the 1964–72 cohort. None of these cohort-to-cohort changes are statistically significant (at $p < 0.05$), however, except the decrease in smoking among 24-year-old men in the 1964–72 cohort. This overall trend in smoking corresponds to that found in other surveys.[10]

One way to illuminate the differences in the schooling–smoking relation by cohort, age, and sex is to examine the predicted probabilities of smoking implied by the regression results. Table 2 shows those predictions for the end values and midpoint of years of schooling, for each cohort/age/sex combination. These predicted probabilities clearly show the dramatic change in the schooling–smoking relation between the pre- and post-'health concern' cohorts. The strong negative relation between schooling and smoking came about primarily from decreases in smoking by the highly educated; smoking probabilities for those

Table 2. Predicted Probability of Smoking at Ages 17 and 24, by Sex, Cohort, and Years of Completed Schooling:[a] White Men and Women Aged 24–75 Years, With 12 to 18 Years of Completed Schooling.

Cohort[b]	Age 17			Age 24		
	12 years schooling	15 years schooling	18 years schooling	12 years schooling	15 years schooling	18 years schooling
			Men			
1921–41	0.26	0.21	0.17	0.67	0.61	0.56
1942–52	0.44	0.34	0.25	0.65	0.54	0.43
1953–63	0.62	0.28	0.08	0.84	0.54	0.21
1964–72	0.48	0.26	0.12	0.70	0.44	0.22
			Women			
1921–41	0.10	0.10	0.11	0.44	0.36	0.29
1942–52	0.16	0.11	0.08	0.47	0.36	0.26
1953–63	0.28	0.14	0.06	0.53	0.46	0.39
1964–72	0.42	0.16	0.05	0.52	0.30	0.15

[a]Based on maximum-likelihood logit regressions of probability of smoking reported in table I. Probabilities are evaluated at mean father's schooling.
[b]Defined by calendar year when age 17.

with only 12 years of schooling are generally as high or higher in the post-'health concern' cohorts as in the pre-'health concern' cohorts. Table 2 also reaffirms that the schooling–smoking relationship observed at age 24, after schooling was completed, could be accounted for by equally strong differences in smoking probabilities among the same individuals at age 17, before they had obtained differential amounts of schooling.

Discussion

The data examined in this paper reject the hypothesis that additional years of schooling play a significant causal role in the schooling–smoking correlation.[i] There are apparently one or more 'third variables' that affect both smoking and

[i]This paper does not explicitly address the possibility that differences in quality of schooling prior to the 12th grade could be the cause of the observed differences in smoking behavior at age 17. Differences in quality, however, are similar to additional years of schooling because both reflect differences in the quantity of education inputs into, the individual. We find no causal relationship between education inputs after the 12th grade (in the form of additional years of schooling) and smoking. To assert a strong causal role for education inputs up to the 12th grade (in the form of 'quality' differences) would then require that causality diminish with increasing schooling and finally cease by the 12th grade. It seems implausible to us to suppose that schooling can increase knowledge,

years of schooling. These data do, however, support the hypothesis that the schooling–smoking relation, and by implication, the effect of any underlying 'third variable', is related to considerations of health consequences of smoking.

What is the third variable that leads to differences in both schooling and smoking? The data do not support the view that differences in 'social class' are the underlying cause. First, the effect of father's schooling is very weak and not statistically significant even in regressions which omit the individual's own schooling. Second, 'class' effects should presumably have been present for the older cohorts as well as the more recent ones, but no significant relation between schooling and smoking emerges until the post-1953 cohorts.

Mental ability is another possible third variable. Those individuals who complete additional schooling are presumably more intelligent. Smoking incidence among high-school students has also been negatively correlated with academic performance, which itself is a correlate of ability.[3] Thus, even though all our sample have the same number of years or schooling at age 17, those of greater mental ability may more rapidly absorb and act upon information about the harmful effects of smoking, as well as obtain more additional schooling. If the schooling–smoking correlation were primarily due to superior mental ability, however, one might expect that it would become weaker over time as knowledge about the harmful effects of smoking became more widely diffused. The analysis by cohort provides no significant evidence of such weakening over time.

Fuchs (1982) suggests that both schooling and smoking behavior are related to individual differences in time discount, i.e., willingness and ability to incur current costs for future benefits. Schooling has long been recognized as a form of investment decisions about cigarette smoking have a similar character. Assuming imperfect capital markets, so that no single marginal rate of time discount would prevail for all persons in all domains, differences in time discount could explain the observed correlation,between schooling and smoking. The data in this study are consistent with this hypothesis, but cannot test it.

Cigarette smoking is undoubtedly an important intervening variable in the correlation between schooling and health. If, as this study suggests, additional years of schooling is not causally related to smoking, identification of the 'third variable' that affects both may provide a key to understanding the schooling–health relation.

---

change preference, increase ability for self-control, or otherwise exert strong influence over smoking behavior until the 12th grade and not thereafter.

References

1. Antonovsky, A. (1967). "Social Class, Life Expectation and Overall Mortality." *Milbank Memorial Fund Quarterly* **Jan.**: 31–37.
2. Auster, R., Leveson, I. and Sarachek, D. (1969). "The Production of Health: An Exploratory Study." *Journal of Human Resources* **4**: 412–436.
3. Borland, B. L. and Rudolph, J. P. (1975). "Relative Effects of Low Socioeconomic Status, Parental Smoking and Poor Scholastic Performance on Smoking Among High School Students." *Social Science and Medicine* **9**: 27–30.
4. Consumer's Union (1954). "Cigarette Smoking and Lung Cancer." *Consumer Report* **19**(Feb.): 54–92.
5. Friedman, G. D., Petitti, D. B., Bawol R. D. and Siegelaub, A. B. (1981). "Mortality in Cigarette Smokers and Quitters." *New England Journal of Medicine* **304**: 1407–1410.
6. Fuchs, V. R. (1982). "Time Preference and Health: An Exploratory Study." In *Economic Aspects of Health*, ed. V. R. Fuchs. University of Chicago Press: Chicago, IL, pp. 93–120.
7. Garrison, L. P. (1981). Studies in the economics of surgery, Ph.D. dissertation, Stanford University, Stanford, CA.
8. Grossman, M. (1972). "On the Concept of Health Capital and the Demand for Health." *Journal of Political Economy* **80**: 223–255.
9. Grossman, M. (1975). "The Correlation between Health and Schooling." In *Household Production and Consumption*, ed. N. E. Terleckyi. Columbia University Press: New York, pp. 147–223.
10. Harris, J. E. (1979). "Cigarette smoking in the United States, 1950–1978." In *USDHEW, Public Health Service, Smoking and Health*, Report of the Surgeon General. DHEW publication no. (PHS)79-50066. GPO, Washington, DC.
11. Harris, J. E. (1980). "Patterns of Cigarette Smoking." In *USDHHS, Public Health Service, The Health Consequences of Smoking for Women*, Report of the Surgeon General. GPO, Washington, DC, pp. 17–42.
12. Harris, J. E. (1981). "On the Mortally Risk of Cigarette Smoking." Presented at the *International Workshop on the Analysis of Actual versus Perceived Risks*, June 1–3, Washington, DC.
13. Lieb, C. W. (1953). "Can the Poisons in Cigarettes be Avoided?" *Reader's Digest* **63**: 45–47.
14. Maccoby, N. and Solomon D. S. (1981). Health Disease Prevention: Multi-Community Studies." In *Public Communication Campaigns*, eds. R. E. Rice and W. J. Paisley. Sage Publications: Beverly Hills, CA, pp. 105–125.
15. Miller, L. M. and Monahan, J. (1954). "The Facts Behind the Cigarette Controversy." *Reader's Digest* **65**(July): 1–6.
16. Newhouse, J. P. and Friedlander, L. J. (1980). "The Relationship between Medical Resources and Measures of Health: Some Additional Evidence." *Journal of Human Resources* **15**: 200–218.
17. Norr, R. (1952). "Cancer by the Carton." *Reader's Digest* **61**: 7–8.
18. Taubman, P. and Rosen, S. (1982). "Healthiness, Education and Marital Status." In *Economic Aspects of Health*, ed. V. R. Fuchs. University of Chicago Press: Chicago, IL, pp. 121–140.

19. Thaler, R. A. and Shefrin, H. M. (1981). "An Economic Theory of Self Control." *Journal of Political Economy* **89**: 392–406.
20. U.S. Department of Health, Education and Welfare, National Clearinghouse for Smoking and Health (1976). Adult Use of Tobacco — 1975. GPO, Washington, DC.
21. U.S. Department of Health, Education and Welfare, Public Health Service (1964). Smoking and Health. Report of the Advisory Committee to the Surgeon General, PHS publication no. 1103. GPO: Washington, DC.
22. Vogt, T. M., Selvin, S., Widdowson, G. and Hulley, S. B. (1977). "Expired Air Carbon Monoxide and Serum Thiocyanate as Objective Measures of Cigarette Exposure." *American Journal of Public Health* **67**: 545–549.

2.3

Reflections on the Socio-Economic Correlates of Health

Income, education, occupation, age, sex, marital status, and ethnicity are all correlated with health in one context or another. This paper reflects on the difficulties encountered in deriving robust scientific conclusions from these correlations or drawing reliable policy applications. Interactions among the variables, nonlinearities, casual inference, and possible mechanisms of action are discussed. Strategies for future work are suggested, and researchers are urged to pay special attention to possible interactions among health, genes, and socio-economic variables.

Income, education, occupation, age, sex, marital status, and ethnicity are all correlated with health in one context or another. Effective health policy requires an understanding of these correlations; such understanding is also relevant for broader economic issues such as productivity, income distribution, labor force participation, and intergenerational transmission of poverty. No one has done more to advance understanding of these correlations than Michael Grossman. His seminal work on the demand for health[1] quickly had a major impact on health economics and has continued to inspire streams of research ever since. In addition to his own exceptional productivity, Grossman has been the foremost mentor of Ph.D. s in health economics. He and his students have investigated almost every

Originally published in *Journal of Health Economics*, 23: 653-661, 2004. Copyright by Elsevier B.V.

aspect of health from infant mortality to substance abuse, with special attention to the roles of education and income in determining health outcomes.

Despite the contributions of Grossman and others, it seems to me that considerable uncertainty remains concerning the socio-economic correlates of health, the extent to which they reflect causal chains, and their implications for policy. There are numerous reasons for this uncertainty. Many of the socio-economic variables are correlated with each other; sometimes it is difficult to estimate the independent relationship of each one with health. To skirt the problem of multi-collinearity, some researchers refer simply to "socio-economic status" (SES), but this blending of income, education, and occupation limits the scientific value and policy applicability of the research. Interactions among the variables are numerous and varied, as are nonlinearities. One of the biggest problems is establishing causality. Moreover, even when a causal connection appears to be particularly robust, the mechanism of action is usually unknown. All of these problems are exacerbated by the fact that health is multi-dimensional. Frequently used measures such as mortality, morbidity, disability, and self-reported health status are usually positively correlated, but sometimes the correlations are weak and occasionally are even negative. For example, holding age constant, women report worse health and greater disability than men but have higher life expectancy. Additional complications arise from possible interactions among genes, changing medical technology, and the socio-economic variables.

This brief overview of my reflections on these matters cannot possibly cover them in depth; it summarizes my views about the state of knowledge in this area and concludes with some suggestions for future research.

Income

Of all the socio-economic variables, the relationship between income and health is probably the most complicated. The correlation can vary from highly positive to weakly negative, depending on context, covariates, and level of aggregation. Even when the positive correlation is strong and stable, the interpretations can include causality running from income to health, from health to income, and/or "third variables" that effect health and income in the same direction.

In high-income countries, researchers usually conclude that the correlation is positive and that the causality runs from higher income to better health. The strength of this effect, however, varies greatly by age, disease, level of income, and other variables. The mechanism(s) through which income might affect health are usually not clearly established. Income can facilitate access to medical care (through insurance or direct purchase), but some of the most carefully controlled studies such as the RAND health insurance experiment do not show significant health effects from better insurance coverage, and universal coverage in European countries does not eliminate the income–health correlation. Income can support acquisition of food, shelter, and other goods and services that contribute to better health, or it can be an indicator of greater efficiency in home production of health (if productivity in the market and in the household are positively correlated). On the other hand, higher income (holding education and other variables constant) may signal longer hours of work, more stress, or participation in dangerous occupations, thus offsetting possible favorable effects of higher income on health.

Some researchers make a distinction between income and wealth. This distinction would be redundant if the two variables were measured comprehensively (including human capital and imputed income), if capital markets worked perfectly, if there were no transaction costs, and if individuals did not engage in peculiar forms of mental accounting. When empirical research produces different results for income and wealth, or for different forms of income, it would be useful to determine why.

The relationship between health and income is particularly strong across countries at below average levels of income. When 149 countries are sorted into quintiles according to Gross Domestic Product per capita in the late 1990s, those in the middle quintile ($3860 average GDP per capita) have 20 years more life expectancy than countries in the lowest quintile ($800 GDP per capita), but only 10 years less than countries in the highest quintile ($20 910 GDP per capita).

The stronger relation across poorer countries may reflect a greater effect of income on health or a greater impact of health on income. Both explanations are probably valid. Higher income in poor countries can increase access to health-enhancing necessities and can support investments in sanitation. Better health means much higher survival rates for infants and children, which raises GDP per capita by increasing the ratio of workers to dependents. Better health among adults increases labor force participation and improves the productivity of those who are at work. Even in high-income countries, a causal chain from health to income is observed when sicker older workers withdraw from work prior to normal retirement, thus reducing their current income as well as their subsequent public and private retirement income.

To see how health and income can be negatively correlated, consider two high-income countries with equal endowments of human, physical, and natural resources but sharply different attitudes toward work. In one country the work week is 35 h, there are many holidays, and four to eight weeks of annual vacation. In the other country, everyone works nearly all the time. The gross domestic product per person would almost surely be higher in the second country, but it would not be surprising if life expectancy were lower. Could this help explain why life expectancy in Italy is higher in the South than the North while income is higher in the North?

Many different "third variables" could be responsible for the positive correlation between income and health, but the obvious ones, such as education, are usually controlled for. Other possibilities, such as the level of seretonin in the brain or the strength of the immune system, are never controlled for. These variables are, no doubt, partly endogenous, but also partly reflect differences in genes, intrauterine developments, and environmental factors in infancy and early childhood. Several additional questions concerning the income-health relationship must be mentioned, albeit all too briefly.

Nominal or real income?

Most health studies use nominal income measures, even when the individuals or populations live in different locations within the US. Significant differences in cost-of-living across these locations suggest that nominal income is an imperfect and probably biased measure of real income. Because the latter is presumably the variable expected to affect health, the former should be deflated by a cross-location cost-of-living index. The presumption of bias arises from the likelihood that nominal income and cost-of-living are positively correlated. If so, the elasticity of health with respect to real income would be greater than for nominal income.

Permanent or transitory income?

Some researchers find that it is permanent income that affects health; other models assume that transitory changes are very important. No one has produced a definitive answer to this question, probably because there isn't one. The answer may vary depending upon the health measure under study, the level of income, the age of the subjects, and other factors.

Absolute or relative income?

For a long time most researchers assumed that the positive correlation between income and health was driven primarily by the poor health of those living in poverty, defined as a very low absolute level of income. As income rose over time, however, the income–health gradient showed little evidence of diminishing. Thus, considerable attention is now given to relative income, i.e., to the fact that those at the bottom of the income distribution have worse health than their more affluent peers regardless of the average level of income. This change in focus requires a reexamination of the mechanisms that were invoked for the income–health gradient when average income levels were much lower. When those in poverty went hungry, the connection between health and income was obvious. Now, when obesity is widespread in the US, especially among low-income individuals, different explanations are required. It may be that having much less income than most of society has adverse effects on health in part through psychological mechanisms. More than 2 centuries ago Adam Smith in *The Wealth of Nations* wrote about the importance of relative income for well-being when he defined "necessaries" as "not only the commodities which are indispensably necessary for the support of life, but whatever the custom of the country renders it indecent for creditable people, even of the lowest order, to be without."

Education

Compared with income, the education–health relationship appears to be much less complicated. Causality running from health to education is possible, but there is less evidence of this effect than in the case of income. A negative correlation between health and education is very unlikely. Moreover, measurement is usually less problematic for education than for income. Michael Grossman, who has led the way in empirical as well as theoretical investigation of the education–health connection concludes that "years of formal schooling completed is the most important correlate of good health" (Grossman 2003, p. 32). Proponents of income can argue that education is serving as a proxy for long-term income, but proponents of education can counter that education's favorable effect on health works, in part, through higher income. The correlation is undoubtedly high in most contexts, but the case for a causal interpretation would be strengthened if certain questions could be resolved.

For example, in cross-section studies, income has sharply diminishing effects on health as income rises, but the apparent effect of additional years of schooling is undiminished at all levels. It is plausible that high school graduates learn something in school that makes them healthier than their peers who dropped out after tenth grade. But is it plausible that adding 2 years of schooling beyond college should have as large a causal effect on health?

The analogy between education's contribution to health and its contribution to higher earnings is also problematic. With respect to earnings, we know that college graduates who majored in science or engineering earn much more than humanities majors, and MBAs make much more than teachers with masters in education. Do similar differences exist in the education–health relationship? Are college graduates who majored in biology healthier than French literature majors? Does a masters degree in computer science confer more health benefits than one in art history? Does the content of schooling matter at all? If not, what is it that schooling does to improve health?

Education and intelligence are usually correlated, but inclusion of a control for intelligence in earnings regressions does not have much effect on the education coefficient. Is the same true for the education–health relationship? One study of health differences among elderly with chronic conditions found that inclusion of intelligence test scores eliminated the significance of the education variable.

Finally, there are large differences among high school students with respect to cigarette smoking, binge drinking, unprotected sex, and other unhealthy behaviors. Participation in these behaviors tends to be negatively correlated with the amount of schooling the students will eventually complete and negatively correlated with adult health. Thus, when we observe a positive correlation between completed education and adult health, we cannot assume that the additional education caused the better health. Some economists claim that teenagers know how much schooling they will complete (and how high their earnings will be) and that those who expect to have high incomes will take better care of their health even as teenagers so they can enjoy the higher income over a longer period. This may be theoretically correct, but probably weak in importance. One could also imagine a theoretical model in which teenagers who know they will have higher incomes in the future engage in more unhealthy behaviors because they will be better able to afford the medical care to deal with the consequences.

An alternative to inferring that schooling is the cause of better health is to posit the existence of one or more "third variables" that explain the correlation. One possibility is time preference. Individuals who have lower rates of time discount (more willing to delay gratification) are more likely to stay in school longer and do (or not do) the things that contribute to better (worse) health. Another possibility is self-efficacy, a concept developed by psychologist Albert Bandura to describe an individual's effective control over his (her) behavior. It is, of course, possible that additional schooling lowers time preference, or increases self-efficacy, thus bringing schooling back as a cause of better health.

To explain the education–health connection, some researchers have proposed that those with more schooling are quicker to act on new health information or take advantage of improvements in medical technology. This seems reasonable, but is it important? The persistence of the negative gradient between education and cigarette smoking many decades after information about the harmful effects of smoking became widespread raises questions about the robustness of this explanation.

In comparisons across low-income countries, women's education is found to be highly correlated with the health of infants and children. Because the level of schooling is usually quite low, it is certainly possible that learning to read and write and receiving some elementary instruction about sanitation and hygiene can have direct health effects. But again one must raise the possibility of omitted variables: those societies that afford greater educational opportunities to women probably also have other customs, traditions, and policies more favorable to women. Such differences would have favorable effects on the health of women and their children independently of the additional schooling.

Occupation

Some occupations are much less healthy than others. For example, work related death rates in construction and transportation are triple the rate for all workers. Death rates in agriculture and mining are even higher — five to six times the national average. In addition to fatal injuries, there are large differences across occupations in non-fatal injuries, exposure to toxic materials, and long-term damage to health through physical and psychological stress. Information about past occupation(s) could be as important as current occupation.

Extensive research on earnings differentials across occupations concludes that (ceteris paribus) riskier occupations pay higher wages. But this fact poses a dilemma for investigators. If occupation is not included in a regression of health on income and education, the coefficients may be biased. But inclusion of occupation as an additional RHS variable is also problematic without more understanding of occupational "choice." The constraints facing a young man born amid the coal mines of West Virginia are undoubtedly different from those confronting a native of Manhattan.

Age

That health decreases with age (on average) is a fundamental fact of biology. Because age is frequently correlated with income, education, and other variables, it is essential to control for age through age-adjustment, or better still, analysis of age-specific data. Interactions between age and other variables such as income and education are often quite important. In particular, the correlation between health and income varies greatly over the life cycle, and not monotonically.

Sex

At the close of the 20th century, the life expectancy of women exceeded that of men in every country. This is attributed to biological differences, but interactions between these differences and the physical and social environment are of major importance. In low-income countries ($1000 Gross Domestic Product per capita or less), the female-male differential in life expectancy is only about 4%. For countries with GDP per capita around $3000, it is 8%, and at $9000 it averages 11%. But the differential does not continue to increase with GDP per capita. In the 30 highest income countries (GDP per capita averaging $21000), the sex differential in life expectancy is only 8%. A similar shift can be observed over time in the female-male differential in life expectancy in high-income countries. Over the past 30 years, the differential has tended to fall, reversing the previous long-term trend toward a higher ratio in the course of economic development. In the US this downward trend occurred at the same time that the female–male education ratio was rising.

Marital Status

In every country, married men and women are healthier than their unmarried peers. Moreover, marital status is usually correlated with income and education. Thus, researchers usually include marital status as a RHS variable when it is available. The presence of a spouse is assumed to make a positive contribution to the household production of health or to increase the demand for health. But there is another possible explanation for the correlation that has the causality running from health to marital status: healthier men and women tend to do better in the marriage market. If that is the case, the typical equation is mis-specified.

Both views come sharply into play when considering the fact that the marital status–health correlation is much stronger for men than women. The household production story would say that wives are much more important for the maintenance of their husband's health than the reverse. The marriage market selection story would say that health is a more important determinant of marital status for men than for women. Panel data might help shed light on this puzzle.

Ethnicity

Ethnic differences in health are extensively discussed but convincing explanations are rare. Because ethnicity is frequently highly correlated with other socio-economic variables, a deeper understanding of ethnic differences could contribute substantially to understanding the relation between socio-economic variables and health.

This understanding will not come easily. Measurement problems abound because classification of an individual in a socially constructed ethnic group can depend on self-identification or on the perception of others. The categories are inherently imprecise, and often include heterogeneous sub-categories. Ethnicity may be a marker for genetic differences, cultural differences, or differential treatment by others. Understanding how the legacy of centuries of slavery, segregation and discrimination may affect the health of blacks in the US today is particularly problematic. Researchers must try to avoid stigmatization or the reinforcement of stereotypes, but must also avoid providing incorrect or incomplete explanations because they are politically correct.

The most challenging ethnic health problem in the US is to explain why black life expectancy is 7 years less than white. The most frequently proposed answers–lower income, less education, and poorer access to medical care–probably have some validity; however, Hispanic-Americans rank lower than blacks on all three measures but do not experience such adverse health outcomes.

Concluding Observations and Suggestions for Research

The focus of most empirical research is on hypothesis testing and determining whether the data are "consistent with the model." Policy makers would benefit from more focus on quantitative estimates of the relation between health and the independent variables.

Most quantitative estimates (and some qualitative inferences) of the relation between socio-economic variables and health are context specific. Policy decisions, therefore, should be based as much as possible on empirical research that covers the relevant contexts.

Even when researchers are confident that they have established a causal connection, they rarely are explicit about the mechanism(s) of action. The elucidation of mechanisms can be enhanced by inclusion of previously omitted variables. For example, if the investigator believes that income increases health through access to medical care, inclusion of one or more measures of access should provide support or refutation of this belief.

Another way of probing for mechanisms is through disaggregation. If the investigator believes that income (or education) affects health through mechanism X, it will usually be possible to draw on medical and epidemiological knowledge to say, "If it is X, the effect will be greater at certain ages than at others, or greater for mortality from certain causes of death than for others." Repeating the analysis with disaggregated data will lend support to or cast doubt on the proposed mechanism.

Most researchers look for regularities in the data, but there may be significant pay-offs to pursuing anomalies. For example, why do Hispanic-Americans have higher life expectancy than blacks despite less education and lower income? Why is the black–white ratio of heart disease mortality at ages 45–74 much higher for females than males even though black–white differentials in hourly earnings and education are smaller for females than males?

Another question deserving careful attention is why the correlation between income and health is so much stronger in cross-section individual data than in cross-area mean data? Are there differences in income distribution across areas (plus nonlinear relationship between income and health) that are concealed in the area means? Or is there more genetic variation (third variable explanations) within than between areas? Or is there more causality from health to income within areas because the between area differences in income are affected by inherited physical capital, industry mix, location, and other income determinants not controlled for in the regressions? Or are all three explanations relevant?

My final suggestion for research is to pay more attention to interactions between genes and socio-economic variables. For example, social scientists have often identified stress as a major cause of bad health, but sceptics have noted that the effects of apparently the same stress vary greatly across individuals. Recent genetic research helps explain why. Among individuals exposed to considerable stress, the probability of depression is very high for those with two short versions of a particular gene, moderately high for those with one short and one long version, and no higher than that of unstressed individuals for those with two long versions. It seems inevitable that similar interactions will be found for many genes and many diseases. Economists seeking to broaden understanding of the socio-economic correlates of health will have to incorporate these interactions into their analyses.

References

1. Grossman, M. (1972). *The Demand for Health: A Theoretical and Empirical Investigation*. Columbia University Press for the National Bureau of Economic Research: New York.
2. Grossman, M. (2003). "Education and Nonmarket Outcomes." In *Handbook of the Economics of Education*, eds. E. Hanushek and F. Welch. North-Holland, Elsevier Science: Amsterdam.

Op-Ed

Social Determinants of Health: Caveats and Nuances

Belief in the importance of the social determinants of health is gaining wide acceptance; this useful development will undoubtedly contribute to better public policy and clinical practice.[1] Although the general concept is not contested, several caveats and nuances should be considered.

First, statements such as "social determinants explain half the variation in health" are neither correct nor incorrect; they are incomplete. Assessments of the relative importance of different determinants depend critically on the health variation to be explained. For instance, if the goal was to explain the sharp increase in life expectancy at birth in the United States during World War II, 0.5% per annum from 1940 to 1945, health determinants could be divided roughly into 3 categories: social (eg, income, education, neighborhood), biological (genes), and medical care (quantity and quality, including state of science and technology). Significant biological changes over such a short period as World War II did not contribute to increase in life expectancy. Absent any major scientific or technological change and the diversion of approximately half of all practicing physicians to military service during the war, medical care would be an unlikely

Originally published in *JAMA*, 317(1):25–26, January 2017. Copyright by American Medical Association.

explanation. That leaves social determinants such as unusual increases in income, decreases in unemployment, and positive shifts in the national psyche inspired by war as the most likely explanations.

Another example of variation is the rapid decline in cardiovascular and cerebrovascular mortality between 1970 and 1980. Again, the period is too short for biological change to have played a role. Some social changes such as a decrease in smoking among men likely contributed. However, smoking among women did not decrease, but vascular mortality among women declined at the same rate as among men. The most likely explanation is medical care, especially more aggressive and effective control of blood pressure. Before the Veterans Administration multisite studies of 1967 and 1970, a systolic blood pressure of 100 mm Hg plus the patient's age was considered normal and did not require treatment.[2,3] As noted in the fourth Joint National Committee,[4] by extending the Veterans Administration practices to other patient populations, gains in hypertension control contributed to a 50% decline in coronary artery disease mortality.[4]

A third example is low infant mortality among Mexican Americans, with a rate slightly less than the rate among non-Hispanic whites.[a] That this could be explained by more or better-quality medical care is unlikely. The percentage of people without health insurance is above average for Mexican Americans, who often live in medically underserved areas. Similarly, the social conditions for Mexican Americans, as reflected in income and education, are worse than for non-Hispanic whites. That leaves a biological explanation as the likely explanation.

When discussing the relative importance of social determinants and medical care for health outcomes, a critical distinction must be made between cross-sectional variation in health at a point in time and changes in health outcomes over time. In studies across states, cities, and other geographical regions, differences in the quantity of medical care are easily controlled for, and the frontier of medical science and technology is, for all practical purposes, similar everywhere. For such cross-sectional variation, the social determinants, such as income, education, and neighborhood and health behaviors such as cigarette smoking, usually provide more explanatory power than differences in medical care. By contrast, variation in health outcomes over time in the United States at present is usually explained

---

[a]US Department of Health and Human Services (HHS) Office of Minority Health. Infant mortality and Hispanic Americans. HHS website. http://minorityhealth.hhs.gov/omh/browse.aspx?lvl=4&lvlid=68. Accessed October 24, 2016.

more by advances in medical science and technology. In recent decades, some social determinants such as a decline in cigarette smoking have contributed to better health outcomes, but some, such as an increase in the prevalence of obesity and the fragmentation of families, have had the reverse effect. Social determinants, as a group, probably explain little of the increase in life expectancy.

In understanding the relative importance of social determinants or medical care in increasing life expectancy over time, it is vital to specify where and when. In the United States in the early decades of the 20th century, before the discovery and diffusion of antibiotics, life expectancy increased rapidly, primarily because of improved sanitation, cleaner drinking water, and improving living standards. Medical care did not have a significant role in the rate of increase of life expectancy from 1900 to 1930 of 3.1 years per decade. By contrast, the increase in life expectancy in the most recent 30 years of 1.5 years per decade was attributable less to social determinants than to better control of high blood pressure and cholesterol levels, substantial advances in perinatal interventions, and superior diagnostic and therapeutic interventions for patients with trauma.

A large number of social variables-income, education, housing, nutrition, occupation, and others-are correlated with life expectancy, and most are highly correlated with each other. This multicollinearity increases the difficulty of allocating scarce resources to derive the most health benefit. The answer may depend on the particular health problem being addressed. For example, if the goal is to close the gap in life expectancy between black and white populations, the most effective interventions may be different from those for closing the gap between rural and urban populations.

Chetty et al.[5] have documented a substantial correlation between income and life expectancy derived from millions of individual observations, but they decline to conclude that this proves a causal mechanism from income to life expectancy. An alternative inference is a causal mechanism from health (life expectancy) to income. Moreover, it is possible that the causal connection runs one way at certain socioeconomic levels and reverses at another.

Years of schooling completed has a strong negative correlation with the probability of smoking, which is highly correlated with life expectancy. But a study of the probability of smoking at age 17 years (when all individuals in the study had approximately the same amount of schooling) revealed an equally high negative correlation between the probability of smoking and years of schooling the individual would have completed by age 24 years.[6] This is evidence against the hypothesis that additional years of schooling is the cause of the differential in the probability of smoking.

Some health outcomes may vary as the result of interactions between 2 or more determinants. Research on such interactions between the genes of individuals and interventions of medical care are proceeding at a rapid pace. But the possibility of interaction with social determinants should also be considered. For example, for a given diagnosis, the appropriate choice between treatment with surgery or medication might depend on the social condition of the patient. Similarly, the best policy choice of public health interventions might depend on the social determinants of the target population.

The increasing recognition by the health care community of the importance of social determinants of health along with biological and medical care is welcomed. The embrace of these insights, however, should be accompanied by an awareness that the relative importance of different determinants depends on the variation in health to be explained. Application of these insights to public health and clinical policies will improve as more is learned about the causal mechanisms between determinants and health, of interactions between determinants, and the size as well as the direction of effects on health.

References

1. Adler, N.E., Glymour, M.M. and Fielding, J. (2016). "Addressing Social Determinants of Health and Health Inequalities." *The Journal of American Medical Association* **316**(16): 1641–1642.
2. Veterans Administration Cooperative Study Group on Anti-hypertensive Agents. (1967). "Effects of Treatment on Morbidity in Hypertension: Results in Patients with Diastolic Blood Pressures Averaging 115 Through 129 mm Hg." *The Journal of American Medical Association* **202**(11): 1028–1034.
3. Veterans Administration Cooperative Study Group on Anti-hypertensive Agents. (1970). "Effects of Treatment on Morbidity in Hypertension II: Results in Patients with Diastolic Blood Pressure Averaging 90 Through 114 mm Hg." *The Journal of American Medical Association* **213**(7): 1143–1152.
4. 1988 Joint National Committee (1988). "The 1988 Report of the Joint National Committee on Detection, Evaluation, and Treatment of High Blood Pressure." *Archives of Internal Medicine* **148**(5): 1023–1038.
5. Chetty, R., Stepner, M., Abraham, S. *et al.* (2016). "The Association Between Income and Life Expectancy in the United States, 2001–2014." *The Journal of American Medical Association* **315**(16): 1750–1766.
6. Farrell, P. and Fuchs, V.R. (1982). "Schooling and Health: The Cigarette Connection." *Journal of Health Economics* **1**(3):217–230.

Op-Ed

Black Gains in Life Expectancy

In recent decades the US black population has experienced substantial gains in life expectancy, now approaching the life expectancy of the white population. Between 1995 and 2014, the increase in black life expectancy at birth was more than double the white increase: a gain of 6.0 years from 69.6 years to 75.6 years for black people compared with a gain of 2.5 years from 76.5 years to 79.0 for white people.[1] The difference in the percent per annum rate of increase was also more than double: 0.44 for black people, 0.17 for white people.

Male life expectancy increased more rapidly than female life expectancy in both races. From 1995 through 2014, life expectancy at birth increased from 65.7 years to 72.5 years among black men, from 73.3 years to 76.7 years among white men, from 73.9 years to 78.4 years among black women, and from 79.6 years to 81.4 years among white women;[1] thus, black men had the largest gains of the 4 race-sex groups, with a rate of increase of 0.52% per annum. Also noteworthy is that between 1990 and 2011, the bottom half of the black survivor distribution gained appreciably more than the top half: 0.65% per annum

Originally published in *JAMA*, 316(18):1869–1870, November 2016. Copyright by American Medical Association.

vs 0.24%. The bottom half, a gain of 8 years of life expectancy, and the top have had a gain of 4 years. In 1990 for black individuals, life expectancy for the top half of the survivor distribution was 30.3 years more than the lower half (84.3 vs 54.0 years); in 2011, the gap was reduced to 26.8 years (88.7 vs 61.9 years).[1]

In a study of changes in black-white differences in life expectancy from 1999 to 2013, Kochanek *et al.* found that the gap in life expectancy closed by 2.3 years, from 5.9 to 3.6 years. The authors reported that greater decreases in cardiovascular disease mortality for blacks accounted for 0.37 years of the total decrease in the gap, cancer accounted for 0.32 years, human immunodeficiency virus (HIV) disease for 0.31 years, unintentional injuries for 0.28 years, and perinatal conditions for 0.14 years. Thus, gains in just 5 causes accounted for almost 60% of the decrease in the black-white life expectancy gap. A study by Firebaugh *et al.* (2014) shifted the emphasis to black-white changes in age of death rather than cause of death. Their study combined all causes of death into just 4 major categories. Because there is an interaction between cause and age, cause of death might have been found to have more influence and age less of an influence if the study had divided cause of death into many more discrete categories.

The potential for further closing the gap in life expectancy between blacks and whites has changed significantly since the 1990s. The death rate for HIV disease has declined so substantially that even elimination of the large racial differential could not have a major effect on the existing life expectancy gap for all causes. Much the same could apply for deaths from perinatal conditions and, to a lesser extent, even to deaths from cardiovascular disease. Although cardiovascular disease is still a major cause of death, the average age of death from this cause has increased appreciably for both sexes, thus reducing the potential for further gains in life expectancy. For instance, in 2014, more than half the deaths from cardiovascular disease in white and black women occurred after age 85 years. Among white men, the median age of death from cardiovascular diseases was 78 years; for black men, it was 68 years.

To make a significant contribution to reducing the current gap between black and white life expectancy, a cause must have substantial number of deaths and a significantly higher age-adjusted death rate for blacks than for whites. Eleven causes of death meet those 2 criteria (Table). For example, diabetes mellitus ranks high on both counts, with a black age-adjusted death rate almost double the white death rate (37.3 vs 19.3 per 100 000 in 2014 and more total deaths, 13 435 among blacks and 59 741 among whites in 2014) than most of the other causes on the list. With a goal of reducing the 17% differential in black-white all-cause deaths,

Table 1. Significant Causes of Death With the Highest Ratio of Deaths of Black to White and Total Number of Deaths From Each Cause, 2014[a]

Cause of death	Total no. of deaths[b]	Age-adjusted death rates per 100 000		Black-white ratio
		Blacks	Whites	
Human immunodeficiency virus infection	6721	8.3	1.1	7.5
Homicide	15 809	17.2	3.0	5.7
Essential hypertension and hypertensive renal disease	30 221	15.6	7.4	2.1
Nephritis, nephrotic syndrome, and nephrosis	48 146	24.6	12.1	2.0
Cancer of prostate	28 344	13.9	7.3	1.9
Diabetes mellitus	76 488	37.3	19.3	1.9
Septicemia	38 940	17.9	10.2	1.8
Cancer of breast	41 678	16.4	11.0	1.5
Cerebrovascular disease	133 103	49.7	35.2	1.4
Cancer of colon, rectum, anus	52 234	18.6	14.0	1.3
Diseases of the heart	614 348	206.3	165.9	1.2

[a]Adapted from[1] (Tables 12 and 16).
[b]Total number of deaths for all races and ethnicities.

it appears that progress in just a few causes probably will not be enough; progress in many causes will be required.

The very high black-white ratio for age-adjusted homicide deaths suggests another opportunity for reducing the racial gap in all-cause deaths, but realization of the opportunity depends more on public health measures such as gun control than on medical care. Essential hypertension, prostate cancer, kidney disease (nephritis, nephrotic syndrome, nephrosis), and septicemia all have high black-white age-adjusted mortality ratios and a substantial number of total deaths, posing a challenge to research, prevention, diagnosis, and therapeutic interventions. Continued progress in preventing and treating heart disease in black men could also make a substantial contribution because of the large number of these men who die young relative to white men and black women.

In 1944, Gunnar Myrdal Nobel Prize winner in Economics, wrote that black-white differences were arguably the United States most important problem. Major advances in life expectancy that bring blacks closer to whites is a significant contribution to its solution.

References

1. Kochanek, K. D., Murphy, S. L., Xu, J. and Tejada-Vera, B. (2016). "Deaths: Final Data for 2014." *National Vital Statistics Report* **65**(4): 1–122.
2. Kochanek, K. D., Arias, E. and Anderson, R. N. (2015). *Leading Causes of Death Contributing to Decrease in Life Expectancy Gap Between Black and White Populations: United States, 1999–2013.* National Center for Health Statistics: Atlanta, GA, November Data brief, 218.
3. Firebaugh, G., Acciai, F., Noah, A. J., Prather, C. and Nau, C. (2014). "Why the Racial Gap in Life Expectancy is Declining in the United States." *Demographic Research* **31**(32): 975–1006.
4. Myrdal, G. (1944). *An American Dilemma: The Negro Problem and Modern Democracy.* Harper & Bros: New York, NY, p. 194.

Part 3

The Cost of Care

Introduction

If there is one red hot health subject that never seems to go away, it is the high cost of medical care. In 1927, Ray Lyman Wilbur, physician-president of Stanford University, became chair of a national committee to look into the high cost of care. The committee was later staffed by Rufus Rorem (1894–1988), one of the first health economists and one of my mentors. He taught me a great deal about health care through stories such as the following: Rufus published an article, "Why Hospital Costs Are So High" and was deluged with requests for reprints from hospital administrators. He then published another article, "How to Keep Hospital Costs From Going Higher." There were no requests for reprints.

The first paper in Part 3 dates back to 1967 when I addressed a National Conference on Medical Care Costs on "The Basic Forces Influencing Costs of Medical Care." I gave reasons for concern about the rise in national health care expenditures from $4 billion in 1929 to over $40 billion in 1965, an inflation-adjusted per capita rate of increase of 3.4 percent per annum. Repeated expressions of concern since 1965 did not do much to slow the rate of growth, it averaged 3.2 percent per annum between 1965 and 2015. The rate of increase has been, on average, lower since 1995 than in 1965–1995; it is a major challenge to economists to determine why. Possible answers include increase in managed care, slower growth of GDP, the 2008 recession, and Obamacare. To the extent that slower growth of health care expenditures is the result of slower growth of GDP that is small comfort because the nation's ability to pay for health care depends on the GDP.

My paper identifies the major factors that influence health care expenditures. On the demand side, they are the price of care relative to other prices, the responsiveness of demand to changes in relative prices (i.e., the price elasticity), changes in income, the income elasticity of demand, health insurance, health of the population, education, and a shift from home production of some health care to market production. On the supply side, there has been dramatic technologic change including antibiotics, drugs to lower blood pressure and cholesterol, and new diagnostic and surgical interventions. Assessments of the relative importance of these diverse factors has not yielded definite answers, and the explanations may vary from one period to another. In my judgment, the most important factors contributing to the growth of expenditures are the growth of private and public health insurance and the development of new medical technologies. As Burton Weisbrod pointed out, these phenomena are partly related. Independent increases in insurance boost the demand for new technologies. Independent innovations increases the demand for health insurance.

Looking toward the future, there will probably be less impetus to growth from increases in insurance because coverage is already widespread. In 2015 approximately 91 percent of Americans had health care insurance, albeit many policies were not comprehensive. The course of scientific advance and the development of new drugs and other technologies is difficult to predict. Other countries have created institutions to evaluate cost-effectiveness of new medical technologies, but so far the U.S. has given mostly lip service to this approach. The Trump Administration has promised "more competition" and "less regulation" as the route to slower growth of health care expenditures. I see little in history to believe that would work, especially since Trump has also promised "health care for all." Competition among hospitals often results in higher expenditures as they try to lure physicians with expensive new technologies. Competition among physicians often result in higher expenditures even at lower fees as physicians resort to "physician-induced" demand in an attempt to maintain income.

The second and third papers serve to illustrate my conclusions about the importance of supply factors in driving expenditures, conclusions not shared by all health economists. I believe that in many local health care markets an increase in the supply of physician specialists does not do much to reduce fees but does increase utilization and expenditures. One way, which I think will command wide agreement, is that it becomes easier to get an appointment, waiting time decreases, thus the effective cost to the patient is less. But beyond that effect, I believe that physicians can increase or decrease the demand for their services by the advice and instructions they give to patients, and this varies depending how busy they are. When supply increases for reasons unrelated to demand, a physician with spare time is more likely to encourage utilization than he/she would with a full practice. The data show that in many markets some specialists are extremely busy while others are working at their specialty at much less than their full capacity. Fees are set and maintained at a level that provides a satisfactory income for those with less than full workloads. Choice of location of specialists is affected by demand for their services but is also influenced by factors similar to those that influence other high income earners: good schools (either public or private), upscale shopping and restaurants, recreational and cultural amenities, and the like. The presence of one or more good hospitals is also a plus. Even if an increase in physician supply should exert downward pressure on fees, the effect on the demand of insured patients would be slight. For example, a $100 decrease in fees is experienced as only a $20 decrease for the patient with 80 percent insurance coverage. I believe the increase in utilization and expenditures associated with an increased supply is mostly the result of "physician-induced" demand.

The fourth paper addresses a question much discussed in health economics of the possible effect on costs of treatment by medical faculty and their residents compared with care from community physicians. Most studies attempted this comparison between "teaching" hospitals and those that were not. Critics easily pointed out that costs could differ for reasons other than teaching status.

My colleagues and I were fortunate to obtain data on costs and outcomes for patients admitted by faculty and others by community physicians in the same hospital. This meant that many of the variables that might vary between hospitals were the same for all the physicians. Results for comparisons of faculty admitted and community physician admitted patients were similar for a study of a 1000 patients in each group and for 51 matched pairs. In general, patients treated by faculty (and residents) had higher costs and fewer in-hospital deaths.

For the 51 pairs of seriously ill patients, matched for age, sex, DRG, and predicted probability of death, the results for costs and outcomes were striking. Average costs per patient were twice as high in the faculty group than those admitted by community physicians. In 44 of the 51 pairs, the faculty patients had higher costs. This was partly the result of longer stays and partly higher costs per day. Outcomes were a different story. The in-hospital death rate was almost twice as high for the community physician patients as for those admitted by faculty. It is relevant to note the differences in DNR (do not resuscitate) notation on the medical charts; 6 of 51 for faculty, 26 of 51 for the community physicians. Difference in code status, however, did not explain the difference in costs or mortality. For

23 pairs with the same code status, the faculty-community cost differential was the same as for the 51 pairs and the faculty patients still had fewer in-hospital deaths. For 48 pairs we were able to follow up the patients for one year, and here is the other striking result. While the in-hospital death rate was almost double for the community physician patients, by 240 days after discharge, the survival rates were equal and continued to be equal to the end of the year at 17 percent of admissions in each service.

The paper concludes with an extensive discussion of the results, including possible patient differences in attitudes toward death and pre-admission care, and differences in attitudes and goals of faculty physicians and their residents. Allowance for such differences pose additional problems for policy makers who want to establish systems that are equitable and efficient, and maintain tolerable opportunities for patient choice when third parties are paying the bill.

My opportunity to present the results of the study to a group of faculty physicians and to a group of community physicians provides an interesting footnote to the study and food for thought. Both groups were pleased with the results. The faculty felt that their higher costs were justified because "they save lives." The community physicians felt that they were providing "appropriate" care given the condition and preferences of their patients.

The two op-eds deal with controlling the cost of health care from different perspectives. The discussion of waste in health care expenditures identifies two definitions: *medical* waste is care that according to current expert opinion offers no benefit to the patient, *economic* waste is care where the expected benefit to the patient is less than expected cost. The first type exists, but, in my opinion, accounts for only a minor share of expenditures. Economic waste is widespread, as one would expect, given fee-for-service payment of physicians and widespread insurance that insulates patients from the cost of care. It is not unreasonable for the patient to want all the care that might do some good, and it is not surprising that most physicians want to provide it. Consideration of uncertainty present in most medical encounters and heterogeneity in patient reactions to an intervention complicates the analysis and tends to increase utilization.

The second op-ed approaches this problem from the point of view of the physician who wants to behave ethically by delivering "appropriate" care. The physician who avoids only "medical" waste will be faithful to the obligation to the individual patient, but the physician who avoids "economic" waste will be serving the interests of all patients and society as a whole. The op-ed concludes by arguing that the physician's practice context will have a big effect on the physician's decision about what is "appropriate" care. If the physician is paid fee-for-service and the patient has open-ended insurance, the pressures are in favor of doing as much as is medically justified. On the other hand, if the patient is part of a defined population that pays an annual fee, and if the physician is in an integrated group practice with responsibility for the health of the defined population, it is more likely that he/she will decide that cost-effective medicine is "appropriate" care.

3.1

The Basic Forces Influencing Costs of Medical Care

Introduction

Until quite recently, an economist was rarely to be found in the company of the nation's leading physicians, and on those few occasions, he was likely to be flat on his back with one or more of his vital organs exposed to public view. It is my intention here to provide exposure of a different sort. The question — The basic forces influencing costs of medical care — is one which almost every physician would be prepared to tackle. My aim is to indicate how an economist goes about answering it. Economics is, above all else, a way of looking at questions. In Lord Keynes's words, "The Theory of Economics does not furnish a body of settled conclusions immediately applicable to policy. It is a method rather than a doctrine,

Originally published in *Report of the National Conference on Medical Care Costs*, pp. 16–31, U.S. Department of Health, Education, and Welfare, U.S. Government Printing Office, Washington, D.C.; reprinted in *The Modern Hospital*, September 1967; reprinted in *Federal Programs for the Development of Human Resources*, Joint Economic Committee, Vol. 2, Washington, D.C., 1968; reprinted in Victor R. Fuchs (ed.) (1972), *Essays in the Economics of Health and Medical Care*, pp. 39–50. New York, NY: Columbia University Press for the National Bureau of Economic Research.

an apparatus of the mind, a technique of thinking, which helps its possessor to draw correct conclusions."

To be sure, even among economists there is not always just one way of looking at things. Winston Churchill used to complain that whenever he asked Britain's three leading economists a question, he received four different answers — two from John Maynard Keynes. Nevertheless, there is a common fund of concepts, a common core of analysis, that nearly all economists use.

The basic analytical approach is a consideration of the factors affecting the demand for medical care and those affecting the supply — demand and supply, the two magic words. Some of us, when visiting hospitals, have discovered that by putting on a white coat and talking rudely to nurses it is easy to pass as a physician. To be mistaken for an economist is often even simpler. All one need do is nod gravely and say "demand and supply."

Definition of terms

Demand for and supply of what? I shall assume that medical care refers to the services rendered by physicians, dentists, and other health professionals, plus all the goods and services consumed in connection with their work, or upon their direction. Thus, the costs of medical care include the costs of hospitals, drugs, and the like. This lumping of diverse health services is a concession to convention and to the limitations of time. Ideally one should apply the demand-supply analysis separately to hospitals, dentists, drugs, and so on because the forces that influence the cost of one type of health service are often different from those that influence another.

What is meant by costs? At least three possible meanings can be distinguished. It could mean price, or cost of production, or expenditures. When people speak of the rising costs of medical care, they frequently are referring to rising expenditures, and this is the way I shall use the term.

Expenditure trends

We all know that these expenditures have been growing rapidly. In round numbers, expenditures for medical care have risen from under $4 billion in 1929 to over $40 billion in 1965 and probably close to $50 billion in 1967. Even as recently as twenty years ago, expenditures were only $10 billion. Of course, expenditures for most other goods and services have also risen; it is therefore more meaningful for some purposes to look at the share of total spending allocated to medical care. This, too, has risen, from under 4 percent in 1929 to about 6 percent in recent years. Nearly all of this relative increase has occurred since 1947.

Before examining the factors responsible for this trend, it is worth noting that there is nothing wrong a priori with changes in industry and sector shares of gross national product. Indeed, such changes seem to be a natural concomitant of economic growth. For instance, the relative importance of agriculture has declined precipitously in most western countries. During the last half of the nineteenth and the first half of the twentieth century there was a significant rise in the relative importance of manufacturing. Now we are witnessing in this country the growth of what I have described elsewhere as the "first service economy."[a] If agriculture's share of GNP falls from over 9 percent to under 4 percent, as it did in the United States between 1947 and 1965, some other industries must show increases. There is no magic in the 4 percent figure for medical care; it is now 6 and it could be 8 or 10.

Reasons for concern about costs

Why then should there be a national conference on the costs of medical care? Let me suggest three reasons for concern.

First, questions arise concerning the contribution that these increased expenditures make to health. Although we spend much more per person for medical care than any other country, we do not enjoy the highest health levels. On the contrary, many European countries have age-specific death rates considerably below our own. The relatively high infant mortality rate in this country is disturbing, and difficult to explain. The disparity in death rates for middle-aged males is even more shocking, and has more serious economic implications. In the United States, of every hundred males who reach the age of forty-five, only ninety will reach fifty-five. In Sweden the comparable figure is ninety-five. During this critical decade when most men are at the peak of their earning power, the U.S. death rate is double the Swedish rate, and higher than that of almost every western nation. It certainly seems legitimate to ask why. This is not necessarily with a view to spending less for medical care — I doubt if anyone can foresee a decline — but with a view to developing more effective use of the resources that we are now devoting to health.

A second reason why we should be concerned about medical care costs is the peculiar structure of the medical care industry. Most industries in the United States consist of profit-seeking firms actively engaged in competition with one

---

[a] Victor R. Fuchs, *The Growing Importance of the Service Industries,* Occasional Paper 96, New York, NBER, 1965.

another. The fundamental rationale of the American economic system is that the hope of profit (and the fear of loss) under conditions of open competition are the best guarantees of efficiency, appropriate price and rate of output, and fair returns to the various factors of production. By contrast, the medical care industry is organized along radically different lines. Nonprofit operations are the rule in the hospital field; there are severe restrictions on entry and competition in medical practice; and advertising and patent control dominate the market for drugs. Thus, there is no a priori basis for believing that the prices and quantities of medical care approach those that would result from perfectly competitive market conditions.

A third reason is that a large and still increasing portion of the cost of medical care is paid by third parties. In particular, the taxpayer is being called upon to pick up a substantial share of the bill. Because payment for medical care is increasingly regarded as a collective responsibility, it is natural and appropriate that there should be collective expressions of concern, such as this conference reflects, about the quantity and quality of medical care, and about its price.

These quantities and prices are determined by demand and supply. Let us consider each side of the equation in turn.

Demand for Medical Care

Economists say that the demand for any good or service depends upon relative prices, income, and tastes.

Price

How does price affect expenditures? Perhaps the most firmly established proposition about the demand for medical care is that it is relatively inelastic with respect to price. If the price rises relative to other prices, the decline in the quantity demanded will be proportionately less than the increase in price. The result is an increase in medical care expenditures. If, other things remaining unchanged, price rises by 10 percent and quantity demanded falls by only 5 percent, expenditures will rise by approximately 5 percent. Some studies suggest that the price elasticity of demand for medical care may be as low as 0.2, i.e., quantity demanded declines by only 2 percent when price rises by 10 percent. But present knowledge does not permit fixing a specific value beyond saying that the elasticity is surely below unity.

An aspect of the price of medical care that is not widely recognized is that it really has two components. One is the nominal price charged by the physician or hospital; the other is the value of the patient's time.[b] For instance, the nominal price of a visit to a physician might be ten dollars, but the trip to and from his office, the wait, and the actual examination will probably take an hour or more. This time might be worth more or less than ten dollars depending upon the alternatives available to the patient.

Once it is understood that the price of medical care includes both components, a number of interesting implications become apparent. Even if no sliding fee scale is used, the total price of medical care tends to vary with earning power. The price is lower for retired people and the unemployed than for those with jobs, generally lower for women than for men, and so on. Also, even when the nominal price is reduced to zero, as under prepayment plans or socialized medicine, the true price is not zero.

Income

One of the factors to be considered in any demand study is real per capita income. During the past twenty years this has risen by over 50 percent, and there is no doubt that the demand for medical care increases with income. What is less clear is whether the demand for medical care is elastic or inelastic with respect to income, i.e., whether a given percentage increase in income leads to more, or less, than the same percentage increase in medical care expenditures, other things remaining the same. This question is only gradually yielding to attack as more and better data become available and analytical techniques are sharpened. Some recent studies suggest that the elasticity may be significantly below unity, and few investigators believe that it is greater than unity. At most, the demand for medical care seems to increase approximately in proportion to income. If this is true, we cannot attribute any of the increase in medical care's *share* of total expenditures to rising income.

Insurance

A special factor that complicates the analysis of the demand for medical care is the growth of insurance and prepayment plans. Once a person is covered by such a plan, the effective price to him of additional units of medical care depends only upon the value of his time. This may explain a large part of the increase in the quantity of medical care demanded, and may also help explain the apparent

---

[b]Gary S. Becker, "A Theory of the Allocation of Time," *Economic Journal,* 75, September 1965, pp. 493–517.

insensitivity of insured consumers to increases in the nominal price of medical care. It is worth noting that hospital care has shown the most rapid rate of increase in expenditures, and it is hospital care that has been most thoroughly covered by insurance and prepayment.

The curious behavior of dental expenditures also offers support for this hypothesis. All the available evidence suggests that at any point in time the demand for dental care is more elastic with respect to income than is the demand for physicians' services.[c] Nevertheless, during these recent decades of sharply rising income, expenditures for dental care have increased less than have expenditures for physicians' services. One possible explanation is the very small role played by insurance and prepayment plans in the dental field. Expenditures for eyeglasses and appliances and for drugs, two other components of medical care that are typically paid for directly by the consumer, have also risen much less rapidly than have expenditures for hospitals or physicians.

This should not come as a surprise. The advocates of insurance and prepayment had something like this in mind. They wanted to remove any financial barriers to obtaining medical care. But it is a basic law of economics that if you lower the price, the quantity demanded will increase. A critic of the British National Health Service put the matter cogently, albeit a bit strongly, in a recent issue of *The Lancet*: "If taxi fares and meters were abolished, and a free National Taxi Service were financed by taxation, who would go by car, or bus, or walk. . . the shortage of taxis would be endemic, rationing by rushing would go to the physically strong, and be more arbitrary than price, and 'the taxi crisis' a subject of periodic public agitation and political debate."[d]

This does not mean that insurance and prepayment should be abandoned. But it does suggest a need to discover techniques — possibly coinsurance, deductibles, or experience rating — to check prices and expenditures without interfering with essential health services.

Tastes

All factors other than income or price that affect demand are put by economists in a catchall category called taste. In the case of medical care, this would include the factors that affect the health levels of the population and the attitudes toward seeking medical care at any given level of health. Taste for medical care, therefore,

---

[c] See Morris Silver's essay "An Economic Analysis of Variations in Medical Expenses and Work-Loss Rates" below.

[d] Arthur Seldon, "National or Personal Health Service," *The Lancet,* 1, March 25, 1967, p. 675.

would be related to: (1) demographic variables, (2) education, (3) environment, (4) ways of living, and (5) the genetic stock of the population.

Research on these matters is only in its infancy, and there are few reliable findings to report. We know that an increase in the proportion of elderly people in the population tends to increase the demand for medical care, other things remaining the same. The effect of increased education is unclear. It probably leads to improved health levels, and thus less need for medical care, but may also lead to greater demand for medical care at any given level of health.

Most observers believe that recent environmental changes, particularly the increase in real income per capita, have contributed to better health status. I think that this inference is incorrect. Some tentative findings from my research suggest that the environmental and life-style changes of the past two decades have had either a neutral or negative impact on health for most of the population. One piece of evidence in support of this hypothesis is the stability of age-adjusted death rates in the United States in the face of large increases in medical care and improvements in medical science.[e]

All these questions, however, are in need of more study. The National Center for Health Statistics is now developing vast new bodies of relevant data. A combined assault on these data by health experts and social scientists could yield information of great importance in our continuing efforts to understand and improve the nation's health.

Accounting illusion

In concluding this discussion of demand, it should be noted that part of the observed increase in medical care costs is an accounting illusion. It does not involve any increase in real costs — only money costs. It is the result of an increase in the proportion of medical care produced and sold in the market, and a decline in the proportion provided outside the market by family, friends, and neighbors. Only the former is included in the GNP. A generation ago, a considerable amount of bed care and associated services for the sick were provided for at home. Surely there is relatively less of this today.

Some of the reasons for this shift other than increases in income and insurance coverage, are: (1) urbanization, (2) the fragmentation of the family, and (3) the increased labor force participation of women. We do not know how much of the increase in observed medical care costs can be attributed to this shift, but it may be substantial. One corollary is that "home care" programs and other current plans

---

[e] See the essay "The Production of Health, an Exploratory Study" below.

to transfer costs back out of the hospital will reduce the money costs of medical care by more than they will reduce real costs.

Supply of Medical Care

I turn now to the supply of medical care. In studying the supply side of an industry there are three main elements to look at. The first is the supply of the factors of production — labor and capital — flowing into the industry. The second is changes in productivity, and the third is the degree of monopoly control, or other market imperfections that may influence the supply actually available to consumers.

Supply of productive factors

With respect to the supply of labor going to the health industry, the crucial question is whether the industry has to pay inordinately high wages in order to attract an increasing fraction of the total labor force. There is some evidence to suggest that the answer to this is "no." In technical terms, the supply of labor for the medical care industry is very elastic.[f] This is true, incidentally, of most other industries as well. Except in the extremely short run, the U.S. labor force is highly mobile and adaptable; studies of interindustry differences in earnings consistently refute the hypothesis that expanding industries must pay unusually high wages to bid away labor from other industries.

Between 1950 and 1960 medical care employment rose by 54 percent, compared with only 14 percent for total employment. Throughout the postwar period the annual rate of increase has been about 5 percent for medical care employment, compared with a little over 1 percent for the economy as a whole. Despite this rapid expansion, wages for medical care personnel seem to have been rising at about the same rate as in many other industries. This last point has not been thoroughly documented, but seems to be a reasonable inference from the data available.

An analysis of the supply of capital to the medical care industry is much more difficult to undertake because most capital is used in hospitals, and most hospitals are nonprofit. Thus, the flow of capital is not determined by the rate of profit (as it is in most industries), but by government decisions and by philanthropy. It is possible, however, to devise methods of financing and reimbursing hospitals that would make the flow of new investment more responsive to market-type

---

[f] It certainly would be in the absence of medical licensure and other restrictions on entry.

mechanisms. The Soviet Union and other socialist nations have been attempting to do precisely this with substantial portions of their "nonprofit" economies.

Productivity

Changes in the supply of any good or service, in the sense of changes in the price-quantity relationships, depend primarily on changes in productivity. It is a commonplace to argue that productivity in medical care has advanced less rapidly than in the economy as a whole; but in the absence of reliable measures of the output of medical care this must remain a matter of speculation.

The development of such measures is an extremely difficult task because of our ignorance concerning the precise contribution of medical care to health. In addition, output is not limited to improvements in health but takes other forms, including validation services and the "hotel" aspects of hospital care.[g]

There is some reason to believe that the available measures understate the true output of the medical care industry. A visit to a physician today is surely more productive than one twenty years ago, and this is even more true of a patient-day in a hospital. On the other hand, it is possible that many of the expensive procedures that are now part of "best practice" techniques are really not worth the money in the sense that their marginal contribution is small and the same amount of resources used in other ways would yield more utility to the consumer.

The common practice of reimbursing hospitals on the basis of their costs, as under Medicare and many other public and private programs, appears to be an open invitation to inefficiency. At best, the ability of hospital management to improve productivity is imperfect because of the independence of the attending staff. Under present arrangements, almost no one has any incentive to be concerned with the efficiency of the hospital as a whole.[h]

Physicians

The physician plays a key role in the supply of all medical care; his decisions and behavior affect almost everything else. Physician supply is now more specialized than formerly. This growth of specialization is often attributed to exogenously determined advances in medical science, but such an explanation ignores the role

---

[g] See the preceding essay in this volume.

[h] With few exceptions, each hospital is independently "owned" and managed. In other industries an exceptionally able manager may gradually come to exercise supervision over an increasingly large pool of resources through the growth of his firm, through mergers, and through establishment of branch plants; this pattern is absent in the hospital field. Also, it is much easier for inefficient management to remain in charge for long periods of time.

played by changes in demand. Two hundred years ago, Adam Smith observed that the division of labor is limited by the extent of the market. The relevant market for any one physician's services has grown tremendously because of the growth of income and population, the increased concentration in urban centers, and improvements in transportation. All these trends would lead to increased specialization, even if medical technology remained static. Moreover, given an increase in real income people want to buy more medical service for any given health condition. One way of buying more service would be to visit several different general practitioners, or to visit the same one several times. Alternatively, one can buy more medical service in each visit through the use of specialists. The specialist in medicine usually has more, not merely different, training than a general practitioner. The more valuable the patient's time, the greater will be the demand for "high powered" doctors. This demand-induced growth of specialization is thus a cause as well as a result of advances in medical science. Without a specialized practice, without the demand for specialized equipment and procedures, these advances would probably come more slowly.

Physicians have frequently been criticized because of their high earnings and their alleged desire to restrict their numbers. Such criticism, it seems to me, does not go to the heart of the matter. Most of the difference between the earnings of physicians and those of other occupations should not be attributed to their control over entry and competition, but to their long hours of work, the lengthy period of education required, and the absence of pensions, paid vacations, and other fringe benefits. Moreover, physicians' earnings account for less than 20 percent of total health expenditures, and whatever the extent of their monopoly return, it could only be a small part of this fraction.

A more valid criticism, it seems to me, can be directed against physicians for their opposition to changes in the methods of producing and financing medical care. The medical profession, or at least a significant and articulate portion of it, seems to believe that there can be rapid and far-reaching technological change without disturbing the traditional organization of medical practice. This belief is irrational. One clear lesson from economic history is that technological innovation means organizational change.

One final aspect of physicians' market control is the extremely narrow range of options available for someone seeking personal medical care. One bit of evidence is the size distribution of earnings in the entire medical care industry which can only be described as unnatural. Nearly all American industries have a distribution which reflects a fairly smooth vertical hierarchy of personnel. There are usually large numbers performing routine functions, and relatively fewer persons at each successive stage of increased power and responsibility. Only in the medical care industry do we find almost a void in the middle of the distribution and a peak at the high end.[i]

Whether consumers would use less expensive medical care personnel, if available, would depend upon a number of factors — the institutional setting and supervision, the presence of a financial incentive, and so on. That it is technically possible for professionals with fewer than ten to twelve years of training beyond high school to render useful medical care has been repeatedly demonstrated in a variety of settings.

As some of my earlier remarks suggested, patients with high incomes and patients with acute conditions would undoubtedly continue to seek the highest possible level of training and experience. But the demand for something less might be large in cases of chronic illness, or in isolated communities, or among those with low incomes.

New medical techniques

One special feature of the supply of medical care is the appearance of radically new medical techniques and procedures. Normally, when economists speak of the supply of a commodity they assume that the quality of the commodity remains unchanged. This is almost never strictly true, even for such staples as coal or wheat, but frequently the change in quality comes gradually and can be objectively measured, and an increase in quality can be thought of as a decrease in price.

In the case of medical care, some of the new procedures (such as renal dialysis and open heart surgery) are so radically different from anything previously available that they cannot conveniently be analyzed in this manner. Part of the increased expenditure for medical care is undoubtedly attributable to the appearance of these new techniques for treating conditions that simply could not be treated before.

Summary of the Demand-Supply Analysis

What conclusions emerge from this analysis of demand and supply? By now it should be clear that cost is the result of many forces, that rising costs are not necessarily bad (or necessarily good), and that economists have some interesting questions to ask, but are far from being able to supply all the answers. Many of the estimates have a large range of uncertainty, but sustained scientific investigation can reduce that range and increase understanding.

---

[i]See "The Distribution of Earnings in Health and Other Industries" by Fuchs, Rand, and Garrett below.

If we take as our analytical task the explanation of why medical care now accounts for 6 percent of gross national product instead of the former 4 percent, the following developments all seem to have played a role:

1. An increase in medical care prices *vis-à-vis* other prices facing a relatively inelastic demand. These price increases are probably related to the institutional rigidities that surround the organization and production of medical care.
2. The growth of insurance, prepayment, and other forms of third-party payment.
3. A shift from nonmarket to market production. If we measured all costs, the increase for medical care would not be as great as the GNP accounts indicate.
4. The introduction of radically new medical techniques and procedures to treat conditions that formerly could not be treated at all.
5. More tentatively, I have suggested that there may be greater need for medical care now to offset changes in the environment and in ways of living that are detrimental to health.

There is, admittedly, considerable question about the relative importance of these various factors, but the new emphasis being given to research on these problems should help us to make the quantitative estimates that are needed for planning and control.

3.2

Surgical Work Loads in a Community Practice

Many physicians and laymen believe that the only solution to the alleged "doctor shortage" is a massive increase in the number of physicians;[5,7,8] other observers, however, have been calling attention to the under-utilization of physicians in those tasks which long years of training have equipped them to perform.[10,20,22] With the social cost of college plus medical school now well in excess of $100,000 per student, it is essential that the question of effective and efficient use of medical manpower receive careful study.

One area of medicine which has long been suspected of harboring underutilization is surgery. According to Longmire,[18] "... in each community in our country there are a few surgeons who are doing all or more than they humanly can do. Many, though, are working at a pace far below their capacity and this is a tremendous waste of highly skilled talent." Bunker[3] has hypothesized that in the United States there may be too many surgeons for the needs of the population and has suggested that this may lead to unnecessary surgery. Fuchs,[9] using aggregate national data, has calculated that even if all operations were done by surgical specialists, their average work load would be below five operations per week, which would fall far below capacity. Maloney[14] and Owens[17] have also

Originally published in *Surgery*, 71(3):315–327, March 1972. Copyright by the C. V. Mosby Company. Written with Edward F. X. Hughes, M.D., M.P.H., John E. Jacoby, M.D., Eugene M. Lewit, B.A.

presented evidence of work loads in this range — Maloney for university surgeons and Owens for general surgeons. Strickler[21] and Phillips[18] have argued the other side of the issue: that there is adequate work for surgeons and even a need for more in certain areas. Riley and associates[19] provide indirect evidence that such a need many exist.

There have been very few attempts to measure the surgical work load of individual surgeons or of populations of surgeons,[11,15,18] and even fewer attempts to carefully distinguish among different types of surgeons and different types of procedures. The current study is an attempt to elicit direct evidence about the alleged underutilization of surgeons by quantifying the in-hospital surgical work load of a population of general surgeons. We first develop a methodology for aggregating different types of surgical procedures and then apply it to a population of general surgeons, in private practice, in a suburban community in the New York metropolitan area. No attempt is made in this present study to measure the nonoperative work loads of these surgeons or to appraise the quality of care they deliver.

Methods

The problem of aggregation. A major problem in measuring surgical work loads is the development of a set of weights to be applied to different procedures so that a meaningful summary index can be calculated. This is a common problem in economics and the customary solution is to use "price weights." A similar approach could be used for surgical procedures by the application of a relative value scale, such as that developed by California Medical Association in the 1950's[6] and subsequently adopted by a number of medical societies.[4]

The California Medical Association established the relative value scale to assist practitioners in arriving at equitable fees. The Association asked practitioners to list their customary fee for a multitude of procedures. After extreme values were discarded, median and modal fees were determined. The median values were then multiplied by a conversion factor such that a small procedure (puncture aspiration of abscess, subsequent) was given unit value and all other procedures expressed as multiples of it.

A surgical relative fee value is intended to encompass all the work associated with a procedure: pre- and postoperative care as well as the actual operation. The question arises, however, whether the relative fees are systematically related to the work involved in different procedures. To answer this question, the following data were collected for 24 general surgical procedures (of graduated complexity) and three miscellaneous categories. These latter categories were designed to encompass all general surgical procedures not included in the previous 24 and were classified as being of minimal (Class I), moderate (Class II), or considerable complexity (Class III).

1. *Operating room (OR) time.* The operating room log book of a major New York teaching hospital was examined to obtain the average OR time for each of the 27 categories. OR time, defined as the time from entrance of the patient to the operating room to his leaving that room, was recorded directly from the log. Data were collected for 20 consecutive operations in each category. For the miscellaneous categories, and the unilateral inguinal herniorrhaphy category, 50 operations were recorded. These additional data were collected because of the diversity within the miscellaneous categories and because the herniorrhaphy category is used as an index in our weighting system. The mean for each category was calculated.
2. *Length of stay.* Total length of hospital stay for each patient whose OR time was recorded was extracted from the hospital discharge record. The mean for each category was calculated.
3. *Relative fees.* The "1960 Relative Value Studies" of the California Medical Association (Committee on Fees of the Commission on Medical Services, 1960) was the source of the relative fee value of each procedure.
4. *Other data.* It was hypothesized that the care of a patient undergoing an operation with a high mortality risk would entail more work than an operation with a lower risk. The lack of comprehensive, comparable data on operative mortality rates, however, precluded the inclusion of this variable in the subsequent analysis.

Table 1 and Fig. 1 reveal an extremely high correlation between the relative fee and OR time ($r = 0.97$). There is a moderate correlation between relative fee and length of stay ($r = 0.40$). From a regression of relative fee on OR time, the elasticity at the mean values was found to be 0.95, indicating an increase of 0.95 percent in relative fee for each 1 percent increase in OR time. The addition of length of stay to the regression equation has very little effect on either the OR time regression coefficient or the total explanatory power.

This evidence indicates that the relative fee value of a given operation is, in fact, a good reflection of the work associated with the procedure and would serve as a satisfactory weighting scale for comparing different procedures. To simplify our weighting scale, the relative fee value for each category was divided by the relative fee value for an adult unilateral inguinal herniorrhaphy (35.0). The resulting quotient expresses the value of each category as a multiple of a herniorrhaphy (see Table 1) and carries the label, "hernia equivalents." Thus, a

Table 1.   Relative Fee, Operating Room (OR) Time, and Length of Stay for 24 Surgical Procedures and 3 Miscellaneous Categories.

Procedure	Relative fee	OR time (min.)	Length of stay (days)	Hernia equivalents		
				Relative fee	OR time	Length of stay
1. Breast biopsy	15	50.2	3.7	0.43	0.57	0.44
2. Rectal fistulectomy	22	41.8	7.7	0.63	0.47	0.92
3. Hemorrhoidectomy	30	39.0	5.7	0.86	0.44	0.68
4. Pilonidal cyst, excision	30	50.8	6.6	0.86	0.57	0.78
5. Inguinal herniorrhaphy, unilateral adult	35	88.4	8.4	1.00	1.00	1.00
6. Phlebectomy, unilateral	40	74.8	1.6	1.14	0.84	0.19
7. Appendectomy	40	79.5	11.3	1.14	0.90	1.34
8. Exploratory laparotomy	40	93.0	30.2	1.14	1.05	3.60
9. Colostomy	45.8	87.5	41.6	1.31	0.99	4.95
10. Amputation of leg	52.5	74.8	71.4	1.50	0.84	8.50
11. Inguinal herniorrhaphy, bilateral adult	52.5	117.9	8.5	1.50	1.33	1.01
12. Thyroidectomy	55	120.0	6.4	1.57	1.36	0.76
13. Bilateral phlebectomy	60	125.5	5.2	1.71	1.42	0.62
14. Splenectomy	60	155.8	25.1	1.71	1.76	2.99
15. Cholecystectomy	62.5	146.5	19.8	1.78	1.66	2.36
16. Vagotomy and pyloroplasty	70	170.8	12.2	2.00	1.93	1.45
17. Radical mastectomy	70	179.8	14.2	2.00	2.03	1.69
18. Gastroenterostomy and vagotomy	75	176.0	20.1	2.14	1.99	2.39
19. Gastrectomy	80	214.0	26.6	2.28	2.42	3.17
20. Colectomy	81.5	198.8	27.2	2.33	2.25	3.24
21. Lobectomy	100	200.0	26.6	2.86	2.26	3.17
22. Abdominal-perineal resection	100	254.5	26.0	2.86	2.88	3.10
23. Peripheral vascular surgery	120	216.2	29.0	3.43	2.44	3.45
24. Aortic-mitral valve replacement	200	423.8	35.7	5.71	4.79	4.25
25. Class I	23.7	49.4	12.1	0.68	0.56	1.44
26. Class II	56.5	125.4	22.6	1.61	1.42	2.69
27. Class III	141.4	368.1	28.9	4.04	4.16	3.44

radical mastectomy with a relative value of 70.0, 2.00 times a herniorrhaphy, is equal to 2.00 hernia equivalents. The unilateral adult inguinal herniorrhaphy category was chosen as the index in our weighting system for several reasons. The procedure is among the most common performed by general surgeons; it is a fairly standard procedure varying little from surgeon to surgeon, or patient to

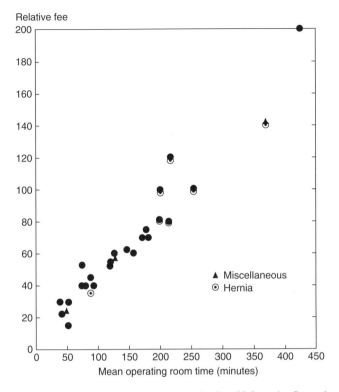

Fig. 1.   Mean Operating Room Time and Relative Fee: 27 Operative Categories.

patient; it is in the middle range of complexity; and it holds a position of special importance in the early operative training of a general surgeon.

This weighting system was then applied to a population of general surgeons to measure their surgical work loads and the relative complexity of the procedures they performed.

The surgical work load of a population of general surgeons. The study population consists of 19 general surgeons in private practice who constitute the entire general surgical staff of a medium-sized, voluntary, nonteaching hospital in a suburban community in the New York metropolitan area. These 19 designated themselves as general surgeons. This designation was confirmed by the New York State Medical Directory,[16] the Directory of Medical Specialists,[1] and existing hospital appointments. Two surgeons at this hospital who concentrated on plastic surgery were not included in the study population; those performing thoracic surgery and colon and rectal surgery were included. The plastic surgeons were not included in the study because their specialized case loads differed qualitatively from the case loads of the general surgeons and did not lend themselves as readily to analysis by our weighting scheme. The case loads of those performing thoracic and colon and rectal surgery entailed what is traditionally interpreted to be general surgery, and they were included in the study.

A listing of all operating room surgical procedures performed by these surgeons in a recent calendar year was obtained from the index hospital and from seven additional institutions to calculate the surgeons' complete hospital surgical work load. Weights were assigned to each procedure according to the relative fee scale[6] and expressed in terms of hernia equivalents. Weekly work loads were calculated on the basis of a 48 week year.

The first secondary procedure performed during each operation was recorded and arbitrarily assigned a relative fee value equal to 20 percent of its value as an independent procedure. This 20 percent value was felt to be a reasonable approximation of the additional work entailed in an operation with a secondary procedure. The data were not sensitive to the magnitude of this arbitrary approximation. The relative fee value for this secondary procedure was added to that for the primary procedure to arrive at a total for the operation. Further secondaries were not included.

Data were obtained on the amount of first assisting at operation by these surgeons. Inspection of the data revealed that in the overwhelming majority of cases first assisting by a general surgeon was not medically indicated and this work was not included in the calculation of surgical work load.[12]

Results

The 19 general surgeons performed 4,178 operations in the calendar year, a work load that was probably at least as large as that of the national average and substantially above the average for New York State.[9] These operations, including 900 secondary Procedures, amounted to 3,952 hernia equivalents (H.E.). The mean H.E. per operation was 0.95, and the median operation had a value of 0.94 H.E. Thus, more than half the operations were less complex than an adult inguinal herniorrhaphy. Variations in complexity are considered after an analysis of variations in work loads.

Variations in work loads. Table 2 and Fig. 2 show that there is very large variation in work loads among the 19 surgeons. The busiest surgeon performed 13.0 H.E. per week, the mean weekly work load was 4.3 H.E., and the median was 3.1 H.E. per week. Thus half of this population of general surgeons performed

Table 2.   Annual Number of Operations and Hernia Equivalents (H.E.) by Surgeon.

Surgeon	Annual no. of operations	No. of operations with secondary procedure	Annual no. of H.E.*	Weekly no. of H.E.[†]	Mean (H.E.*) per operation	S.D. of mean	Coefficient of variation
A	569	131	625	13.0	1.10	0.63	56.9
B	562	128	460	9.6	0.82	0.59	72.0
C	451	52	353	7.4	0.78	0.57	73.4
D	275	48	296	6.2	1.08	0.65	60.0
E	300	67	278	5.8	0.93	0.65	69.7
F	274	46	266	5.5	0.97	0.57	58.6
G	249	46	245	5.1	0.98	0.62	63.0
H	177	56	191	4.0	1.08	0.70	64.6
I	178	21	176	3.7	0.99	0.68	68.5
J	121	22	147	3.1	1.22	0.63	52.2
K	165	25	143	3.0	0.87	0.63	72.6
L	139	21	129	2.7	0.92	0.63	68.4
M	133	18	122	2.5	0.92	0.61	66.0
N	121	51	116	2.4	0.96	0.71	73.5
O	127	19	111	2.3	0.88	0.55	62.8
P	136	83	111	2.3	0.82	0.67	81.3
Q	98	23	92	1.9	0.94	0.62	66.7
R	47	8	48	1.0	1.01	0.73	72.4
S	56	35	43	0.9	.77	0.33	42.8
Total	4,178	900	3,952				
Mean	200	47	208	4.3	0.95		
Median	165	46	147	3.1	0.94		
Weighted mean[‡]					0.96		

*Primaries +0.2 secondary procedures.
[†] Based on a 48 week year.
[‡] Weight = annual number of H.E.

less operative work per week than the equivalent of 3.1 inguinal herniorrhaphies. The work was distributed among the surgeons in such a way that the bottom 50 percent of the surgeons performed 25 percent of the work, the upper 25 percent performed 50 percent of the work, and the upper 10 percent performed 25 percent of the work.

The importance of weighting operations is demonstrated by comparisons between surgeons. For instance, surgeons A and B performed almost exactly the same number of operations but surgeon A's work load measured in hernia equivalents was more than one third greater. Surgeon C performed 64 percent more operations than did surgeon D but his work load was only 19 percent greater.

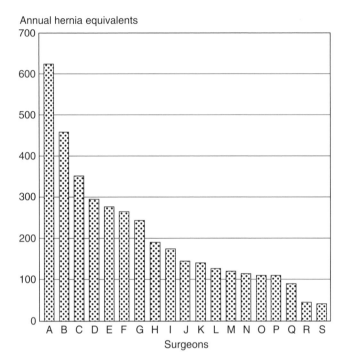

Fig. 2.   Annual Hernia Equivalents, by Surgeon.

What surgeon characteristics are associated with different work loads? Table 3 compares groups of surgeons classified by professional accreditation, number of hospital affiliations, and age.

Six surgeons were certified by the American Board of Surgery, five were Fellows of the American College of Surgery (approved residency training without Board Certification), six were Fellows of the International College of Surgery (variable surgical training), and two had no evidence of similar accreditation. No attempt was made to further analyze accreditation in terms of number of years of residency. Board Certified surgeons have a mean weekly work load of 6.0 H.E., two thirds greater than non–Board Certified surgeons with 3.6 H.E. per week. When non–Board Certified surgeons are categorized by their respective subgroups, it appears that the most productive group of all is nonaccredited surgeons. The two nonaccredited surgeons are performing three times more H.E. than the FICS surgeons, more than two times more than the FACS surgeons, and 42 percent more than the Board Certified surgeons.

Table 3. Work Loads of Surgeons Classified by Professional Accreditation, Number of Affiliations, and Age.

Classes	Annual no. of H.E. per surgeon	S.D.	Weakly no. of H.E.	Mean H.E. per operation per surgeon	S.D. of mean
Professional accreditation:					
Board certified ($n = 6$)	286	177.6	6.0	0.98	0.10
Non-Board certified ($n = 13$)	172	123.2	3.6	0.94	0.12
FACS ($n = 5$)	148	90.8	3.1	1.03	0.12
FICS ($n = 6$)	114	45.2	2.4	0.90	0.08
None ($n = 2$)	406	75.7	8.4	0.80	0.03
Number of affiliations:					
2 ($n = 4$)	156	135.6	3.2	0.92	0.10
3 ($n = 5$)	143	37.4	3.0	0.96	0.08
4 ($n = 5$)	211	167.1	4.4	0.94	0.19
≥ 5 ($n = 5$)	312	183.7	6.5	0.97	0.08
Surgeons age:					
≥ 65 ($n = 2$)	95	73.5	2.0	0.99	0.31
55-64 ($n = 7$)	156	65.4	3.2	0.95	0.07
45-54 ($n = 5$)	229	164.8	4.8	0.94	0.07
35-44 ($n = 5$)	305	200.0	6.4	0.96	0.14

Owing most likely to the small sample size (2) of the nonaccredited surgeons, none of the differences between this group and the others are significant at five percent by the Mann-Whitney U test.

The difference in work loads between the Board Certified surgeons and the FICS surgeons is significant at the five percent level.

The volume of surgical work load was inversely related to age of the surgeon. Surgeons aged 35 to 44 years performed twice as much surgery as those aged 55 to 64 and more than three times as much as those over 65. These differences, however, are not statistically significant at the five percent level.

The number of hospital affiliations of a surgeon was positively correlated with his work load. Surgeons with five or more affiliations did twice as much work as those with two or three affiliations, and 50 percent more than those with four. Of these differences only that between those surgeons with three and those with five or more affiliations was significant at five percent.

To determine the net influence on annual work load of each of the above variables (accreditation, age, and affiliations), a multiple regression technique was employed. The estimated equation was

$$\ln Y = \begin{matrix} 14.9 + 1.29 \ln X_1 - 2.83 \ln X_2 - 0.809 X_3 \\ (0.51) \qquad (1.00) \qquad (0.53) \end{matrix}$$

$\overline{R}^2 = 0.39$ (standard errors of the regression coefficients in parentheses). All variables except Board Certification are expressed in natural logarithms. $Y =$ annual H.E.; $X_1 =$ number of affiliations; $X_2 =$ surgeon's age; $X_3 =$ dummy variable for Board Certification.

The results of this equation are for the most part consistent with the previous findings. The coefficients of affiliation and age are significant at the one percent level. In a double log equation of this kind, the coefficients may be interpreted as elasticities. Thus a one percent increase in a surgeon's age is associated with a 2.8 percent decrease in his annual work load, and a one percent increase in the number of affiliations is associated with a 1.3 percent increase in work load. The coefficient of board certification is not significant at the five percent level and the negative sign is unexpected. This may be the result of a negative correlation between age and certification.

Variations in complexity of operations. Although a few surgeons had a mean H.E. per operation substantially above or below the mean for the group, most recorded very similar values for their average operation and for the standard deviation of the mean (Table 2). The mean operative value for 11 of the 19 surgeons deviated from the population mean by less than 0.10 H.E.

It should be noted that the distribution of operations by degree of complexity departs substantially from a normal distribution for the population as a whole as well as for individual surgeons. As shown in Fig. 3, the distribution is multipeaked and skewed to the right. Less than 1.5 percent of the procedures are valued at greater than 2.5 H.E., the equivalent of a colectomy. These larger procedures were scattered among surgeons of all degrees of accreditation. Of the 15 surgeons who performed operations of greater complexity than 2.5 H.E., 12 did fewer than 6 in the year. The existence of this small number of complex procedures scattered in this population raises questions for Surgical training and quality of care that will be discussed in the next section.

Table 3 shows that the mean H.E. per operation did not vary much with professional accreditation, number of affiliations, or surgeon's age. Figure 4 shows some differences in the over-all distribution between Board Certified and non–Board Certified general surgeons. The former have a smaller fraction of their operations in the range of 0.2 to 0.7 H.E. and slightly more from 0.9 to 2.0 H.E. These distributions are significantly different at the 1 percent level by the

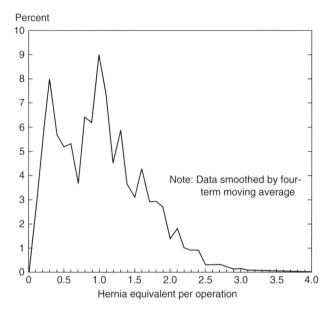

Fig. 3.   Distribution of All Operations by Complexity.

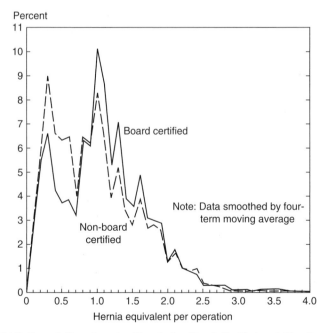

Fig. 4. Distribution of Operations by Complexity: Board Certified and Non-Board Certified Surgeons.

Table 4.   Complexity of Operations by 19 Surgeons in Hospitals Classified by Size and Control.

Class	Annual no. of H.E.* per hospital	S.D.	Mean H.E. per operation per hospital	S.D. of mean
Number of beds[†]:				
≤100 (*n* = 2)	65	72.12	1.00	0.25
100-200 (*n* = 4)	888	665.57	0.92	0.06
Type of hospital:				
Proprietary (*n* = 2)	518	568.51	1.02	0.23
Voluntary (*n* = 4)	661	792.91	0.91	0.07
Government (*n* = 2)[‡]	134	98.99	1.04	0.20

*Primaries +0.2 secondary procedures.
[†] Acute hospitals only.
[‡] Nonacute hospitals.

Kolmogorov–Smirnov test. The distribution of procedures greater than 2.0 H.E. among the two groups, however, is almost identical, with the tail of the curve for the Board Certified surgeons being slightly longer.

The data generated about this population of general surgeons permit comparisons of some properties of the surgeons' work in the various hospitals. Table 4 shows that the mean H.E. per operation is slightly larger (1.00 H.E.) in acute hospitals with less than 100 beds than in acute hospitals with 100 to 200 beds (0.92 H.E.). This difference in size of operations by hospital is confirmed in Fig. 5, which shows the percentage distribution of operations by hospital size. The hospitals of less than 100 beds had less surgery below 1 H.E. and more surgery in the more complex range of 1.5 to 2.5 H.E. than the larger hospitals. These differences are significantly different at the 1 percent level by the Kolmogorov-Smirnov test. Of note is the fact that no surgery of complexity greater than a colectomy was performed in the smaller hospitals.

Table 4 shows that the two nonacute government hospitals have a mean H.E. per operation slightly greater than the two acute proprietary hospitals and the four acute voluntary hospitals. The percentage distributions of operations by hospital type (not shown) confirm the finding that the most complex surgery is performed in the government hospitals but show that the proprietary hospitals are doing more complex surgery than the voluntary. These differences are significant at the one percent level by the Kolmogorov-Smirnov test.

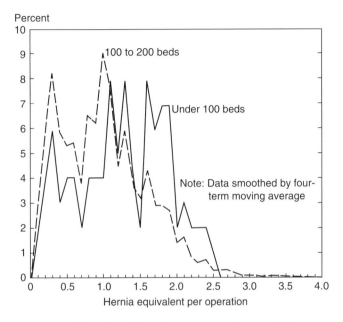

Fig. 5.   Distribution of Operations by Complexity: Hospital Size.

Discussion

This study describes and analyzes the annual in-hospital surgical work loads of 19 general surgeons practicing in a suburban community in the New York metropolitan area. The mean weekly work load of 4.3 H.E. and especially the median value of 3.1 H.E. suggest substantial underutilization of costly and highly specialized medical skills.

The problem of determining underutilization of surgeons is complicated by the lack of an adequate standard of what comprises a well-balanced, productive surgical work load. During this study, the authors asked many surgeons in different practice settings what they considered a desirable surgical work load. Consistently, the surgeons stipulated 10 H.E. per week. They felt that a work load of this magnitude would provide an adequate technical challenge and still leave time for continuing education and leisure. Phillips'[18] data support this standard. Assuming the mean operation in his work load had the same H.E. value as in our population, Phillips and colleagues averaged 10.3 H.E. per week. He felt this work load fulfilled his skills and still left time for other interests.

The fact that a work load of 10 H.E. per week is not an unrealistic burden is further suggested by the work of Masson and colleagues (Masson, 1971), who measured the work loads of two productive surgeons and concluded a standard of 15 H.E. per week still left time for substantial extramural activities.

In the population studied, only one surgeon operated more than 10 H.E. per week, and only one other approximated that value. The mean work load of the population is less than one-half the standard and the median about a third.

Other findings of interest in this study are: (1) Though Board Certified surgeons as a whole had a larger work load than noncertified surgeons, their work loads were smaller than those of the nonaccredited surgeons. (2) Surgeons in the youngest age group had the largest work loads. (3) Board Certified surgeons had slightly more complex work loads than non–Board Certified, but complex procedures were scattered throughout the population of general surgeons. (4) More complex surgery was being performed in the smaller acute hospitals.

One must be careful not to overgeneralize the results of this study. It was performed on only one population of 19 general surgeons in a state known to have a general surgeon/population ratio 64 percent[23] in excess of the national norm. Before generalized conclusions about surgical underutilization can be drawn, further research must be performed on larger and geographically stratified populations.

This study also focuses on only the utilization of a surgeon's operating time. To draw conclusions about the utilization of a surgeon's total professional time would be inappropriate. To answer the question of how surgeons are spending their nonoperative time, the authors of this study are planning time studies of members of this population and survey studies of this and larger groups of surgeons in various practice settings.

This population of surgeons is the first to have been so extensively studied. The results provide impressive support for the suggestive findings of other investigators. The similarity to Fuchs'[9] findings has already been mentioned. Owens (1970) found that surgical specialists were performing one to four major operations per week. Maloney[14] found that university geographic full-time surgeons were operating 3.5 times a week, whereas strict full-time surgeons reported 2.2 operations per week. Masson and associates[15] found a population of general surgeons performing 3.8 operations per week. Subjective evidence of underutilization from surgeons themselves was reported by both Owens and Maloney. In the *Medical Economics* survey Owens stated, "most (surgical specialists) felt they could do more — typically, at least five more major operations a week." Maloney stated "it was an almost universal complaint among strict full-time surgeons that they had inadequate clinical material to maintain their professional competence." Wolfe and colleagues (Strickler, 1968), in their study of a Saskatchewan group practice, reported the general surgeon there, earning a very good living, "estimated that he could have handled three times as much work as he actually carried out." That the problem of underutilization is not universal, however, is illustrated by the work loads of Phillips[18] and the data generated by Riley and co-workers.[19] The latter showed that 65 percent of rural family practitioners in upstate New York performed hospital surgery and concluded: "There is significant demand for surgical and obstetrical practice in the rural region of New York State, and at present a large portion of the responsibility for providing these services lies with the family doctor." It appears that geographic distribution of general surgeons may be a factor in determining underutilization.

This investigation raises a number of questions for study for those concerned with the delivery of surgical care in the United States.

1. Might there not be widespread underutilization of general surgeons? Is underutilization a function purely of oversupply or does it stem in part from uneven geographic distribution?
2. Does underutilization of general surgeons jeopardize quality of care? Do surgical skills atrophy with underutilization? This problem of quality of care is highlighted by a surgeon with a low work load performing one radical mastectomy or portacavals shunt a year.
3. Is a surgeon with a low work load more susceptible to the temptation to operate in equivocal therapeutic situations and run the risk of unnecessary surgery?
4. Might not surgical residency programs be training too many general surgeons and, in addition, overtraining these general surgeons for the job they will do (mean operation, 0.95 H.E.)? Taylor[22] has stressed the need for residency reform to prepare for "the job to be done," and Longmire[18] has actually called for a reduction of 100 in the number of senior residency positions offered.
5. Since complex procedures were scattered in small numbers throughout the population of general surgeons, could the quality of surgical care delivered by this and other populations of surgeons be improved by a pattern of regional organization in which all complex surgery would be referred to one hospital, and performed by highly trained, full-time surgeons?

This study indicates that a group of general surgeons is underutilizing highly trained skills. Other data suggest that this is not an atypical situation. One must be careful not to misinterpret this study. It is not a call for more surgery and does not mean to imply that high work loads per se mean quality surgery. Academic surgery has for decades stressed that surgical intervention is only one in an armamentarium of therapies available to the surgeon. It has advocated operating only when precise indications are present and has stressed the importance of preoperative diagnosis and postoperative care. This advocacy has gone far to raise the level of surgical care in this country.

From this study, we believe there is a need for surgical services in the United States to be further investigated and rationalized. The American Surgical Association and the American College of Surgeons are now beginning to look at the problems of the delivery of surgical services in the United States with the hope of raising the accessibility and quality of surgical care available to all (American College of Surgeons and the American Surgical Association, 1971). It is to the credit of the specialty of surgery that these efforts are being undertaken, and it is to be hoped they will add credence to Bunker's (1970) point hat an "important corrective force . . . (in improving the delivery of surgical services). . . is the growth and maturity of surgery as a specialty."

This study focused on the field of general surgery. The methodology developed for this study is applicable to other specialties, and it is hoped that it will be applied. Other surgical specialties and some medical specialties may also evidence under- and inefficient utilization of valuable skills.

We are indebted to Drs. Kurt Deuschle, Charles Goodrich, David Lyall, and Robert Brown and Mr. Arthur Selvan for help in completing this study. We also thank Ms. Carol Breckner and Ms. Phyllis Goldberg for research assistance, Mr. Irving Forman for technical assistance, and Ms. Maria Perides for secretarial assistance. We are also indebted to many others who must remain anonymous.

References

1. American Board of Medical Specialists (1970–1971). *Directory of Medical Specialities*. Vol. 14.
2. American College of Surgeons and the American Surgical Association (1971). "The Study on Surgical Services for the United States." *Bulletin of the American College of Surgeons* **56**: 14.
3. Bunker, J. P. (1970). "Surgical Manpower: A Comparison of Operations and Surgeons in the United States and in England and Wales." *The New England Journal of Medicine* **282**: 135.
4. Bureau of Medical Care Insurance, The Council Committee on Economics (1965). *Relative Value Scale*, 2nd edn. Medical Society, State of New York.
5. Carnegie Commission on Higher Education (1970). *Higher Education and the Nation's Health*. McGraw-Hill Book company, Inc.: New York.
6. Committee on Fees of the Commission on Medical Services (1960). *Relative Value Studies*, 3rd edn. California Medical Association: USA.

7. Editorial (1970a). "The Need for More Physicians." *The Journal of the American Medical Association* **213**: 1027.

8. Editorial (1970b). "M.D.'s Needed." *New York Times*, May 20.

9. Fuchs, V. R. (1969). "Improving the Delivery of Health Services." *The Journal of Bone and Joint Surgery* **51A**: 407.

10. Ginzberg, E. (1966). "Physician Shortage Reconsidered." *The New England Journal of Medicine* **275**: 85.

11. LeRiche, H. and Stiver, W. B. (1959). "The Work of Specialists and General Practitioners in Ontario." *Canadian Medical Association Journal* **81**: 37.

12. Lohrenz, F. N. and Payne, R. (1968). "The Physician-Assistant — Surgical." *Group Practice* **17**: 13.

13. Longmire, W. P. (1965). "Problems in the Training of Surgeons and in the Practice of Surgery." *American Journal of Surgery* **110**: 16.

14. Maloney, J. V. Jr. (1970). "A Report on the Role of Economic Motivation in the Performance of Medical School Faculty." *Surgery* **68**: 1.

15. Masson, P. G., Moody, T. C. and Stubbs, J. D. (1971). *Planning and Control for Community Hospitals: A Case Study of the Cambridge Hospital.* Sloan School of Management, M.I.T.: Cambridge, MA.

16. Medical Society of New York (1968–1969). *Medical Directory of New York State*, Vol. 52. Medical Society of the State of New York: New York: USA.

17. Owens, A. (1970). "General Surgeons: Too Many in the Wrong Places." *Medical Economics* **47**: 128.

18. Phillips, R. (1968). "Analysis of a Rural Surgical Practice." *American Journal of Surgery* **115**: 795.

19. Riley, G. J., Wille, C. R. and Haggerty, R. J. (1969). "A Study of Family Medicine in Upstate New York." *The Journal of the American Medical Association* **208**: 2307.

20. Roemer, M. J. and Duboise, D. M. (1969). "Medical Costs in Relation to the Organization of Ambulatory Care." *The New England Journal of Medicine* **280**: 988.

21. Strickler, J. H. (1968). "How Many Surgeons Are Needed?" *Minnesota Medicine* **51**: 331.

22. Taylor, H. C. (1965). "Objectives and Principles in the Training of the Obstetrician-Gynecologist." *American Journal of Surgery* **110**: 35.

23. Where Four Specialties Are Concentrated (1970). *Hospital Physician* **6**: 75.

24. Wolfe, S., Badgley, R. F. and Kasius, R. V. (1968). "The Work of a Group of Doctors in Saskatchwan." *The Milbank Memorial Fund Quarterly* **46**: 103 pt. I.

3.3

The Supply of Surgeons and the Demand for Operations

This paper presents a multiequation, multivariate analysis of differences in the supply of surgeons and the demand for operations across geographical areas of the United States in 1963 and 1970. The results provide considerable support for the hypothesis that surgeons shift the demand for operations. Other things equal, a 10 percent increase in the surgeon/population ratio results in about a 3 percent increase in per capita utilization. Moreover, differences in supply seem to have a perverse effect on fees, raising them when the surgeon/population ratio increases. Surgeon supply is in part determined by factors unrelated to demand, especially by the attractiveness of the area as a place to live.

Inequality in the distribution of physicians across the United States and the possible influence of physician supply on the demand for their services are subjects of continuing interest to economists and health policy-makers. If physicians choose their locations partly for reasons unrelated to demand, and if, given their locations, they can increase or decrease the demand for their services independently of changes in price, the implications for economic analysis and for public policy are profound. Some economists[3,6] have reported evidence in support of the demand-shifting hypothesis, but others are skeptical.[12] Many physicians believe that they have almost unlimited power to shift demand. This belief

Originally published in *The Journal of Human Resources*, 13(Suppl.): 35–56. Copyright by University of Wisconsin Press.

is based on introspection, clinical experience, and the correlation between supply and utilization, but skeptics offer several alternative explanations for the correlation.

The principal purpose of this paper is to shed some light on this question through multiequation, multivariate analysis of differences in the supply of surgeons and the demand for operations across geographical areas of the United States. In-hospital operations seem particularly well suited for analysis of demand-shifting because several of the problems that have hampered previous studies can be avoided or minimized. The following section discusses the hypothesis of demand-shifting and indicates why this study provides a good test of it. The analytical framework and data are then described, followed by a section reporting the empirical results and a concluding section which considers some implications.

The "Demand-shifting" Hypothesis

Standard economic analysis assumes that the supply and demand schedules in any market are independent. Given an exogenous increase in supply, a new equilibrium is reached by moving down the (constant) demand curve, as shown in Figure 1A. The demand-shift hypothesis asserts that "given an exogenous shift in the supply of physicians from S_1 to S_2, the physicians induce a shift in demand from D_1 to D_2" (see Figure 1B).

Another way of viewing demand-shifting is presented in Figure 1. The benefits from increases in the quantity of medical care, either to an individual

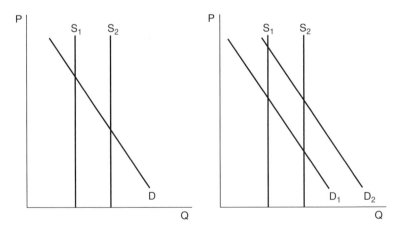

Fig. 1.   (A) No Demand Shifting. (B) Demand Shifting.

patient or to a population, can be assumed to increase at a decreasing rate, hence the falling marginal benefit curve *MB*. For simplicity, let us assume that the cost of medical care to the patient (financial cost, time costs, risk, etc.) increases at a constant rate, shown by the marginal cost curve *MC*. If patients had full information and full control over the quantity of care, they would choose quantity *Q*. The fact that the quantity may be determined by the physician does not in itself imply demand-shifting. The physician, acting as an unbiased agent of the patient, may also choose quantity *Q*. If, however, the physician chooses and the patient accepts a quantity of care greater than or less than *Q*, we would say that there has been demand-shifting.

Note that demand can be shifted either up (to the right) or down (to the left). Let us assume that, other things equal, physicians prefer to come as close to *Q* as possible, that is, they derive utility from ordering the amount of care that equates marginal cost and marginal benefit for their patients.[a] Let us also assume that physicians derive utility from income and that work (at least beyond some level) is a source of disutility. If the physician/population ratio is relatively high in an area (for reasons unrelated to demand), they may push quantity to the right of *Q* in order to keep prices and incomes from falling drastically. If there are relatively few physicians in an area, and if they cannot or do not raise price to an equilibrium level, they may push quantity to the left of *Q* in order to avoid excessive work. This latter situation, sometimes characterized as "excess demand," has been offered as an explanation for the observed correlation between supply and utilization.[4] It would be described in Figure 1A by a price that is *below* the intersection of S_1 and demand. A shift of supply to the right results in higher utilization because it takes care of some of the excess demand.

Note that the presence of demand-shifting should not be equated with "unnecessary care." If "necessary care" is defined as *Q* in Figure 2, demand-shifting to the *left* implies that some patients are not getting the care they should, and does not imply that any patients are getting unnecessary care. Moreover, necessary care may be defined differently than the quantity that maximizes the patient's utility (i.e., *Q*). If, for instance, it is defined as the quantity that maximizes the patient's health regardless of cost, the optimum would clearly be to the right of *Q*, and such demand-shifting would not necessarily imply "unnecessary care."

This study of in-hospital operations provides a sharp test of demand-shifting for several reasons. First, operations are typically well-defined procedures; it is,

[a]For fuller discussion of physician-maximizing behavior, see Evans,[3] Sloan-Feldman,[12] Reinhardt,[11] and Green.[7]

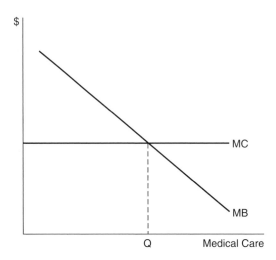

Fig. 2. Alternative Way of Viewing Demand Shifting.

therefore, possible to get a direct measure of quantity. There is some variation in average complexity of operations (as measured by the California Relative Value Scale) across geographical areas; the coefficient of variation for 11 frequently performed procedures is 6 percent. A count of operations, however, is likely to be a much better measure of quantity of medical care than a count of office visits, which may vary greatly with respect to length, number of tests and X-rays, etc. Furthermore, variations in average complexity can be studied separately.

A second reason why operations should provide an interesting study of demand-shifting is that we can rule out "excess demand" (i.e., demand-shifting to the left) as an important explanation for any observed relation between supply and utilization. Excess demand may exist for house calls and other types of services rendered by general practitioners, where price seems to be below its equilibrium level and nonprice rationing is observed, but such phenomena are rare in surgery. Economists and physicians who have studied surgical markets have reported that the average number of operations per surgeon (150 to 200 per year) is far below the level that surgeons consider a "full workload" (about 400 to 500 per year).[5,8,14] The average workload is less that half that recorded in group-practice settings such as the Group Health Cooperative (Seattle) and the Mayo Clinic (Rochester, Minnesota), and below the quantity that surgeons would be willing and able to perform at the going price. The data used in this paper reveal that even in nonmetropolitan areas where the surgeon/population ratio is very low, the average surgeon performs only about 250 operations per year. A recent SOSSUS report noted, ". . . we have failed to identify large or small areas of this country that are significantly under-supplied with personnel suitably qualified to carry out surgery".[13]

The "cost of time" explanation is also likely to be less relevant for operations than for physician office visits. This explanation for the correlation between supply and utilization asserts that equilibrium is achieved by a change in the total price to the patient, including the cost of time. Where the physician population is higher, the time costs to the patient of search, travel, and waiting are all reduce, which is equivalent to a decline in price. Thus Figure 1A is said to adequately describe the market for physician services if price is correctly specified. There is, therefore, no need to introduce demand-shifting as an explanation. Time costs are undoubtedly important for the average ambulatory visit, but are likely to be less relevant for in-hospital operations because the psychic costs of surgery and the time costs of hospitalization are likely to be large relative to the time costs of search, travel and waiting. Thus, this study avoids an ambiguity inherent in many previous studies of demand-shifting;

Finally, given widespread insurance coverage for in-hospital surgery (about 80 percent of the population), the absence of accurate price data may cause fewer problems than in studies of demand for out-patient services which have lower insurance coverage.

Although an interarea analysis focused on surgical operations seems to offer several advantages, there are potential problems as well. First, there is probably a significant amount of "border-crossing" by surgical patients. Whereas most outpatients obtain care from nearby physicians, it is not unusual for patients to travel considerable distances for in-hospital surgery. Such "border-crossing" is likely to be particularly relevant for residents of nonmetropolitan areas who frequently go to metropolitan areas for their operations. According to American Hospital Association data (1972), the rate per thousand population of operations (excluding births) in metropolitan area hospitals was 1.75 times the rate in nonmetropolitan area hospitals. Health Interview Survey data (1970), based on the *residence* of the patient rather than the location of the hospital, indicate a (nonobstetrical) operation rate for metro residents only 1.10 times the rate for nonmetro residents. Using this information plus the metro/nonmetro population ratio of 2.33, we can calculate that nonmetro residents obtain about 30 percent of their operations in metro areas (assuming no movement of metro residents to nonmetro areas for in-hospital surgery).[b] Thus, if there is an effect of supply on demand, the demand in nonmetro areas may be affected by the supply in the adjacent metro area as well as by the supply in the nonmetro area itself.

There is probably much less unreciprocated border-crossing from one geographical division to another. A comparison of the surgical utilization rates in the HIS data for 1970 with AHA data for 1972 shows four divisions (New England, East North Central-East, South Atlantic-Upper, and Pacific) with rates above the U.S. average for both measures, and five divisions (East North Central-West, South Atlantic-Lower, East South Central, West South Central, and Mountain) with rates below the U.S. average, according to both measures. There are two divisions (Middle Atlantic and West North Central) which show rates above the U.S. average by location of hospital (AHA data) and below the U.S. average by residence (HIS data). This suggests that there may be some unreciprocated border-crossing into these two divisions for surgery. However, it should be noted that both these divisions had rates above the U.S. average in the HIS data for 1963, so it may be that some of the discrepancy in 1970 is the result of sampling variability.[c]

Another possible source of difficulty is that a significant amount of surgery (fragmentary data suggest about 20 percent [Ref. 13, Table 13, p. 39]) is performed by physicians who are not "surgical specialists" — primarily general practitioners and surgical residents. The location of surgical residents is highly correlated with that of surgeons, but the location of general practitioners is

---

[b]Let X_n = number of operations performed in nonmetro areas; R_n = number of operations performed *on residents* of nonmetro areas; P_n = population of nonmetro areas; and X_m, R_m, P_m = the same for metro areas.

$$X = X_m/P_m \div X_n/P_n \quad R = R_m/P_m \div R_n/P_n \quad P = P_m/P_n$$

given $X = 1.75$, $R = 1.10$, $P = 2.33$, and assuming that no metro residents are operated on in nonmetro areas. Solve for X_n/R_n.

$$R_m/R_n = RP$$

$$X_m/X_n = XP$$

$$(R_m + R_n)/R_n = 1 + RP$$

$$(X_m + X_n)/X_n = 1 + XP$$

$$X_n/R_n = (1 + RP)/(1 + XP) = (1 + 2.563)/(1 + 4.078) = .70$$

[c]The coefficient of rank correlation of surgical utilization (adjusted for demographic characteristics) between 1963 and 1970 across the divisions is only .42.

not, and some attempt will be made to take account of their supply in the analysis.

Not only are some operations performed by "nonsurgeons," but surgical specialists typically do not limit their practice to performing operations. Thus, this study is concerned with only a portion (albeit the major portion) of the demand for "surgeons' services," and would result in an understatement of "demand-shifting" if, as seems likely, it is easier and more attractive for surgeons to shift the demand for office procedures and tests than for in-hospital operations.[d]

One problem that is perennial in attempts to estimate demand-shifting is that of simultaneity. Strong demand for surgery in an area may attract surgeons, rather than surgeons stimulating demand. I will attempt to deal with this problem by using "predicted" physician supply rather than actual supply. The predictions will be based on a regression that incorporates "taste" variables that affect surgeon location.

The Analytical Framework and Data Base

The general framework of this paper is similar to that used by Fuchs and Kramer[6] to analyze interarea variations in the demand for, and supply of, physicians' services. A demand equation is specified which includes variables usually thought to determine demand (e.g., demographic characteristics, income, price), and then "predicted" physician supply is added. This predicted supply is obtained by regressing the surgeon/population ratio on a set of variables believed to determine physician location. The physician-location decision is of interest in its own right, given the wide variation in the physician/population ratio across areas.

Cross-section regressions are run for 1963 and for 1970, and in a few instances the observations for the two years are pooled. The Health Interview Survey (HIS), which is the source for the surgical utilization data, provides information for 22 areas (metropolitan and nonmetropolitan areas in each of 11 divisions)[e] that cover the entire population. These areas are the units of

---

[d]In-hospital procedures are typically monitored by hospital audit committees. Also, such procedures expose the patient to much greater risk.

[e]The East North Central area is divided into an eastern section (Ohio and Michigan) and a western section (Indiana, Illinois, and Wisconsin). The South Atlantic is divided into an upper section (Delaware, Maryland, District of Columbia, Virginia, and West Virginia) and a lower section (North Carolina, South Carolina, Georgia, and Florida).

observation for some of the regressions. Other regressions are run on a more detailed breakdown of the HIS data in which individuals are cross-classified by age (six classes), sex, race (white and nonwhite), and education of head of family (five classes), and the 22 areas. Regressions across these cells permit much finer control of demographic variables and also permit testing of Pauly's suggestion that demand-shifting might be more important for some groups (e.g., the poorly educated) than for others.[10]

The possibility of border-crossing from nonmetro to metro areas is allowed for by including an additional predicted supply variable for each of the nonmetro areas. This variable is based on the ratio of the number of surgeons in the adjacent metro area to the total population of the division. Also, some regressions are run across only the metro areas or only the nonmetro areas. Per capita income and surgical prices are deflated by a general price index for each division, adjusted for metro-nonmetro differences, and all nominal dollar values for 1963 are inflated to 1970 price levels.

The utilization rates were calculated from the Health Interview Survey (for 1963 and 1970) conducted by the National Center for Health Statistics. The data represent a probability sample of households including all living civilian noninstitutionalized individuals. In 1970 interviews were conducted with approximately 37,000 households containing about 116,000 individuals, and in 1963 with 42,000 households containing 134,000 individuals. Surgical rates were obtained in response to the following questions: "Was the respondent hospitalized at any time during the last 12 months?" and, if an operation was performed, "What was the name of the operation?" For each hospitalization, only the first operations were included; the number of second and third operations was small. Deliveries, abortions, and other obstetrical procedures were excluded from the analysis because they are primarily a function of conception rates.

Although the Health Interview Survey data are representative of the nation's population, they are subject to recall error by the individual or proxy respondent. Hospitalization and operations are reported with greater accuracy than simple episodes of illness, but an overall rate of underreporting of 10 percent remains. Moreover, this underreporting is not uniformly distributed among the population. Whites tend to report hospitalization more accurately than do nonwhites; higher education is also associated with more accurate reporting, as is higher income (controlling for education).

The physician supply data come from the AMA *Distribution of Physicians in the U.S.* and are reasonably accurate. Most of the other data come from the

Table 1.   Summary Statistics.

Symbol	Units	Mean		Standard deviation[a]		Coefficient of variation (%)	
		1963	1970	1963	1970	1963	1970
Q^*	Operations per 100,000	4871	5558	668	567	13.7	10.2
S^*	Surgeons per 100,000	26.9	30.5	10.0	9.5	37.2	31.1
INC^*	$000 per capita	2.97[b]	3.35[c]	.36	.33	12.1	9.9
$HOTEL^*$	Dollars per capita	37.4	47.3	10.9	15.1	29.1	31.9
$NRMET$	Fraction	.139	.129	.237	.232	171.2	179.8
$\%WYTE$	Percent	88.5	87.8	7.6	6.6	8.6	7.5
GP^*	GPs per 100,000	36.4	26.3	6.1	5.2	16.8	19.8

Source: See text.
[a] Across 22 areas.
[b] 1965.
[c] 1969.

Bureau of the Census and the Bureau of Labor Statistics. The principal variables (summary statistics in Table 1) are:

Endogenous

Q^* Number of operations per 100,000 population.

S^* Number of surgical specialists per 100,000 population. These are office-based patient-care physicians, both board-certified and nonboard-certified. The MD supply is adjusted to take account of doctors of osteopathy.

$METS^*$ This variable is used only for the nonmetro areas and takes a value of zero for the metro area. It is based on the predicted number of surgeons in the metro area divided by the total population of the division. It is included to allow for the possible effect of the surgeon supply in a metro area on the demand in the nonmetro area in the same division.

Exogenous

INC^* Real income per capita (in thousands of dollars). The income data were obtained from *Distribution of Physicians in the U.S.* Data for 1969 were used for 1970, and 1965 data for 1963. Nominal per capita income was deflated by a divisional price index derived by Williamson[15] from BLS data for large metro areas. Prices in nonmetro areas were assumed to be .87 of the prices in the metro areas (the cost-of-living differential reported by the BLS). The all-commodity CPI was used to adjust for intertemporal change.

*HOTEL** Per capita receipts (dollars per person) of hotels and motels in the division.[f] The same value was used for the nonmetro and metro areas in a division. This variable is used as a measure of the "attractiveness" of the area. The "services" component of the CPI was used to adjust for intertemporal change.

NONMET A dummy variable denoting nonmetro area.

NRMET The fraction of the population in a nonmetro area living in counties that were designated as "potential" SMSAs or that had population in excess of 50,000. This variable took a value of zero for the metro areas.

% WYTE Percent of the area's population that is white.

*GP** Number of general practitioners per 100,000 population.

In addition to the above variables, some attempts were made to use an endogenous price-of-surgery variable. This was based on American Medical Association data for nine divisions in 1970 reporting the average price of an initial office visit, a follow-up office visit, and a follow-up hospital visit (all for surgeons). An average of these three prices was calculated and then deflated by the Williamson-BLS divisional price index for all commodities. The surgical price index never had any effect in either the demand or location regressions.

A variable measuring the percent of the division's population with surgical insurance was also tried without any appreciable effect. This variable, obtained from the Health Insurance Institute, is probably not measured accurately.[g]

In the regressions across the cells, dummy variables are included for the demographic characteristics — age, sex, race, and education of head of family — that are used to form the cells,

Regression Results

Surgeon location

Table 2 presents the results for the surgeon-location regressions.[h] Representative runs for each year across the 22 areas are shown. The fits are extremely good (R^2 as high as .96) and the coefficients are relatively insensitive to changes in specification. The principal conclusion is that the "taste" variables have a very strong influence on surgeon location.

---

[f]Nevada was excluded because its huge gambling-based receipts did not seem relevant.

[g]The number shown for the Middle Atlantic division is larger than the division's population.

[h]All regressions use population weights.

Table 2.   Results of Surgeon-Location Regressions Across States, 1963 and 1970.

	$\overline{R}^2$	S.E.[a]	NONMET	NRMET	HOTEL*	%WYTE	$\hat{Q}^*$	GP*
1970	.93	2.5	−25	14	.16	.24		
			(11.8)	(3.2)	(4.4)	(2.7)		
		3.0	−28	18	.17	.27	−.002	
			(4.8)	(1.9)	(3.6)	(2.2)	(.5)	
	.93	2.5	−25	13	.17	.26		−.05
			(9.3)	(2.8)	(4.1)	(2.3)		(.3)
1963	.96	2.1	−24	10	.12	.14		
			(12.7)	(2.7)	(2.7)	(2.2)		
		4.3	−28	14	.22	.29	−.005	
			(4.7)	(1.6)	(1.6)	(1.4)	(.9)	
	.95	2.2	−24	11	.12	.12		.03
			(11.4)	(2.6)	(2.4)	(1.3)		(.2)

Notes: t-statistics in parentheses. Regressions weighted by population ∗ indicates predicted value.
[a]Standard error of the regression.

The NONMET dummy variable is highly significant in all runs with a value usually close to −25. The preference for nonmetropolitan-like areas is also revealed by the NRMET variable, with a coefficient of about 14. This indicates that nonmetro areas with 100 percent of their population in counties that are nearly like metropolitan counties have, ceteris paribus, 14 more surgeons per hundred thousand than nonmetropolitan areas with no population in such counties. The preference of surgeons for metropolitan living may reflect the professional attraction of the "medical environment" as well as their preference as consumers. Potential demand, however, as measured by predicted utilization ($\hat{Q}^*$) has virtually no effect on location.

That surgeons live in areas that most people consider desirable to visit and vacation in is demonstrated by the HOTEL* variable. This coefficient (usually highly significant) shows the increase associated with an increase of one dollar per capita in receipts of hotels and motels. The elasticity at the means is approximately .2.

The coefficient of %WYTE is always positive and usually statistically significant, but varies somewhat depending upon the specification. A value of .20 implies an elasticity of .6 at the means. The GP* coefficient is not significant and does not have any appreciable effect on those that are. Some attempts were made to incorporate predicted price into the location regressions. Its coefficient was always insignificant.

Table 3.   Results of Demand Regressions Across Areas, 1963 and 1970.

	S.E.	$\hat{S}^*$	$MET\hat{S}^*$	INC*	%WYTE	GP*
1970	407	60	30	230		
		(3.1)	(2.0)	(.6)		
	419	60	30	223	1	
		(3.0)	(1.7)	(.5)	(.0)	
	536			753	2	
				(2.1)	(.1)	
	412[a]	54	26	263		
		(2.8)	(1.7)	(.7)		
	367[a]	43	44	801		−57
		(2.4)	(2.9)	(2.0)		(2.5)
1963	523	44	41	768		
		(1.4)	(1.7)	(1.4)		
	539	42	37	705	5	
		(1.3)	(1.3)	(1.2)	(.3)	
	573			909	16	
				(2.5)	(.9)	
	524[a]	43	41	797		
		(1.4)	(1.7)	(1.5)		
	538[a]	42	43	856		−6
		(1.3)	(1.7)	(1.4)		(.3)
Addendum		S*	METS*			
OLS						
1970	411	65	34	239		
		(3.8)	(2.4)	(.6)		
	368	55	51	756		−54
		(3.4)	(3.5)	(1.9)		(2.3)
1963	520	59	51	633		
		(2.2)	(2.4)	(1.2)		
	535	59	52	676		−4
		(2.1)	(2.3)	(1.2)		(.2)

[a]*GP** added as an instrument.

Demand

Table 3 presents the results for the demand regressions across the 22 areas. Table 4 presents similar runs across the cells. The latter regressions permit much finer control of the demographic variables, but do not, of course, allow for any additional variation in those variables which are only available for the areas. The fits of the demand equations are not as good as those for the surgeon-location equations, and the size and significance of the coefficients are more sensitive to variations in specification. In general, the results support the view that an exogenous change in surgeon supply *does* affect the demand for operations. Each additional surgeon in an area, ceteris paribus, is associated with an increase of

Table 4.   Results of Demand Regressions Across Cells, 1963 and 1970[a].

	$\hat{S}^*$	$MET\hat{S}^*$	INC^*	GP^*	$PR\hat{I}CE$
Part A (area values)					
1970	62	27	−83		
	(3.4)	(2.2)	(.2)		
	42	44	633	−68	
	(2.1)	(3.2)	(1.4)	(2.9)	
1963	49	34	300		
	(2.4)	(2.6)	(.8)		
	42	37	550	−18	
	(2.0)	(2.7)	(1.3)	(1.4)	
Part B (division values)					
1970	29		78		
	(1.2)		(.2)		
	33		68		−2(−.03)[b]
	(1.0)		(.2)		(.2)
1963	56		−40		
	(2.1)		(.1)		
	80		−211		−9(−.19)[b]
	(2.1)		(.5)		(.9)

[a] Age, sex, race, education dummy variables included; regression coefficients are presented in Table 5.
[b] Elasticities at means.

between 40 and 60 operations per year. The elasticity at the means for a coefficient of 50 is about .28. Use of the two-stage procedure does reduce the relation between supply and utilization. In OLS regressions (shown at the bottom of Table 3), the surgeon-supply coefficient is from 8 to 40 percent larger than in the two-stage runs.

The regressions in Part B of Table 4 were run across cells with 11 division values instead of 22 area values. The predicted surgeons were obtained from a regression across the divisions of S^* on $HOTEL^*$, $\%WYTE$, and the percent of the division's population living in metropolitan areas ($\% MET$). The fit was good ($\overline{R}^2 = .80$) and the coefficient for $\%MET$ (.24) was the equivalent of the $NONMET$ dummy coefficient in the area-location regressions. The relative price of surgery was included in the cell-division regressions, but was never significant.

The income coefficient is always positive in the demand equations, but usually not statistically significant unless predicted surgeon supply is omitted. One surprising finding is the statistically significant negative coefficient for GP^* in 1970. One possible explanation is that where GPs are numerous, they can provide continuing nonsurgical care for various conditions which might otherwise be treated by surgery. However, this variable was insignificant in 1963. The

Table 5.   Regression Coefficients of Demographic Variables in Demand
Regressions Across Cells (Area Values).[a]

	1970		1963	
	(1)	(2)	(1)	(2)
Female	710	704	476	475
	(4.6)	(4.6)	(3.7)	(3.7)
Age 0–9	−1812	−1801	−1488	−1483
	(7.3)	(7.3)	(7.2)	(7.2)
10–19	−2165	−2149	−1917	−1905
	(8.8)	(8.8)	(8.8)	(8.8)
35–49	1490	1487	1202	1188
	(5.8)	(5.9)	(5.6)	(5.6)
50–64	1290	1293	1291	1273
	(4.7)	(4.8)	(5.5)	(5.5)
65+	2526	2512	1441	1432
	(7.9)	(7.9)	(5.3)	(5.3)
Nonwhite	−1498	−1542	−1754	−1733
	(6.2)	(6.4)	(8.6)	(8.4)
Education 0–8	−627	−472	−673	−510
	(2.1)	(1.6)	(2.5)	(1.9)
9–12	162	183	−140	−112
	(.6)	(.7)	(.5)	(.4)
15–16	−807	−813	−691	−705
	(2.3)	(2.3)	(2.1)	(2.1)
17+	−642	−674	−804	−809
	(1.6)	(1.7)	(2.1)	(2.1)

[a] (1) No other right-hand-side variables.
(2) INC^*, $\hat{S}^*$, $MET\hat{S}^*$, and GP^* included as right-hand-side variables.

coefficients for the demographic characteristics are presented in Table 5. They
are usually very significant and virtually unaffected by the inclusion or exclusion
of the area variables.

It is possible that the effect of predicted supply on demand reported in Table 3
and Part A of Table 4 is really the effect of the metro-nonmetro distinction on both
supply and demand. To test for this possibility, similar two-stage regressions were
run for just the metro areas and just the nonmetro areas, with 1963 and 1970
pooled in order to have a reasonable number of observations.[i]

The results for the demand regressions across the areas are reported in Table 6
and those for the regressions across cells in Table 7. The principal coefficient of
interest is for predicted supply ($\hat{S}^*$), and we see that this coefficient is generally

[i]Equality of slope coefficients between 1963 and 1970 was tested for both S^* and Q^* regressions and
the null hypothesis was not rejected in any equation.

Table 6.   Results of Separate Demand Regressions Across Metro Areas and Nonmetro Areas, 1963 and 1970 Pooled.

	S.E.	S*	INC*	YEAR	%WYTE	GP*	METS*
Metro areas	463	76	259	404			
		(2.1)	(.5)	(1.4)			
	466	91	478	258	−20		
		(2.3)	(.9)	(.8)	(1.0)		
	444	116	1111	−521		−47	
		(2.8)	(1.6)	(.9)		(1.8)	
Nonmetro areas	466	85	1187	−223			
		(3.0)	(2.7)	(.9)			
	468	84	745	−56	16		
		(3.0)	(1.1)	(.2)	(.9)		
	477	82	1311	−330		−9	
		(2.7)	(2.2)	(.7)		(.3)	
	476	79	1107	−189			9
		(1.9)	(2.0)	(.6)			(.2)
	468	65	424	84	21		24
		(1.5)	(.5)	(.2)	(1.1)		(.6)
	489	78	1223	−285		−8	7
		(1.8)	(1.7)	(.6)		(.2)	(.2)

Table 7.   Results of Demand Regressions Across Cells, Separate for Metro Areas and Nonmetro Areas, 1963 and 1970 Pooled.

	$\hat{S}$*	INC*	YEAR	GP*	METS*
Metro areas	25	98	612		
	(1.0)	(.3)	(3.2)		
	82	1087	−477	−54	
	(2.6)	(2.3)	(1.1)	(2.9)	
Nonmetro areas	90	481	35		
	(3.5)	(1.3)	(.2)		
	82	760	−202	−21	
	(3.0)	(1.5)	(.6)	(.8)	
	65	310	142		25
	(1.5)	(.7)	(.6)		(.7)
	58	587	−93	−20	24
	(1.3)	(1.0)	(.2)	(.8)	(.7)

larger and more statistically significant in these regressions than in those that included both metro and nonmetro areas. For the five metro regressions in the two tables, the median coefficient for $\hat{S}$* is 82, and for the 10 nonmetro regressions the median is 80. These coefficients imply an elasticity at the means of approximately .53 for the metro areas and .27 for the nonmetro areas. The difference in elasticity reflects the much lower surgeon/population ratio in the nonmetro areas.

The nonmetro regressions were run with an exogenous *METS** variable, as well as without; this coefficient was not statistically significant. A variable designed to measure the possible impact of border-crossing in metro areas also had no significant effect. The only variable except predicted supply which came close to consistently significant results is *GP** in metro areas. The negative coefficient is similar in size to that reported in Tables 3 and 4 for 1970. In general, the separate regressions strongly support the demand-shift hypothesis and reject the hypothesis that the metro-nonmetro distinction explains the observed relation between predicted supply and utilization.

Interaction with education

Mark Pauly has suggested that the ability of physicians to shift demand for their services might vary for different groups in the population. In particular, he hypothesized that the effect might be inversely related to the level of education. Table 8 reports the results of regressions directed to this question. The regressions are run across the cells grouped by education, with 1963 and 1970 pooled. The

Table 8.   Results of Demand Regressions Across Cells by Education, 1963 and 1970 Pooled[a].

	$\hat{S}^*$	$MET\hat{S}^*$	INC^*	$YEAR$
Part A (area values)				
Education 0–8	73	41	−155	442
	(3.0)	(2.5)	(.3)	(1.9)
9–14	54	28	98	497
	(2.9)	(2.3)	(.3)	(2.8)
15 +	25	14	462	226
	(.7)	(.6)	(.7)	(.7)
All	56	30	95	433
	(4.2)	(3.5)	(.4)	(3.5)
Part B (division values)				
Education 0–8	41		253	434
	(1.2)		(.5)	(2.0)
9–14	49		−97	587
	(2.0)		(.2)	(3.5)
15 +	8		247	365
	(.2)		(.4)	(1.2)
All	41		68	503
	(2.3)		(.2)	(4.2)

[a]Dummy variables for age, sex, race, and education (where applicable) included; coefficients not shown.

effect of predicted supply on demand does seem to be largest for the low-education class and smallest for the high-education class. The differences between the coefficients, however, are not statistically significant.

Complexity, urgency, and necessity

Eleven frequently performed procedures[j] that account for 42 percent of all nonobstetrical operations were scaled for "complexity," "urgency," and "necessity." The complexity scale is based on the California Relative Value Scale. The urgency and necessity scales are based on replies by physicians to a mailed questionnaire asking them to choose a statement which best characterizes their impression of the operations being performed in each category (see Ref. 1).

Indexes of complexity, urgency, and necessity were calculated for each cell and then regressed on the demographic dummy variables, income per capita, and predicted surgeon supply, with the results as shown in Table 9. There seems to be some positive relation between complexity and surgeon supply, but the coefficient is not statistically significant. The surgeon-supply coefficient in the urgency index regression is large and statistically significant. Each additional surgeon per 100,000 population in an area lowers the urgency index by 1 percent — a large

Table 9. Results of Regressions of Indexes of Complexity, Urgency, and Necessity Across Cells (Area Values), 1970.[a]

	$\hat{S}^*$	$MET\hat{S}^*$	INC^*
Complexity	.31	.24	1.3
	(1.4)	(1.6)	(.3)
Urgency	−.98	−.12	12.8
	(2.2)	(.4)	(1.5)
Necessity	−.26	−.01	4.9
	(1.3)	(.0)	(1.3)

Note: All three indexes were rescaled to have means of 100. The standard deviations across areas (controlling for age, sex, race, and education) are: complexity, 6.1; urgency, 13.8; and necessity, 4.7

[a]Dummy variables for age, sex, race, and education included; coefficients not shown.

---

[j]The 11 selected operations are appendectomy, cataract removal, cholecystectomy, dilation and curettage (excluding abortions), hemorrhoidectomy, hernia repair, hysterectomy, lumbar laminectomy for disc, prostatectomy, tonsillectomy, and varicose-vein stripping.

change, given the relatively small variation in the urgency index across areas. The necessity index also shows an inverse relation with surgeon supply, but the effect is smaller than for the urgency index and not statistically significant.

The effect of supply on price

The effect of predicted supply on quantity (and complexity) provides some evidence in support of the hypothesis that surgeons shift the demand for their services. Confidence in this conclusion would be increased if changes in supply also resulted in changes in price in the same direction. This question is investigated with regressions across the 11 divisions.

The surgical price index is derived from AMA data reporting average fees by specialty and division for initial and follow-up office visits and follow-up hospital visits in 1970. There is reasonably high correlation among these different fees.[k] An average of the three types of fees is taken to be representative of the relative price of surgery across divisions. This index is deflated by the Williamson-BLS divisional price index for all commodities, as shown in Table 10.

The surgical price index in both deflated and undeflated form is regressed on predicted surgeon supply and predicted demand and on the observed values

Table 10.   Divisional Price Indexes: Surgical Visits and all Commodities (U.S. = 100).

	Surgical price index[a] (1)	Williamson-BLS index[b] (2)	Deflated surgical price index (1)÷(2) (3)
New England	108.1	107.9	100.2
Middle Atlantic	121.9	107.8	113.1
East North Central	87.5	101.0	86.6
West North Central	86.5	100.2	86.3
South Atlantic	94.2	94.8	99.4
East South Central	83.1	92.6	89.7
West South Central	89.6	91.1	98.4
Mountain	77.8	99.5	78.2
Pacific	111.1	100.9	110.1

[a]Source: American Medical Association, Profile of Medical Practice, 1972, pp. 81, 83, 85.
[b]Source: Williamson [15, mimeo version, pp. 79–80]. Division values are population weighted means of Williamson's state data.

---

[k]The coefficients of rank correlation across the nine divisions are: IOV and FOV .77; IOV and FHV .67; FOV and FHV .90.

Table 11. Regressions of Surgical Price on Supply and Demand Across Divisions, 1970.

2SLS	$\hat{S}^*$	$\hat{Q}^*$
Deflated surgical price	1.47	.01
	(1.2)	(.3)
Surgical price	1.55	.02
	(.9)	(.6)
OLS	S^*	Q^*
Deflated surgical price	2.01	−.01
	(2.7)	(.6)
Surgical price	2.83	−.01
	(3.5)	(.9)

of these variables. The predicted values of the endogenous variables are obtained from regressions with *INC**, *%MET, HOTEL**, and *GP** as instruments.

The results (Table 11) reveal a *positive* effect of supply on price; this is clearly contrary to conventional market behavior. By contrast, the effect of demand on price is quite small. A coefficient of 1.5 for supply is equivalent to an elasticity of .5 at the means of the variables. Inasmuch as predicted price had no effect in the surgeon-supply equation, we can reject the view that the high correlation between price and surgeon supply[1] reflects a causal relation running from price to supply.

Discussion and Summary

The small number of observations and potential measurement error in some of the data require us to regard the results reported in this paper as less than definitive. In particular, better price data and a more robust demand specification would serve to increase confidence in the findings. The shortcomings notwithstanding, the cumulative impact of the various statistical experiments casts serious doubt concerning the stability of the demand function for operations when there is an exogenous shift in the supply of surgeons. The hypothesis that an increase in the supply of surgeons results in an increase in demand is strongly supported by the following findings:

1. "Predicted" supply consistently has a positive effect on demand in a variety of specifications.

---

[1] $r = .78$ for undeflated price, and .71 when the surgical price index is deflated by the Williamson-BLS index.

2. The effect is present in both 1970 and 1963 even though the quantity measure is subject to substantial sampling error and the correlation between years is not very high.

3. The effect is present and even stronger when metro areas and nonmetro areas are studied separately.

4. The supply effect on demand is inversely correlated with the level of education.

5. The supply effect is stronger for procedures deemed less urgent and less necessary by physicians.

6. Supply has a positive effect on price, not a negative one.

Can these results be reconciled with "normal" market behavior without recourse to demand-shifting? They can, but it takes some straining to do so. One possible explanation is that surgeon quality is positively correlated with the surgeon/population ratio and that higher quality induces additional demand much as a decrease in price does.[m]

I agree that quality is probably correlated with quantity, but it seems doubtful that the quality effect would be strong enough to explain the observed differences in utilization or price. One indicator of "quality" is the percentage of surgeons who are subspecialists, such as opthalmologists, orthopedists, and the like, rather than general surgeons. This percentage is highly correlated with the surgeon/population ratio across divisions ($r = .72$), but the elasticity is only .15. Let us assume this captures only half of the quality difference so that the full elasticity of quality with respect to S^* is .3. Let us also assume that the elasticity of demand with respect to quality is .3 (about triple the probable elasticity of demand with respect to price). The "quality effect" would then yield an elasticity of demand with respect to supply of .09, considerably less than the elasticity actually observed. Furthermore, it should be noted that "better quality" surgeons frequently recommend *less* surgery than do their colleagues with less training.

I believe that the "stylized facts" revealed in this paper can be summarized as follows: Surgeons have considerable discretion in choice of location and their distribution is determined partly by their preferences as consumers. Thus geographical areas differ in their surgeon/population ratio for reasons unrelated to the inherent demand for operations. Where surgeons are more numerous, the demand for operations increases. Other things equal, a 10 percent higher surgeon/population ratio results in about a 3 percent increase in the number of operations and an *increase* in price. Thus, the average surgeon's workload decreases by 7 percent, but income per surgeon declines by much less.

---

[m]This explanation was suggested by Sherwin Rosen.

These findings do leave one troublesome question. If surgeons can raise prices where they are more numerous, why don't they raise them even higher where the surgeon/population ratio is lower? One possible answer is that their incomes are already satisfactory because of their higher (but not excessively high) workloads, and they have less incentive to induce additional demand.

The implications for national policy of these results seem striking. If the surgeon/population ratio should increase (this seems likely if no action is taken), the result will probably be higher rather than lower fees, and also more operations. The marginal benefit of these operations relative to marginal cost is not addressed in this paper, but recent studies by physicians raise serious doubts, at least for some procedures.[2,9]

One clear limitation of this study is the omission of that portion of the surgeons' workload unrelated to in-hospital operations. As suggested previously, the surgeons' ability to shift the demand for out-patient services is probably greater than for operations. Thus the total impact of supply on demand may be larger, and the implied difference in income per surgeon smaller, than that observed in this study. Indeed, while the weakness of some of the data and the tentative character of the conclusions need to be stressed, it should also be noted that some of these weaknesses serve to understate rather than exaggerate the extent to which surgeons can shift the demand for their own services.

References

1. Bombardier, C., Fuchs, V. R., Lillard, L. A. and Warner, K. E. (1977). "Socioeconomic Factors Affecting the Utilization of Surgical Operations." *New England Journal of Medicine* **297**(13): 699–705.
2. Bunker, J. P., Barnes, B. A. and Mosteller, F. (1977). *Costs, Risks, and Benefits of Surgery.* Oxford University Press: New York.
3. Evans, R. G. (1974). "Supplier-Induced Demand: Some Empirical Evidence and Implications." In *The Economics of Health and Medical Care*, ed. M. Perlman. Macmillan: London, pp. 162–173.
4. Feldstein, M. S. (1970). "The Rising Price of Physicians' Services." *Review of Economics and Statistics* **52**(2): 121–133.
5. Fuchs, V. R. (1969). "Improving the Delivery of Health Services." *Journal of Bone and Joint Surgery* **51-A**(2): 407–412.
6. Fuchs, V. R. and Kramer, M. J. (1973). *Determinants of Expenditures for Physicians' Services in the United States 1948–68.* National Bureau of Economic Research/HEW: New York.
7. Green, J. (1978). "Physician-Induced Demand for Medical Care." *Journal of Human Resources* **13**: 21–34.
8. Hughes, E. F. X., Fuchs, V. R., Jacoby, J. E. and Lewit, E. M. (1972). "Surgical Workloads in a Community Practice." *Surgery.*

9. Paradise, J. L. *et al.* (1978). "Limitation of Sore-Throat History as an Indication for Tonsillectomy." *New England Journal of Medicine* **298**: 409–413.
10. Pauly, M. V. (1978). "Doctors and Their Workshops." Unpublished manuscript.
11. Reinhardt, U. (1977). *Parkinson's Law and the Demand for Physicians' Services.* Princeton University, mimeographed.
12. Sloan, F. and Feldman, R. (1977). "Monopolistic Elements in the Market for Physicians' Services." Paper presented at the *Federal Trade Commission Conference on Competition in the Health Care Sector*, June 1–2, Washington.
13. SOSSUS. (1976). *Surgery in the United States: A Summary Report of the Study on Surgical Services for the United States,* I. Sponsored jointly by the American College of Surgeons and the American Surgical Association.
14. Watkins, R. N., Hughes, E. F. X. and Lewit, E. M. (1976). "Time Utilization of a Population of General Surgeons in a Prepaid Group Practice." *Medical Care* **14**(10): 824–838.
15. Williamson, J. G. (1977). "Unbalanced Growth, Inequality, and Regional Development: Some Lessons from American History." In *Proceeding of the Symposium of a National Policy Toward Regional Change: Alternatives to Confrontation.* LBJ Library: Austin, Texas, September 24–25.

3.4

Case Mix, Costs, and Outcomes Differences between Faculty and Community Services in a University Hospital

To gain insight into the possible consequences of prospective payment for university hospitals, we studied 2025 admissions to the faculty and community services of a university hospital, measuring differences in case mix, costs, and mortality in the hospital. The faculty service had more of the patients with costly diagnoses, but even after adjustment for diagnosis-related groups (DRGs), costs were 11 percent higher on the faculty service (95 percent confidence limits, 4 to 18 percent). The percentage differential was greatest for diagnostic costs. The differential was particularly large — 70 percent (95 percent confidence limits, 33 to 107 percent) — for patients with a predicted probability of death of 0.25 or greater.

The in-hospital mortality rate was significantly lower on the faculty service after adjustment for case mix and patient characteristics ($P < 0.05$); the difference was particularly large for patients in the high-death-risk category. Comparision of a matched sample of 51 pairs of admissions from the high-death-risk category confirmed the above results with respect to costs and in-hospital mortality, but follow-up revealed that the survival rates were equal for the two services at nine months after discharge.

The effect of prospective payment on the cost of care will be closely watched; we conclude that it will also be important to monitor the effect on outcomes, including hospital mortality rates.

Originally published in *New England Journal of Medicine*, 310(19):1231–1237, May 1984. Copyright by Massachusetts Medical Society. Written with Alan M. Garber, M.D., Ph.D., and James F. Silverman, M.D.

Prospective payment is a cornerstone of federal and state plans to control health-care costs.[1] It is also perceived as a threat to the financial viability of academic medical centers, whose costs per admission exceed those of community hospitals.[2,3] Many investigators attribute higher costs to the distinctive mix of patients cared for in teaching hospitals.[4] These patients undergo extensive diagnostic investigation, receive more aggressive treatment, and stay in the hospital longer — in part because they often present with more complex problems than their counterparts in nonteaching hospitals. Each hospital's case mix changes little from year to year.[5] If academic medical centers continue to serve patients like those they have admitted in the past and to provide them with the same level of care, their revenues will depend on the case-mix adjustment applied to prospective payment.

The case-mix measure that will be applied under Medicare — the use of diagnosis-related groups (DRGs) — is already in use in Maryland and New Jersey.[6] DRGs are groupings of diagnostic categories drawn from the *International Classification of Diseases* (ninth edition, *Clinical Modification*) and modified by the inclusion of major surgical procedures, patient age, and the presence of important complications or concurrent illnesses.[7] Currently there are 467 DRGs, chosen to minimize the variance in costs within each group.[8] Teaching hospitals anticipating DRG-based payment schedules will find little reassurance in previous studies of the relation between hospital costs and case mix. These studies have shown that teaching hospitals have higher costs even when case mix is held constant.[8,9,10] There has been little discussion of the contribution, if any, of higher costs to better patient outcomes. Both policy makers and the hospitals need to know the causes of these cost differences and their implications.

We explored these issues by comparing patients who were admitted to the faculty and community services of a major university-affiliated hospital, measuring the contribution of case mix and other patient characteristics to differences in costs between the two services. We identified subsets of patients with particularly large cost differences and explored the possible causes of those differences, Finally, we investigated whether higher expenditures were associated with differences in outcomes and explored the implications for hospital costs and performance under prospective payment. By studying differences within a single hospital, we implicitly held constant wage rates, costs of materials and supplies, laboratory fees, pharmacy prices, quantity and quality of nursing, and similar factors that confound comparisons between different hospitals.

Methods

Sample and data base

The basic population consisted of all the admissions of patients 45 years of age and over at the Stanford University Hospital during 1981. The sample was limited to admissions of patients whose illnesses placed them in DRGs meeting these criteria: (1) the DRG had to have accounted for at least 20 admissions to each of the faculty and community services; and (2) there had to have been 10 or more deaths in the DRG in 1981. The second criterion ensured adequate variation in survival for the purposes of analysis of outcome.

Full-time faculty members served as attending physicians for the patients admitted to the faculty service. All other patients were admitted to either the community teaching or the community non-teaching service. Referring community physicians selected cases having particular educational value for the teaching service; these included some of the sickest community-service patients with some of the most complicated diseases. House staff and students cared for these patients under the supervision of community physicians. Their freedom to order tests or diagnostic procedures for these patients was more limited than on the faculty service. The nonteaching service consisted of the two thirds of community-service patients who received no routine house-staff care. The 43 admissions that lacked a specification of physician type were excluded, to leave a final sample of 1007 faculty-service and 1018 community-service admissions in 12 DRGs. These DRGs accounted for 16.2 percent of all admissions and 29.5 percent of all costs of patients 45 years of age and over.

The data were generated from a data base known as the "Care Monitoring System." This system uses discharge data from medical records, including information about patient demographics, physician activity, outcomes, diagnoses, and procedures. The data are classified by DRG, and the medical-record data are merged with the financial record, which assigns charges according to service unit. For this study, the service units were aggregated to form three categories: routine (including room and central service), diagnostic, and therapeutic services. The allocation of charges was made by one of us, who is the hospital chief of staff (J.F.S.), by review of the cost centers (e.g., radiology) and service units (e.g., chest x-ray films). Thus, respiratory-therapy charges were assigned to the therapeutic-service category, clinical laboratory studies to the diagnostic category, radiology-chest x-ray films to the diagnostic category, and radiology-angioplasty to the therapeutic category. Costs here refer to patient charges rather than to the actual value of resources used. Because the ratio of resource costs to charges varies according to type of charge, differences in charges may either overestimate or underestimate cost differences if the distribution of charges according to type varies greatly between the faculty and community services. To determine whether this was a serious problem, separate cost/charge ratios were calculated for the routine, diagnostic, and therapeutic categories, and these ratios were applied separately to the faculty and community services in accordance with the distribution of charges in each service. When this result was compared with the actual charge data used, the difference was less than one percentage point for the average DRG and less than one tenth of one percentage point for the comparison of 51 matched pairs discussed below. Thus, charges are used throughout as an index of costs.

Predicting hospital outcome (survival)

The method of maximum likelihood was used to estimate a multiple logistic equation relating the probability of death during hospitalization to a number of personal characteristics. The dependent variable took the value of one if admission terminated in death, and the value of zero otherwise. Independent variables were age and dummy variables (each observation takes a value of one or zero) for sex, urgency of admission, race, area of residence, previous discharge, and each of the 12 DRGs. A predicted probability of death was computed for each patient by applying the estimated logistic equation to the values of the variables for the patient.

Cost and survival adjustment

We determined the contribution of patient mix to observed differences in costs and survival by adjusting for DRG alone and for DRGs with personal characteristics, These adjustments are analogous to indirect age adjustments. To adjust costs for DRGs and other characteristics, we first derived a measure of predicted costs. In the first stage, linear regressions were estimated with the natural logarithm of costs as the dependent variable and the following as exogenous variables: dummy variables for sex, religion, type of insurance, urgency of admission, race, location of residence, previous discharge, age category, and DRG. To adjust for DRG alone we performed similar regression analyses omitting the other variables. The regression coefficients were then applied to obtain the predicted cost for each admission. The geometric means of the ratio of actual to predicted costs (i.e., adjusted-cost ratios) were computed for the faculty-service and the community-service patients separately. Finally, the adjusted cost was calculated as the adjusted cost ratio for faculty-service (or community-service) patients multiplied by the mean costs for both groups combined. The formula for adjusted costs for the faculty service was

$$\text{Adj.costs} = \exp\left[\sum_{i=1}^{N_r} \frac{\log C_i - \log \hat{C}_i}{N_r}\right] (\bar{c}),$$

where C_i are the actual costs for the ith faculty-service patient, $\bar{C}_i$ are that patient's predicted costs, $\bar{c}$ is the mean cost for faculty- and community-service patients combined, and N_r is the total number of faculty-service patients in the group.

Outcomes were adjusted in an analogous manner. To obtain the predicted risk of death for an individual patient, adjusting for personal characteristics as well as DRGs, we used the value of the predicted probability of death for that patient. The adjusted-risk ratio for any group of patients was defined as the proportion of the group who actually died divided by the mean predicted probability of death for the group. The adjusted risk was simply the adjusted-risk ratio for either a community or faculty group multiplied by the percentage of the combined population who died. Statistical significance was determined by testing for differences in means for costs and differences in proportions for mortality, using a two-tailed test.

Matched observations in patients with a high death risk

All patients whose predicted probability of death was equal to or greater than 0.25 were identified for chart review and follow-up. This included 60 faculty-service and 140 community-service patients. Pairs consisting of one patient from each service were then matched by age, sex, and DRG. Close matches were found for 55 pairs of patients, but 4 pairs were excluded because medical records could not be located for one member of the pair. The remaining 51 pairs were compared for costs and outcomes, their medical charts were reviewed, and their survival status during the year after discharge was ascertained.

Results

Patients admitted to the faculty and community services differed in several important respects, as shown in Table 1. The former were much more likely to be admitted for cardiac surgery or treatment of lymphoma or leukemia. A disproportionate number of patients on the community service had diagnoses of cerebrovascular disorders, chronic obstructive pulmonary disease, or heart failure

Table 1.   Percentage Distribution of Admissions According to Diagnosis-related Group
(DRG), Patient Characteristics, and Type of Physician.

Characteristics	Faculty physicians 1007	Community physicians 1018
number of admissions	percent	
DRG		
014 Cerebrovascular disorders	4.6	15.3
082 Respiratory neoplasms	6.1	6.9
087 Pulmonary edema and respiratory failure	2.0	2.3
088 Chronic obstructive pulmonary disease	5.0	10.8
089 Simple pneumonia	2.6	6.2
105 Cardiac-valve procedure	19.2	5.7
107 Coronary bypass	37.2	23.2
127 Heart failure and shock	4.9	14.8
172 Digestive-tract cancer	2.5	4.0
203 Pancreatic or hepatobiliary cancer	2.4	2.8
274 Malignant breast disorders	2.7	2.9
403 Lymphoma or leukemia	11.0	5.0
Emergency status		
Elective	5.1	3.6
Urgent	54.9	28.2
Emergent	40.0	68.2
Discharge within past six months		
Yes	18.6	22.5
No	81.4	77.5
Residence distance*		
<30 minutes	12.4	55.3
31–60 minutes	20.2	14.5
61–120 minutes	27.7	18.6
≥121 minutes	38.0	6.7
Unknown	1.7	4.9
Sex		
Female	34.9	46.6
Male	65.1	53.4
Age		
45–64	57.6	34.7
65–74	31.5	31.2
≥75	10.9	34.1

*Approximate travel time to hospital.

and shock. The faculty-service patients were substantially younger (seven years, on average), less likely to have been admitted on an emergency basis, and much less likely to live within a half hour's drive of the hospital. The distributions (not shown in the table) of patients according to race, religion, and insurance coverage were similar in the two services, except that those on the community side included a larger percentage of Medicare patients, reflecting the difference in age distribution.

Costs

Table 2 shows that costs were higher on the faculty service in nine of the DRGs. The overall cost differential of 59.6 percent was substantially reduced to 10.8 percent (95 percent confidence limits, 3.7 to 18 percent) when costs were adjusted for differences in the distribution of cases across the 12 DRGs. Additional adjustment for the socioeconomic characteristics of the patients had virtually no effect on the overall cost differential of over $1,200 per case. Similarly, the exclusion of 16 outliers (costs in excess of $100,000) had very little effect on the differential. Adjusted average length of stay did not differ significantly between

Table 2. Cost Per Admission and Hospital Mortality According to Type of Physician.[*]

Diagnosis-related group (DRG)	Cost per admission		Hospital deaths per 100 admissions	
	Faculty	Community	Faculty	Community
	dollars			
014 Cerebrovascular disorders	9,097[†]	4,865[†]	19.6	21.8
082 Respiratory neoplasms	5,274	4,439	14.8	28.6
087 Pulmonary edema and respiratory failure	13,688[‡]	4,903[‡]	30.0	17.4
088 Chronic obstructive pulmonary disease	8,872	7,539	6.0	7.3
089 Simple pneumonia	7,630	8,379	7.7	14.3
105 Cardiac-valve procedure	25,054	22,924	4.7	8.6
107 Coronary bypass	19,159	18,075	2.1	3.0
127 Heart failure and shock	5,163	4,364	12.2	14.6
172 Digestive-tract cancer	7,684	4,713	8.0	26.8
203 Pancreatic or hepato-biliary cancer	5,846	4,217	16.7[‡]	48.3[‡]
274 Malignant breast disorders	4,063	4,259	11.1	26.7
403 Lymphoma or leukemia	9,452	10,341	10.8	19.6
All 12 DRGs	15,313[§]	9,592[§]	7.2[§]	14.9[§]
All adjusted for DRG mix	13,096[†]	11,815[†]	8.6[†]	13.0[†]
All adjusted for DRG mix and other characteristics	13,071[†]	11,840[†]	9.2[‡]	12.3[‡]

[*] In all tables, "cost" is based on charges; see text.
[†] P < 0.01.
[‡] p < 0.05.
[§] P < 0.001.

the two services; adjusted cost per day was significantly higher on the faculty service.

Patients were assigned to four risk categories on the basis of their predicted probability of death. These categories corresponded to values of 0.25 or higher (9.9 percent of the admissions), between 0.15 and 0.24 (22.9 percent), between 0.05 and 0.14 (27.6 percent), and less than 0.05 (39.6 percent). Table 3 shows that the cost differential was small and statistically insignificant for patients with low predicted probability of death. It was largest among the most seriously ill patients — those who, at the time of admission, had an estimated probability of death of 0.25 or greater. Among such patients, those treated by faculty had costs that were 70 percent higher (95 percent confidence limits, 33 to 107 percent) than those treated by community physicians, after adjustment for case mix as measured by DRGs. When costs were disaggregated into three major categories, the adjusted percentage differential was greatest for diagnostic costs and smallest for routine costs.

Table 3.   Adjusted Costs According to Type of Cost, Predicted Probability of Death, and Type of Physician.[*]

Type of cost	Type of physician	Predicted probability of death[†]				
		<0.05	0.05–0.14	0.15–0.24	>0.25	All
Total	Faculty	17,781	12,081[‡]	7,955	7,976[§]	13,096[¶]
	Community	17,048	10,449[‡]	7,103	4,697[§]	11,815[¶]
Diagnostic	Faculty	3,613	3,408[§]	2,044[‡]	1,757[§]	2,985[§]
	Community	3,353	2,506[§]	1,603[‡]	843[§]	2,420[§]
Routine	Faculty	9,328	6,131	4,204	4,815[¶]	6,795
	Community	9,135	5,495	4,285	3,089[¶]	6,529
Treatment	Faculty	4,591	2,697	1,560	1,803[‡]	3,209
	Community	4,391	2,386	1,404	973[‡]	2,993
Faculty-community differential (%)[‖]						
Total		4.3	15.6	12.0	69.8	10.8
Diagnostic		7.8	36.0	27.5	108.4	23.3
Routine		2.1	11.6	−1.9	55.9	4.1
Treatment		4.6	13.0	11.1	85.3	7.2

[*]Costs ore adjusted far DRG mix.
[†]Estimated with a logistic regression.
[‡]P < 0.05.
[¶]P < 0.01.
[§]P<0.001.
[‖] 100 × (faculty − community) ÷ community.

Table 4. Deaths Per 100 Admissions According to Predicted Probability of Death and Type of Physician.

	Types of physician	Predicted probability of death*				
		<0.05	0.05–0.14	0.15–0.24	>0.25	All
Unadjusted	Faculty	2.0	8.8	16.1	23.3	7.2[†]
	Community	3.8	9.7	21.4	34.3	14.9[†]
Adjusted for DRG	Faculty	2.1	8.8	16.2	22.8	9.2[§]
& other charac-teristics[‡]	Community	4.5	9.6	20.9	34.6	12.3[§]

*Estimated with a logistic regression.
[†]$P < 0.001$.
[‡]Urgency of admission, age, sex, race, residence, and discharge during the previous six months.
[§]$P < 0.05$.

Mortality

Faculty-service patients incurred higher costs, but Tables 2 and 4 show that they also had better outcomes as measured by deaths per 100 admissions. In-hospital mortality rates were higher for patients on the community service in 11 of the 12 DRGs. Even after adjustment for DRGs and socioeconomic characteristics, the community-service patients were 34 percent (95 percent confidence limits, 1 to 66 percent) more likely to be dead at discharge. Disaggregation according to predicted probability of death shows that the survival difference was most pronounced for the high-risk patients, the same ones who had the largest differential in costs.

Analysis of the relation between the cost and mortality differentials reveals substantial differences across the 12 DRGs. In one set of DRGs (089, 105, 107, 274, and 403) there was a large mortality differential and virtually no difference in cost. In a second set (082, 172, and 203), there were large differentials in both costs and mortality. And in a third set (014, 087, 088, and 127), there was a large cost differential, but adjusted mortality rates were similar on the two services. Interestingly, the distribution of patients according to service and DRG appears to be responsive to these cost-mortality trade-offs. In the first set of DRGs, in which the faculty service had substantially lower mortality with no increase in cost, this service accounted for 63 percent of the admissions. By contrast, in the third set of DRGs, in which the faculty service had substantially higher costs without lower mortality, only 27 percent of the patients were treated by faculty physicians. In the intermediate set of DRGs, admissions were more equally divided, with 44 percent cared for on the faculty service.

Matched pairs

The results of a comparison of matched observations shown in Table 5 strongly support the conclusions drawn from the larger sample and offer additional insights concerning the differences between the two services. The 51 admissions to the faculty service were matched by DRG, age, and sex with 51 admissions to the community service. The patients came from the following DRGs (numbers of pairs shown in parentheses): 014 (5), 082 (16), 087 (5), 172 (4), 203 (14), and 274 (7). All patients had a death risk of 0.25 or higher. Within this matched group the average cost was more than twice as high in the faculty service. Moreover, this difference was not attributable to a few large outliers. In 41 of the 51 pairs, the patient on the faculty service had the higher costs. Much of the difference in cost per admission was associated with longer stays on the faculty service;

Table 5.   Results of Analysis of 51 Matched Pairs.

Characteristic	Faculty physician	Community physician	Faculty minus community*	95% confidence limit*
Average age (yr)	68.7	69.7		
Average predicted probability of death (%)	31.9	32.8		
Cost per admission ($)	8,809[†]	3,132[†]	5677	±4318
Length of stay (days)	12.2[†]	5.9[†]	6.3	±5.0
Cost per day ($)	797[†]	578[†]	219	±193
Death in hospital (%)	27.5[†]	49.0[†]	−21.5	±19.2
"Do not resuscitate" code	11.8[‡]	51.0[‡]	−39.2	±18.4
Local residence	41.2[‡]	76.5[‡]	−35.3	±19.5
Matched by code status (23 pairs)				
Cost per admission ($)	10,756	3,722		
Probability of death (%)	30.2	30.4		
Death in hospital (%)	17.4	34.8		
Matched by residence (22 pairs)				
Cost per admission ($)	11,476	3,570		
Probability of death (%)	29.9	29.8		
Death in hospital (%)	31.8	40.9		
Survival for at least one year (48 pairs) (%)	16.7	16.7		

*Difference and confidence limits are shown when difference is statistically significant ($P < 0.05$).
[†]$P < 0.05$.
[‡]$P < 0.001$.

however, cost per day was also significantly higher on that service. The difference in outcomes, as measured by status at discharge, was also substantial: the death rate was almost twice as high among patients on the community service.

Although these patients had been carefully matched according to several criteria, review of their medical charts revealed a large difference in the proportion who had a "DNR" ("Do not resuscitate") notation on their charts. Only 6 of the 51 patients admitted to the faculty service had a DNR notation, as compared with 26 on the community service. This could reflect objective differences in the medical condition of the patients that were not accounted for by DRG, age, sex, and predicted probability of death, or it could reflect subjective differences in patient or physician attitudes. Also, the low use of the DNR code on the faculty service may result from administrative difficulties faced by house officers who must obtain approval from the faculty supervisor in order to put this notation on the chart. The difference in code status is large, but it does not explain the differences in costs and outcomes. For 23 pairs in which the faculty and community patients had the same code status (in 21 the code was "resuscitate"), the faculty-community differentials were similar to those for all the pairs. Among the 23 pairs, 19 of the faculty-service patients had higher costs.

A much higher percentage of the community-service patients were local residents (who could drive to the hospital in less than 30 minutes). We were able to match 22 pairs according to residence zone (19 were in the "local" zone), but this matching did not reduce the cost differential. Among the 22 pairs, 18 of the faculty-service patients had higher costs. The differential in mortality was smaller than for all the pairs, but the faculty-service patients still had lower death rates,

There is no doubt that a higher percentage of the patients on the faculty service were discharged alive, but there is considerable interest in knowing how much longer they lived. The last line of Table 5 and Figure 1 provide answers to that question. For 48 pairs it was possible to ascertain whether the patient lived for at least one year after discharge or, if not, what the date of death was. The percentage surviving for one year was quite low, and it was equal for the two services. Figure 1 shows that there was still a considerable difference in survival rates six months after discharge, but by the end of nine months the difference between the two services had disappeared.

Discussion

Our study, like studies comparing community and teaching hospitals,[9,10] found that adjustment for case mix eliminated much of the cost differential between faculty and community service in this hospital, Nevertheless, admissions to the

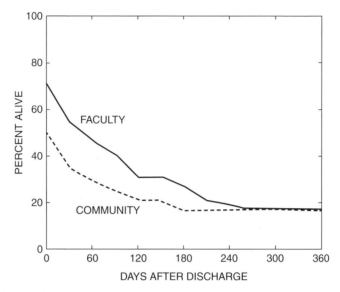

Fig. 1.   One-year Survival Curves for 48 Matched Pairs of Patients, One of Each Pair Admitted to The Hospital's Faculty Service and the Other to Its Community Service.

faculty service generated higher costs within DRGs that could not be explained by other observed patient characteristics. These higher costs were accompanied by lower hospital mortality. Both cost and mortality differences were greatest for the high-risk group of patients.

A number of plausible explanations could be offered for these findings, with distinct and sometimes contradictory implications for health-care financing and for the costs of medical education. These may be divided into explanations based on differences in physician attributes and practice patterns, and those based on differences in patient populations.

Physician differences

The differential in adjusted costs probably reflects in part the greater impact on the faculty service of the hospital's role as a training institution and referral center. House staff and medical students have major responsibilities for the care of patients on the faculty service. They have no role with respect to two thirds of the patients on the community service, and when they care for community-service patients, house officers have less autonomy than on the faculty service. These trainees, who learn by doing procedures and interpreting diagnostic tests, may order such studies more readily because of their putative educational value. The greater use of diagnostic services by trainees may also reflect their unwillingness or inability to rely as heavily as the more seasoned private physicians on the clinical examination.[11]

Physician attitudes toward death may also have contributed to the more aggressive care on the faculty service. An unwillingness to allow patients to die may have driven some house officers to press for more care, even when it led to little or no improvement in patient outcome. Private physicians, who knew their patients better, may have been more aware of the patients' own wishes concerning continued life support. In many cases, the patients' preferences may not have been known to the faculty physicians, who would have treated aggressively when in doubt. Finally, the inexperience of house officers and medical students may have led them to provide some services that had few benefits for the patient.

Patient differences

Despite efforts to control for diagnosis and other patient characteristics, there may have been systematic differences between the patients on the two services in their medical condition, extent of workup before admission, or attitudes toward death. Chart review suggested that among the seriously ill patients, those admitted to the community service were more frequently admitted for purely supportive care and were less likely to receive extensive diagnostic workups or to be admitted to the intensive-care unit. Since the severity or stage of illness can vary considerably within the high-risk DRGs, control for DRG does not eliminate this source of variation in service intensity. A single DRG can include both a patient presenting with a metastasis and an unknown primary tumor, who receives an extensive diagnostic workup, and a moribund patient admitted for terminal care. Moreover, physicians on the community service typically cared for patients whom they had followed for long periods before hospitalization; thus, they may have been better able to avoid duplication of tests performed outside the hospital and to minimize other costs associated with the workup of new patients.

Patient attitudes can also contribute to variation in the type and quantity of services provided. Patients having the same morbidity and the same prognosis will not seek the same care if their attitudes toward death and toward medical intervention differ. A patient who is emotionally prepared to die may not consent to intubation, mechanical ventilation, and cardiac resuscitation, though his equally ill fellow patient may desire such measures. The much higher proportion of "DNR" orders on the community service probably reflects such patient preferences, in addition to possible differences in prognosis and physician attitudes.

Many studies of hospital costs have assumed that hospital output could be represented by the volume of services provided.[2] Such an approach has been justly criticized because inappropriate and ineffective care add to such "output." Patients seek improvements in personal welfare from a hospital, not the tests and treatments themselves; improvement in patient welfare, however, is difficult to measure. Hospital survival is undoubtedly an important component of welfare, and according to this criterion, patients on the faculty service did better. In the matched sample of patients for whom follow-up data were available, the faculty-service patients also had longer out-of-hospital survival. The distribution among DRGs and the variation in other patient characteristics could only partially explain their lower mortality rates. Like the cost differentials, the outcomes deviated most for the group of patients with the highest risk and were likely to reflect differences in practice patterns as well as in the types of patients seen on each service.

The more extensive use of diagnostic procedures and the more intensive care provided on the faculty service may have reduced mortality while generating higher costs. Because the patient populations may have differed, these results do not prove that faculty physicians reduced mortality by providing more care. But, if patients on the faculty service were less likely to die simply because they were better risks, why did the faculty service attract them? It is unlikely that chance alone could cause so marked a disparity in patient populations. One possible explanation is that community physicians waited longer to admit their patients to the hospital than did their faculty counterparts. By substituting outpatient for inpatient services, they may have increased the proportion of their patients who were in the final stages of illness, while reducing hospital costs. Just as an all-inclusive measure of costs of illness, including outpatient services, might have shown less discrepancy between the faculty and community services, better control for stage of illness might have reduced the mortality differential.

Patient perceptions of the difference in practice styles may underlie systematic differences in the patient populations of the faculty and community services. Patients who desired or were likely to benefit from more care may have sought, or may have been referred to, members of the faculty. Not only did differences in underlying disease contribute to the mortality differences, but they appeared to determine what kind of care was appropriate. Notably, in the DRGs that included mainly faculty-service patients, those patients had lower mortality than community-service patients, with similar costs. In the DRGs with mostly community-service patients, those patients had lower costs than faculty-service patients, with similar mortality. It is as if most of the patients were assigned to the service that would provide the best balance of costs and benefits. Neither the faculty nor the community medical practice was necessarily better or worse, merely different. There is no reason to expect or to desire patients with diverse conditions and attitudes to receive the same care or to have the same outcomes.

We have studied only one hospital, and therefore our results may not be generalizable. On the other hand, the differences we observed between the faculty and community services in the same hospital are likely to understate the differences between separate teaching and community hospitals. In the hospital we studied, the same advanced, specialized facilities were available to the faculty-service and community-service patients, and house staff participated in the care of some community-service patients. Furthermore, faculty and community physicians in this hospital undoubtedly interacted more closely than faculty and community physicians in separate hospitals, contributing to a more homogeneous style of medicine. On the other hand, mortality differences in the 12 DRGs we studied were greater than in other DRGs, which had lower death rates.

It is difficult to ascertain whether the aggressive care on the faculty service contributed to the lower in-hospital mortality; it is even more difficult to judge whether the reduced mortality was justified by the cost. In the matched sample of seriously ill patients, more than half were discharged alive, but less than one fifth survived for as long as one year. The absence of relevant data on the postdischarge experience precludes our drawing strong inferences from the survival curves shown in Figure 1. We did not investigate the quality of life for the survivors, nor did we ascertain their source of postdischarge care or its cost. Many of the faculty-service patients presumably returned to their home communities after discharge and were cared for by their community physicians.

Even if the extra costs on the faculty service are attributable to the education of house staff and students, without corresponding patient benefits, these activities may be worthwhile. In that case, the question is not whether such care should continue, but whether it should be financed with patient-care revenues. If, on the other hand, these services have few educational benefits and little value to the patient, other methods of training physicians should be investigated. But if more intensive care helps some patients while educating house staff, effort should be devoted to identifying the patients most likely to benefit from such care. These are the patients who are likely to suffer most from prospective payment.

Under a prospective-payment plan, hospitals will have incentives to manipulate discharge diagnoses to fit patients into DRGs with higher payment schedules, to perform surgical procedures that shift patients to other DRGs, to limit hospital stays, and to minimize daily expenditures.[12] Institutions that continue to practice the high-cost medicine that is typical of the faculty service will incur financial penalties. Less aggressive services will become more common. Institutions will face the difficult challenge of both limiting expenditures and continuing to provide costly care to patients for whom it is appropriate. If hospital services become more homogeneous, we may see hospital mortality rise, Undoubtedly, policy makers will closely monitor the effects of prospective payment on expenditures; an important potential consequence of prospective payment will be overlooked if they do not also monitor hospital mortality rates.

We are indebted to Byron Wm. Brown, Jr., for advice on statistical methods, and to Judy Anderson and Leslie Perreault for research assistance.

References

1. Iglehart, J. K. (1982). "The New Era of Prospective Payment for Hospitals." *New England Journal of Medicine* **307**: 1288–1292.
2. Sloan, F. A., Feldman, R. D. and Steinwald A. B. (1983). "Effects of Teaching on Hospital Costs." *Journal of Health Economics* **2**: 1–28.
3. Watts, C. A. and Klastorin, T. D. (1980). "The Impact of Case Mix on Hospital Cost: A Comparative Analysis." *Inquiry* **17**: 357–367.
4. Ament, R. P., Kobrinski, E. J., and Wood, W. R. (1981). "Case Mix Complexity Differences Between Teaching and Nonteaching Hospitals." *Journal of Medical Education* **56**: 894–903.
5. Lave, J. R. and Lave, L. B. (1971). "The Extent of Role Differentiation Among Hospitals." *Health Services Research* **6**: 15–38.
6. Iglehart, J. K. (1983). "Medicare Begins Prospective Payment of Hospitals." *New England Journal of Medicine* **308**: 1428–1432.
7. Hornbrook, M. C. (1982). "Hospital Case Mix: Its Definition, Measurement and Use. II. Review of Alternative Measures." *Medical Care Research and Review* **39**: 73–123.
8. Thompson, J. D., Fetter, R. B. and Mross, C. D. (1975). "Case Mix and Resource Use." *Inquiry* **12**: 300–312.
9. Becker, E. R. and Steinwald, B. (1981). "Determinants of Hospital Casemix Complexity." *Health Services Research* **16**: 439–458.
10. Thompson, J. D., Fetter, R. B. and Shin, Y. (1978). "One Strategy for Controlling Costs in University Teaching Hospitals." *Journal of Medical Education* **53**: 167–175.
11. Mariz, E. W. and Ptakowski, R. (1978). "Educational Costs to Hospitalized Patients." *Journal of Medical Education* **53**: 383–586.
12. Simborg, D. W. (1981). "DRG Creep: A New Hospital-Acquired Disease." *New England Journal of Medicine* **304**: 1602–1604.

Op-Ed

Eliminating "Waste" in Health Care

President Obama is the most recent in a long line of US presidents to seek reductions in health care spending through elimination of "waste." However, the stakes this time are unusually high — the president has reported that eliminating waste is needed to fund two-thirds of the approximately $900 billion needed (over 10 years) for expanded health care coverage.[1] To achieve this goal requires defining waste, identifying contexts in which it occurs, determining why it occurs, and implementing policies that prevent reoccurrence.

Defining waste in medical care is not simple. Consider, for example, a patient who has experienced frequent, intermittent headaches for several weeks. Her physician thinks it is unlikely that the headaches are caused by a brain tumor or lesion (less than 1 chance in 10). A magnetic resonance imaging scan would provide more definite information. If the physician orders the scan, is that waste? What if the chances were 1 in 100 or 1 in 1000? What if the patient is so anxious about the headaches that she has difficulty with daily functions? Should that affect the definition of waste? As another example, consider 10 members of a college football team who are found to have a disease that has 2 possible interventions. Bed rest, fluids, and over-the-counter medications for relief of symptoms would result in recovery of all 10 patients in about 2 weeks; administration of a new,

Originally published in *JAMA*, 302(22):2481–2482. December 2009. Copyright by American Medical Association.

expensive drug would likely cure 7 patients within 2 or 3 days, send 1 patient to the hospital, and have no effect on the others. Is it wasteful to give the drug — or not to give it?

These examples lead to considering 2 possible definitions of waste in medical care. Medical waste is defined as any intervention that has no possible benefit for the patient or in which the potential risk to the patient is greater than potential benefit. Economic waste is defined as any Intervention for which the value of expected benefit is less than expected costs. The proportion of care deemed wasteful using the medical definition is much smaller than that deemed wasteful using the economic definition. Medical waste could occur only if the physician is misinformed, if the patient is misinformed and the physician succumbs to patient demands, or if the physician behaves unethically. Economic waste is much more common because of third-party payment. A conscientious clinician treating an insured patient would tend to recommend any intervention with a potential benefit greater than the potential risk.

Two ubiquitous aspects of medical care make identification of waste particularly problematic. First, there is little certainty in medicine. Implicitly, if not explicitly, physicians are usually dealing with probabilities. Many interventions appear to have been wasteful in retrospect, but that is not the correct criterion; only prospective probability of success is relevant. The oft-heard promise "we will find out what works and what does not" scarcely does justice to the complexity of medical practice. Some interventions are undoubtedly useless, but those that might help some patients are much more common. Second, patients differ in unpredictable ways. The same drug given to patients with the same diagnosis often has different effects, ranging from rapid cure to serious adverse reaction.

Any effort to reduce costs on a large scale requires consideration of economic waste. Where in medical practice is economic waste likely to be found? Almost everywhere. Some patients do not receive sufficient screening because of lack of insurance, inertia, or fear, but for the US population as a whole, the error is probably on the side of excess screening. On a per capita basis, patients in the United States receive almost 3 times as many magnetic resonance imaging scans as those in Canada.[2] Are the benefits of extra scans enough to justify the extra cost? Repeated testing is another area with high potential for economic waste. There is usually little scientific foundation for the appropriate interval between tests and even less economic analysis of benefits and costs of alternative intervals.

For a variety of reasons, including pressure from patients, physicians prescribe brand-name drugs when generic medications would be as effective or no drug at all would be best. An analogous situation may be the choice between a high-cost device or procedure and a less expensive alternative. For example, high-cost drug-eluting stents may be the better choice for some patients, but others would do just as well with less expensive bare-metal stents.[3,4]

Some patients are hospitalized for what might be wasteful reasons. For example, the patient's insurance coverage might be better in hospital, compensation to the physician for dealing with a complex case on an outpatient basis may be inadequate, or readmission may occur because of poor coordination between inpatient and outpatient care or because the discharged patient lacks social support. Another example is the excess ordering of tests because of "defensive medicine" practiced out of fear of litigation for missing a diagnosis.

Identification of waste is difficult, but eliminating it is more difficult. Every dollar of waste is income to some individual or organization. Insured patients want all the care that might do some good; fee-for-service payment to clinicians also can lead to economic waste.[5] The combination of insurance and fee-for-service can be wasteful because neither the patient nor the physician has an incentive to consider cost. Some see the solution in making the patient cost-conscious through large deductibles and co-payments. That may work for high-income individuals, but the average person who lives from paycheck to paycheck could not handle the typical medical bill. Moreover, the average patient in the United States is a poor judge of what care is needed and the quality of that care. The idea of sick patients shopping for the lowest-price medical care (the way they buy automobiles) is a fantasy that will not contribute to informed elimination of waste. There seems to be no alternative to relying on physicians to practice more cost-effective care.

There are 3 requirements for physicians to practice cost-effective care. First, physicians need information about effectiveness and costs; the range of possible diagnostic and therapeutic interventions available in all but the simplest cases is staggering. The provision of such information in a timely and easily accessible form is a public good that can only be provided by a large, publicly funded but quasi independent organization.[6] Second, physicians require access to an infrastructure that provides specialized technology and personnel appropriate for cost-effective care, for example, a multidisciplinary, team approach to the care of patients with diabetes. Third, information and infrastructure will often be wasted unless physicians are provided with incentives that reward cost-effective decisions.

President Obama is correct about possible cost reductions through elimination of waste — if the economic definition is what he has in mind. But the president should not underestimate the challenge of implementing policies that lead to such elimination.

Financial Disclosures: Dr Fuchs reported receiving financial support for his research from the Blue Shield of California Foundation and the Robert Wood Johnson Foundation.

Additional Contributions: I also thank Pat A. Basu, MD, MBA (Department of Radiology, Stanford University School of Medicine), Alan S. Go, MD (Comprehensive Clinical Research Unit, Kaiser Permanente of Northern California), and Cynthia Yock, MS (Stanford Health Policy, Stanford University), for helpful comments. No compensation was given for their contributions.

References

1. Obama seeks out skeptics at Montana town hall. (2009). CNN Web site. http://www.cnn.com/2009/POLITICS/08/14/obama.health.care/index.html. August 18, 2009. Accessibility verified November 10.
2. Medical Imaging in Canada 2007. (2009). Canadian Institute for Health Information Web site, http://secure.cihi.ca/cihiweb/products/MIT_2007_e.pdf. Accessed October 7.
3. Bertrand, O. F., Faurie, B., Larose, E. *et al.* (2008). "Clinical Outcomes After Multilesion Percutaneous Coronary Intervention: Comparison between Exclusive and Selective Use of Drug-Eluting Stents." *Journal of Invasive Cardiology* **20**(3): 99–104.
4. Yan, B. P., Ajanl, A. E., New, G. *et al.* (2008). "Melbourne Interventional Group Investigators. Are Drug-Eluting Stents Indicated in Large Coronary Arteries? Insights from a Multi-centre Percutaneous Coronary Intervention Registry." *International Journal of Cardiology* **130**(3): 374–379.
5. Emanuel, E. J. and Fuchs, V. R. (2008). "The Perfect Storm of Overutilization." *The Journal of the American Medical Association* **299**(23): 2789–2791.
6. Emanuel, E. J., Fuchs, V. F., and Garber, A. M. (2007). "Essential Elements of a Technology and Out comes Assessment Initiative." *The Journal of the American Medical Association* **298**(11): 1323–1325.

The Doctor's Dilemma — What Is "Appropriate" Care?

Most physicians want to deliver "appropriate" care. Most want to practice "ethically." But the transformation of a small-scale professional service into a technologically complex sector that consumes more than 17 percent of the nation's gross domestic product makes it increasingly difficult to know what is "appropriate" and what is "ethical." When escalating health care expenditures threaten the solvency of the federal government and the viability of the U.S. economy, physicians are forced to reexamine the choices they make in caring for patients.

In an effort to address this issue, physicians' organizations representing more than half of all U.S. physicians have endorsed a "Physician Charter" that commits doctors to "medical professionalism in the new millennium." The charter states three fundamental principles, the first of which is the "primacy of patient welfare." It also sets out 10 "commitments," one of which states that "while meeting the needs of individual patients, physicians are required to provide health care that is based on the wise and cost-effective management of limited clinical resources."

Originally published in *New England Journal of Medicine*, 365(7):585–587, August 201. Copyright by Massachusetts Medical Society.

How can a commitment to cost-effective care be reconciled with a fundamental principle of primacy of patient welfare?

The dilemma arises for two main reasons. First, recent decades have witnessed a flood of new, expensive medical technologies (drugs, imaging devices, surgical procedures) that are of varying degrees of value to patients. A few are true breakthroughs, with strong favorable effects on mortality and morbidity. Others make a meager contribution, at best, to health outcomes. Moreover, technologies that may provide high value for carefully selected patients are often used indiscriminately for a much larger cohort of patients. Second, health insurance, private or public, has become so widespread that 90 percent of the country's health care bill is paid by third parties, not by the patient receiving the service.

What is a conscientious physician to do? Some new cancer drugs cost thousands of dollars per month for a single patient. The bills for many surgical procedures run to five or even six figures. Noninvasive imaging devices can offer information to assist in diagnosis, at a cumulative cost in the billions of dollars. U.S. patients, on average, get almost three times as many magnetic resonance imaging scans as Canadian patients; there is no evidence that this large differential can be explained by national differences in the medical condition of patients or that it results in significant national differences in health outcomes. So what level of utilization deserves to be called "appropriate"?

If insurance were not widespread, many physicians would be reluctant to order an expensive intervention unless it offered a good chance of substantial benefit — that is, unless it was cost-effective. Indeed, without U.S.-style cost-insensitive insurance, many expensive diagnostic and therapeutic innovations would not be developed and brought to market.[1] The insured patient, on the other hand, will usually want any and all care that might possibly be of net benefit, regardless of cost. The physician may recognize that the intervention under consideration is not cost-effective but may recommend it anyway, for a variety of reasons: to keep the goodwill of the patient, to protect against a malpractice suit, or in the belief that the "primacy of patient welfare" makes the denial of such care "inappropriate" and "unethical."

The doctor's dilemma is the nation's problem. Some policy experts think that if patients had "more skin in the game" — that is, had less insurance — the problem would be solved. It would not. Even the most ardent advocates of deductibles and copayments acknowledge the need for an annual cap on patients' payments, beyond which insurance takes over completely. There is no consensus on the right level for the cap, but it is generally recognized that the average U.S. household, with large debts and minimal financial assets, could not handle much more than $5,000. But the extreme skew in annual health care expenditures, with 5 percent of individuals accounting for 50 percent of spending in any given year, means that many health care decisions, and especially those involving big-ticket interventions, will be made by and for patients whose costs have exceeded the cap.

Another popular "solution" is to eliminate care that does more harm than good — that is, "unnecessary" care. Such elimination would be desirable, but the potential savings from this source are smaller than is usually claimed. It is true that after the fact, many interventions turn out to be useless or even harmful for some patients. But the heterogeneity of patient populations and uncertainty about the response of individual patients to an intervention means that it is often difficult or impossible to determine in advance which ones will prove to help particular patients and which will turn out to have been unnecessary.

There is no escaping the fact that many interventions are valuable for some patients even if, for the population as a whole, their cost is greater than their benefit. Under what circumstances are they likely to be ordered, and when are they likely to be withheld? The context within which the physician practices, his or her assumption about the behavior of other physicians, and the economic and health consequences of ordering all the care that might do some good versus practicing cost-effective medicine will affect the physician's choice. If the physician is paid on a fee-for-service basis and the patient has open-ended insurance, the scales are tipped in favor of doing as much as possible and against limiting interventions to those that are cost-effective. In that setting, who would benefit from the resources that are saved by practicing cost-effective medicine is not obvious to the physician.

In contrast, if the physician is practicing in a setting that has accepted responsibility for the health of a defined population and the organization receives an annual fee per enrollee, the chances of the physician's practicing cost-effective medicine are substantially increased, even though all patients are insured. The physician's colleagues are practicing the same way, and the resources saved can be used for the benefit of the defined population, which includes the physician's patient. In Canada, which has universal insurance, per capita spending on health care is only 55 percent of the U.S. level because there is a limited overall budget, and all physicians in the system recognize the need for prudence in making decisions about care.

In short, when physicians are collectively caring for a defined population within a fixed annual budget, it is easier for the individual physician to resolve the dilemma in favor of cost-effective medicine. That becomes "appropriate" care. And it is an ethical choice, as defined by philosopher Immanuel Kant, because if all physicians act the same way, all patients benefit.[2]

References

1. Weisbrod, B. (1991). "The Health Care Quadrilemma: An Essay on Technological Change, Insurance, Quality of Care, and Cost Containment." *Journal of Economic Literature* **29**: 523–552.
2. Kant, I. (1949). In *Critique of Practical Reason and Other Writings in Moral Philosophy*, trans. L. W. Beck. University of Chicago Press: Chicago.

Part 4

International Comparisons

Introduction

Probably the most important and simplest way to appreciate the high cost of health care in the United States is to compare it with costs in other high income democracies. The first three papers and the op-ed in Part 4 make such comparisons. In the U.S., health care consumes approximately 18 percent of the GDP; in other high spending countries, the share is approximately 12 percent. Given U.S. GDP of over $18 trillion, the extra spending in the U.S. amounts to more than *one trillion dollars* per year. This *excess* is far more than the U.S. spends on national security or on education. It amounts to more than $3,000 per man, woman, and child, or about $10,000 per three-person household. In my opinion, there are no more important tasks for health economics and health policy than to determine *what* the public derives from this extra spending, evaluate it, and explain *why* the U.S. has a system that generates such high spending.

The first paper compares per capita expenditures for physician services in the U.S. and Canada. Comparisons between these two countries are particularly meaningful because the two countries are similar in many economic, social, and cultural dimensions and in the training of their physicians. They have, however, very different systems of health care–government plays a much greater role in Canada. The paper takes the ratio of per capita physician expenditures of U.S. to Canada of 1.72 and decomposes it in different ways. Surprisingly, there were more physicians per capita in Canada; the U.S./Canada ratio was 0.88. Thus, expenditures per physician were almost twice as high in the U.S. as in Canada.

Classification of physicians between general and specialist is not the same in the two countries; but it is fairly certain that the shortfall in the U.S. is in primary care physicians; the per capita number of specialists is probably higher in the U.S.

The greater supply of specialists in the U.S. is supported by a classification of physician expenditures by type. For procedures, the U.S./Canada ratio was 2.78; for evaluation and management it was 1.16. Expenditures are equal to price multiplied by quantity. For prices of procedures, the U.S./Canada ratio was 3.34; for evaluation and management the price ratio was 1.82. Again, defects in the data warrant not taking these statistics as precise measurements, but it is surely true that the U.S. spends relatively more on procedures and Canada relatively more on evaluation and management. By dividing the expenditure ratios by the fee ratios we derived the quantity of services ratios of 0.83 for procedures and 0.64 for evaluation and management. These ratios seem low, but I think it is reasonable to conclude that the higher expenditures for physician services in the U.S. were attributable to higher fees in the U.S., not to more services. According to the most recently available statistics, there are now more physicians per capita in the U.S. than Canada; the ratio is 1.10. The ratio for expenditures per capita is 1.82.

It is also worth noting that high fees for procedures in the U.S. do not translate into an equal differential in physician income because U.S. physicians have higher expenses, including liability insurance, non-physician personnel, cost of billing and collecting fees, and rent and office amenities. To supplement the U.S./Canada comparison, we analyzed the Iowa/Manitoba per capita expenditure ratio, 1.08, and carried out decompositions similar to those for the national comparisons. Iowa had many fewer physicians than Manitoba, but other results were qualitatively similar with high fees for procedures in Iowa playing a major role.

Some of the higher expenditures in the U.S. are what economists call "transfers" to distinguish them from "real costs," that is, resources that could have been used to produce goods and services that add to the GDP. When a drug company uses its monopoly power to extract a higher price from patients, the first effect is simply to transfer money from the patient to the drug company. This may mean more money for the company executives and possibly for the shareholder and less for the patient. The company will claim that it will use the extra money for research, which they may or may not do and may or may not be a good use of the money from a social point of view. Moreover, the extra revenue could be used by the company for advertising and other marketing activities, which again may or may not be socially desirable.

The higher fees paid to physician specialists can also be thought of primarily as "transfers"– from patients and taxpayers to physicians. Analysis of the effects are tricky. If fees and incomes are reduced for physicians, but remain high for top lawyers, bankers, stock traders, CEOs, and entrepreneurs, the supply of physician-specialists could be affected. On the other hand, if top incomes fall everywhere, there would be less effect on supply. Moreover, a decline in fees may not result in lower incomes if there are fewer specialists with higher average workloads.

The second paper compares and decomposes the U.S./Canada ratio of expenditure per capita for care in acute care hospitals of 1.26. A similar analyses was applied to a comparison of California to Ontario; that ratio for hospital expenditures was 1.23. Admission per capita were higher in Canada and especially in Ontario. On the other hand, expenditures per admission were higher in the U.S. and especially California, more than offsetting the higher admission rates in Canada and Ontario. The higher expenditures per admission in the U.S. and California was partly explained by more expensive case mix, a larger share of expenditures for inpatient care as opposed to outpatient care, and more resources used per DRG case adjusted admission. Length of stay was much shorter in the U.S. and California, but the occupancy rates of 65 percent in the U.S. and 64 percent in California were sub-optimal and added to the costs in those hospitals through higher overhead costs per patient day. After all adjustments for many factors, including inpatient share of expenditures, case mix and prices of resources per adjusted admission (the real cost) ratios were 1.24 for U.S./Canada and 1.46 for California/Ontario.

To understand, the higher health care expenditure in the U.S. as a problem in efficiency, it is important to distinguish the efficiency of individual physicians and hospitals and the efficiency of health care systems as a whole. For example, there are ten times as many open heart surgical units in California as in Ontario. The population ratio is now like 3 to 1. When the lithotripter was developed to treat kidney stones without surgery, many California hospitals rushed to buy one. In Lower Ontario, it was decided to buy one for the region; it had a volume of 50 cases a week. Each California hospital was happy to get 5 cases per week. The higher volume is probably much more efficient, even after accounting for higher travel costs and possibly waiting lists in Ontario.

The most important conclusion from the decomposition is that the U.S. hospitals use more resources on average to treat admissions. We believe this happens because 1) U.S. hospitals must keep more extensive records for billing and liability concerns; 2) amenities, which on average, are at a higher standard. These include more space and privacy for patients, visitors, and staff; 3) greater concentration in a few hospitals of expensive specialized procedures in Canada compared with large number of U.S. community hospitals that strive to provide a wide variety of specialized services.

The third paper, written for a lay audience, summarizes my conclusions about why the U.S. spends so much more than other countries for health care: higher prices for drugs and other manufactured health care inputs, higher fees to physician-specialists, higher administration costs for selling, billing, and collecting insurance, and most important of all, a more expensive mix of health care including more use of technology.

The op-ed focuses on reasons why the U.S. has a health care system that differs from those in Canada, the United Kingdom, and other OECD countries. The reasons include more distrust of government in the U.S., weaker support for equality of income and services, and heterogeneity of the population. Also, there are many important differences between the Canadian and U.S. political systems, including U.S. "checks and balances," long expensive election campaigns, powerful congressional committees, gerrymandering. Even when the opposition to comprehensive health reform is a minority, it can find many ways to block reforms.

The fourth paper in Part 4, prepared as an invited lecture in Malaysia, discusses in non-quantitative language for a lay audience why health policy comes to the fore in developed countries, what forms the problems take, and how governments try to deal with them.

4.1

How Does Canada Do It?
A Comparison of Expenditures
for Physicians' Services in the
United States and Canada

As a percentage of the gross national product, expenditures for health care in the United States are considerably larger than in Canada, even though one in seven Americans is uninsured whereas all Canadians have comprehensive health insurance. Among the sectors of health care, the difference in spending is especially large for physicians' services. In 1985, per capita expenditure was $347 in the United States and only $202 (in U.S. dollars) in Canada, a ratio of 1.72. We undertook a quantitative analysis of this ratio.

We found that the higher expenditures per capita in the United States are explained entirely by higher fees; the quantity of physicians' services per capita is actually lower in the United States than in Canada. U.S. fees for procedures are more than three times as high as Canadian fees; the difference in fees for evaluation and management services is about 80 percent. Despite the large difference in fees, physicians' net incomes in the United States are only about one-third higher than in Canada. A parallel analysis of Iowa and Manitoba yielded results similar to those for the United States and Canada, except that physicians' net incomes in Iowa are about 60 percent higher than in Manitoba. Updating the analysis to 1987 on the basis of changes in each country between 1985 and 1987 yielded results similar to those obtained for 1985.

We suggest that increased use of physicians' services in Canada may result from universal insurance coverage and from encouragement of use by the larger number of physicians who are paid lower fees per service. U.S. physicians' net income is not

Originally published in *New England Journal of Medicine*, 323(13):884–890, September 1990. Copyright by Massachusetts Medical Society. Written with James S. Hahn, A.B.

increased as much as the higher U.S. fees would predict, probably because of greater
overhead expenses and the lower workloads of America's procedure-oriented physicians.
(N Engl J Med 1990; 323: 884–90.)

AMERICAN interest in the Canadian health care system is growing rapidly for
two principal reasons.[1–3] First, costs have escalated in the United States to such an
extent that health care now accounts for approximately 11.5 percent of the gross
national product, whereas in Canada the comparable figure is about 9 percent.
Second, one in seven Americans has no health insurance, and tens of millions
of others have incomplete coverage; in contrast, Canada provides comprehensive,
first-dollar health insurance to all its citizens. If U.S. spending could be held to
the Canadian percentage, the savings would amount to more than $100 billion
a year.

There have been numerous descriptions of the evolution of national health
insurance in Canada and of the current federal-provincial system.[4–6] A detailed
statistical analysis of trends in Canada and the United States has identified
prospective global budgets for hospitals and negotiated fee schedules for
physicians' services as major reasons for lower spending in Canada.[7] Other
studies have focused on hospital costs,[8,9] drug prices,[10–12] the use of surgical
services,[13,14] and administrative costs.[15]

This study concentrates on per capita expenditures for physicians' services
because in this important sector the ratio between U.S. and Canadian spending is
particularly large (1.72 in 1985). In other words, after adjustment for population
size and the overall purchasing power of the Canadian dollar, Americans spend
72 percent more than Canadians for physicians' services. The comparable ratio
for hospital expenditures is 1.34, and for all other health expenditures combined
it is 1.30.

How does Canada do it? Do Canadians receive fewer physicians' services?
Are the higher U.S. expenditures attributable entirely to higher fees? Do higher
fees result from the use of more resources to produce a given quantity of services
(more physicians, nurses, equipment, and the like), or do they reflect higher
prices for those resources (higher physicians' net incomes, nurses' salaries, and
the like)?

Our principal objective was to provide quantitative answers to these
questions. Our analysis of the ratio between the United States and Canada was
supplemented by a parallel comparison of Iowa and Manitoba. The state and the
province have small, relatively homogeneous populations, and we had special
access to data for the two regions. Our analysis of the ratio between Iowa and
Manitoba in per capita expenditures for physicians' services (1.51) served as a
check on the comparison between the United States and Canada and helped to

sharpen our understanding of the reasons for the differences between countries in spending, fees, and use. The effect of physicians' services on the health of Americans and Canadians is not addressed in this paper.

Methods

Data on health care expenditures, the number of physicians who care for patients, vital statistics, and socioeconomic variables for the United States, Canada, Iowa, and Manitoba for 1985 were gathered from published sources,[16-34] and the appropriate ratios were calculated. All data in Canadian dollars were converted to U.S. dollars according to the purchasing-power-parity exchange rate of $1 U.S. equals $1.22 Canadian. This rate, calculated each year by the Organization for Economic Cooperation and Development, is based on the relative prices of the same comprehensive basket of goods and services in the two countries. All dollar amounts mentioned in this paper are in U.S. dollars. Total expenditures for physicians' services were allocated to procedures or to evaluation and management according to a formula based on the distribution of specialists in each country (or region). Details of the allocation are available elsewhere.*

Fees

The necessary data on physicians' fees were not available — except from Manitoba — in published form. We therefore relied on data made available to us on a confidential basis by the Health Insurance Association of America, California Blue Shield, Iowa Blue Cross and Blue Shield, and Health and Welfare Canada. Fees in the United States for surgery (33 procedures) and evaluation and management (22 kinds of visits that we combined in five broad categories to achieve comparability with the Canadian data) are based on billed charges reported to the Health Insurance Association of America by its members. The association did not have data for ancillary services; charges for radiology (eight procedures) and anesthesiology (eight procedures) were therefore obtained from California Blue Cross and adjusted to the levels of the association by comparing surgery fees from both sources. Billed charges for Iowa for the same procedures and visits were provided by Iowa Blue Cross and Blue Shield. A list of the procedures and types of visits according to CPT-4 code (Current Procedural

---

*See NAPS document no. 04801 for 20 pages of supplementary material. Order from NAPS c/o Microfiche Publications, P.O. Box 3513, Grand Central Station, New York, NY 10163–3513. Remit in advance (in U.S. funds only) $7.75 for photocopies or $4 for microfiche. Outside the U.S. and Canada add postage of $4.50 ($1.50 for microfiche postage).

Terminology, fourth revision), as well as the precise methods we used to calculate the fee ratios, is available elsewhere.*

All U.S. and Iowa charges were reduced by 20 percent to measure the fees actually received by American physicians more accurately, There are services that are provided but never paid for; there are differences between what is billed and what insurance companies will allow; preferred-provider and health maintenance organizations extract explicit or implicit discounts from billed charges; physicians who accept Medicare assignment may receive less than their usual fee; and Medicaid is frequently the lowest payer of all. A survey of the Medical Group Management Association for 1985 reported that fee-for-service cash collections were 15 percent less than gross fee-for-service billed charges.[35] It is widely believed that the collection ratio for such groups is higher than the ratio for physicians in solo practice or small partnerships. A sample of Medicare-approved charges for 30 major services and procedures showed a median difference from Health Insurance Association of America billed charges of −23 percent.[36] Reducing U.S. billed charges by 20 percent therefore appeared appropriate. No such adjustment was necessary for Canada because bills are paid fully and promptly by the provincial governments according to predetermined, annually negotiated rates.

Fees in Manitoba were taken from the physicians' manual of the Manitoba Health Services Commission and included an adjustment for services provided in rural areas. Because overall Canadian fees were unavailable, Manitoba fees were adjusted to an all-Canada level according to a ratio of benefit rates between Canada and Manitoba that we calculated using provincial data assembled by Health and Welfare Canada. Because there is considerable interest in the United States in reimbursement for procedures as compared with reimbursement for evaluation and management, we calculated separate fee ratios for the two categories of services.

Quantity of services per capita

In principle, the quantity of services per capita is the sum of all the visits, tests, operations, and other services provided by physicians. Because comprehensive data to measure these services directly were not available, we estimated the ratios between the United States and Canada and between Iowa and Manitoba by dividing the ratio of expenditures per capita by the appropriate fee ratio. Because expenditures equal the product of fees and the quantity of services, this method provided an indirect measure of the relative quantity of services provided.

Price of resource

Physicians' services are produced through the use of resources such as physicians, nurses, equipment, and office supplies. We estimated the ratio of the prices of these resources for the United States and Canada (and for Iowa and Manitoba) from physicians' net incomes, nurses' salaries, and other relevant data. The overall ratio was a weighted average (weighted according to expenditures) of the price ratios for four categories of resources: physicians, other personnel, office, and equipment and supplies. This average was then adjusted to take liability-insurance premiums into account.

Quantity of resources

Of the four categories of resources listed above, we only had data on quantity for the number of physicians. We therefore estimated the ratio of the quantity of resources per capita for the United States and Canada (and for Iowa and Manitoba) by dividing the ratio of expenditure per capita by the ratio of the price of resources. Because expenditures equal the product of the price of resources and the quantity of resources, this method provided an indirect measure of the quantity of resources.

Results

Table 1 presents selected background statistics for each country and for Iowa and Manitoba in order to put the data on expenditures in context. Most of the populations of the United States, Canada, and Manitoba are urban, whereas more than half of Iowa's population is rural, which helps to explain the low number of physicians per capita in that state. Despite its huge territory, 90 percent of Canada's population lives in a narrow band of land just north of the border with the United States. Manitoba, like Canada in general, has a large area, most of which is thinly populated. More than half of Manitoba's population and more than three quarters of its physicians live in one city, Winnipeg. The elderly are relatively more numerous in the United States and in Iowa; were all other things equal, this would lead to a slightly higher use of medical services. The higher per capita gross national product in the United States would tend to increase health care expenditures per capita, mostly through higher incomes for physicians, nurses, and other personnel.

The differences in the number of physicians per capita, both in the aggregate and according to the type of physician, are worthy of special note. On a per capita basis there are more physicians who care for patients in Canada than in the United

Table 1.   Selected Background Statistics, 1985.*

Variable	United States	Canada	Iowa	Manitoba	Ratio of United States to Canada	Ratio of Iowa to Manitoba
Population (000s)	283,739	25,358	2,905	1,070	—	—
Percent rural	26.3	24.3	52.3	28.8	—	—
Percent in cities of ≥ 100,000	25.4	34.5	10.5	55.5	—	—
Percent over 65 years old	12.0	10.4	14.2	12.5	—	—
Births (per 1000)	15.8	15.1	14.3	16.0	—	—
Gross national (domestic) product per capital[†]	16,703	14,801	14,490	13,791	1.13	1.05
Patient-care physicians (per 1000)[‡]	1.81	2.05	1.21	2.02	0.88	0.60
Private-practice general practitioners and family physicians	0.24	0.90	0.29	0.88	0.26	0.33
Other[‡]	1.57	1.15	0.92	1.14	1.37	0.81
Short-term general hospitals (per 1000)[§]						
Beds	4.20	4.43	5.22	4.89	0.95	1.07
Admissions	140	136	142	153	1.03	0.93
Days	994	1,293	1,084	1,317	0.77	0.82
Life expectancy at birth (yr)						
Men	71.2	72.9	73.1	72.9	0.98	1.00
Women	78.2	79.7	80.2	79.7	0.98	1.01
Infant mortality (per 1000)	10.6	8.0	9.5	9.9	1.33	0.96

*Data were collected from references 16 through 29. Calculations in this and the subsequent tables were performed with unrounded numbers.
†Values are in 1985 U.S. dollars. Canadian figures were adjusted according to the purchasing-power-parity exchange rate. $1.00 U.S. equals SI.22 Canadian.
‡Values include interns and residents.
§Canadian data include rehabilitation units.

States, and many more in Manitoba than in Iowa. The disparity with respect to general practitioners and family physicians is very large. In most specialties and subspecialties, however, the ratio between the United States and Canada is much greater than 1. Rates of hospital admission are similar in the two countries; the average length of stay is considerably longer in Canada, partly because some of Canada's short-term general hospitals include rehabilitation units.

Canada does better than the United States with respect to life expectancy and infant mortality, but Iowa does slightly better than Manitoba. There is no reason to believe that access to or the quality of medical care in Iowa is superior to the U.S. average or that care in Manitoba suffers in comparison with care in the rest of Canada. The reversal in ratios therefore suggests that these differences in gross measures of health are determined largely by nonmedical factors, such as personal behavior, the environment, and genetic endowment.

The data on per capita health expenditures (Table 2) show that the ratios between the United States and Canada and between Iowa and Manitoba are much

Table 2.   Health Expenditures per Capita, According to Type of Expenditure, 1985.*

Expenditure	United States	Canada	Ratio of United States To Canada	Iowa	Manitoba	Ratio of Iowa to Manitoba
	dollars			*dollars*		
Total	1, 780	1, 286	1.38	1, 432	1, 326	1.08
Physicians	347	202	1.72	240	159	1.51
Procedures	193	69	2.78	130	51	2.54
Evaluation and management	154	133	1.16	110	107	1.02
Hospitals	698	520	1.34	541	519	1.04
All other[†]	735	564	1.30	651	648	1.01

*Values are in 1985 U.S. dollars. Data were collected from references 20 and 30 through 34.
[†]includes expenditures for nursing homes and other institutions, drugs, dentists' services, other professional services, public health, appliances, prepayment administration, construction, research, home care, ambulance services, other personal health care, and miscellaneous expenses.

greater for physicians' services than for hospital services or other expenditures. They also show that within the category of physicians' services, procedures account for nearly all the higher spending in the United States. To understand the difference between the ratios for procedures and for evaluation and management, it is necessary to examine the ratios for fees and for the quantity of services separately.

Fees

Physicians' fees for procedures are approximately 234 percent higher in the United States than in Canada (Table 3); the difference between Iowa and Manitoba is about 199 percent. By U.S. standards, fees for procedures are exceedingly low in Canada. For example, in Manitoba in 1985 total obstetrical care was reimbursed at $245; the fee for a hernia repair was $186 and for a cholecystectomy $311. Canadian surgical fees are much lower across the board than U.S. fees: for the United States and Canada, 27 of the 33 ratios for surgical procedures are between 2.0 and 4.5; and for Iowa and Manitoba, 29 of the 33 ratios are between 1.75 and 4.25.

Fees for evaluation and management are also higher in the United States than in Canada, but the ratios are much smaller: 1.82 for the United States and Canada, and 1.72 for Iowa and Manitoba. Canadian fees for hospital visits are particularly low; in Manitoba physicians received only $7.20 for a "moderate" hospital visit in 1985 (a visit limited in scope and duration).

The overall fee ratio was moderately sensitive to our allocation of expenditures between procedures and evaluation and management. For instance,

Table 3. Physicians' Fees, 1985.*

Service[†]	Ratio of United States to Canada	Ratio of Iowa to Manitoba
Surgery	3.21	2.76
Anesthesiology	3.73	2.86
Radiology	3.59	4.19
Procedures (weighted average)	3.34	2.99
Moderate office visit	1.56	1.44
Extensive office visit	1.55	1.50
Moderate hospital visit	4.77	3.56
Extensive hospital visit	2.57	2.70
Consultation	1.60	1.64
Evaluation and management (weighted average)	1.82	1.72
All services[‡]	2.39	2.18

*Values are in 1985 U.S. dollars.
[†]"Moderate" visits were limited in scope and duration. "Extensive" visits were longer and broader in scope.
[‡]Values are weighted averages of the procedures and evaluation-and-management ratios.

if the true share of procedures were five percentage points larger than our estimate, the overall fee ratio between the United States and Canada would increase from 2.39 to 2.47. If the share were five percentage points smaller, the ratio would be 2.32. The exchange rate also affected the fee ratio. If we had used the market rate ($1.00 U.S. equals $1.36 Canadian), which reflects capital movements and speculation as well as the relative purchasing power of the two currencies, the overall fee ratio would be 2.68. Finally, the relation between the fee ratio and our assumption of a 20 percent discount from billed charges for U.S. fees should be noted. If we had assumed a 25 percent discount, the overall ratio would be 2.24; a 15 percent discount would yield a ratio of 2.54.

Quantity of services per capita

Table 4 provides striking refutation of the hypothesis that lower spending in Canada is achieved by providing fewer services. On the contrary, the ratio between the United States and Canada for all services is 0.72, and between Iowa and Manitoba the ratio is 0.69. The disparity in use is much greater for evaluation and management than for procedures. These results are sensitive to possible biases in the fee ratios, but the conclusion that the rate of use is greater in Canada than in the United States appears robust. For instance, if the overall

Table 4. Estimation of the Ratios of Quantity of Physicians' Services per Capita, 1985.

Service	Ratio of United States to Canada	Ratio of Iowa to Manitoba
Procedures		
Expenditures per capita (Table 2)	2.78	2.54
Fees (Table 3)	3.34	2.99
Quantity of services per capita*	0.83	0.85
Evaluation and management		
Expenditures per capita (Table 2)	1.16	1.02
Fees (Table 3)	1.82	1.73
Quantity of services per capita*	0.64	0.60
All services		
Expenditures per capita (Table 2)	1.72	1.51
Fees (Table 3)	2.39	2.18
Quantity of services per capita*	0.72	0.69

*Values are expenditures per capita divided by fees.

fee ratio between the United States and Canada were 2.0 instead of 2.39, the ratio of the quantity of services per capita would be 0.86, still well under 1.0. These results are not sensitive to assumptions about the exchange rate because using a different rate would change the expenditures and fee ratios in equal proportion; the ratio of the quantity of services per capita would not be affected.

Prices of resources

As a share of total expenditures, the most important resource in both countries is the physician; the physician's net income is 52 percent of gross income in the United States and 66 percent in Canada. In 1985 net income per office-based physician was $112,199 in the United States and $73,607 in Canada.[37,38] After adjustment for differences in the mix of specialties, U.S. incomes were 35 percent higher than those in Canada, and 61 percent higher in Iowa than in Manitoba (Table 5). The price ratio for other personnel was based on the full-time compensation of a registered nurse.[16,39-41] The price of occupying and maintaining an office varies greatly depending on geographic location, and direct estimates were unobtainable. We assumed that the price increases as the relative wealth of an area increases; our calculations were therefore based on regional and state per capita income weighted according to the number of physicians in the area. We assumed that the real prices of equipment and supplies used by

Table 5.   Estimation of the Prices of Resources, 1985.

Resource	Ratio of United States to Canada	Ratio of Iowa to Manitoba
Net income per physician*	1.35	1.61
Other resources		
Compensation rate of other personnel	1.09	0.98
Office	1.15	1.05
Medical supplies, equipment, and other	1.00	1.00
All resources[†]	1.24	1.37
All resources, as adjusted for liability insurance	1.30	1.43

*Adjusted for mix of specialties.
[†]Weighted average of all ratios.

physicians are roughly the same in both countries; the ratio was therefore assumed to be 1.0.

We calculated the price ratio for all resources as an expenditure-weighted average of the ratios for the four categories, using the average of U.S. and Canadian weights. Liability insurance is an important item of expenditure for U.S. physicians, but their Canadian counterparts do not incur a similar expense; estimates of liability expenses for Canadian physicians are less than 1 percent of gross receipts. We did not consider expenditures on liability insurance to reflect any real resource used in the practice of medicine; thus, liability insurance was treated as a tax on the prices of all resources. The ratios of resource prices were therefore increased by the share of all expenditures attributable to liability-insurance premiums. We concluded that the prices of resources are moderately higher in the United States than in Canada (Table 5), but the ratio is small as compared with the fee ratio of 2.39. Most of the excess of U.S. over Canadian fees must be attributable to the fact that Americans use more resources to produce a given quantity of services.

Ratio of quantity of resources to quantity of services

The results of our estimation of the ratios of resources to services (Table 6) were extraordinary, It appears that the United States uses 84 percent more real resources than does Canada to produce a given quantity of physicians' services. The difference between Iowa and Manitoba is somewhat smaller, with a ratio of 1.53.

Table 6. Estimation of the Quantity of Resources Relative to the Quantity of Services, 1985.

Variable	Ratio of United States to Canada	Ratio of Iowa to Manitoba
Expenditures per capita (Table 2)	1.72	1.51
Prices of resources (Table 5)	1.30	1.43
Quantity of resources per capita*	1.32	1.06
Quantity of services per capita (Table 4)	0.72	0.69
Ratio of quantity of resources to quantity of services	1.84	1.53

*Values are expenditures per capita divided by the prices of resources.

Table 7. Summary and Update of Estimates.

Variable	1985 Ratio of United States to Canada	1985 Ratio of Iowa to Manitoba	1987 Ratio of United States to Canada
Expenditures per capita	1.72	1.51	1.75
Fees	2.39	2.18	2.61
Quantity of services per capita	0.72	0.69	0.67
Prices of resources	1.30	1.43	1.32
Ratio of quantity of resources to quantity of services	1.84	1.53	1.98

Summary and update

The study's most important results are summarized in Table 7, First, higher expenditures on physicians' services per capita in the United States were entirely explained by higher fees; in fact, the quantity of services per capita is actually lower in the United States than in Canada. Second, the higher fees were attributable primarily to the fact that Americans use more resources to produce a given quantity of services. Third, a small portion of the higher U.S. fees was reflected in higher prices of resources, especially physicians' net incomes. Fourth, the results of the comparison between Iowa and Manitoba were similar to those of the comparison between the United States and Canada, except that a larger proportion of the higher fees in Iowa reflected higher physicians' net incomes. Finally, updating the analysis to 1987 with data on changes in each country from 1985 to 1987 yielded results similar to those obtained for the 1985 comparisons between countries.

Discussion

Two striking conclusions emerged from our statistical analysis of the difference between the United States and Canada in spending for physicians' services. First, the data firmly reject the view that Canadians save money by delivering fewer services. On the contrary, the quantity of services per capita is much higher in Canada than in the United States. Second, as compared with Canada, the United States uses appreciably more real resources to produce a given quantity of services. We will discuss eight possible explanations for these findings: the effects of insurance on demand, the effects of physicians on demand, billing costs, amenities, other administrative costs, overhead accounting, the workloads of procedure-oriented physicians, and the quality or intensity of care.

Effects of insurance on demand

Canadians have universal coverage and face no out-of-pocket expenses, whereas U.S. patients pay coinsurance rates ranging from 0 (full insurance) to 100 percent (for the uninsured). Thus, lower rates of use in the United States must reflect in part the price sensitivity of the demand for physicians' services. If, on average, Americans face the equivalent of 25 percent coinsurance, the results of the Rand Health Insurance Experiment predict that there will be 27 percent fewer visits and 33 percent less outpatient expenditure per capita than if they had full coverage.[42] We found that the use of evaluation and management services in the United States was 36 percent less than in Canada, and the difference between Iowa and Manitoba was 40 percent. Another source has estimated per capita contacts with a physician at 7.1 in Canada in 1985 and at 5.4 in the United States in 1986.[43]

Effects of physicians on demand

To the extent that higher rates of use in Canada are not fully explained by more complete insurance coverage, they may be explained by demand induced by Canadian physicians.[44] The number of general practitioners and family physicians is very high in Canada, and their fee per visit is low. They may thus be more inclined to recommend additional evaluation and management services.

Billing costs

In each Canadian province there is only one source of payment for physicians' services. Physicians typically submit one bill, and payment is usually punctual and complete. In contrast, American physicians must bill a myriad of private and public third-party payers, and often must also bill patients directly. Numerous complex forms must be filled out, there are frequently delays in payment as well as disagreements concerning the amount to be paid, and collection efforts impose additional costs. The differences in billing undoubtedly account for some of the additional resources reflected in the U.S. data, but we do not know exactly how much. The order of magnitude can be inferred from the fact that approximately 16 percent of the gross receipts of physicians are devoted to personnel who are not medical doctors. If one fourth of those personnel are needed for billing tasks that are not required in the Canadian system, then 4 percent of U.S. expenditures can be explained by this factor. There are also additional billing costs for physicians' time, computers, stationery, and postage.

Amenities

Fragmentary data from one Canadian province and the American Medical Association suggest that U.S. physicians spend considerably more than their Canadian counterparts for rent and related office expenses, possibly twice as much. It is unlikely that this large difference is primarily the result of higher prices for identical offices. Some portion, probably a considerable portion, reflects a higher level of amenities in the average U.S. office. This may take the form of a more desirable location, more space per patient, newer furnishings, or more elaborate decor. Why would this occur? One reason is that real per capita income in the United States is 10 to 15 percent higher than in Canada; Americans are therefore accustomed to a somewhat higher level of amenities in most aspects of life. But the income difference would probably explain only about a 10 to 15 percent difference in amenities. More important may be the fact that competition for well-insured patients is more intense in the United States, especially among procedure-oriented physicians, many of whom have lower workloads than they desire. Physicians usually do not compete for insured patients by lowering fees, but they can try to attract such patients by offering a higher level of amenities.

Other administrative costs

There are numerous other costs incurred by many U.S. physicians that are lower or nonexistent for their Canadian counterparts. For instance, concern over possible malpractice suits (much rarer in Canada) may cause U.S. physicians to keep additional notes and records, or to undertake other activities that require their time and other resources but that are not reflected in the measures of quantity of services. (If concern over possible malpractice suits leads U.S. physicians to order additional visits and tests, the ratio between resources and services is not affected, because both the additional services and resources required to produce them are accounted for.) Other administrative costs that are more likely to be incurred by American than Canadian physicians involve maintaining contractual relations with preferred-provider organizations, dealing with third-party use reviews, and marketing.

Overhead accounting

Overhead makes up 48 percent of expenditures in the United States, but only 34 percent in Canada.[37,38] Some of this difference undoubtedly reflects the greater use of resources in the United States, as discussed above. Some, however, may reflect more stringent scrutiny of overhead accounting by the Canadian government, because the overhead percentage is part of the background for negotiations between the provincial governments and physicians' organizations over fees. This constraint is not present in the United States. If identical accounting practices were applied in both countries, the overhead percentages might be slightly closer to each other and the difference in net income might be slightly larger. Such an adjustment would increase the ratio of the price of resources in the two countries by a few percentage points and decrease the ratio of resources to services by an equivalent amount.

Workloads of procedure-oriented physicians

There can be little doubt that the average Canadian physician who specializes in procedures does more of them during a year than his or her counterpart in the United States. We estimated that there are about 40 percent more procedure-oriented physicians in the United States than in Canada (relative to the population), but the number of procedures performed appears to be about 20 percent higher in Canada. For some specialties the difference in workloads may be of the order of magnitude of two to one. This explanation is not as relevant for the comparison between Iowa and Manitoba, because the per capita supply of procedure-oriented physicians is about the same in both places. The difference in the supply of physicians may help explain why the ratio of resources to services is much higher between the United States and Canada than between Iowa and Manitoba.

Quality or intensity of care

The most uncertain and potentially controversial explanation concerns possible differences in quality or intensity of care. This question required that evaluation and management and procedures be considered separately. We estimated that approximately two thirds of the evaluation and management services in Canada are delivered by general practitioners and family physicians, and one third is delivered by internists, pediatricians, psychiatrists, and other specialists. In the United States the proportions are reversed. Should this be interpreted as a difference in quality of care? Some would argue that care provided by physicians with specialty training should be considered as "more" care. But there are others who believe that in most cases the quality of care provided by general practitioners or family physicians is as high, and may even be superior because of their greater familiarity with the patient and his or her circumstances. The question of intensity of care arises because of the possibility that some of the additional evaluation and management services provided in Canada are for patients with minor problems such as colds or upset stomachs. Some visits of this type may be deterred in the United States because insurance coverage is not as complete and because patients have been urged by employers and insurance companies not to visit physicians for minor problems. If the category of moderate office visits included fewer patients with minor problems in the United States, an adjustment for intensity would result in a slight increase in the ratio of the quantity of services per capita and a slight decrease in the ratio of resources to services.

With respect to procedures, the question of possible differences in the quality of care arises for other reasons. The technical competence of the specialists performing the procedures in the two countries is probably not an issue. A comparison of surgical mortality in Manitoba and New England concluded that the differences were small.[45] Timeliness and convenience, however, may differ. Because on a per capita basis there are so many more procedure-oriented specialists in the United States than in Canada, it is likely that Americans with insurance find it easier to have procedures performed when and where they want. From the patient's perspective, this may offer an additional source of satisfaction with the service provided. Whether such differences exist, how large they are, and how they are valued by patients are subjects for further research. These issues are much more muted in the comparison between Iowa and Manitoba than in that between the United States and Canada, because there are so few physicians per capita in Iowa as compared with Manitoba.

This discussion points up the need for additional studies to determine the magnitude of the many factors affecting fees, use of services, and use of resources to produce those services. Further refinements in the ratios of physicians' fees and the prices of resources would be particularly valuable, given the central role of these ratios in the statistical analysis. Such studies and refinements, however, are not likely to alter the principal lesson of this paper: U.S. fees are more than double those of Canada, but physicians' net incomes are only about a third higher. The disparity is explained in part by much greater overhead expenses in the United States and in part by the lower workloads of American procedure-oriented physicians as compared with their Canadian counterparts.

We are indebted to Evelyn Shapiro for valuable advice on all aspects of health care in Canada; to Allan Detsky, M.D., Ph.D., Joseph Newhouse, Ph.D., Douglas Owens, M.D., David Redelmeier, M.D., and Noralou Roos, Ph.D., for helpful comments on specific points; and to the Health Insurance Association of America, Iowa Blue Cross and Blue Shield, Blue Shield of California, and several people in Canada for making data available to us on a confidential basis.

References

1. Iglehart, J. K. (1990). "Canada's Health Care System Faces Its Problems." *New England Journal of Medicine* **322**: 562–568.
2. Doherty, K. (1989). "Is the Canadian System as Good as It Looks for Employers?" *Bus Health* **7**(7): 31–34.
3. Moloney, T. W. and Paul, B. (1989). "A New Financial Framework: Lessons from Canada." *Health Affairs (Millwood)* **8**(2): 148–159.
4. Andreopoulos, S. ed. (1975). *National Health Insurance: Can We Learn from Canada?* Wiley: New York.
5. Evans, R. G. and Stoddart, G. L. eds. (1986). "Medicare at Maturity: Achievements, Lessons, and Challenges." In *Proceedings of the Health Policy Conference on Canada's National Health Care System.* University of Calgary Press: Calgary, AB.
6. Iglehart, J. K. (1986). "Canada's Health Care System." *New England Journal of Medicine* **315**: 202–208, 778–784, 1623–1628.
7. Barer, M. L. and Evans, R. G. (1986). "Riding North on a South-Bound Horse? Expenditures, Prices, Utilization and Incomes in the Canadian Health Care System." In *Proceedings of the Health Policy Conference on Canada's National Health Care System, –Medicare at Maturity: Achievements, Lessons, and Challenges*, eds. R. G. Evans and G. L. Stoddart. University of Calgary Press: Calgary, AB, pp. 53–163.
8. Detsky, A. S., Stacey, S, R. and Bombardier, C. (1983). "The Effectiveness of a Regulatory Strategy in Containing Hospital Costs: The Ontario Experience, 1967–1981." *New England Journal of Medicine* **309**: 151–159.

9. Detsky, A. S., Abrams, H. B., Ladha, L. and Stacey, S. R. (1986). "Global Budgeting and the Teaching Hospital in Ontario." *Medical Care* **24**: 89–94.

10. Fulda, T. K. and Dickens, P. F. (1979). "Controlling the Cost of Drugs: The Canadian Experience." *Health Care Financing Review* **1**(2): 55–64.

11. McRae, J. J. and Tapon, F. (1985). "Some Empirical Evidence on Post-patent Barriers to Entry in the Canadian Pharmaceutical Industry." *Journal of Health Economics* **4**: 43–61.

12. Scherer, F. M. (1985). "Post-patent Barriers to Entry in the Pharmaceutical Industry." *Journal of Health Economics* **4**: 83–87.

13. McPherson, K., Strong, P. M., Epstein, A. and Jones, L. (1981). "Regional Variations in the use of Common Surgical Procedures: Within and Between England and Wales, Canada and the United States of America." *Social Science & Medicine* **15**: 273–288.

14. Vayda, E., Mindell, W. R. and Rutkow, I. M. (1982). "A decade of surgery in Canada, England and Wales, and the United States." *Archives of Surgery* **117**: 846–853.

15. Himmelstein, D. U. and Woolhandler, S. (1986). "Cost without Benefit: Administrative Waste in U.S. Health Care." *New England Journal of Medicine* **314**: 441–445.

16. American Hospital Association (1986). *Hospital Statistics*. American Hospital Association: Chicago.

17. American Medical Association (1986). *Physician Characteristics and Distribution in the U.S.* American Medical Association: Chicago.

18. Health and Welfare Canada (1988). *Active Civilian Physicians by Type of Physician, Canada, by Province, December 31, 1987.* Health and Welfare Canada: Ottawa, ON.

19. Iowa Development Commission (1987). *Statistical Profile of Iowa.* Iowa Development Commission; Des Moines.

20. Statistics Canada (1989). *Canadian Economic Observer, Historical Statistical Supplement, 1988/89.* Catalog 11–210. Statistics Canada: Ottawa, ON.

21. Statistics Canada (1985). *Canada Year Book 1985.* Statistics Canada: Ottawa, ON.

22. Statistics Canada (1988). *Canada Year Book 1988.* Statistics Canada: Ottawa, ON.

23. Statistics Canada (1987). *Hospital Annual Statistics, 1984–1985.* Catalogue 83–232 annual. Statistics Canada: Ottawa, ON.

24. Statistics Canada (1988). *Life Tables, Canada and Provinces, 1985–1987.* Catalogue S41–044. Statistics Canada: Ottawa, ON.

25. Statistics Canada (1988). *Postcensal Annual Estimates of Population by Marital Status, Age, Sex, and Components of Growth for Canada, Provinces, and Territories.* June 1, 1985, Vol. 3, 3rd issue. Catalogue 91–210 annual. Statistics Canada: Ottawa ON.

26. Bureau of the Census (1987). Statistical abstract of the United States: 1987. 107th ed. Government Printing Office: Washington, D.C.

27. *Idem.* (1988). Statistical abstract of the United States: 1988. 108th ed. Government Printing Office: Washington, D.C.

28. *Idem.* (1989). Statistical abstract of the United States: 1989. 109th ed. Government Printing Office: Washington, D.C.

29. *Idem.* (1986). City and county data book. Government Printing Office: Washington, D.C.

30. 1987. National Health Expenditures in Canada, 1975–1985 (1987). Health and Welfare Canada: Ottawa, ON.

31. Levit, K. (1985). "Personal Health Expenditures by State, 1976–1982." *Health Care Financing Review* **6**(4): 1–49.

32. Organisation for Economic Co-operation and Development. (1987). National accounts. Vol. 1. Main aggregates, 1960–1985. Organisation for Economic Co-operation and Development: Paris.

33. Department of Commerce, Bureau of Economic Analysis. (1988). Survey of current business, May 1988. Government Printing Office: Washington, D.C. No. 337–790.

34. Waldo, D., Levit, K. R. and Lazenby, H. (1986). "National Health Expenditures, 1985." *Health Care Financing Review* **8**(1): 1–21.

35. Medical Group Management Association (1986). *The Cost and Production Survey Report: 1986 Report.* Medical Group Management Association: Denver.

36. Health Care Financing Administration (1985). *Average Allowed Charges for Selected Procedure Codes by Type of Service, 1985: Part B Medicare Annual Data Procedure File.* Health Care Financing Administration: Baltimore.

37. Health and Welfare Canada (1988). *Physicians' Income by Specialty Study 1985.* Health and Welfare Canada: Ottawa, ON.

38. American Medical Association (1987). *SMS detailed tables.* AMA Center for Health Policy Research: Chicago.

39. Department of Commerce, Bureau of the Census (1985). *Current Population* survey, Public Use Tape.

40. Health and Welfare Canada (1988). *Salaries and Wages in Canadian Hospitals, 1962–1985.* Health and Welfare Canada: Ottawa, ON.

41. Statistics Canada (1987). *Annual Return of Hospitals — Hospital Indicators, 1984–1985.* Catalogue 83–233. Statistics Canada: Ottawa, ON.

42. Manning, W. G., Newhouse, J. P., Dunn, N. *et al.* (1987). "Health Insurance and the Demand for Medical Care: Evidence from a Randomized Experiment." *The American Economic Review* **77**: 251–277.

43. Sandier, S. (1989). "Health Services Utilization and Physician Income Trends." *Health Care Financing Review* **11**(1): 33–48.

44. Ginzberg, E. (1969). *Men, Money, and Medicine.* Columbia University Press: New York.

45. Roos, L. L., Fisher, E. S., Sharp, S. M., Newhouse, J. P., Anderson, G. and Bubolz, T. A. (1990). "Postsurgical Mortality in Manitoba and New England." *The Journal of the American Medical Association* **263**: 2453–2458.

4.2

Hospital Expenditures in the United States and Canada

Background. Expenditures per capita for hospitals are higher in the United States than in Canada. If the United States had the same spending pattern as Canada, the annual savings in 1985 would have exceeded $30 billion.

Methods. We used data from published sources, computer files, and institutional reports to compare 1987 costs for acute care hospitals on three levels: national (the United States vs. Canada), regional (California vs. Ontario), and institutional (two California hospitals vs. two Ontario hospitals). Expenditures per admission were adjusted for the case mix of patients, prices of labor and other resources, and outpatient visits.

Results. The United States had proportionately fewer hospital beds than Canada (3.9 vs. 5.4 per 1000 population), fewer admissions (129 vs. 142 per 1000 population), and shorter mean stays (7.2 vs. 11.2 days). Higher costs per admission in the United States were explained in part by a case mix that was more complex by 14 percent and by prices for labor, supplies, and other hospital resources that were higher by 4 percent. Hospitals in the United States provided relatively less outpatient care, particularly in emergency departments (320 vs. 677 visits per 1000 population). After all adjustments, the estimate of resources used for inpatient care per admission was 24 percent higher in the United States than in Canada and 46 percent higher in California than in Ontario. The estimated differences between the two pairs of California and Ontario hospitals were 20 and 15 percent.

Conclusions. Canadian acute care hospitals have more admissions, more outpatient visits, and more inpatient days per capita than hospitals in the United States, but they spend appreciably less. The reasons include higher administrative costs in the United States and more use of centralized equipment and personnel in Canada.

Originally published in *New England Journal of Medicine*, 328(11):772-778, March 1993. Copyright by Massachusetts Medical Society. Written with Donald A. Redelmeier, M.D.

Expenditures for hospital care were substantially higher in the United States than in Canada in 1985 after adjustment for population size and the difference in currencies. Hospital costs, along with physicians' services[1] and the cost of administering health insurance plans,[2,3] were the principal factors contributing to the high expenditures for health care in the United States as compared with Canada. If hospitals in the United States followed the same spending pattern as their Canadian counterparts, the savings would have exceeded $30 billion in 1985. By 1989, both the relative and the absolute differences in spending had widened.[4,5]

Why are hospital expenditures greater in the United States? A study of patients 65 years of age or older concluded that admission rates and case mix were similar in the two countries, but that the cost per patient was much lower in Canada.[6] Other studies have focused on global budgeting and regulation as the principal mechanism of cost control in Canada.[7–9] Patterns of medical practice may differ because of the higher incidence of malpractice suits in the United States.[10] Also, the health care needs of the two populations may be dissimilar because of differing cultures and lifestyles.[11]

What factors contribute to the higher expenditures for hospital care in the United States? Do Americans have higher admission rates or longer hospital stays? Do U.S. hospitals treat patients with more complex diseases? Do they pay higher wages or higher prices for drugs and other resources? Do they provide more outpatient care? To answer these questions, we examined hospital costs for 1987 on three levels: national (comparing the United States with Canada); regional (comparing California, the largest state, with Ontario, the largest province); and institutional (comparing two hospitals in California with two in Ontario). The goal was to measure and explain differences in the use of resources to treat comparable patients. We did not examine the effects of differences in hospital expenditures on outcomes for patients.

Methods

Background data

Details of the definitions, sources, and statistical adjustments are available from the National Auxiliary Publications Service.[a] General background data, information on health care expenditures, and 1987 hospital data for the

---

[a]See NAPS document no. 05003 for 13 pages of supplementary material. Order from NAPS c/o Microfiche Publications, P.O. Box 3513, Grand Central Station, New York, NY 10163-3513. Remit in advance (in U.S. funds only) $7.75 for photocopies or $4 for microfiche. Outside the U.S. and

United States, Canada, California, and Ontario were gathered from published sources.[12–33] This study focused on acute care hospitals; extended care facilities, long-term chronic care units, and nursing homes were excluded. Canadian institutions report on a fiscal-year basis (April 1 to March 31), whereas U.S. institutions report on a calendar-year basis (January 1 to December 31); we adjusted the financial data for Canada to account for the three-month time difference. Canadian dollars were converted to U.S. dollars at the purchasing-power exchange rate of $1.23 Canadian to $1 U.S.; all dollar amounts mentioned in this article are expressed in 1987 U.S. dollars.

Adjustment for case mix

To adjust for case mix, we classified the patients in the United States according to diagnosis-related group (DRG) and the patients in Canada according to case-mix group (CMG). In 1987 these two systems were similar in design and definition.[32] We explored possible differences in coding between the two countries by identifying 100 pairs of DRGs and CMGs for which both complicated and uncomplicated versions of the same diagnosis have been defined and by comparing the proportions of patients classified as having the complicated type. To quantify the overall case mix, we analyzed the complete distribution of diagnoses using weights based on DRG-specific charges in California. A second summary measure was obtained with weights based on CMG-specific resource estimates in Ontario. The results obtained with the two weighting approaches were averaged to yield the case-mix ratios used in our adjustments.

Adjustment for prices of resources

Comparisons of wages were based on the earnings of full-time workers plus their fringe benefits. Because the comparisons differed depending on the level of skill required by the occupation, ratios were assessed at three different wage levels: high (head nurses and general-duty staff nurses), medium (laboratory technicians and x-ray technicians), and low (hospital cleaners and food-service helpers). To obtain a ratio for wages in general, we calculated a weighted average of the wage ratios for the three occupational categories. Weights of 50, 25, and 25 for the high, medium, and low wage categories, respectively, were estimated from the distribution of earnings of hospital employees according to occupation.[33]

Canada, add postage of $4.50 ($1.75 for microfiche postage). There is a $15 invoicing charge for all orders filled before payment.

Alternative averages based on weights of 60, 20, and 20, and on 40, 30, and 30 were also calculated.

The price ratio for pharmacy supplies was derived from an analysis by Schieber et al.[30] The price ratio for nonmedical resources (such as electricity, water, and telephone service) was assumed to be the same as the ratio found by the Organization for Economic Cooperation and Development to apply to all goods and services — i.e., the purchasing-power parity exchange rate. To determine the overall relative price of hospital resources, the ratios for labor and non-labor resources were averaged, with weights of 0.67 for labor resources and 0.33 for nonlabor resources used to reflect an average of their relative contribution to total hospital costs in the United States and Canada.[12,13]

Adjustment for outpatient care

To adjust for hospital outpatient services, we developed a model in which "total admission equivalents" were estimated as the sum of hospital admissions, visits to the emergency department, and other outpatient visits (with the last two of these weighted according to their relative costs). When hospital admissions were divided by total admission equivalents, the quotient indicated the proportion of total expenditures that was related to inpatient service; for example, a hospital with 8000 admissions and 2000 additional admission equivalents (representing emergency and outpatient visits) would have 10,000 total admission equivalents and an inpatient share of total expenditures of 80 percent.

Emergency and outpatient visits were converted to admission equivalents on the basis of data from the American Hospital Association for individual states in 1987. We used multivariate regression to analyze these data for the 48 contiguous states and estimated the marginal costs of an average visit to the emergency department and an average outpatient visit, relative to the cost of an average admission. We then applied these estimates to Canadian hospitals, assuming that the difference between the two countries in the use of resources for each outpatient service was similar to the difference in resource use for an inpatient admission. The results of the regression model for California and Ontario were compared with estimates provided by the American Hospital Association and the Ontario Ministry of Health; the results obtained for the four specific hospitals were reviewed by the administrators of the respective facilities.

Specific institutions

Background data for the four study hospitals came from published sources, computer files, and confidential reports. The Stanford University Medical Center and the Sunnybrook Health Science Center are large tertiary care hospitals located in northern California and southern Ontario, respectively. In 1987, both had trauma units, academic teaching programs, and extensive referral networks. St. John's Hospital and Wellesley Hospital are community-oriented hospitals in southern California and southern Ontario, respectively. Both had active obstetrics programs, small intensive care units, and large general medical programs. At all four facilities we evaluated case mix, relative prices, and the inpatient share of expenditures with the same methods used in the national and regional comparisons.

Specific services

To examine the use of resources, we obtained confidential departmental reports detailing clinical activity at each of the four hospitals. Many services could not be compared at each of the four hospitals because of differences in accounting and reporting, but for this study we selected 12 well-specified diagnostic services chosen to illustrate diverse aspects of care, including routine and high-technology procedures.

Results

Table 1 shows selected socioeconomic factors that affect hospital expenditures. As compared with Canada, the United States had a higher percentage of persons 65 years of age or older and a smaller proportion living in cities with more than 100,000 residents. The crude death rate was higher in the United States than in Canada, but a smaller proportion of deaths occurred in hospitals. The birth rate was higher in the United States, and a higher percentage of American newborns weighed less than 2500 g. The homicide rate and the incidence of the acquired immunodeficiency syndrome were much higher in the United States. The differences between California and Ontario were proportionately similar, except that there were fewer elderly patients in California.

The background statistics for acute care hospitals are shown in Table 2. Expenditures per capita were 26 percent higher in the United States, although the number of beds per capita, the number of admissions per capita, and the average stay were all greater in Canada. In the United States (and California) more of the beds were in small and medium-sized hospitals, and a much smaller percentage of beds were in hospitals with more than 500 beds. The greatest difference in age-specific admission rates was in the rate for children: an American child was nearly 50 percent less likely to enter a hospital than a Canadian child. Occupancy rates were appreciably lower in

Table 1.   Background Data on Selected Variables for the United States and Canada, 1987.*

Variable	United States	Canada	California	Ontario	Ratio, U.S. to Canada	Ratio, California to Ontario
Population (thousands)	245,807	25,637	28,314	9,270	—	—
Age ≥ 65 yr (%)	12.3	11.1	10.6	11.3	1.11	0.94
Residents of cities ≥ 100, 000 (%)	25.3	34.6	40.4	48.2	0.73	0.84
No. of deaths per 1000	8.7	7.3	7.6	7.5	1.19	1.01
Deaths occurring in hospitals (%)†	61.8	72.1	59.4	71.6	0.86	0.83
No. of births per 1000	15.7	14.7	18.2	14.7	1.07	1.24
Infants weighing <2500 g at birth (%)‡	6.9	5.7	6.0	5.4	1.21	1.11
No. of AIDS cases per 100, 000§	8.3	2.4	16.4	2.8	3.46	5.86
No. of homicides per 100,000‖	8.3	2.5	10.8	2.2	3.32	4.91
No. of physicians providing patient care per 1000‖	1.86	2.14	2.09	2.22	0.87	0.94
Gross domestic product per capita ($)**	18,338	17,211	21,114	19,619	1.07	1.08
Health expenditures per capita ($)††	1,987	1,435	2,365	1,464	1.38	1.62

*Data were obtained from official records in the United States and Canada.[12–21]

†Excludes deaths occurring in private homes, nursing homes, and convalescent homes and those of patients dead on arrival at the hospital.

‡As reported by the U.S. Bureau of the Census[12] and the Office of the Registrar General of Ontario.[16]

§As reported by the Department of Health and Human Services[17] and Health and Welfare Canada.[18]

¶Refers to murders, manslaughters, and infanticides, as reported in official records.[12,13,16,19]

‖Refers to active civilian physicians rendering patient care.

**Refers to gross domestic product, gross state product, or gross provincial product, as appropriate, expressed in 1987 U.S. dollars.

††Canadian dollars have been converted to 1987 U.S. dollars according to the purchasing-power parity exchange rate, in which $1 U.S. equals $1.23 Canadian.

American hospitals, but annual admissions per bed were higher. The rate of visits per capita to the emergency department in the United States was less than half that in Canada; the rate of other outpatient visits was approximately equal.

Expenditures per admission were 39 percent higher in the United States than in Canada, and they were 63 percent higher in California than in Ontario (Tables 2 and 3). Measuring the real cost in resources of treating comparable

Table 2. Comparison of Data on Acute Care Hospitals in the United States and Canada, 1987.*

Variable	United States	Canada	California	Ontario	Ratio, U.S. to Canada	Ratio, California to Ontario
Expenditures per capita ($)	621	492	628	512	1.26	1.23
No. of hospital beds per 1000 population[†]	3.90	5.43	2.92	4.84	0.72	0.60
Distribution of beds according to hospital size (%)						
Small (<200 beds)	34.4	28.5	36.3	23.1	1.21	1.57
Medium (200–500 beds)	44.3	38.0	49.6	40.6	1.17	1.22
Large (>500 beds)	21.3	33.5	14.1	36.4	0.64	0.39
No. of admissions per 1000, according to age[‡]						
All ages	129	142	106	141	0.91	0.75
≤ 14 yr	49	87	36	85	0.56	0.42
15–24 yr	102	124	102	120	0.82	0.85
25–44 yr	109	118	90	114	0.92	0.79
45–64 yr	147	153	114	151	0.96	0.75
≥ 65 yr	327	325	294	351	1.01	0.84
Inpatient days per 1000	929	1590	678	1495	0.58	0.45
Mean length of stay (days)	7.2	11.2	6.4	10.6	0.64	0.60
Occupancy rate (%)	65	81	64	85	0.80	0.76
No. of admissions per bed	33	26	36	30	1.27	1.20
Emergency visits per 1000[§]	320	677	280	645	0.47	0.43
Other outpatient visits per 1000[¶]	683	670	607	736	1.02	0.82
Expenditures per admission ($)	4,814	3,463	5,903	3,629	1.39	1.63

*Data were obtained from various sources.[22–33]

[†]Refers to registered beds, as reported by the American Hospital Association[22] and Statistics Canada.[23]

[‡]Excludes normal newborns and includes patients transferred from another facility.

[§]Defined as outpatient visits to a hospital facility with 24-hour staffing and offering immediate care.

[¶]Each visit by an outpatient to a unit of the hospital counted as one outpatient visit.

inpatients, however, requires accounting for possible differences in the case mix of patients, in wage rates and prices of other resources paid by hospitals, and in the relative allocation of hospital resources to inpatient and outpatient care.

The diagnostic case mix (as determined by studying DRGs and CMGs) was 14 percent more complex in the United States than in Canada (Table 3). This result was moderately sensitive to the weighting system: an index based only on DRG-specific charges in California suggested that the U.S. case mix was 16

Table 3. Accounting for Ratios of Expenditures per Admission in the United States and Canada, 1987.

	Ratio, U.S. to Canada	Ratio, California to Ontario
Expenditures per admission*	1.39	1.63
Diagnostic case mix[†]	1.14	1.11
Expenditures per adjusted admission[‡]	1.22	1.46
Prices of resources[§]	1.04	1.05
Resources per adjusted admission[¶]	1.17	1.39
Inpatient share of expenditures[‖]	1.06	1.05
Inpatient resources per adjusted admission**	1.24	1.46

*From Table 2.

[†] A measure of the relative complexity of case mix as calculated from data in various sources.[25,27,28]

[‡] Calculated by dividing expenditures per admission by the diagnostic case mix.

[§] A measure comparing prices for labor and nonlabor resources (see Table 4).

[¶] Calculated by dividing expenditures per adjusted admission by prices of resources.

[‖] Represents the proportion of total expenditures used in inpatient care, as calculated from the data in Table 2 and provided by the American Hospital Association.[22]

**Calculated by multiplying resources per adjusted admission by the inpatient share of expenditures.

percent more complex, whereas an index based only on Ontario CMG-specific resource estimates suggested that the U.S. case mix was 12 percent more complex. Adjustment for case mix reduced the difference in expenditures per admission.

The adjustment for case mix did not take into account possible differences in coding practices between the two countries, nor did it reflect possible differences in severity within a given diagnostic group. One test of case mix showed that for each of 100 pairs of DRGs in which complicated and uncomplicated versions of the same diagnosis have been defined, the proportions classified as complicated were virtually identical in the two California and two Ontario hospitals.

The second adjustment considered the prices of the resources purchased by hospitals. Prices were, on average, slightly higher in the United States (Table 3). Persons working in high-wage occupations (such as staff nurses and head nurses) were paid considerably more there, but those in occupations at the other end of the wage scale (such as cleaners and food aides) received higher wages in

Table 4.   Estimation of the Prices of Resources Used in Acute Care Hospitals in the United States and Canada, 1987.

Variable	Ratio, U.S. to Canada	Ratio, California to Ontario
Wage level of occupation		
High*	1.18	1.23
Medium†	0.93	0.93
Lov‡	0.86	0.78
Pharmaceutical products§	1.07	1.07
Other goods and services¶	1.00	1.00
Labor resources‖	1.04	1.04
Nonlabor resources**	1.02	1.02
All resources††	1.03	1.03
All resources, adjusted for liability insurance	1.04	1.05

*Based on wages of head nurses and general-duty staff nurses.

†Based on wages of laboratory technicians and x-ray technicians.

‡Based on wages of housekeeping cleaners and food-service aides.

§Derived from data in Schieber et al.[30]

¶Assumed to be equal to 1.00.

‖Calculated as the weighted average of high, medium, and low occupational wage levels.

**Calculated as the weighted average of prices for pharmaceutical products and other goods and services.

††Calculated as the weighted average of labor resources and nonlabor resources.

Canada (Table 4). The overall price ratio depended on the choice of weights used to average the ratios for specific resources, but even substantial changes in weights resulted in shifts in the overall ratio of only about 2 percent in either direction. Adjustment for prices of resources lowered both the expenditure ratio between the United States and Canada and that between California and Ontario (Table 3).

The third adjustment attempted to account for differences in the proportion of overall hospital resources devoted to inpatient care. The higher number of visits to emergency departments in Canada and Ontario suggested that in hospitals there the inpatient share of total expenditures was smaller. We estimated that the relative expenditures related to one inpatient admission were equivalent in cost to 28 emergency department visits (95 percent confidence interval, 14 to 42) or 77 outpatient visits of other types (95 percent confidence interval, 47 to 107). When they were applied to the data on admissions, emergency department visits, and other outpatient visits, these results yielded inpatient shares of 80 percent for the United States and 75 percent for Canada. The adjustment for the inpatient share of expenditures was the most difficult of the three adjustments to calculate, and alternative models and assumptions might yield different ratios.

The net result after adjustment for case mix, prices of resources, and inpatient share showed that hospitals in the United States used 24 percent more real resources per adjusted admission than Canadian hospitals; the difference between California and Ontario on this measure was 46 percent (Table 3).

The two pairs of California and Ontario hospitals are compared in Table 5. The lengths of stay and occupancy rates were much lower at the California hospitals; the number of admissions per bed was considerably higher at Stanford than at Sunnybrook, but at St. John's and Wellesley it was approximately equal. The two California hospitals had substantially fewer visits to the emergency department than their Ontario counterparts, although the proportion admitted was similar at all four facilities. The expenditures per admission before the three adjustments were 23 percent higher at Stanford than at Sunnybrook and 22 percent higher at St. John's than at Wellesley. Part of this difference was

Table 5.   Comparisons of Individual Hospitals in California and Ontario, 1987.[*]

Variable	Stanford	Sunnybrook	St. John's	Wellesley	Ratio, Stanford to Sunnybrook	Ratio, St. John's to Wellesley
No. of beds	631	620	550	510	1.02	1.08
Admissions (thousands)	22.7	16.4	15.6	14.6	1.38	1.07
Emergency visits (thousands)	27.2	38.8	22.8	40.8	0.70	0.56
% of Emergency patients admitted[†]	17.2	18.6	20.7	16.5	0.92	1.25
Other outpatient visits	161	277	147	137	0.58	1.07
Inpatient days (thousands)	143	201	103	173	0.71	0.60
Mean stay (days)	6.3	12.3	6.6	11.9	0.51	0.55
Occupancy rate (%)	62	89	51	93	0.70	0.55
No. of admissions per bed	36	26	28	29	1.36	1.00
Total expenditures (millions of $)	209	123	108	82	1.71	1.31
Expenditures per admission ($)	9,216	7,501	6,898	5,643	1.23	1.22
Diagnostic case mix	—	—	—	—	1.07	1.04
Expenditures per adjusted admission	—	—	—	—	1.15	1.17
Prices of resources	—	—	—	—	1.11	1.05
Resources per adjusted admission	—	—	—	—	1.04	1.11
Inpatient share of expenditures	—	—	—	—	1.15	1.04
Inpatient resources per adjusted admission	—	—	—	—	1.20	1.15

[*]The notes to Table 3 explain the calculation of the variables at the bottom of the table for which only ratios are presented.

[†]Figures for 1991 were used in these calculations.

explained by a more complex case mix of patients, and part by higher prices of resources. The prices at Stanford were particularly high because of higher wages in the Stanford area in relation to California as a whole. The outpatient share of expenditures was higher in the two Ontario hospitals. After all adjustments, the two California hospitals used 20 percent (for Stanford vs. Sunnybrook) and 15 percent (for St. John's vs. Wellesley) more resources per adjusted admission.

Does the use of more resources per admission by the two California hospitals result in more services to patients? When 12 diagnostic services were studied, the results indicated that American patients received more of certain services but that Canadian patients received more of others (Table 6). The most common biochemical test, the serum electrolyte assay, was performed less often in the

Table 6.   Selected Diagnostic Services per Admission at the Four Hospitals, 1987.[*]

Diagnostic procedure	Stanford	Sunnybrook	St. John's	Wellesley	Ratio, Stanford to Sunnybrook	Ratio, St. John's to Wellesley
no. of procedures per admission						
MRI scanning of the head[†]	0.007	0.000	0.031	0.000	—	—
Echocardiography	0.09	0.06	0.10	0.07	1.49	1.44
Blood culture	0.65	0.46	0.28	0.37	1.41	0.76
Ventilation-perfusion lung scanning[‡]	0.018	0.014	0.011	0.017	1.29	0.63
Arterial blood gas measurement	2.99	2.71	0.98	0.39	1.11	2.52
Electrocardiography[§]	1.05	0.95	1.05	1.03	1.11	1.02
Computed tomography of body	0.22	0.22	0.16	0.15	1.00	1.07
Electroencephalography	0.032	0.040	0.023	0.060	0.80	0.38
Chest radiography[¶]	0.46	0.66	0.39	0.56	0.69	0.69
Urinalysis[‖]	0.96	1.42	0.56	1.20	0.67	0.47
Serum electrolyte assay[**]	4.03	6.36	2.20	6.27	0.63	0.35
Prothrombin-time assay[††]	1.09	1.79	0.45	0.67	0.61	0.66

[*]Data shown are not adjusted for case mix.
[†]MRI denotes magnetic resonance imaging.
[‡]Represents either ventilation scanning, perfusion scanning, or combined ventilation-perfusion scanning.
[§]Excludes measures obtained during electrophysiologic testing.
[¶]Includes radiology of the thoracic cage, regardless of the number of views, and excluding portable radiography.
[‖]By standard dipstick examination.
[**]Includes measurements of serum sodium, potassium, chloride, and bicarbonate concentrations.
[††]May or may not include measurement of partial-thromboplastin time.

two California hospitals than in the two Ontario hospitals. The discrepancy in the two most common lung tests represented a noteworthy difference in practice patterns: patients in the two California hospitals had more arterial blood gas tests, but fewer chest films, than their counterparts in Ontario. There were only three procedures — magnetic resonance imaging of the head, echocardiography, and arterial blood gas measurements — for which both the Stanford-Sunnybrook and St. John's-Wellesley service ratios exceeded the overall case-mix ratios. On balance, the results do not support the hypothesis that the two California hospitals provided more diagnostic services during an admission than their counterparts in Ontario.

Discussion

Canadians spent appreciably less than Americans for acute hospital care in 1987, but they did not have fewer beds, fewer admissions, or shorter stays. The difference arises entirely in expenditures per admission, which were 39 percent higher in the United States. American hospitals had a more complicated mix of patients (as measured by DRGs), and they paid slightly more than Canadian hospitals for the resources used to provide care. The estimated inpatient share of total expenditures was higher in the United States, resulting in a difference of 24 percent between the countries in the quantity of resources per adjusted admission. The comparisons between California and Ontario were similar to the national ratios, but the difference of 46 percent in the quantity of resources per adjusted admission was considerably larger. By contrast, comparisons of specific institutions in California and Ontario yielded differences of 20 percent and 15 percent at the pair of tertiary care hospitals and the pair of community care hospitals, respectively.

What explains the apparently greater use of inpatient resources per adjusted admission in the United States? We do not think it is simply a problem of inadequate adjustment. The DRG system is far from a perfect measure of severity, but there is no evidence that within each DRG the illnesses in the United States were more acute than those in Canada. Indeed, some analysts have suggested that the prospective payment system of Medicare invites "DRG creep" in the United States, with a bias toward upgrading the classification of severity in order to obtain more reimbursement.[34] We also have confidence in the adjustment for the prices of resources. The ratio between the U.S. and Canada for hourly compensation in manufacturing has been estimated as 1.04, the same ratio that we found for the compensation of hospital employees.[35] Other investigators, using data from 1981 and 1985, concluded that hospital wages in the United States were actually lower than those in Canada.[36] If we overestimated the wage ratio, then the difference in resources used per patient was even larger than that reported here. The greatest uncertainty concerns the adjustment for inpatient share, but it is worth noting that for California, Ontario, and the four institutions the inpatient share was within 5 percent of the values available from other sources.

It is widely believed that American hospitals provide services more intensively. This is certainly true if the unit of comparison is a patient-day; however, the higher intensity per patient-day may be offset by the length of the average stay in Canadian hospitals — more than 50 percent longer. As is true of physicians' services, Americans receive a different mix of services but not necessarily more of them. The longer stays in Canadian hospitals imply that Canadian patients have more frequent evaluation of their vital signs, more dressing changes, and more of other services that are provided on a daily basis. Direct measures of the quantity of 12 diagnostic services provided per admission at Stanford as compared with Sunnybrook and at St. John's as compared with Wellesley do not support the hypothesis that when comparable inpatients are treated, American hospitals provide more diagnostic services.

If U.S. hospitals do not deliver more clinical services per admission, what consumes the extra resources? We did not obtain data with which to answer this question, but there are three possibilities: administrative costs, other nonclinical services, and less intensive use of clinical equipment and personnel.

Hospitals in the United States must keep more extensive records in order to facilitate billing to the state and federal governments, insurance companies, and patients, and in anticipation of malpractice suits. According to Woolhandler and Himmelstein,[3] in 1987 these administrative costs accounted for 20 percent of hospital expenditures in California but only 9 percent in Canada. If their results are correct and are representative of the corresponding country and region, we can calculate the increased costs for non-administrative resources per admission as 10 percent for the United States as compared with Canada and as 28 percent for California as compared with Ontario. Thus, roughly half the differences reported in Table 3 would be explained by administrative costs. These costs may, however, be proportionately higher in California than in the rest of the United States; if so, the difference between the United States and Canada in nonadministrative resources per admission would be more than 10 percent.

In addition to administration, hospitals provide other nonclinical services that are frequently referred to as "hotel services" or "amenities." Most American hospitals compete for well-insured patients, raising the possibility that they provide these services at a quantity and quality greater than is found in Canada.

Reliable, comparable data to test this possibility are not available, but there are several reasons for doubting that such services contribute substantially to higher costs per admission in the United States. First, patients in the United States have shorter average stays; therefore, they require fewer meals, less waste disposal, and less laundry service per admission. Second, these services are usually performed by low-wage workers, whose salaries tend to be lower in the United States than in Canada. Finally, the nonlabor resources consumed in these activities, such as the food supplies and cleaning products, represent only a small fraction of total hospital expenditures.[31]

Is it possible to deliver the same clinical service and to use fewer resources? In Canada, specialized procedures are performed in a relatively small number of large hospitals, whereas in the United States most community hospitals provide a wide variety of tertiary care services. For example, after adjustment for differences in population size, in 1987 there were 3 times as many hospitals with units providing open-heart surgery in California as in Ontario, 5 times as many with magnetic resonance scanners, and 10 times as many with extracorporeal lithotriptors. One consequence is much fuller use of capacity in Canada. The lithotriptor at Wellesley Hospital is used to treat almost 50 patients a week. At Stanford, as at many American hospitals, the average use is less than 1/10 as much. Among the more than 100 hospitals in California offering open-heart surgery, half have fewer than 200 procedures performed per year.[37] Canadian centralization, reliance on referral, and establishment of waiting lists result in less idle time for high-cost equipment and associated personnel.

Hospitals in the United States may also use relatively more resources to provide routine clinical services. The tremendous emphasis on early discharge in American hospitals creates a need for additional equipment and personnel ready to provide routine laboratory, radiologic, and other services on short notice. By contrast, the relatively long stays in Canadian hospitals are conducive to a queuing approach that probably results in better use of capacity. In the United States and California, the majority of patients are in small-to-medium-sized hospitals that do not have the relative efficiencies associated with the frequent performance of routine services. Also, greater variability in occupancy rates in American hospitals from day to day and from week to week makes it more difficult for them to schedule equipment and personnel with maximal efficiency.

Canadian patients pay a price for their higher-capacity use of equipment and personnel. The more centralized hospital system can cause delay or inconvenience in obtaining access to specialized services.[38,39] In some cases this results in a delay of discharge.[40] On the other hand, the quality of care in American hospitals may suffer when complex procedures are performed relatively infrequently in smaller hospitals.[41]

After all adjustments, we found that in 1987 the United States devoted more real resources to inpatients of acute care hospitals, after standardization for case mix, than did Canada. Our comparisons of a limited number of diagnostic procedures per admission in the four study hospitals did not support the hypothesis that American hospitals deliver more clinical services. We believe that the most likely explanations for the difference include higher administrative costs for billing and record keeping in American hospitals and more intensive use of centralized equipment and personnel in Canada.

We are indebted to Dr. Wade Aubry, Mr. Peter Ellis, Dr. Robert Fredricks, Prof. Morley Gunderson, Mr. Chris Helyar, Mr. David Hopkins, Mr. Terry Long, Mr. Cyril Nair, Mr. Scott Rowand, Mr. Narendra Shah, Prof. Evelyn Shapiro, Ms. Joanne Spetz, Blue Shield of California, the California Association of Hospitals and Health Systems, the Ontario Ministry of Health, Stanford University Medical Center, Sunnybrook Health Science Center, St. John's Hospital, and the Wellesley Hospital for their assistance in obtaining and interpreting data, and to Prof. George Pink, Prof. Noralou Roos, and Drs. Claire Bombardier, Allan Detsky, Alan Garber, John Hornberger, Douglas Owens, and Miriam Shuchman for reviewing earlier versions of this manuscript.

References

1. Fuchs, V. R. and Hahn, J. S. (1990). "How Does Canada Do It? A Comparison of Expenditures for Physicians, Services in the United States and Canada." *New England Journal of Medicine* **323**: 884–890.
2. Himmelstein, D. U. and Woolhandler, S. (1986). "Cost Without Benefit: Administrative Waste in U.S. Health Care". *New England Journal of Medicine* **314**: 441–445.
3. Woolhandler, S. and Himmelstein, D. U. (1991). "The Deteriorating Administrative Efficiency of the U.S. Health-Care System." *New England Journal of Medicine* **324**: 1253–1258.
4. AHA (1990). *Hospital Statistics 1990–91 edition.* American Hospital Association: Chicago.
5. Statistics Canada (1991). *Hospital Statistics Preliminary Annual Report 1989.* Canadian Government Publishing Center: Ottawa, ON.
6. Newhouse, J. P., Anderson, G. and Roos, L. L. (1988). "Hospital Spending in the United States and Canada: A Comparison." *Health Affairs (Millwood)* **7**(5): 6–16.
7. Detsky, A. S., Stacey, S. R. and Bombardier C. (1983). "The Effectiveness of a Regulatory Strategy in Containing Hospital Costs: The Ontario Experience, 1967–81." *New England Journal of Medicine* **309**: 151–159.

8. Detsky, A. S., Abrams, H. B., Ladha, L. and Stacey, S. R. (1986). "Global Budgeting and the Teaching Hospital in Ontario." *Medical Care* **24**: 89–94.

9. Evans, R. G., Lomas, J. Barer, M. L., Labelle, R. J., Fooks, C., Stoddart, G. L., Anderson, G. M., Feeny, D., Gafni, A., Torrance, G. W. and Tholl, W. G. (1989). "Controlling Health Expenditures — The Canadian Reality." *New England Journal of Medicine* **320**: 571–577.

10. Coyte, P. C., Dewees, D. N. and Trebilcock, M. J. (1991). "Medical Malpractice — The Canadian Experience." *New England Journal of Medicine* **324**: 89–93.

11. Lipset, S. M. (1990). *Continental Divide*. Routledge: London.

12. Bureau of the Census (1990). *Statistical Abstract of the United States: 1990*. 110th edn. Government Printing Office: Washington, D.C.

13. Statistics Canada (1991). *The Canada Year Book 1990*. Statistics Canada: Ottawa, ON.

14. Statistics Canada (1988). *The Canada Year Book 1988*. Statistics Canada: Ottawa, ON.

15. Statistics Canada (1991). *Vital Statistics*. Vol. 3. Statistics Canada: Ottawa, ON.

16. Office of the Registrar General of Ontario (1990). *Vital Statistics for 1987*. Government Printing Office: Ottawa, ON.

17. Centers for Disease Control and Prevention (1988). Cases of specified notifiable diseases, United States, weeks ending December 26, 1987 and December 20, 1986 (51st week). *MMWR – Morbidity and Mortality Weekly Report* **36**: 827–829.

18. Health and Welfare Canada (1988). *Canadian Diseases Weekly Report* **14**: 15.

19. State of California Department of Finance (1990). *California Statistical Abstract, 1990*. Government Printing Office: Sacramento, CA.

20. Treasurer of Ontario and Minister of Economics (1990). *1990 Ontario Budget*. Queens Printer for Ontario: Toronto.

21. Levit, K. R. (1985). "Personal Health Care Expenditures, by State: 1966–82." *Health Care Financing Review* **6**(4): 1–49.

22. AHA (1988). *Hospital Statistics 1988 edition*. American Hospital Association: Chicago.

23. Statistics Canada (1989). *Hospital Statistics Preliminary Annual Report 1987*. Canadian Government Publishing Center: Ottawa, ON.

24. Statistics Canada (1990). (Catalogue 82-003S.) *List of Canadian Hospitals 1989*. Canadian Centre for Health Information: Ottawa, ON.

25. Office of Statewide Health Planning and Development (1990). *Aggregate Hospital Discharge Data Summary January 1, 1987-December 31, 1987*. Government Printing Office: Sacramento, CA.

26. Statistics Canada (1991). *Hospital Annual Statistics 1987–88: Outpatient Services*. Canadian Government Publishing Center: Ottawa, ON.

27. National Center for Health Statistics (1989). *National Hospital Discharge Data Survey: Annual Report 1987*. Series 13. No. 99 (DHHS publication no. (PHS) 89–1760). Government Printing Office: Hyattsville, MD.

28. Hospital Medical Records Institute (1987). *Length of Stay Database by CMG*. Hospital Medical Records Institute: Don Mills, ON.

29. U.S. Department of Labor (1990). *Industry Wage Survey: Hospitals, March 1989* (Bulletin 2364). Bureau of Labor Statistics: Washington, DC.

30. Schieber, G. J., Poullier, J. P. and Greenwald L. M. (1991). "Health Care Systems in Twenty Four Countries." *Health Affairs (Millwood)* **10**(3): 22–38.

31. Donham, C. S. and Maple, B. T. (1989). "Health Care Indicators." *Health Care Financing Review* **11**(3): 113–132.

32. Helyar, C. (1991). *Notebook on Data for Quality Measurement.* Hospital Medical Records Institute: Don Mills, ON.

33. Bureau of the Census (1988). *Current Population Survey Public Use Tapes.*

34. Steinwald, B. and Dummit, L. A. (1989). "Hospital Case-Mix Change: Sicker Patients or DRG Creep?" *Health Affairs (Millwood)* **8**(2): 35–47.

35. Capdevielle, P. (1988). "International Differences in Employers' Compensation Costs." *Monthly Labor Review* **111**: 44–46.

36. Haber, S. G., Zwanziger, J., Anderson, G., Thorpe, K. E. and Newhouse, J. P. (1992). "Hospital Expenditures in the United States and Canada: Do Hospital Worker Wages Explain the Differences?" *J Health Econ* **11**(4): 453–465.

37. Office of Statewide Health Planning and Development (1991). *Annual Report of Hospitals 1990: Licensed Services and Utilization Profiles.* Government Printing Office: Sacramento, CA.

38. Katz, S. J., Mizgala, H. F. and Welch, H. G. (1991). "British Columbia Sends Patients to Seattle for Coronary Artery Surgery: Bypassing the Queue in Canada." *The Journal of the American Medical Association* **266**: 1108–1111.

39. Naylor C. D. (1991). "A Different View of Queues in Ontario." *Health Affairs (Millwood)* **10**(3): 110–128.

40. Iglehart, J. K. (1990). "Canada's Health Care System Faces Its Problems." *New England Journal of Medicine* **322**: 562–568.

41. Hughes, R. G., Hunt, S. S. and Luft, H. S. (1987). "Effects of Surgeon Volume and Hospital Volume on Quality of Care in Hospitals." *Medical Care* **25**: 489–503.

4.3

Why Do Other Rich Nations Spend So Much Less on Healthcare?

The U.S. delivers roughly three times as many mammograms, two-and-a-half times as many MRI scans, and a third more C-sections per capita than the average OECD country.

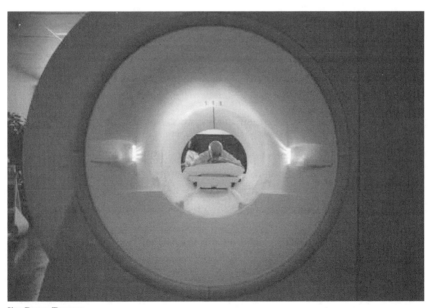

Jim Bourg/Reuters

Despite the news last week that America's healthcare spending will not be rising at the sky-high rate that was once predicted, the fact remains that the U.S. far outspends its peer nations when it comes to healthcare costs per capita. This year the United States will spend almost 18 percent of the gross domestic product (GDP) on healthcare — six percentage points more than the Netherlands, the next highest spender. Because the U.S. GDP in 2014 will be approximately 17 trillion dollars, those six percentage points over the Netherlands amount to one trillion dollars in additional spending. The burden to the average household through lost wages, insurance premiums, taxes, out-of-pocket care, and other costs will be more than $8,000.

Why does the United States spend so much more? The biggest reason is that U.S. healthcare delivers a more expensive mix of services. For example, a much larger proportion of physician visits in the U.S. are to specialists who get higher fees and usually order more high-tech diagnostic and therapeutic procedures than primary care physicians.

Compared with the average OECD country, the U.S. delivers (population adjusted) almost three times as many mammograms, two-and-a-half times the number of MRI scans, and 31 percent more C-sections. Also, the U.S. has more stand-by equipment, for example, 1.66 MRI machines per 6,000 annual scans vs. 1.06 machines. The extra machines provide easier access for Americans, but add to cost. Similarly, occupancy rates in U.S. acute care hospitals are much lower than in OECD countries, reducing the likelihood of delays in admissions, but building that extra capacity adds to cost. Aggressive treatment of very sick elderly also makes the mix expensive. In the U.S. many elderly patients are treated in intensive care units (ICUs), but in other countries they would receive only palliative care. More amenities such as privacy and space in hospitals and more attractive clinics also add to U.S. costs.

While the U.S. mix of services is disproportionately tilted toward more expensive interventions, the other OECD countries emphasize a "plain vanilla" mix. Compared with the U.S., the average OECD country has 30 percent more physician visits and more than 30 percent more hospital days per capita.

The complexity of private-sector insurance is not in the public interest. Each company offers many plans that differ in coverage, deductibles, co-pays, premiums, and other features that make it difficult for buyers to compare the prices of different policies.

One reason for the more expensive mix in the U.S. is it produces more income for drug manufacturers, specialist physicians, and others who have considerable influence on policy. Second, some patients prefer the more expensive mix, just as some prefer to shop at Whole Foods rather than Walmart. Third, some workers mistakenly believe that employers pay for their healthcare and that more expensive means better care. Health economists believe that the premiums for employer-sponsored insurance come out of potential wages. Similarly, the extra money the government spends for health could be used for education, infrastructure, the environment, and other public investment, but these alternatives are not readily apparent or agreed upon. Does the more expensive mix result in better health outcomes? There are no definitive studies to answer this question. Superficially, it appears that the systems in the other countries are more effective because their life expectancy is higher. But their advantage may be attributable to non-medical factors such as significantly lower poverty rates.

A second important reason for higher healthcare spending in the U.S. is higher prices for inputs such as drugs and the services of specialist physicians. The prices of branded prescription drugs in the U.S. are, on average, about double those in other countries. The fees of specialist physicians are typically two to three times as high as in other countries. The lower prices and fees abroad are achieved by negotiation and controls by governments who typically pay for about 75 percent of all medical care. Government in the U.S. pays about 50 percent, which would still confer considerable bargaining power, but the government is kept from exerting it by legislation and a Congress sensitive to interest-group lobbying.

The third and last important reason for higher spending in the U.S. is high administrative costs of insurance. This includes private insurance which covers more than half the insured population. Each year scores of insurance companies must estimate appropriate premiums for plans they wish to sell to several million employers plus 20 to 30 million individuals. In addition, hospitals, clinics, and individual physicians incur substantial costs in billing for each test, visit, and procedure regardless of whether they are covered by private or public insurance or self-pay. Many of our peer countries have lower administrative costs through more coordination, standardization, and in some countries a single national system or several regional healthcare-insurance systems, even when the provision of care is primarily a private-sector responsibility.

The complexity of private-sector insurance is not in the public interest. Each company offers many plans that differ in coverage, deductibles, co-pays, premiums, and other features that make it difficult for buyers to compare the prices of different policies. For most goods and services, wider choice for consumers is assumed to contribute to well-being. In the case of health insurance, however, the fact that the customer knows more than the insurance company about his or her likely use of care results in adverse selection. If the company sets a premium based on average utilization, the company will lose money on the high users and will lose as customers those who expect to use less than the average. It is not efficient or fair to allow a family to choose a plan with generous maternity benefits when they are planning to have a baby and then switch to a plan with no maternity benefits when they are not.

If we turn the question around and ask why healthcare costs so much less in other high-income countries, the answer nearly always points to a larger, stronger role for government. Governments usually eliminate much of the high administrative costs of insurance, obtain lower prices for inputs, and influence the mix of healthcare outputs by arranging for large supplies of primary-care physicians and hospital beds while keeping tight control on the number of specialist physicians and expensive technology. In the United States, the political system creates many "choke points" for diverse interest groups to block or modify government's role in these areas.

For those who would like to limit government control, there is an alternative route to more efficient healthcare through "managed competition," proposed by Alain Enthoven, a Stanford University Business School Professor, more than 25 years ago. It is based on integrated group practice, which brings the insurance function, physicians, hospital, drugs, and other elements of care into a single organization that takes responsibility for the health of a defined population for an annual risk-adjusted per capita payment. Examples include the Group Health Cooperative of Puget Sound in Seattle and the Kaiser Permanente organizations in California.

Such organizations deliver high-quality care at lower costs, and some employers offer such a plan as one option, but most don't. And even those employers that do offer a low-cost integrated group practice as an option typically pay the same percentage subsidy of premium regardless of whether the employee chooses an expensive plan or the low-cost plan. For managed competition to be most effective, employees should be required to pay the marginal excess of a high-cost plan over the low-cost plan. For one large employer who did follow this approach, 71 percent of the hourly paid men chose the low-cost integrated group practice while 63 percent of the salaried men chose one of the more expensive plans. (This statistic comes from a study in progress by Enthoven and myself.)

With regard to healthcare, the United States is at a crossroads. Whether the Affordable Care Act will significantly control costs is uncertain; its main thrust is to reduce the number of uninsured. The alternatives seem to be a larger role for government or a larger role for managed competition in the private sector.

Even if the latter route is pursued, government is the only logical choice if the country wants to have universal coverage. There are two necessary and sufficient conditions to cover everyone for health insurance: Subsidies for the poor and the sick and compulsory participation by everyone. Only government can create those conditions.

4.4

The Challenges to Health Policy in Modern Economies

The Honorable Prime Minister of Malaysia, YAB Dato Seri Dr. Mahathir bin Mohamad; Yang Amat Berbahagia Mulia RajaTun Mohar, Chairman of the Board of Trustees of the Program for the Prime Minister of Malaysia's Fellowship; other Trustees of the Fellowship Program; distinguished guests; ladies and gentlemen.

It is a high honor and a great privilege to be invited to present the Perdana Lecture this morning. I have chosen the subject, "The Challenges to Health Policy in Modern Economies," for two reasons. First, Malaysia is on its way to becoming a modern economy. There were some major bumps in the road in 1997, and there will be other bumps in the years ahead. That is the nature of modern economies. But there can be little doubt that Malaysia will become a modern economy. Second, the question of health policy for Malaysia is up for re-examination and possible fundamental change. This is appropriate and timely, now, while it is possible to anticipate economic, social, demographic and health changes that will occur as Malaysia becomes a modern economy. The goal should be to formulate a health policy appropriate for the conditions that will prevail ten or twenty or thirty

Originally published in *The 1997 Syarahan Perdana Lecture*, Kuala Lumpur, Malaysia.

years down the road. The greatest challenge is to have the courage and the wisdom to make policy, not only for today, but for the future.

My remarks are organized around four questions. First, what are the characteristics of modern economies? Second, why does the health sector's share of the gross domestic product tend to increase in modern economies? Third, what are the special health problems of modern economies? And fourth, what are the similarities and the differences, in health care policies among nations with modern economies?

Exhibit 1 lists some of the most important characteristics of modern economies, characteristics that are particularly relevant to health, medical care, and health policy.

EXHIBIT 1

Characteristics of Modern Economies of Particular Relevance to Health Policy

- High and rising Gross Domestic Product per capita
- Changing distribution of employment by sector: i) Agriculture declines, ii) Service sector rises, iii) Industry rises and then declines
- Women's share of work force increases
- High and rising life expectancy
- Low fertility
- Changing age distribution of the population
- High and increasing proportion of Gross Domestic Product devoted to health care

---

The defining characteristic of a modern economy is a high gross domestic product which tends to increase over time. The second characteristic, the one that has been said to be the most important concomitant and the most predictable aspect of economic progress, is the tendency for employment to move from agriculture to industry and then to the service sector. This generalization was first made by Alan G.B. Fisher in 1935, and made again by Colin Clark in 1940. In *The Service Economy* (1968), I developed the generalization more systematically and more empirically; similar investigations have been carried out in many other countries with similar conclusions. (See the Appendix for a more detailed discussion of sector shares of employment.)

The third characteristic is that women's share of paid employment increases. This is directly related to the change in the sectoral distribution of employment in at least two important ways. First, the service sector, which includes wholesale and retail trade, business and financial services, insurance, personal, professional, and repair services, and government administration and services, has always been more hospitable to female employment than has been industry. This is true in every economy including Malaysia; women are disproportionately employed in the service sector. But women's participation in the work force in the course of economic development also increases for other reasons, including the spread of education and the increase in wages which makes the time of women more valuable. For a variety of economic and social reasons, women choose to participate in the work force. But as women participate in the work force in large numbers, the demand for services to be provided by the market increases. More meals are purchased outside the home instead of being prepared in the home; more personal services are demanded of the market; more health services are obtained outside the home instead of being produced at home. In every country, we find that the higher women's participation in the work force, the greater the demand for market-produced services.

The fourth characteristic of all modern economies is a high and rising life expectancy. In Malaysia, life expectancy is high — not as high as many OECD countries, but much higher than it was — and it is increasing faster than in most modern economies.

Low fertility is another characteristic of modern economies. Malaysia is still in transition from a tradition of high fertility; fertility is falling but it is still quite high relative to the United States and other OECD countries. One hesitates to make an absolute prediction, but it is very likely that fertility will continue to fall as Malaysia moves toward becoming a modern economy.

The consequence of high life expectancy and low fertility is a dramatic change in the age distribution of the population. The percentage of the population who are elderly (65 and above) increases substantially and the percentage who are young (15 and below) decreases. The change in the age distribution is attributable much more to the decline in fertility than to the increase in life expectancy. High life expectancy accompanied by high fertility will not result in a large percentage of the population over 65. High life expectancy *with* low fertility will result in the elderly accounting for ten, fifteen, or even twenty percent of the population. In Malaysia, the percentage is very low at the present time, no more than 4 percent. This is an entirely different world from the one Malaysia is heading toward.

The seventh and last characteristic in Exhibit 1 is a high and increasing proportion of gross domestic product devoted to health care. The typical range of most modern economies is between eight and ten percent.The United States devotes 14 percent of the gross domestic product to health care. That is, one out of every seven dollars of the total production of the country is for hospitals, physicians, drugs, nursing homes, and so on. In Malaysia, the percentage is three or four, less than half that of most OECD countries. But again, there is every reason to think that this will change as Malaysia becomes a modem economy.

Exhibit 2 lists some of the principal reasons why the health sector's share of the GDP tends to increase in modern economies.

EXHIBIT 2
Why Health Sector's Share of GDP Tends to Increase in Modern Economics

- Rising expectations of population
- Social changes
- Disparate effects of technological change in health care and other/sectors
- Political pressure for a more egalitarian society
- The elderly use much more medical care

First, the expectations of the population with regard to health and medical care increase. As income rises, people want more, and better, medical care. They want to live longer, they want to live better, and they want to use some of their higher income for that purpose. As people become more educated, they develop new awareness of and interest in various aspects of health and medical care. Communication improves; television and other media begin to provide more information about health problems and about the new kinds of medical care that are becoming available. I believe that there is also a psychological change that takes place as a nation moves from a traditional to a modern economy. To generalize, a certain amount of fatalism is often characteristic of a traditional economy. There is an inclination to accept life as it is, and to accept disability and death as part of life. As a nation moves toward a modern economy, this mind set changes; there is no longer the same willingness to accept disability and death as inevitable. In the course of developing the modern economy, technology has been developed, transportation has improved, the flow of information has increased. Increasing control over the material world leads to a mind set that says, "I do not have to accept illness and disease as something that simply happens to me; maybe it is something that I can change."

Second, social changes are taking place. One of the most important is the increase in women's participation in the paid work force. When women are employed in the market, they do not have the same time or energy to provide the health services they might have provided in an earlier time, such as care of children, the elderly, and husbands. When women are out of the home and in the workforce, those services are not as readily available; therefore, more health services are demanded of the organized economy and the health sector's share of the GDP increases. In part, it is an accounting illusion because when women provide services at home, the value of those services is *not* included in the GDP but when services are bought in the market place or provided by the government, the value *is* included in the GDP.

Other social changes typically take place with the development of a modern economy. These can generally be characterized as a weakening of families and communities as sources of social support. In a traditional society, the family and the community (or village) are very important sources of social support. In a modern, urban economy, there is less social support and therefore more care demanded of the organized health care sector.

A third reason is that technological change has occurred differently in health care than in other sectors. In most industries, technological change takes two forms. One is the development of new and better products. But a second, very important, part of technological change is to improve the processes of production, to increase efficiency and reduce the cost of existing products. In contrast, the thrust of technological change in health care in modern economies has been almost entirely in the first direction — in the development of new and better services and products. Research institutes and universities, drug companies and equipment manufacturers, and medical science in general are dedicated to the first kind of technological change. There is very little of the other kind of technological change to reduce costs and increase efficiency of producing existing services and products. It has occurred on occasion. For example, antibiotics were a technological change of the first kind that not only contributed to better health but also actually reduced the cost of care. But antibiotics appeared a long time ago, and most technological change in medicine since then has not led to lower costs. Wonderful new surgical techniques, new diagnostic techniques, new transplant techniques, and so forth have, of course, been introduced. But these usually increase expenditures on health care. This disparate type of change, of the first form but not of the second, contributes to an increase in the health sector's share of the GDP.

Fourth, nearly all modern economies are characterized by strong political pressures for a more egalitarian society. These pressures are particularly evident in health care, with most countries raising the standard of health care that is provided to persons of all socioeconomic classes, including the lowest. Even in the United States, which does not have national health insurance, there is much greater equality in health care than in other goods and services.

Finally, the elderly use much more medical care than do other age groups. It probably reaches an extreme in the United States, where an enormous amount of health care resources is devoted to people 65 and over. The per capita consumption of medical care by the elderly is more than three times that of the rest of the population. I have a friend who says, "After 60, it's patch, patch, patch." I mentioned this once to a very vigorous woman who died at the age of 96, and she corrected me. She said, "After 80, it's patch, patch, patch." The point is well taken; individuals do vary in their need for care. But at a certain age, which varies from individual to individual, there is hardly a part of the body that can't benefit from repair or replacement. Given insurance, either government or private, and given a mindset that seeks to postpone disability and death as long as possible, the capacity of older men and women to consume medical care is limited only by the imagination and ingenuity of physicians and scientists.

In modern economies, some health problems become less important, but others loom ever larger. (See Exhibit 3.)

EXHIBIT 3
Health Problems of Modern Economies

- Increasing importance of chronic illness
- Physical factors in death and disability
- Psycho-social factors in death and disability
- Special problems of elderly

One of the biggest changes is from acute to chronic diseases such as arthritis diabetes, mental illnesses, low back problems, and so on. The growing importance of chronic problems requires rethinking all aspects of healthcare: financing, training, organization, and delivery. The role of the patient in the care process is usually much more important for chronic than for acute illness. If someone has an inflamed appendix, he is rushed to the hospital, put under anesthesia, and has an operation. Assuming that all goes well, in a short time the patient is discharged, no worse for the incident. The same is true if a raging infection develops. Antibiotics, administered through an IV, will usually bring the infection under control. In either case, no action or knowledge is required of the patient. By contrast, patients with chronic illnesses must understand the nature of their problems, take their medications properly, watch their diet and exercise, and understand how to monitor their situations. Patients with chronic illnesses require education and motivation. Neither of these is particularly necessary for the patient with the inflamed appendix or raging infection.

It is also important to consider what kinds of organizations, including the deployment of facilities and personnel, would be most cost-effective in dealing with people with different chronic illnesses. The answer varies according to the illness and the state of the relevant technology. For example, what is the most cost-effective way of caring for diabetics? Should every diabetic be cared for by an endocrinologist, perhaps even a sub-specialist in diabetes? Effective? Probably yes. Cost-effective? Probably no. Another possibility is to have diabetics cared for by general practitioners. A third possibility is to create specialized diabetes clinics, staffed primarily by nurses and other personnel who are not physicians but who have received specialized training to provide comprehensive care for diabetics. This staff would work under the supervision of a skilled endocrinologist who monitors the literature, establishes the protocols, and supervises the care. Some countries, such as England, are finding that the third approach is the most cost-effective way to treat diabetics. That could change if the technology changes. The key point is that when a health care system is established, it should have appropriate incentives, information, and infrastructure so that it can adapt to changes in health problems and health care technology.

Certain physical factors in death and disability become more important in modern economies. One such category is accidents involving automobiles, trucks, and other forms of transportation. Another is cigarette smoking, which can be a terrible scourge. If only one thing could be done to improve the health of the population, it would be to eliminate cigarette smoking. Diets change in the course of economic development — and not always for the better. People tend to eat fewer fresh vegetables and fruits and more meat. They may consume too much fat, which contributes to heart disease, cancer, and other diseases that are not as prevalent in more traditional societies. Exercise patterns change because work becomes more sedentary. If people do not exercise sufficiently, they are likely to develop health problems. In the workplace itself there can be accidents, and industry has learned how to guard against such accidents. But a new kind of problem that we are becoming more aware of is associated with repetitive functions. If the same person is doing the same thing day after day, hour after hour, various things can happen to the muscular-skeletal system. If may affect the back, but very often affects the hands or arms or shoulders; it may require surgery.This can occur in white collar, blue collar, and even professional occupations.

Also important are the "psycho-social" factors in death and disability. I do not want to place undue emphasis on the distinction between physical factors and psycho-social factors because the most important fact about the human anatomy is that the head is connected to the body. Physical factors can find expression in psychological and mental problems, and psychological and mental problems can find expression in physical illness. But certain psycho-social stresses that affect health are characteristic of modern economies. There is, for instance, an increase in the tensions associated with urbanization; the pace of work tends to increase and there is more pressure at work, even though people do not work harder in the sense of lifting heavier loads. Support systems in the community and in the family tend to weaken or even disappear. Some people develop a sense of alienation, of isolation, of what the French call anomie. Material wealth increases, but so may loneliness and despair. The poet, Edna St. Vincent, put it succinctly and beautifully:

> Love cannot fill the thickened lung with breath,
> Or cleanse the blood, or mend the broken bone.
> But many a man is making friends with death
> For lack of love alone.

Then, too, there are the special problems of the elderly. Along with an increase in demand for diagnostic and therapeutic interventions, the elderly often need rehabilitation services. Many of the elderly will suffer strokes. These strokes will not kill or even necessarily permanently paralyze them. But they will leave them with functional losses which may be reversed with appropriate rehabilitation services. The second type of service which we see ever greater need for in the United States is "assistance with daily living," (ADL). In modern economies, many people live into their 80s and 90s and many need assistance with bathing, dressing, eating, and transportation. Rehabilitation services and ADL are two huge industries waiting to be born as a nation develops a modern economy.

I now consider the similarities and the differences in health care policies in modern economies. (See Exhibit 4.)

EXHIBIT 4
Similarities and Differences in Health Care Policies in Modern Economies

- Health care is not an ordinary commodity
- Tendency toward convergence of systems based on three functions: finance, purchasing, and delivery
- Attempts to curb growth of health care expenditures : limit demand; limit supply

---

The French essayist, Montaigne, made an interesting general comment about similarities and differences. He wrote, "If our faces were not all alike, we would not be able to distinguish human beings from other animals. But if our faces were not all different, we would not be able to distinguish one human being from another." This is a good beginning for trying to understand the similarities and the differences among health care systems in different countries. Some things are so similar as to be almost uniform. And some things are very different. It is useful to try to identify the forces that drive similarities and differences, and to discover the consequences of different approaches.

One important similarity is that no modern economy treats health care as an ordinary commodity. By ordinary, I mean a commodity that is subject to the free interplay of supply and demand in the market. No matter how committed the country is in general to the idea of free markets and capitalism, government plays a substantial role in health care; in many countries that are otherwise regarded as capitalistic, the government plays a major role. In this respect, the United States stands at one extreme with the least government involvement of any modern economy. Even in the United States, however, almost half of all health care is paid for directly by the government. A substantial part of the rest is subsidized by the government through the tax-deductibility of employer contributions to private insurance. Not only is the U.S. government heavily involved in the purchase of health care through Medicare, Medicaid, and insurance for government workers, but it is also heavily involved in the supply of health care through the subsidization of the training of physicians and other health personnel. The government subsidizes construction of hospitals. Every state government in the U.S. licenses physicians and nurses. The Food and Drug Administration controls what drugs can be prescribed by physicians. In other modern economies, governments are more involved than in the U.S., running national health insurance programs, employing physicians and other personnel, owning hospitals, and in other ways.

Governments differ in how they intervene in health care. Some fund health care through direct taxes. Others create or encourage social insurance funds, financed by employer and employee contributions. Others make more use of tax subsidies in order to keep the appearance of private initiative, but if the tax subsidy is very large, the government is, in fact, dictating the outcome.

A second similarity, which has only recently become apparent, is a tendency toward convergence of health care systems in modern economies. This convergence is based on three functions and the articulation among those functions. The first function is finance. Every country must have a system of raising money to pay for health care, whether it is through private insurance, compulsory social insurance, or taxes. Whatever the method, there must be a system for gaining control of resources. At the opposite end of health care, there must be a system for delivery of services to patients through physicians, clinics, hospitals, and so on. This function is the organization and management of health care at the retail level, where care is provided to patients.

Between finance and delivery there is a third function, that of purchasing. It is the organization and management of health care at the wholesale level. It is composed of the institutions and mechanisms that move the money from the finance system to the delivery system. In the United States,"managed care organizations" have arisen to provide the interface between the raising of money and the delivery of care to patients. In England, the Thatcher reforms called for "purchasing authorities" to perform this function. The term "internal markets" came into use.

The convergence of health care systems toward this three-function organizational form — financing, purchasing, and delivery — is evident in many countries, although the language used to describe the phenomenon varies. In Germany, for example, there is extreme reluctance to use the word "markets" in connection with health care. Of course, market forces are at work in German health care, but they are not explicitly acknowledged. In the United States, by contrast, there are those who delight in discussing health care in a market idiom, while there are others who would prefer to follow the German example.

The third similarity that I found during a two-month visit to Western Europe last fall is a preoccupation with the cost of health care. In every country, I heard the same statement, "Our health care costs are too high," followed by the same question, "How can we keep costs from going higher?" Government officials, in particular, are very concerned about health care costs because in every country health care is a big part of the budget. European governments that want to join the European Monetary Union (EMU) are desperate to keep their budgets under control. They know that if health care costs grow too rapidly, their budgets will go into deficit and they will not be allowed into the EMU.

The main differences among countries can be found in the broad strategies employed to keep health care expenditures in check. Some countries emphasize the demand side; some emphasize the supply side. The demand side emphasis, not surprisingly, is most evident in the United States. Americans believe that insurance makes patients unconcerned about the price and utilization of care. The remedy is sought in making patients more cost-conscious. The principal methods of accomplishing this are deductibles and copayments. A deductible is a fixed amount which the patient must pay each year before insurance begins to pay. A copayment requires the patient to pay either a fixed dollar amount per service or a percentage of the cost of each service. In many other countries, such as England, curbs on expenditures are sought by limiting supply. The government limits the number of physicians, especially the number of specialists. It limits the number of hospitals, and it restricts the introduction and diffusion of new technologies. High-cost technologies are tightly rationed, and patients must wait to have access to them. Each country seeks its own approach to limiting health care expenditures in the light of its history, culture, and political climate.

In summary, Malaysia is on its way to becoming a modern economy. Almost all of the necessary ingredients are either in place or could easily be put into place. In the course of becoming a modern economy, there will be certain predictable changes that Malaysia can anticipate and for which it can plan. It is highly likely that the age distribution of the population will change, with the elderly becoming a much larger fraction over time. This won't happen right away. Thus, Malaysia is now in a very advantageous demographic situation. It is a young country, just at the beginning of this demographic transition. The problems of the elderly are not currently of great concern; there is time to put into place systems which will be appropriate at the time these problems become apparent.

There will be social changes involving families and communities that will increase the demand for health care. There will be new kinds of health problems: chronic illness and problems arising from changes in the physical and psycho-social environment. In creating a new health care system, Malaysia, like all countries, faces certain constraints and certain choices. An old German prayer says, "God, give me the courage to change those things that can be changed. Give me the fortitude to accept those things that cannot be changed. And give me the wisdom to know the one from the other." This is what should guide Malaysia in the development of a health care system.

Finally, it must be recognized that there are other issues that a country has to think about besides health policy. It is important that a country's health policy be consistent with the other goals and values of the society. In Western Europe, for example, many countries attach a great deal of importance to what they call social solidarity. They devise their health policies to help feed and reinforce social solidarity. In the United States, the emphasis is not on social solidarity but on individualism, freedom, and choice. This difference in emphasis results in a different approach to health policy. Or consider the difference between the United States and Canada. These two countries share an unarmed 3,000 mile border. There is a huge amount of trade back and forth, and a huge amount of visiting. The same language (English) is spoken in both countries except in Quebec (French). The same religions and many of the same ethnic backgrounds can be found in both countries. Nevertheless, the founding document of the United States, the Declaration of Independence, sets the standard and the goal for the country — "Life, liberty, and the pursuit of happiness." Just across the border, the founding goal is "Peace, order, and good government." It is not, therefore, surprising that Canada's approach to health policy is very different from the approach to health policy in the United States. Even though the technology is the same, the training of physicians and nurses is the same, and the economic forces that are at work are the same, the approaches to health policy are very different. The bottom line is that health care is more than a technical issue that physicians, economists, and other specialists can resolve. An essential ingredient is political leadership. To develop appropriate health policy, a country needs political leaders who have the vision and understanding of the economic and social forces at work and the ability to make health policy consistent with the other values and goals of the society.

Many people believe that the 21st century will be an Asian century. The Prime Minister of Malaysia has imaginatively said, "Let it be a world century." So be it. But even in a world century, Asia will play an increasingly important part. And Malaysia can play an increasingly important part within that Asian-World century. I hope that this country will have the courage, wisdom, and imagination to take a leadership role. I hope that Malaysia can develop a pluralistic, dynamic economy and an efficient, humanistic health care system which can be a model for the world.

Appendix

Sector Shares of Employment and Gross Domestic Product Per Capita U.S. from 1870 to 1978 and OECD Countries in 1970.

Figure A.1 shows agriculture's share of total employment plotted against GDP per capita measured in 1995 U.S. thousands of dollars.

Two sets of data are plotted: a time series for the U.S. covering the period from 1870 until 1978 (open circles) and a cross-section of OECD countries for a single year, 1970 (solid dots). Separate curves are fitted to each data set. The thicker line describes the U.S. historical relationship and the thinner line describes the OECD relationship in 1970. It is easy to see that the relationship in the U.S. historical data is almost identical to that in the OECD cross-sectional data. This is remarkable. In economic analysis, when functions are fit to both cross-sectional data and to time-series data, it is rare to get practically the same fit for both kinds of data.

Parenthetically, Malaysia currently has a GDP per capita of about U.S. $4500 but only about 20% of the work force is in agriculture. According to either one of the curves in Figure A.1, a 20% share would be expected for a country with a GDP per capita of about $7,000. It would appear that Malaysia is ahead of the curve in terms of its share in agriculture relative to the reported GDP per capita.

Figure A.2 shows the relationship between the service sector's share of employment and GDP per capita.

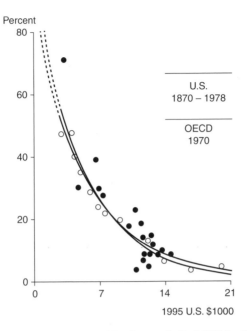

Fig. A.1. Agriculture's Share of Employment by Real GDP Per Capita.

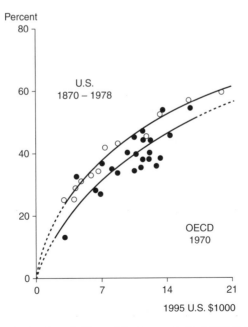

Fig. A.2. Service Sector's Share of Employment by Real GDP Per/Capita.

For the U.S. and OECD data sets, the curves for the agriculture and service sectors were estimated as a system using exponential functional forms and a maximum likelihood iterative procedure. The curves are similar, albeit not as close as for agriculture. For any given level of GDP per capita, the service sector's share is smaller in the OECD countries than it is in the U.S. I believe that the primary explanation for the difference is the very large role that manufacturing plays in the exports of many of the OECD countries, which requires more employment in manufacturing and proportionately less in the service sector. Again, if we ask about Malaysia, the statistics show that Malaysia has over 40% of employment in the service sector. Either one of the curves in Figure A.2 suggests that such a large share for the service sector might be expected in a country with a GDP per capita of seven or eight thousand dollars.

Industry's share of employment, derived by subtracting the estimated agriculture and service shares from 100%, is plotted against GDP per capita in Figure A.3.

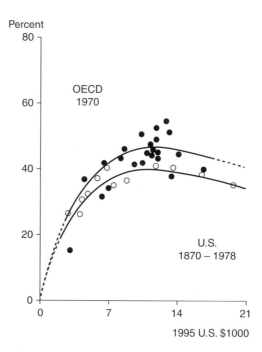

Fig. A.3.   Industry's Share of Employment by Real GDP Per Capita.

We see again a slight difference between the OECD and U.S. curves — the former is a bit higher-but again they have essentially the same shape and reach their peaks at approximately the same level of GDP. Somewhere around $11,000 per capita in 1995 US dollars, industry's share is at a maximum; after that, industry's share declines. Malaysia's share is consistent with the estimated functions.

Op-Ed

How and Why US Health Care Differs From that in Other OECD Countries

United States health care, often hailed as "the best health care system in the world," is also faulted for being too costly, leaving many millions of individuals uninsured, and having avoidable lapses in quality. Criticism often draws on comparisons with other countries of the Organisation for Economic Co-operation and Development (OECD). This Viewpoint also makes such comparisons, over a broad range of variables, and reaches one inescapable conclusion — US health care is very different from health care in other countries. Potential reasons for the differences are discussed, leading to the conclusion that future efforts to control cost, provide universal coverage, and improve health outcomes will have to consider the United States' particular history, values, and political system.

US vs OECD: Health Expenditures and Outcomes

Compared with the average OECD country, US health care expenditures differ in 3 important ways.[1] First, as a percentage of gross domestic product, US

Originally published in *JAMA*, 309(1):33–34, January 2013. Copyright by American Medical Association.

expenditures are twice as high. Second, the US share of health expenditures funded by government is much lower, 46% vs 75%. Third, the mix of services provided (technology intense vs more basic care) is very different (eTable, available at http://www.jama.com).

The larger role of government in health in OECD countries and the difference in mix of services are the main proximate explanations for the higher level of spending in the United States. Because funding in most OECD countries is usually through a tax-supported system, administrative costs are usually much lower than in the United States, with its fragmented sources of funding and payment. Also, the OECD countries use the concentration of funding to negotiate aggressively with drug companies and physicians and to control investment in hospitals and equipment. The United States could try to use the buying power of Medicare in a similar way, but legislation and political pressure prevent such an approach. The OECD countries provide more physicians and more acute care hospital beds, whereas the United States provides much more high-tech services, such as magnetic resonance imaging (MRI) scans and mammograms, proportionately more specialists, more amenities (privacy and space in hospitals), and more standby capacity as evident in a higher ratio of MRI scanners available to MRI scans performed. The greater number of physician visits and hospital days in OECD countries does not result in higher spending because of differences in services provided during a visit or a hospital day. In general, the United States has an expensive mix, whereas the OECD countries have an inexpensive one.

The effect of these differences in mix and total expenditures on health outcomes is uncertain. Measured by life expectancy, the OECD countries do slightly better than the United States, but firm conclusions are elusive because life expectancy depends on many factors in addition to medical care. For instance, the percentage of population in poverty is much higher in the United States than in the OECD countries (17% vs 9%), and poverty is a predictor of early death. Health is probably distributed less equally in the United States than in the OECD countries because the United States has more individuals without insurance and greater income inequality.

Why the Differences?

Three basic differences between the United States and most other OECD countries might explain why health policy differs. First, US individuals appear more distrustful of government, a distrust that has deep historical roots. It was an armed rebellion against the government of King George III that led to the founding of the United States. It was Thomas Jefferson, a principal founding father, who said, "That government is best which governs least." The initial antigovernment sentiment has received recurrent "booster shots" from waves of immigrants who came to the United States seeking freedom. Their willingness to risk life in a new land was frequently fueled by negative experience with government in their home country, a government that oppressed them because of their political beliefs, religion, ethnicity, or social class. Medicare and Medicaid appear to be an exception to distrust of government, but these programs provide insurance for populations that were not and could not be served by private insurance. A Pew public opinion survey of a representative sample of US individuals about their attitude toward elected officials showed more than twice as many negative as positive views.[2]

Closely related to the weaker support for government action in the United States is a reluctance to achieve more equal outcomes for the population through redistributive public policy. Although US individuals have always rejected European-style class distinctions that required deference and subservience,[3] the declaration that "all men are created equal" did not carry any suggestion of equality of outcomes, such as in income or health. The income tax is less progressive in the United States than in most OECD countries, and the redistributive effect is augmented in the OECD countries by more egalitarian transfers of money and services. In response to a Pew survey,[2] 4 of 5 US individuals agreed that "everyone has it in their own power to succeed." Only 1 in 5 agreed that "success in life is pretty much determined by forces outside our control." Whether this view reflects reality is another matter. It is attitude and beliefs that shape voting behavior.[4]

Heterogeneity of the US population tends to strengthen resistance to redistribution. Diversity of race, religion, ethnic origin, and sometimes language contribute to a weaker sense of empathy for less fortunate members of society, whose identity may differ greatly from one's own. In more homogeneous nations, such empathy is more likely to be experienced and acted upon. Weak support for redistribution at the national level in the United States stands in sharp contrast with redistribution within self-defined more homogeneous groups (for example, Mormon Relief Societies, Jewish homes for the aged in almost every major city, and the founding of Baptist, Catholic, Lutheran, Methodist, and other sectarian hospitals).

The third, and probably most important, difference between the United States and most OECD countries is the political system. Many observers attribute US failure to enact comprehensive health care reform to the opposition of "special interests," such as pharmaceutical and device manufacturers, insurance companies, physicians (especially those in high-income specialties), and hospitals. But all countries have special interests; only in the United States have they been particularly successful in blocking comprehensive reform. This success can be explained in part by noting that the US political system is different from the parliamentary systems of most OECD countries in ways that make special interests more effective. Some of these differences are built into the US Constitution, including the checks and balances provided by 2 separate houses of Congress with their powerful committees, plus an independent executive branch with veto power. Some differences have evolved over time, such as expensive primary election battles, long election campaigns, and the Senate filibuster. Thus, the US system provides many "choke points" for special interests to block or reshape legislation. Also, in recent years, contributions from special interest groups significantly influence who runs for office, who gets elected, and how elected officials vote.

Lessons for Future Reform

President Obama's Affordable Care Act (ACA), if fully implemented, would involve significant redistribution with tens of millions of poor and sick persons obtaining health insurance paid for by others. If the ACA is pared back, there will be less redistribution and tens of millions of persons would not have coverage, and the more difficult task of controlling health costs would remain. This review suggests a strategy for obtaining further reform.

First, government's role should be limited to what is necessary, not just desirable. Efficiency and equity in financing require a dedicated tax to fund basic care for all.[5] Second, provision of basic coverage for all should not require equality for obtaining additional coverage. As in Australia, Israel, the Netherlands, and Switzerland, individuals should be free to purchase more than basic care. Third, reform should have features that would appeal to some special interests, or to some elements within each special interest group (for example, some physicians or some health plans). Comprehensive health care reform in the United States is necessary to avoid a financial disaster, but enactment of such reform will require attention to US history, values, and politics.

References

1. OECD iLibrary (2012). OECD Health Statistics. http://www.oecd-ilibrary.org/social-issues-migration-health/data/oecd-health-statistics_health-data-en.
2. The Pew Research Center for The People & The Press (2012). The 2005 Political Typology Survey. http://www.pewtrusts.org/uploadedFiles/wwwpewtrustsorg/Reports/Public_opinion_and_polls/PRC_ politicaltypology_0505,pdf.

3. St. John de Crévecoeur, J. H. (1782). "What Is an American?" *Letter III, Letters From an American Farmer*. http://nationalhumanitiescenter.org/pds/makingrev/independence/text6/crevecoeuramerican.pdf.
4. Bundorf, M. K. and Fuchs, V. R. (2008). "Public support for national health Insurance: the roles of attitudes and beliefs." *Forum for Health Economics & Policy.* **10**(1): 1–4.
5. Fuchs, V. R. and Shoven, J. B. (2010). *The Dedicated VAT Solution.* SIEPR Policy Brief: Stanford, CA.

Part 5

Health Insurance

Introduction

Health care expenditures in the United States, 18 percent of GDP, greatly exceed spending on food or clothing or transportation or other items of consumption. Moreover, the amount of care consumed varies greatly across individuals in any given year and usually varies greatly over time for any given individual. While nearly one-quarter of the population has no contact with a physician or a hospital in a given year, about 5 percent account for about 50 percent of total expenditures.

The result of this uncertainty is great demand for health care insurance in all high income countries. Except in the United States, health insurance is usually universal or close to it. Government typically plays a big role. In the United States about 90 percent of the population has some insurance, half of it employment-based. The extent of coverage and access to care varies more than in other high income democracies. In theory, and in many other countries in practice, universal coverage is not that difficult to achieve; there are only two necessary and sufficient conditions: *Subsidies* for individuals too poor or too sick to pay for insurance at an actuarially appropriate premium, and *compulsion* to ensure that the rest of the population acquires insurance and provides their fair share of subsidies. In other high income democracies, strong egalitarian pressures plus a willingness to use government to require participation result in universal coverage. In the United States, weaker support for redistribution and a desire to limit the role of government has prevented this result.

The first paper in Part 5, "From Bismarck to Woodcock: The 'Irrational' Pursuit of National Health Insurance," was prepared for a conference celebrating George Stigler's 65th birthday. He was one of my principal mentors at Columbia University and a Nobel Prize winner for his theoretical and empirical research on industrial organizations. According to Stigler (1911–1991), "If an economic policy has been adopted by many countries ...it is fruitful to assume that the real effects were known and desired." (1977) Given the criticisms of national health insurance by some American economists (Martin Feldstein and Milton Friedman are quoted), the paper asks why is it so popular and durable in other countries? Many possible answers are discussed, including egalitarian pressures and a desire to have more control over physicians and hospitals. I am most impressed by its role in redistributing money to the sick by paying for their care. Health insurance functions like an offset to an unjust tax. I also see a national health plan fulfilling the need for a unifying symbol when monarchy and religion have become weaker.

The second paper, by Kate Bundorf and me, addresses the opposite question: Why, given the popularity of national health insurance in other countries, does the United States resist this policy? It is possible that the U.S. political system, with its many checks and balances, enables special interests who would be adversely affected by national health insurance to choke off such legislation. But it is also possible that there is insufficient support for the required subsidies and compulsion.

We explore this possibility by examining replies to a national telephone survey of 2,000 adults conducted by The Pew Research Center for the People and the Press in early December 2004. Some of the sample (28 percent) could not be contacted. Additionally, 55 percent of the contacts declined to be interviewed; and 6 percent did not complete the interview, leaving a final response rate of 31 percent. Pew reweighted the responses to match national estimates of the U.S. population based on sex, age, education, race, Hispanic origin, region and distribution across Republican and Democratic counties.

There were many questions in the survey, frequently asked in pairs, and balanced by another pair of questions aimed at the same attitude. Probably the most important results are that the population is evenly divided about government economic intervention, shows a slightly favorable attitude toward government redistribution, but less than half of those interviewed have favorable attitudes toward *both* redistribution and economic intervention. Results from *voters* might differ from those interviewed, but the survey results imply that a substantial majority supporting both subsidies and compulsion is probably lacking.

In 2006, The Brookings Institution Hamilton Project invited four proposals for health insurance reform. As one of the four, Ezekiel Emanuel (1957–) and I submitted the third paper in Part 5. The paper describes our proposal in considerable detail. In summary, our proposal had the following essential elements.

1) **Universal coverage** for a comprehensive set of health care benefits. In addition to the ethical and political advantages of a universal system, it is much less costly to administer. In the U.S. system at least $300 billion of resources are used for administration each year; these resources could be used to deliver care to patients, or to meet other public and private demands. In our plan, individuals could buy additional health care and pay the full cost, including costs of administration.

2) **Financing by a dedicated value-added tax**. The tax, which is collected from business firms, works like a consumption tax, which most economists think is more efficient and more equitable than an income or a payroll tax. "Dedicated" means that the proceeds must be used for health care, and the universal system must be fully paid by the value-added tax.

3) **Free choice of health plan** every year by beneficiaries. Health plans would be paid a fixed amount per year for each enrollee in their plan, risk-adjusted to equalize for plans that get an above or below average share of sicker enrollees.

4) **The health plans would not compete with each other through price**, but they would be rivals in the quality of services offered. Such rivalry would extend to their ability to attract high quality personnel and their ability to organize and deliver cost-effective care.

Rivalry between plans and per capita payment instead of fee-for-service would help to curb expenditures. Moreover, integration of the insurance function with hospitals, multi-specialty physician groups, and other personnel results in good quality care at below average cost. This is not just speculation; plans of this type already exist.

The op-ed in Part 5 discusses an additional problem standing in the way of national health insurance legislation: Large number of Americans believe that they already have health insurance at little or no costs to themselves. Many workers believe that their employer is providing health insurance as a "fringe benefit" at no cost to the worker except for a possible co-insurance as a small part of the premium. Many citizens who have health insurance provided by government believe that at least part of it is free to them. These beliefs are encouraged by employers, union leaders, politicians, and (sadly) much of the media with the seemingly benign phrase "shared responsibility." In fact, virtually all health economists who have studied employment-based insurance have concluded that insurance is part of total compensation. Its only difference from wages is that the premium is not taxable as income to the worker. This makes it attractive to employees, especially those in high tax brackets, but the result is a Federal deficit, a decrease in other federal spending, or an increase in other taxes. Politicians may tell their supporters that they are "giving" them health insurance, but government has no resources to "give" insurance; they must obtain the funds by taxes or borrowing. "Shared responsibility" is a ruse or a misunderstanding. All the cost of health insurance is ultimately borne by the public in the form of lost wages, higher prices or higher taxes; record corporate profits suggests that the cost of health care is probably not coming out of profits.

What is the effect of insurance on expenditures for health care? What is its effects on health outcomes? Attempts to answer these questions by comparing the insured with the uninsured cannot yield reliable answers because the two groups differ in many other ways, only some of which are known and only some of those can be controlled for. A solution was sought in the Rand Health Insurance research (1971–1982), a randomized controlled experiment, which I think was the best designed and executed social experiment ever conducted in the United States.

Large numbers of individuals and families were randomly assigned to different insurance plans or no insurance at all. They were followed for several years with close observation of their utilization of medical care and changes, if any, in their health. A major finding that did not surprise economists was that the more comprehensive the insurance, the greater the utilization of care. For many conceptual and technical reasons a precise quantitative description of this relationship is not possible, but the investigators concluded that there was a modest increase in utilization (and expenditures) (one to two percent) for every decrease in price to patients of ten percent as result of more insurance. Individuals with free care used 25 percent more than individuals who paid 25 percent of their bills (with an upper limit depending on income).

Clear cut examples of effects on health are more difficult to discern. My reading of the results is that there were no major increases in health associated with the increased utilization, but there are others who believe there were some favorable effects.

In thinking about the effects of medical care on health it is important to distinguish between the total (average) effect and the marginal effect. For example, if there were no medical care available in the United States, life expectancy would undoubtedly fall precipitously. That is the total effect. On the other hand, during World War II approximately one half of practicing physicians were diverted to military service, with little observable effect on the nation's life expectancy. In fact, between 1940 and 1945 life expectancy *rose* by an unprecedented rate, 0.5 percent per annum. This increase was probably attributable to a sharp fall in unemployment, a sharp increase in income, and a boost to national morale attributable to the war effort. It would probably be wrong to attribute a positive effect on life expectancy to a decrease in physician supply, but a negative effect of this marginal change was probably small.

A recent attempt to measure the effects of health insurance in a controlled experiment (the Oregon experiment) has yielded results that seem to me more ambiguous than the Rand experiment. Oregon wanted to increase the number of poor covered by Medicaid, but didn't have enough money to enroll all who were eligible. They held a lottery, gave insurance to the winners, and gave nothing to the losers, who they treated as "controls." The first few years of the experiment, in my opinion, yield little in the way of substantial improvements in the health of the lottery winners. Those that were favorable largely took the form of "better mental health," "felt more financially secure," and the like.

How should we think about these results? My view is that the lottery winner or anyone that gets free health insurance is getting two things: 1) a grant of money equal to the average cost of the insurance, and 2) and a requirement that the winner buy a prescribed health insurance policy; in the Oregon case participation in the Medicaid program. Suppose that instead, lottery winners were given free *service station* insurance to cover gasoline, oil, tires, brakes, lights, battery and other necessary car maintenance and repair. Is there any doubt that the winners would on average experience "more financial security," "better mental health," and the like relative to the lottery losers? The quantitative results might not be the same as with Medicaid because the latter would cover cases with extraordinary high expenses not experienced by car owners. It is possible that the lottery losers (the control group) also received care for major health problems at government hospitals or through free care programs. This would decrease the possibility that winners of the Oregon lottery would show much better health outcomes than the losers.

Another consideration in comparing Medicaid with service station insurance for lottery winners is that many visits for medical care can be postponed, whereas a poor individual frequently needs a car to get to work. Fixing an engine that won't start, replacing a worn out tire, or even the need for "gas money" could pose an urgent threat to mental health or financial security.

Another type of empirical evidence that has been invoked in favor of health insurance that seems to me informative but not dispositive is comparison between the U.S. health care system and those of other high income countries. The raw results are lower expenditures in other countries and higher life expectancies. The expenditure result can be explained by the other governments using other methods of control including hard bargaining with drug companies and physicians, controls over financing of facilities and equipment, and controls over technology. The better results for life expectancy do not tell us anything definitive about the effects of health insurance on health outcomes. Many other countries provide more and better *social services*. Moreover, the percent in poverty is higher in the United States as measured by percent with incomes below one-half the median. Those non-medical factors probably have more effect on health outcomes than differences in medical care.

5.1

From Bismarck to Woodcock: The "Irrational" Pursuit of National Health Insurance

Uniformity of practice seldom continues long without good reason,

— Samuel Johnson, 1775

If an economic policy has been adopted by many communities, or if it is persistently pursued by a society over a long span of time, it is fruitful to assume that the real effects were known and desired.

— George Stigler, 1975

Almost a century ago Prince Otto Eduard Leopold von Bismarck, the principal creator and first chancellor of the new German nation-state, introduced compulsory national health insurance to the Western world. Since then, nation after nation has followed his lead until today almost every developed country has a full-blown national health insurance plan. Some significant benchmarks along the way are the Russian system (introduced by Lenin after the Bolshevik Revolution), the British National Health Service (Beveridge and Bevan, 1945), and the Canadian federal-provincial plans (hospital care in the late 1950s, physicians' services in the late 1960s). In nearly all cases these plans built on

Originally published in *Journal of Law and Economics*, 19(2):347–359, August 1976. Copyright by The University of Chicago Press.

previous systems of medical organization and finance that reflected particular national traditions, values, and circumstances.[1]

In some health plans, such as those in the communist countries, the government has direct responsibility for providing services. In others, the production of medical care is still at least partially in the private sector, but the payment for care is through taxes or compulsory insurance premiums which are really ear-marked taxes. Even in the United States, the last major holdout against the world-wide trend, government funds pay directly for almost half of all health care expenditures and pay indirectly for an appreciable additional share through tax exemptions and allowances.[a] Moreover, most observers believe it is only a question of *when* Congress will enact national health insurance, not *if* it will.

Almost as obvious (to many economists) as the rise of public subsidy of health insurance is the "irrational" aspect of such programs. Health insurance, in effect, reduces the price the consumer faces at the time of purchase of medical care and therefore induces excessive demand. Because the direct cost to the consumer is less than the true cost to society of providing that care, he tends to over-consume medical care relative to other goods and services. This misallocation of resources results in a significant "welfare loss," which Martin Feldstein has estimated at a minimum of $5 billion per annum in the United States.[2]

Not only does society seem to be irrationally bent on encouraging people to overuse medical care, but in the free market for health insurance people also tend to buy the "wrong" kind. Most economists agree that to the extent that health insurance serves a useful purpose it is to protect consumers against large, unexpected bills for medical care. All insurance policies are actuarily "unfair," that is, they carry a load factor for administrative costs, but, if consumers are risk averse, it is worthwhile for them to pay these costs in order to protect themselves against unpredictable (for the individual) large losses. It follows, therefore, that consumers should prefer major medical (catastrophe) insurance, that is, plans with substantial deductibles or co-payment provisions for moderate expenses but ample coverage for very large expenses. Instead, we observe a strong preference for "first dollar" or shallow coverage. Of the privately held hospital insurance policies in the United States, the number covering the first day of hospitalization are several times greater than the number covering long-term stays.

Another apparent irrationality with respect to health insurance was alleged by Milton Friedman in a *Newsweek* column in April, 1975. He noted that Leonard Woodcock, President of the United Automobile Workers (UAW), is leading the

---

[a]For a discussion of why the United States is the last to adopt national health insurance, see p. 306–307 *infra*.

drive for universal comprehensive national health insurance despite the fact that such a measure is

> ... against the interest of ... members of his own union, and even of the officials of that union. ... The UAW is a strong union and its members are among the highest paid industrial workers. If they wish to receive part of their pay in the form of medical care, they can afford, and hence can get, a larger amount than the average citizen. But in a governmental program, they are simply average citizens. In addition, a union or company plan would be far more responsive to their demands and needs than a universal national plan, so that they would get more per dollar spent.[3]

Friedman says that Woodcock is an "intelligent man," and therefore finds his behavior a "major puzzle."

From Bismarck to Woodcock, it seems that economists are drowning in a sea of irrationality. But other economists warn us against jumping to the "irrationality" conclusion. In particular, George Stigler has taught us to look beyond the surface appearance of political actions in search of their actual consequences and of the interests that they serve. He writes,

> It seems unfruitful ... to conclude from the studies of the effects of various policies that those policies which did not achieve their announced goals, or had perverse effects ... are simply mistakes of the society.[4]

In short, when confronted with some consistent and widespread behavior which we cannot explain, we should not blithely assume that it is attributable to lack of information or bad judgment. We should be wary of what might be called the "fallacy of misplaced ignorance." It may be that the behavior we observe is more consistent with the self-interest of particular individuals or groups than it first appears.

It is to George Stigler that we are also indebted for the "survivor principle," one of his many contributions to the study of industrial organization.[5] The basic notion is simple: if we want to learn something about the relative efficiency of differently sized firms in an industry, Stigler tells us to look at that industry over time and notice which size classes seem to flourish and which do not. Can the "survivor principle" be applied to institutions as well? If so, national health insurance seems to pass with flying colors. No country that has tried it has abandoned it, and those that have tried it partially usually expand it. It may not be unreasonable to infer, therefore, that national health insurance does serve some *general* interests. That is, there may be some *welfare gains* lying below the surface that more than offset the losses so apparent to many economists. An exploration of some of the special or general benefits that might explain the widespread pursuit of national health insurance follows.

The U.S. Already Has Implicit National Health Insurance

Some of the observed behavior would seem less irrational if we assume that the U.S. already has *implicit* national health insurance, especially for catastrophic illness. If it is true that most uninsured people who need care can get it one way or another — through government hospitals, philanthropy, or bad debts — then it may be rational for people to buy only shallow coverage, or indeed, not to buy any insurance at all. To suggest that there is implicit insurance in the United States covering nearly everyone is not at all to suggest that there is equal access to equal quality care. We know that so-called free care may often have some stigma attached to it, may be less pleasant and less prompt, and may fail in other ways as well. But it cannot be denied that a good deal of medical care is delivered every year in the United States to persons who do not have explicit insurance or the money to pay for it.

Those persons without explicit insurance are essentially free riders. Those who do carry extensive insurance, such as the automobile workers, in effect pay twice — once through the premiums for their own insurance and again through taxes or inflated costs to cover care for those without explicit insurance. If this is a significant factor, it could be perfectly rational for the automobile workers to support *universal compulsory* insurance. Why society provides implicit or (in most countries) explicit coverage for all remains to be explained.

An Attempt to Control Providers

Another reason why the UAW leaders and others may favor a single national health plan is the hope of gaining some control over the providers of medical care — the hospitals and the physicians. In recent years one of the major frustrations faced by the auto workers and other groups with extensive insurance coverage is the rapid escalation in the price of medical care. They may believe that only a single source national health insurance plan will be in a position to control provider behavior and stop the escalation in costs. Moreover, there is strong evidence that they are not alone in this view. One of the puzzles for economists has been to explain the traditional opposition of the medical profession to legislation which, at least in the short run, increases the demand for their services. This opposition probably stems in part from the belief that national health insurance would ultimately result in an increase in government control over providers.

Tax Advantages

Why do people buy shallow coverage — where the administrative load is high and the risk element relatively small? One reason is that when the premium is paid by the employer the implicit income is free of tax. Even health insurance premiums paid by the individual are partially deductible from taxable income. If the tax laws allowed employers to provide tax-free "food insurance," we would undoubtedly see a sharp increase in that type of fringe benefit. But again the explanation is not very satisfactory. Why do the tax laws encourage the purchase of medical care but not food, clothing, or other necessities? In an attempt to answer this question, we should consider some of the characteristics of medical care and health insurance that are different from conventional commodities.

Externalities

One explanation for the popularity of national health insurance that has great appeal for economists at the theoretical level is that there are substantial external benefits associated with the consumption of medical care. If this were true, then governmental subsidy of care need not be irrational; indeed it might be irrational not to provide that subsidy. The best example of potential externalities is the prevention or treatment of communicable diseases such as tuberculosis. In earlier times these diseases constituted a very significant portion of overall health problems, but are much less important today. Furthermore, if a concern with externalities were the chief motivation, it would be logical and feasible to subsidize those services (for example, venereal disease clinics) which are clearly addressed to the communicable diseases. However, even economists who are strong advocates of national health insurance, such as Lester Thurow, do not rely on the externality argument, Thurow writes, "Once a society gets beyond public health measures and communicable diseases, medical care does not generate externalities."[6]

Mark Pauly has called attention to one special kind of externality which probably is operative. It involves the satisfaction people get from knowing that someone else who is sick is getting medical attention.[7] This satisfaction could be purchased by voluntary philanthropy, but the total amount so purchased is likely to be less than socially optimal since each individual's giving tends to be based on his or her private satisfaction, ignoring the effects on others. The solution may be compulsory philanthropy, that is, tax-supported programs.

A Matter of "Life or Death"

Another explanation for national health insurance that has great appeal at the theoretical level but carries less conviction empirically is that "the market should not determine life or death." This theme is advanced by Arthur Okun in his new book, *Equality and Efficiency, the Big Tradeoff*, and is a basic tenet of those who argue that "health care is a right."[8] There is considerable logic in the argument that society may be unwilling to accept the consequences of an unequal distribution of income for certain kinds of allocation decisions, such as who serves in the army during wartime, who gets police protection, and who faces other life-threatening situations. It may be easier and more efficient to control such allocations directly than to try to redistribute money income (possibly only temporarily) to achieve the desired allocation.

Although this explanation has a certain theoretical appeal, one problem with it is that the vast majority of health services do not remotely approach a "life or death" situation. Moreover, the ability of medical care to make any significant contribution to life expectancy came long after Bismarck and Lenin advocated national health insurance. Even today, when some medical care is very effective, it is possible that housing, nutrition, and occupation have more influence on life expectancy than does medical care, yet we allow inequality in the distribution of income to determine allocation decisions in those areas. According to Peter Townsend, there is no evidence that the British National Health Service has reduced class differences in infant mortality, maternal mortality, or overall life expectancy.[9] If equalizing life expectancy were society's goal, it is not at all clear that heavy emphasis on national health insurance is an optimal strategy.

The emphasis on medical care rather than other programs that might affect life expectancy is sometimes defended by the statement that it is more feasible. Although diet or exercise or occupation may have more effect on life expectancy than does medical care, it may be technically simpler to alter people's consumption of medical care rather than to alter their diet, etc. It has also been argued that it is politically more feasible to push medical care rather than alternative strategies. The distinction between technical and political feasibility is not, of course, clear-cut because the former depends in part on what we are willing to do in the way of permitting government to intrude on personal decisions — a political question. However, to the extent that the popularity of national health insurance is said to be attributable to its political feasibility, we have really not explained much. Its political popularity is precisely the question we started with.

The Growth of Egalitarianism

Life expectancy aside, one way of interpreting the growth of national health insurance is an expression of the desire for greater equality in society. British economists John and Sylvia Jewkes have written,

> The driving force behind the creation of the National Health Service was not the search for efficiency or for profitable social investment. It was something quite different: it was a surging national desire to share something equally.[10]

An American economist, C. M. Lindsay, has developed a theoretical model which analyzes alternative methods for satisfying the demand for equality of access to medical care. Among other things, he shows that if this demand for equality is widespread, there are externalities similar to those discussed by Pauly in connection with philanthropy. Thus a free market approach will result in less equality than people really demand. He also shows that the British National Health Service can perhaps best be understood as an attempt to satisfy this demand for equality. He concludes, ". . . the politician's sensitive ear may read the preferences of his constituents better than the econometrician with his computer".[11]

Why the demand for equality has grown over time and why it should find expression in medical care more than in other goods and services are not easy questions to answer. Is there really more altruism in society now than before? Were Bismarck and Lenin the most altruistic political leaders of their time? Is it simply the case that equality is a normal "good," that is, we buy more of it when our income rises? If this is the explanation, what are the implications for equality in a no-growth economy?

Perhaps there has been no real increase in altruism at all. Perhaps what we observe is a response to an increase in the ability of the less well-off to make life miserable for the well-off through strikes, violence, and other social disruptions. In this view health insurance is part of an effort to buy domestic stability. It may be that industrialization and urbanization make us all more interdependent, thus increasing the power of the "have-nots" to force redistributions of one kind or another. Or perhaps there has been a decline in the willingness of the "haves" to use force to preserve the status quo.

Such speculations, if they contain some validity, would explain a general increase in egalitarian legislation, but they would not help much in explaining why this legislation has focused heavily on medical care. Indeed, is it not curious that society should choose to emphasize equality in access to a service that makes little difference at the margin in life expectancy or to economic or political position and power? A cynic might argue that it is not curious at all since it is precisely because medical care does not make much difference that those with power are willing to share it more equally with those with less. Indeed, one might argue that the more a society has significant, enduring class distinctions, the more it needs the symbolic equality of national health insurance to blunt pressures for changes that alter fundamental class or power relationships.

One egalitarian goal that has always had considerable acceptance in the United States is equality of opportunity. Thus, a popular argument in favor of national health insurance is that it would help to equalize access to medical care for children. Some recent theoretical work on the economics of the family, however, calls into question the effectiveness of such programs. Gary Becker has argued that the thrust of programs aimed at increasing investment in disadvantaged children can be blunted by parents who can decrease their own allocation of time and money to their children as investment by the state increases.[12] The increase in the welfare of the children, therefore, may be no greater than if a cash subsidy equal to the cost of the program were given directly to the parents. The ability of the "head" to reallocate family resources may not, however, be as unconstrained as Becker's model assumes. There may be legal or social constraints, or there may be a desire on the part of the head to maintain the child's obedience, respect, or affection. Thus the importance of the reallocation effect is an empirical question, about which at present we know virtually nothing.

Paternalism[b]

An argument advanced by Thurow in favor of transfers in kind — such as national health insurance — is that some individuals are not competent to make their own decisions. He writes,

> Increasingly we are coming to recognize that the world is not neatly divided into the competent and the incompetent. There is a continuum of individuals ranging from those who are competent to make any and all decisions to those who are incompetent to make any and all decisions.[c]

---

[b]I am grateful to Sherman Maisel for suggestions concerning this section.
[c]Lester C, Thurow, *supra* note 7, at 193.

Thurow argues that if society desires to raise each family up to some minimum level of *real* welfare, it may be more efficient to do it through in-kind transfers than through cash grants. Even if we agree with this general argument, it does not follow as a matter of logic that subsidizing medical care brings us closer to a social optimum. It may be the case, for instance, that the "less able" managers tend to *overvalue* medical care relative to other goods and services, in which case Thurow ought to want to constrain their utilization rather than encourage it.

More generally, there is the question whether government will, on average, make "better" decisions than individuals. As Arrow has stated in a slightly different context, "If many individuals, given proper information, refuse to fasten their seat belts or insist on smoking themselves into lung cancer or drinking themselves into incompetence, there is no reason to suppose they will be any more sensible in their capacity as democratic voters."[13] Two arguments have been suggested to blunt Arrow's critique. The first is that the "less able" are less likely to vote; therefore the electoral process produces decisions that reflect the judgment of the more able members of society. Second, it has been suggested that there is considerable scope for discretionary behavior by elected representatives; they do not simply follow the dictates of their constituents.[14] It may be that their judgment is generally better than that of the average citizen.

An Offset to an "Unjust Tax"[d]

Suppose the U.S. were defeated by an enemy in war and had to pay an annual tribute to the enemy of $100 billion. Suppose further that the enemy collected this tribute by a tax of a variable amount on American citizens chosen at random. The U.S. government might decide that this tribute tax was unjust and that it would be more equitable for the federal government to pay the tribute from revenues raised by normal methods of taxation. If the enemy insisted on collecting the tribute from individual citizens on a random basis, the government could choose to reimburse those paying the tribute.

Some observers believe there is a close parallel between the tribute example and expenditures for medical care. They see ill health and the consumption of medical care as largely beyond the control of the individual citizen — the cost is like an unjust tax — and the purpose of national health insurance is to prevent medical expenditures from unjustly changing the distribution of income. There is, of course, the question whether, or how much, individuals can influence and control the amount of their medical expenditures. Putting that to one side,

---

[d]I am grateful to Seth Kreimer for suggestions concerning this section.

however, and assuming that the analogy is a good one, there are still some questions that arise.

One might ask why the government has to intervene to protect people against the tribute tax. Why couldn't citizens in their private lives buy insurance against being taxed for tribute? The total cost and the probabilities are known; therefore private insurance companies could easily set appropriate premiums. One answer might be that this is also inequitable to the extent that some people can afford the insurance more easily than others. The government could easily remedy this, however, by some modest changes in the distribution of income.

Another problem, of course, is that some people might not buy the insurance. They would be "free riders" because if they were hit with a big tribute tax they would be unable to pay and others would have to pay in their place. Furthermore, they would be wiped out financially, so that society would have to support their families.

To be sure, the government could both redistribute income to take care of the premium and make insurance compulsory, but that becomes almost indistinguishable from a national insurance plan. The only difference then would be whether there is a single organization, the government, underwriting the insurance, or whether there are several private insurance companies.

In the tribute tax example we have assumed that the probability of loss would be identical across the population, but this is clearly not true for health insurance. One argument advanced in support of national health insurance is that it does not require higher-risk individuals to pay higher premiums. A counter argument is that individuals do have some discretion concerning behavior that affects health and concerning the utilization of medical care for given health conditions. National health insurance, it is alleged, distorts that behavior. A related argument is that medical care will always have to be rationed in some way and that national health insurance requires the introduction of rationing devices other than price and income. These devices carry their own potential for inequity and inefficiency.

The Decline of the Family

Illness is as old as mankind, and, while frequently in the past and not infrequently today, there is little that can be done to change the course of disease, there is much that can be done to provide care, sympathy, and support. Traditionally most of these functions were provided within the family. The family was both the mechanism for *insuring* against the consequences of disease and disability and the locus of the *production* of care. The only rival to the family in this respect until modern times was the church, a subject to be considered below.

With industrialization and urbanization, the provision of insurance and of care tended to move out of the family and into the market. Thus, much of the observed increase in medical care's share of total economic activity is an accounting illusion. It is the result of a shift in the production of care from the home, where it is not considered part of national output, to hospitals, nursing homes and the like, where it is counted as part of the GNP. Unlike the production of bread, however, which also moved from the family to the market (and stayed there), medical care, or at least medical insurance, increasingly became a function of the state.

One possible explanation is that the state is more efficient because there are significant *economies of scale.* With respect to the production of medical care, the economies of scale argument can fairly safely be rejected. Except for some exotic tertiary procedures, the economies of scale in the production of physicians' services and hospital services are exhausted at the local or small region level. For the insurance function itself, there may be significant economies of scale. Definitive studies are not available, but the proposition that a single national health insurance plan would be cheaper to administer than multiple plans cannot be rejected out of hand.[e] To be sure, a single plan would presumably reduce consumer satisfaction to the extent that the coverage of the plan would represent a compromise among the variety of plans different individuals and groups might prefer.

The relationship between the declining importance of the family and the growing importance of the state is complex. Not only can the latter be viewed as a consequence of the former, but the causality can also run the other way. Every time the state assumes an additional function such as health insurance, child care, or benefits for the aged, the need for close family ties becomes weaker. Geographic mobility probably plays a significant role in this two-way relationship. One of the reasons why people rely more on the state and less on their family is that frequently the family is geographically dispersed, The other side of the coin is that once the state assumes responsibilities that formerly resided with the family, individuals feel freer to move away from the family, both literally and figuratively.

It has often been alleged that these intra-family dependency relationships are inhibiting and destructive to individual fulfillment. Whether a dependency

---

[e] See Maurice LeClair, The Canadian Health Care System, in National Health Insurance: Can We Learn from Canada? 11, 16 (Proc. of Sun Valley Forum on Nat'l Health 1974 Symposium, Spyros Andreopoulos ed. 1975). LeClair writes that the experience in Saskatchewan clearly indicated economies of scale in the administration of a virtually universal plan. See also further comment on this point by LeClair, *id.* at 24.

relationship with the state will prove less burdensome remains to be seen. There is also the question whether the efficient provision of *impersonal* "caring" is feasible.

The Decline of Religion

In traditional societies when the family was unable to meet the needs of the sick, organized religion frequently took over. Indeed, practically all of the early hospitals in Europe were built and staffed by the church and served primarily the poor. The development of strong religious ties, with tithes or contributions frequently indistinguishable from modern taxes, can be viewed as an alternative mechanism for dealing with the philanthropic externalities discussed previously. Moreover, at a time when technical medical care was so ineffective, religion offered a particular kind of symbolic equality — in the next world if not in this one. Thus, the decline of organized religion, along with the weakening of the family, may have created a vacuum which the state is called upon to fill.

The "Political" Role

When refugees from the Soviet Union were interviewed in Western Europe after World War II, they invariably praised the West and disparaged life in Russia — with one notable exception. They said they sorely missed the comprehensive health insurance provided by the Soviet state.[15] It may be that one of the most effective ways of increasing allegiance to the state is through national health insurance. This was undoubtedly a prime motive for Bismarck as he tried to weld the diverse German principalities into a nation. It is also alleged that he saw national health insurance as an instrument to reduce or blur the tension and conflicts between social classes.

We live at a time when many of the traditional symbols and institutions that held a nation together have been weakened and have fallen into disrepute. A more sophisticated public requires more sophisticated symbols, and national health insurance may fit the role particularly welt.

Why Is the U.S. Last?

One rough test of the various explanations that have been proposed is to see if they help us understand why the U.S. is the last major developed country without national health insurance. Several reasons for the lag can be suggested. First, there is a long tradition in the U.S. of distrust of government. This country was largely settled by immigrants who had had unfavorable experiences with governments in

Europe and who had learned to fear government rather than look to it for support and protection. Second, it is important to note the heterogeneity of our population compared to some of the more homogeneous populations of Europe. We are certainly not a single "people" the way, say, the Japanese are. Brian Abel-Smith has noted, for instance, that the U.S. poor were often Negroes or new immigrants with whose needs the older white settlers did not readily identify.[f]

The distrust of government and the heterogeneity of the population probably account for the much better developed non-governmental voluntary institutions in the U.S. Close observers of the American scene ever since de Toqueville have commented on the profusion of private non-profit organizations to deal with problems which in other countries might be considered the province of government. These organizations can be viewed as devices for internalizing the philanthropic externalities discussed earlier in this paper, but the organizations are frequently limited to individuals of similar ethnic background, religion, region, occupation, or other shared characteristic.

Another possible reason for the difference in attitudes between the U.S. and Europe is the greater equality of opportunity in this country. In the beginning this was based mostly on free or cheap land, and later on widespread public education. Moreover, the historic class barriers have been weaker here than in countries with a strong feudal heritage. To cite one obvious example, consider the family backgrounds of university faculties in Sweden and the U.S. Sweden is often hailed as the outstanding example of a democratic welfare state, but the faculty members at the leading universities generally come from upper-class backgrounds. By contrast, the faculties at Harvard, Chicago, Stanford, and other leading American universities include many men and women who were born in modest circumstances. With greater equality of opportunity goes a stronger conviction that the distribution of income is related to effort and ability. Those who succeed in the system have much less sense of noblesse oblige than do the upper classes in Europe, many of whom owe their position to the accident of birth. In the U.S., even those who have not succeeded or only partially succeeded seem more willing to acquiesce in the results.

Summing Up

The primary purpose of this inquiry has been to attempt to explain the popularity of national health insurance around the world. My answer at this point is that probably no single explanation will suffice. National health insurance means

---

[f] Abel-Smith, B. *supra* note 1.

different things to different people. It always has. Daniel Hirschfield, commenting on the campaign for national health insurance in the United States at the time of World War I, wrote:

> Some saw health insurance primarily as an educational and public health measure, while others argued that it was an economic device to precipitate a needed reorganization of medical practice. . . . Some saw it as a device to save money for all concerned, while others felt sure that it would increase expenditures significantly.[16]

Externalities, egalitarianism, the decline of the family and traditional religion, the need for national symbols — these all may play a part. In democratic countries with homogeneous populations, people seem to want to take care of one another through programs such as national health insurance, as members of the same family do, although not to the same degree. In autocratic countries with heterogeneous populations, national health insurance is often imposed from above, partly as a device for strengthening national unity. The relative importance of different factors undoubtedly varies from country to country and time to time, but the fact that national health insurance can be viewed as serving so many diverse interests and needs is probably the best answer to why Bismarck and Woodcock are not such strange bedfellows after all.

References

1. Abel-Smith, B. (1964). "Major Patterns of Financing and Organization of Medical Care in Countries Other than the United States." *Bulletin of the New York Academy of Medicine* **40**(7): 540-559.
2. Feldstein, M. S. (1973). "The Welfare Loss of Excess Health Insurance." *The Journal of Political Economy* **81**: 251.
3. Friedman, M. (1975). "Leonard Woodcock's Free Lunch." *Newsweek*.
4. Stigler, G. J. (1975). *The Citizen and the State: Essays on Regulation.*
5. Stigler, G. J. (1958). "The Economies of Scale." *The Journal of Law and Economics* **1**: 54-71.
6. Thurow, L. C. (1974). "Cash Versus In-Kind Transfer." *American Economic Review* **64**(2): 190-195
7. Pauly, M. V. (1971). *Medical Care at Public Expense: A Study in Applied Welfare Economics.* Praeger: New York.
8. Okun, A. M. (1975). *Equality and Efficiency: The Big Tradeoff.* Brookings Institution Press: Washington, D.C.
9. Townsend, P. (1974). "Inequality and the Health Service." *Lancet,* **1**: 1170–1190.
10. Jewkes, J. and Jewkes, S. (1963). *Value for Money in Medicine.* Blackwell: Hoboken, NJ.

11. Lindsay, C. M. "Medical Care and the Economics of Sharing." *Economica* **36**(144): 351-362.
12. Becker, G. S. and Tomes, N. (1976). "Child Endowments, and the Quantity and Quality of Children." *The Journal of Political Economy* **84**(2): S143-S162
13. Arrow, K. J. (1973). "Government Decision Making and the Preciousness of Life." *Ethics of Health Care* **33**: 45 (Papers of the *Conference on Health Care and Changing Values*, Institute of Medicine, Laurence R. Tancredi ed.)
14. Breton, A. (1974). *The Economic Theory of Representative Government*. Palgrave Macmillan: Basingstoke, UK.
15. Field, M. G. (1967). *Soviet Socialized Medicine*. The Free Press: New York.
16. Hirschfield, D. S. (1970). *The Lost Reform; The Campaign for Compulsory Health Insurance in the United States*. Harvard University Press: Cambridge, MA.

5.2

Public Support for National Health Insurance: The Roles of Attitudes and Beliefs

The U.S. is the only developed country without some form of national health insurance. Yet, public opinion polls have consistently reported solid majorities in favor of such a system. In this paper, we examine whether attitudes toward different roles of government and beliefs that may be related to those attitudes are consistent with widespread support for national health insurance. Our analysis is based on the premise that a system of national health insurance would require government redistribution and government intervention in health care markets. We find that people who have favorable attitudes toward government economic intervention are 27 percentage points more likely and those with favorable attitudes toward government economic intervention are 18 percentage points more likely to favor national health insurance than those with unfavorable attitudes. The most intense support for national health insurance, strongly favoring as opposed favoring it, is among people with favorable attitudes toward both roles of government. Consistent with research from other social programs, we find that the beliefs regarding racial minorities, as well as beliefs regarding individual control over life, limit support for national health insurance in the U.S. On the other hand, negative beliefs regarding businesses are an important source of support for national health insurance. We conclude that significant changes in either attitudes and beliefs or their relationship with support for national health insurance are probably necessary to create a strong majority in support of such legislation.

Keywords: Public opinion; universal coverage; health care reform; redistribution.

Originally published in *Forum for Health Economics and Policy*, 10(1): Article 4, 2007. Copyright by The Berkeley Electronic Press. Written with M. Kate Bundorf.

Introduction

Numerous attempts were made during the 20th century to enact a system of universal health insurance in the U.S. Theodore Roosevelt's 1912 presidential campaign platform included a system of compulsory health insurance. In the 1940s, Harry Truman advocated a comprehensive health insurance program modeled after Social Security. While the enactment of the Medicare and Medicaid programs in the 1960s dramatically expanded publicly financed insurance, the legislation fell far short of providing universal coverage. Both the Nixon administration in the 1970s and the Clinton administration in 1990s proposed major initiatives to expand health insurance coverage, primarily by mandating that employers provide coverage for workers. None of these attempts were successful, leaving the U.S. as the only developed country without a system of national health insurance. Many Americans — over 46 million in 2005 — are uninsured[7]

Public opinion polls over the last 20 years have consistently found that a solid majority of Americans favor enacting some form of national health insurance.[4,5] Why does the U.S. lack a system of national health insurance despite widespread public support for it? Two types of explanations exist for this apparent paradox. First, the barriers to implementing a system of national health insurance that exist in the U.S. may ultimately override the preferences of the American public. Powerful interest groups historically have opposed national health insurance.[20,25] The fragmented structure of U.S. political institutions, with the separation of powers among the three branches of government, may shift power away from the government and toward these special interests.[22] Others point to the absence of a significant socialist party that keeps the idea of national health insurance on the policy agenda under the U.S. two-party system.[15] Finally, the failure to enact national health insurance in the U.S. may be due not to fundamental differences between the U.S. and other countries in interests or institutions, but to the unique sequence of historical events that led to the formation of the current system.[11,16,26]

An alternative explanation is that favorable public opinion does not necessarily reflect strong public support for national health insurance. Arguments of "American exceptionalism" attribute the lack of national health insurance to the individualistic and anti-government attitudes of the American public.[12] Although Americans may support universal coverage, they may oppose the extent of government intervention that it would require. Other research points to a lack of consensus among supporters in their preferred policy, reducing the likelihood of success of any single proposal.[5] Finally, the intensity of the preferences of those who oppose national health insurance may exceed that of those who favor it. As stated by Machiavelli, "The reformer has enemies in all those who profit from the old order and only lukewarm defenders in all those who profit from the new order," an observation which has a psychological basis in prospect theory which proposes that the aversion to a loss is greater than the desire of a gain of the same magnitude.[13]

The objective of this paper is to determine whether attitudes among the American public toward different roles of government are related to support for national health insurance. Our analysis is based on the premise that a system of national health insurance would require a greater role of government in both redistributing resources and intervening in health care markets. Because the uninsured are heterogeneous, including both those who cannot afford health insurance and those who can afford coverage but choose not to purchase it,[6] a system of national health insurance would require subsides for low income families who are unable to purchase coverage as well as compulsion for higher income families who are unwilling to acquire health insurance. Subsidies require redistribution from those with higher incomes to those with lower incomes. Compulsion requires government intervention in health care markets. A system which redistributed from the healthy to the sick would also likely require intervention on the part of the government in health care markets. Of course, the extent and exact form of redistribution generated by a system of national health insurance would depend in large part on the design of the system.

In our analysis, we examine whether attitudes toward government redistribution and government economic intervention are related to support for national health insurance. We hypothesize that the importance of attitudes toward both roles of government is a feature that distinguishes national health insurance from other social policies. This hypothesis is consistent with evidence that the attitudes and perceptions that motivate support for federal action in health care differ from those that motivate support for more overtly redistributive policies.[24]

We also examine how particular beliefs are related to support for national health insurance. A growing body of evidence indicates that racial and ethnic heterogeneity, both within the U.S. and across countries, is associated with lower levels of income redistribution and public spending.[1,3,14,17,19] Individual views regarding the causes of poverty are also associated with support for redistributive social programs.[2,3,8] Because a system of national health insurance would likely require significant redistribution, we examine the relationship between support for national health insurance and beliefs regarding individual control over life as well as beliefs regarding racial minorities and immigrants.

We also examine the relationship between support for national health insurance and beliefs regarding the importance of religion. Religious beliefs may affect support for national health insurance through multiple mechanisms. Religion may predispose one toward being more altruistic and, thus, to have a more favorable attitude toward redistribution. However, the dominant American religious tradition places a strong emphasis on individual responsibility and a lack of reliance on government, suggesting that religious beliefs may be negatively associated with support for national health insurance. Others have also argued that, because religious involvement functions as insurance against the monetary and psychic costs of adverse life events, it serves as a substitute for social spending.[23] In this case, religious affiliation may be negatively correlated with support for national health insurance.

Finally, we examine a set of beliefs that may influence attitudes toward government economic intervention. In particular, we propose that people with negative beliefs regarding businesses may have more favorable attitudes toward government economic intervention as a mechanism to counteract negative effects of corporations. Similarly, those who have more favorable beliefs regarding politicians may have more confidence in government-run programs.

Data

The primary data source for our analysis is the December 2004 Political Typology Survey conducted by The Pew Research Center for the People and the Press. The survey includes questions about a variety of beliefs and attitudes as well as positions on policies and political issues. The data are based on telephone interviews of a randomly selected sample of 2,000 adults living in the continental U.S. conducted between December 1 and 16, 2004 (Princeton 2004). The contact rate (the proportion of working numbers where a request for interview was made) was 72%, the cooperation rate (the proportion of contacted numbers where consent for an interview was initially obtained) was 45%, and the completion rate (the proportion of initially cooperating and eligible interviews that were completed) was 94%. The overall response rate was 31% (Princeton 2004). We weight our estimates to correct for survey non-response using weights which balance the interviewed sample to match national estimates of the distribution of the population based on sex, age, education, race, Hispanic origin, and region (U.S. Census definitions) as well as the distribution of the population across Republican and Democratic counties.

While the survey was also conducted in 1994 and 1999, we focus on 2004 primarily because, unlike earlier years, it includes a question about support for national health insurance. We use the earlier surveys to examine time trends in particular attitudes and beliefs that were highly correlated with support for national health insurance in 2004.

Measure of support for national health insurance

The measure of support for national health insurance is based on a question, "Do you strongly favor, favor, oppose, or strongly oppose the U.S. government guaranteeing health insurance for all citizens, even if it means raising taxes?" In most analyses, we consider those who indicated they either strongly favor or favor the policy as favoring national health insurance. In some analyses, however, we differentiate between those who strongly favor and those who favor to measure the intensity of support.

Measures of attitudes toward different roles of government

Measures of attitudes toward government economic intervention and government redistribution are based on a series of questions in which respondents considered two statements representing opposing views on a particular issue and indicated which statement best describes their own views. We identified two questions corresponding to each attitude. For attitudes toward government redistribution, one question asked respondents to choose between the statements "Poor people have hard lives because government benefits don't go far enough to help them live decently" and "Poor people today have it easy because they can get government benefits without doing anything in return". The other asked them to choose between the statements "The government should do more to help needy Americans, even if it means going deeper into debt" and "The government today can't afford to do much more to help the needy". These questions focus on redistribution based on income. Unfortunately, the survey does not contain questions related to redistribution based on health status.

For attitudes toward government economic intervention, one question asked respondents to choose between the statements "Government often does a better job than people give it credit for" and "Government is almost always wasteful and inefficient." The other asked them to choose between "Government regulation of business is necessary to protect the public interest" and "Government regulation of business usually does more harm than good." Appendix Table 1 includes the full text and the distribution of responses for each question.

Measures of beliefs

From questions in which respondents read pairs of statements and indicated which best describes their own view, we developed measures of five beliefs: (1) businesses are too powerful/too profitable; (2) politicians are out of touch with voters/don't care about people like me; (3) an individual is in control of his or her life; (4) racial discrimination is not a barrier to blacks/immigrants are a burden on society; and (5) religion is important. We identified two pairs of statements related to each belief. The full text and the distribution of responses for each question are presented in Appendix Table 2.

Prevalence of Support for National Health Insurance, Attitudes toward the Roles of Government, and Beliefs

Consistent with other public opinion polls, a solid majority of survey respondents (68%) indicated they either favored or strongly favored national health insurance even if it meant raising taxes (Table 1).

People were relatively evenly divided in their attitudes toward government redistribution and government economic intervention (Table 1). Over half of respondents indicated favorable attitudes toward government redistribution on each measure. Fifty-five percent indicated that government benefits do not go far enough to help poor people, and 60% indicated that the government should do more to help needy Americans. Close to half of respondents indicated favorable attitudes toward government economic intervention on each measure. Forty-seven percent indicated that government often does a better job than people give it credit for, and 53% indicated that government regulation of business is necessary to protect the public interest.

People varied in the five beliefs that we examined (Table 2). Negative beliefs regarding politicians and businesses were prevalent. Seventy percent of respondents indicated that they believe that elected officials lose touch with people quickly, and 65% indicated that elected officials do not care what people like them think. Eighty-one percent of respondents indicated that they believe that too much power is concentrated in the hands of a few large companies, and 57% indicated that they believe that businesses are too profitable.

A belief in individual control over life was also widely held among survey respondents. Eighty-one percent of survey respondents indicated that they believe that everyone has it in their own power to succeed, and 69% of respondents indicated that they believe that most people can get ahead if they work hard. Nearly two-thirds of respondents indicated that they believe that the failure of

Table 1. Prevalence of Support for Policies and Attitudes toward Government.

	N	Proportion
Policies		
Favor the U.S. government guaranteeing health insurance for all citizens, even it it means raising taxes	1,902	0.68
Favor making it more difficult for a woman to get an abortion	1,824	0.40
Favor allowing gays and lesbians to marry legally	1,869	0.34
Favor an increase in the minimum wage from $5.15 hour to $6.45 an hour	1,944	0.88
Favor limiting the amount that patients can be awarded in medical malpractice lawsuits	1,877	0.68
Attitudes toward Government Redistribution		
Poor people have hard lives because government benefits don't go far enough	1,873	0.55
The government should do more to help needy Americans	1,882	0.60
Attitudes toward Government Economic Intervention		
Government often does a better job than people give it credit for	1,914	0.47
Government regulation of business is necessary to protect the public interest	1,866	0.53

Source: December 2004 Pew Political Typology Survey conducted by The Pew Research Center. Estimates are weighted to be nationally representative.

Table 2. Prevalence of Beliefs.

	N	Proportion
Beliefs regarding politicians		
Elected officials in Washington lose touch with the people pretty quickly	1,887	0.70
Most elected officials don't care what people like me think	1,934	0.65
Beliefs regarding businesses		
Too much power is concentrated in the hands of a few large companies	1,878	0.81
Business corporations make too much profit	1,890	0.57
Beliefs regarding individual control over life		
Everyone has it in their own power to succeed	1,969	0.81
Most people who want to get ahead can make it if they're willing to work hard	1,945	0.69
Beliefs regarding racial minorities and immigrants		
Blacks who can't get ahead in this country are mostly responsible for their own condition	1,880	0.64
Immigrants today are a burden on our country because they take our jobs, housing, or health care	1,872	0.46
Beliefs regarding religion		
Religion is a very important part of my life	1,981	0.75
It is necessary to believe in God in order to be moral and have good values	1,959	0.51

Source: December 2004 Pew Political Typology Survey conducted by The Pew Research Center. Estimates are weighted to be nationally representative.

blacks to get ahead was their own responsibility rather than the result of racial discrimination. Forty-six percent of respondents indicated that they believe that immigrants are a burden on our country. Finally, a belief in the importance of religion was widespread; 75% of respondents indicated that religion was an important part of their lives. Fifty-one percent indicated they believe that it is necessary to believe in God in order to be moral and have good values.

Relationship between Support for National Health Insurance and Attitudes Toward the Different Roles of Government

Support for national health insurance is highly correlated with attitudes toward both government redistribution and government economic intervention. Figures 1 and 2 present the proportion favoring national health insurance, distinguishing between those who strongly favor and those who favor the policy, for each measure of attitudes toward the different roles of government.

People with favorable attitudes toward government redistribution are more likely to support national health insurance than those with less favorable attitudes. Fifty-nine percent of those who believe that "poor people have it easy today because they can get government benefits without doing anything in return" favor national health insurance compared to 76% of those who believe "poor people have hard lives because government benefits do not go far enough..." ($p < = 0.01$). Fifty-eight percent of those who believe that "the government today can't afford to do much more to help the needy" favor national health insurance compared to 75% of those who believe that "the government should do more to help needy Americans, even if it means going deeper into debt" ($p < = 0.01$). In addition, the difference in support between those with unfavorable land favorable attitudes toward government redistribution is driven by differences in the extent to which people strongly favor national health insurance (as opposed to favor it).

The results are similar for the variables measuring attitudes toward government economic intervention. Those with more favorable attitudes toward government economic intervention based on either measure are more likely to favor national health insurance than those with unfavorable attitudes. The difference in the proportion who support national health insurance is greater for the variable measuring attitudes toward government regulation (difference = 0.17, $p <= 0.01$) than for the variable measuring attitudes toward the efficiency of government (difference = 0.07, $p <= 0.05$). Attitudes toward government

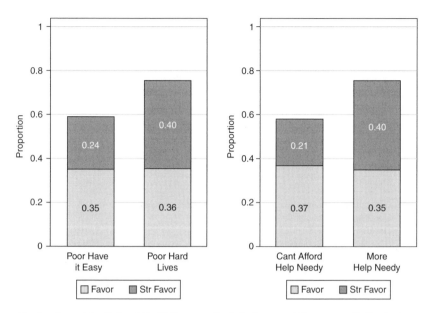

Fig. 1. Support for National Health Insurance by Attitudes toward Government Redistribution.

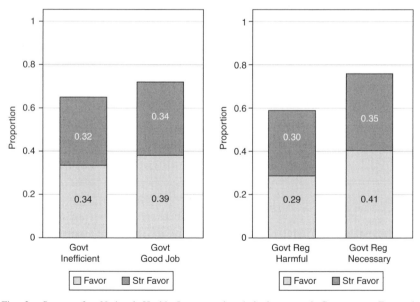

Fig. 2. Support for National Health Insurance by Attitudes toward Government Economic Intervention.

redistribution have a stronger relationship with intensity of support for national health insurance than attitudes toward government economic intervention.

We next examine the extent to which the different attitudes are independently associated with support for national health insurance and whether the relationships are correlated with other demographic and socioeconomic characteristics. Table 3 presents summary statistics for control variables that we include in multivariate models, including income, education, age, sex, race, and ethnicity. In Table 4,

Table 3.   Study Sample.

Variable[a]	N	Mean
Government Economic Intervention I — Favorable Attitudes	1,808	0.31
Government Economic Intervention — Mixed	1,808	0.39
Government Redistribution — Favorable Attitudes	1,793	0.41
Government Redistribution — Mixed	1,793	0.35
Blacks Responsible for Own Condition AND Immigrants a burden	1,787	0.32
Blacks Responsible for Own Condition OR Immigrants a burden	1,787	0.51
Individual has Control over Life	1,923	0.61
Individual has Control over Life — Mixed	1,923	0.31
Businesses — Positive Beliefs	1,802	0.13
Businesses — Mixed Beliefs	1,802	0.34
Politicians — Positive Beliefs	1,844	0.15
Politicians — Mixed Beliefs	1,844	0.32
Belief in the Importance of Religion	1,943	0.46
Belief in the Importance of Religion — Mixed	1,943	0.36
Male	2,000	0.48
Income < $30,000	2,000	0.31
Income >= $30,000 & < $75,000	2,000	0.36
Income >= $75,000	2,000	0.21
Income — Don't Know/Missing	2,000	0.12
Age 18–25	2,000	0.15
Age 26–40	2,000	0.28
Age 41–64	2,000	0.40
Age 65 and over	2,000	0.16
Age — Don't Know	2,000	0.02
Education; <= High School Graduate	2,000	0.44
Education: > High School Graduate to Bachelor's Degree	2,000	0.45
Education: > Bachelor's Degree	2,000	0.11
Black	2,000	0.12
Race Unknown	2,000	0.02
Hispanic	2,000	0.10
Ethnicity Unknown	2,000	0.01

[a]Mixed indicates that the respondent indicated a favorable attitude on one question regarding the attitude and an unfavorable attitude on the other.
Source: December 2004 Pew Political Typology Survey conducted by the Pew Research Center. Estimates are weighted to be nationally representative.

Table 4. The Relationship between Support for National Health Insurance and Attitudes toward Government.

	(1)	(2)	(3)	(4)	(5)
	Redistribution	Economic Intervention	Both Attitudes	Demographics	Attitudes and Demographics
Redistribution — Favor	0.270 [0.031]**		0.268 [0.031]**		0.274 [0.032]**
Redistribution — Mixed[a]	0.190 [0.032]**		0.197 [0.033]**		0.204 [0.033]**
Economic Intervention — Favor		0.204 [0.030]**	0.184 [0.031]**		0.182 [0.031]**
Economic Intervention — Mixed[a]		0.070 [0.030]*	0.053 [0.031]		0.048 [0.031]
Male				−0.044 [0.023]	−0.017 [0.024]
Age 18–25				−0.021 [0.039]	−0.046 [0.039]
Age 26–40				−0.010 [0.028]	−0.038 [0.030]
Age 65 plus				−0.043 [0.034]	−0.027 [0.036]
Hispanic				−0.009 [0.046]	−0.020 [0.047]
Hispanic — Unknown				−0.045 [0.197]	−0.158 [0.204]
Black				0.042 [0.039]	−0.012 [0.043]
Race-Unknown				0.090 [0.119]	0.114 [0.134]
Income <$30,000				0.037 [0.030]	0.021 [0.031]
Income> = $75,000				−0.051 [0.031]	−0.044 [0.031]
Income — Don't Know				−0.009 [0.040]	0.004 [0.044]
Education: < = High school Grad.				−0.047 [0.026]	−0.069 [0.028]*
Education:> Bachelor's Degree				0.076 [0.032]*	0.019 [0.032]
Constant	0.507 [0.025]**	0.595 [0.023]**	0.429 [0.030]**	0.727 [0.027]**	0.491 [0.040]**
Observations	1725	1745	1618	1902	1618
R-squared	0.050	0.030	0.080	0.010	0.090

Standard errors in brackets.

*significant at 5%;

**significant at 1%.

[a]Mixed indicates that the respondent indicated a favorable attitude on one question regarding the attitude and an unfavorable attitude on the other.

Note: Estimates are weighted to be nationally representative.

we present results from models of the relationship between favoring national health insurance and attitudes toward government redistribution and government economic intervention. The dependent variable is a binary indicator of whether the respondent favors national health insurance. For each attitude, we combined responses from the two sets of statements into a single variable by coding those indicating a favorable attitude in both questions as having a favorable attitude, those indicating an unfavorable attitude in both questions as having an unfavorable attitude, and those indicating a favorable attitude in one set of statements and an unfavorable attitude in the other as mixed.

We focus on the comparison between people indicating a favorable and those indicating an unfavorable attitude. Specifying the variables in this way allows us both to estimate a more parsimonious model by reducing the number of measures and to create a less noisy measure of each attitude. For each attitude, we treated the variable as missing if the response was missing for either question pair. We used linear probability rather than maximum likelihood logit or probit models to facilitate the interpretation of the magnitude of the effects. The results of nonlinear models do not differ substantively from those reported here.

People with favorable attitudes toward government redistribution are 27 percentage points more likely ($p < = 0.001$) to favor national health insurance than those with unfavorable attitudes (Table 4 — Model 1). Similarly, people with favorable attitudes toward government economic intervention are 20 percentage points more likely ($p < = 0.001$) to favor national health insurance (Table 4 — Model 2). The two attitudes'are independently associated with favoring national health insurance. When we include both in the model (Table 4 — Model 3), neither the magnitude of the effect of either nor its statistical significance changes much.

Demographic and socioeconomic characteristics, in contrast, are not highly correlated with one's support for national health insurance. In Model 4 (Table 4), the coefficients on the variables measuring demographic and socioeconomic characteristics are small, particularly when compared to those of the attitude variables, and generally are not statistically significant. The only variable that has a statistically significant effect is the indicator of a relatively high level of education. Those with formal schooling exceeding a bachelor's degree are 7 percentage points more likely to favor national health insurance than those with either some college or a bachelor's degree ($p < = 0.05$).

The estimates of the relationship between attitudes toward government redistribution and government economic intervention are not sensitive to controlling for demographic characteristics. The coefficients on the variables

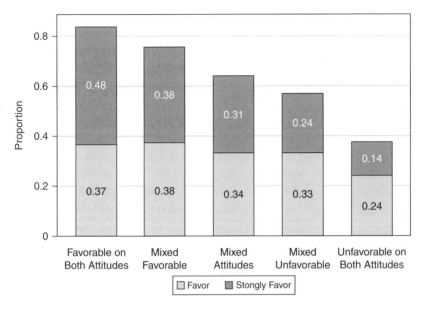

Fig. 3.   Support for National Health Insurance by Attitudes toward Both Roles of Government.

measuring attitudes and their statistical significance are virtually identical in the model including the demographic controls (Table 4 — Model 5) and the model without these controls (Table 4 — Model 3).

The level and the intensity of respondents' support for national health insurance are correlated with the extent to which they have favorable attitudes toward both government redistribution and government economic intervention (Figure 3). We categorized respondents into five groups based on the extent to which they had favorable attitudes toward both roles of government. The two extreme groups are those who had favorable attitudes toward both roles of government and those who had unfavorable attitudes toward both. The middle category (Mixed Attitudes) includes people who indicated either that they were mixed on both attitudes or that they had a favorable attitude toward one role of government and an unfavorable attitude toward the other. People who indicated a favorable attitude toward one role of government and a mixed attitude on the other were categorized as "mixed favorable." Those with an unfavorable attitude toward one and a mixed attitude toward the other were categorized as "mixed unfavorable." To compare the intensity of support across categories, we distinguished those strongly favoring from those favoring national health insurance.

Among those with a favorable attitude toward both government redistribution and government economic intervention, 85% support national health insurance. In contrast, among those with an unfavorable attitude toward both, 38% support national health insurance. Differences in the distribution of responses are statistically significant ($p < = 0.001$). The proportion favoring national health insurance rises continuously from those who have unfavorable attitudes toward both roles of government to those who have favorable attitudes toward both, with the increase driven primarily by the percentage of respondents within each category reporting that they strongly favor national health insurance. This percentage increases from 14% among those who have unfavorable attitudes toward both government redistribution and government economic intervention to 48% among those have favorable attitudes toward both ($p < = 0.001$). In contrast, the proportion reporting they favor national health insurance, but not strongly, does not differ significantly across the categories.

Relationship Between Support for National Health Insurance and Beliefs

Some, but not all, of the beliefs that we examined are correlated with one's position on national health insurance (Table 5). We use an approach similar to that which we used to examine the relationship between support for national health insurance and attitudes toward the different roles of government to examine this correlation. From questions in which respondents were presented with pairs of statements and asked which best describes their own view, we identified two questions related to each belief and combined the responses to the two questions into a single categorical variable based on whether the respondent indicated a similar belief in both pairs. The survey questions we used to develop these variables are presented in Appendix Table 2. We then estimated models of the relationship between support for national health insurance and these measures of beliefs using ordinary least squares. Once again, the results are not substantively different if we estimate nonlinear models. We present in Table 5 only the comparison between those who indicate having the belief on both questions and those who indicate not having the belief on both questions. In other words, the table leaves out the comparison between those who have "mixed beliefs" although this category is included in the empirical models.

The belief most strongly correlated with favoring national health insurance is that businesses are too powerful and too profitable. In Table 5, Column 1, we present the results of the model including all the different beliefs, but no control variables. Individuals with this belief are 35 percentage points more likely to

Table 5.   The Relationship between Support for National Health Insurance and Beliefs.

	(1) All beliefs	(2) All Beliefs and control variables
Racial Discrimination not a Problem for	−0.130	−0.117
Blacks/Immigrant are a Burden on the Economy	[0.038]**	[0.039]**
Individual has Control over Life	−0.107	−0.104
	[0.039]**	[0.039]**
Religion is Important	−0.045	−0.038
	[0.033]	[0.035]
Politicians Care/Don't Lose Touch	0.035	0.029
	[0.038]	[0.038]
Businesses are Too Powerful/Profitable	0.352	0.353
	[0.041]**	[0.042]**
Constant	0.620	0.634
	[0.063]**	[0.072]**
Observations	1493	1493
R-Squared	0.09	0.1

Standard errors in brackets.
*Significant at 5%;
**Significant at 1%.
Note: Models include a mixed cateogry for each belief. All belief comparisons are the effect relative to not holding that belief. Column 2 includes controls for sex, age, race, ethnicity, income, and education. Estimates are weighted to be nationally representative.

favor national health insurance than those who do not have this belief. Beliefs regarding individual control over life and racial minorities and immigrants are also correlated with one's position on national health insurance. Those who believe an individual is in control of his or her life are 11 percentage points less likely to favor national health insurance than those without this belief ($p <= 0.01$). Those who indicate both that racial discrimination is not a barrier to blacks and that immigrants are a burden on society are 13 percentage points less likely to favor national health insurance ($p <= 0.01$). In contrast, beliefs regarding politicians and the importance of religion are not strongly associated with one's position on national health insurance. Once again, controlling for demographic characteristics (Table 5 — Column 2) has little effect on these results.

In Figures 4–6, we focus on those beliefs that are highly correlated with support for national health insurance in the multivariate models and examine the intensity of support for national health insurance for each component of the combined measures of beliefs. For beliefs regarding both business and individual control over life, each of the underlying variables exhibits a similar relationship with support for national health insurance ($p <= 0.01$) (Figures 4 and 5). In the

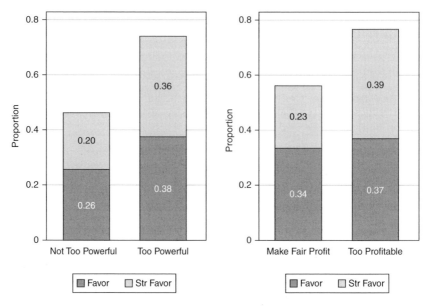

Fig. 4.   Support for National Health Insurance by Beliefs regarding Businesses.

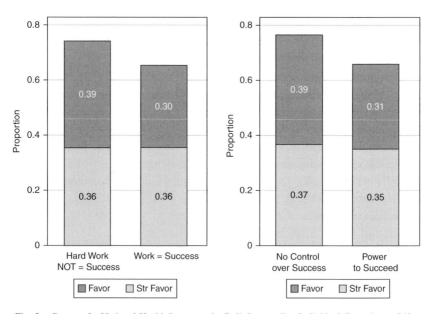

Fig. 5.   Support for National Health Insurance by Beliefs regarding Individual Control over Life.

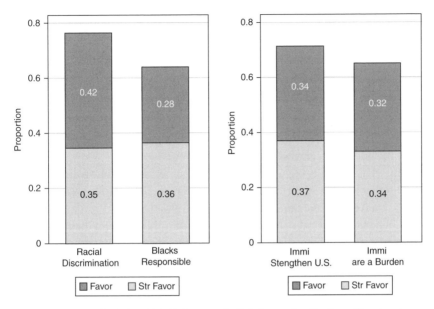

Fig. 6.   Support for National Health Insurance by Beliefs regarding Blacks and Immigrants.

case of beliefs regarding individual control over life, the difference between those who do and do not hold this belief in support for national health insurance is driven primarily by differences in the extent to which they strongly favor national health insurance (Figure 5). In other words, people who believe that an individual has control over his or her life exhibit less intense support for national health insurance than those who do not. Figure 6 suggests that beliefs regarding racial minorities are more strongly associated with one's position on national health insurance than beliefs regarding immigrants. In fact, the relationship between beliefs regarding immigrants and support for national health insurance is not statistically significant at conventional levels in the unadjusted model ($p <= 0.12$). In contrast, people who believe that racial discrimination prevents blacks from succeeding are not only more likely to favor national health insurance, but are more likely to strongly favor it ($p <= 0.01$).

Historical Trends in Attitudes and Beliefs that are Related to Support for National Health Insurance

Between 1994 and 2004, attitudes toward the different roles of government changed in ways that are more favorable for support for a system of national health insurance (Table 5). In 2004, people were more favorably disposed toward both government economic intervention and government redistribution than they were in 1994. The proportion of the population indicating that "government is almost always wasteful and inefficient" declined from 66% in 1994 to 45% in 2004. The proportion indicating that "government regulation of business is necessary to protect the public interest" increased from 41% in 1994 to 49% in 2004. While the proportion indicating that "poor people have it easy because they can get government benefits without doing anything in return" did not exhibit a consistent time trend, the proportion indicating that "the government should do more to help needy Americans..." increased from 48% to 57%.

The data provide less evidence of changes in underlying beliefs that are correlated with support for national health insurance. Beliefs regarding business stayed relatively constant throughout the period as did beliefs regarding the extent of individual control over life. However, trends in beliefs regarding blacks and immigrants are less favorable for the prospects for national health insurance. The proportion of the population indicating that they believe that "blacks who can't get ahead in this country are mostly responsible for their own condition", a belief that is negatively correlated with support for national health insurance, increased from 54% in 1994 to 60% in 2004. While the proportion of the population indicating they believe that "immigrants are a burden..." declined substantially, this belief is not highly correlated with support for national health insurance.

Relationship between Support for Other Types of Policies and Attitudes toward Government

Our analysis is based on the premise that a system of national health insurance would require a greater role for the government both in redistribution and in intervening in health care markets, and we find that attitudes toward these different roles of government are highly correlated with support for national health insurance among the American public. In this section, we examine whether these correlations are unique to national health insurance. Our hypothesis is that attitudes toward both roles of government are unlikely to be correlated with support for other types of policies that do not require both extensive redistribution and intervention in markets by the government. The survey included questions on whether the individual favors four other policies: 1) making it more difficult to get an abortion, 2) allowing gays and lesbians to marry, 3) increasing the minimum wage, and 4) limiting medical malpractice awards. The prevalence of support for these policies ranged from 34% for allowing gays and lesbians to marry legally to 88% for increasing the minimum wage (Table 1).

Table 6.   Trends in Attitudes and Beliefs.

Percent either agreeing or strongly agreeing with each statement	2004	1999	1994
Government is almost always wasteful and inefficient	45	51	66
Government regulation of business is necessary to protect the public interest	49	48	41
Poor people today have it easy because they can get government benefits without doing anything in return	52	45	53
The government should do more to help needy Americans, even if it means going deeper into debt	57	57	48
Too much power is concentrated in the hands of a few large companies	77	77	76
Business corporations make too much profit	54	52	52
Everyone has it in their own power to succeed	78	80	79
Most people who want to get ahead can make it if they're willing to work hard	68	74	68
Blacks who can't get ahead in this country are mostly responsible for their own condition	60	59	54
Immigrants today are a burden on our country because they take our jobs, housing and healthcare	44	44	63

Source: Estimates are collected from 3 public reports available from the Pew Research Center for the People and the Press including "The People, The Press, & Politics: The New Political Landscape" (1994), "Retro-Politics The Political Typology: Version 3.0" (1999), and "Beyond Red vs. Blue (2005). Discrepancies in estimates from 2004 between Tables 5 and 1 are due to differences in the treatment of missing data.

Table 7.   The Relationship Between Other Policies and Attitudes Toward Government.

Attitude	(1) Favor making it more difficult to get an abortion	(2) Favor allowing gays and lesbians to marry	(3) Favor an increase in the minimum wage	(4) Favor limiting medical malpractice awards
Redistribution — Favor	−0.196 [0.034]**	0.198 [0.032]**	0.194 [0.023]**	−0.189 [0.031]**
Redistribution — Mixed	−0.12 [0.035]**	0.081 [0.032]**	0.146 [0.025]**	−0.089 [0.030]**
Economic Intervention — Favor	0.006 [0.034]	0.027 [0.032]	0.063 [0.022]**	0.055 [0.033]
Economic Intervention — Mixed	0.019 [0.032]	0.014 [0.030]	0.037 [0.020]	0.045 [0.031]
Observations	1568	1591	1641	1609
R-squared	0.05	0.12	0.09	0.06

Standard errors in brackets.
*Significant at 5%;
**Significant at 1%.
Note: Models include controls for sex, age, race, ethnicity, income, and education. Estimates are weighted to be nationally representative.

Attitudes toward government redistribution are highly correlated with support for each policy (Table 7). People who have favorable attitudes toward government redistribution are less likely to favor making it more difficult to get an abortion, are more likely to favor legalizing gay and lesbian marriage, are more likely to favor increasing the minimum wage, and are less likely to favor limiting medical malpractice awards than those with unfavorable attitudes. Attitudes toward government economic intervention, in contrast, are correlated only with support for increasing the minimum wage. People who have favorable attitudes toward government economic intervention are more likely to favor the minimum wage than those who have unfavorable attitudes. The magnitude of the effect however, is much smaller for support for the minimum wage (0.06) than for support for national health insurance (0.18).

Discussion

A system of national health insurance will require both government intervention in health care markets and government redistribution of resources across individuals of differing socioeconomic and health status. In this study, we find that people with favorable attitudes toward government redistribution and government economic intervention are significantly more likely to favor national health insurance than those with unfavorable attitudes toward these roles of government. These attitudes are more closely associated with one's position on national health insurance than are demographic and socioeconomic characteristics. In multivariate models, characteristics such as age, gender, income, race, and ethnicity are not strongly associated with whether one favors national health insurance. Only education is associated with favoring national health insurance, with those with relatively high levels of formal education more likely to favor it. Yet, the magnitude of the effect for education is relatively small, particularly compared to those of attitudes toward the different roles of government. This finding is consistent with research from the 1980s documenting that individual characteristics such as race, income, education, and age, which are highly correlated with support for other types of policies, are less strongly associated with popular support for government involvement in health care.[24]

We also find that those who have favorable attitudes toward both roles of government indicate the strongest support for national health insurance. These individuals are the most likely to "strongly favor" rather than "favor" national health insurance. We interpret this as evidence of limitations of the intensity of support for national health insurance among many Americans, and this interpretation is consistent with research demonstrating that the proportion favoring national health insurance declines substantially when individuals are told that extending coverage will require substantial increases in taxes.[5]

Yet, our findings indicate that these attitudes toward the different roles of government are not highly correlated. Each attitude has an independent effect of support for national health insurance in the multivariate model. This implies that the relatively high level of overall support for national health insurance may be limited by the extent to which people have favorable attitudes toward both roles of government.

Finally, our results suggest that the strong association between attitudes toward both roles of government is somewhat unique to support for national health insurance. While attitudes toward government redistribution are highly correlated with one's position on a range of policies, attitudes toward government economic intervention were correlated only with support for an increase in the minimum wage. In addition, the magnitude of the effect of attitudes toward government economic intervention was small in the case of support for increasing the minimum wage (0.06) compared to support for national health insurance (0.18). This finding is consistent with earlier research indicating that the reasons that people support federal involvement in health care differ from the reasons they support other types of policies, particularly those that are primarily redistributive.[24]

Support for national health insurance is also strongly associated with certain beliefs. The belief most strongly associated with favoring national health insurance was that businesses are too powerful and too profitable. While our study provides no direct evidence on why this is the case, the institutional features of the U.S. system provide two potential mechanisms. First, employer-sponsored health insurance is the predominant form of coverage in the U.S. Second, most health insurance, particularly for the under 65 population is provided by private insurers. Thus, support for national health insurance in response to negative beliefs regarding businesses may be related to the role of businesses in either providing health insurance to workers or selling insurance products in the marketplace.

Interestingly, while similar proportions of survey respondents expressed negative beliefs regarding business and politicians, beliefs regarding businesses were much more highly correlated with favoring national health insurance than those regarding politicians. This suggests that negative views regarding the private sector are a stronger motivation for favoring national health insurance than positive views regarding politicians.

The belief that an individual has control over his or her life was widely held among survey respondents and strongly associated with a lower likelihood of supporting national health insurance, consistent with the individualistic attitudes of Americans as an explanation for the lack of national health insurance. People who believe that racial discrimination does not play an important role in the progress of blacks are less likely to favor national health insurance. The importance of beliefs about individual control and about racial minorities in this study is consistent with explanations offered by Alesina and Glaeser about why European countries do more to reduce poverty than does the United States.[3] Heterogeneity of the population and distrust of government as barriers to national health insurance in the United States have also been stressed by Fuchs (1976, 1991).

Somewhat surprisingly, we found no evidence that a belief that religion is important is associated with favoring national health insurance. While our findings provide no direct evidence on why this is the case, religion in our study is not precisely identified. Probably those who believe that religion is important include some individuals who are strongly opposed to government interventions in the economy and some who strongly support public funding of social programs. The fact that our measure is highly correlated with support for policies that are much more obviously associated with religious beliefs provides support that the variable is indeed capturing this belief. Our results may differ from those of Scheve and Stasavage (2006) either because we focus on health insurance, rather than social insurance more broadly or because we use a different measure of religious beliefs than they do.

We do not doubt that the opposition of special interest groups and the peculiarities of American political institutions pose obstacles to the enactment of national health insurance, but we conclude that significant changes in either attitudes and beliefs or their relationship to support for national health insurance are probably necessary to create a strong majority in support of such legislation. Our analysis provides mixed evidence on the extent to which attitudes and beliefs have changed in ways that are favorable for support for national health insurance since 1994, the last major attempt to enact such a plan. On one hand, attitudes toward government economic intervention, and to a lesser extent, government redistribution, have become more favorable. On the other hand, we found little change between 1994 and 2004 in the prevalence of beliefs that are highly correlated with support for national health insurance.

We believe that such changes in attitudes and beliefs are possible. The same American public that voted for conservative, business-oriented governments in the 1920s embraced sweeping major shifts in economic and social policy in the 1930s. The civil rights legislation in the 1960s provides another example of major social change. We suspect, however, that the types of changes that are necessary to create strong support for a system of national health insurance are likely to be caused by significant external events. Different types of events, however, may facilitate a system of national health insurance through different mechanisms. Some events may fundamentally change people's attitudes toward the different roles government. For example, a terrorist event, such as 9–11, may change people's attitudes toward government intervention in markets, strengthening support for national health insurance. Other events, in contrast, may weaken the link between attitudes toward government intervention and support for national health insurance. For example, a public health crisis may generate greater support for government intervention in health care markets, even among people with unfavorable attitudes toward government intervention more generally. In summary, we think that national health insurance will come to the United States some day, but probably only in the wake of major political, economic, or social trauma, or in response to a public health crisis, continued erosion of employment-based insurance, or financial melt-down of Medicare.

Appendix Table 1. Summary of Statements used in Constructing Variables on Attitudes toward Government Economic Intervention and Government Redistribution.

Attitude toward Government Economic Intervention		Proportion
Statement Pair #1		
Unfavorable Attitude	1) Government is almost always wasteful and inefficient OR...	0.45
Favorable Attitude	2) Government often does a better job than people give it credit for	0.50
Missing		0.05
Statement Pair #2		
Favorable Attitude	1) Government regulation of business is necessary to protect the public interest OR...	0.49
Unfavorable Attitude	2) Government regulation of business usually does more harm than good	0.44
Missing		0.07
Attitude toward Government Redistribution		
Statement Pair #1		
Unfavorable Attitude	1) Poor people today have it easy because they can get government benefits without doing anything in return OR...	0.52
Favorable Attitude	2) Poor people have hard lives because government benefits don't go far enough to help them live decently	0.42
Missing		0.06
Statement Pair #2		
Favorable Attitude	1) The government should do more to help needy Americans, even if it means going deeper into debt OR...	0.57
Unfavorable Attitude	2) The government today can't afford to do much more to help the needy	0.37
Missing		0.05

Appendix Table 2.   Summary of Statements used in Constructing Variables on Beliefs.

Beliefs regarding Businesses		Proportion
Statement Pair #1		
Have Belief	1) Too much power is concentrated in the hands of a few large companies OR...	0.77
Do Not Have Belief	2) The largest companies do NOT have too much power	0.17
Missing		0.06
Statement Pair #2		
Have Belief	1) Business corporations make too much profit OR...	0.54
Do Not Have Belief	2) Most corporations make a fair and reasonable amount of profit	0.40
Missing		0.06

Beliefs regarding Politicians		Proportion
Statement Pair #1		
Have Belief	1) Elected officials in Washington lose touch with the people pretty quickly OR...	0.66
Do Not Have Belief	2) Elected officials in Washington try hard to stay in touch with voters back home	0.28
Missing		0.06
Statement Pair #2		
Have Belief	1) Most elected officials don't care what people like me think OR...	0.63
Do Not Have Belief	2) Most elected officials care what people like me think	0.33
Missing		0.03

Beliefs regarding Individual Control over Life		Proportion
Statement Pair #1		
Have Belief	1) Everyone has it in their own power to succeed OR...	0.78
Do Not Have Belief	2) Success in life is pretty much determined by forces outside of our control	0.19
Missing		0.03
Statement Pair #2		
Have Belief	1) Most people who want to get ahead can make it if they're willing to work hard	0.68
Do Not Have Belief	2) Hard work and determination are no guarantee of success for most people	0.30
Missing		0.03

(Continued)

Appendix Table 2. *(Continued)*

Belief that Religion is Important		Proportion
Statement Pair #1		
Have Belief	1) Religion is a very important part of my life, OR...	0.74
Do Not Have Belief	2) Religion is not that important to me	0.25
Missing		0.01
Statement Pair #2		
Have Belief	1) It IS necessary to believe in God in order to be moral and have good values OR...	0.50
Do Not Have Belief	2) It IS NOT necessary to believe in God in order to be moral and have good values	0.48
Missing		0.02

Beliefs regarding Racial Minorities and Immigrants		Proportion[1]
Statement Pair #1		
Have Belief	1) Blacks who can't get ahead in this country are mostly responsible for their own condition OR...	0.60
Do Not Have Belief	2) Racial discrimination is the main reason why many black people can't get ahead these days	0.34
Missing		0.06
Statement Pair #2		
Have Belief	1) Immigrants today are a burden on our country because they take our jobs, housing and healthcare OR...	0.44
Do Not Have Belief	2) Immigrants today strengthen our country because of their hard work and talents	0.51
Missing		0.06

References

1. Alesina, A., Baqir, R. and Easterly, W. (1999). "Public Goods and Ethnic Divisions." *The Quarterly Journal of Economics* **114**(4): 1243–1284.
2. Alesina, A. and Ferrara, E. L. (2005). "Preferences for Redistribution in the Land of Opportunities." *Journal of Public Economics* **89**: 897–931.
3. Alesina, A. and Glaeser E. (2004). *Fighting Poverty in the U.S. and Europe*. Oxford University Press: Oxford.
4. Blendon, R. J. and Benson J. M. (2001). "Americans' View on Health Policy: A Fifty-Year Historical Perspective." *Health Affairs (Millwood)* **20**(2): 33–46.
5. Blendon, R. J., Benson, J. M. and Desroches, C. M. (2003). "Americans' Views of the Uninsured: An Era for Hybrid Proposals." *Health Affairs*.

6. Bundorf, M. K. and Pauly, M. V. (2006). "Is Health Insurance Affordable for the Uninsured?" *Journal of Health Economics* **25**(4): 650–673.

7. DeNavas-Walt, C., Proctor, B. D. and Lee, C. H. (2006). *Income, Poverty, and Health Insurance Coverage in the United States: 2005.* Current Population Reports, P60-231. U.S. Census Bureau, Washington D.C., pp. 1–86.

8. Fong, C. (2001). "Social Preferences, Self-Interest, and the Demand for Redistribution." *Journal of Public Economics* **82**(2): 225–246.

9. Fuchs, V. R. (1976). "From Bismarck to Woodcock: The 'Irrational' Pursuit of National Health Insurance." *The Journal of Law and Economics* **19**(2): 347–359.

10. Fuchs, V. R. (1991). "National Health Insurance Revisited." *Health Affairs* **10**(4): 7–17.

11. Hacker, J. S. (1998). "The Historical Logic of National Health Insurance: Structure and Sequence in the Development of British, Canadian, and U.S. Medical Policy." *Studies in American Political Development* **12**(1): 57–130.

12. Jacobs, L. R. (1994). "The Politics of American Ambivalence Toward Government." In *The Politics of Health Care Reform: Lessons from the Past, Prospects for the Future*, eds. J. A. Monroe and G. S, Belkin. Duke University Press: Durham, NC. p. 375.

13. Kahneman, D. and Tverksy, A. eds. (2000). *Choices, Values, and Frames.* Cambridge University Press: New York.

14. Luttmer, E. F. P. (2001). "Group Loyalty and the Taste for Redistribution." *Journal of Political Economy* **109**(3): 500–528.

15. Maioni, A. (1997). "Parting at the Crossroads: The Development of Health Insurance in Canada and the United States, 1940–1965." *Comparative Politics* **29**(4): 411–431.

16. Mayes, R. (2005). *Universal Coverage: The Elusive Quest for National Health Insurance.* The University of Michigan Press: Ann Arbor, MI.

17. Orr, L. L. (1976). "Income Transfers as a Public Good." *American Economic Review* **66**(3): 359–371.

18. Princeton Survey Research Associates International (2004). *Methodology: December 2004 Typology*, Pew Research Center, pp. 1–7.

19. Poterba, J. M. (1997). "Demographic Structure and the Political Economy of Public Education." *Journal of Analysis and Policy Management* **16**(1): 48–66.

20. Quadagno, J. (2004). "Why the United States Has No National Health Insurance: Stakeholder Mobilization Against the Welfare State: 1945–1996." *Journal of Health and Social Behavior* **45**: 25–44.

21. Rhoades, J. A. and Cohen, S. B. (2006). *The Long-Term Uninsured in America, 2001–2004: Estimates for the U.S. Population under Age 65.* Agency for Healthcare Research and Quality: Rockville, MD. pp. 1–7.

22. Rosenau, P. V. (1994). "Impact of Political Structures and Informal Political Processes on Health Policy: Comparison of the United States and Canada." *Policy Studies Review* **13**(4): 293–314.

23. Scheve, K. and Stasavage, D. (2006). "Religion and Preferences for Social Insurance." *Quarterly Journal of Political Science* **1**(3): 255–286.

24. Schlesinger, M. and Lee T. K. (1993). "Is Health Care Different? Popular Support of Federal Health and Social Policies." *Journal of Health Politics, Policy and Law* **18**(3): 551–628.
25. Starr, P. (1982). *The Social Transformation of American Medicine*. Basic Books: New York.
26. Tuohy, C. H. (1999). *Accidental Logics: The Dynamics of Change in the Health Care Arena in the United States, Britain, and Canada*. Oxford University Press: New York.

5.3

A Comprehensive Cure: Universal Health Care Vouchers

The Universal Healthcare Voucher System (UHV) achieves universal health coverage by entitling all Americans to a standard package of benefits comparable to that received by federal employees. Enrollment and renewal are guaranteed regardless of health status, as is the individual's right to buy additional services beyond the standard benefits with after-tax dollars. Health plans would receive a risk-adjusted payment based on their enrollment. UHV is funded entirely by a dedicated value-added tax (VAT) with the rate set by Congress. A VAT of approximately 10 to 12 percent would insure all Americans under age 65 at a cost no greater than current public and private health care expenditures.

UHV offers true universality, individual choice, effective cost control, and competition based on quality of care and service. To foster accountability and efficient administration, the voucher system creates a National Health Board and twelve regional boards with a governance structure and reporting requirements similar to the Federal Reserve system. The National Board establishes the overall rules and procedures and sponsors an independent Institute for Technology and Outcomes Assessment, which will slow the rate of growth of expenditures by encouraging cost-effective innovations. In each region a Center for Patient Safety and Dispute Resolution replaces the dysfunctional malpractice system. UHV is relatively simple compared with other reforms that have similar objectives. Most importantly, it is congruent with basic American values: equality of opportunity and freedom to pursue personal goals.

Originally published in the Hamilton Project, July 2007. Copyright by The Brookings Institution. Written with Ezekiel J. Emanuel, M.D., Ph.D.

Introduction

The American health care system is a dysfunctional mess. The problems are well known. There are coverage problems: tens of millions are uninsured, others have poor coverage, and millions receive Medicaid, which looks comprehensive on paper but, because of extremely low reimbursement, is served by few providers. In addition, as costs rise there has been — and will continue to be — a steady drop in employer-based insurance. There are cost problems: the rise in health care costs exceeds the economy's rate of growth by 2.5 to 4 percentage points each year.[3] Economists predict that health care will consume one of every five dollars of output in the entire economy by 2016 (CMS, 2005). Medicare is going bankrupt. Given present trends, it will consume all taxes collected under current law in slightly more than fifty years (Federal Hospital Insurance and Federal Supplementary Medical Insurance Trust Funds, 2007). There are serious quality problems: it has become part of the conventional wisdom that 100,000 Americans die each year from medical errors, that only 55 percent of proven-effective therapies are administered to patients who need them, and that fewer than 25 percent of doctors and hospitals have installed electronic medical records, despite their advantages for quality and efficiency.[6,19,25] Paradoxically, the huge amount of money the United States is currently spending on health care should be sufficient to provide high-quality care for all Americans.

Myriad reforms of the health care system have been proposed; they can be grouped into three broad categories.[2,21,22] First are incremental reforms, such as expanding the existing State Children's Health Insurance Program (SCHIP) to cover all uninsured children, expanding Medicare to cover people between fifty-five and sixty-five, or providing tax breaks to individuals to buy health coverage. These reforms do not try to solve any single problem entirely, much less seek to change the fundamentals of the health care system. Rather, they try to make headway mainly by expanding coverage.

Second are individual mandates. Having been enacted in Massachusetts and proposed in California and Pennsylvania, this is the health care reform of the moment.[13] It is a "fill-in-the-cracks" approach. It aims for nearly 100 percent coverage by requiring that individuals buy insurance. To enable them to do so, these plans typically expand Medicaid, create new health-purchasing mechanisms such as Massachusetts's Health Care Connector or some other form of insurance exchange, and provide income-linked subsidies so that all can afford health insurance.[7] Like incremental reforms, individual mandates aim at extending coverage but, because they keep the current health care financing and delivery systems in place, do not address the problems of cost and quality.

Single-payer plans have long been proposed (Physicians for a National Health Program[23]). *Single payer* is a capacious term that could refer to any plan that relies on tax revenue to finance health care, but in the U.S. context the term is associated with a distinctive approach to reform modeled on Medicare or on the Canadian health care system. Advocates of a single-payer plan would eliminate private insurance and for-profit providers and would use the expected large savings from reduced sales and administrative costs to achieve universal coverage and expand the range of services provided. Most of the single-payer plans currently proposed enshrine fee-for-service payment for physicians and call for negotiated budgets with hospitals.

Although incremental reforms, individual mandates, and single-payer plans all address some of the key problems of the American health care system, all have important operational and political flaws.[11] To address the problems of coverage, cost, and quality in a sustainable, plausible manner, we offer a fourth alternative: universal health care vouchers. But before considering this alternative, it is worth asking what, if anything, can be learned from these other proposals.

It is hard to see what can be learned from proposals for incremental reform. These proposals would not achieve universal coverage, they would increase rather than decrease health care expenditures, and they would leave the current dysfunctional system essentially unchanged.

Individual mandates stress the value of the insurance exchange. If we as a nation decide to retain private health care delivery financed by health plans and insurance companies, then using such arrangements to create extremely large purchasing pools can reduce insurance underwriting, sales, and marketing costs. It can also permit community rating, in which premiums are the same for everyone rather than being adjusted for age, health risk, or other factors. But *voluntary* exchanges such as Massachusetts's Health Care Connector are inherently unstable. As the experience of the now defunct PacAdvantage in California and other voluntary insurance exchanges has shown, they lead to adverse selection: the enrollees are disproportionately the sicker patients whose higher costs set off a vicious cycle of ever-higher premiums and reductions in enrollment.[20] This suggests that any workable system needs to have *mandatory* enrollment and risk adjustment of premiums so that an insurance company will be fairly compensated if its average enrollees are in particularly poor health. Moreover, because individual mandates by themselves do not fundamentally change the health care delivery system, they can do little to stem cost increases or improve quality of care.

Advocates of single-payer plans argue that a central financing mechanism can achieve tremendous administrative savings and, by removing employers from the business of providing health insurance for their employees, can generate substantial labor efficiencies, thus stimulating the economy. But these savings change only the level of expenditures — they do not affect the rate of increase over time. Lowering the steep slope of the upward curve of health care spending can only be achieved by changing the delivery system to provide incentives, information, and infrastructure for more integrated and cost-effective delivery of care. This reform is impossible within a single-payer system bent on minimizing administrative costs while leaving the fee-for-service reimbursement system in place.

The Essential Elements of Universal Health Care Vouchers

How can we integrate central financing of health care with large purchasing pools to gain the advantages of single-payer plans and individual mandates while avoiding their disadvantages? We propose universal health care vouchers as the comprehensive cure for the ailing American health care system.[8] Universal health care vouchers involve a ten-step therapy (see also Table 1).

1. Guaranteed health care for all Americans. All U.S. residents would receive a voucher good for the acquisition of health coverage through a qualified health plan or insurance company. At first, those who currently receive coverage through Medicare, Medicaid, SCHIP, or another government program would choose whether to stay with their current program or join the voucher system. Unlike a health savings account, the voucher would not provide a specified dollar amount to be used to buy individual medical services over the year, but instead would convey the right to enroll in a health plan that covers a set of standard benefits. In other words, it would be an insurance voucher, not a cash voucher. The recipient would pay nothing directly for the voucher itself or for the benefits that it covers; financing would be accomplished through a dedicated value-added tax (VAT) described below. There would be no deductibles and minimal copayments.

2. Comprehensive benefits. The voucher would cover a set of comprehensive benefits modeled on the generous benefits that federal employees, including members of Congress, receive today through the Federal Employees Health Benefits (FEHB) program.[a] To qualify for participation in the voucher program,

---

[a]FEHB program includes coverage for preventative screenings, brand name and generic prescription drugs, dental care, home and office visits, physical and occupational therapy, and mental health inpatient and outpatient care. The plan also allows patients to choose their own doctors and hospitals, requires no referral for specialist visits, and charges low copayments. See FEHB 2007 for a full set of benefits.

Table 1. Ten Main Features of the Proposed Universal Health Care Voucher System.

Feature	Description
Guaranteed health care for all	Each household would receive a voucher for coverage through a qualified health plan or insurance company. The voucher would not be a cash voucher denominated in dollars to buy health services, but rather would be an insurance voucher entitling the holder to enrollment in a health plan of the holder's choice.
Standard health benefits	Standard benefits would be generous, modeled on services currently received by members of Congress and other federal employees through the Federal Employees Health Benefits program.
Freedom of choice	Voucher holders would be able to choose from among several health plans. Plans would be required to accept any enrollee without exclusions for preexisting conditions and with guaranteed renewability.
Freedom to purchase additional services	Voucher holders could choose to buy, with after-tax dollars, additional services and amenities such as wider selection of physicians, coverage of complementary medicines, or additional mental health benefits.
Funding through a dedicated value-added tax (VAT)	Financing for the vouchers would come from a dedicated VAT of about 10 to 12 percent on purchases of goods and services. Revenue from the tax could not be diverted to other uses such as defense or Social Security.
End of employer-based insurance	The tax exemption for employer-based health insurance would be eliminated. Employers would probably stop offering health insurance, and wages would rise in line with the current cost of health insurance.
Phasing out of Medicare, Medicaid, SCHIP, and other government health programs	No one receiving benefits from Medicare, Medicaid, SCHIP, or any other government program would be forced out, but there would be no new enrollees. Current enrollees would have the option of joining the voucher system. Over about fifteen years these programs would shrink in size and eventually disappear.
Independent oversight	A National Health Board and twelve regional health boards would be created on the model of the Federal Reserve System. Members of the National Board and chairs of the regional boards would be nominated by the President and confirmed by the Senate for long (e.g., ten-year) terms; the other regional board members would be named by the National Health Board. Dedicated funding would make the boards independent of annual congressional appropriations and help insulate them from political lobbying.
Cost and quality control measures	A new Institute for Technology and Outcomes Assessment would assess the effectiveness and cost of new drugs, medical devices, diagnostic tests, and other interventions on the basis of both existing research and new studies commissioned by the Institute. The Institute would also assess the outcomes of patients in the different health plans. Results of the assessments would be publicly disseminated in ways that protect patient confidentiality. To ensure objectivity and independence, the Institute would be funded by a dedicated share of the VAT revenue, estimated at 0.5 percent.

(Continued)

Table 1. (*Continued*)

Feature	Description
Patient safety and dispute resolution measures	Each regional health board would create a regional Center for Patient Safety and Dispute Resolution to receive and evaluate claims of injury by patients; compensate those patients found to have been injured by medical error; and, when appropriate, discipline or disqualify from practice physicians providing poor-quality care. The regional centers would also evaluate interventions to enhance patient safety and would coordinate and fund implementation of valuable interventions by health plans, hospitals, physicians, and others. Physicians would likely pay greatly reduced premiums to cover those (probably rare) malpractice awards in cases that go to court. The centers would be funded by a dedicated 2.5 percent of the VAT revenue.

health plans and insurance companies would have to agree to provide these standard benefits for the value of the voucher. Those that qualify, however, would otherwise be free, for the most part, to structure their businesses as they see fit. They could shrink (within limits) or expand their physician and hospital networks. They could offer different drug formularies, more disease management programs, or a larger or smaller choice of specialists or specialty hospitals, or make other modifications. They could even offer, at an additional charge, benefits not covered by the voucher. But, other than copayments, they could not charge voucher holders for coverage of the standard benefits.

3. Freedom of choice. Like today's programs with individual mandates, the voucher system would establish an insurance exchange in each region of the country to facilitate enrollment by individuals and families in the health care plan of their choice. All Americans except those who prefer to remain in Medicare, Medicaid, or SCHIP would receive their coverage by enrolling through the insurance exchange. Participating health plans and insurance companies would be private and would not be run by the government. In most regions, consumers would have freedom of choice among several qualified health plans or insurance companies; probably five to eight, but as many as twenty or more in some locales. They would be free to change plans each year or to select a three-year enrollment option that would provide them with some additional benefits. Americans who fail to enroll themselves in a health plan or insurance program would be assigned to one, on an equitable basis, by the exchange in their region.

To participate in the voucher system, health plans and insurance companies would have to guarantee enrollment and renewability every year for all applicants without consideration of their medical history: they could not turn anyone away for any reason and could not refuse to cover preexisting conditions. They would have to provide aggregate data on their own past performance, including patient satisfaction, disenrollment rates, hospitalization and mortality rates for various conditions (such as diabetes, emphysema, and heart attacks), patient outcomes for various conditions, and other quality measures.

Regional health boards would certify that each health plan and insurance company has a sufficient network of hospitals and physicians and adequate financial reserves, and that the plan or company is in fact providing the standard benefits. The regional boards would pay each plan and company a risk-adjusted premium for each person or family enrolled. To minimize the financial incentive for plans and companies to cherry-pick the healthiest patients and avoid enrolling sicker ones, the government would adjust the premium for age, sex, smoking status, preexisting conditions, and other factors, as determined by the National Health Board.

4. Freedom to purchase additional services. Individuals and families would be free to purchase additional health care services or amenities that are not part of the standard health benefits. These might include greater choice of physicians and hospitals, access to a wider range of drugs or more brand name drugs, wider choice of eyeglasses, more mental health benefits, or even a "concierge medicine" package that eliminates time limits on office visits and provides for physicians to make house calls. However, payments for this additional coverage would not be tax deductible; they would be paid for with after-tax dollars, as is the case for food, clothing, and other consumer goods.

5. Funding by a dedicated VAT. Funding for the vouchers would come entirely from a dedicated value-added tax (VAT), similar to a sales tax on purchases of goods and services. Initially the VAT would be about 10 to 12 percent on all purchases subject to the tax. All the money raised, and only that money, would be used to support the voucher system. Thus there would be a direct connection between the VAT rate and the level of services included in the core benefits — the more generous the benefits, the higher the tax rate would have to be. Congress would have the power to set and adjust the VAT rate.

6. An end to employer-based insurance. The current tax benefit for employer-based health insurance would be eliminated. Since all workers would now receive vouchers for the standard health benefits, they would no longer look to their employers for health insurance and would likely demand higher wages instead. Employer competition for workers would push up wages in those firms that previously provided insurance. Some employers might still provide extended coverage for services not included in the standard benefits as a fringe benefit to attract or reward workers. This could be done in either of two ways: the employer could offer a specific dollar amount to its workers to pay for certain noncovered services (a defined contribution), or the employer could purchase an insurance plan on the workers' behalf. In either case, these added benefits would be taxed like other compensation rather than being exempt from tax as employer-provided health benefits are today.

7. Phasing out of Medicare, Medicaid, SCHIP, and other government health insurance programs. Americans whose health care is currently paid through Medicare, Medicaid, SCHIP, or another government health insurance program would not be forced to switch to the voucher plan. Initially, the voucher system would cover the 210 million Americans who are insured through their employers, self-insured, or uninsured. The 41 million Americans aged sixty-five and older enrolled in Medicare and the 50 million Americans who receive Medicaid, SCHIP, or other means-tested government health benefits[16] would have a choice: to remain in their government-funded program or to join the voucher system. However, there would be no new enrollees in Medicare, Medicaid, SCHIP, or other current programs. Americans who turn sixty-five after the voucher system goes into effect would remain in the voucher system. Similarly, those now receiving Medicaid or SCHIP would have to switch permanently to the voucher system if they get a job or otherwise become ineligible for their current program. Thus, over time, fewer and fewer people would participate in these government-run health programs. Within essentially fifteen years, all Americans would receive the same standard benefits within the same health care delivery system. There would be one universal health care voucher system — a public guarantee with private provision of services — for all Americans regardless of age, income, employment, health, or marital status.

8. Independent oversight. To reduce political interference and allow tough administrative choices to be made, a National Health Board and twelve regional health boards would be established, modeled on the Federal Reserve System. Members of the National Health Board and the chairs of each regional health board would be nominated by the president and confirmed by the Senate for a long fixed term (say, ten years), which could be renewed only once. The terms of the National Health Board members would be staggered, with the term of only one member expiring in any given year. This board would appoint the members of the regional health boards to similarly staggered terms of the same length.

The administrative budgets of the National Health Board and the regional health boards would be funded from the dedicated VAT, not by an annual appropriation by Congress. The National Health Board would have responsibility to

- define and regularly adjust the standard health benefits to reflect changes in standards of care, advances in technology, and fiscal realities;
- conduct research to determine the risk adjustments necessary for the premiums paid to health plans;
- determine payment differences based on geography;
- sponsor research on quality, outcomes, and performance of the health care system;
- oversee and coordinate the regional health boards; and
- report regularly to Congress and the American public on the health care system.

Within their geographic regions, the twelve regional health boards would have responsibility to

- oversee the insurance exchanges;
- certify and oversee the participating health plans and insurance companies and ensure that they have sufficient financial reserves and medical resources to provide the health services offered in the standard benefits package;
- manage the enrollment of individuals and families in health plans and insurance companies and assign to a health plan those who do not enroll on their own;
- pay the health plans and insurance companies the risk-adjusted premiums on their enrollees' behalf; and
- collect, analyze, and disseminate information on the quality of health care delivered by the individual health plans and insurance companies.

9. Cost and quality control mechanisms. An Institute for Technology and Outcomes Assessment would be created to judge the value of new drugs, medical devices, tests, and other interventions and to assess patient outcomes under the system. This Institute would be responsible for

- systematic review of research studies and other data on the effectiveness of different drugs, devices, new technologies, and other interventions;
- comparison of the effectiveness and costs of drugs, devices, diagnostic tests, and other interventions;
- commissioning of research studies to compare drugs, devices, diagnostic tests, and other interventions;
- collecting data from health plans and insurance companies on patient outcomes and on the drugs, medical technologies, and interventions used; and

- disseminating data on technology and outcomes assessments to health plans, physicians, patients, drug and technology manufacturers, and the general public, while respecting patient confidentiality.

To ensure the independence and objectivity of the Institute's work, funding would come from a fixed share (estimated at 0.5 percent) of the total revenues of the dedicated VAT. In addition, its operations would be overseen by an independent board appointed by the National Health Board.

10. Centers for patient safety and Dispute resolution. Each regional health board would create a regional center for patient safety and dispute resolution. These centers would be responsible for

- receipt and adjudication of patient complaints about medical errors and injuries;
- compensation of patients where it is found that their injuries were caused by medical error;
- discipline, disqualification, and prohibition from practice of physicians and other health professionals who injure patients or violate established safety procedures;
- development of programs to promote patient safety; and
- coordination with health plans, hospitals, physicians, visiting nurses, and others to implement interventions proven to enhance patient safety.

Patients who believe they have been injured and are not satisfied by the center's resolution of their complaint would still be able to sue for malpractice.

Funding for the centers and for compensation to injured patients would come from the dedicated VAT. Since the current malpractice system costs about $20 billion a year,[5] approximately 2.5 percent of the VAT's total revenues would be required. With the centers paying for initial investigation, adjudication, and compensation, physicians would not have to pay malpractice premiums. They could still retain insurance in case patients are dissatisfied with the resolution by the centers and elect to sue, but only a small amount of insurance should be necessary.

Economics of Universal Health Care Vouchers

We believe that any comprehensive health care reform proposal should meet two basic criteria. First, current national health expenditures should not have to increase to cover all Americans. That is, the initial cost of the new health system should not exceed the amount being spent on health care at this time. The system does not need more money — it needs to spend the money more efficiently. Second, the rate of increase in health care spending over time should reflect the growth of the economy and the public's willingness and ability to pay for health care services.

Would instituting a universal health care voucher system increase or decrease national health care costs at the time it is instituted? In 2005, the annual premium for the FEHB program varied by state, but the premium in the high-end Blue Cross-Blue Shield preferred provider plan that serves as the basis for the voucher system's proposed standard benefit was $4,728 for individuals and $10,824 for families. Table 2 indicates that the total cost (using the 2005 premiums) for all Americans except those in Medicare would be $778 billion.

Many who are currently uninsured are young, healthy individuals — self-defined "invincibles" — who choose not to insure themselves. But others are

Table 2. Projected Costs of the Proposed Universal Health Care Voucher System[a] Compared to Current System Costs.[b]

a. Universal Health Care Vouchers			
Group served	Number	Average annual premium	Total annual costs
Individuals	15.2 million	$4,728	$71.9 billion
Families	65.2 million[c]	$10,824	$705.7 billion
Total non-Medicare population	257.6 million	NA	$778 billion
Increase for extra use by uninsured and Medicaid populations	25 percent of population	Added costs per person: 26 percent more than the average	$50 billion
Total non-Medicare	257.6 million	NA	$828 billion[d]
b. Current Employer-Based System			
Type of insurance	Total annual costs		
Medicaid	$260 billion[e]		
Private Health Insurance	$694 billion		
Total non-medicare	$954 billion		

[a] 2005 rates and expenditures. Annual premium is based on FEHB Blue Cross-Blue Shield standard national plan. Using government Employees Health Association (GEHA) high national benefit plan (2005 annual premiums are $4,728 for individuals and $10,824 for families) the total non-Medicare costs would be $778 billion. Adding $50 billion for extra use by the Medicaid and currently uninsured populations yields $828 billion.

[b] using estimates from 2005 according to figures cited in Ref. 3.

[c] The average family size is 3.7 persons.

[d] See Footnote 2 in the text for the calculation of this figure.

[e] Excludes payments for nursing homes.

uninsured because they are unhealthy and cannot obtain insurance, or have low incomes and cannot afford it, or both. The Medicaid population tends to be sicker than the federal employee population, and therefore their costs are likely to be higher. A study by the Urban Institute estimates that, for an equivalent level of coverage, the uninsured and Medicaid populations incur about 26 percent higher costs per person than employed populations with private insurance.[15] The uninsured and Medicaid populations under age sixty-five account for about 25 percent of the total U.S. population under age sixty-five. Costs under the voucher system would therefore be higher than the $778 billion calculated based on premium rates for the FEHB program. This increase raises the total estimate to $828 billion.

This is a large sum, but it needs to be compared with current health spending for the same population. In 2005 (the most recent year for which data are available), federal and state governments spent $260 billion on Medicaid, not counting what they spent on nursing home care. In 2005, the total expenditure for private health insurance was $694 billion; this figure excludes out-of-pocket expenses for prescriptions, dental services, and other products.[3] These two figures sum to $954 billion (in 2005 dollars) for the 257.6 million Americans not currently receiving Medicare. This means that universal health care vouchers would not increase total national expenditure on health care, yet would cover everyone with essentially the same plan that covers members of Congress, even taking into account the higher use by the currently uninsured and Medicaid populations.

Much of the $828 billion would replace existing spending, both private and public. Moving Medicare, Medicaid, and SCHIP beneficiaries into the voucher plan would yield further savings. First, the need for safety-net providers for the uninsured — county hospitals, community clinics, and the like — would be obviated because all Americans would have health coverage. This should reduce the health care expenditures of municipal and state governments. Second, the responsibility of state and municipal governments for funding of health care for their own employees would be eliminated, thus saving these governments even more. For instance, in 2006 almost 3 percent of Maryland's state budget went to health insurance for state workers.[18] This would be saved. Third, as new enrollment in Medicaid and SCHIP stops, and as current beneficiaries get jobs or choose to enroll in the voucher plan and cease to be eligible for these programs, their funding demands should decline. In Maryland in 2006, Medicaid accounted for 17 percent of the state budget and SCHIP for 2 percent.[b,c] Thus the combination of eliminating state responsibility for employee health insurance and phasing out Medicaid and SCHIP would save states about 20 percent of their budgets. Although states and municipalities may choose not to reduce taxes by the full amount they save — they may instead reallocate some of the savings to other activities, such as education — their citizens should see substantial declines in state and municipal taxes along with improvements in services. The federal government would also realize substantial savings from phasing out Medicaid and SCHIP.

The total phasing out of Medicare would constitute yet another important change in taxes. With no new enrollment, the number of Medicare enrollees would decrease by about 5 or 6 percent a year because of mortality, and the program would draw to a close in a few decades. This would allow Medicare taxes — currently 2.9 percent of payroll — to be phased out. There would also be a decrease in the general federal revenue devoted to Medicare to make up for shortfalls in the trust fund. In short, the phase-out of Medicare would rapidly result in a substantial reduction in Medicare expenditure.

How are the $126 billion savings possible? First, underwriting, sales, and marketing costs would be significantly lower under the voucher system than under the current system of employer-based insurance and self-insurance. In addition, employers would save the cost of administration of health benefits. Also, although the FEHB program is generous, some Americans have even more generous benefit packages. They would be entitled to fewer benefits than they currently receive through their employer-based insurance and would have to pay for any additional services. That additional cost is not included in the above figures.

> with no restrictions or enrollment requirements, and no exclusions for preexisting health conditions, a universal voucher system would guarantee that every American has health coverage—not 96 or 97 percent, but 100 percent.

---

[b]The uninsured and Medicaid populations are about one-quarter of the insured population, and therefore the fraction of costs attributable to these groups is assumed to be approximately one-quarter of the $778 billion for the insured population, or $194 billion, augmented by 26 percent because of the higher cost per person of these populations, for a total of $245 billion. Adding the extra $50 billion in costs for this population ($245 billion minus $125 billion) to the $778 billion for the insured population results in a total of $828 billion.

[c]Maryland budget figures according to the Department of Health and Mental Hygiene.[18]

Comparing Universal Health Care Vouchers with Individual Mandates and Single-payer Plans

Table 3 summarizes the principal differences between the proposed universal health care voucher system and proposals for individual mandates and single-payer systems. Unlike individual mandates, universal health care vouchers would simply and efficiently achieve universal coverage without the costly administration of income-based subsidies. The poor and the sick would be implicitly subsidized by the difference between the value of the voucher to them and the amount of VAT they pay. Also, unlike mandates, a voucher system would not prop up an inefficient and inequitable employment-based insurance system, nor would it require beneficiaries to change health plans when their income, employment, marital status, or other characteristics change. Finally, because the voucher system would be universal no coverage denial, it would not be subject to the adverse selection problem in which a disproportionate share of higher users of care are drawn into the system while the better insurance risks make other arrangements. Individual mandates by themselves remain subject to this serious problem.

One very important difference between a universal voucher system and single-payer systems currently proposed is that the latter promise an open-ended entitlement that is often not tied directly to adequate funding. In the voucher system, by contrast, expenditure and revenue are explicitly connected through the dedicated tax. Also, single-payer systems generally provide only a monetary promise; they do not guarantee access to care. Many Medicare beneficiaries today have difficulty finding a physician to accept them as a patient. In a voucher system, everyone would be enrolled in a plan that is held responsible for providing care to its enrollees.

A universal voucher system would make plans accountable for quality and service by allowing only qualified plans to enroll patients.

Finally, a crucial difference between a voucher system and the other two models is that neither of the other two models makes a significant effort to improve efficiency in the organization and delivery of care. The projected universal voucher system, by contrast, would make plans accountable for quality and service by allowing only qualified plans to enroll patients. Paying a risk-adjusted fee per enrollee (that is, capitation) creates a strong financial incentive for insurance companies to be efficient in care delivery. In short, the projected universal voucher system would be more than just a funding mechanism. It would create a positive

Table 3. Comparison of the Proposed Universal Health Care Voucher System with Other Proposals.

Criterion	Universal health care vouchers	Individual mandates	Single-payer plans
Universal coverage	True universal coverage of all Americans.	Falls short of universal coverage. Requires everyone to have insurance coverage through an employer, government, or self-purchase, but some people will evade mandates and others will be exempted because coverage is unaffordable.	True universal coverage of all Americans.
Choice	Every American has a choice of health plan, hospital, and physicians.	Many people insured through their employer continue to have no choice of health plan. People insured through Medicaid still have very limited choice.	Every American has a choice of hospital and physicians but is enrolled in a single nationwide plan.
Role of employers	Employers are taken completely out of the health care system. Consequently, wages increase and strikes over health care disappear. Neither workers nor employers any longer make job decisions based on health insurance considerations.		
Cost control	Controls costs through several mechanisms: a dedicated tax that limits what can be spent; competition between health plans; greater cost-consciousness on the part of individuals buying additional services; systematic technology assessment that eliminates practices of marginal or no value; and incentives that shift R&D by drug and medical device companies toward more cost-effective interventions.		
Administrative efficiency	Administrative costs are about 10 percent of total health care spending. Administrative savings are achieved by reducing insurance underwriting, sales, and marketing, and through administration cuts by employers. The elimination of the administrative burden of Medicaid, and of the income-linked determination of subsidies would also create administrative efficiencies.		
Technology and outcomes assessment	Creates an Institute for Technology and Outcomes Assessment to evaluate the effectiveness and cost of drugs, devices, and new technologies and to evaluate patient outcomes and the quality performance of health plans and insurance companies.		
Delivery system	Provides strong incentives, through financing and data collection by the regional health boards, for health plans to integrate care across hospitals, physicians, and other providers.		

(*Continued*)

Table 3.   (*Continued*)

Criterion	Universal health care vouchers
Employers remain involved in health care as they are now. Employers who drop insurance coverage for their workers may pay a penalty.	Employers are taken completely out of the health care system.
No cost control mechanism.	Controls costs through negotiation of fees, prices, and budgets with physicians, hospitals, drug companies, and other providers; and through restrictions on the supply of medical technologies.
Administrative costs exceed 15 or 20 percent, with no administrative savings. The need to determine incomes and the level of subsidies provided to individuals to buy health insurance would increase costs.	Administrative costs of about 3 to 4 percent. Administrative savings are achieved by removing employers as well as all insurance companies and for-profit providers from the health care system.
No systematic effort to assess technology or outcomes.	No systematic effort to assess technology or outcomes.
Same health care delivery system as at present. No financial or other incentive to create accountable health plans or integrate care.	Same health care delivery system as at present. No financial or other incentive to create accountable health plans or integrate care.

dynamic that moves the entire system toward more efficient use of resources and higher-quality care.

What Would the Health Care Experience Be Like Under a Universal Voucher System?

Initially, all Americans who are not in Medicare, Medicaid, or SCHIP would be notified by their regional health board that they can now choose their health plan or health insurance company through the insurance exchange. Through mailings, the Internet, and other mechanisms, potential enrollees would be informed about the different plans available in their geographic area. Charts would identify the similarities and differences in the various plans: what local hospitals each plan uses, the physicians participating in the plan, the copayments required, and other relevant information. Americans would also be instructed on how to enroll. People with coverage today would be able to keep their current doctor, and many aspects of their plan would remain the same.

As stated above, Medicare, Medicaid, SCHIP, and other government health programs would initially remain in place, but participants in these programs would be notified that they could now switch to the voucher system. Those who prefer not to switch would just stay in their current program.

For most Americans, enrollment in a health plan under the universal health care voucher system would feel much like what they currently experience through their employer-based coverage, with four important differences. First, they would have a wider choice of health plans. Today most Americans who are covered by their employer have no choice of health plan.[16] They are told who will provide their coverage and what will be covered. Those currently uninsured would experience a new freedom to choose a health plan.

Second, Americans would no longer have to be screened to determine their premiums or to determine what will be excluded from coverage for the first year. No health plan or insurance company would be allowed to subject Americans to pretesting or to deny coverage on the basis of preexisting conditions. No one could be denied enrollment or renewal of coverage for any reason. Instead of health plans choosing their enrollees, as is effectively the case today, enrollees would be allowed to choose their health plan.

Third, enrollees would pay nothing directly for the set of standard health benefits. The universal health care voucher would cover the full cost. There would be no premiums deducted from paychecks or paid for out of pocket. There would be no deductibles, and many people would find their copayments to be less than what they are currently paying.

Finally, enrollees could decide whether they want to buy additional services or insurance coverage, and how much they are willing to pay for them.

Workers who currently receive health coverage through their employer — whether they work in a factory, an office, or a government agency — would see more money in their paycheck as employers compete for their labor by offering higher wages instead of health benefits. Fringe benefits such as health coverage are, after all, just another form of compensation.[12] When employers stop offering health insurance, the money that before went into health insurance premiums would be offered instead to workers as higher salaries to induce them to stay with the company. How much would workers' pay rise? It would primarily depend on how much of current workers' compensation is in the form of health insurance.

Conversely, Americans would for the first time pay a VAT. Over time, as Medicare and Medicaid are phased out and their beneficiaries are enrolled in the voucher system, it would increase from the initial 10 to 12 percent to approximately 15 percent. The new tax would be offset by the higher wages mentioned above, however, and by reductions in other taxes. Each year the federal government would pay less and less for Medicare, Medicaid, SCHIP, and other programs, reducing the strain on federal finances. Similarly, states would pay less and less for Medicaid, SCHIP, and other need-based programs, and payments for state workers' health insurance would be eliminated; as calculated above, elimination of state expenditures devoted to these programs would reduce total state government spending by about 20 percent. Finally, as mentioned above, state and local funding of safety-net providers — including county hospitals, community health clinics, and other programs — could be phased out, clearing the way for further tax reductions. These safety-net providers would be integrated into the health plan packages approved by the regional health boards.

People with diabetes, emphysema, and other chronic conditions would probably experience much better coordination of care: more home visits from nurses to be sure they are taking their medicine and following the treatment plan, and more telephone calls and other reminders to check on their diet and their use of medications and vaccines. They also would probably observe a greater effort to involve them in exercise, smoking cessation programs, and other preventive activities. Capitation payment to the health plans leads them to emphasize keeping enrollees well.

Potential concerns about universal health care vouchers

Three main obstacles stand in the way of enacting a universal health care voucher system. First is the perception on the part of many that a VAT would be regressive and would hurt the poor. Although this contention is widely repeated, it is simplistic at best, and simply bad economics at worst. The fairness of any tax proposal cannot be properly evaluated by considering only the tax. The benefits that the tax would pay for must also be considered — as well as the costs and benefits of alternative policies, or of doing nothing. The current system, is structured largely around the generous tax benefits, worth about $200 billion in 2007, given to employer-based insurance. The system is heavily biased toward the rich and against the less well off.[24] Not only do the rich receive a bigger tax break, but the working poor often pay Medicare and other taxes yet receive no health coverage in return. Under the universal health care voucher system, everyone would pay the VAT in proportion to their consumption.

The essential point, however, is that less-well-off Americans — as well as all those who are sick and therefore need more health care services — would generally receive much more in benefits than they would pay in taxes. Health coverage for a family today costs about $11,000 a year. The poor, the near poor, and many other people earning less than the median income would not pay anywhere near that much in value-added taxes. Consequently, the value of the health coverage they receive would greatly exceed what they pay in tax for that coverage. That is the hallmark of progressivity.

A second obstacle is the danger that insurance companies and health plan sponsors might find ways to cherry-pick (or lemon-drop) prospective customers in a system that allows all Americans to choose among competing health plans. It could be profitable for a health plan or insurance company to avoid sick patients and attract young, healthy ones. Sick patients might be discouraged from signing up, for example, if a hospital network failed to include a cancer center, offered only second-rate mental health services, or did not contract with the best diabetes doctors.

Fortunately, there are ways of preventing this outcome. The key is risk adjustment. The regional health boards would pay health plans more per patient if they enroll older, sicker patients on average, and less if they enroll young, healthy people. Some health care systems in the United States and health authorities in some other countries, such as the Netherlands and Israel, already have relevant experience with what does and does not work. This experience could be applied to the voucher system. Admittedly, risk adjustment is still an imperfect science. The National Health Board would need to conduct research into improving adjustment methods. In the meantime, however, there could be some form of reinsurance. For instance, regional health boards could provide "stop-loss" coverage, so that any plan that spends more than $100,000 on a single patient is not held liable for the full cost; the regional health board would pick up the excess. But however it is accomplished, some form of risk adjustment is critical to a stable, efficient, and fair program and to ensuring that the system focuses resources on providing the best health care for people who are sick, not on coddling the worried well.

The final hurdle that universal health care vouchers must overcome is political. The voucher program constitutes a comprehensive reform of the U.S. health care system. It would mean change in the way health care insurance is financed, change in the role of employers, change in the way the system is administered, change in the way Americans enroll, change in the way the system delivers care, and change in the way technology is developed and evaluated. Such far-reaching change is sure to create uncertainty, and uncertainty makes people cautious. Overcoming such inertia and innate risk aversion is a challenge facing any serious health care reform. What ultimately emerges will depend on a balance of factors: how bad the system has become, how willing people are to try something new, and how much comfort they can be given that what is being proposed has a good chance of being better.

Advantages of universal health care vouchers

Compared with the current health care system, the universal health care voucher system offers advantages in almost every area: coverage and choice, administrative efficiency, cost control, quality, and impact on the economy.

Coverage and Choice. With no restrictions or enrollment requirements, and no exclusions for preexisting health conditions, a universal voucher system would guarantee that every American has health coverage — not 96 or 97 or even 99 percent of Americans, but 100 percent. Even those who fail to sign up for a health plan would be assigned a plan and would be covered. There would be no gaps.

Americans would enjoy both continuity of coverage and choice. As long as they wanted to stay in a health plan or with a particular physician, they could do so. They could not be denied coverage or denied renewal of their plan. Their employer could not switch plans or force them to change physicians or hospitals. Each individual would decide whether and when to switch health plans, physicians, or hospitals and whether or not to buy additional services beyond those in the standard health benefit. Each household would be allowed to weigh whether a wider choice of physicians or coverage for complementary medicine is worth the money that could otherwise be spent on, say, sending their children to a private college or buying a new car.

Administrative Efficiency. Eliminating the employer from health coverage and removing the burden of Medicaid administration on states would create significant administrative savings and efficiencies, as described above. Putting all Americans — initially everyone except those who choose to remain in Medicare, Medicaid, SCHIP, or another government program — into the insurance exchange would save tens of billions of dollars that are now spent on insurance underwriting, sales, and marketing. Since the voucher system would require no determination of eligibility for participation or for subsidies based on income, its adoption would produce additional billions in administrative savings. Employers also would save billions because they would no longer need such large human resources departments to manage health benefits, track health contributions, and hire consultants to evaluate various insurance options. Once phase-in is complete, states would no longer have to administer Medicaid, and providers would no longer have to bill Medicaid, producing still more efficiency.

The universal voucher system would lead to a reduction in the number of health plans and insurance companies. There are more than one thousand such companies that operate today; these would probably consolidate to fewer than one hundred or so companies nationwide, with many fewer in any one city or region.

This would lead to significant savings in billing costs at hospitals and physicians' offices. As Medicare, Medicaid, SCHIP, and other government programs are phased out, hospitals, physicians' offices, home health agencies, and others would realize additional administrative savings because they would be dealing with even fewer billing systems.

The administrative costs of the universal voucher system would not be as low as those of a single-payer system. Expenditures for the Institute for Technology and Outcomes Assessment (an estimated 0.5 percent of costs) and for the Centers for Patient Safety and Dispute Resolution (2.5 percent), as well as for the national and regional health boards, would probably amount to 10 percent of the system's total cost. Even with these costs, however, more than $100 billion in administrative savings would be realized each year.

Cost Control. Another major advantage of the universal voucher system would be effective cost control, which would ensure the financial sustainability of the entire health care system. This would be achieved without price controls or the centralized management of local spending constitutive of current single-payer proposals. There would be five separate cost-control levers. First, and most effectively, the yield from the VAT would determine how much could be spent on the vouchers. This would provide a hard budget constraint on cost increases. Of course, revenue collected by the VAT would rise as the economy grows; but if the public wanted health care spending to grow even more rapidly because it wanted additional services, it would have to persuade Congress to increase the tax rate. Americans' aversion to tax increases should thus hold health care costs down, but the system would allow Congress to enact increases when the public deems the added expenditure is worth it.

Second, competition among health plans would restrain costs. Currently, competition among health plans is perverse. Plans do not compete to offer a package of services for a fixed price. Instead, all too frequently they compete to avoid sick patients. Under the universal voucher plan, because health plans and insurance companies would have the same risk-adjusted fixed payment per enrollee for a standard set of benefits, with no opportunity to charge enrollees more for those benefits, they would have to compete for enrollees. They would therefore have a strong financial incentive to be efficient. The likely result would be innovations in the management of chronic illnesses, where 70 percent of health care spending occurs.[1] Because hospitalization is so expensive, health plans would probably find ways to keep patients with chronic conditions healthier and out of the hospital. Similarly, they would have a strong incentive to eliminate duplicate testing and expensive medicine that adds little benefit.

Third, those Americans who want additional services would have to pay for them with after-tax dollars. They would therefore have an incentive to spend judiciously to receive value for their money.

Fourth, the independent Institute for Technology and Outcomes Assessment would evaluate the effectiveness, cost, and value of new technologies and new applications of existing technologies. Data developed by the Institute would ensure that any new procedures added to coverage under the standard benefit package would be cost-effective; the data would also provide vital information for health plans and insurance companies as they design more efficient and effective care. Data from the Institute would ensure that any cost cutting that harms patients would be detected. Health plans could also cover only cost-effective, proven care without fear of litigation since the Centers for Patient Safety and Dispute Resolution that adjudicate claims of medical error would not view use of evaluations by the Institute as a medical error. This would provide a safe harbor for actual implementation of cost-effective care by health plans.

Finally, the Institute's reports would send a signal to drug and medical device companies to focus their research and development on cost-effective interventions. Right now the new interventions that these companies develop are typically expected to hit the market in ten years. Companies thus face uncertainty about what interventions will be covered by health insurers ten years hence, and at what price. They therefore try to recoup their costs as fast as possible through high prices. The Institute would provide more reliable and predictable information on future coverage decisions, emphasizing that cost-effective interventions — those that really improve survival or quality of life, or that save money without reducing the quality of care — will be covered. This would lead to a shift in research priorities and hold down costs in the future.

No single cost-control mechanism is likely to be effective in restraining the rise in health care expenditure, but these five different mechanisms all pulling in the same direction should together make a difference.

Improved Quality. The universal voucher system would also improve quality and patient safety, especially through innovation in health care delivery. Today we know two things about quality: that the current system does not consistently deliver high-quality care, and that health plans and current practitioners do not know the best way to deliver high-quality care. Innovation in health care delivery is needed.

Hospitals and health professionals today have few financial or other incentives to implement patient safety measures. The universal voucher system would provide strong incentives for health plans and insurance companies to develop infrastructure that improves quality. Monitoring of outcomes by the Institute for Technology and Outcomes Assessment and monitoring of health plan performance by the National Health Board would provide significant incentives for health plans to invest in information technologies, including computer order entry systems for physicians, electronic medical records, and other ways to share data. The regional Centers for Patient Safety and Dispute Resolution would develop and finance interventions to improve patient safety.

The voucher system would end the malpractice nightmare in which thousands of patients who are injured are never compensated while a few patients reap outsized rewards, and in which doctors practice defensive medicine while paying large malpractice premiums. To cut through this morass, the voucher system's Centers for Patient Safety and Dispute Resolution would adjudicate all patient claims of injury and compensate quickly and fairly those who have actually suffered harm. The money would come not from malpractice premiums but from the VAT. This would largely free physicians from the malpractice burden, but in exchange they would have to agree that the bad physicians who cause a disproportionate amount of malpractice injury will be drummed out of the profession.

In short, unlike individual mandates or single-payer plans, the universal voucher proposal deals with both malpractice and patient safety more broadly. Many interventions that would improve patient safety have not been implemented, despite substantial evidence that they really reduce infections, reduce complications, and save money and lives. There are many reasons for this inaction, but surely one of them is that no organization exists today with the muscle and money to push for change. The voucher plan would provide both the impetus and the money to develop interventions and implement them.

Economic Improvement. The universal voucher system would help the economy. Most obviously, it would relieve businesses of the burden of financing and administering their employees' health insurance, thus making them more efficient and competitive. Employers would also be relieved of obligations for their retirees' health coverage, and they could reduce spending on human resources departments and consultants, freeing resources to invest in their core business. They would no longer have to cope with the unpredictability of future health care cost increases, and they could once again base hiring decisions on demand for their output and on worker productivity, not on the basis of future health care costs. This should boost employment.

Lower-income Americans — as well as those who are sick and need more health care — woul receive much more in benefits than they would pay in taxes.

The voucher system would also be a huge benefit for workers. Their health care coverage would be guaranteed, not tied to their job and possibly lost if they are laid off. Strikes over health benefits would disappear. The phenomenon of job-lock, in which workers stay in jobs where they are no longer happy or productive so as not to lose their insurance coverage, would vanish. Although they would pay a new tax, the VAT, workers would at the same time see their Medicare taxes, federal income taxes, and state taxes decline, and they would receive a pay increase. Over time, with effective cost control, pay increases would once again reflect increases in productivity and not be held down by increases in health care premiums.

Other Advantages. Two of the biggest advantages of the universal voucher proposal are implicit rather than explicit. The first is that the plan is comparatively simple. The second is that it coheres with American values.

Nothing that changes the way $1 out of every $7 is raised and spent in the U.S. economy is going to be very simple, but the universal voucher program has relatively few moving parts. It envisages one standard benefits plan for all Americans. It involves no income-linked subsidies, and thus none of the complex administration that such subsidies require. It relies on just one funding source, the VAT, rather than on many different streams — employer contributions, worker premiums, out-of-pocket costs, Medicare taxes, and other state and federal taxes. Each region of the country would have just one insurance exchange. The number of health plans and insurance companies nationwide would be substantially reduced. Employers would be freed of responsibility for financing health care. Administration of the system would be handled by one national board and twelve regional health boards. No other health care proposal that seeks significant improvement is as simple. Such simplicity makes incentives clearer and more effective instead of confusing and counter-productive.

The universal voucher system's biggest advantage, however, may be the way it reflects core American values: equality of opportunity and individual freedom. The United States is different from many other Western countries that emphasize an egalitarian ethos. A universal health care voucher system would promote equality of opportunity: its standard benefits would be provided to everyone, funded by a tax that everyone pays. At the same time, it would let individual freedom flourish: it would use market mechanisms — competition — to foster quality and efficiency in health plans and in hospital and physician delivery of services. It would give people a choice of health plans, physicians, and hospitals operating in the private sector, and the option to spend their own money to buy more coverage for amenities and a wider range of services. This balance of equality of opportunity with market mechanisms and individual freedom is quintessentially American.

If Americans want a health care financing system that can achieve universal coverage, with multiple cost-control mechanisms and incentives to improve quality, and one that can do so in a sustainable way, the universal health care voucher system is the best option.

References

1. Agency for Healthcare Research and Quality. (2002). *Health Care Costs Fact Sheet.* Department of Heath and Human Services: Washington, D.C. http://www. ahrq.gov/news/costsfact. pdf.
2. Butler, S. (2001). "Reforming the Tax Treatment of Health Care to Achieve Universal Coverage." *Covering America: Real Remedies for the Uninsured.* June. Economic and Social Research Institute: Washington, D.C. http://www.esresearch. org/RWJ11PDF/full_document.pdf.
3. Catlin, A. Cowan, C. Heffler, S. and Washington, B. (2007). "National Health Spending in 2005: The Slowdown Continues." *Health Affairs* **26**(1): 142–153.
4. Centers for Medicare and Medicaid Services (CMS). (2005). *National Health Expenditure Projections, 2006–2016.* Centers for Medicare and Medicaid Service: Baltimore, MD. http://www.cms.hhs.gov/NationalHealthExpendData/downloads/ proj2006.pdf.
5. Congressional Budget Office (CBO). (2004). *Limiting Tort Liability for Medical Malpractice.* Congressional Budget Office: Washington, D.C. http://www. cbo.gov/ftpdocs/49xx/doc4968/01-08-MedicalMalpractice.pdf.
6. Kohn, L. T., Corrigan, J. M. and Donaldson, M. S. eds; Committee on Quality of Health Care in America, Institute of Medicine. (2000). *To Err is Human: Building a Safer Health System.* National Academy Press: Washington, D.C.
7. Enthoven, A. and Kronick, R. (1989). A Consumer-Choice Health Plan for the 1990s: Universal Health Insurance in a System Designed to Promote Quality and Economy. *New England Journal of Medicine* **320**: 29–37, 94–101.
8. Emanuel, E. J. and Fuchs, V. (2005a). "Health Care Vouchers: A Proposal for Universal Coverage." *New England Journal of Medicine* **352**: 1255–1260.
9. Federal Employees Health Benefits (FEHB). (2007). *Service Benefit Plan.* Federal Employees Health Benefits: Washington, D.C. http://www.fepblue.org/ benefits/benefits07/benftaagso-07.html.
10. Federal Hospital Insurance and Federal Supplementary Medical Insurance Trust Funds (2005). *Boards of Trustees Annual Report.* Washington D.C.
11. Fuchs, V. and Emanuel, E. J. (2005). "Health Care Reform: Why? What? When?" *Health Affairs* **24**(6): 1399–1414.
12. Gruber, (2000). "Health Insurance and the Labor Market." In *Handbook of Health Economics*, Vol. 1, eds. A. J. Culyer and J. P. Newhouse. Elsevier Science: New York, NY. pp. 645–706.

13. Gruber, (2006). "The Massachusetts Health Care Revolution: A Local Start for Universal Access." *The Hastings Center Report* **36**(5): 14–19.

14. Hall, R. E. and Jones, C. I. (2007). "The Value of Life and the Rise in Health Spending." *The Quarterly Journal of Economics* **122**(1): 39–72.

15. Holahan, J. Bovbjerg, R. R. and Hadley, J. (2006). *Caring for the Uninsured in Massachusetts: What Does it Cost, Who Pays, and What Would Full Coverage Add to Medical Spending.* Urban Institute: Washington, D.C.

16. Kaiser Family Foundation and Health Research and Educational Trust. (2006). *Employer Health Benefits: 2006 Annual Survey.* Health Research and Educational Trust: Chicago. http:// www.kff.org/insurance/7527/upload/7527.pdf.

17. Krugman, P. and Wells, R. (2006). The Health Care Crisis and What to Do About it. *New York Review of Books* 53(5).

18. Maryland. (2006). Fiscal 2006 State Budget Highlights. http://dbm.maryland.gov/ dbm_publishing/public_content/dbm_taxonomy/budget/publications/budge_highlights/ fy2006budhighlights.pdf.

19. McGlynn, E. A., Asch, S. M., Adams, J., Keesey, J., Hicks, J., DeCristofaro, A. and Kerr, E. A. (2003). "The Quality of Health Care Delivered to Adults in the United States." *New England Journal of Medicine* **348**: 2635-2645.

20. PacAdvantage. (2006). Press release: PacAdvantage Will No Longer Provide Access to Health Insurance Offerings. PacAdvantage: San Francisco. http://www. pacadvantage.org/ documents/brokers/Final PA News Release.pdf.

21. Palmisano, D. J., Emmons, D. W. and Wozniak, G. D. (2004). "Expanding Insurance Coverage Through Tax Credits, Consumer Choice, and Market enhancements: The American Medical Association Proposal for Insurance Reform." *The Journal of the American Medical Association* **291**(18): 2237–2242.

22. Pauly, M. V. (2001). An adaptive credit plan for covering the uninsured. In *Covering America: Real Remedies for the Uninsured.* Economic and Social Research Institute: Washington, DC. http://www.esresearch.org/RWJ11PDF/full_ document.pdf.

23. Physicians for a National Health Program. (2003). "Proposal of the Physicians' Working Group for Single-Payer National Health Insurance." *The Journal of the American Medical Association* **290**(Aug): 798–805. http://www.pnhp.org/physician sproposal/proposal/Physicians%20ProposalJAMA.pdf.

24. Sheils, J. and Haught, R. (2004). "The Cost of Tax-Exempt Health Benefits in 2004." *Health Affairs* http://content.healthaffairs.org/ cgi/ content/full/ hlthaff.w4.106v1/DC1.

25. Wachter, R. M. and Shojania, K. G. (2004). *Internal Bleeding: The Truth Behind America's Terrifying Epidemic of Medical Mistakes.* Rugged Land Press: New York.

Who Really Pays for Health Care? The Myth of "Shared Responsibility"

When asked who pays for health care in the United States, the usual answer is "employers, government, and individuals." Most Americans believe that employers pay the bulk of workers' premiums and that governments pay for Medicare, Medicaid, the State Children's Health Insurance Program (SCHIP), and other programs.

However, this is incorrect. Employers do not bear the cost of employment-based insurance; workers and households pay for health insurance through lower wages and higher prices. Moreover, government has no source of funds other than taxes or borrowing to pay for health care.

Failure to understand that individuals and households actually foot the entire health care bill perpetuates the idea that people can get great health benefits paid for by someone else. It leads to perverse and counterproductive ideas regarding health care reform.

Originally published in *JAMA*, 299(9):1057–1059, March 2008. Copyright by American Medical Association. Written with Ezekiel J. Emanuel, M.D., Ph.D.

The Myth of Shared Responsibility

Many sources contribute to the misperception that employers and government bear significant shares of health care costs. For example, a report of the Centers for Medicare & Medicaid Services states that "the financial burden of health care costs resides with businesses, households, and governments that pay insurance premiums, out-of-pocket costs, or finance health care through dedicated taxes or general revenues."[1] A New America Foundation report claims, "There is growing bipartisan support for a health system based on shared responsibility — with the individual, employers, and government all doing their fair share."[2]

The notion of shared responsibility serves many interests. "Responsibility" is a popular catchword for those who believe everyone should pull their own weight, while "sharing" appeals to those who believe everyone should contribute to meeting common social goals. Politicians welcome the opportunity to boast that they are "giving" the people health benefits. Employers and union leaders alike want workers to believe that the employer is "giving" them health insurance. For example, Steve Burd, president and chief executive officer of Safeway, argued that decreasing health care costs is critical to his company's bottom line — as if costs come out of profits.[3] A highly touted alliance between Wal-Mart and the Service Employees International Union for universal coverage pledged that "businesses, governments, and individuals all [must] contribute to managing and financing a new American health care system."[4]

The Massachusetts health care reform plan is constructed around "shared responsibility." The rhetoric of health reform proposals offered by several presidential candidates helps propagate this idea. Hillary Clinton, for instance, claims that her American Health Choices plan "is based on the principle of shared responsibility. This plan ensures that all who benefit from the system contribute to its financing and management."[5] It then lists how insurance and drug companies, individuals, clinicians, employers, and government must each contribute to the provision of improved health care.

With prominent politicians, business leaders, and experts supporting shared responsibility, it is hardly surprising that most Americans believe that employers really bear most of the cost of health insurance.

The Health Care Cost-Wage Trade-off

Shared responsibility is a myth. While employers do provide health insurance for the majority of Americans, that does not mean that they are paying the cost.

Wages, health insurance, and other fringe benefits are simply components of overall worker compensation. When employers provide health insurance to their workers, they may define the benefits, select the health plan to manage the benefits, and collect the funds to pay the health plan, but they do not bear the ultimate cost. Employers' contribution to the health insurance premium is really workers' compensation in another form.

This is not a point merely of economic theory but of historical fact. Consider changes in health insurance premiums, wages, and corporate profits over the last 30 years. Premiums have increased by about 300% after adjustment for inflation. Corporate profits per employee have flourished, with inflation-adjusted increases of 150% before taxes and 200% after taxes. By contrast, average hourly earnings of workers in private nonagricultural industries have been stagnant, actually decreasing by 4% after adjustment for inflation. Rather than coming out of corporate profits, the increasing cost of health care has resulted in relatively flat real wages for 30 years. That is the health care cost-wage trade-off.[6]

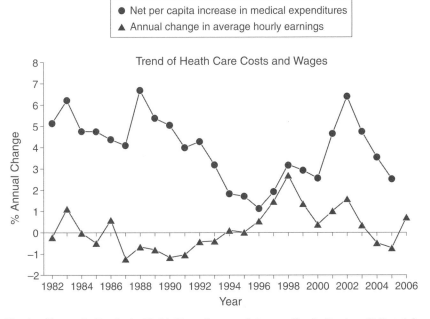

Fig. 1.   Changes in Per Capita Health Expenditures and Average Hourly Earnings (Adjusted for Inflation), 1982–2005.

Source: Data are from the Council of Economic Advisers[6] and Catlin *et al.*[7]

Even over shorter periods, workers' average hourly earnings fluctuate with changes in health care expenditures (adjusted for inflation) (Figure). During periods when the real annual increases in health care costs are significant, as between 1987 and 1992 and again between 2001 and 2004, inflation-adjusted hourly earnings are flat or even declining in real value. For a variety of reasons, the decline in wages may lag a few years behind health care cost increases. Insurance premiums increase after costs increase. Employers may be in binding multiyear wage contracts that restrict their ability to change wages immediately. Conversely, when increases in health care costs are moderate, as between 1994 and 1999, increases in productivity and other factors translate into higher wages rather than health care premiums.

The health care cost-wage trade-off is confirmed by many economic studies.[8–11] State mandates for inclusion of certain health benefits in insurance packages resulted in essentially all the cost of the added services being borne by workers in terms of lower wages.[12] Similarly, using the Consumer Expenditure Survey, Miller[13] found that "the amount of earnings a worker must give up for gaining health insurance is roughly equal to the amount an employer must pay for such coverage." Baicker and Chandra[14] reported that a 10% increase in state health insurance premiums generated a 2.3% decline in wages, "so that [workers] bear the full cost of the premium increase." Importantly, several studies show that when workers lose employer-provided health insurance, they actually receive pay increases equivalent to the insurance premium.[8,12]

In a review of studies on the link between higher health care costs and wages, Gruber[15] concluded, "The results [of studies] that attempt to control for worker selection, firm selection, or (ideally) both have produced a fairly uniform result: the costs of health insurance are fully shifted to wages."

The Cost-Public Service Trade-off

A large portion of health care coverage in the United States is provided by the government. But where does government's money for health care come from? Just as the ultimate cost of employer-provided health insurance falls to workers, the burden of government-provided health coverage falls on the average citizen. When government pays for increases in health care costs, it taxes current citizens, borrows from future taxpayers, or reduces other state services that benefit citizens: the health care cost-public service trade-off.

Health care costs are now the single largest part of state budgets, exceeding education. According to the National Governors Association, in 2006, health care expenditures accounted for an average of 32% of state budgets, while Medicaid alone accounted for 22% of spending.[16] Between 2000 and 2004, health care expenditures increased substantially, move than 34%, with Medicaid and SCHIP increasing more than 44%.[7] These increases far exceeded the increase in state tax receipts. In response, some states raised taxes, others changed eligibility requirements for Medicaid and other programs, and still others reduced the fees and payments to physicians, hospitals, and other providers of health care services.

However, according to a Rockefeller Institute of Government study of how 10 representative states responded, probably the most common policy change was to cut other state programs, and "the program area that was most affected by state budget difficulties in 2004 was public higher education. . . . On average, the sample states projected spending 4.5% less on higher education in FY 2004 than in FY 2003, and raised tuition and fees by almost 14% on average."[17] In other words, the increasing cost of Medicaid and other government health care programs are a primary reason for the substantial increase in tuition and fees for state colleges and universities. Middle-class families finding it more difficult to pay for their children's college are unwittingly falling victim to increasing state health care costs. Not an easy — but a necessary — connection to make.

Policy Implications

The widespread failure to acknowledge these effects of increasing health care costs on wages and on government services such as education has important policy implications. The myth of shared responsibility perpetuates the belief that workers are getting something while paying little or nothing. This undercuts the public's willingness to tax itself for the benefits it wants.

This myth of shared responsibility makes any reform that removes employers from health care much more difficult to enact. If workers and their families continue to believe that they can get a substantial fringe benefit like health insurance at no cost to themselves, they are less likely to consider alternatives. Unless this myth is dispelled, the center-piece of reform is likely to be an employer mandate. This is regrettable and perpetuates the widely recognized historical mistake of tying health care coverage to employment. Furthermore, an employer mandate is an economically inefficient mechanism to finance health care. Keeping employers in health care, with their varied interests and competencies, cost control, efficient insurance exchanges, value-based coverage, delivery system reform, and many other essential reforms.[18,19] Employers should be removed from health care except for enacting wellness programs that directly help maintain productivity and reduce absenteeism. Politicians' rhetoric about shared responsibility reinforces rather than rejects this misconception and inhibits rather than facilitates true health care reform.

Not only does third-party payment attenuate the incentive to compare costs and value, but the notion that someone else is paying for the insurance further reduces the incentive for cost control. Getting Americans invested in cost control will require that they realize they pay the price, not just for the deductibles and co-payments, but for the full insurance premiums too.

Sustainable increases in wages require less explosive growth in health care costs. Only then will increases in productivity show up in higher wages and lower prices, giving a boost to real incomes. Similarly, the only way for states to provide more support for education, environment, and infrastructure is for health care costs to be restrained. Unless the growth in Medicaid and SCHIP are limited to — or close to — revenue increases, they will continue to siphon money that could be spent elsewhere.

Conclusion

Discussions of health care financing in the United States are distorted by the widely embraced myth of shared responsibility. The common claim that employers, government, and households all pay for health care is false. Employers do not share fiscal responsibility and employers do not pay for health care — they pass it on in the form of lower wages or higher prices. It is essential for Americans to understand that while it looks like they can have a free lunch — having someone else pay for their health insurance — they cannot. The money comes from their own pockets. Understanding this is essential for any sustainable health care reform.

References

1. Centers for Medicare & Medicaid Services. *Health Expenditures by Sponsors: Business, Household and Government.* http://www.cms.hhs.gov/NationalHealth ExpendData/downloads/bhg08.pdf.
2. Gallagher, C. and Harbage, P. (2007). *Growing Support for Shared and Personal Responsibility in Health Care.* New America Foundation: Washington, D.C. http://www.newamerica.net/publications/policy/growing_support_shared_and_ personal_responsibility_health_care.
3. Burd, S. (2006). "Meeting the US Health Care Challenge. US Chamber of Commerce CEO Leadership Series: Event summary." http://www.uschamber.com/ NR/rdonlyres/ekv73cduc6ygrheayctrps464scv17isnos4gi3zpp4vadkukz7ycircw3mwi ey5qvh5nlisfeq3pgtj7nns7xrslhg/CEOSeriesSafeway.pdf.

4. Kavilanz, P. B. (2007). "Wal-Mart, Union Push Universal Health Care." http://money.cnn.com/2007/02/07/news/companies/walmart_healthcare/index.htm.

5. Hillary Clinton for President. *American Health Choices Plan.* http://www.hillaryclinton.com/feature/healthcareplan/americanhealthchoicesplan.pdf.

6. Council of Economic Advisers. (2007). *Economic Report of the President.* US Government Printing Office: Washington, D.C. Appendix B: Tables 3, 47, and 90. http://www.whitehouse.gov/cea/pubs.html.

7. Catlin, A. Cowan, C. Hartman, M. and Heffler, S.; National Health Expenditure Accounts Team (2008). "National Health Spending in 2006: A Year of Change for Prescription Drugs." *Health Affairs (Millwood),* **27**(1): 14–29.

8. Eberts, R. W. and Stone, J. A. (1985). "Wages Fringe Benefits, and Working Conditions: An Analysis of Compensating Differentials," *Southern Economic Journal* **52**: 274–280.

9. Sheiner, L. (1999). *Health Care Costs, Wages, and Aging.* Federal Reserve Board of Governors: Washington, D.C. http://www.federalreserve.gov/pubs/feds/1999/199919/199919pap.pdf.

10. Royalty, A. B. (2003). *A Discrete Choice Approach to Estimating Workers' Marginal Valuation of Fringe Benefits.* Indiana University-Purdue University: Indianapolis. http://liberalarts.iupui.edu/~anroyalt/wfdiscch _j03.pdf.

11. Madrian, B. C. (2006). *The US. Health Care System and Labor Markets.* National Bureau of Economic Research: Cambridge, MA. January 2006. NBER Working Paper No. 11980. http://www.nber.org/papers/w11980.

12. Gruber, J. (1994). "The Incidence of Mandated Maternity Benefits." *The American Economic Review* **84**(3): 622–641.

13. Miller, R. D. Jr. (2004). "Estimating the Compensating Differential for Employer-Provided Health Insurance." *International Journal of Health Care Finance and Economics* **4**(1): 27–41.

14. Baicker, K. and Chandra A. (2005). *The Labor Market Effects of Rising Health Insurance Premiums.* National Bureau of Economic Research: Cambridge, MA: NBER Working Paper No. 11160. http://www.nber.org/papers/w11160.

15. Gruber, J. (2000). "Health Insurance and the Labor Market." In *Handbook of Health Economics.* Vol 1, A. J. Culyer and J. P. Newhouse JP, eds. Elsevier Science: New York, NY.

16. *The Fiscal Survey of States.* National Governors Association and National Association of State Budget Officers: Washington, D.C. June 2007. http://www.nasbo.org/Publicatians/PDFs/Fiscal%20survey%20of%20the%20states%20june%202007.pdf.

17. Fossett, J.W. and Burke, C.E. (2004). *Medicaid and State Budgets in FY 2004: Why Medicaid Is so Hard to Cut.* Rockefeller Institute of Government: Albany, NY. http://www.nysl.nysed.gov/scandoclinks/ocm56501455.htm.

18. Blumenthal, D. (2006). "Employer-sponsored Health Insurance in the United States — Origins and Implications." *New England Journal of Medicine* **355**(1): 82–88.

19. Galvin, R.S. and Delbanco, S. (2006). "Between a Rock and a Hard Place: Understanding the Employer Mind-set." *Health Affairs (Millwood)* **25**(6): 1548–1556.

Part 6

Demography and Aging

Introduction

Health care differs from other consumption goods and services in many ways; one of the most important is the increase in utilization at older ages. Precise figures are not available, but it is safe to assume that per capita expenditures for health care by those 65 and older are at least double and possibly as high as triple the expenditures of those under age 65. The ratio is particularly high for long-term care in nursing homes and home care. The ratio is probably higher in the United States than in countries that have universal coverage because Medicare provides universal coverage in the U.S. at ages 65 and older; virtually all of the uninsured in the U.S. are under age 65. The increase in utilization of care by the elderly comes at a life-cycle stage when the income of most elderly decreases because of a big decrease in employment.

The increase in utilization combined with the decrease in income poses a significant financial problem which is exacerbated by demographic change. Karen Eggleston (19) and I analyze this change in the first paper of Part 6, "The New Demographic Transition: Most Gains in Life Expectancy Now Realized Late in Life." We explore how gains in life expectancy at birth are realized by different ages of the U.S. population. We find that at the beginning of the 20th century about 80 percent of the additional years of life were lived *before* age 65, but in recent years, almost 80 percent of the additional years of life were lived *after* age 65. During the intervening decades there have been large decreases in mortality of infants and children and most of the gains for adults have been below age 65.

Thus future gains in life expectancy must inevitably be realized by adults who are 65 or older.

The next three papers in Part 6 address this demographic future, with different emphasis in the analyses but similar conclusions. They share the view that there are a few options available to avert the coming financial problems of the elderly. They are not "either or" solutions; all possibilities could be pursued with mutual benefit. In my opinion, all *should* be pursued simultaneously. Each solution will be disruptive, but the total disruption will be less than if the problem were solved by pursuing one solution alone.

One possibility is to slow the rate of growth of health care spending per person 65 and over. If that rate were no higher than the rate of growth of GDP, the other possible solutions would be needed less. In the short-run it will be relatively easy to achieve this goal because the above 65 group will be adding individuals at the youngest ages, the baby boomers of the 1950s who will just be turning 65. The "young" old consume much less health care than the "old" old. But this "solution" will be a demographic delusion. Per capita expenditures on care for the elderly may slow for a while, only to be followed by large increases as the baby boomers move into their late 70s, 80s, and 90s.

The fundamental driving force behind increased spending is new medical technology and expanding use of existing technology — drugs, diagnostic interventions, surgical procedures. If U.S. medical care were locked in to pre-World War ii levels of science and technology, health expenditures would probably be a lot less than they are today, but so would life expectancy. To slow the growth of spending in a sustainable way, it will be necessary to devise institutions and incentives that limit the development and diffusion of medical innovations to those that yield high value per dollar of expenditure. The extensive use of many technologies (e.g., MRI scans) often do not meet this test. Other industries do not suffer from the same problem because executives in those industries realize that consumers will be applying a cost-benefit calculation before buying a new technology. Patients and drug companies do not have the same incentive because of health insurance.

A second possible solution is to increase employment rates of those who are under age 65 and those above that age. Although Americans are healthier than in the past and most jobs are less physically demanding, age-specific employment rates are lower now than in previous generations. Many existing laws discourage workers from staying in the work force and discourage employers from hiring older workers. These laws could be changed. Some experts believe that continued employment (possibly part-time or in less stressful occupations) would actually contribute to better health of workers and more life satisfaction. The solution that seems to offer the most promise is increased savings prior to age 65. Every one percent increase in savings would increase income available after retirement by four times as much as a one percent increase in employment income of the elderly, assuming historical rate of return.

Each of the three papers presents data and analyses that are still relevant today. The first emphasizes the change in economic position of the elderly relative to children. From a time when poverty was rampant among the elderly, the combination of Medicare, Medicaid, and Social Security plus changes in family structure that hurt children have reduced the percent elderly in poverty to below the percent of children in poverty. This paper makes three controversial recommendations:

(1) Periodically revise the definition of who is "old" and deserving of special social consideration. Let the increase in life expectancy be the guide. Instead of always thinking of age as years since *birth*, it is sometimes useful to think of the age of a cohort as the average of years until *death*. In 1950 life expectancy in the U.S. at age 65 was 13.9 years, in 1970 it was 15.2 years, in 1990, 17.2, and in 2010, 19.1

(2) Develop more flexible labor market arrangements, especially for the elderly.

(3) Develop a more appropriate balance between health care for the dying and care for the rest of the population. The increase in the number of palliative and hospice care programs is a step in that direction.

The paper "'Provide, Provide:' The Economics of Aging "gives away its preferred solution in the title, which is also the title of a poem by Robert Frost. The principal contributions of this paper are:

(1) Defines and estimates for various years the "full income" of the elderly.

(2) Decomposes the change in health care consumption of the elderly into a) age-specific consumption per older person, b) number of elderly, and c) age distribution of the elderly. Growth of age-specific consumption is most important.

(3) Measures full income inequality before age 65 and after. Most important result is that inequality after age 65 is much less than under age 65. Medicare makes a substantial contribution to equality after age 65. The more *voluntary* the addition to savings, the greater will be the increase in income inequality among the elderly.

The next paper in this Part pursues the full income approach, labeling it "holistic." The big advantage of considering health spending and other income of the elderly together is that it forces consideration of both terms simultaneously. Action in one area has repercussions in the other area. Modest tweaking with benefits and subsidies within each program separately may incorrectly suggest that all can be saved simultaneously. They cannot without significant slowing in the growth of Medicare expenditure per beneficiary, increasing employment rates, and more savings prior to retirement.

Slowing the rate of growth of Medicare expenditures per beneficiary will require attention to the development and diffusion of new medical technologies (i.e., drugs, diagnostic and surgical procedures, devices). The op-ed argues that as long as patients have insurance coverage, physicians are paid fee-for-service, and payers of health care do not bargain vigorously with suppliers, medical innovation in the U.S. is likely to continue as before. Pleas for value-based innovations and patient care are likely to fall on deaf ears. The country needs an independent organization to evaluate the cost-effectiveness of new technology, and enough patients covered by per capita reimbursement instead of fee-for-service to create a market for innovations that lower cost (holding quality of care constant) as well as innovations that increase quality.

6.1

The New Demographic Transition: Most Gains in Life Expectancy Now Realized Late in Life*

The original "demographic transition" describes a process that began in Europe by the early 1800s with decreases in mortality followed, usually after a lag, by decreases in fertility.[13,28] According to Lee and Recher (2011), p. 1, "this historical process ranks as one of the most important changes affecting human society in the past half millennium." The increase in life expectancy associated with this demographic transition has been accompanied by rising levels of per capita output, which have in turn spurred further improvements in population health through better nutrition and living standards[3,15] and, especially since World War II, through advances in medical care.[12] At the same time, increases in life expectancy have resulted in a higher proportion of each cohort living long enough to participate in the production of goods and services. Reductions in fertility are also closely linked to higher labor force participation rates among women.[11,18,22]

Originally published in *Journal of Economic Perspective*, 26(3):1–22, 2012. Copyright by American Economic Association. Written with Karen N. Eggleston.
*To access the Appendix, visit http://dx.doi.org/10.1257/jep.26.3.137.

During the original demographic transition, mortality decline prior to fertility decline often led to larger cohorts concentrated in working ages; this transitional change in the age structure of the population provided a boost to income that has been called a "demographic dividend".[6] Swift (2011) documents a significant two-way positive relationship between life expectancy and GDP per capita between 1820 and 2001 for 13 high-income countries.

Now, the United States and many other countries are experiencing a new kind of demographic transition. Instead of additional years of life being realized early in the lifecycle, they are now being realized late in life. At the beginning of the twentieth century, in the United States and other countries at comparable stages of development, most of the additional years of life were realized in youth and working ages; and less than 20 percent was realized after age 65. Now, more than 75 percent of the gains in life expectancy are realized after 65 — and that share is approaching 100 percent asymptotically. The choice of age 65 to illustrate this new demographic transition is somewhat arbitrary, but if we used 60 or 70 instead, the results would be qualitatively similar.

The new demographic transition is a *longevity* transition: How will individuals and societies respond to mortality decline when almost all of the decline will occur late in life? This issue is broader and more far-reaching than the issue of cohort size in each age group, with its usual focus on the prospective retirement of the unusually large "baby boomer" cohort, and has important socioeconomic implications independent of patterns of fertility.

When the gains in life expectancy occur mainly towards the end of life, they contribute more to the age bracket that is traditionally mostly retired rather than to the age bracket in prime working years. Retirees are highly dependent on transfers from the working population for living expenses, including large consumption of medical care. Thus, gains in life expectancy concentrated at the end of life can unsettle an economy's balance between production and consumption in ways that pose a long-run challenge for public policy. The obvious changes needed (at least "obvious" to many economists) would be to raise productivity, the savings rate, and the age of retirement, but how to accomplish such goals is controversial and uncertain.

This paper covers the years 1900–2007 for the United States and 16 other "developed countries," chosen for the continuity of their mortality data: Australia, Belgium, Canada, Denmark, England and Wales, Finland, France, Iceland, Italy, Netherlands, Northern Ireland, Norway, Scotland, Spain, Sweden, and Switzerland. We focus on demographic statistics including life expectancy at birth and at age 65, the percent of each birth cohort expected to survive to age 65, and the share of the increase in life expectancy at birth realized after age 65. For the U.S. economy, we also calculate expected labor force participation for each birth cohort, which allows us to investigate how changes in mortality affect labor force participation and work-life as a share of life expectancy. Results on the longevity transition and expected labor force participation for the United States and other high-income countries are followed by consideration of economic and social changes in China and other countries that are experiencing an earlier stage of the original demographic transition. The paper concludes with a brief discussion of the long-run implications of the new demographic transition.

The Longevity Transition

To examine long-term trends in life expectancy at birth, we draw upon the life tables in the Human Mortality Database, which offers high-quality demographic data for selected countries and regions compiled by a respected group of demographers at (http://www.mortality.org). We first extract data on life expectancy at birth; in particular, we calculate "period" life expectancy, which is the projected average age of death for a cohort if it experienced the age-specific death rates prevailing at the year of birth. We also look at rates of survival from birth to age 65 and life expectancy at age 65. We use the five-year period life tables since 1900 (or earliest available year) for each of the 17 countries or regions in the Human Mortality Database that have data extending back at least 70 years. The five-year intervals help to smooth annual fluctuations in demographic trends.

We calculate changes for nine overlapping 20-year intervals: 1907–1927, 1917–1937, and so on up to 1987–2007.[a] (The years ending in "7" are chosen to represent mid points of each of our five-year intervals.) To calculate the change in years lived past 65, we first multiply survival to 65 by life expectancy at age 65 for each five-year period and then take differences across 20-year intervals. Finally, we calculate the change in years lived past 65 as a percentage of change in life expectancy at birth for each country for each of the nine 20-year intervals.

---

[a] For our detailed underlying data on the five-year averages for each country, see the online Appendix with this paper at (http://e-jep.org). Online Appendix tables 1–3 show the decreases in the coefficient of variation across the 17 high-income countries for the demographic variables portrayed in Figures 1 and 2. To include data for the United States prior to 1933 (when the Human Mortality Database series begins for the United States), we use life table data from U.S. National Vital Statistics Reports, derived from death registration states for the period 1900 to 1928, and for the whole United States thereafter (all races combined). For a small share of observations at the beginning of the century — Australia, Canada, and Northern Ireland in 1900–1919; Spain in 1900; and the United States in 1905, 1915, and 1925 — we use imputed values from regressions with year and country fixed effects and country-specific linear time trends.

Figure 1(a) shows that life expectancy at birth has increased almost continuously for well over a century in high-income countries. Much of this rise in life expectancy was due to a particularly large fall in death rates for infants, children, and young adults, resulting in a sharp rise in the percentage of a cohort surviving to age 65, as indicated in Figure 1(b). Survival rates from birth to age 65 more than doubled over the twentieth century from 40.9 percent in 1900-04 to 83.3 percent in 2005–09 in the United States. Similarly, survival rates from birth to age 65 in 16 high-income comparators increased from 42.0 to 87.8 percent over the same period.

The other major demographic change that contributes to the longevity transition is an increase in life expectancy at age 65, an increase which has become larger in recent decades as shown in Figure 2(a). The interaction between the increase in life expectancy at age 65 and the increase in the percentage of the cohort that survives to age 65 has resulted in an exceptionally large increase in the share of the gain in life expectancy that is realized after age 65. As can be seen in Figure 2(b), that share was only about 20 percent during each 20-year period at the beginning of the twentieth century, but it was 76 percent in the United States and 78 percent for the 16-country mean by the end of the century, and is approaching 100 percent asymptotically. Our results here are quite similar to, and extend over time, those of Lee and Tuljapurkar (1977) based on the 1995 survival profile of the United States.

We can illustrate the shift in survival improvement toward older ages by comparing the age distribution of mortality decline between the first half and second half of the twentieth century for a region with particularly reliable long-run data: England and Wales. Figure 3 shows that between 1900–1904 and 1950–1954, declines in death rates were largest for infants and children, whereas between 1950–54 and 2000–2004, declines were most salient for those over age 70. This pattern of age-specific mortality decline across the twentieth century was similar for Sweden, another country where reliable long-run data is available.[b]

The actual survival of a given birth cohort will differ from the estimates of life expectancy at birth when survival is changing over time. Remember, estimates of life expectancy at birth (what we earlier called "period" life expectancy) are based on the age-specific death rates prevailing at that year of birth. For example, in 1900–1904, life expectancy at birth in England and Wales was 48.6 years.

---

[b]For details on Sweden, see the online Appendix. Figure 3 shows a slight increase in death rates for the oldest [90+] age groups between 1900–1904 and 1950–1954, perhaps because of small numbers, less-reliable data, and/or survival of a less-healthy cohort to those ages.

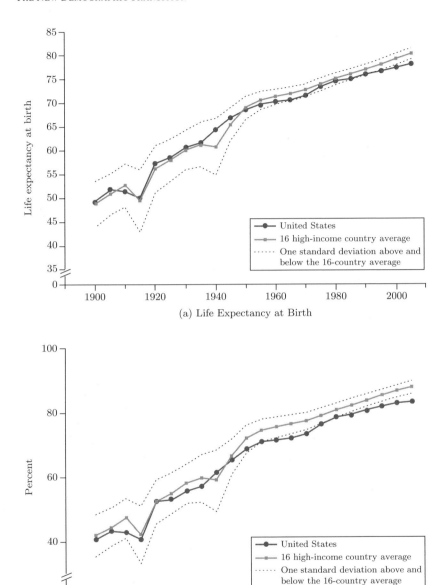

(a) Life Expectancy at Birth

(b) Percent of Birth Cohort Expected to Survive to Age 65

Fig. 1.   Life Expectancy at Birth and Survival to Age 65, Since 1990 (*in the United States and 16 other high-income countries*).
Source: Authors' calculations using data from the Human Morality Database and other sources as detailed in the online Appendix.

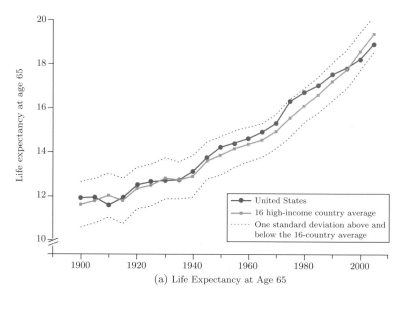

(a) Life Expectancy at Age 65

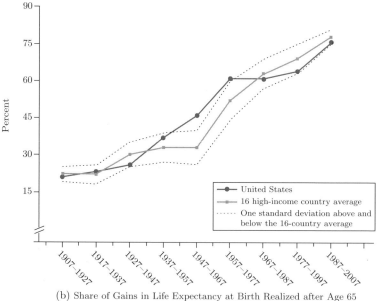

(b) Share of Gains in Life Expectancy at Birth Realized after Age 65

Fig. 2.   Life Expectancy at Age 65 and Gains in Life Expectancy Realized after Age 65 Since 1990
(*in the United States and 16 other high-income countries*).
Source: Authors' calculations using data from the Human Mortality Database and other sources as
detailed in the online Appendix.

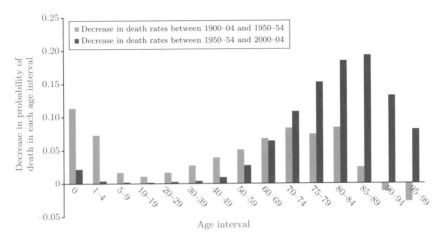

Fig. 3.   Decrease in Death Rates by Age Group in England and Wales, 1900–1904 to 1950–54 and 1950–1954 to 2000–2004.
Source: Authors' calculations using data from the Human Mortality Database.

In contrast, the cohort born in 1900–1904 had a cohort, life expectancy (actual mean age of death) of 53.8 years, since they experienced part of the increase in survival shown in Figures 1–3. The cohort born only 17 years later experienced a cohort life expectancy of 62.4 years, whereas "period" life expectancy at birth did not reach that level until 1935–1939.[c]

Nevertheless, we find that estimates based on cohort life tables prepared by the Social Security Administration[4] exhibit a similar trend towards survival gains realized late in life: for men, the share of life expectancy increases realized after age 65 was 28 percent between the 1900 and 1920 birth cohorts, rising to a projected 62 percent between the 1980 and 2000 birth cohorts. For women, the share of life expectancy gains realized after age 65 increased from 30 percent (between the 1900 and 1920 birth cohorts) to an estimated 69 percent (between the 1980 and 2000 birth cohorts).

The century-long demographic trends shown in Figures 1 and 2 have been similar in all 17 countries with available data. From a U.S. perspective, the main difference is lagging survival to 65 compared to the other 16 countries (the U.S. line is below the 16-country average in Figure 1(b)); also, the United States experienced a larger rise in female life expectancy at age 65 between the 1940s

---

[c] Survival gains have been so dramatic that period and cohort survival significantly differs. For example, age-specific death rates for England and Wales in 1900–1904 would have led to only 43.7 percent of women and 36.4 percent of men surviving to 65. But of the cohort born in 1900–1904, 61.3 percent of women and 49.6 percent of men actually survived to age 65.

and 1970s than the other countries. The relative differences among countries have decreased over time, especially for life expectancy at birth and survival to age 65.

The Longevity Transition and Expected Labor Force Participation

One of the most significant economic effects of the longevity transition is on expected lifetime labor force participation, partly in terms of total years in the workforce and especially in terms of years in the workforce as a fraction of expected years of life. Two factors affecting the connection from life expectancy to years of work are 1) whether the growing numbers of elderly are healthy enough to work and 2) the economic, social, and political pressures for a period of retirement at the end of life.

Greater longevity can have opposing effects on age-specific health status. If improved survival is correlated with reductions in morbidity for the elderly, then illness may be compressed into the end of life, as posited by the "compression of morbidity" hypothesis.[16] On the other side, medical interventions do tend to keep alive those who are in worse health,[47] which suggests the possibility that the longer-lived elderly could be sicker for a longer period. The net effect of rising longevity on age-specific morbidity is an empirical question. According to the National Long-Term Care Survey, the share of elderly Americans with severe disabilities decreased from 26.2 to 19.7 percent between 1982 and 1999.[33] Reference 35 find a strong within-country correlation between declining mortality and improved self-assessed health for several European countries. Thus, the empirical record suggests that better health in terms of both improved survival and reduced morbidity could tend to raise age-specific rates of labor force participation. Changes in occupational structure which lower the physical demands of work also can increase participation.

Higher incomes tend to increase the demand for leisure, in the form of fewer hours of work per week and, especially recently, as a block at the end of life.[10,37] Furthermore, several factors might give rise to a negative interaction between improved survival and employment, at least for some subgroups. For example, the reduced selection effect of mortality might also increase the proportion of the cohort that is less valued in employment (because of less stamina, ambition, education, and the like), reducing age-specific labor force participation. Alternatively, if firms have pyramid-like organizational structures with many jobs at entry and fewer at higher levels in the hierarchy — such as the military's "up or out" policy regarding age and promotion of officers — then increases in survival will lead to crowding at higher levels of the pyramid and lower rates of participation. Moreover, a sharp rise in employment rates for women, at wages that were often below those paid to men, might have led to some decrease in the demand for men's labor.

On net, which of these forces have predominated over the past century, and which are likely to predominate in the future? Estimates of what we call "expected labor force participation" can help answer this question.

Calculating expected labor force participation

We define "expected labor force participation" (XLFP) as the total years an individual is expected to participate in the labor force, based on period estimates of survival, and labor force participation by gender and age. That is

$$XLFP_{jt} = \sum_{i=1}^{100} \pi_{ijt} L_{ijt},$$

where L_{ijt} is the labor force participation rate for age i and gender j in year t, weighted by probability of survival to age $i(\pi_{ijt})$. It is necessary to examine men and women separately because of the large upsurge in female labor force participation between the 1950s and 2000.[11,20,21] Our calculations rely on labor force participation rates from decennial censuses (1900–1930) and the Current Population Survey (1942–2007). As in the earlier estimates of life expectancy, we can calculate both "period" expected labor force participation, which is based on the age-specific labor force participation rates prevailing at a certain point of time, or the actual realized labor force participation rates for a birth cohort; these estimates will differ when age-specific labor force participation rates are changing over time.

Changes in lifetime expected labor force participation can be decomposed into two factors: changes in survival to given ages and changes in age/sex-specific rates of labor force participation. For example, we calculate the effect of improving survival, holding age-specific labor force participation rates constant at their 2007 values. We also calculate the effect of changing rates of labor force participation, holding survival rates constant.[d]

Our work is related to the literature on expected lifetime work hours[24] and work-life expectancy,[41] including the work-life estimates for the U.S. population

---

[d]These are decompositions 1B and 2B, respectively, in Table 7 of the online Appendix. Alternative calculations, using 1900 as the base year (decompositions 1A and 2A), show similar results.

from the 1950s through the early 1980s from the Bureau of Labor Statistics.[e] As far as we are aware, this paper is the first to produce work-life estimates for the United States covering the period 1900 to 2007, decompose those changes into survival and age/sex-specific labor force participation effects, and to estimate work-life expectancy relative to life expectancy at birth for a broader range of countries in recent decades.

U.S. expected labor force participation since 1900

In the early twentieth century, most of the increase in life expectancy arose from the dramatic decrease in mortality at young ages. This change first increased the years of youth dependency for these cohorts, and then increased expected labor force participation — the expected number of years that an individual will be in the labor force if he or she participates at the average labor force participation rate for each sex and age in a given year.

Figure 4(a) shows that years of expected labor force participation at birth for U.S. males increased by a third — from about 30 to 40 years — between 1900 and 1950. For the most recent half century, however, increases in survival have been offset by decreasing age-specific labor force participation rates for men, causing expected lifetime labor force participation to be relatively constant at about 40 years. Because life expectancy at birth has continued to increase, male expected labor force participation as a fraction of expected years of life has declined, as shown in Figure 4(b). Table 1 shows that in the United States between 1900 and 2000, male labor force participation increased from 30 to 40.5 years, female participation from 6.4 years to 34.4 years, and for the total population from 18.5 to 37.4 years. This increase in years of expected labor participation is two-thirds of the total gain in life expectancy at birth of 28.2 years over the twentieth century.

How much of this change is attributable just to longer life expectancies? If we hold age-specific rates of labor force participation constant but allow survival rates to grow at the actually observed pace, the rise in life expectancy alone would have increased expected labor force participation by 13.3 years for males and by 10.8 years for females since 1900 (as shown in Table 1). The effect of mortality decline was concentrated in the first half of the twentieth century. Indeed, for men, if we hold age-specific labor force participation rates constant

---

[e]In other pre-existing work in this area,[26] update worklife estimates for the U.S. based on 1998–1999 labor force participation rates. Reference 36 use a regression framework. In related research,[24] estimates lifetime working hours for U.S. men born between 1840 and 1970 and for the U.S. population born between 1890 and 1970.

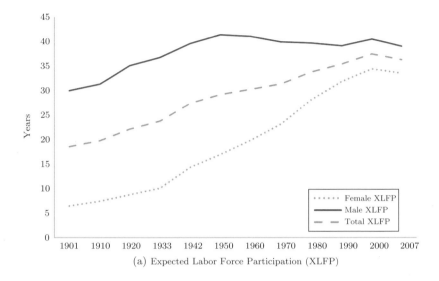

(a) Expected Labor Force Participation (XLFP)

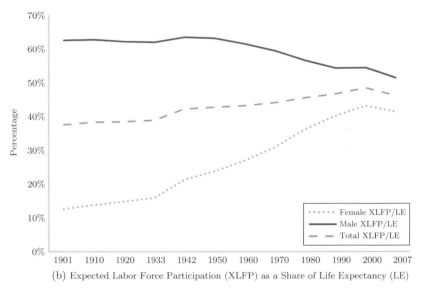

(b) Expected Labor Force Participation (XLFP) as a Share of Life Expectancy (LE)

Fig. 4.   U.S. Expected Labor Force Participation Since 1990 and as a Share of Life Expectancy at Birth.
Source: Authors' calculations using data from the Human Mortality Database and other sources as detailed in the online Appendix.

Table 1.   Expected Labor Force Participation in the United States, by Sex, 1900–2007.

	Men					Women		
Year	Male XLFP	Male XLFP holding LFP constant	Male XLFP adjusted for hours worked	Male XLFP/ LE_0	Male XLFP adjusted for hours/LE_0	Female XLFP	Female XLFP holding LFP constant	Female XLFP/ LE_0
1900	30.0	25.7	37.28	62.6%	77.9%	6.4	22.7	12.7%
1910	31.3	27.1	39.96	62.8%	80.2%	7.4	24.1	13.9%
1920	35.1	30.4	37.65	62.2%	66.8%	8.7	26.3	14.9%
1933	36.7	32.3	40.40	62.0%	68.2%	10.0	28.3	16.0%
1942	39.5	34.1	42.66	63.5%	68.5%	14.3	30.1	21.3%
1950	41.3	35.6	38.22	63.2%	58.4%	16.9	31.3	23.8%
1960	41.0	36.3	36.79	61.5%	55.2%	19.8	32.0	27.0%
1970	39.9	36.4	34.67	59.5%	51.7%	23.1	32.2	31.0%
1980	39.6	37.4	n.a.	56.6%	n.a.	28.1	32.8	36.3%
1990	39.1	37.9	n.a.	54.4%	n.a.	31.8	33.1	40.3%
2000	40.5	38.7	n.a.	54.5%	n.a.	34.4	33.3	43.2%
2007	39.0	39.0	n.a.	51.6%	n.a.	33.5	33.5	41.5%
Change, 1900 to most recent	**9.0**	**13.3**	**−2.6**	**−11.0%**	**−26.1%**	**27.1**	**10.8**	**28.8%**

	Total (men and women)				
Year	Total XLFP	Total XLFP holding LFP constant	Total XLFP adjusted for hours worked	Total XLFP/LE_0	Total XLFP adjusted for hours/LE_0
1900	18.5	24.2	n.a	37.6%	n.a.
1910	19.8	25.6	n.a.	38.4%	n.a.
1920	22.1	28.4	n.a.	38.5%	n.a.
1933	23.7	30.3	29.0	39.0%	47.5%
1942	27.4	32.2	29.2	42.3%	45.1%
1950	29.1	33.6	29.0	42.8%	42.5%
1960	30.2	34.2	28.8	43.2%	41.2%
1970	31.3	34.4	28.9	44.2%	40.7%
1980	33.8	35.2	n.a.	45.7%	n.a.
1990	35.4	35.6	n.a.	46.8%	n.a.
2000	37.4	36.0	n.a.	48.6%	n.a.
2007	36.3	36.3	n.a.	46.3%	n.a.
Change, 1900 to most recent	**17.7**	**12.0**	**n.a.**	**8.7%**	**n.a.**

Sources: Author calculations based on survival data from the Human Mortality Database (1933–2007), supplemented by data for death registration states for 1900–1920; and labor force participation rates from decennial censuses (1900–1930) and the Current Population Survey (1942–2007). Adjustments for hours worked draw from Hazan (2009).[24] See the online Appendix for details.

Notes: Expected Labor Force Participation (XLFP) is calculated as the total years an individual is expected to participate in the labor force based on period estimates of labor force participation and survival by gender and age. XLFP for a given year represents the expected number of years that an individual would be in the labor force if he or she participates at the average LFP rate for each age in that given year. LE_0 is life expectancy at birth. "XLFP holding LFP constant" uses 2007 age- and sex-specific labor force participation rates, but allows survival to each age to vary as it actually did between 1900 and 2007.

but allow survival rates to vary in calculating expected labor force participation ("male XLFP holding LFP constant"), the ratio of years of expected labor force participation to life expectancy at birth was relatively constant at 54 percent from early in the twentieth century until about 1970 (not shown in the table). At that point, it began a slow but seemingly inexorable decline, now falling to about 50 percent.

Actual years of expected labor force participation, reflecting both survival effects and changes in age-specific labor force participation rates, have also begun to decline. As shown in both Table 1 and Figure 4(b), the ratio of years of expected labor force participation to life expectancy at birth ($XLFP/LE_0$) has declined for U.S. men from 62.6 percent in 1900 to 51.6 percent in 2007. That same ratio for women increased from 12.7 percent in 1900 to 43.2 percent in 2000, before declining slightly to 41.5 percent by 2007. For the overall U.S. population, years of expected labor force participation divided by life expectancy at birth peaked at 48.6 percent in 2000 and declined slightly to 46.3 percent by 2007.

Since 1950, increases in survival and declines in age-specific participation rates of men tended to offset one another. For example, between 1950 and 2007, labor force participation rates of men ages 45–54 declined from 95.8 percent to 88.2 percent, but survival to age 50 increased from 84.1 to 92.2 percent, so the total expected years in the labor force between ages 45 and 55 remained eight years.[f] For women, increases in years of expected labor force participation mostly reflect increases in age-specific rates of labor force participation, especially after 1950. Accordingly, for women, if we hold age-specific labor force participation rates constant but allow survival rates to vary in calculating expected labor force participation ("female XLFP holding LFP constant"), the ratio of years of expected labor force participation to life expectancy at birth has declined slowly but steadily from about 45 percent in the first few decades of the twentieth century to about 40 percent (not shown in the table).

The increase in female labor force participation since the late 1950s could be considered primarily a one-time substitution from unpaid home production to paid work outside the home.[11,21] If so, then the decrease in years of expected labor force participation for Women in the United States since 2000 would reflect completion of the one-off change and the beginning of a similar trend as seen for men — that is, a decline of years in the labor force as a share of life expectancy at birth.

---

[f]For the detailed data behind these calculations across the range of ages, for both men and women, see online Appendix Table 7, which offers alternative decompositions of changes in both male and female labor force participation. Online Appendix Table 7 also shows that holding age-specific labor force participation rates constant (at either their 1900 or 2007 values) would have led to a larger increase in male expected labor force participation than actually observed.

Taking into account the decrease in the intensive margin — annual hours worked per full-time worker — tends to reinforce the conclusion that expected work life has declined as a fraction of life expectancy at birth. Reference 24 estimated lifetime work hours over the past century conditional on survival to age five. We adapt Hazan's data to life expectancy at birth to calculate years of expected labor force participation adjusted for hours worked and show the results in Table 1 (the online Appendix available with this paper at (http://e-jep.org) has details of our calculations).

Calculation of a century-long trend in expected years of labor force participation in other high-income countries is not possible because there is no reliable source for internationally comparable labor force participation rates before 1980. Given the similarities in trends of both survival and labor force participation across these countries for the available years, we suspect the trend of declining expected labor force participation as a share of life expectancy at birth that we found for the United States reflects a broad and robust trend that countries experience as they reach high life expectancy levels. Indeed, with the sole exception of the Netherlands, the ratio of years of expected labor force participation to life expectancy at birth has declined since 1980 for males in all other high-income countries in our analyses.[g] Adjusting for a decline in work hours would reinforce this trend.

Demographic Transition Across Stages of Economic Development

The demographic transition traces out a pathway, with many societies arrayed along earlier phases of the transition roughly and imperfectly in accordance with their per capita incomes. Many developing countries are currently experiencing the original demographic transition. For example, Table 2 shows that between 1990 and 2010, the share of years lived past 65 as a percentage of increase in life expectancy at birth was only a little over one-third in Vietnam and Brazil, and less than one-quarter in Bangladesh — comparable to levels a century earlier in today's high-income countries.

Improving health and increasing life expectancy at birth clearly can contribute to better living standards for the world's poor (World Health Organization, 2002).

---

[g]The online Appendix tables provide calculations of expected labor force participation across 15 countries since 1980; see Appendix Table 8 in the online Appendix available with this paper at (http://e-jep .org). Reference 9, p. 17 examines the age at which male mortality was 1.5 percent in 1977 and 2007, finding that at that age almost 90 percent of UK men were employed in 1977, but by 2007, only 30 percent were.

Table 2. The Longevity Transition in Asia and Select Developing Countries.

| Country | Change in years lived past 65 as a percentage of change in life expectancy at birth, 1990–2010 | |
	Males	Females
Japan	72.7%	87.0%
South Korea	45.4%	57.1%
China	51.9%	40.6%
Philippines	26.2%	36.0%
Indonesia	26.1%	35.7%
Brazil	34.2%	35.0%
Vietnam	32.5%	34.7%
India	23.6%	25.8%
Bangladesh	20.7%	25.4%

Source: Authors' calculations based on the life tables for each country prepared by the International Programs Center of the U.S. Bureau of the Census in its International Data Base.

Data on labor force participation for developing countries is not always reliably comparable across countries and over time. Nevertheless, the importance of improved survival for gains in expected labor force participation at early stages of the longevity transition can be illustrated with extant data. For example, in 1980 only 70 percent of Indonesian men survived to age 45; by 2007, 90 percent did. This improved survival added 10 years to expected labor force participation rates for Indonesian males between 1980 and 2007. As a result, expected labor force participation rates for Indonesian males rose to 43.7 years, which was 64.5 percent of life expectancy at birth in 2007.

China and India are especially important cases to consider, given their large populations and relatively rapid economic development. In India, the share of years lived past 65 as a percentage of increase in life expectancy at birth was only one-quarter (as shown in Table 2) in the most recent 20-year period. For China, that share was 52 percent for men and 41 percent for women in the 1990–2010 period.

China's position reflects the rapidity of its demographic transition since the early 1970s and its achievement of relatively high levels of health despite low per capita income by the end of the Mao era.[2,43] Indeed, despite the higher death rates associated with the Great Leap Famine of 1959–1961, China's growth in life expectancy from approximately 35–40 years in 1949 to 65.5 years in 1980 ranks as the most rapid sustained increase in documented global history.[h] These earlier health improvements and growth of the working-age population contributed to China's unprecedented economic growth for the past quarter-century. Wang and Mason (2008) estimate that between 1982 and 2000, about 15 percent of China's rapid growth in output per capita stemmed from the demographic dividend. (Bloom and Williamson (1998) estimate that one-quarter to one-third of the growth rates in the "East Asian miracle" stemmed from the demographic dividend.) Although the pace of mortality decline in China has slowed, it continues: Chinese life expectancy increased between 1990 and 2010 from 69.9 to 76.8 years for women and from 66.9 to 72.5 years for men.

With a rapid demographic transition to relatively low mortality and low fertility, China's population is now aging.[39] Many policy challenges loom as China establishes social and economic institutions commensurate with its transition to a middle-income, market-based economy with a large elderly population.[8,14] One additional challenge for China in reducing the growth-slowing potential of the new demographic transition is China's increasing burden of chronic disease. Fueled by rapid urbanization, increases in high-fat and calorie-rich diets, reductions in physical activity, unabated male smoking and other factors, prevalence of chronic disease in China has quickly caught up with that of high-income countries. For example, the age-standardized prevalence of diabetes among adults in China was 9.7 percent in 2007-2008, more than three times reported prevalence in 1994,[46] comparable to the U.S. rate of 8.3 percent overall in 2010 and 11.3 percenramong adults,[9] and higher than the OECD average.[38]

The timing and the rapidity of the longevity transition have varied across countries and regions. For example, in Japan between 1950 and 1970, only 13.1 percent of increase in male life expectancy at birth was realized after age 65; for women, that figure was 17.3 percent. During the 1990 to 2009 period, Japan led the world in the new demographic transition, with the share of gains in life expectancy at birth realized after age 65 reaching 72.7 percent for men and 87 percent for women (again, as shown in Table 2).

The original and the new demographic transitions are inextricably intertwined with the evolution of social and economic institutions.[1] Evidence is mounting that no society at an advanced stage of economic development can presume that

---

[h]Miller *et al.* (2012) assess the relative importance of various explanations proposed for these gains, including better nutrition, widespread public health interventions, improved access to medical care, and increases in educational levels. They find that gains in education and public health campaigns jointly explain 25–32 percent of the crude death rate decline under Mao, and similar proportions of the dramatic reductions in infant and under-five mortality in that period.

further gains in longevity will contribute to growth of per capita income under currently prevailing institutions. For example, Lee and Mason (2011) compare the "average age of consumption" to the "average age of labor income"[i] across a large group of countries for which they and their international collaborators have collected detailed generational accounts, including the value of assets and transfer wealth from social support programs (but not including bequests or value of nonmarket labor). They find that for developing countries, net transfers flow strongly downward from older to younger ages. However, in a "sea change" analogous to what we call the new demographic transition, "the direction of intergenerational transfers in the population has shifted from downward to upward, at least in a few leading rich nations" including Germany, Austria, and Japan (Lee and Mason, 2011, p. 116). Although the Lee-Mason estimates are cross-sectional, the link to the longevity transition is clear: for the 13 countries that overlap between their dataset and ours, there is a strong negative correlation (-0.89) between the share of gains in life expectancy over the past 20 years that were realized after age 65 and the current number of years by which the average age of income exceeds the average age of consumption. In other words, the more the gains in life expectancy are concentrated in traditional retirement years, the closer the intergenerational transfers are to being upward rather than downward.

For a broader group of 107 countries, Bloom *et al.* (2010) calculate counterfactual annual growth rates of per capita income between 1960 and 2005, using 2005–2050 projections of demographics. The results vary depending on the level of economic development. They find that in most non-OECD countries, declining youth dependency would more than offset increasing old-age dependency. However, about half of countries would have grown more slowly using 2005–2050 projections of demographics. Among 26 OECD countries analyzed, 25 of them (Turkey is the exception) would have had lower economic growth — averaging 2.1 rather than 2.8 percent per year — under the counterfactual of 2005–2050 demographic change.

Policy Implications of the New Demographic Transition

Historically, adults produced more than they consumed and supported children. With such a pattern in place, the increase in proportion of the population in older

---

[i]They construct the average ages of consumption and labor income as follows: "The average age of consumption is calculated by multiplying each age by the aggregate consumption at that age, summing these products over all ages, then dividing by the total amount of consumption at all ages. An equivalent calculation gives the average age of labor income" (Lee and Mason, 2011, p. 123).

years implied by the demographic transition might have been thought to shift out the social budget constraint as people expanded their number of years worked. However, "a funny thing happened along the way: societies invented retirement... and the economic consequences of population aging are now viewed with alarm" (Lee and Mason, 2011, p. 115).

Retirement, a relatively new phenomenon in human history, can be viewed as a response to many economic and social changes. Contributing factors include the shift from self-employment on farms or small businesses to wage and salary status; more rapid technological change, resulting in more rapid obsolescence of human capital (alongside compensation packages that often underpay at the beginning and overpay at the end of a career, as discussed in Lazear (1981)); the introduction of a variety of health and welfare programs which assist the elderly but also discourage work; an income-driven increase in the demand for leisure, with the diminishing marginal value of an even shorter work week overtaken by the efficiency gains of a block of leisure at the end of life; and, in times of high unemployment, public concern about job opportunities for younger workers.

Will the new demographic transition inevitably lead to slower economic growth? As people foresee longer lives, they might choose to work longer, save more, and/or invest in human capital in sufficient amounts and innovative enough ways that longer lives continue to contribute to increased prosperity. In this spirit, Bloom et al. (2010) assert that "the problem of population ageing is more a function of rigid and outmoded policies and institutions than a problem of demographic change per se" (p. 607).

It is not clear, however, that the United States or other high-income countries even further along in the new demographic transition are reshaping their policies and institutions sufficiently in response to the longevity transition. Although both the United States and France have increased the age of retirement or age to qualify for early retirement, social welfare systems across the high-income countries of the world continue to give strong incentives for earlier, rather than later, retirement.[19] Between 1965 and 2005, the correlation between change in male life expectancy at birth and change in retirement age is actually negative: −0.21 (Bloom et al., 2010, p. 591). This trend cannot continue indefinitely: longer and longer retirement lives are not consistent with continued increases in per capita income unless there are significant increases in savings, investment, and productivity. It is ironic that the same phenomenon that led to higher GDP per capita — namely higher life expectancy — could now lead to lower GDP per capita.

Successful navigation of the new demographic transition calls for a combination of policies to give incentives for more savings and investment (including in human capital) earlier in the lifecycle and for additional work later in the lifecycle. Two forces in particular might move the society in that direction: improvement in health, and reductions in the transfers that the elderly can expect to receive from the young.

Public policy should encourage higher labor force participation for the elderly, both by reducing the disadvantages that employers face when employing older workers and by providing enhanced incentives to individuals to continue to work. "People cannot expect to finance 20–25 year retirements with 35-year careers," Shoven noted.[23] "It just won't work. Not in Greece [or] the United States . . . Eventually, we are going to have to increase retirement ages." However, increasing labor force participation for the 65-plus age group alone probably won't make a big difference: even a doubling of those rates from their 2007 levels of 12.6 for women and 20.5 for men would not bring the U.S. ratio of expected labor force participation to life expectancy at birth back to its 2000 level. Increased labor force participation by men in the 50–64 age bracket is also needed.

Public policy might also seek to improve productivity, with an emphasis on education and building human capital early in the lifecycle, and on investment to reduce morbidity and improve the ability to work later in life. Whether compression of morbidity later in life will continue depends on whether improvements in medical technology and in die socioeconomic determinants of health are offset by adverse trends such as increasing obesity. A potentially promising focus here would be to consider investments in public health and medical technologies that reduce morbidity and improve quality of life, as well as more focus on medical innovations that reduce costs of care. (One example of a policy consistent with both objectives would be expansion of palliative care as a substitute for what can otherwise be extremely expensive end-of-life care in a hospital — especially in countries where the concept of hospice services is relatively new, such as China.)

Finally, increased savings, investment, and capital formation could help in fueling endogenous growth.[32,40] U.S. personal savings rates have been low for many decades. Increasing the savings rate of individuals before they retire would ameliorate the potential adverse impact of longevity on economic growth. Countries will need to make fiscally realistic structural changes to entitlement programs — such as Medicare and Social Security in the United States — to support acceptable living standards and improvements in health.

High-income societies are now facing a new demographic transition: the longevity transition. They must decide how to respond to mortality decline when almost all of the decline will occur late in life. Additional increases in life expectancy will result in further declines in expected labor force participation as a percentage of life expectancy at birth unless there is a significant rise in labor force participation rates across both middle and older ages. Of course, increased life expectancy has great value independent of its relationship to per capita income.[37] The original demographic transition gave society a "demographic gift" of higher per capita incomes[7] without much need for a policy response, but the new demographic transition requires politically difficult policies if societies wish to preserve a positive relationship running from increased longevity to greater prosperity.

References

1. Aoki, M. (2011). "The Five-Phases of Economic Development and Institutional Evolution in China and Japan." Presidential Lecture at the 16th World Congress of the International Economic Association.

2. Banister, J. (1987). *China's Changing Population.* Stanford University Press: Stanford, CA.

3. Barker, D. J. (l990). "The Fetal and Infant Origins of Adult Disease." *British Medical Journal* **301**(6761): 1111.

4. Bell, F. C. and Michael, L. M. (2005). *Life Tables for the United States Social Security Asia 1900–2100.* Actuarial Study No. 120, Social Security Administration Office of the Chief Actuary, SSA Pub. No. 11–11536. Available at: http://www .socialsecurity). gov/OACT/NOTES/s2000s.html.

5. Bloom, D. E., David, C. and Günther, F. (2010). "Implications of Population Ageing for Economic Growth." *Oxford Review of Economic Policy* **26**(4): 583–612.

6. Bloom, D. E., David, C. and Jaypee, S. (2003). *The Demographic Dividend: A New Perspective on the Economic Consequences of Population Change.* Monograph Reports, MR-1274. RAND Corporation: Santa Monica, CA. http://www.rand. org/pubs/monograph_reports/MR1274.

7. Bloom, D. E. and Williamson, J. G. (1998). "Demographic Transitions and Economic Miracles in Emerging Asia." *World Bank Economic Review* **12**(3): 419–455.

8. Chen, Q., Karen, E. and Ling, L. (2011). "Demographic Change, Intergen-erational Transfers, and the Challenges to Social Protection Systems in China." *Demographic Transition and Inclusive Growth in Asia.* Edward Elgar: Cheltenham, UK.

9. Centers for Disease Control and Prevention (CDC) (2011). "National Diabetes Fact Sheet, 2011." CDC: Atlanta, GA. http://www.cdc.gov/diabetes/pubs/pdf/ ndfs_2011.ndf.

10. Costa, D. L. (1998). *The Evolution of Retirement: An American Economic History, 1880–1990.* University of Chicago Press: Chicago, USA.

11. Costa, D. L. (2000). "From Mill Town to Board Room: The Rise of Women's Paid Labor." *Journal of Economic Perspectives* **14**(4): 101–122.

12. Cutler, D., Deaton, A. and Lleras-Muney, A. (2006). "The Determinants of Mortality." *Journal of Economic Perspectives* **20**(3): 97–120.

13. Davis, K. (1945). "The World Demographic Transition." *Annals of the American Academy of Political and Social Science* **237**(1): 1–11.
14. Eggleston, K. N. and Tuljapurkar, S. eds. (2010). *Aging Asia: Economic and Social Implications of Rapid Demographic Change in China, Japan, and South Korea.* Shorenstein APRC; distributed by Brookings Institution Press: Washington, D.C.
15. Fogel, R. W. (1994). "Economic Growth, Population Theory and Physiology The Bearing of Long-term Processes on the Making of Economic Policy." *American Economic Review* **84**(3): 369–395.
16. Fries, J. F. (1980). "Aging, Natural Death, and the Compression of Morbidity." *New England Journal of Medicine* **303**(3): 130–135.
17. Fuchs, V. R. (1999). "Provide, Provide: The Economics of Aging." In *Medicare Reform: Issues and Answers,* eds. A. J. Retten-maier and T. R. Saving. University of Chicago Press: Chicago, USA, pp. 15–36.
18. Galor, O. and Weil, D. N. (1996). "The Gender Gap, Fertility, and Growth," *American Economic Review* **86**(3): 374–387.
19. Gruber, J. and Wise, D. A. (1998). *Social Security Programs and Retirement around the World.* University of Chicago Press: USA.
20. Goldin, G. (1986). "The Female Labor Force and American Economic Growth: 1890 to 1980." In *Long-Term Factors in American Economic Growth,* Conference on Income and Wealth, Volume 51, eds. Stanley Engerman and Robert Gallman. University of Chicago Press: USA, pp. 557-604.
21. Goldin, C. (1990). *Understanding the Gender Gap: An Economic History of American Women.* Oxford University Press: New York.
22. Guinnane, T. W. (2011). "The Historical Fertility Transition: A Guide for Economists." *Journal of Economic Literature* **49**(3): 589–614.
23. Haven, C. (2011). "Stanford Economist: How Do We 'Get off This Path of Deficits as Far as the Eye Can See?'" *Stanford Report,* August 2, http://news. stanford.edu/news/2011/august/shoven-debt-qanda-080211.html.
24. Hazan, M. (2009). "Longevity and Lifetime Labor Supply: Evidence and Implications." *Econometrica* **77**(6): 1829–1863.
25. Human Mortality Database. University of California, Berkeley and Max Planck Institute for Demographic Research. Available at: www.mortality.org.
26. Hunt, T., Pickersgill, J. and Rutemiller. H. (2001). "Recent Trends in Median Years to Retirement and Worklife Expectancy for the Civilian U.S. Population (Prepared Using 1998/99 BLS Labor Force Participation Rates)." *Journal of Forensic Economics* **14**(3): 203–227.
27. Lazear, E. P. (1981). "Agency, Earnings Profiles, Productivity, and Hours Restrictions." *American Economic Review* **71**(4): 606–620.
28. Lee, R. D. (2003). "The Demographic Transition: Three Centuries of Fundamental Change." *Journal of Economic Perspectives* **17**(4): 167–190.
29. Lee, R. D. and Reher, D. S. (2011). "Introduction: The Landscape of Demographic Transition and Its Aftermath." *Population and Development Review* **37**(Issue Supplement s1): 1–7.

30. Lee, R. D. and Mason, A. (2011). "Generational Economics in a Changing World." *Population and Development Review* **37**(Issue Supplement s1): 115–142.
31. Lee, R. D. and Tuljapurkar, S. (1997). "Death and Taxes: Longer Life, Consumption, and Social Security." *Demography* **34**(1): 67–81.
32. Lucas, R. E. (1988) "On the Mechanics of Economic Development." *Journal of Monetary Economics* **22**(1): 3–42.
33. Manton, K. G. and Gu, X. (2001). "Changes in the Prevalence of Chronic Disability in the United States Black and Nonblack Population above Age 65 from 1982 to 1999." *Proceedings of the National Academy of Science of the United States of America* **98**(11): 6354–6359.
34. Miller, N. G., Eggleston, K. N. and Qiong, Z. (2012). "Understanding China's Mortality Decline under Mao: A Provincial Analysis, 1950–1980." Unpublished paper.
35. Milligan, K. and Wise, D. A. (2011). "Social Security and Retirement around the World: Historical Trends in Mortality and Health, Employment, and Disability Insurance Participation and Reforms — Introduction and Summary." NBER Working Paper 16719.
36. Millimet, D. L., Nieswiadomy, M., Hang, R. and Slottje, D. (2003). "Estimating Worklife Expectancy: An Econometric Approach." *Journal of Econometrics* **113**(1): 83–113.
37. Murphy, K. M. and Topel, R. H. (2006). "The Value of Health and Longevity." *Journal of Political Economy* **114**(4): 871–904.
38. OECD (2011). *Health at a Glance 2011: OECD Indicators.* Organization for Economic Cooperation and Development: Paris, France. http://www.oecd.org/dataoecd/6/28/49105858.pdf.
39. Peng, X. (2011). "China's Demographic History and Future Challenges." *Science* **333**(6042): 581–587.
40. Romer, P. M. (1990). "Endogenous Technological Change." *Journal of Political Economy,* **98**(5), Part 2: *The Problem of Development: A Conference of the Institute for the Study of Free Enterprise Systems,* pp. S71–S102.
41. Smith, S. J. (1982). "New Worklife Estimates Reflect Changing Profile of Labor Force." *Monthly Labor Review* **105**(3): 15–20.
42. Swift, R. (2011). "The Relationship between Health and GDP in OECD Countries in the Very Long Run." *Health Economics* **20**(3): 306–322.
43. Wang, F. (2011). "The Future of a Demographic Overachiever: Long-Term Implications of the Demographic Transition in China." *Population and Development Review* **37**(Supplement): 173–190.
44. Wang, F. and Mason, A. (2008). "The Demographic Factor in China's Transition." In *China's Great Economic Transformation,* eds. L. Brandt and T. G. Rawski. Cambridge University Press: Cambridge, MA, pp. 136–166.
45. World Health Organization (2002). *Macroeconomics and Health: Investing in Health for Economic Development: Report of the Commission on Macroeconomics and Health:* World Health Organization WHO: Geneva.
46. Yang, W., Lu, J., Weng, J., Jia, W., Ji, L., Xiao, J., Shan, Z., Liu, J., Tian, H., Ji, Q., Zhu, D., Ge, J., Lin, L., Chen, L., Guo, X., Zhao, Z., Li, Q., Zhou, Z., Shan, G. and He,

J. (2010). "Prevalence of Diabetes among Men and Women in China." *New England Journal of Medicine* **362**(12): 1090–1101.

47. Zeckhauser, R. J., Sato, R. and Rizzo, J. (1985). "Hidden Heterogeneity in Risk: Evidence from Japanese Mortality." In *Health Intervention and Population Heterogeneity: Evidence from Japan and the United States.* National Institute for Research Advancement: Tokyo, Japan, pp. 23–131.

6.2

"Though Much Is Taken": Reflections on Aging, Health, and Medical Care

Though much is taken, much abides (Alfred, Lord Tennyson).

Less than one score years ago this nation brought forth a new system of financing health care for the elderly — Medicare. This system, conceived as part of a broad thrust toward a "Great Society" and dedicated to the proposition that high-quality medical care should be freely available to all persons aged 65 and over, is now the subject of intense reexamination. It is altogether fitting and proper that this be done. The rapid rate of growth of health care expenditures, the growing resistance to further increases in governmental taxes or deficits, and the changing circumstances of the elderly make this an appropriate time to ask (and attempt to answer) basic questions about the economic and social forces that affect this age group and this program.

Projections of Medicare outlays and revenues indicate very large future deficits in the Hospital Insurance trust fund and the Supplementary Medical Insurance trust fund. A wide range of possible solutions to this problem have been proposed, including modification of benefits, changes in methods of

Originally published in *The Milbank Memorial Fund Quarterly. Health and Society*, 62(2): 142–166, Spring 1984. Copyright by Milbank Memorial Fund and Massachusetts Institute of Technology.

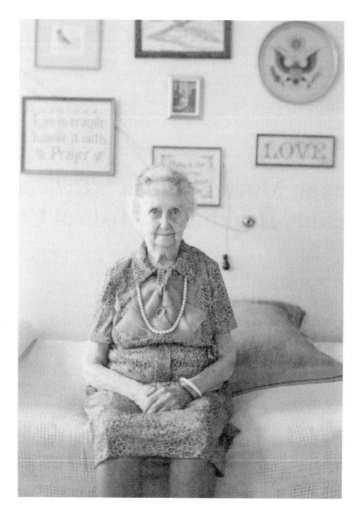

reimbursement, and discovery of new sources of funds. This paper attempts to place the Medicare issue in a broad context by identifying major economic and social trends that concern the elderly and by briefly considering the causes and consequences of these trends. I do not discuss Medicare directly, but the questions raised and the data presented will, I hope, contribute to the formulation of improved public policies regarding health care for the elderly.

I begin by supposing that a policy maker with a strong interest in the elderly had disappeared in 1950 and had only recently returned. What would he or she most need to know about the elderly with respect to their current situation and the changes of recent decades? In my judgment there are six areas that are of critical importance: the number of elderly; their health status; use of medical care; labor force participation; income; and their living arrangements. I discuss the most dramatic changes in these areas during the past three decades, indicate how current policies may have contributed to these changes, and suggest the need for reconsideration of those policies.

The Number of Elderly

Almost every article and book about the elderly begins by noting that the percentage of the population over age 65 has grown appreciably over time. Why is there so much interest in this percentage? First, it is assumed that most men and women aged 65 and over are not at work; therefore, part of the working generation's output must be transferred to the elderly through Social Security payments, private pension plans, direct provision of services, or other means. The higher the percentage of elderly, the greater the amount that must be transferred. Second, it is assumed that health deteriorates with age and that the consumption of medical care increases. Furthermore, it is argued that even though the decline in labor income, the deterioration in health, and the increased use of medical care are, for the most part, foreseeable, many elderly cannot or do not adequately provide for old age by saving or by acquiring a health insurance policy when young that would protect them later in life. (Imperfections in insurance markets, problems of adverse selection, and high administrative and sales costs are said to contribute to this outcome.) Finally, the rise in the number of elderly increases their political power. This increase, coming at a time when economic resources are often allocated through the ballot box rather than the market place, raises the possibility of bitter political conflict between the elderly and other groups in society.

The definition of old age — that is, the age of eligibility for retirement and Medicare benefits — is a critical variable in the development of viable programs for the elderly. Consider, for instance, a hypothetical population in which the birth rate equals the death rate and everyone dies at 80 years of age. If every man and woman works from ages 20 to 65 and then retires, the ratio of workers to retirees will be three to one. If, however, the retirement age is 70, there will be five workers for every retiree, thus permitting a substantial increase in benefits or decrease in taxes, or both.

It is conventional to define the elderly with reference to the number of years since birth, but this is largely a concession to administrative convenience rather than the logical result of a closely reasoned argument. Individuals "age" at very different rates and, in theory at least, the elderly could be defined in terms of years until death, e.g., those men and women who will die within some specified time. For instance, we could look at the proportion of the population that will die within one year (the crude death rate). According to this measure the proportion has *decreased* since 1950. To be sure, it doesn't make much sense to define infants, children, and young adults as "elderly," even if they are close to death. But a count of persons aged 65 and over who will die within the next several years is informative because much of the interest in the elderly revolves around their need for medical care and other special services. From a different perspective, a count of persons aged 65 and over who are not in the labor force is revealing because it shows the portion of the population that must live on transfer payments, income from capital, or dissaving.

These alternative views of who is old yield different trends in the relative importance of the elderly, as may be seen in Table 1, The first row shows the familiar increase in the proportion of the population aged 65 and over, from 8.2 percent in 1950 to 11.3 percent in 1980, The second row, however, shows that if we define the elderly as persons aged 65 and over who will die within five years, this number as a percent of the total population has increased relatively slowly since 1950 and has hardly grown at all since 1965. Sharp declines in age-specific death rates at ages 65 and above have offset the effect of the increase shown in the first row. On the other hand, if we define the elderly as persons aged 65 and over who are out of the labor force (row 3), that proportion has grown even more rapidly than the percent over age 65.

Table 1. The "Elderly" as a Proportion of the Total Population: Alternative Definitions.

Definition	1950 (%)	1965 (%)	1980 (%)
(1) Age 65 and over	8.2	9.5	11.3
(2) Age 65 and over and within 5 years of death[a]	2.6	3.0	3.1
(3) Age 65 and over and not in the labor force	6.2	7.9	10.0

[a]Estimated by author.

Sources: U.S. Bureau of the Census, *Current Population Reports,* Series P-25, No. 310, June 1965, Table 1; No. 519, April 1974, Table 2; No. 917, July 1982, Table 2 (Washington). U.S. Bureau of the Census, *Historical Statistics of the United States, Colonial Times to 1970* (Washington, 1975), Pt. 1, Series B189–192. U.S. Bureau of the Census, *Statistical Abstract of the United States, 1982–83* (Washington, 1982), Table 109. Employment and Training Administration, *Employment and Training Report of the President, 1981* (Washington, 1981). Table A-2.

The Health of the Elderly

One of the big surprises of recent years has been the sharp reduction in age-specific mortality of older persons. Between 1965 and 1980 life expectancy at age 65 jumped from 14.6 to 16.4 years. This was a much bigger increase than was expected, based on extrapolation of either the 1935–1965 or 1950–1965 trends (see Table 2). The improvement is attributable primarily to a decrease in the risk of death from heart disease or cerebrovascular disorders (strokes), as may be seen in Table 3. Why death rates from these causes have plummeted is not well understood. Analysts who are technologically inclined attribute most of the reduction to better control of hypertension, special coronary care units in hospitals, open heart surgery, and similar medical innovations. Other observers credit changes in diet, smoking, exercise, and other aspects of personal behavior. We do not know the true explanation; there is probably some validity to both points of view.

Are people escaping fatal heart attacks and strokes only to spend more years in poor health? That question is difficult to study because measures of morbidity and disability lack the objectivity of mortality statistics, but in my judgment the answer is no. Restricted-activity days and bed-disability days per hundred persons aged 65 and over were about the same in 1980 as in 1965 (Reference 14, 119). The percent of persons reporting activity limitations due to chronic conditions rose somewhat from 1970 to 1980, but it is doubtful that this is the result of greater

Table 2.   Life Expectancy at Age 65, Selected Years 1935 to 2000.

	1935	1950	1965	1980	2000
Actual	12.5	13.9	14.6	16.4	
Predicted from 1935–1950 trend			15.5		
Predicted from 1935–1965 trend				15.8	
Predicted from 1950–1965 trend				15.3	
Predicted from 1935–1980 trend					18.5
Predicted from 1950–1980 trend					18.3
Predicted from 1965–1980 trend					19.1

Sources: National Center for Health Statistics, *Health, United States, 1982* (Washington, December 1982), Table 10. National Center for Health Statistics, *Vital Statistics of the United States, 1965* (Washington, 1967), Mortality, Pt. A, Table 5–4. U.S. Bureau of the Census, *Historical Statistics of the United States, Colonial Times to 1970* (Washington, 1975), Pt. 1, Series A-133. Dublin, L., *Health Progress 1936–1945, A Supplement to Twenty-Five Years of Health Progress.* (New York: Metropolitan Life Insurance Company, 1948), table 6. U.S. Bureau of the Census, *Statistical Abstract of the United States 1982–83* (Washington, 1982), p. 71.

Table 3. Age-specific Death Rates from Heart and Cerebrovascular Diseases and Other Causes, 1965 and 1980.

Age	Cause	1965	1980	Change 1965 to 1980 (percent per annum)
		(Deaths per 100,000)		
65–74				
	Heart and cerebro-vascular diseases	2057	1433	−2.4
	Other causes	1606	1535	−0.3
75–84				
	Heart and cerebro-vascular diseases	5261	4065	−1.7
	Other causes	3098	3113	0.0
85 and over				
	Heart and cerebro-vascular diseases	13256	9229	−2.4
	Other causes	6813	5261	−1.7

Source: National Center for Health Statistics, *Health, United States, 1982* (Washington, December 1982), tables 9, 16, 19.

morbidity. For instance, the percent of elderly persons reporting hypertension without heart involvement rose from 6.4 to 13.1 (Reference 14, 121), but it is unlikely that hypertension actually increased. Indeed, direct measures of blood pressure among the elderly over the same period show declines in average levels and a large decline in the percent of the population aged 65 to 74 with systolic pressure of 160 or more or diastolic pressure of 95 or more (Reference 9, 1982a). Taking all the available mortality and morbidity data into account, I conclude that the health status of the elderly at any given age has improved in recent decades and that this improvement is primarily the result of lowered incidence or severity of heart disease and cerebrovascular disease.

Death rates from all other causes at ages 65 to 84 were virtually the same in 1980 as in 1965. This relative stability presents a major puzzle. During those years Medicare substantially improved access to health care for the elderly, especially the poor. Also, there were many significant medical advances including new drugs, improved surgical procedures, and enhanced diagnostic techniques. It is difficult to believe that these achievements had no beneficial effect. Age-adjusted death rates from malignant neoplasms (cancer) actually rose between 1965 and 1980 among the elderly, possibly as a result of increases several decades ago in cigarette smoking and environmental hazards. It is encouraging to note that cancer mortality has declined for males aged 35 to 44; perhaps similar declines will begin to show up at older ages as the cohorts with fewer cigarette smokers reach that point in the life cycle.

Will life expectancy at older ages continue to increase at a rapid rate? Some experts say no, arguing that there is a biologically determined average limit for the species of about 85 years.[2] Other observers contend that recent large declines in the death rate for the aged 85 + group is evidence against the existence of that limit.[12] Both groups agree that additional declines in mortality at ages 65 to 84 are possible or even likely; it would, therefore, be prudent to consider the possibility of such declines in planning future programs for the elderly.

Health Care Utilization

The role of additional medical care in improving the health of the elderly is a matter of some dispute. What is beyond dispute is the increased consumption of medical services by the elderly. Between 1965 and 1981 there was a large increase in health expenditures at all age levels, but the *share* accounted for by persons aged 65 and over jumped from 23.8 percent to 32.7 percent. This shift has helped to fan the Medicare financial crisis; it is, therefore, important to examine it in some detail. Two factors are responsible and they have been about equal in importance: first, the *number* of elderly grew more rapidly than the rest of the population; second, the change in *per capita* health expenditures by the elderly outpaced the rate for persons under age 65 (see column 1 of Table 4). The relative importance of these factors was not the same among the subperiods, however, as may be seen in columns 2–4. Not surprisingly, per capita expenditures among the elderly rose rapidly in the years immediately after the enactment of Medicare (1965–1970). From 1970 to 1976 per capita expenditures rose at about the same rate for both age groups; divergent trends in population accounted for nearly all of the differential change in expenditures, During 1976–1981, however, a large differential in the growth of per capita expenditures again emerged. This gap, combined with a continuing difference in population trends, resulted in a total differential change in expenditures of 3.8 percent per annum. This was larger than the difference between the elderly and the rest of the population in the five years immediately following the introduction of Medicare!

The last eight rows of Table 4 provide additional detail regarding the surge of spending on the elderly. We see that there was a very sharp *deceleration* in public spending on persons under age 65, while the trend increased slightly for the elderly. Private spending, on the other hand, held steady for persons under 65 and accelerated sharply for those over that age. With respect to type of expenditure,

Table 4.   Rates of Change of Health Care Expenditures, by Age, 1965–1981 (percent per annum).

		1965–81 (1)	1965–70 (2)	1970–76 (3)	1976–81 (4)
Real[a] health care expenditures					
	65 +	8.0	9.2	6.9	8.2
	<65	5.3	6.6	5.0	4.4
	Differential	2.7	2.6	1.9	3.8
Population					
	65 +	2.2	1.7	2.4	2.4
	<65	0.9	1.0	0.9	0.9
	Differential	1.3	0.7	1.5	1.5
Real[a] health care expenditures per capita					
	65 +	5.8	7.5	4.5	5.8
	<65	4.3	5.6	4.1	3.5
	Differential	1.5	1.9	0.4	2.3
Public	65 +	10.5	21.8	5.3	5.7
	<65	7.2	11.3	6.9	3.5
Private	65 +	1.6	−4.3	3.0	6.2
	<65	3.5	4.1	3.1	3.5
Physicians	65 +	5.5	5.3	4.2	7.5
	<65	4.1	5.3	3.4	3.9
Hospitals	65 +	6.8	9.4	5.4	6.2
	<65	5.8	8.3	5.3	4.0

[a] Adjusted for inflation by the Gross National Product deflator.
Sources: U.S. Bureau of the Census, *Current Population Reports,* Series P-25, No. 519, April 1974, Table 2; No. 917, July 1982, Table 2 (Washington). Council of Economic Advisers, *Economic Report of the President, 1982* (Washington, 1982), Table B-3. Fisher, C.R., Differences by Age Groups in Health Care Spending, *Health Care Financing Review* 1(4), 1980, pp. 65–90. Table A. Provisional data from the Health Care Financing Administration.

it was physicians' services that experienced the most rapid increase among the elderly.

What accounts for these divergent trends? One possibility is that increasing competition among physicians for patients led more of them to concentrate on the older men and women in their practice. Another possibility is that the new medical and surgical interventions have been particularly applicable to older persons. These speculations indicate why it is so difficult to predict expenditures on medical care, either in the aggregate or for particular age groups or particular types of service. Sudden advances in medical technology — new drugs, new diagnostic techniques, new surgical procedures — can dramatically alter utilization. In addition, modifications in insurance coverage, or in reimbursement methods, or in the number of physicians can alter the balance of demand and supply, thus inducing changes in the way physicians treat patients and the way patients use physicians. Whatever the cause, the upsurge in per capita expenditures of the elderly is a major factor in the prospective deficits in Medicare.

Does utilization rise with age?

Analysts interested in projecting future health care utilization by the elderly have frequently noted that the age distribution within the group aged 65-and-over is shifting toward the older ages and that utilization (as reflected by Medicare reimbursements) rises steadily with age (see first three columns of Table 5). Under the assumption that the cross-sectional age-spending relationship holds constant over time, the effect of the change in age distribution is estimated by applying the cross-sectional data on age-specific expenditures to the change in the age distribution.

Although this procedure is widely used, implicitly if not explicitly, it is incorrect. To the extent that the change in the age distribution is the result of rising life expectancy (i.e., falling age-specific death rates), the cross-sectional differences in expenditures by age *overestimate* the changes that would result from an aging population. Health care spending among the elderly is not so much a function of time since birth as it is a function of time to death. The principal reason why expenditures rise with age in cross-section (among persons aged 65 and over) is that the proportion of persons near death increases with age. Expenditures are particularly large in the last year of life, and, to a lesser extent, in the next-to-last-year of life. Among Medicare enrollees in 1976, the average reimbursement for

Table 5.   Reimbursement per Medicare Enrollee by Age and Sex, 1976 (dollars).

	Actual			Adjusted for survival status		
	All (1)	Men (2)	Women (3)	All (4)	Men (5)	Women (6)
67–68	518	578	471	624	654	595
69–70	555	613	511	649	667	630
71–72	603	674	551	679	704	660
73–74	657	717	613	712	713	705
75–79	736	793	699	732	716	742
80–84	818	854	798	717	679	741
85+	866	937	832	595	594	595

Source: Health Care Financing Administration, Office of Research and Demonstrations, *Health Care Financing Program Statistics* (Baltimore, August 1982), Medicare Summary, Use and Reimbursement by Person, 1976–1978, pp. 53, 61. Adjusted expenditures calculated by author.

those in their last year of life was 6.6 times (and in their next-to-last-year of life 2.3 times) as large as for those who survived at least two years.[6] As age-specific death rates fall over time, there will be fewer people in the last year of life in any age category, and this will tend to reduce age-specific health care expenditures.

Age-sex-specific expenditures adjusted for age-sex differences in death rates can be calculated by a method analogous to the indirect method of calculating age-sex-adjusted death rates. Suppose that each person's expenditures depended only on their survival status, e.g., last year of life, next-to-last year, or "survivor." We can estimate a "predicted" expenditure for each age-sex group by multiplying the proportion in each survival status by the all-group average expenditure for each survival status and summing across the three statuses. The higher the death rate of the group, the higher would be its "predicted" expenditures. The ratio of actual to "predicted" expenditures for a group tells us whether expenditures are relatively high or low after adjusting for its death rate. This ratio multiplied by the average expenditure for all groups yields the adjusted expenditure for the group.[a]

As may be seen in the last three columns of Table 5 and in Figure 1, adjustment for age-sex differences in survival status eliminates most of the age-related increase in expenditures, especially the very high expenditures in the group aged 85-and-over. It also eliminates the excess of male over female expenditures at given ages. The only reason why older men use more medical care than older women at any given age is because a higher proportion of the men are in their last year of life.

I do not claim that there is *no* effect of aging on health care utilization apart from the proximity to death, but much of the apparent effect is attributable to the relationship between age and mortality.

This observation would be of little consequence if mortality rates were constant over time, but they are not. Between 1965 and 1978 the age-adjusted death rate of persons aged 65 and older fell from 65 per 1,000 to 53 per 1,000. If age-specific death rates continue to fall at this rate, 75-year-olds

---

[a]Let X = expenditures per person

   N = number of persons

   P = predicted expenditures per person

   X′ = expenditures adjusted for age-sex differences in survival status

   g = age-sex group g

   t = all age-sex groups

   s = survival status s

   u = all survival statuses

$$X'_{ug} = \frac{X_{ug}}{P_{ug}} X_{ut} \quad \text{where} \quad P_{ug} = \frac{\sum_s X_{st} N_{sg}}{\sum_s N_{sg}}$$

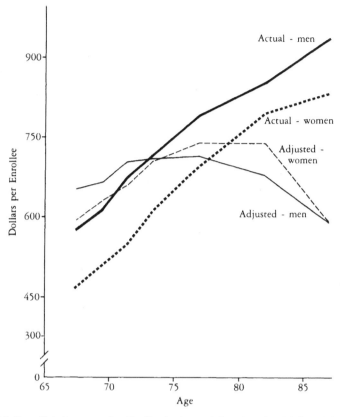

Fig. 1. Medicare Reimbursement Per Enrollee by Age and Sex, Actual and Adjusted for Survival Status, 1976.

in 1987 will face the same probability of death as 71-year-olds faced in 1965.

How much health care will 75-year-olds utilize in 1987? The answer will depend upon many factors, including changes in medical technology, the strengthening or weakening of family support systems, and revisions in Medicare reimbursement policies. But to the extent that fewer 75-year-olds will be in the last or next-to-last year of life, a simple extrapolation from past utilization of 75-year-olds is inappropriate.

Manton (1982, 205) reaches a similar conclusion from a model that emphasizes the distinction between the hypothetical age trajectory of mortality risk for individuals and the age trajectory for a cohort. He writes: "As mortality rates decline at a given age, there would be some compensating decline in the rate of utilization of certain health services (e.g., nursing home care) before that age. In fact, such models might be used as the basis for improving projections of health service utilization by providing estimates of the likely change in health-service-utilization rates associated with a given mortality reduction."

The relationships between utilization, age, and survival status will depend on the *reasons* for the lower death rate. If mortality falls because people are living healthier lives or because of more effective preventive measures, the conventional extrapolations will overestimate health care utilization, as demonstrated above. On the other hand, if the lower death rates are the result of ever more complex technological interventions, the rising cost of such interventions will tend to offset the fact that fewer persons are in the last year of life.

Labor Force Participation

Between 1950 and 1980 the labor force participation rate of men aged 65 and over fell from 46 percent to 19 percent. Participation rates of men aged 55 to 64 have also dropped sharply in recent years, from 83 percent in 1965 to 72 percent in 1980. What accounts for these striking declines? Many explanations have been offered, including poor health, mandatory retirement rules, age discrimination, rising wages, and improved social security benefits.

Health

When older men are surveyed about their labor force status, those not participating frequently cite ill health as the reason. These replies have been viewed with some skepticism because ill health may be offered as a socially acceptable reason for not working when the true explanation lies elsewhere. A longitudinal analysis of retirement patterns, however, revealed that poor health is a good predictor of which men currently at work will not be working four years later.[3] This relationship does *not*, however, explain why participation, by older men is so much lower now than it was 30 years ago. As noted, the health of the elderly has probably improved, and the occupational structure has shifted away from blue collar jobs requiring heavy physical exertion. Thus, at any given age probably fewer men are compelled to leave the labor force for health reasons now than in earlier decades. Therefore, we must look to other factors.

Mandatory retirement and age discrimination

According to some popular discussions, men stop working because of mandatory retirement or because they are victims of age discrimination. In my judgment neither of these explanations has been a significant factor in the long-term downward trend in labor force participation. First, about half of all currently retired men were never subject to mandatory retirement rules.[13] Furthermore, many workers retire before the mandatory age, many retire willingly at the mandatory age, and some are not working for other reasons such as ill health.

Mandatory retirement rules are usually part of a total labor contract, either explicit or implicit, that provides workers with stable or even rising wages until retirement, even though their productivity may decline during their last years of employment. If older workers are being paid more than they're currently worth, when they lose their jobs through mandatory retirement they obviously have difficulty obtaining a new job at their old wage rate.

The gap that develops between the wages of some older workers and their productivity is one reason why we hear complaints about "age discrimination." It is obvious that many employers prefer younger to older workers, but this is not discrimination in an economic sense if age affects productivity or labor costs. For instance, the older worker may expect a higher wage even though his productivity does not justify the wage differential. Even if there is no wage-productivity gap, the fringe benefits of older workers are often relatively high, especially for health insurance, life insurance, and pension benefits. As the share of fringe benefits in the total compensation package increases, it becomes increasingly uneconomic for firms to hire older workers. If there appears to be more age discrimination now than there was 30 years ago, it is probably because of the changes in wages and fringe benefits that make it less attractive to hire older workers.

Decline of self-employment

One factor that probably does contribute to the downward trend in participation by older men is the declining importance of self-employment. Self-employed men are more likely to continue working at older ages than are wage-and-salary workers, holding constant education, age, health, wages, and other relevant variables.[3] Wage-and-salary workers typically face more rigidity in hours and wages, while the self-employed find it easier to reduce their hours of work without changing their occupation or job. The proportion of workers who are self-employed has declined drastically throughout the twentieth century because of the shift of employment from agriculture to industry and service. Even within each sector, self-employment has declined in relative importance as small farms and small businesses find it increasingly difficult to compete with larger enterprises.

Real wages

Some economists argue that the growth of real wages in the economy as a whole is a major reason for the decline in labor force participation of older men, although this conclusion does not flow directly from economic theory. An *increase* in participation would be equally consistent with theory because the higher the wage, the higher the price of not working. But higher wages also mean higher income and the income effect increases the demand for leisure. It is difficult to predict whether the price or income effect will dominate.

For women of prime working age higher real wages have resulted in more labor force participation, not less. In the case of older men, however, it appears that the income effect is larger than the price effect. This would explain why the labor force participation of older men has declined in the United States as real income has risen. One problem with this explanation is that participation rates of older men in Europe are as low as in the United States, even though real income is not as high. To be sure, these countries typically have generous public pension plans that facilitate retirement. But why do they have such plans? The increasing number of elderly may be the answer, partly because of the political power that numerical strength confers and partly because younger workers want the older ones to leave the labor market.

Number of elderly

The growth in the proportion of elderly probably contributes to their low participation rate. When there are relatively few older people, the population has a pyramid-like age structure similar to the hierarchical structure of most organizations; the relatively few older workers can more easily progress up the organizational ladder. Currently in the United States and in most European countries the age distribution is more rectangular in shape, but organizations still have a pyramid-like hierarchy with fewer and fewer openings the higher up one goes. Thus, if most older workers stayed in the labor force, they would find it impossible to move up within their organizations.

Social security

Probably one of the most important reasons why the labor force participation of older men has declined so rapidly is the unusual growth of Social Security benefits. Between 1970 and 1980 average retirement benefits (adjusted for inflation) increased by more than 3 percent per annum, while hourly earnings did not even keep pace with inflation. There is no doubt that public policy has made it increasingly attractive for older people to stop work — by increasing retirement benefits relative to wages, by offering an early retirement option at 62, and by withholding benefits from eligible retirees at the rate of 50 cents per dollar of earnings on earnings above a prescribed rate.

The trend toward earlier retirement, combined with greater life expectancy, will place a tremendous burden on those workers who remain in the labor force (as already noted). To reverse this trend, however, will probably require major changes in the structure of jobs and labor markets as well as changes in the structure of Social Security retirement benefits.

Income

From a purely financial perspective, today's older Americans are much better off than their predecessors. They have more income and more wealth (adjusted for inflation) than any previous generation of elderly. Their real income has risen not only in absolute terms but also relative to the income of the working population, primarily because of the rapid growth of Social Security retirement benefits. It is true that household income, when the householder is aged 65 or over, is only half of that in the age range 45 to 64, but this figure must be adjusted for household size. In 1980 the households of the elderly had on average only 1.74 persons, compared with 2.83 persons when the householder is 45 to 64. Taxes also make a big difference. The elderly's taxes (federal and state individual income taxes, property taxes on owner-occupied housing, and payroll taxes) are estimated to be only 13 percent of their income, while the 45 to 64 age group pay taxes equal to about 25 percent of income (U.S. Bureau of the Census, 1983). Thus, the *after-tax* income *per household member* of the elderly is almost equal to that of the 45 to 64 age group.

Not only does the *average* older person receive an after-tax income comparable to that he or she received at younger ages, but income is more *equally* distributed after age 65 than before that age. Consider the following analysis of incomes based on the Retirement History Survey, a longitudinal study of approximately 11,000 individuals.[5] In 1968 when the respondents were 58 to 63 years of age and most were still in the labor force, the wealthiest 10 percent of the sample had a mean income of $65,363 (all figures in 1982 dollars), while the poorest 10 percent received only $1,838. By 1978, however, at ages 68 to 73, with most of the sample in retirement, the mean income of the wealthiest 10 percent had *fallen* to $52,117 while the poorest 10 percent showed a *rise* in income to $4,070. The principal reason for the narrowing of inequality after age 65 is that

Social Security benefits become more important and labor income less important, and the former is distributed much more equally than the latter.

The improvement in the income position of the *poor* elderly has been particularly striking. As recently as 1970 one out of four persons aged 65 and over was below the poverty level, while the proportion among persons under 65 was about one in eight. In 1982 the proportion was the *same* for both age groups — about one in seven.

To be sure, money income is only one measure of economic well-being, but consideration of other factors tends to strengthen the impression that the elderly are, on average, about as well-off as other age groups. For instance, persons over age 65 are more likely to own a house free and clear of any mortgage. Also, the elderly receive a disproportionate share of non-cash transfers such as subsidized housing, transportation, and medical care. Because they are typically not in the labor force they have more time for home production activities such as gardening, repair, and maintenance; they experience fewer work-related expenses, such as commuting and meals away from home; and they have the opportunity to move to a less costly area of the country.

One disadvantage faced by the elderly is the small size of the typical household. In 1980, 44 percent of their households had only one person, and 46 percent had only two. Small households are usually not as efficient as larger ones in the use of space, equipment, food, heat, and light. The difficulties and disadvantages of doubling up with another older person in order to gain the economies of a larger household are, however, apparently considerable. Fewer than 2 percent of elderly households include members who are unrelated, despite efforts by social agencies to encourage shared housing.

Although most of the elderly receive an after-tax income that compares favorably with what they earned while at work, there is a dramatic change in the *source* of income after age 65. From ages 25 to 54, earnings account for more than 90 percent of the total, and between 55 and 64 they still account for 78 percent of income. For people over 65, however, earnings provide only 20 percent. Social Security retirement benefits are the most important other source, with capital income such as interest and dividends next in importance, followed by government employee pensions, private pensions, and public assistance.

Does the source of income matter? I think it does. Social Security retirement benefits and other annuity-like income does not flow from *assets* that the older person can pass on to children or consume at a pace that he or she determines. In an earlier era the aged had less total income relative to younger people than they do today, but more of it came from farms or small businesses or bits of real estate that they *owned*. Ownership usually contributes to a sense of power and control and can affect intra-family relationships. A recent analysis of frequency of visits by children to their elderly parents found that the number of visits was positively related to the parents' bequeathable wealth (e.g., stocks, bonds, bank accounts, real estate), but not to non-bequeathable wealth (e.g., Social Security, private pensions).[1] If seniors today are "doing better and feeling worse," it may in part be because of this loss of control over their economic assets.

Living and Dying

A wide variety of demographic, social, and economic forces have resulted in major changes in how the elderly live and die. For instance, the male-female differential in death rates and the tendency of older widowed and divorced men to choose younger wives when they remarry create a large surplus of unmarried women above the age of 65. This surplus has grown in recent decades because female life expectancy has grown much more rapidly than male. In 1980 there were almost four unmarried women aged 65 and over for every unmarried man of that age, a steep increase from a ratio of less than two to one in 1940. The greatest change occurred among the widowed. In 1940 there were approximately two elderly widows for every widower, but by 1980 there were more than five. The huge rise in the number of elderly widows has been accompanied by a dramatic change in their living arrangements. In 1950 one in four was living alone; the other three were living with children, other relatives, or friends. By 1980 two out of three widows aged 65 and over were living alone, and only one in three was sharing living quarters with someone else. Most elderly men are married. Even at ages 75 and above, two out of three men are living with their wives, but only one woman in five has a husband.

There has been a great deal of hand-wringing about the decline of three-generation households, but historians have hastened to point out that in western Europe and the United States the three-generation household has always been the exception, not the rule. We can accept their conclusion that most households did not contain an aged mother or father, but it does not follow that only a small fraction of aged men and women lived with their children. When mortality is high and the population is growing rapidly, it is possible for *most of the elderly* to live with their children even though only a *minority of children* have elderly parents living with them. For example, if each woman has two daughters, and if half of the women survive into old age, only one daughter in four would have her mother living with her, even if every one of the survivors were living with a daughter. As an indication of how longer life expectancy and falling birth rates have raised the mother-to-daughter ratio, the number of women aged 65 and over relative to those aged 35 to 44 *doubled* between 1950 and 1980.

In addition to these demographic changes, rising real income contributes to the decrease in the number of mothers who double up with their children.[8] Americans of all ages have always put a high value on autonomy; therefore, the rising income of recent decades and the particularly rapid rise in the income of the elderly have made it possible for an ever higher percentage of them to maintain their own households, health permitting.

Health is also an important factor in living arrangements. In earlier times, poor health was often the reason why older men and women moved in with their children. At present, poor health often results in a move to a nursing home. The number of elderly in nursing homes increased at an astonishing 7 percent per annum between 1963 and 1977, to a total of over 1.1 million. On any given day 5 percent of all elderly live in nursing homes, and between 20 and 25 percent will do so at some point in their lives. Of those who do enter, only one in four returns to a private or semiprivate residence; one-half are transferred to another health facility (usually a short-term general hospital), possibly to die or to return to the nursing home.

Why have nursing homes become so important? Rising income, the increased propensity to live alone, higher mother-to-daughter ratios, and higher labor force participation rates by young and middle-aged women are all part of the answer. There are many more elderly people who need care and attention, and relatively fewer children who are providing it within the home. Public policy also influences the decision because frequently nursing home care is paid for by government (57 percent of the total in 1981), but the cost of home care is borne mostly by the family through out-of-pocket expenditures and the foregone earnings of the caregiver.

Economic and social factors also affect the location and manner of death. According to a report from the National Center for Health Statistics (1982b), 62 percent of deaths of persons aged 65 and over occur in a hospital or medical center, often at great cost. In some cases the patient is hospitalized because there is a reasonable chance to postpone the death through the kinds of medical intervention that are only possible within a hospital setting. In other cases, however, the patient is taken to the hospital to die because public and private insurance pays more fully than if the dying person is cared for at home. And in still other cases, there is no one close enough, either geographically or emotionally, to offer any alternative to hospitalization.

The cost of caring for very ill patients can vary enormously, depending upon the patient and the physician.[4] In some cases the intensive application of modern technology can prolong life for one or two months or perhaps even more. This type of decision has traditionally been left to the patient and his or her physician, but exploding costs may lead to a reexamination of that position. At a minimum, there will be a search for less costly alternatives, and a closer examination of the factors that influence such decisions.

A Final Note

The data presented in this paper and the accompanying discussion are meant to be suggestive, not definitive. Large gaps in our understanding of the aging process and of the determinants of labor force participation, health care utilization, and other key variables make it difficult to draw firm conclusions. It may be useful, however, to state explicitly some of the major themes that are implicit in the preceding pages. Most important is the need to recognize that the "Medicare problem" reflects the intersection of two larger sets of issues. First, there are a range of questions concerning the elderly in general: questions of retirement benefits, age of eligibility, wages and hours of work, and the like. Second, there are questions concerning the financing, organization, and delivery of health care for persons of all ages. Any Medicare "solution" that fails to consider these larger issues will probably turn out to be counter-productive.

Also implicit in this paper is the need to recognize that resources devoted to the elderly are resources that could be used to help children, teenagers, minorities, and other groups with special claims to public attention. To say this is not to deny that there are many elderly who are poor, sick, lonely, or otherwise disadvantaged. But the growing political power of the elderly suggests the possibility of disproportionate attention to this group at a time when many small children are neglected or abused, when the schools are at a low ebb, and when teenage suicide is at epidemic proportions. Twenty years ago the plight of the elderly was palpable. Today the most pressing social needs may lie elsewhere. The "good society" needs to balance its efforts, to make hard choices among many worthwhile objectives.

These considerations, and the data presented in this paper, lead me to hazard three inferences that have direct relevance for policy. First, we need to periodically revise our definition *who is old*. One way to do this is to focus on changes in life expectancy at older ages. For instance, in 1935 when the age of eligibility for Social Security retirement benefits was set at 65, life expectancy at that age was 12.5 years. In 1984 the average 72-year-old has that same life expectancy. From that point of view it is not unreasonable to say that if age 65 marked the entry into old age in 1935, in 1984 old age begins at 72.

Second, we need to develop *more flexible labor market arrangements* to facilitate the continued labor force participation of older men and women. Unless this happens, the ratio of workers to retirees will become so small as to pose a grave threat to our economy and our society. Simply passing laws against mandatory retirement and age discrimination will not solve the problem. We need to develop more flexibility in hours of work, in wages (to accommodate possible age-related declines in productivity), and in amount of responsibility (to speed the movement of younger men and women into positions of leadership within organizations).

Finally, and this may prove to be the most difficult task of all. we need to reach a social consensus concerning what is *appropriate care for the dying.* At present the United States spends about 1 percent of the gross national product on health care for elderly persons who are in their last year of life. This is much more than the nation spends on institutional care for the mentally ill and the mentally retarded of all ages, more than private and public expenditures for basic and applied research in all fields, and more than the total expenditures of all the private colleges and universities in the country. On the other hand, it is less than is spent on alcohol, and not much more than is spent on tobacco.

How much *should* be spent on care for the 1.3 million elderly persons who die each year? For most goods and services our society answers this question by saying "Let the market decide." According to economic theory the free choice of knowledgeable buyers paying with their own money for services rendered by competitive suppliers should result in a socially efficient allocation of resources. It will not necessarily be a "fair" allocation, but this problem is supposed to be addressed through redistribution of income, not direct subsidization of particular services.

This free-market approach is not likely to work well for the seriously ill. Patients and their families are often under great emotional stress and they typically have little previous experience with the complex technical choices that must be made. The hospitals and physicians who serve them often have considerable monopoly power. Furthermore, even in the absence of public subsidies, private insurance would push utilization beyond the point where benefits are equal to cost. The problem of distributive justice is not amenable to solution through conventional income redistribution methods because the amount society would want to give to an individual would depend on how much care they needed. Some economists would prefer an indemnification plan that provides old people with additional income when they become sick and lets them decide how much to spend for medical care. This plan may be a delight to some theorists, but it would be a nightmare for most patients and physicians.

It is possible to nibble at the edges of the problem by providing more information to patients, by fostering more competition among providers, by financing alternative modes of care for the dying, and by increasing deductibles and coinsurance. The fundamental problem, however, will remain. One of the biggest challenges facing policy makers for the rest of this century will be how to strike an appropriate balance between care for the dying and health services for the rest of the population.

References

1. Shleifer, A. and Summers, L. (1985). "The Strategic Bequest Motive." *Journal of Political Economy* **93**(6): 1045–1076.
2. Fries, J. F. (1980). "Aging, Natural Death, and the Compression of Morbidity." *New England Journal of Medicine*, **303**(3): 130–135.
3. Fuchs, V. R. (1982). "Self-Employment and Labor Force Participation of Older Males." *Journal of Human Resources*, **17**(3): 339–357.
4. Garber, A. M., Fuchs, V. R. and Silverman, J. F. (1984). "Case Mix, Costs, and Outcomes: Differences between Faculty and Community Services in a University Hospital." *New England Journal of Medicine* **310**: 1231–1237.
5. Hurd, M. and Shoven, J. (1984). The Economic Status of the Elderly: 1969–1979. In *Horizontal Equity, Uncertainty, and Measures of Well-Being*, eds. T. Smeeding and M. H. David. National Bureau of Economic Research and University of Chicago Press: Chicago.
6. Lubitz, J. and Prihoda, R. (1982). Use and Costs of Medicare Services in the Last Years of Life. *Health Care Financial Review* **5**(3): 117–131.
7. Manton, K. G. (1982). "Changing Concepts of Morbidity and Mortality in the Elderly Population." *Milbank Memorial Fund Quarterly/Health and Society* **60**(2): 183–244.
8. Michael, R. T., Fuchs, V. R. and Scott, S. R. (1980). "Changes in the Propensity to Live Alone: 1950–1976." *Demography* **17**(1): 39–56.
9. National Center for Health Statistics (1981). "Hypertension in Adults 25–74 Years of Age, United States, 1971-1975." *Vital and Health Statistics*, Series 11, No. 221. National Center for Health: Washington, D.C.
10. National Center for Health Statistics (1982a). "Blood Pressure Levels and Hypertension in Persons Ages 65–74 Years: United States, 1976–1980." *Advancedata* No. 84. Public Health Service: Hyattsville, MD.
11. National Center for Health Statistics (1982b). "Advance Report of Final Mortality Statistics, 1979." *Monthly Vital Statistics Report* **31**(6 Supplement).
12. Schneider, E. L. and Brody, J. A. (1983). "Aging, Natural Death, and the Compression of Morbidity: Another View." *New England Journal of Medicine* **309**(14): 854–855.
13. Schulz, J. H. (1976). *The Economics of Aging.* Wadsworth: Belmont, CA.

14. U.S. Bureau of the Census (1982). *Statistical Abstract of the United States, 1982–1983.* U.S. Bureau of the Census: Washington, D.C.

15. U.S. Bureau of the Census (1983). "Estimating After-Tax Money Income Distributions Using Data from the March Current Population Survey, Table I." *Current Population Reports.* Special Studies, Series P-23, No. 126, U.S. Bureau of the Census: Washington, D.C. p. 12.

6.3

"Provide, Provide": The Economics of Aging

"May you live to a hundred and twenty." This traditional Jewish blessing was inspired by the last chapter of the Torah, which describes the death of Moses at that age with "his eyes undimmed and his vigor unabated" (Deut. 34:7). Unlike Moses, many people experience a more troubled old age. In addition to the loss of family and friends and a diminution of status,[a] nearly all older persons face two potentially serious economic problems: declining earning power and increased utilization of health care. The decline in earning power is attributable to physiological changes[b] and to obsolescence of skills and knowledge, and is exacerbated by public and private policies that reduce the incentives of older persons to continue working and increase the cost to employers of employing older workers. Increased utilization of health care is undertaken to reduce or offset the effects of declining health.

The two economic problems of earnings replacement and health care payment are usually discussed separately, but there are several reasons why they should be considered together. First, there are often trade-offs between the two. Money is money, and for most people there is never enough to go around. This is self-evident

---

Originally published in Andrew Rettenmaier and Thomas R. Saving (eds.) (1999), *Medicare Reform: Issues and Answers*, pp. 15–36. Chicago, IL: University of Chicago Press. Copyright by The University of Chicago.
[a]My wife tells participants in her preretirement workshops that it is often painful to go from *Who's Who* to "Who's he?"

[b]For example, loss of strength, dexterity, stamina, sensory perceptions, cognitive functions.

where private funds are concerned. Low-income elderly, for instance, frequently must choose between expensive prescription drugs and an adequate diet.

For middle-income elderly, the choice may be between more expensive Medigap insurance and an airplane trip to a grandchild's graduation. Difficult choices are also apparent with respect to public funds. The same tax receipts that could be used to maintain or increase retirement benefits could be used to fund additional health care, and vice versa. In discussing these trade-offs, one health policy analyst asserts that people would gladly give up other goods and services for medical care that cures illness, relieves pain, or restores function (Ref. 9, p. 213). But the reverse is also possible. Some people may be willing to forgo some health insurance to maintain access to other goods and services.

A second reason for looking at the two problems together is that they pose similar questions for public policy: How much should each generation provide for its own needs in old age, and how much should be provided to them by their children's generation? How much provision should be voluntary, and how much compulsory? How much intra-generational redistribution is appropriate after age 65? How well can private markets serve the elderly's desire for annuities and health insurance, and when are public programs more efficient?

Finally, the magnitude of the problem of health care payment is approaching that of earnings replacement in economic importance and by 2020 will far exceed it. Declining health after age 65 results in substantial increases in the use of prescription drugs, hospital admissions, repair or replacement of parts of the body, rehabilitation and physical therapy, and assistance with daily living. New technologies offer great promise for mitigating the health problems of aging, but often at considerable expense. Overall, per capita health care expenditures after age 65 are more than three times greater than before 65.[14]

This paper focuses primarily on the apparently relentless increase in consumption of health care by older Americans. If consumption continues to increase at the same rate as in the past, it will amount to 10 percent of the GDP by 2020, more than double the 1995 share. If the government's share of the total (about 63 percent) remains unchanged, the tax burden on younger cohorts will increase proportionately. Concomitantly, if the private share remains unchanged, income available to the elderly for other goods and services will be less in 2020 than in 1995. Although the emphasis of the chapter is on aggregate and average results for the elderly, income inequality among the elderly is also examined and compared with inequality at younger ages. The chapter concludes with a discussion of changes that might avert the economic and social crises foreshadowed by the data.

Consumption of Health Care and Income Available for Other Goods and Services

Sources and methods

The estimates presented in Table 1 were calculated from data obtained from a wide variety of sources. To summarize, the population data and projections (middle series) are from the Bureau of the Census. Medicare expenditures on the elderly were obtained from the Health Care Finance Administration. Total personal health care expenditures were estimated by applying ratios of total personal health care to Medicare expenditures, as presented in Ref. 14. Projected expenditures were obtained by extrapolating trends in age-specific constant-dollar expenditures and population projections.

Income available for other goods and services was estimated by subtracting personal income taxes and private health care expenditures from personal income. Taxes paid by the elderly were calculated by Ref. 6 using the NBER tax model. Private expenditures for Health care (supplementary insurance premiums plus out-of-pocket payments) were estimated using the ratios of private to total expenditures calculated by Ref. 14. Personal income was obtained from the March (of the following year) supplement of the Current Population Survey (CPS).[c] Unfortunately, there is strong evidence of underreporting of income in the CPS. The Census Bureau, using comparisons of CPS money income with independent estimates, has calculated that CPS income for the total population in 1990 was 88 percent of income calculated from independent sources. The extent of underreporting varies greatly depending on the source of the income. For example, the CPS wage and salary income is estimated to be 97 percent of the figure obtained from independent estimates, but CPS income from interest is only 51 percent of the independent estimate, and income from dividends, only 33 percent.

To show the possible effects of underreporting, two estimates of income available for other goods and services are presented, CPS and CPS-Adjusted. The adjustments were made by applying the Census Bureau estimates of underreporting by source of income (for all ages) to each source of income for the elderly. The adjustment factors for 1995 were the ratios of the 1990 independent estimates to the CPS incomes; for 1985, an average of the 1983 and 1987 ratios; and for 1975, the 1979 ratios.[1] The deductions for taxes and private health care expenditures are identical for both estimates of income.

---

[c] All summary measures of income were obtained from individual records, appropriately weighted to take account of oversampling in the CPS. The data were extracted using CPS Utilities (1997).

Table 1.   Consumption of Health Care and Income Available for Other Goods and Services. Americans Ages 65 and Over.

	1975	1985	1995	2020	2020
Population[a]					
Millions	22.7	28.5	33.5	53.2	53.2
As percent of total population	10.5	11.9	12.8	16.5	16.5
Medicare[b]					
Per person (dollars)	1,473	2,713	4,114	14,309[c]	11,107[d]
Total (billions)	33	77	138	762	591
As percent of GDP	0.8	1.3	1.9	5.24	4.51
Total personal health care[e]					
Per person (dollars)	3,485	6,088	9,231	29,445[c]	24,391[d]
Total(billions)	79	174	310	1.567	1.298
As percent of GDP	1.9	3.0	4.3	10.8	9.9
Income available for other goods and services[f]					
CPS					
Per person (dollars)	9,241	10,492	11,203	9,803[g]	9,059[h]
Total(billions)	210	299	376	522	482
As percent of GDP	5.0	5.2	5.2	3.6	3.7
CPS-ADJUSTED					
Per person (dollars)	13,054	16,188	15,367	14,233[g]	9,162[h]
Total (billions)	296	462	515	758	488
As percent of GDP	7.1	8.1	7.1	5.2	3.7

Note: All dollar amounts in 1995 dollars adjusted by the GDP implicit deflator.

[a] Population data and projections for 2020 from the U.S. Census Bureau, middle series.

[b] Health Care Financing Review Statistical Supplement 1997.

[c] Estimated from extrapolation of trend in age-specific rate of expenditures 1975–95 and Census Bureau population projections.

[d] Estimated from extrapolation of trend in age-specific rate of expenditures 1985–95 and Census Bureau population projections.

[e] Estimated from relationship between total personal health care and Medicare in 1977 (for 1975) and 1987 (for 1985, 1995, and 2020).[14]

[f] Estimated from personal income (Current Population Survey, March 1976, 1986, 1996) less laxes[6] less private health care expenditures (ratios of private to total personal health care from Ref.14

[g] Estimated from extrapolations of 1975–95 trends in personal income and private health care expenditures.

[h] Estimated from extrapolations of 1985–95 trends in personal income and private health care expenditures.

Results

The most striking result of the extrapolations is that even the more conservative one shows health care for the elderly requiring one-tenth of the GDP by 2020. Per capita consumption of health care will reach $25,000 in 1995 dollars.[d] A second important result is the dramatic effect of rising health care expenditures on income available to the elderly for other goods and services. The absolute level of residual income (in constant dollars) is projected to be lower in 2020 than in 1995; expressed as a share of GDP, the projected decrease will be even greater. This projection is based on the projections for total health care expenditures and the assumption that the ratio of private to total expenditures will be 37 percent, the same as in 1995. The projections for 2020 are not unqualified predictions. Their principal purpose is to show what will happen if the rate of health care consumption of the elderly does not slow and the rate of growth of their income does not accelerate.

Comparison of CPS and CPS-Adjusted income estimates indicates that the former may significantly understate the income of the elderly. The adjustment procedure outlined above results in an adjusted income that is 32 percent above the CPS level in 1975. The differential between adjusted and unadjusted is 38 percent in 1985 and 25 percent in 1995.[e] The adjustment process affects income available for other goods and services more than it does total income (in percentage terms) because the same amount for private health care expenditures is deducted from both the adjusted and unadjusted total incomes.

Differences by age

Table 2 reproduces the key statistics of Table 1 for three age groups (65–74, 75–84, and 85+) in 1995. Total personal health care expenditures rise sharply with age. with the oldest group consuming three times as much per person as those 65–74, and almost twice as much as those 75–84. Because persons 85 and over have such high health care expenditures (a significant portion of which must be privately financed), they have relatively little income left for other goods and services. The elderly can, of course, draw down their assets to purchase medical care and other goods and services, but the importance of this source should not be exaggerated. Only minimal financial assets are available to most of the elderly, and their willingness or ability to use their housing equity is apparently limited. Uncertainty about the length of life is a significant factor in the economic behavior of the elderly. According to one study, the annuity-like character of

---

[d] All dollar figures in this paper are in 1995 dollars, using the GDP implicit price deflator as the source of adjustment.

[e] If underreporting by source of income is different for the elderly than for the population as a whole, these adjustments may be too large or too small. Also, there is no certainty that the independent estimates are correct. Therefore, both CPS and CPS-Adjusted are shown throughout the paper.

Table 2.   Consumption of Health Care and Income Available for Other Goods and Services in 1995 by Age.

	65–74	75–84	85+
Population (millions)	18.8	11.1	3.6
Medicare			
Per person (dollars)	3,097	4,958	6,781
Total (billions)	58	55	25
Total personal health care			
Per person (dollars)	6,183	10,572	19,358
Total (billions)	116	118	70
Income available for other goods and services			
CPS			
Per person (dollars)	13,392	9,544	5,202
Total (billions)	251	106	19
CPS-ADJUSTED			
Per person (dollars)	17,726	13,417	9,254
Total (billions)	333	150	34

Sources and Notes: See Table 1.

Social Security, Medicare, and Medicaid benefits has resulted in an increase in the propensity of older Americans to consume out of their remaining lifetime resources.[10]

Decomposition of change in personal health care consumption of the elderly

Between 1975 and 1995, personal health care consumption of the elderly rose 6.82 percent per annum in constant dollars. The average annual rate of change between 1985 and 1995 was 5.77 percent. As shown in Table 3, these rates of change can be decomposed into three components: (1) the change in age-specific consumption per person, (2) the change in the number of elderly, and (3) the change in the age distribution of the elderly. The results of this decomposition indicate that for both time periods, the highest rate of change was in per person age-specific consumption, which was more than twice as important as the rate of change in the number of elderly. Changes in the age distribution within the 65 + population were of minor significance.[f]

The Census Bureau middle series projection of the rate of change in the number of elderly between 1995 and 2020 of 1.85 percent per annum is very close to the rate of change from 1975 to 1995. Furthermore, I estimate that rates

---

[f]Interactions among these terms were minuscule.

Table 3. Decomposition of Constant Dollar Rate of Change of Total Personal Health Care Consumption of Older Americans (Percent per Annum).

	1975–95	1985–95	1995–2020	1995–2020
Age-specific consumption per older person	4.65	3.89	4.65[a]	3.89[b]
Number of elderly	1.95	1.61	1.85[c]	1.85[c]
Age distribution of elderly	0.22	0.27	−0.01[d]	−0.01[d]
Total Change	6.82	5.77	6.49	5.73

[a]The 1975–95 trend.
[b]The 1985–95 trend.
[c]Based on U.S. Census Bureau projections.
[d]Estimated from U.S. Census Bureau age-specific projections and age-specific expenditures in 1995.

of change of the age distribution *within* the 65+ population will have virtually zero effect on health care spending; that is, the increase in the number of old-old (85+), who are the largest consumers of health care, will be offset by a large increase in the number who are 65 to 74. By assuming the same rates of increase of age-specific health care consumption per person as prevailed in the 1975–95 and 1985–95 periods, we can project two health care consumption total rates of change for 1995 to 2020. Extrapolation from the longer period yields a projected rate of change in health care consumption of 6.49 percent per annum: the ten-year extrapolation yields a rate of 5.73 percent per annum.

The actual level of health care spending in 2020 is subject to considerable uncertainly. The rate of growth from 1985 to 1995 was slower than in the previous decade, and it is possible that there will be additional slowing in the decades ahead. On the other hand, several special circumstances were at work during the 1985–95 period, such as the introduction of DRG (diagnosis-related group) hospital reimbursement for Medicare patients, the spread of managed care (mostly for people under age 65, but with spillover effects at all ages), the squeezing of physician incomes, and the shortening of lengths of hospital stay. It may be difficult to push these interventions much further, in which case the 1985–95 trend may understate future rates of change.

Expectations at Age 65: Life, Work, and Income

Since 1975, life expectancy at age 65 has risen appreciably, especially for men. This change in life expectancy has not been accompanied by any increase in paid work by older men, and by only a small increase for women. Thus, the number of years when income must come from sources other than employment has grown, and employment's share of total income was less in 1995 than in 1975. Tables 4 and 5 summarize these trends. The first row of Table 4 presents life expectancy at age 65, a familiar statistic calculated from age-specific mortality rates in the year indicated. It is the mean years of life remaining for the cohort that reached age 65 (in, say, 1995) if it experienced the age-specific mortality that prevailed in 1995. Expected years of work is conceptually similar: it is obtained by combining age-specific rates of work with age-specific survival rates. It shows the years of work that the cohort that reached age 65 (in, say, 1995) would experience if the age-specific work rates and the mortality rates prevailing in 1995 continued through the lifetime of that cohort. The expected years of work are not forecasts, any more than the life expectancies are forecasts. The values could be used for forecasting purposes, however, by making assumptions about future trends in age-specific mortality and age-specific work rates.

Years of life expected at age 65 increased at a rapid pace from 1975 to 1995, more rapidly for men than for women, although the latter still enjoyed a 3.3 years' advantage over men in 1995. In contrast to life expectancy, expected years of work remained relatively constant, at about two years for men and one year for women (full-time equivalents). The number of expected years *not* at work (row 1 minus row 2) rose appreciably for men from 11.7 in 1975 to 13.7 in 1995. Women also show an increase in years *not* at work, from 17.3 to 17.8 years.

The change in life expectancy, unaccompanied by an equivalent increase in expected years of work, results in the elderly relying more on sources of income other than employment in 1995 than in 1975. Part A in Table 5 shows the share of income derived from employment for all elderly, including those living in families with one or more members under age 65. These younger family members are more likely to be in the labor force, and this tends to increase the share of income derived from employment. Part B is limited to individuals 65 and over who do

Table 4.   Expected at Age 65.[a]

Expected	Men			Women		
	1975	1985	1995	1975	1985	1995
Years of life	13.7	14.6	15.6	18.0	18.6	18.9
Years of work (FTE)[b]	2.0	1.7	1.9	0.7	0.7	1.1
Years not at work	11.7	12.9	13.7	17.3	17.9	17.8

[a]Based on survival rates and age-specific rates in the year indicated.
[b]Assuming a full-time work year of 2,000 hours.

Table 5.   Sources of Income of the Elderly (Ages 65+) in 1975, 1985, 1995.

	Part A			Part B		
	Families with any elderly			Families with only elderly		
	1975	1985	1995	1975	1985	1995
CPS						
Mean income[a]	11,818	15,004	16,587	11,475	15,011	16,486
Percent from						
Employment[b]	26	19	21	13	9	11
Interest and dividends[c]	18	26	17	22	30	20
Pensions[d]	12	14	16	14	15	18
Social Security[e]	40	39	40	48	45	46
Other[f]	3	2	5	3	1	5
CPS-Adjusted						
Mean income[a]	15,630	20,700	20,751	15,743	21,369	21,008
Percent from						
Employment[b]	21	14	19	11	6	10
Interest and dividends[c]	30	38	29	35	42	32
Pensions[d]	12	15	14	13	16	15
Social Security[e]	34	31	33	39	34	37
Other[f]	3	2	5	3	1	5

Note: All dollar amounts in thousands of 1995 dollars adjusted by the GDP implicit deflator.

[a]Family income (from all sources) divided equally among all family members.

[b]Includes wages and salaries and nonfarm and farm self-employment income.

[c]Includes rental income.

[d]Private and public employee pensions and annuities.

[e]Social Security retirement, supplementary security, and railroad retirement.

[f]Consists primarily of various social insurance and public assistance payments.

not have any family members under age 65. Both CPS and CPS-Adjusted data are shown.

Mean family income per capita is approximately the same in families with and without members under age 65, but employment's share of total income is only half as large when no family members are under age 65. The employment percent of income is lower in 1995 than in 1975 independent of the presence of family members under age 65, and this is true for both the unadjusted and adjusted data. The exceptionally low shares of employment income in 1985 are attributable to low labor force participation and to the unusually high income from interest and dividends in that year. For example, in 1985 the yield on triple-A corporate bonds was 11.4 percent compared with 7.6 percent in 1995.[g] The effect of high interest rates in 1985 is particularly strong for the CPS-Adjusted data because underreporting of interest is estimated to be considerably larger than

---

[g]These are nominal yields that reflect the impact of inflation on interest rates.

underreporting of income from most other sources. Pension income was more important in 1995 than in 1975, while Social Security declined slightly in relative importance.

Income Inequality Before and After Age 65

Contrary to what many believe,[h] income inequality among the elderly is substantially *less* than at younger ages. To measure inequality, family income is divided equally among family members to obtain individual personal income. The individuals in each of eleven age groups are then arrayed from the lowest to the highest personal income, grouped by decile, and the means of each decile calculated. The ratio of the mean of the eighth to the mean of the third decile is used to measure inequality. This comparison of the 10 percent of individuals who are in the middle of the upper half of the distribution with the 10 percent who are in the middle of the bottom half yields a robust measure of income inequality. It is relatively free of the problems of mismeasurement of income at the extremes of the distribution that can play such a large role in measures such as the Gini coefficient.

Tables 6, 7, and 8 show the mean income of the eighth and third deciles and their ratios for CPS and CPS-Adjusted data for 1995,1985, and 1975. The underreporting adjustment has a greater impact at older than at younger ages because income sources such as interest and dividends (which have a high rate of underreporting) constitute a greater proportion of total income of the elderly. For the same reason, the underreporting adjustment among the elderly makes more of a difference for the eighth than for the third decile. The most important finding, however, is that in 1995 income inequality at ages 65 and over is substantially less than at younger ages in both the unadjusted and adjusted measures. Indeed, in 1995 the largest inequality among the elderly (2.43 at ages 65–74) was *less* than the smallest inequality among those under 65 (2.78 at ages 41–48).

The smaller inequality after age 65 is attributable lo Social Security. If income from this source is subtracted from the mean income of the eighth and third deciles in 1995, the ratios for the remaining income soar to 6.31 (CPS) and 6.60 (CPS-Adjusted) at ages 65–74, compared with 2.43 and 2.73 when all sources are included. At older ages the leveling effect of Social Security is even greater. For those 85+ in 1995, the eighth/third decile ratios after subtracting Social Security

---

[h]Richard Disney (1996) states, "The income distribution of the elderly (65+) is more unequal than that of those under 65"(11). The author relies on Michael Hurd's review article (1990), which summarizes the results of earlier studies based on data for 1967, 1979, and 1984.

Table 6.   Mean Income* of 8th and 3rd Deciles, by Age, 1995.

Age	CPS			CPS-Adjusted		
	8th decile	3rd decile	8th/3rd ratio	8th decile	3rd decile	8th/3rd ratio
0 to 8	13,286	3,527	3.77	14,260	3,754	3.80
9 to 16	15,126	4,674	3.24	16,375	5,062	3.23
17 to 24	18,890	5,638	3.35	20,058	5,986	3.35
25 to 32	22,876	6,815	3.36	24,374	7,277	3.35
33 to 40	22,213	7,586	2.93	23,902	8,118	2.94
41 to 48	27,030	9,909	2.73	29,665	10,686	2.78
49 to 56	31,355	10,710	2.93	34,607	11,769	2.94
57 to 64	28,108	9,285	3.03	32,396	10,428	3.11
65 to 74	20,068	8,264	2.43	24,610	9,005	2.73
75 to 84	16,988	7,697	2.21	20,442	8,427	2.43
85+	16,191	7,081	2.29	20,315	7,575	2.68
median <65			3.13			3.17
median > = 65			2.29			2.68

*Family income divided equally among all family members.

Table 7.   Mean Income* of 8th and 3rd Deciles, by Age. 1985

Age	CPS			CPS-Adjusted		
	8th decile	3rd decile	8th/3rd ratio	8th decile	3rd decile	8th/3rd ratio
0 to 8	12,195	3,730	3.27	12,630	3,942	3.20
9 to 16	14,028	4,602	3.05	14,672	4,991	2.94
17 to 24	18,411	6,143	3.00	19,358	6,481	2.99
25 to 32	21,696	6,942	3.13	22,692	7,234	3.14
33 to 40	20,705	7,550	2.74	21,778	7,968	2.73
41 to 48	23,594	8,740	2.70	25,054	9,306	2.69
49 to 56	26,603	9,708	2.74	29,357	10,930	2.69
57 to 64	24,575	8,626	2.85	30,087	10,379	2.90
65 to 74	19,059	7,617	2.50	25,885	8,937	2.90
75 to 84	16,644	6,986	2.38	23,374	8,078	2.89
85+	16,789	6,570	2.56	23,392	7,771	3.01
median <65			2.92			2.92
median >= 65			2.50			2.90

Note: All dollar amounts in thousands of 1995 dollars adjusted by the GDP implicit deflator.
*Family income divided equally among all family members.

income are 11.70 (CPS) and 12.52 (CPS-Adjusted), compared with 2.29 and 2.68 when income from all sources is considered (see Table 9). Table 9 shows that Social Security's share of total income rises steadily with age, reaching about 90 percent for those in the third decile at ages 85+ and about 50 percent for those in the eighth decile. To be sure, these calculations undoubtedly overstate

Table 8.   Mean Income* of 8th and 3th Deciles, by Age, 1975.

Age	CPS			CPS-Adjusted		
	8th decile	3rd decile	8th/3rd ratio	8th decile	3rd decile	8th/3rd ratio
0 to 8	10,525	3,866	2.72	11,093	4,219	2.63
9 to 16	11,495	4,163	2.76	12,322	4,547	2.71
17 to 24	16,227	6,203	2.62	17,369	6,731	2.58
25 to 32	17,225	6,741	2.56	18,503	7,233	2.56
33 to 40	15,036	6,050	2.49	16,035	6,511	2.46
41 to 48	18,375	7,548	2.43	19,896	8,221	2.42
49 to 56	22,172	8,771	2.53	24,302	9,893	2.46
57 to 64	20,679	7,537	2.74	24,225	9,063	2.67
65 to 74	14,811	6,273	2.36	19,540	7,522	2.60
75 to 84	12,965	5,886	2.20	17,335	7,066	2.45
85+	12,763	5,310	2.40	16,478	6,577	2.51
median <65			2.59			2.57
median > = 65			2.36			2.51

Note: All dollar amounts in thousands of 1995 dollars adjusted by the GDP implicit deflator.
*Family income divided equally among all family members.

the extent of inequality that would exist if there were no Social Security program. Current work and savings patterns and living arrangements are influenced by the existence of Social Security; in its absence, these patterns would change. The levels of inequality now observed for individuals in their fifties and early sixties probably offer a better indication of income inequality after age 65 in a world without Social Security.

Relative inequality by age changed markedly during the period from 1975 to 1995, as can be seen in Figures 1 and 2 for CPS and CPS-Adjusted data, respectively. Inequality has risen appreciably at every age below 65 but has not risen for the elderly, and at some ages has actually fallen. Similar analyses that adjust for family size by using the ratio of family income to the poverty cutoff for each family yield the same conclusion.

Effects of Medicare on Inequality

Not only is income more equally distributed after 65 than before that age. but the Medicare program makes an additional large contribution to equality in economic well-being among the elderly. Medicare serves as a health insurance policy given to every American 65 and over. Its value each year is approximately equal to the average reimbursement per beneficiary, which amounted to $4,114 in 1995 (Table 1). Because average reimbursement is predictably related to age, the value

Table 9. Sources of Income of the Elderly by Age in 1995, 8th and 3rd Deciles.

	65–74		75–84		85+	
CPS	8th	3rd	8th	3rd	8th	3rd
Mean income[a]	20,068	8,264	16,988	7,697	16,191	7,081
Percent from						
Employment[b]	23	11	14	5	12	4
Interest and dividends[c]	15	5	15	5	18	3
Pensions[d]	22	5	19	4	12	1
Social Security[e]	35	76	46	85	51	91
Other[f]	5	4	6	2	8	2
CPS-Adjusted						
Mean income[a]	24,610	9,005	20,442	8,427	20,315	7,575
Percent from						
Employment[b]	20	11	13	6	10	4
Interest and dividends[c]	26	8	25	9	30	6
Pensions[d]	20	5	17	4	10	1
Social Security[e]	30	72	40	80	42	88
Other[f]	5	4	6	2	8	2

Note: All dollar amounts in thousands of 1995 dollars adjusted by the GDP implicit deflator.
[a]Family income (from all sources) divided equally among all family members.
[b]Includes wages and salaries and nonfarm and farm self-employment income.
[c]Includes rental income.
[d]Private and public employee pensions and annuities.
[e]Social Security retirement, supplementary security, and railroad retirement.
[f]Consists primarily of various social insurance and pubic assistance payments.

of the policy in 1995 could also be viewed as ranging from $3,097 for beneficiaries ages 65 to 74 to $6,781 for those ages 85 and older (Table 2).

Beneficiaries do pay directly for a small portion of Part B of the policy, but this is a minor offset to the value of the Medicare policy and is outweighed by the additional sales and administrative costs the elderly would have to bear if they bought a comparable policy in the private market.

If a cash transfer equal to the cost of Medicare were made to the elderly, no doubt some might choose to buy more of other goods and services instead of health insurance. Nevertheless, for the elderly as a whole, the value of the existing compulsory system may be equal to or greater than its cost because adverse selection and moral hazard would probably make a purely voluntary system unworkable. If those who did buy insurance voluntarily were above-average consumers of health care, the premium would not cover expenses and the market would tend to break down. Also, some who did not buy insurance might be relying on a socially provided "safety net" if they needed a great deal of care, thus further jeopardizing the availability of insurance for all.

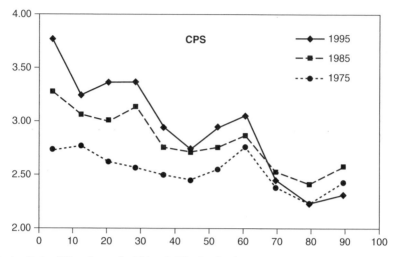

Fig. 1.   Ratio of Mean Income* of 8th to 3rd Deciles, by Age.
*Family income divided equally among all family members.

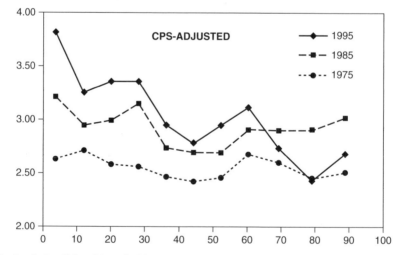

Fig. 2.   Ratio of Mean Income* of 8th to 3rd Deciles, by Age.
*Family income divided equally among all family members.

When the value of Medicare is added to money income, the effect is to appreciably reduce inequality in the economic well-being of seniors.

The magnitude of this effect is shown in Table 10. It is particularly large for those 85, reflecting the greater value of Medicare relative to money income for older persons. The egalitarian thrust of Medicare reimbursements is modified

Table 10. Inequality among the Elderly in 1995, with and without the Value of Medicare.

	65–74	75–84	85+
CPS			
Mean income plus Medicare*			
8th decile	23,165	21,946	22,972
3th decile	11,361	12,655	13,862
Ratio of 8th to 3th decile	2.04	1.73	1.66
Ratio without Medicare	2.43	2.21	2.29
CPS-Adjusted			
Mean income plus Medicare*			
8th decile	27,707	25,400	27,096
3rd decile	12,102	13,885	14,356
Ratio of 8th to 3rd decile	2.29	1.90	1.89
Ratio without Medicare	2.73	2.43	2.68

*Mean income from Table 6; Medicare expenditures from Table 2.

slightly by the fact that average lifetime reimbursements per beneficiary tend to be larger for beneficiaries who live in higher-income areas, as identified by zip codes.[12]

The government also subsidizes health insurance for Americans under age 65, primarily through the tax treatment of employer contributions to premiums, but the thrust of this subsidy is much less egalitarian than that of Medicare. Many low-income workers do not benefit at all because they are not covered by private insurance. Also, workers with higher earnings tend to have more insurance than those with lower earnings. Moreover, the cash value of the tax subsidy depends on the tax bracket of the recipient — the higher the bracket, the greater the subsidy. Finally, the average value of the subsidy is small relative to the money income of persons under 65. For these reasons, the addition of the health insurance subsidy to money income for persons under 65 has a much smaller effect on economic inequality than Medicare does for persons 65 and over.

Possible Changes

The prospect of the elderly's health care consuming one-tenth of the GDP is likely to arouse considerable concern among policy makers, the public, and the elderly themselves. This is a larger share of GDP than most nations currently spend, or are planning to spend, on health care for citizens of all ages. Also, in some of these countries the elderly make up a larger percentage of the population than the 16.5 percent projected by the Census Bureau for the United States in 2020.

Although 10 percent of GDP is an enormous amount, there is no physical law or economic principle that says a nation cannot devote that amount of resources to health care for the elderly, if it chooses. No one questions the amount spent by the elderly on videotapes or computers, for example, because they are spending their own money. Similarly, if the elderly were paying for their own health care, either out of current income or with funds that they had put aside for this purpose before age 65, the public policy picture would be entirely different. Presently, however, almost two-thirds of the funds must be raised by taxes — taxes that are borne primarily by men and women under age 65. Such a large tax burden poses problems for the economy as a whole and could also contribute to intergenerational tension and hostility. Moreover, if the government's share of the elderly's health care bill remains the same (or decreases), the huge absolute rise in private expenditures will leave the elderly with an ever-decreasing ability to purchase other goods and services.

What economic changes could alter these results? The answers lie in three directions: (1) a decrease in the rate of growth of age-specific health care expenditures, (2) an increase in the amount of paid work by persons 65 and older, and/or (3) an increase in the savings rate of persons under age 65.

Age-specific expenditures

The increase in health care expenditures for persons 65 and over is *not* primarily a demographic phenomenon (Table 3). There has been and will continue to be some growth in the number of elderly, but more than two-thirds of expenditure growth has come from an increase in age-specific expenditures. Why did older persons use so much more health care in 1995 than in 1975 or 1985? Certainly not because they were sicker in 1995. On the contrary, most experts believe that the elderly are healthier now than at any previous time. The most objective evidence of this comes from mortality rates. Age-specific mortality of the elderly was appreciably higher in 1975 than in 1995 — and most people are sick before they die.[i]

There is substantial consensus among health care experts that the driving force behind increasing health expenditures is new technology — new methods of diagnosis, new drugs, new surgical procedures, and the like. In a survey of fifty leading health economists in 1995, more than four out of five agreed with the statement "The primary reason for the increase in the health sector's share of GDP over the past 30 years is technological change in medicine".[8]

---

[i]Paradoxically, good health can often lead to greater health care utilization by the elderly. Those in good health may be deemed better candidates for expensive surgical procedures that would be regarded as medically inappropriate for persons of similar age who are in poor health.

Can the pace of technological change in medicine be slowed? Public policy can affect the development and diffusion of new medical technologies in three ways. First, the government has a huge effect on the demand for medical care through Medicare, Medicaid, and other public programs. What the government pays for and how much it pays directly influence the adoption of new technologies by health care providers and indirectly influence the amount and direction of private R&D. Second, the government heavily subsidizes the training of specialists and subspecialists, who then become important agents in the process of technology development and diffusion. Finally, the government influences technology through direct subsidization of medical research. In my judgment this is probably the least important influence, as evidenced by the lower levels of technology utilization in Canada and Western Europe compared with the United States. The results of U.S. government-subsidized research are known in all these countries, but the lower percentage of physicians who are specialists and the limitations in government funding of health care facilities and programs result in less use of expensive technology and in a lower rate of health care spending.

The example of other countries shows that public policy can slow the pace of technological change and diffusion. But does the United States want to do that? Technological innovations have contributed to longer and especially better quality of life for many older Americans. Some current research suggests that new medical technology has been cost-effective — its benefits exceed its costs. Some technological innovations lower the cost of treating a patient with a particular disease. It is a grave mistake, however, to think that lowering the cost per unit will lead to lower overall expenditures. The experience in medical care to date (and in many other industries such as personal computers) is that total expenditures increase even as cost per unit goes down. If the growth of medical expenditures continues, however, who will pay for the increase? What new sources of funds could become available to help the elderly finance medical care and also maintain their access to other goods and services?

More work and more saving

One possibility is greater participation in paid work by older men and women. As seen in Table 4, employment after age 65 was about the same in 1995 as in 1975 despite substantial improvement in the health of the elderly and longer life expectancy.[j] According to one authority on retirement, better health has not prevented a long-term trend toward early retirement (Ref. 2, p. 195). Another recent study, however, states that this trend ended abruptly in 1985[13]

---

[j]At any given point in time, persons in poorer health tend to retire earlier.[5]

(forth-coming). Table 4 does show a small increase in years of work expected at age 65 between 1985 and 1995. Although the health of the elderly is improving, there are two major impediments to working after age 65. First, older workers are discouraged by the high marginal tax rates implicit in means-tested benefit structures. Second, employers often find older workers add disproportionately to their health insurance and pension costs. To increase labor force participation after age 65, policy makers will need to address both of these obstacles.

Because their own employment income accounts for a relatively small part of the total income of the elderly (10 percent in 1995), there would have to be a substantial increase in labor force participation to make a significant impact on the ability of the elderly to pay for more medical care and maintain access to other goods and services. Another possibility is for those who will reach 65 in 2020 or beyond to begin now to substantially increase their rate of saving. Income from savings (interest, dividends, and pensions) is more than four times as important as employment as a source of income after age 65. Thus, a substantial increase in this source would have a major effect on the financial condition of the elderly.

One probable side effect of an increase in the relative importance of income from employment and savings would be somewhat more income inequality among the elderly. The more voluntary the additional savings and the more individual discretion over the way the savings are invested, the greater will be the increase in inequality. But voluntary or compulsory, individually controlled or not, the clearest implication of the projections for 2020 is the need for additional savings.

This was the advice given by Robert Frost in 1936 in his poem "Provide, Provide." a portion of which follows:

> ...
> Die early and avoid the fate.
> Or, if predestined to die late,
> Make up your mind to die in state.
>
> No memory of having starred
> Atones for later disregard
> Or keeps the end from being hard.
>
> Better to go down dignified
> With boughten friendship at your side
> Than none at all. Provide, provide!*

---

*From "Provide, Provide," from *The Poetry of Robert Frost,* edited by Edward Connery Lathem, copyright 1936 by Robert Frost, © 1964 by Leslie Frost Ballentine, © 1969 by Henry Holt and Co., Inc. Reprinted by permission of Henry Holt and Company, Inc.

References

1. Bureau of the Census. *Money Income of Households, Families, and Persons in the United States: 1980, 1987, 1991, and 1992.* Tables A2 and Cl.
2. Costa, D. L. (1998). *The Evolution of Retirement: An American Economic History, 1880–1990.* University of Chicago Press: Chicago.
3. CPS Utilities (1997). *March CPS Utilities, 1964–1996.* Release 96.1. Unicon Research Corporation: 1640 Fifth Street, Santa Monica, CA 90401, 310-393-4636.
4. Disney, R. (1996). *Can We Afford to Grow Older? A Perspective on the Economics of Aging.* MIT University Press: Cambridge, USA.
5. Dwyer, D. S. and Mitchell, O. (1998). "Health Problems as Determinants of Retirement: Are Self-Rated Measures Endogenous?" NBER Working Paper 6503 (April).
6. Feenberg, D. (1998). Personal communication.
7. Frost. R. (1988). "Provide, Provide." In *The Norton Anthology of Modern Poetry,* 2d ed., eds. R. Ellman and R. O'Clair. W. W. Norton: New York, p. 263.
8. Fuchs, V. R. (1996). "Economics, Values and Health Care Reform." *American Economic Review* **86**(1): 1–24.
9. Glied, S. (1997). *Chronic Condition: Why Health Reform Fails.* Harvard University Press: Cambridge, MA.
10. Gokhale, J., Kotlikoff, L. and Sabelhaus, J. (1996). "Understanding the Postwar Decline in U.S. Saving: A Cohort Analysis." *Brookings Papers on Economic Activity* **1**: 315–407.
11. Hurd, M. (1990). "Research on the Elderly: Economic Status, Retirement. and Consumption and Saving." *Journal of Economic Literature* 28(2): 565–637.
12. McClellan, M. and Skinner, J. (1997). "The Incidence of Medicare," NBER Working Paper No. 6013 (April), p. 21.
13. Quinn, J., Burkhauser, R., Cahill, K. and Weathers, R. (Forthcoming). "The Microeconomics of the Retirement Decision in the United States." OECD Working Paper, Paris.
14. Waldo, D. R., Sonnefeld, S. T., McKusick, D. R. and Arnett III, R. H. (1989). "Health Expenditures by Age Group. 1977 and 1987." *Health Care Financing Review* **10**(4, summer): 116–120 (See Table 4, p. 118).

6.4

The Financial Problems of the Elderly: A Holistic View

"Grow old along with me! The best is yet to be," wrote Robert Browning in his poem *Rabbi Ben Ezra*. A century later, Robert Butler, a former director of the National Institute of Aging, took a more dismal view of aging, epitomized in the title of his book *Why Survive? Being Old in America* (1975). Why the change in perspective? One possible reason is that an elderly person was a rarity in Browning's time; as the twentieth century drew to a close, however, mortality tables showed that three out of four Americans would reach the biblical "three score and ten." Just being old no longer carries any special distinction.

A Japanese statesman-scholar, Wataru Hiraizumi, recently provided a provocative insight into the effect of an increase in the proportion of elderly persons in a society. Recalling his first few weeks in France in the 1950s, he says, "I suddenly saw the reason for a singular uneasiness. ... It was the presence of a seemingly inordinate number of old people.... They looked vigilant, severe, and vaguely ill-tempered" (2000). He attributed this to the fact that in France at that time more than 11 percent of the population was over 65, whereas in the Japan he had recently left, elderly persons were barely 5 percent of the population.

Probably an even more important reason for the change from Browning to Butler is that improvements in the material condition of America's elderly have been surpassed by rapidly rising expectations. Although today's elderly persons are on average healthier and wealthier than any previous generation in the nation's history, their desires and expectations regarding life in retirement are outpacing the ability of society to fulfill them. Nowhere is this more evident than with respect to health and medical care.

Recent decades have witnessed an unprecedented number of advances in medical technology that, albeit costly, have contributed to longer, better-quality lives for many older Americans. Ten of the most important, as indicated in Fuchs and Sox (2001), are

Balloon angioplasty with stents
Blood-pressure-lowering drugs
Cataract extraction with lens implant
Cholesterol-lowering drugs
Coronary artery bypass graft
Hip and knee replacement
MRI and CT scanning
Mammography
New drugs for depression
New drugs for ulcers and acid reflux

Thanks in part to such innovations (and in part to declines in cigarette smoking), the overall age-adjusted death rate has decreased by 20 percent since 1980. But some major causes of death, such as cancer and diabetes, show little or no decline in mortality. When medical care could do little to extend life for anyone, not much was expected of it. In an era of great progress, however, expectations of further gains accelerate. The more medical care does to keep people alive and healthier, the more is demanded of it.

Moreover, despite the gains in health and wealth, many Americans still experience a troubled old age. In addition to the inevitable loss of family and friends, diminution of status, and existential concerns, many elderly persons face two potentially serious financial problems: lower income and greater expenditures for medical care. Physiological changes are the primary cause of both lower earnings and poorer health. Earnings are also affected adversely by obsolescence of skills and knowledge and by public and private policies that reduce the incentives of older persons to continue working and increase the cost to employers of employing older workers.

These financial problems have been widely discussed in recent years; the chapters in this volume provide additional food for thought. Unfortunately, most policy discussions of the financial problems of elderly persons tend to focus on only one program at a time. Thus, there is a plethora of papers on Social Security, Medicare, Medicaid, employment-based pensions, Medigap insurance, and so on. Sometimes these sharply focused studies are required by legislative or administrative exigencies, but I believe a holistic view is a necessary complement to such fragmented analyses.

A Holistic View

A holistic view focuses simultaneously on the financing of health care and the financing of other goods and services. It also focuses on the expenditures of the elderly that are self-financed as well as on those that are financed by transfers from the young. A holistic view cautions against policy proposals that claim we can patch existing public programs for elderly persons without major changes in policies and behavior. These limited proposals usually include means testing benefits, subsidies, modest increases in taxes, and various administrative maneuvers. When they are examined one program at a time, such proposals may seem reasonable and feasible. The entire package, however, applied to all programs for elderly persons, is likely to create large disincentives for work and saving before retirement and require huge transfers that will ultimately be rejected by taxpayers.

At one time it was reasonable to treat, the problem of earnings replacement separately from the problem of paying for health care. Health care expenditures of elderly persons were small relative to expenditures on other goods and services, and a holistic approach was not essential. Now, however, health care expenditures equal or exceed expenditures for all other goods and services for many elderly persons, and given the trends of recent decades, this may be true for the elderly as a group within twenty years.

Artificial separation of the problem of earnings replacement from that of health care payment ignores the fact that there are often tradeoffs between the two. Money is money, and for most elderly persons there is never enough to go around. This is self-evident where private funds are concerned. Low-income elderly persons, for example, frequently must choose between prescription drugs and an adequate diet. For middle-income elderly persons, the choice may be between more expensive Medigap insurance and an airplane trip to a grandchild's wedding. Difficult choices are also apparent with respect to public funds. The same tax receipts that could be used to maintain or increase retirement benefits could be used to fund additional health care, and vice versa. Policy analysts who fail to understand that a large increase in Medicare spending will jeopardize the government's ability to fulfill its Social Security commitments ignore the realities of economics and politics.

A holistic approach not only requires analyses that encompass different government programs but also must involve examination of the two-way interactions between changes in the private sector and public programs. For instance, from 1993 to 2000 the share of employers providing health insurance for retirees declined from 40 percent to less than 25 percent.[2] This change may suggest that government provision of health insurance for retirees should expand, but such expansion could result in further decreases in private coverage.

Another significant trend in the private sector that has major implications for the future financial problems of elderly persons is the shift in private pensions from defined benefit to defined contribution. This change works well for retirees when the stock market is rising briskly, but it looks less attractive when the stock market flattens or goes into decline. Moreover, the 401(k) plans and IRAs that have supplanted the traditional retirement plans typically do not call for automatic annuitization upon retirement. This can be advantageous to retirees who would like access to their money but can be problematic for them and for taxpayers if they lose their retirement savings in bad investments or spend them at too rapid a rate. Furthermore, if annuitization is voluntary, the terms available are likely to suffer from the problem of adverse selection. Hurd and McGarry (2002) have shown that the ability of individuals to predict their longevity is significantly greater than could be expected from chance. For this reason, some compulsory annuitization is probably as necessary as some compulsory enrollment in health insurance.

Full Income

To provide a holistic framework for addressing the financial problems of elderly persons, it is useful to think of the "full income" (or its equivalent, "full consumption") of the elderly. I define *full income* as the sum of personal income and health care expenditures not paid from personal income. Two critical questions can be addressed within this framework: (1) How much of the elderly's full income is devoted to health care and how much to other goods and services? (2) How much of the elderly's full income is provided by transfers from the population under age 65 (Social Security retirement payments, Medicare, and similar programs) and how much is provided by elderly persons themselves (earnings, pensions, income from savings, and the like)?

Using data from the Current Population Survey (CPS) (*U.S. Department of Commerce and U.S. Department of Labor 1997*), the Medicare Current Beneficiary Survey (*Health Care Financing Administration 1997*), and other sources, with adjustments for underreporting, I estimate that 35 percent of the elderly's full income in 1997 was devoted to health care and 65 percent to other goods and services (see the right-hand column of Table 1). I also estimate that 56

Table 1. Americans Age 65 or Older, Sources and Uses of "Full Income" in 1997 (percentage distribution).

| | Source | | |
Use	Under age 65	Age 65 or older	Total
Health care	27	8	35
Other	29	36	65
Total	56	44	100

Source: Fuchs 2000.

Table 2. Projected Uses and Sources of "Full Income" in 2020 under Alternative Assumptions about Gap between Growth of Health and Other.

| | Gap (percent per annum) | | | |
	0	1	2	3
Use				
Health	35	40	46	52
Other	65	60	54	48
Source				
<65	56	58	60	62
≥ 65	44	42	40	38

Source: Fuchs 2000.
Note: Assuming that the share of Health and the share of Other provided by <65 remain constant.

percent of full income was provided by transfers from the "young" and 44 percent by elderly persons themselves (see the bottom row of Table 1).

Probably the most important information in Table 1 is the disaggregation of full income by use *and* source found in the interior of the table. We see that elderly persons are much more dependent on transfers for health care expenditures than for other goods and services. Of the 35 percent of full income that goes for health care, more than three-fourths (27 divided by 35) is provided by the young, as opposed to less than half (29 divided by 65) for other goods and services. This fact combined with the tendency for spending on health care to grow more rapidly than spending on other goods and services will pose major problems for policymakers and elderly persons within two decades.

Table 2 shows what the uses and sources of full income would be in 2020 if the generations under 65 continue to bear the same share of health care and "other" as in 1997. If health care spending does not grow more rapidly than "other" (the first column of Table 2), the shares of uses and sources will be identical to those shown in Table 1. If health care spending grows 3 percent per annum more rapidly than "other" (the last column in Table 2), we see that the health share of full income would jump from 35 to 52 percent and the young would provide 62 percent of full income instead of the 56 percent provided in 1997. These calculations are all per capita; that is, they do not take into account the fact that the ratio of elderly to those under age 65 will be higher in 2020 than it was in 1997. Thus, the figures in Table 2 underestimate the potential increased dependency of the elderly on transfers from the young.

Will spending on health for elderly persons grow faster than spending on other goods and services? This question cannot be answered with certainty, but it would be prudent to assume that it will. Over the period 1970–2000, Medicare expenditures per elderly person enrollee grew approximately 2.8 percent per annum faster than GDP per capita (excluding health care expenditures). The growth of the nonhealth economy is an indicator of the rate at which expenditures on "other" could grow. The "gap" of 2.8 percent per annum is attributable primarily to technological advances such as those listed above. Will the pace of technological advance in medicine slow in the next two decades? Not likely. There are currently seven hundred new drugs in development for the diseases of aging, and as the elderly's share of the health care market increases, the share of medical R&D focused on elderly persons is likely to grow.

In theory, advances in medical technology do not necessarily lead to higher expenditures, but in practice that is usually the way it works. The last major exception to this rule occurred a half century ago with the introduction and rapid diffusion of antibiotics. But antibiotics were a very special kind of medical advance. They were given to patients who had life-threatening infections, most of whom who were in otherwise good health. Many beneficiaries were children and young adults who, once the infection was cured, went on to live many years without requiring major medical intervention. By contrast, advances in medical technology that extend life or improve quality of life for older Americans do not offer that same prospect of reducing overall utilization of medical care. Indeed, many expensive interventions, such as open-heart surgery, will only be undertaken on patients who are otherwise in reasonably good health. Moreover, antibiotics were very inexpensive to produce and dispense. By contrast, many of the products currently under development in the biotech and bioengineering laboratories are likely to be expensive to produce and implement.

Implications for Policy

The coming increase in the absolute and relative number of elderly persons will unquestionably increase the burden on the working population and require an increase in taxes. But if the scenario sketched out in Table 17.2 materializes, that is, if health care expenditures for elderly persons grow 2 to 3 percent per annum more rapidly than expenditures on other goods and services, the burden on the young is likely to be unbearable. There seem to be only two possible escapes from this bleak scenario: slow the rate of growth of health care expenditures, or require elderly persons to assume more of the responsibility for paying for their health care.

Slowing the growth of health care expenditures may not be feasible, and even if it is feasible, it may not be desirable. Although advances in technology are the driving force behind the growth of medical expenditures, many of these advances contribute significantly to longer, better-quality lives. Politicians in both parties strongly support increased spending for medical research, and private decision makers in the drug and biotech industries are betting tens of billions of dollars each year that the money to pay for advances in medical technology will be forthcoming. Many economists now assert that the advances of recent decades, albeit expensive, are "good buys" and see no reason why that will not be true of future advances as well.

If health care expenditures for elderly persons continue to grow rapidly, however, and if the ability to finance these expenditures by transfers from the young reaches its limit, the only alternative is for elderly persons to pick up a larger share of the bill. If these payments must come from incomes that grow at only a modest pace, elderly persons will become increasingly "health care poor." Indeed, many are already in that unhappy condition. Although eligible for MRIs, angiograms, bypass surgery, and other high-tech diagnostic and surgical interventions, they do not have the resources to purchase a new mattress, to heat their house to a comfortable temperature in winter, to take a taxi to the doctor, or to access other goods and services that would make life more bearable.

Elderly persons must have additional personal income in order to avoid the scenario in which more and more of them will become "healthcare poor." They need more income from *savings* (including pensions and investments) and from *earnings,* which means they will have to work more both before and after age 65. Why do millions of Americans reach age 65 so heavily dependent on transfers from the young? One possibility is that their income over the life cycle was so low that they could barely meet everyday expenses, let alone save for retirement. This explanation is undoubtedly correct for some low-income elderly, but analyses of longitudinal data by Venti and Wise (1998) show that inequality in savings for retirement varies greatly even among those with the same earnings prior to retirement. This conclusion holds after adjustments for special factors that affect the ability to save and for differences in investment returns.

Savings income

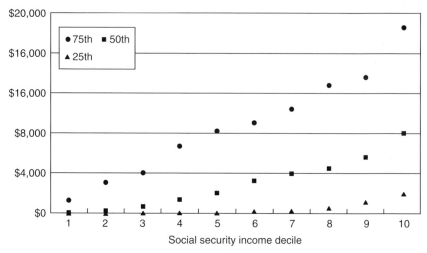

Fig. 1. Savings Income by Social Security Income Decile, Americans Aged 65 and Older, 1997. Symbols Represent Percentiles.
Source: Fuchs 1999a.

An examination of CPS data on sources of income provides additional evidence concerning the question of the relation between saving and income. To obtain the statistics shown in Figure 1, everyone 65 and over was sorted into deciles based on their Social Security income, an ordering that is probably similar to one based on lifetime earnings.[a] Within each decile individuals were sorted by savings income (pensions, interest, dividends, and rent) and the 25th, 50th, and 75th percentiles were identified. The results reveal that although savings income tends to be positively correlated with Social Security income, there is great variation *within each decile*. Many elderly persons in the lower deciles have substantial savings income, whereas many in the higher deciles have very little. Consider the striking differences among workers in the middle range of income, that is, Social Security deciles 5 and 6. Those are the quintessential "average workers." At least one-fourth of them have virtually no savings income, but another fourth have savings income of over eight thousand dollars per year. It is clear from these data that when saving is voluntary, many individuals do not save. To provide higher income for future elderly persons and to reduce inequality among them, it will be necessary to introduce some form of compulsory saving.

---

[a] All household income was assumed to be shared equally among the members of the household.

The other major potential source of increase in income for elderly persons is more paid work. In the late 1990s, mean hours of work per man age 60 was only 1,495 per year, at age 65 only 701 hours, and at age 70 only 358 hours.[b] The comparable figures for women were 926, 423, and 150 hours per year, respectively. Given that most Americans at these ages are in reasonably good health and suffer from fewer physical limitations than earlier cohorts, there seems to be ample potential for more work.

Since 1975 life expectancy at age 65 has risen appreciably, especially for men. This change, unfortunately, has not been accompanied by any increase in paid work by older men and by only a small increase for women. Thus, the number of years when income must come from sources other than employment has grown, and employment's share of total income was less in 1995 than in 1975. Table 3 provides a useful summary of how work has failed to keep pace with increases in life expectancy.

The first row of Table 3 presents life expectancy at age 65, a familiar statistic calculated from age-specific mortality rates in the year indicated. It is the mean years of life remaining for the cohort that reached age 65 (in, say, 1995) if it experienced the age-specific mortality that prevailed in 1995. Expected years of work is conceptually similar; it is obtained by combining age-specific rates of work with age-specific survival rates. It shows the years of work that the cohort that reached age 65 (in, say, 1995) would experience if the age-specific work rate and the mortality that prevailed in 1995 continued through the lifetime of that cohort. The expected years of work are not forecast, anymore than the life expectancies are forecast. The values could be used for forecasting purposes,

Table 3. Expected at Age 65.

Expected	Men			Women		
	1975	1985	1995	1975	1985	1995
Years of life	13.7	14.6	15.6	18.0	18.6	18.9
Years of work (FTE)[a]	2.0	1.7	1.9	0.7	0.7	1.1
Years not at work	11.7	12.9	13.7	17.3	17.9	17.8

Source: Fuchs 1999b.
Note: Based on age-specific mortality and employment rates in the year indicated.
[a] Assuming a full-time work year of 2000 hours.

---

[b] These figures were calculated from the 1996–98 Current Population Surveys. They reflect the total annual hours worked for each age-sex group divided by the total number in the group regardless of labor force status.

however, by making assumptions about future trends in age-specific mortality and in age-specific work rates.

Inspection of Table 3 reveals that years of life expected at age 65 increased at a rapid pace from 1975 to 1995, more rapidly for men than for women, although the latter still enjoyed a 4.3 year advantage over men in 1995. In contrast to life expectancy, expected years of work remained relatively constant, at about 2 years for men and 1 year for women (full time equivalents). The number of years *not* at work (row 1 minus row 2) rose appreciably for men from 11.7 in 1975 to 13.7 in 1995. Women also show an increase in years *not* at work, from 17.3 to 17.8 years. Health care and consumption of other goods and services in these years not at work must be financed by the accumulated savings of the elderly or by transfers from the young.

To make paid work for older Americans more attractive, there must be a reexamination of all policies that create high implicit marginal tax rates on earnings and employment as well as a review of employment laws, which often make it more costly for employers to hire or retain older workers. In addition to providing more income, there could be additional benefits to elderly persons from making work more feasible and desirable. Work often provides satisfaction, identity, and an opportunity to maintain or develop relationships. Moreover, staying active usually contributes to better health. We should recall the words of another English poet, Alfred Tennyson, who in contemplating Ulysses in retirement has the aging hero say, "How dull it is to pause, to make an end, to rust unburnished, not to shine in use! As though to breathe were life."

References

1. Butler, R. N. (1975). *Why Survive? Being Old in America.* Harper and Row: New York.
2. Freudenheim, M. (2000). *New York Times* **31**: 38.
3. Fuchs, V. R. (1999a). "Health Care for the Elderly: How Much? Who Will Pay for It?" *Health Affairs* **18**(1): 11-21.
4. Fuchs, V. R. (1999b). Provide, Provide: The Economics of Aging. In *Medicare Reform: Issues and Answers*, eds. A. Rettenmaier and T. R. Savings. University of Chicago Press: Chicago.
5. Fuchs, V. R. (2000). "Medicare Reform: The Larger Picture." *Journal of Economic Perspectives* **14**(2): 57-70.
6. Fuchs, V. R. and Sox, Jr. H. C. (2001). "Physicians' Views of the Relative Importance to Patients of Thirty Medical Innovations: A Survey of Leading General Internists." *Health Affairs* **20**(5): 30-42.

7. Health Care Financing Administration (Office of Strategic Planning) (1997). Medicare Current Beneficiary Survey. http://www.hcfa.gov/surveys/mcbs/Default. htm.

8. Hiraizumi, W. (2000). "Mass Longevity Transforms Our Society." *Proceedings of the American Philosophical Society* **144**(4): 361–383.

9. Hurd, M. D. and McGarry, K. (2002). "The Predictive Validity of Subjective Probabilities of Survival." *Economic Journal* **112**: 966-985.

10. U.S. Department of Commerce (Bureau of the Census) and U.S. Department of Labor (Bureau of Labor Statistics) (1997). Current Population Survey. http://www.bls.census.gov/cps/cpsmain.htm.

11. Venti, S. F. and Wise, D. A. (1998). "The Cause of Wealth Dispersion at Retirement: Choice or Chance?" *American Economic Review* **88**(2): 185–191.

Op-Ed

New Priorities for Future Biomedical Innovations

Since 1900, life expectancy at birth has increased by an unprecedented 30 years in the United States and other developed countries. Before World War II, most of the gains resulted from improvements in nonmedical factors: nutrition, sanitation, housing, and public health measures. Since World War II, however, biomedical innovations (new drugs, devices, and procedures) have been the primary source of increases in longevity. These innovations have also been the most important reason why health care expenditures have grown 2.8 percent per year more rapidly than the rest of the economy over the past 30 years.[1] Will the future simply be a rerun of recent decades? Probably not. Current demographic, social, and economic forces will create new priorities for future biomedical innovations: more emphasis on improving quality of life and less on extending life, and more attention to value-enhancing innovations instead of pursuit of any medical advance regardless of its cost relative to its benefit.

Society may not pursue further gains in life expectancy as vigorously as we've done in the past, because there has been a dramatic shift in the age at which the increased years of life are realized (see bar graph). In the early decades of the 20th century, approximately 80 percent of the gains in life expectancy were realized before the age of 65 years and only 20 percent at 65 years or older. Now the situation is reversed — almost 80 percent of recent gains in life expectancy

Originally published in *New England Journal of Medicine*, 363(8):704–706, August 2010. Copyright by Massachusetts Medical Society.

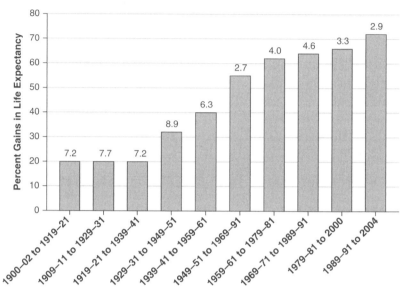

Percent Gains in Life Expectancy Realized at 65 Years of Age or Older during Overlapping Periods. The value at the top of each bar is the number of years by which life expectancy increased during the period.

are realized at an age of 65 years or older. The main reason for the change is the sharp decline in rates of death at younger ages; thus, an ever larger percentage of each birth cohort survives to at least 65 years of age. At the beginning of the 20th century, given the age-specific mortality rates of that time, only 41 percent of the birth cohort could expect to reach 65 years of age. By the end of the century, survivorship until 65 years had doubled, to more than 81 percent.[2] When survivorship to 65 years of age was low, gains in life expectancy meant keeping more Americans alive during their working years. Now, further gains in life expectancy will mostly mean keeping more Americans alive while they are retired and dependent on indirect transfers of funds from younger workers for much of their living expenses, health care, and social services. At 65 years of age or older, 4 of 5 men and 9 of 10 women are not in the labor force, and almost 4 of 10 have a physical or mental disability. Moreover, almost half of all patients in hospital beds are 65 years of age or older.[3] The U.S. entitlement programs for the elderly will be major contributors to huge federal deficits for the foreseeable future — deficits that are often invoked as reasons not to spend federal dollars providing health insurance to all Americans.

A diminished focus on developing innovations that increase life expectancy could and should be accompanied by greater pursuit of innovations, such as joint replacement, that improve the quality of life for both the elderly and the near-elderly. The potential market for quality-of-life enhancement among Americans 55 years of age or older is huge: 3 of 10 such Americans have difficulty stooping or bending, 1 of 10 has difficulty reaching or grasping, 4 of 10 usually sleep less than 7 to 8 hours in a 24-hour period, 15 percent have difficulty carrying 10 lb (4.5 kg), nearly one third have some hearing impairment, one fifth have lost all their natural teeth, and 1 of 4 has difficulty walking a quarter of a mile (0.4 km).[4]

Along with the shift in emphasis to developing future innovations that enhance quality of life, there is a growing need for a shift to value-conscious innovation instead of fostering the "progress at any price" attitude that has dominated biomedical innovation until now. The economy cannot continue to cope with the rapid increase in health care expenditures, an increase that is fueled in large part by innovations produced in an environment that ignores cost. The problem is not just federal health care expenditures. State and local governments, hard-pressed to meet their obligations under Medicaid and other health care programs, are forced to cut back support for education, repair of roads and bridges, and other critical expenditures. And the private sector is also under duress (see line graph). A rapid increase in the cost of employment-based health insurance is the major reason why the wages of the average worker have been relatively stagnant for three decades.[5]

To understand the differences between the present environment for biomedical innovations and a value-conscious one requires thinking of three effects of every innovation: its effect on the quality of care (including reductions in mortality and morbidity rates, relief of pain, and improvement of other types of care that patients desire), its effect on the cost of care (the resources used to develop it and provide it to patients, relative to those used for current practice), and its effect on the value of care (changes in quality relative to changes in cost). Until now, most biomedical innovations have been evaluated (if at all) only in terms of their effect on the quality of care. Cost is usually ignored, which means that value is ignored as well. There have been a few key innovations that increase quality of care and decrease the cost of care, resulting in unambiguously positive value; examples are antibiotics and diuretics. Most innovations, however, increase both quality of care and costs. Their effect on value depends on the relative sizes of these increases. In a value-conscious environment, some of the most

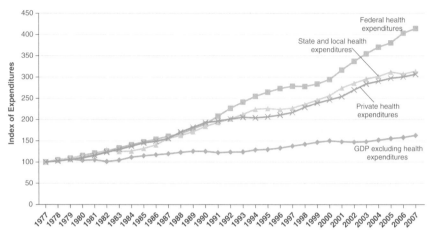

Indexes of Health Expenditures and the Gross Domestic Product (GDP) Excluding Health Expenditures, per Capita, Adjusted for Inflation, 1977–2007.
The index value at 1977 was set at 100.

popular innovations would meet a reasonable value standard, but many probably would not.

An additional important result of a value-conscious environment would be the encouragement of innovations whose main effect is to substantially decrease cost while holding quality constant or reducing it only slightly. Such innovations are common in other industries but rare in medicine. If some of the resources devoted to marginal advances in the quality of care were reallocated to the development of innovations that reduced the cost of care, the problem of paying for high-value advances in quality for the entire population would be much easier to address.

Despite passage of the Patient Protection and Affordable Care Act, there is still need for health care reform that will slow the rate' of growth of expenditures. Regardless of whether that reform involves a much larger role for government or is more market-oriented, a shift in emphasis toward more value-conscious innovations is necessary and perhaps inevitable.

References

1. Pauly, M. V. (2005). "Competition and New Technlogy." *Health Affairs (Millwood)* **24**: 1523–1535.
2. National Center for Health Statistics (2007). *United States Life Tables, 2004*. Centers for Disease Control and Prevention: Atlanta.

3. Bureau of the Census (2009). *Statistical Abstract of the United States*. Goverment Printing Office: Washington, DC.

4. Schoenborn, C. A. and Heyman, K. M. (2009). "Health Characteristics of Adults Age 55 Years and Over: United States, 2004–2007." *National Health Statistics Report* **16**: 1–31.

5. Emanuel, E. J. and Fuchs, V. R. (2008). "Who Really Pays for Health Care? The Myth of "Shared Responsibility." *The Journal of the American Medical Association*, **299**: 1057–1059.

Part 7

Health Policy and Health Care Reform

Introduction

Throughout a long career in health economics, I have not spent much time (or ink) in partisan policy disputes. I have, however, been deeply interested in health policy and in reform of what seems to me to be a dysfunctional health care system in the United States. The first two papers in Part 7 offer extended statements about policy and reform. The first was prepared when I had been in the health field only a little over a decade; the second after 30 years.

The first paper, the E.S. Woodward Lectures in Economics delivered at the University of British Columbia, November 1 and 2, 1978, tried to provide a diverse audience with a broad description of health care, to illustrate how economics offers insights about the field, and to use health as a quintessential example of economic problems in a post-industrial society. In this paper I discuss the many determinants of health and give reasons for the rapid growth of expenditures for health care. The growth of government is singled out for special analysis because the proper role of government is central to the debate between the Right and Left about health care. The Right stresses the efficiency of a decentralized market-price system as opposed to a centralized command and control system. The Right also believes that there is an important connection between property rights and human rights: Milton Friedman's argument about "the fragility of freedom." But the Right seems to lack a plausible view of the historical development of society. Asked to explain the popularity of national health insurance in high income democracies, the Right says "people are stupid" or that it is achieved and sustained by "special interests" rather than the general interest. It is difficult to see who those "special interests" might be; the drug companies and the specialist physicians make much more money in the U.S. system. A more plausible explanation might be that national health insurance meets society's needs better than other ways of organizing medical care. That those needs are political, social, and psychological as much as physiological is one the paper's themes.

I credit the Left for keeping before us a vision of a just society. The Left's weakness is not an inability to identify important problems, it is their proposed solutions. Who among us does not think that health is better than illness, life better than death? But to state worthwhile goals is one thing, to have good ideas about how to reach them is another. For some on the Left, the solution is always to spend more — more hospitals, more physicians, more drugs. This at a time when most U.S. hospitals have excess capacity, when many specialists do not have full workloads in their speciality, when overuse and misuse of drugs are a major cause of death, and when the U.S. spends 18 percent of GDP on health care while our peer countries spend 12 percent.

The second paper, my presidential address to the American Economic Association in 1995, traces the development of modern health economics since its origins in the 1960s. Despite the rapid growth of the field, and a growing consensus among experts about answers to positive questions, public debates about health care reform generate more heat than light. I report the results of a mail survey that I conducted among leading economic theorists, leading practicing physicians, and leading health economists. The response rates were high — 63 percent, 89 percent, and 88 percent respectively. The participants were asked whether they agree or disagree with each of 20 relatively short statements, with a "no opinion" option. Ten percent of the replies were "no opinion." Three scholars who had no connection with the survey were asked to identify the statements as "positive" or "policy-value." With very high agreement, the experts thought that seven of the statements were positive, 13 were "policy-value." The paper provides detailed results. A summary of my conclusions follows:

1) Neither the economic theorists nor the practicing physicians consistently answered the positive questions the way health economists did. For example, 83 percent of the theorists agreed with the statement "Widespread use of currently available screening and other diagnostic techniques would result in a significant (more than 3 percent) reduction in health care expenditures (from what they would otherwise be) five years from now." Among the health economists, only 11 percent agreed, among the practicing physicians, 32 percent. Among practicing physicians, 64 percent agreed with the statement

"The high cost of health care in the U.S. makes U.S. firms substantially less competitive in the global economy," but only 17 percent of economic theorists and only 9 percent of health economists. My conclusion: To make good judgements about positive questions of health policy, it is not enough to know economics *or* health care institutions and technology, both kinds of knowledge are needed.

2) Most of the differences in responses, especially among health economists were the result of differences in values. For the values questions answered by the health economists, the mean difference between agree and disagree was 33.9%; the mean difference for positive questions was 71.6% (chi-square of the difference between of type question, 5.5)

Answers to survey were analyzed to discover any other empirical regularities to see if they shed additional insight as to why public debate about health policy is so contentious and uninformative. It seems to me that health economists have not been successful in conveying their agreement on positive questions to the media and public. More important, many key policy choices involve values, and here disagreement is widespread within each of the three groups.

The paper concludes with my policy recommendations, based on my analysis and values:

1) A broad-based tax dedicated to health care to provide every American with a voucher for participation in a basic health plan.
2) Provision of care through integrated health plans paid primarily by capitation.
3) A large private center for technology assessment financed by a small levy on health care spending.

In reviewing these two papers on health policy and health care reform, I began to realize how my views on these subjects have evolved over time. One big change is an increased appreciation of how difficult it is to grasp essential features of health economics. Also, I more fully realize how much views about health policy depend on values rather than objective analyses.

A third change in my thoughts about medical care is to be more tolerant of and sympathetic to my colleagues in the medical school who teach the students so many things that seem to me to be wrong or incomplete. I now see that they face the alternative of saying "we don't know." I suspect that this answer does not satisfy most patients or most students, so they are offered some plausible story which might be the correct one but often isn't.

I am also more sensitive to how difficult it is for a conscientious physician to practice "appropriate" care when the presence of insurance creates a large gap between what is appropriate for the physician's own patient and what is best for society as a whole, including taxpayers and others who must pay for the care.

Perhaps the most important change in my views concerns the proper role for government in health care. Fifty years ago, I was concerned about the constant expansion of government at the expense of the family as a strong social institution. I still have this concern, but the U.S. spends 18 percent of GDP for health care; other high income democracies spend 12 percent. Most of the trillion dollar excess results from resistance to a bigger role for government, I think we pay too big a price for that resistance. If the price of having smaller government were small, I would probably be inclined to support such a policy if problems of equity could be dealt with. But when the cost of smaller government exceeds one trillion dollars per year, support for such a policy seems too much.

The third paper resulted from an invitation from the American Association of Medical Colleges to give the Alan Gregg Lecture at their annual meeting on November 6, 2011. It was an opportune time for me because I was becoming increasingly aware that successful health care reform depends critically on the support and ability of physicians. The academic medical centers in this country achieve great heights in research and in some aspects of patient care, but for most part are locked into a structure of education and training that hasn't changed much in 100 years. Given the rapid changes that are occurring in finance, organization and delivery of care (discussed in the op-ed in this Part), the academic centers should reinvent themselves to produce physicians better equipped for the world they will practice in. Given the criticism explicit and implicit in my remarks to the AAMC, the reception to my Lecture was encouraging. Several academic medical centers are reexamining their education mission, from changes in the criteria they use to select students into medical school to the content, length, sequence, and other aspects of their training regimes. Academic medical centers are like huge ships in the ocean: they change direction slowly and that is not necessarily a bad thing.

The fourth paper was written in response to my receiving the John R. Commons Award in 2001 from the International Honor Society for Economists, Omicron Delta Epsilon, in recognition of achievements and service to the economics profession. In the paper I address questions about the effect of economic research on public policy. My answer is that it is greater than one might think, but it's complicated. Sometimes the effect is not seen until many decades after the publication of the research. Adam Smith and Karl Marx are outstanding examples. There is a "market for messages"; if and when a researcher's message gets translated into policy usually depends when political, social, and economic conditions create a receptive market for that message. The paper points out that quite often an important contribution of economic research is to keep bad policies from being enacted. Communication between economists and media needs improvement on both sides. Some economists should try to write and speak more clearly; some media should invest in staff that understand enough economics to provide clear accurate translations of research results. Some media should stop emphasizing only the research results that support their political agenda and give equal space to results that question it.

7.1

Economics, Health, and
Post-Industrial Society

Two hundred years ago the industrial revolution was figuratively and literally beginning to pick up steam. In a few Western countries agricultural advances, which came faster than population growth, enabled some men and women to escape from grinding poverty. Life for most, however, was still "nasty, brutish, and short." Infant mortality rates of 200 or 300 per 1000 births were the rule, and life expectancy in Western Europe was not very different from what it had been under the Romans. The great majority of men and women worked on farms, producing barely enough to feed themselves plus a small surplus for the relatively few workers engaged in the production of other goods and services. Widows and orphans, the sick, the elderly, and the destitute relied primarily on family and church for help in their time of need.

Agriculture continued to dominate employment for another century; as recently as 1877, half the United States labor force was still engaged in farming. Then, very quickly, in less than "thirty minutes" if we think of recorded history as a "day," most of the countries of Western Europe and North America became industrialized. But the process of economic development did not stop with industrialization. As Colin Clark noted so accurately in 1940: "The most important

Originally published in *The E. S. Woodward Lectures in Economics*, presented at the University of British Columbia, November 1–2, 1978; reprinted in *Milbank Memorial Fund Quarterly. Health and Society*, 57(2):153–182, Spring 1979. Copyright by The University of British Columbia.

concomitant of economic progress is the movement of labor from agriculture to manufacture, and from manufacture to commerce and services." By 1957, the United States had become the world's first "service economy" — that is, the first nation in which more than half of the labor force was engaged in producing services rather than goods.

Today, many Western societies can be described as "post-industrial".[2] Such societies are characterized by a variety of special features — affluence, urbanization, infant mortality rates of 10 to 15 per 1000, high female labor force participation, low fertility, decreased importance of family and traditional religions, increased importance of the state, long life expectancy, and, of course, a substantial change in the locus of economic activity. The hospital, the classroom, and the shopping center have replaced the coal mine, the steel mill, and the assembly line as the major work sites of modern society. "Industrial man" has been succeeded by "post-industrial person," but the import of this transformation for society has not yet been fully analyzed.

In these lectures I shall focus on one of the largest and fastest growing industries in post-industrial society — medical care — and on a range of problems specifically related to medicine and health. I will use the discipline of economics to provide some insights concerning these problems, and will also attempt to use the health field to illuminate more general problems of post-industrial society. In this last respect I wish to ally myself with the first Woodward Lecturer, H. Scott Gordon, who wrote in 1971: "I have never regarded economics as a discipline that is inherently narrow." At the same time, I am aware of the limits of economics — both those limits that stem from shortcomings in current theoretical and empirical knowledge and those limits that are inherent in any science of man.

For instance, it should be clear that economics alone does not, indeed should not, tell us whether it is better to devote resources to extending the life of an 80-year-old man with terminal cancer or to reducing the risk of birth defects in a population of newborns. What economics does do is help us arrange the relevant information in a systematic way and make explicit the choices that individuals and society face. Therein lies much of its unpopularity. Economics earns the label "the dismal science" because it constantly reminds us that we have been turned out of the Garden of Eden. Many persons prefer to pretend that choices do not have to be made; many like to believe that they are not being made at present.

These lectures will not offer that kind of comfort or reassurance; neither will they supply simple answers to the major policy issues of the day. They are, rather, one man's attempt to report some key findings from more than a decade of research in health economics, and to offer some generalizations from these findings. I am aware, and you are forewarned, that such generalizations, based on only one aspect of society, must necessarily be speculative.

Lecture I: The Determinants of Health

In this first lecture I will review some major results concerning the determinants of health, especially the roles played by medical care, income, and education. We will see that changes in health are much more dependent on non-medical factors than on the quantity of medical care. Nevertheless, medical care has become one of the largest industries in modern society. The second part of this lecture discusses some of the reasons for this rapid growth.

Medical care

One of the first things economics does is to sensitize us to the distinction between *inputs* and *outputs* — that is, in the present context, to the difference between *medical care* and *health*. This perspective can be found in the wise observations of René Dubos and has been ably articulated in Canada by Refs. 6, 15. It remained for economists, however, to develop the matter systematically and quantitatively in multivariate analyses that examine the effect on health of medical inputs, income, education, and other variables.

The basic finding is: when the state of medical science and other health-determining variables are held constant, the marginal contribution of medical care to health is very small in modern nations. Those who advocate ever more physicians, nurses, hospitals, and the like are either mistaken or have in mind objectives other than the improvement of the health of the population. The earliest studies that reported this conclusion were greeted with skepticism in some quarters because the analyses typically relied on mortality as the measure of health. Mortality, it was said, is a rather crude index of health. It was suggested that more sophisticated measures would reveal the favorable effects of greater numbers of physicians, nurses, and hospital beds. A recent Rand study, however, based on six sensitive indicators of ill health (elevated cholesterol levels, varicose veins, high blood pressure, abnormal chest X-ray, abnormal electrocardiogram, and an unfavorable periodontal index) provides striking confirmation of the results based on mortality.[17] Variations in the amount of health resources available across 39 metropolitan areas of the United States had no systematic effect on these health measures taken alone or in linear combination.

Examples of the distinction between medical care and health can be drawn from many countries other than the United States. In Great Britain, for instance, the National Health Service (NHS) has undoubtedly served to sharply reduce class differences in access to medical care, but the traditionally large class differentials in infant mortality and life expectancy are no smaller after three decades of the NHS. Also, despite free access to medical care, time lost from work because of sickness has actually increased greatly in Britain in recent decades. The number of sick days depends on many factors in addition to health, but these data hardly support the notion that there has been a large payoff from the NHS in that area.[24] The discrepancy between health and medical care is even sharper in the USSR. In recent years there apparently has been a deterioration in health as measured either by infant mortality or life expectancy, even though the Soviet medical care system is said to have expanded.[5]

There are several reasons why an increase in medical resources, given a reasonable quantity as a base, does not have much effect on health. First, if physicians are scarce, they tend to concentrate on those patients for whom their attention is likely to make the most difference. As doctors become more plentiful, they naturally tend to spend more time on patients less in need of attention. Second, patients also alter their behavior, depending upon how easy or difficult it is to get to see a physician. When physicians are more numerous, patients tend to seek attention for more trivial conditions. Third, many of the most effective interventions, such as vaccinations or treatment of bacterial infections, require only modest amounts of resources. Quite often, one "shot" goes a long way. On the other hand, the long-term benefits of some of the most expensive procedures, such as open-heart surgery or organ transplants, are still in doubt. Fourth, there is the problem of "iatrogenic disease" — illness that arises as a result of medical care. Because medical and surgical interventions are more powerful than ever before, they carry with them greater risk. Sometimes too much care, or the wrong care, can be more deleterious to health than no care at all. Finally, it is abundantly clear that factors other than medical care (e.g., genes, environment, life-style) play crucial roles in many of the most important health problems.

Income and inequality

For most of man's history, income has been the primary determinant of health and life expectancy — the major explanation for differences in health among nations and among groups within a nation. A strong income effect is still observed in the less-developed nations, but in the United States the relation between income and life expectancy has tended to disappear. This is true when health is measured by mortality, or by indicators such as high blood pressure, varicose veins, elevated cholesterol levels, and abnormal X-rays or cardiograms, or by subjective evaluation of health status. Other things equal, there is no longer a clearly discernible effect of income on health except at the deepest levels of poverty. I regard the disappearance of the income effect as an important aspect of post-industrial society, but the fact is not widely known, and the implications are rarely discussed. To realize one such implication, consider how attitudes toward economic growth might differ, depending upon whether further growth was or was not expected to reduce mortality.

The favorable effect of economic growth and technological change on *average* life expectancy is well known. Less appreciated is the extent to which growth has also reduced *inequality* in life expectancy across individuals and groups. The principal reason for the reduction is that general economic growth, even if unaccompanied by any reduction in income inequality, has more favorable effects on the health of the very poor than on those who have already reached a level of living well above subsistence. A second reason is that many effective medical discoveries of the past half-century, such as antibiotics, have been relatively low in cost and widely available.

Consider the following statistics taken from U.S. life tables for the white population. At the turn of this century, given the age-specific death rates then prevailing, one-fourth of a newborn cohort of males would die before the age of 23. On the other hand, one-fourth could expect to live beyond the age of 72. In other words, the variation in life expectancy was great. One simple measure of variation is the interquartile ratio — i.e., the difference between the age of death at the third quartile and at the first quartile divided by the median age at death. For white males in 1900, this variation was 86 percent [(72–23)/57], but by 1975 it had fallen to 26 percent. This large reduction is attributable in part to drastic declines in infant and child mortality, but even if one looks at years of life remaining at age 20, the interquartile ratio fell from 59 percent to 35 percent between 1900 and 1975. White females experienced a similar decline in variation in life expectancy. Furthermore, nearly all of the decline occurred before the advent of Medicare and Medicaid.

Not only has the distribution of life expectancy become much more nearly equal within the white population, but the difference between white and non-white life expectancy has also been reduced substantially in this century. In 1900, life expectancy for whites was 47 percent higher than for non-whites. In 1975, the differential was 8 percent! The overall reduction in inequality of life expectancy bears a strong relationship to reduction in inequality by income class. In 1900, those with short life expectancy were disproportionately from the lower half of the income distribution. Now, with the correlation between income and life expectancy much weaker, we can say that with respect to the most precious good of all, life itself, the United States is approaching an egalitarian distribution.

Education

Despite the general trend toward equality in life expectancy, there is one factor — education — that consistently appears as a significant correlate of good health. The same research by health economists that reveals the small marginal contributions of medical care and of income to health reports a strong positive relation between health and years of schooling. In the United States, regardless of the way health is measured (e.g., mortality, morbidity, symptoms, or subjective evaluation), and regardless of the unit of observation (e.g., individuals, city or state averages), years of schooling usually emerges as the most powerful correlate of good health. Michael Grossman, an economist who has done extensive research on this question, has tended to interpret this relationship as evidence that schooling increases the individual's efficiency in producing health, although he recognizes that some causality may run from better health to more schooling.[13] The way schooling contributes to efficiency in producing health has never been made explicit, but Grossman has speculated that persons with more education might choose healthier diets, be more aware of health risks, obtain healthier occupations, and use medical care more wisely.

I accept the "efficiency" hypothesis, but I think that it explains only a part of the correlation. One reason for my skepticism is that Grossman did not find any favorable effect of IQ on health, holding constant schooling and other variables. If more years of schooling increases efficiency in producing health, it seems that a higher IQ ought to work in the same direction. Furthermore, recent research on surgical utilization casts doubt on the proposition that the better educated individuals use medical care differently than do the less educated. While the probability of surgery is much lower for the highly educated than for the rest of the U.S. population, a new study by Garrison (1978) shows that the highly educated who do undergo surgery enter the hospital at the same stage of disease as do the less educated. He also finds that the better educated patients choose the same kinds of physicians, have about the same length of stay, and, apart from the fact that their general health is a little better than average, have about the same outcomes from surgery. Thus, at least in the context of in-hospital surgery, there is little support for the "efficiency" effect in the use of medical care.

The most plausible explanation for the lower surgery rates of the highly educated is that they have less need for surgery, i.e., they are in better health.

The question remains, Why? One explanation that I favor is that both schooling and health are manifestations of differences among individuals in the willingness and/or ability to invest in human capital. Both schooling and health-related activities involve incurring current costs for the sake of future benefits, and it seems quite clear that individuals differ in the "rate of return" that will induce them (or their parents) to undertake such investments. There are numerous possible reasons for such differences. For instance, some individuals have much better access to capital than do others. Even holding access to capital constant, individuals differ in their skills of self-control and in their ability to visualize the future.

Recent preliminary research gives modest support for this view. A colleague and I surveyed a group of young adults to ascertain their rate of time discount, measured by the extra money they would require to wait for a money award in the future rather than collecting a smaller sum in the present. My colleague was interested in the pattern of the rates, i.e., how they changed with length of time involved, the size of the award, etc. I added a few questions about the respondents' health and then looked at the relation between health and discount rate across individuals. I found a strong, statistically significant, negative correlation between the rate of discount and the subjective assessment of health. For the 25 percent of the sample with the lowest discount rates, the probability of being in excellent health was 63 percent; for the quarter with the highest rates, the probability was only 32 percent.

Some recent statistics from England seem to provide additional support for my view of the correlation between health and schooling. A study of cigarette smoking revealed that among men in social class I (highly educated) the proportion who smoked fell almost by half between 1958 and 1975. In contrast, among men in social class V (poorly educated) the proportion scarcely changed. It seems unlikely that this difference in behavior arises primarily because the men in class V have not heard about the dangers of smoking or do not understand the implications for health. It is more likely that they are unwilling (or unable) to give up a present pleasure for a distant and uncertain benefit. I suspect that if one compared these two groups of men with regard to other aspects of behavior that involve explicit or implicit rates of time discount (e.g., saving, buying on credit), one would find similar differences.

Progress in medical science

This discussion of the determinants of health should not close without some consideration of the effects of progress in medical science. Economics not only

cautions us to distinguish between inputs and outputs but also calls attention
to the distinction between the marginal product of an additional unit of input,
holding constant the production function, and the shift of that function through
technological progress. In the first instance, we ask what will be the effects on
health of an increase in the quantity of physicians, nurses, and hospitals, assuming
no change in the way care is delivered. In the second, we ask what will be the
effects on health of an advance in medical science, assuming no change in the
quantity of physicians, nurses, and hospitals.

With respect to the latter question, it seems to me that the "medical care
doesn't matter" argument is overstated by some writers. To be sure, medical
progress was slow until well into the twentieth century, but from about 1935 to
about 1955, a period which marked the introduction of anti-infectious drugs, major
improvements in health were recorded in all industrial nations. The decreases in
mortality were far greater than could be attributed to general economic advance,
increases in the *quantity* of medical care, or similar changes.

The only reasonable explanation, in my view, is that advances in medical
knowledge changed the structural relations governing the production of health.
In a study of changes in infant mortality in 15 Western nations between 1937 and
1965, for instance, I estimated that the change in structure accounted for at least
half of the large decline in infant mortality over that period.[7]

The application of medical and public health knowledge also improved health
in the less developed countries, and at unprecedented speed. In a sample of 16
less developed countries studied by demographer Sam Preston, life expectancy
was only 39 years in 1940, but rose to 60 years by 1970.[19] He and I estimated
that about two-thirds of the increase was attributable to better health technology
and similar structural changes and only one-third to a rise in per capita income.
By contrast, in the United States the same change in life expectancy — from 39
to 60 years — required three-quarters of a century, from 1855 to 1930, because
health technology was developing so slowly at that time.

It remains true that advances in medical science do not come at a steady
or predictable pace. During the 1960s many "breakthroughs" were hailed, and
expenditures for medical care rose appreciably, but the favorable consequences
for health were quite limited. In recent years, however, U.S. death rates, especially
from heart disease, have decreased rapidly. For men and women at most ages, the
probability of death from arteriosclerotic heart disease in 1975 was 20 percent to
25 percent lower than in 1968. Analysts who are technologically inclined attribute
most of this large decrease to better control of hypertension, special coronary
care units in hospitals, open-heart surgery, and similar medical innovations. Some
observers are more prone to credit changes in diet, smoking, exercise, and other

aspects of personal behavior. We do not know the true explanation; I suspect that there is some validity to both points of view.

The growth of medical care

While the pace of medical advance has been highly uneven, the growth of expenditures for medical care has been unrelenting. For at least the past three decades (and probably for much longer) the share of gross national product (GNP) devoted to medical care has steadily increased in the United States and many other countries. Today, in every post-industrial society, health care absorbs a substantial portion of the nation's resources; in several, the share devoted to health is rapidly approaching 10 percent. In the remainder of this lecture I will consider several possible explanations for the rapid growth of health care as an industry. In so doing, I will make a few remarks regarding the growth of services in general, and I will offer some speculations concerning medical care as a substitute for family and religion.

Income and productivity

One popular, but I believe exaggerated, explanation for the relative growth of service employment is the growth of per capita income. With respect to health care, higher income is clearly not a *direct* causal factor. Precise estimates of the income elasticity of the demand for health care differ, but almost all investigators agree that it is well below unity — i.e., people behave as if health care is a "necessity." It follows, therefore, that the direct effect of a rise in per capita income should be a *decrease* in health care's share of real GNP. Some services other than health may be considered as "luxuries," i.e., they have income elasticities greater than one, but it is interesting to note that according to the U.S. national income accounts there has been only a small increase in the service sector's share of gross product measured in *constant dollars*.[7] To be specific, during the past 30 years, while service employment was growing from 46 percent to 61 percent of total employment, the share of real output (1972 dollars) originating in the service sector changed only from 51 percent to 56 percent. If services had the high income elasticity of demand that is often ascribed to them, the growth of service output would surely have been more rapid.

The differential trends in employment and real output are the result of a relatively slow growth of output per worker in services. In this respect, health care has been no exception. Labor input per patient, especially in hospitals, has grown at an extremely rapid rate. In 1976, there were 304 full-time equivalent employees per 100 patients in the U.S. short-term hospitals compared with 178 per 100 patients in 1950.

Taken at face value, these data suggest that there has been a *decrease* in productivity, but that is highly problematical. The character of hospital *activity* has changed greatly since 1950. Each patient now has many more laboratory and X-ray tests, more complex surgery is performed, and new treatment approaches, such as intensive care units, have proliferated. I use the word "activity" rather than "output" deliberately, because we are far from knowing how much this increased activity has resulted in better health. Some changes in medical technology, such as the anti-infectious drugs mentioned previously, have clearly raised productivity enormously, but the only thing we know with certainty about some of the other technological changes is that they have greatly raised expenditures.

One reason why it is so difficult to measure productivity in medical care is that the consumer is an integral part of the production process. Health depends not only on how efficiently the physicians and nurses work, but also on what the patient does. Similar problems arise in attempts to measure change in real output and productivity in education, social services, police protection, entertainment, and many other service industries. As more and more of the work force becomes employed in industries whose output cannot be accurately measured, the "real" GNP will become increasingly unreliable as the measure of the welfare of society. We will probably be forced to abandon faith in a single summary index for measuring long-term changes or for international comparisons. Instead, welfare comparisons will be sought through mortality and morbidity indexes, crime rates, reading ability, and other more direct indicators of well-being.

Medical technology

The rapid growth of medical technology — the vast expansion in the character and scope of interventions that physicians can undertake — has been a major factor in the growth of health expenditures in recent decades. Familiar examples include renal dialysis, open-heart surgery, organ transplants, and high-energy cancer treatments. These innovations, attributable in large part to the investment in medical research of the past quarter-century, may or may not make major contributions to improved health, but relative ineffectiveness does not deter their use.

In the past I have referred to the proclivity of physicians to employ new technologies simply because they exist as the "technological imperative".[7] Recent economic research, however, provides a different explanation for the emphasis on expensive treatments that yield little in lives saved, while preventive activities with high potential yield per dollar of expenditures are denied resources. Such behavior may be fully consistent with consumer sovereignty (i.e., willingness to pay) even in a population with uniform incomes and preferences. The reason is that the amount most people are willing to pay for a given reduction in the probability of death is positively related to the *level* of the probability. Thus, a person facing almost certain death would usually be willing to pay a great deal for even a small increase in the chance of survival; that same person, facing a low probability of death, would not pay nearly as much for the same increase in survival probability. If one infers the "value of life" from the amount the person is willing to pay for the change in the probability of survival, it is clear that the value of life varies for the same individual, depending upon the circumstances.

Imagine, if you will, a cancer treatment program that costs $1 million per life saved, and another program to lower the probability of getting cancer that costs only $500,000 per life saved. People might be more willing to pay for the *treatment,* if sick, than to pay for the *prevention,* if well. This behavior is not necessarily "irrational," nor need it be the result of some "death-denying" psychological quirk. We do not think it odd that a thirsty man will pay a large amount for a small drink of water if there is very little available, but is not willing to pay much for a drink when water is plentiful and he is not particularly thirsty.

The medical profession has been frequently criticized for failing to allocate resources so as to maximize the number of lives saved, but some of this criticism may be unjustified — at least in the sense that the emphasis on heroic efforts in life-threatening situations at the expense of preventive measures may be a reasonable response to consumer preferences. If we seek a health care system that does what people want it to do (regardless of whether that preference is expressed in the market or through political processes), we should expect considerable inequality at the margin in costs per life saved. To the extent that we deem this an undesirable outcome, the way to guard against it is to rule out the *possibility* of relatively high-cost interventions. If the intervention is unknown, society may, in some sense, be better off. For instance, suppose the very expensive cancer treatment did not exist. People might be more likely to avail themselves of the cancer prevention program. Perhaps even more to the point, suppose a project to develop a cancer treatment with the characteristics described above was being considered. It could be socially advantageous *not* to support the research, even though, once completed, the results would be used.

Government, family, and religion

The growth of government, the decline in importance of the family, and the weakening of traditional religion are three closely related factors that I believe have also contributed substantially to the growth of the health care industry. The growing importance of government will be discussed in some detail in the next lecture. At this point I want to call attention to the fact that subsidization of health care by government induces additional demand. Nearly all health economists believe that the *price* elasticity of demand for care is smaller than one, but none believes that it is zero. It follows, therefore, that a reduction in the price of care at the point of decision through public (or private) insurance increases the quantity demanded. To get some feel for the possible magnitude of this effect, let us assume that the total price (including money, time, and psychic costs) of care has been reduced by one-half as a result of government intervention, and let us also assume that the price elasticity of demand is −0.5. If nothing else changed, the increase in quantity demanded would be two-fifths. A decline in price of three-fourths with an elasticity of −0.28 would produce approximately the same change.[a] These examples suggest that the government's effect on price has probably been a major factor in increased utilization.

The effects of the decline of the family and of traditional religion are more difficult to quantify, but I offer a few examples to convey the flavor of the argument. Consider nursing homes. In the United States they are by far the fastest growing component of the health care sector; their share of total spending climbed from less than 2 percent in 1960 to almost 8 percent in 1977. Nursing home expenditures now exceed spending for drugs or for dentists' services; the only larger categories are hospitals and physicians' services. But what is a nursing home and what services does it provide? I would argue that it provides very little that was not provided in the past at home by the family. Indeed, in some cases it does not provide as much.

To be sure, the growth of nursing homes is attributable in part to growth in the relative number of the aged. But more important, in my opinion, is the growth in female labor force participation and the mobility of the population. Elderly widows comprise the bulk of the nursing home population, and there has been tremendous increase in the percentage of widows 65 and over who live alone. In 1950 that figure was 25 percent; in 1976 it was 65 percent. True enough, rising income makes living alone possible and helps pay for nursing home care; however, a considerable amount of what we think of as an *increase* in health care is not an increase at all, but rather a substitute for care that was formerly provided within the family.

---

[a]The change in quantity is equal to the product of the change in price and the elasticity of demand, where the changes between period 1 and period 2 are measured as percentages according to the following formula: $(2 - 1) \div (2 + 1) \div 2$.

The same may be said about the growth of child care and many other services. Contrary to the assumption underlying the national income accounts, these services do not represent a completely new addition to the nation's output; they are in part simply a transfer from home production to the exchange economy. The rise of female labor force participation and the growth of service employment are bound together in a nexus of mutual reinforcement. Each is both cause and consequence of the other.

Not only does purchased medical care in part take the place of the family, but I believe that it is also frequently a modern substitute for religion. This is most obvious in the case of mental illness, and the similarity between psychiatry and religion has been frequently discussed. It needs to be emphasized, however, that many visits to physicians who are not psychiatrists are undertaken for reasons other than specific diagnostic or therapeutic intervention. The patient may be seeking sympathy, or reassurance, or help in facing death (his own or that of someone close to him). The patient may want to unburden himself to an authority figure who will keep his secrets confidential. There may be a desire to find someone to assume responsibility for a difficult decision, or there may be a need for validation of a course of action already decided upon. The ability to state "The doctor says I should (or shouldn't) do this" often is worth a great deal.

In an earlier day, priests, ministers, and rabbis met many of these demands. For some persons they still do, but today many find a white coat more reassuring than a black one, a medical center more impressive than a cathedral. One striking change is in the customary site of death. In an earlier day dying was usually a private affair, attended by family and friends, and legitimized by priest or shaman or witch doctor. Today, in most Western nations, more than half of all deaths occur in hospitals. The physician is now our chief ambassador to death.

The analogy I have drawn between medical care and religion may be regarded as disparagement of care by those who share Marx's opinion of religion as the "opium of the people." But it is well to remember that in the very same passage Marx also called religion the "heart of a heartless world... the spirit of spiritless conditions." Despite the many criticisms that can be raised about medicine today — its high cost, its preoccupation with technology, its fragmentation into specialties and subspecialties — the truth is that for many people it is the "heart of a heartless world... the spirit of spiritless conditions."

Lecture II: The Growth of Government

In the previous lecture I presented an economist's view of the determinants of health and discussed the growth of medical care into one of the largest industries in modern society. In this lecture I will consider the tremendous expansion of government in the health field, and will use health as a test case to appraise Right-wing and Left-wing approaches to economic policy. Finally, I will articulate my own values and judgments, bearing in mind the focus of the Woodward Lecture series on economic freedom and contemporary economic problems.

The extension of the scope of government in the health field, like the extension of government in many other aspects of post-industrial society, is too obvious to require elaboration. I shall, therefore, move immediately to a consideration of possible explanations.

One likely reason is the ever-increasing complexity of modern life. Consumers are now faced with a bewildering array of goods and services and they feel a great need for information about them. There can be significant economies of scale in the provision of information about the quality of beef, the purity of drugs, and the safety of airlines; thus, it may be more efficient to have a single agency, the government, provide that information.

Many observers also believe that urbanization and the growth of population and income have increased the importance of *externalities,* so that there is legitimate scope for the government to do more than simply provide information. An externality in health exists if Brown's consumption or other actions have favorable (or unfavorable) effects on Smith's health, but these effects are not reflected in the prices Brown faces and there is no feasible way for Brown and Smith to make a private arrangement that would cause Brown to take these effects into account.

Familiar examples in this category include vaccinations (positive externality) and air pollution (negative externality). When externalities exist, the solution most economists prefer is to use subsidies or taxes to bring private costs (or benefits) into line with social costs (or benefits). Direct regulation that compels or forbids certain activities outright should generally be avoided unless the costs of administering the subsidies or taxes are unreasonably high.

A special kind of externality discussed by Calabresi and Bobbitt (1978) in their recent book *Tragic Choices* concerns society's unwillingness to "see" some of its members (typically the very poor) take unusual risks or pursue degrading activities. An example is the inhibition to the sale of kidneys or other organs by living donors. Calabresi and Bobbitt refer to society's unwillingness to countenance behavior that is an "affront to values" as a "moralism." Is it really "moral," however, to force an already disadvantaged person to be more disadvantaged by denying him the opportunity to do that which he thinks it is to his advantage to do? It seems to me that inhibitions of this character might more accurately be described as "estheticisms"; that is, they are really matters of taste.

The importance of taste and social conventions in these matters is nicely illustrated by the fact that society readily permits individuals to work in coal mines and to pursue other activities that are far more dangerous to health than is the absence of one kidney.

Or consider public policy with respect to abortions. At one time most governments forbade them. More recently we have seen governments encourage abortion through subsidies. Someday governments may compel an abortion rather than allow the birth of a horribly deformed child, either because the public does not want to have to support the child, or simply because it upsets people to see or hear about the child. In each case the majority in society uses government to influence the behavior of others, always in the name of "morality," but probably because such behavior affects the majority through tangible or psychological externalities. One can speculate that such psychological externalities have grown in importance with urbanization, affluence, and, especially, more rapid, widespread, and vivid communications.

A pure libertarian, confronted with these alternative governmental policies toward abortion, would say: "A plague on *all* your houses." The libertarian position is that the government should not forbid abortions, should not subsidize them, should not compel them — in short, should do nothing to interfere with the right of the individual to do as he or she pleases — unless the action harms someone else. Ah, there's the rub. What constitutes harm? The libertarian would not allow murder, robbery, or rape. Many libertarians would go along with economically sound measures to deal with air pollution. But what if I find abortion, or prostitutes soliciting on the street, more offensive than air pollution, and most voters feel as I do? The distinction between physiological and psychological harm is rather fragile; the head is connected to the body, and we now know that there are important interchanges between the psyche and the soma. This discussion illustrates the importance of widely shared values for the smooth functioning of a democratic society. As Tawney[23] has written: "The condition of effective action in a complex civilization is cooperation. And the condition of cooperation is agreement, both to ends to which effort should be applied, and the criteria by which its success is to be judged."

In post-industrial society, governments clearly go far beyond providing information or dealing with obvious externalities. In the United States, especially, the government, in the name of health and safety, now undertakes detailed regulation and control of thousands of products and activities. One possible reason for the proliferation of government interventions is that they serve as a form of "pre-commitment" concerning certain kinds of behavior. In other words, Smith may vote for laws that force persons in Brown's circumstances to behave in ways contrary to Brown's preference in order to pre-commit himself (Smith) if his circumstances should change to those of Brown. Smith, then, might think that if he were to become poor he would be tempted to sell a kidney. He might therefore now vote to make such sales illegal in order to prevent himself from ever taking such action.

I believe that health insurance can in part be regarded as a form of pre-commitment; the insured is pre-committing himself or herself to disregard price in making decisions about the utilization of care. Economists have had a great deal of difficulty explaining the popularity of "first dollar" coverage in health insurance policies. It is easy to see why risk-averse individuals might want to insure against large medical bills, but why would they want to bear the administrative costs and the excess utilization costs associated with insurance for small bills that they could pay out of their normal income? One possible answer is that they do not want money costs to influence their decisions about the utilization of care. *Compulsory* health insurance can be viewed as pre-commitment to buy insurance regardless of changes in income or other circumstances.

Conventional economic analysis regards "pre-commitment" as irrational; why should anyone ever want to gratuitously restrict his options? Economist Richard Thaler has suggested an answer: "pre-commitment" may be a rational strategy for dealing with problems of self-control.[21] Such problems can arise when there is tension between alternative behaviors that have very different implications for our welfare in the short and long run. For instance, in the short run I may get pleasure from smoking or from spending, but I also know that in the long run I will suffer from the effects of smoking or from a lack of savings. I may pre-commit myself by taking a job where smoking is prohibited, and I may join a Christmas Club.

The financial field offers numerous examples of pre-commitment strategies including front-end loaded life insurance policies and mutual fund plans, passbook loans, and prepayment of real estate taxes to banks. Even installment buying has a pre-commitment aspect as evidenced by the many consumers who pay high consumer loan interest rates while maintaining low-yielding savings accounts.

Government regulation may also be a strategy to reduce the opportunity to make decisions that turn out badly. Consider airline safety. Instead of the current practice of setting a single standard of safety, the government could merely provide information about the safety standards adhered to by different airlines and let individuals choose among airlines on the basis of safety, price, and so on. There are costs associated with making airlines safer; one could imagine consumers being offered a choice between a high price/high safety airline and a low price/low safety line. Conventional economics tells us that the larger the range of choice, the greater is consumer welfare. But many (perhaps most) people would not like to make this kind of choice; they prefer to have the Federal Aviation Authority set a single minimum "safe" standard which all scheduled airlines must meet. In so doing, they seek to minimize the regret or guilt that they might experience if there is a crash.

There has been some discussion in economics about the "costs" of decision-making, but these costs have generally been assumed to be experienced in the process of *making* the decision, i.e., acquiring the information and taking time to think about alternatives. Having the government set a single safety standard clearly reduces those costs. The point at issue here, however, is that there are psychic costs associated with having *made* a decision that turns out badly, and individuals may very well opt for government regulations that preclude such decisions.

The growth of government can also be viewed as a substitute for family or church as the principal institution assisting individuals who experience economic or social misfortune. Private insurance could conceivably do the same job, but problems of "free riders" (those who don't buy insurance and then need help anyway), adverse selection (the tendency for the poorer risks to buy the insurance), or excessive sales and administrative costs may make universal, compulsory programs the more sensible way to proceed. Moreover, a principal thrust of many government programs is to combine insurance with *redistribution.* Indeed, I believe that an unrelenting pressure for a more egalitarian society is one of the most important explanations for the growth of government in health and other areas.

The conditions of modern life seem to compel a more equal sharing of material goods and political power. In *Equality and Efficiency: The Big Tradeoff,* Arthur[18] assumes that this occurs because people have a "preference" for equality. Perhaps some do, but it is also possible that many who have power and goods would rather not share them; their ability to maintain inequality, however, may vary with circumstances. It seems to me that, the more affluent and the more complex a society becomes, the more it depends on the willing, cooperative, conscientious efforts of the people who work in that society and the more difficult it is to obtain satisfactory effort through the use of force.

When the main task at hand consisted of hauling large blocks of stone from the river to the pyramid, it was a relatively simple matter to rope a dozen slaves together and use a whip and the threat of starvation to secure compliance. In feudal societies, the predominantly agricultural work force was kept in line despite huge inequalities in income through force, the need for protection, the limited mobility of the poor, and through the promise of Heaven and the threat of Hell. But when a nation's workers are airplane mechanics, teachers, and operating-room nurses, for example, it is clear that such techniques will not do. A few dissatisfied air-traffic controllers can change the pace of a continent. Even such low-paid work as the changing of tires in a tire store involves considerable potential for danger and disruption. It would be very expensive to check every bolt on every wheel, but the management lives in fear that a few carelessly tightened bolts will allow a wheel to fall off and result in a million-dollar damage suit against the company. Furthermore, in the affluent post-industrial society virtually all persons live above a subsistence level — and will be maintained at above subsistence whether they work or not.

The problem of getting everyone to "go along" is compounded by the declining force of religion, nationalism, and other traditional control structures. Calls to serve "God and Country" do not meet with as enthusiastic a response as they once did, whether that service is military or some onerous and not particularly rewarding civilian task. A weakening of hierarchical structures is evident wherever we look — in the family, in the church, in the school, in the workplace. Romantics of the Right yearn for a return to the "good old days," but such yearning is not likely to avail much against economic growth and technological change. As Macrae (1976) has so aptly noted in *America's Third Century*:

> It is pointless to say ... that society must therefore return to being ruled by the old conventions, religious restrictions, craven obedience to the convenience of the boss at work. Individuals will not accept these restrictions now they see that wealth and the birth control pill and transport technology make them no longer necessary. . ..

The preoccupation with equality, or the *appearance* of equality, is evident in many discussions about health. With respect to the British National Health Service, for instance, economists Jewkes and Jewkes (1963) have argued that: "The driving force behind [its] creation ... was not the search for efficiency or for profitable social investment. It was something quite different: it was a surging national desire to share something equally." As noted in my first lecture, the results of the NHS seem consistent with that view.

Or think of the buckets of ink that have been spilled over regional inequality in the physician/population ratio in Canada, the United States, and most other countries. In the United States, at least, this interminable discussion has proceeded without any evidence that health is adversely affected by a low physician/population ratio. Indeed, in the United States one cannot even show that the number of physician visits per capita is significantly lower in areas that have been identified as "medically underserved." Moreover, the oft-heard argument that an overall increase in the number of physicians will result in a reduction in regional inequality seems to be without empirical foundation.

The more one examines this issue the more puzzling it appears. Nearly everyone says regional inequality in physician supply is bad, but no one quite explains why. Nearly everyone says it should be reduced, but not much is done about reducing it. In California, for a long while we had the spectacle of the state's political leaders voicing loud complaints about how difficult it was to get physicians to settle in rural areas, at the same time setting fee schedules for Medical (Medicaid) patients that reimbursed rural physicians at a lower rate than their urban counterparts. In my view, national health insurance and other governmental interventions in health are best viewed as political acts undertaken for political and social objectives relatively unrelated to the health of the population. This seems to be an inescapable conclusion from the evidence now available.

Theories of the right and left

The discussion of the proper role of government in society is central to the debate between the ideologues of the Right and the Left, a debate that seems to me to capture a degree of attention far in excess of the merits of the theories propounded by either side. The positions of the arch conservatives and the radicals are usually clear-cut and often provocative. In my judgment, however, they are ultimately unsatisfactory either as analyses of how we have come to our present position or as prescriptions for where we ought to go from here. I shall try to illustrate my proposition with references to health and medical care, but I believe the same critique is valid in a more general framework.

I begin with the Right. And I admit at the outset that some of its favorite themes seem to have considerable value. For one thing, it is the Right that regularly reminds us of the efficiency of a *decentralized* price system as a mechanism for allocating scarce resources. Frankly, it is a shame that we need to be reminded of this — surely, theory and experience combine to teach us that the alternative (some sort of centralized control) will usually be much less efficient.

Second, we should be indebted to the Right for reminding us, in the words of a Milton Friedman lecture title, of "the fragility of freedom." Accustomed as we are to freedom of speech, press, religion, and more, we are too prone to take them for granted — to imagine that they are the normal and expected state of affairs — rather than, as any comprehensive view of past or contemporary societies reveals, a precious exception. When conservatives insist that there are important complementarities between property rights and human rights, we ignore them at our peril.

So much for their good points; where does the Right go wrong? One big problem is that the Right, with the notable exception of Schmupeter (1942), seems to lack any plausible view of the historical development of society. This is nicely illustrated if one looks at the Right's analysis of the growth of national health insurance around the world.

How does the Right deal with such a phenomenon? The first response (and often the last) is to castigate it as one more deplorable trend toward socialism. When pressed for an explanation of the trend, the Right offers two types of theories. First, there is the "people are stupid" explanation. The same people who are supposedly so knowledgeable when running businesses or choosing occupations or spending money are presumed foolish, irrational, or worse when they must make choices about government policy. This is not very convincing. If there is some widespread behavior that we do not understand, let's not automatically attribute it to the other fellow's ignorance or irrationality.

Not all conservatives subscribe to the "people are stupid" theory. A substantial number try to explain the growth of national health insurance and similar (in their view) misguided legislation as the triumph of special interests over the general public interest. The research strategy is to identify the special groups that gain from policies that seem to result in a general welfare loss (and many economists believe national health insurance fits that category because it encourages excessive utilization). A second task is to figure out how the special groups are able to assert and maintain their interest over that of the majority. Sometimes this strategy is useful, but with respect to the growth of national health insurance, it has not been notably successful. Indeed, in the United States, one special interest group that has benefited greatly from Medicare and Medicaid has been the physicians, and they were in the forefront of the groups that opposed such legislation.

What the Right apparently cannot accept, but neither can it refute, is the hypothesis that national health insurance comes to developed countries not out of ignorance, not out of irrationality, not at the behest of narrowly defined special interest groups, but because most of the people want it, because it meets certain needs better than alternative forms of organization. That these needs are often political, social, and psychological rather than physiological is one of the principal themes of these lectures.

Another problem with the Right is its failure to apply its own economic reasoning to institutions and to goals. For instance, granted that the market is an efficient institution for allocating most goods and services, the extension of the market mechanism to all aspects of human society at the expense of other institutions such as the family may well run into diminishing returns. For the market to be most effective it needs complementary inputs from other institutions, just as capital needs labor and land.

Or consider the Right's preoccupation with the goal of freedom. It is easy to agree that certain basic freedoms of thought and expression are essential to a good society, but more difficult to accept George Stigler's position that freedom should always dominate other goals. He writes (1958 and 1975; italics mine): "The supreme goal of the Western world is the development of the individual: the creation for the individual of a *maximum* area of personal freedom, and with this a corresponding area of personal responsibility." It seems to me odd that an economist would want to maximize personal freedom or any other single goal rather than to find an optimum balance among various goals. Surely, the law of decreasing marginal utility must apply to freedom as well as to other goals, and one suspects that there is increasing marginal disutility to the personal responsibility that Stigler notes is a corollary of freedom. It is reasonable to suppose that there is some *combination* of freedom and responsibility that is optimal, although that optimum probably varies among individuals, depending on their ability to benefit from freedom and to handle responsibility.

Let us turn now to the Left. And let us again begin on a positive note. We should be grateful to the Left for two reasons. First, it reminds us that a decentralized price system isn't *always* the best way to allocate scarce resources. There are things such as externalities and transaction costs that may mean that some allocation problems are better handled by institutions other than the market.

More important, the Left at its best makes a contribution by keeping before us a vision of a just society. Like the prophets of old, it scolds, it warns, it preaches. And so it should. The Left reaffirms in secular form the ancient cry for justice. The big problem with the Left is not its inability to identify important problems. It is its analysis of the causes and its proposed solutions that must give one pause. Who among us would not like to see a world free of war, poverty, racism, sexism, and ignorance? Or, to narrow it down to the field of health, who among us does not think that health is better than illness, life better than death? But to state worthwhile goals is one thing; to have some good ideas about how to reach them is another.

Consider Leftist critiques of health and medical care. First, there is the naive reformist position, typified by, say, Galbraith (1958). According to this view, the problem is one of insufficient public funds. If only we had more hospitals, more physicians, more medical schools, and so on, the problem would be solved. This at a time when, in the United States, there is excess hospital capacity in every major metropolitan area, when general surgeons are carrying what they themselves agree is only 40 percent of a reasonable workload (and there is widespread suspicion that many of the operations should not be done), and when iatrogenic illness (arising out of the medical care process itself) is a major problem! That so many on the Left can still believe so many shibboleths is a tribute to the triumph of ideology over analysis.

There is another type of Leftist critique, however, which is slightly more sophisticated and far more radical. Far from simply prescribing "more medical care," these Leftist critics argue that the "system" is at fault. The trouble, we are told, is that providers are oriented to profits rather than to health, that if only we made the system more "democratic," placed public health at top priority, put physicians on salaries, and so on, all would be well. Would it? Right now in the United States about 95 percent of the hospital industry is in the hands of nonprofit organizations, either public or private, yet the escalation in costs in these hospitals has been tremendous, and the emphasis on complex, esoteric technology great. When we look at other systems with other forms of organization and reimbursement, such as in England or Russia, do we see more emphasis on preventive medicine, more action on environmental health problems, more consumer control of the medical care process? The answer is overwhelmingly negative. Indeed, even in China and Cuba, which have done some fine things in delivering simple but effective medical care to the general population, a basic health problem like cigarette smoking is left virtually untouched. Some say this is because certain Communist leaders are avid smokers, or because tobacco is an important crop. Whatever the reason, it is a strange way for these governments to fulfill their self-proclaimed responsibility for the health of the people.

Because the Left is so eager to attribute the problems of the world to capitalism, it ignores some basic observations about human behavior. Most of the health problems that it identifies existed before capitalism and persist in non-capitalist countries. Many problems arise from the conflict between health and other goals, rather than from the evil or selfish intent of physicians. Personal behavior and genetic endowment are far more important to health than is medical care — whatever the system. Even when medical care is relevant, health is rarely something one person can *give* to another. It comes, if at all, from the efforts of physician and patient working together, often in the face of uncertainty and fear.

One of the strongest generalizations warranted by a comparative study of medical care in modern nations is the inability of planning agencies, insurance funds, hospital boards, and other lay authorities to completely control the medical profession. In country after country, the introduction of national health insurance was marked by significant concessions to physicians with respect to methods and levels of reimbursement, procedures for reviewing the quantity and quality of care, geographical and specialty choice, and control over allied (competing?) professions.

What's the problem? In part, the power of physicians derives from their ability to withhold what is sometimes an essential service. A strike by physicians may not be as threatening as one by coal miners in winter, or bartenders on New Year's Eve, but it is not negligible. Emigration by physicians is a more distant, but probably more effective, threat against unacceptable pressure. Because medical skills are more easily transferred from one country to another than are those of most other professions, and because physicians earn a high income, their return to migration is large relative to costs.

In my opinion, more subtle factors are also at work. The effectiveness of medical care depends in considerable measure on a bond of mutual confidence between physician and patient. Too much external control can break that bond. Moreover, physicians, like priests or magicians, can fill their roles effectively only if set apart from the common run of mankind. A medical profession that was completely subservient to lay authority would be, in several respects, a less effective profession. This is not to say that fee-for-service reimbursement never leads to over-utilization, or that licensure laws are completely in the public interest, or that present institutional arrangements are ideal. It is to say that many of the most difficult problems of health and medical care transcend particular forms of economic and political organization — a conclusion that the Left leaves out.

Concluding Remarks

These lectures are drawing to a close. The time has come for me to restate my own conclusions and value judgments as clearly as possible. What speculative generalizations do I draw from a broad economic study of health and medical care in modern society? First, I am impressed by the widespread confusion between process and product, the tendency to identify medical care with health, even though the connection is a fairly limited one. I wonder if that same confusion does not exist in other aspects of society, for example, schooling vis-á-vis wisdom, litigation vis-á-vis justice, or police activity vis-á-vis public safety? In the case of medical care and national health insurance, it seems clear to me that institutions often serve purposes other than those that are explicitly articulated. From the health insurance of Bismarck's administration to the Professional Standards Review Organizations of Nixon's, we can see sharp differences between the stated and the actual intent of health legislation.

The growth of big government in modern society stands as a major challenge for social analysis. My reading of its role in health and medical care leads me to emphasize two factors — the decline of other institutions and the pressure for a more egalitarian society. It seems clear to me that the success of the market system in the Western world was attributable in no small measure to the existence of strong non-market institutions such as the family and religion. The fruits of the market system — science, technology, urbanization, affluence — are undermining these institutions, which were the foundations of the social order. Human beings need more than an abundance of material goods. They need a sense of purpose in life — secure relationships with other human beings — something or someone to believe in. With the decline of the family and of religion, the inability of the market system to meet such needs becomes obvious, and the state rushes in to fill the vacuum. But it does so imperfectly because it is so large and so impersonal.

The affluence and complexity of modern life also contribute to the pressure for more equality, and government is now the chief institution for undertaking redistributive functions. This is not to suggest that the pressure for equality is always met quickly and fully. On the contrary, much legislation is designed to give symbolic recognition of the ideal of equality, but does not involve significant redistribution. This is not necessarily to be condemned; a preoccupation with equality and the neglect of other goals can be socially harmful. It is useful to recall Lord Acton's comment on the French Revolution (1907): "The finest opportunity ever given to the world was thrown away because the passion for equality made vain the hope of freedom."

For all its weakness, the family is probably still the greatest single barrier to equality in post-industrial society. As long as mothers and fathers pass on to their offspring their own particular genetic endowment, their own special heritage and values, attempts to achieve complete equality will be frustrated. At some point we shall have to ask whether that last increment of equality is worth the loss of so valuable an institution as the family — one that can stand as a refuge from impersonal markets and authoritarian government.

Government also grows because the majority frequently sees no feasible alternative for dealing with the complexity and interdependence of modern life. Thus, it seems to me that the fulminations of the Right against the ever-increasing role of government are often misdirected. The constant assertions that this or that regulation or subsidy is irrational and inefficient often fall on deaf ears because the majority doesn't see it that way. As I have tried to show with illustrations from health, some individual governmental interventions can perhaps be justified economically — because of economies of scale, or because of externalities (tangible or psychological), or as precommitment strategies, or as techniques for shifting responsibility, or as redistributive mechanisms introduced to buy social tranquility. The point that I think needs emphasis is that the cumulative impact of the growth of government is to weaken (and ultimately destroy) other useful institutions such as the market, family, and private associations of a religious, fraternal, and philanthropic character. Thus, we should be wary of the constant expansion of government, and especially centralized government, not only because any particular proposed expansion is "inefficient" — it may well pass a comprehensive cost-benefit test for a majority of the population — but because there are other goals besides efficiency.

For me the key word is *balance*, both in the goals that we set and in the institutions that we nourish in order to pursue these goals. I value freedom *and* justice *and* efficiency, and economics tells me that I may have to give up a little of one goal to insure the partial achievement of others. Moreover, I believe the best way to seek multiple goals is through a multiplicity of institutions — the market, government, the family, and others. No single institution is superior for all goals. Also, diversification, be it of institutions, genes, or security holdings, is the best assurance of stability and survival in the face of an uncertain future. Above all, we must avoid concentration of power. In the spirit of the lowered aspirations of our time, I conclude that, although diffusion of power may keep us from reaching Utopia, it also limits the harm that may befall us.

References

1. Lord Acton. (1907). "History of Freedom in Christianity." In *History of Freedom and Other Essays*, eds. Figgis, J. N. and Laurence, R. V. Arno Publishers: New York, p. 57 (reprinted in 1971).
2. Bell, D. (1973). *The Coming of Post-Industrial Society*. Basic Books, Inc.: New York.
3. Calabresi, G. C. and Bobbitt, P. (1978). *Tragic Choices*. W. W. Norton: New York.
4. Clark, C. (1940). *The Conditions of Economic Progress*. Macmillan: London.
5. Davis, C. and Feshbach, M. (1978). "Life Expectancy in the Soviet Union." *The Wall Street Journal* June 20, p. 20.
6. Dubos, R. (1959). *The Mirage of Health*. Harper: New York.
7. Fuchs, V. R. (1968). "The Growing Demand for Medical Care." *The New England Journal of Medicine* **279**(4): 190–195.
8. Fuchs, V. R. (1974). "Some Economic Aspects of Mortality in Developed Countries." In *The Economics of Health and Medical Care*, ed. Perlman, M., (Proceedings of a Conference Held by the International Economic Association at Tokyo). Macmillan: London, pp. 174–193.
9. Fuchs, V. R. (1978). The Service Industries and U.S. Economic Growth Since World War II. In *Economic Growth or Stagnation?* ed. Backman, J. Bobbs-Merrill: Indianapolis, IN.
10. Galbraith, J. K. (1958). *The Affluent Society*. Houghton Mifflin Co: Boston, MA.
11. Garrison, L. (1978). Studies in the Economics of Surgery. Unpublished Ph.D. Thesis, Stanford University, Stanford, CA.

12. Gordon, H. S. (1971). Social Institutions, Change and Progress. *The E. S. Woodward Lectures in Economics.* University of British Columbia: Vancouver, B.C., Canada, p. ix.

13. Grossman, M. (1976). "The Correlation between Health and Schooling." In *Household Production and Consumption,* ed. Terleckyj, N. E. National Bureau of Economic Research. Vol. 40, Studies in Income and Wealth. Columbia University Press: New York, pp. 147–223.

14. Jewkes, J. and Jewkes, S. (1963). *Value for Money in Medicine.* Blackwell: Oxford, England.

15. Lalonde, M. (1974). *A New Perspective on the Health of Canadians.* Government of Canada: Ottawa, ON, Canada.

16. Macrae, N. (1976). *America's Third Century.* Harcourt Brace Jovanovich: New York, p. 90.

17. Newhouse, J. P. and Friedlander, M. J. (1977). *The Relationship between Medical Resources and Measures of Health: Some Additional Evidence.* Rand Corporation Document R-2066-HEW (May). The Rand Corporation: Santa Monica, CA.

18. Okun, M. (1975). *Equality and Efficiency, the Big Tradeoff.* The Brookings Institution: Washington, D.C.

19. Preston, S. H. (1979). "Causes and Consequences of Mortality Declines in Less Developed Countries During the Twentieth Century." In *Population and Economic Change in Developing Countries,* ed. Easterlin, R., National Bureau of Economic Research, New York. University of Chicago Press: Chicago, p. 111.

20. Schumpeter, J. S. (1942). *Capitalism, Socialism and Democracy.* Harper and Brothers: New York.

21. Shefrin, H. M. and Thaler, R. (1977). An Economic Theory of Self-Control. Working Paper 208. National Bureau of Economic Research, New York.

22. Stigler, G. J. 1958 and (1975). "The Goals of Economic Policy." (First published as a pamphlet by the University of Chicago Law School, March, 1958. Printed in the *Journal of Business* **169**(July), 1958). Reprinted in *The Journal of Law and Economics* **18**(2): 283–292.

23. Tawney, R. H. (1926). *Religion and the Rise of Capitalism.* Harcourt Brace and Company: New York.

24. Townsend, P. (1974). "Inequality and the Health Service." *The Lancet* **1**: 1179-1189.

7.2

Economics, Values, and Health Care Reform[*]

Interest in health economics has soared over the past three decades, stimulated by intellectual innovations, greater availability of data, and, most importantly, a surge in health care spending from 6 to 14 percent of GDP.[a] An 11-fold increase[b] in the number of Ph.D.s has enabled many professional schools, government agencies,[c] and research institutes to add health economists to their staffs. Nevertheless, the health care debate of 1993–1994 benefited much less than it could have from the results of their research.

Originally published in *American Economic Review*, 86(1): 1–24, March 1996. Copyright by American Economic Association.
[*]Presidential Address delivered at the one-hundred eighth meeting of the American Economic Association, January 6, 1996, San Francisco, CA.

Department of Economics and Department of Health Research and Policy, Stanford University, Stanford, CA 94305, and the National Bureau of Economic Research. For helpful comments on an earlier draft and/or assistance with the survey of health economists, economic theorists, and practicing physicians, I wish to thank Philip Alper, Byron Wm. Brown, David Druker, Alain Enthoven, Beverly Fuchs, Alan Garber, Claire Gilchrist, Shelley Horowitz, John Jacoby, Seth Kreimer, Rachelle Marshall, Mark McClellan, Paul Milgrom, Robert Mnookin, Roger Noll, Mitchell Polinsky, James Poterba, Donald Redelmeier, Diane Reklis, Paul Romer, Gordon Rosenberg, Nathan Rosenberg, Harold Sox, Amos Tversky, and Richard Zeckhauser. Financial support from The Robert Wood Johnson Foundation and the Andrew W. Mellon Foundation is also gratefully acknowledged.
[a]For a short introduction to the field of health economics, see Fuchs (1987). For a thorough review of the health economics literature prior to 1963, see Klarman (1965).
[b]There were 132 dissertations completed in 1990–1994, compared with only 12 in 1960–1964. The number of dissertations in all fields of economics increased by 2.5 times during that 30-year interval.
[c]Examples include the Congressional Budget Office, the General Accounting Office, the Office of Management and Budget, and the Office of Technology Assessment.

In this lecture I identify the primary sources of modern health economics and describe interactions between the discipline and the field of health, drawing heavily on my personal experience. I then turn to the question of why economists did not have more impact on health care reform. I report and analyze the answers of health economists, economic theorists, and practicing physicians to a survey I conducted in 1995. My principal conclusion is that value differences among economists, as well as among all Americans, are a major barrier to effective policy-making. I discuss the implications of the importance of values for economics and conclude the lecture with my recommendations for health care reform — recommendations based on my values as well as my understanding of health economics.

The Past

In 1963, a seminal paper by Kenneth Arrow discussed risk aversion, moral hazard, asymmetrical information, philanthropic externalities, and numerous other topics that have since played major roles in health economics research.[d] He saw that *uncertainty* about health status and about the consequences of care was the key to understanding the health sector from both positive and normative perspectives. As Arrow wrote, "Recovery from disease is as unpredictable as its incidence" (1963, p. 951).

At the same time that Arrow was depicting the theoretical landscape, Martin Feldstein was pioneering in the application of quantitative methods such as 2-stage least squares, principal component analysis, and linear programming to the estimation of production functions and other important economic aspects of medical care. His numerous papers analyzing the British National Health Service formed the basis for his Ph.D. thesis at Oxford University.[22]

A third line of work that has had a significant influence on health economics also began in the early 1960's with the National Bureau of Economic Research Conference on Investment in Human Beings (1962) and Gary S. Becker's treatise on human capital (1964). The NBER conference volume included Mushkin's paper (1962), "Health As an Investment," and a few years later the application of the human capital model to health was given its fullest development by Grossman (1972).

Predating and postdating the theoretical and econometric innovations of the 1960's is a stream of research that focuses on health care institutions, technology, and policy. As early as 1932, Davis and Rorem (1932) were writing about the crisis in hospital finance. Significant contributions to this genre have been made

---

[d]This is Arrow's most frequently cited single-authored paper (Intriligator, 1987, p. 687).

by Henry Aaron, Alain Enthoven, Rashi Fein, Eli Ginzberg, Herbert Klarman, Dorothy Rice, Anne Scitovsky, Anne and Herman Somers, Burton Weisbrod, and many others. Although they are all economists, much of their work does not appear in economics journals, but rather in books and in publications such as the *New England Journal of Medicine, Journal of the American Medical Association, Milbank Memorial Fund Quarterly,* and *Health Affairs.*

In recent decades several leading health economists have addressed theoretical, empirical, and policy questions in various aspects of their research (e.g., Joseph Newhouse, Mark Pauly). Health economics has also been enlivened and enriched by contributions from economists who are primarily specialists in other fields such as industrial organization, labor, finance, and public economics (e.g., Sherwin Rosen, Richard Zeckhauser). There has also been a welcome infusion from another direction, namely physicians who have earned Ph.D.s in economics and who now contribute to the economics literature (e.g., Alan Garber, MarkMcClellan).

Parenthetically, all this name-dropping has a point. I want to underscore the varied intellectual, methodological, and ideological sources that have contributed to the health economics enterprise. Research has often been described as lonely work, and in one sense it is. But in another sense it is the most collective of all human activities. Philosopher Susan Haack (1995) sees scientific research as analogous to an attempt by many participants to fill out a huge crossword puzzle. We have clues; we try out possible answers; we check to see whether they fit together. Occasionally, an Arrow or a Becker comes up with one of the really big answers that runs across the puzzle and makes it easier to discover the smaller words that intersect it. If several of the small answers don't fit, however, we may have to modify or even reject the larger one. It is good to remember that all answers are provisional until the puzzle is completed — and it never will be.[e]

Although I have mentioned only American economists, note should be taken of many fine health economists in England, Canada, and other high-income countries. There is, however, less of a global intellectual community in this field than in some other branches of economics[f] — or in other fields of health[g] — because most health economics research is applied and is (or is

---

[e] In an extension of the crossword puzzle analogy suggested by Richard J. Zeckhauser in a 1995 personal communication, it seems that economics might make more progress if theorists didn't tend to concentrate on the lower left-hand corner of the puzzle while empiricists work the upper right-hand corner.

[f] The relatively new International Health Economics Association will hold its inaugural conference in Vancouver in May 1996.

[g] The *Journal of the American Medical Association* has twenty international editions published weekly in eleven languages, with 40 percent more recipients than the regular U.S.-based edition (George D. Lundberg and Annette Flanagin, 1995).

perceived to be) country specific. More than 60 years ago Hamilton (1932) noted that "The organization of medicine is not a thing apart which can be subjected to study in isolation. It is an aspect of culture whose arrangements are inseparable from the general organization of society" (p. 190). On the whole I agree with Hamilton; there are, however, important economic questions concerning technology assessment and disease prevention that are common to all high-income countries. This type of research does not receive support commensurate with its importance because funding sources, both public and private, tend to focus on national problems.

My involvement in health economics grew out of my research on the service industries.[27,28] It was motivated in part by a desire to gain a better understanding of the postindustrial society that was emerging in the United States and other developed countries.[26,33] The growth of the service economy and improved methods of contraception were bringing women into paid employment and dramatically changing gender roles and relationships. Lower fertility and longer life expectancy were transforming the age distribution of the population, and this transformation, along with the fragmentation of the family and the declining influence of traditional religion, were creating new social and economic conditions. The health sector, with its nonprofit institutions, professional dominance, sharply skewed distribution of demand, and the critical importance of the consumer in the production process, seemed like a fruitful area for investigation. I was particularly interested in trying to understand the determinants of health and the determinants of health care expenditures.

With regard to health, my research has led me to emphasize the importance of nonmedical factors such as genetic endowment, the physical and psychosocial environment, and personal behaviors such as cigarette smoking, diet, and exercise. Over time, advances in medical science contribute significantly to reductions in morbidity and mortality; at any given point in time, however, differences in health levels within or between developed countries are not primarily related to differences in the quantity or quality of medical care.[h]

With respect to expenditures on medical care, my research has led me to emphasize the importance of supply factors, especially technology and the number and specialty mix of physicians.[i] To be sure, conventional demand factors such as price, income, and insurance play significant roles, but in my judgment

---

[h]For an explanation, see Fuchs (1994, pp. 108–10); also see Fuchs (1974a, Ch. 2, 1974b, 1993); Refs. 9, 10, 68, 74 and 78.

[i]See Fuchs and Kramer (1973), Fuchs (1978b, 1990), Fuchs and Silverman (1984), Fuchs and Halm (1990), Redelmeier and Fuchs (1993).

concentration on them to the exclusion of (partly exogenous) supply factors misses a big part of the expenditures story. Despite many attempts to discredit it,[j] the hypothesis that fee-for-service physicians can and do induce demand for their services is alive and well.[k]

My views about health and health care expenditures have been formed not only through research but also through close interaction with medical scientists, practicing physicians, and other health professionals. Since 1968 I have maintained a regular medical school faculty appointment in addition to my appointment in economics, and have participated every year in a wide variety of health-related activities. This dual life would have gained approval from John Stuart Mill who, in *The Principles of Political Economy* (1848, reprinted 1987), wrote, "It is hardly possible to overrate the value... of placing human beings in contact with persons dissimilar to themselves, and with modes of thought and action unlike those with which they are familiar ... Such communication has always been ... one of the primary sources of progress" (p. 581).

The proposition that the discipline of economics has a great deal to contribute to health and medical care is not one likely to require elaborate defense before this audience. (I have had audiences that were less receptive to this notion.) It might, however, be useful to report briefly just what it was in economics that I found to be most relevant in the invasion of alien turf. (To avoid undue suspense, let me say at once that it was *not* game theory.)

In my experience, the most important contribution we make is the economic point of view, which may be summed up in three words: scarcity, substitutability, and heterogeneity. This economic point of view stands in stark contrast to the romantic and mono-technic points of view that I found prevalent among health professionals and health policymakers. The romantic point of view refuses to accept the notion that resources are inherently scarce; any apparent scarcity is attributed to some manmade problem, such as capitalism or socialism, market failure or excessive government interference. In the 1960's and 1970's, many physicians said that there was no need to limit expenditures for medical care if only we would cut defense spending. In 1996, when health care expenditures are almost four times as large as the defense budget, this argument is not heard as often. Because it denies the inevitability of choice, the romantic point of view is increasingly seen as impotent to deal with the problems of health care.[l]

---

[j] See Dranove and Wehner (1994).
[k] See Gruber and Owings (1996).
[l] As a sign of the times, Sweden, Norway, Finland, and the World Health Organization are sponsoring the first international conference on priorities in health care in October 1996.

To be sure, it is not clear whether economic research or the force of circumstances is bringing about the change in point of view. I suspect that there is a synergistic relationship in which the former provides the language to give expression to the latter. Or, as Max Weber (1915; reprinted 1946) wrote, material and ideal interests are the tracks on which society rides, but ideas throw the switches (p. 280).

The monotechnic point of view, found frequently among physicians, engineers, and others trained in the application of a particular technology fails to recognize the diversity of human wants, or acknowledge the difference between what is technically best and what is socially desirable.[m] "Optimal" care is defined as the point where the marginal benefit is zero, ignoring the fact that resources used for health care have alternative uses that might yield greater benefit. The "production" of health is viewed narrowly as a function of inputs of medical care, and the appropriate input mix is assumed to be determined by technology without regard to relative prices, explicit or implicit. For example, Feldstein found that average lengths of stay in British hospitals were uniform across regions despite large regional differences in the pressures for admission.[n]

The monotechnic view often fails to consider the heterogeneity of preferences, even though for many health problems there are alternative interventions: one drug versus another, drugs versus surgery, or even "watchful waiting" versus any intervention. Under the influence of economists and other behavioral scientists, physicians are now making such choices with more attention to patient differences in time preference, attitudes toward risk, tolerance of pain, functional needs, and other characteristics.

Among our specific tools, one of the most useful is the idea of the margin. The key to gaining acceptance for this principle is to have people realize that most decisions involve a little more or a little less, and that they will make better decisions if they look at the costs and benefits associated with having a little more or a little less. This formulation is more effective than postulating "maximization," which economists find useful for classroom or research purposes, but sounds unreal to most noneconomists.

David M. Eddy's research on the frequency with which women should get Pap smears provides a fine example of the use of marginal (or incremental) analysis to assist in medical decision-making. This screening test for cervical cancer is of proven safety and effectiveness, and before Eddy's work appeared most experts

---

[m]Economists fall into their own monotechnic trap when they offer policy advice under the assumption that efficiency is society's only goal.
[n]See Feldstein (1967).

recommended that women obtain this test annually. Using mathematical models and clinical studies of the natural history of the disease, Eddy (a physician with extensive training in operations research and economics) calculated the incremental cost of 1 additional year of life expectancy with screening regimes ranging from once every 6 months to once every 5 years. The results were striking. *Some* screening has a high yield at low incremental cost, but as the frequency of screening is increased from once every 2 years to once a year the incremental cost rises to close to $1 million per additional year of life expectancy.[15–17,o]

The impact of Eddy's research on health policy is worth noting. The American Cancer Society accepted his conclusions and the Society's recommendation to screen once every 3 years made the front page of the *New York Times*. The U.S. Surgeon General, the U.S. Preventive Services Task Force, and the American College of Physicians supported this position, and many individual physicians changed their practice accordingly. Intense opposition came from the American College of Obstetricians and Gynecologists and the American Society of Cytology. The contending groups finally negotiated a compromise along the following lines: "Pap smears should be done annually; after two or more negative examinations the frequency can be decreased."[p]

The economist's distinction between movement along a function and a shift in the function is a very useful one. It is particularly applicable in discussing the relationship between medical care and health. At any given time in developed countries the effects of additional medical care on health are usually small, but over time advances in medical science have had significant effects on health.[q] Or consider the relationship between infant mortality and per capita income. At any given time income is a good predictor of infant mortality, especially post-neonatal mortality (28 days to one year). In log-log regressions across the 48 states in 1937 and 1965, the income elasticity of post-neonatal mortality was -0.53 (0.11)

---

[o]To put this in perspective, consider the choice between tissue plasminogen activator (TPA) and its cheaper alternative, streptokinase, as the treatment to dissolve a clot during a heart attack. The latest studies suggest that the incremental cost of TPA rather than streptokinase is $33,000 per year of life extended (Mark *et al.*, 1995). In the United States TPA is usually the treatment of choice, but Canadians use streptokinase.

[p]Eddy's analysis focuses on the incremental benefit and cost of more services to all the patients in a population. Another important example of margin is the cost and benefit of extending a (usually) once-in-a-lifetime service such as coronary bypass surgery to more and more patients.

[q]Antibiotics, drugs for hypertension, surgery for trauma, and care of infants born prematurely are examples of outstanding successes.

and −0.49 (0.12) respectively.[r] The decline in post-neonatal mortality between 1937 and 1965, however, was consistent with an elasticity of −2.00. There was undoubtedly a shift in the function associated with the introduction of antibiotics and other advances in medical science.[30] In 1991 the elasticity was −0.73 (0.12) but the change from 1965 to 1991 was consistent with an elasticity of −1.08, suggesting a further shift in the function, but not nearly so large as the shift between 1937 and 1965.

Economists have much to contribute to the health field. What can they expect in exchange? The most immediate benefit to me was the pressure to make my lectures and research results accessible, relevant, and credible to intelligent but untutored and often unsympathetic audiences. I was obliged to write clearly and simply and to reconsider assumptions and conclusions in economics that I might otherwise have accepted too readily. My experience was in accord with that of[52] who wrote, "Some experience with popular lecturing has convinced me that the necessity of making things plain to uninstructed people was one of the very best means of clearing up the obscure corners in one's own mind."

For example, one of the questions that troubled me for a long time is why there is such a strong correlation between health and years of schooling. I originally believed that this was another manifestation of the productivity-enhancing effect of education. Schooling could increase an individual's knowledge about the health effects of personal behavior and medical care options or could enable a person to better process and act upon information about health.[47] Or schooling could increase an individual's ability to develop strategies of self control.[73] I began to doubt the schooling-causes-health hypothesis, however, when it was observed that the favorable effect of an additional year of schooling on health does not diminish with increased years of schooling. It is just as strong for those with more than a high school education as for those with less and continues right through graduate school on up to the doctoral level.[47,s] I began to suspect that perhaps the correlation was the result of some underlying difference among individuals that affects both schooling and health.

To explore this question I examined survey data on smoking behavior collected by colleagues in the Stanford Heart Disease Prevention Program as part of a health education experiment designed to alter smoking and other risks for heart disease.[58] Identical regressions of smoking on schooling were estimated

---

[r]Standard errors of the regression coefficients shown in parentheses. Mortality rates arc 3-year averages centered on the years shown. Regressions are weighted by state population.
[s]This is in sharp contrast to the effects of income and medical care on health — their marginal products diminish rapidly over the ranges usually found in high-income countries.

at age 17 and at age 24, with schooling measured in both cases as the number of years the individual would eventually complete. The most striking result was the absence of any increase in the size of the schooling coefficient between the ages of 17 and 24. The additional schooling could not be the cause of the differential smoking behavior (and by extension the differential health associated with smoking) at age 24 because the differences in smoking were already evident at age 17, before the differences in schooling had emerged.[21,t]

In my judgment, the most likely explanation for the high correlation between health and schooling is that both reflect differences in time preference.[34] Both health and schooling are aspects of investment in human capital; differences among individuals in time preference that are established at an early age could result in different amounts of investment in health and education.[u]

Although I believe there have been many fruitful interactions between economics and health, the political debate over health care reform in 1993–1994 benefited much less than it could have from the insights of economists. Possible explanations for the failure of health economics research to have more impact on policy are explored in the next section.

The Present

George Stigler's Presidential Address to the American Economic Association in December 1964 was distinctive in its emphasis on prophecy over preaching. To be specific, Stigler predicted that economics was "at the threshold of its golden age" (1965, p. 17) because "the age of quantification is now full upon us" (p. 16). The growth of empirical estimation was, for Stigler, "a scientific revolution of the very first magnitude" (p. 17). He believed that empirical research would have an impact on policy far beyond anything possible from theory alone because "a theory can usually be made to support diverse policy positions. Theories present general relationships, and which part of a theory is decisive in a particular context is a matter of empirical evidence" (p. 13).

---

[t]It is worth noting that the negative relation between schooling and smoking is only evident for cohorts that reached age 17 after the information about the effects of smoking on health became available. It is also of interest that the relationship has not diminished for more recent cohorts even though the information about the negative consequences of smoking has become more widely available.

[u]There are alternative or complementary "third variable" explanations possible; compare Albert Bandura's (1991) concept of self-efficacy.

With regard to health care, Stigler's prediction of a vast expansion in empirical research has been amply fulfilled. During the past 30 years economists have published thousands of empirical articles on various aspects of health and medical care. But the shallow and inconclusive debate over health policy in 1993–1994 contradicts his expectation that this research would narrow the range of partisan disputes and make a significant contribution to the reconciliation of policy differences.[v] What went wrong?

One possibility is that the research was inconclusive. If health economists cannot agree among themselves, why should their research have a salutary effect on public policy? Second, even if the research were conclusive, it would not be of much help to policy if the results were not adequately disseminated to a wider audience. A third possible explanation is that the policy debate foundered on differences in values, differences which could not be reconciled by empirical research, however conclusive and however well disseminated.

To gain some insight into these matters, I prepared a 20-question survey concerning health economics and health policy and sent it to health economists, economic theorists, and practicing physicians. The health economists were those whom I considered to be the leading people in the field, plus some of the more promising recent Ph.D.s. There were 46 respondents (response rate 88 percent). The theorists were also leaders in the field; I was assisted in selecting them by two eminent theorists.[w] There were 44 respondents (response rate 63 percent). The practicing physicians were reached through my personal contacts, and include colleagues and friends of those contacts. Nearly all are in private practice, not teaching, research, or administration. They are located on both the east and west coasts in small towns and large cities. The practice settings vary from solo to a group of over 100 physicians, and in organizational form from traditional fee-for-service to capitation. They include generalists, surgical specialists, and nonsurgical specialists. There were 42 physician respondents (response rate 89 percent).

The participants were asked to indicate whether they agree or disagree with each of 20 relatively short statements; they were also given the option of answering "no opinion." Ten percent of the health economists' replies were "no opinion"; the theorists used that option 19 percent of the time, and the physicians 11 percent. Participants were also invited to qualify any of their replies by jotting

---

[v] Stigler's optimism regarding the impact of empirical research on policy may have had more vindication in other fields, but my research into family issues (Fuchs, 1983) and gender issues (Fuchs, 1988a) do not lead me to such a conclusion.

[w] In order to keep a clear distinction between health economists and theorists, I excluded any theorist who had done a substantial amount of work on health care.

comments on the back of the survey. The percentage of replies that were qualified was 8, 5, and 3 for the health economists, theorists, and physicians, respectively. Participants were told to assume that the statements refer to the United States in 1995, other things held constant. For statements with more than one part, "agree" would indicate that the respondent agreed with all parts of the statement. The order of the questions was determined randomly, and respondents were guaranteed anonymity.

Three experts[x] from three different universities who were not participants in the survey were asked to identify which of the 20 questions were relatively value-free ("positive" questions) and which had substantial value aspects ("policy-value" questions). Their independent replies were almost unanimous in identifying seven of the questions as "positive," and thirteen as "policy-value." Table 1 shows the percent agreeing for each question, with the two types of questions grouped separately. Question numbers refer to the ordering of the questions in the survey. The policy-value questions are presented in three groups: four that pertain directly to national health insurance, three that pertain directly to health insurance company underwriting, and all others. Questions for which the percentage agreeing differs significantly from a 50–50 split (by a chi-square test) are identified with asterisks.

We see in Table 1 that the degree of consensus on positive questions among health economists is extremely high.[y] In six of the seven cases the hypothesis that the observed split differs from a 50–50 split simply by chance is rejected with $p < 0.01$ and the seventh with $p < 0.05$. There is also a high degree of consensus among economic theorists, but for two of the questions (12 and 13) the majority of theorists gave replies opposite to the majority of health economists. Consensus among the physicians on the positive questions was more rare. In no case did the split differ from 50–50 with $p < 0.01$, and in only three cases was the split significant at $p < 0.05$. For one question (4) the majority of physicians gave replies opposite to the majority of health economists.[z]

---

[x] An empirical researcher who specializes in public economics, a law professor who teaches a course in health-policy and who has read widely in philosophy, and a theorist who specializes in law and economics.
[y] The fact that there is perfect unanimity for only one of the seven positive questions should not be a cause for surprise. Even physics has its dissenters. Steven Weinberg (1995), winner of the Nobel Prize in Physics, has noted "If you had a law suit that hinged on the validity of the unified weak and electromagnetic theory, you could probably find an expert witness who was a Ph.D. physicist with a good academic position who would testify that he didn't believe in the theory" (p. 12).
[z] I believe the health economists' majority responses are correct for all seven questions.

Table 1.   Percentage Agreeing with Positive and Policy-Value Questions.[a]

Survey question number[b]	Question	Health economists $(n \leq 46)$	Economic theorists $(n \leq 44)$	Practicing physicians $(n \leq 42)$
A. *Positive Questions:*				
4	The high cost of health care in the United States makes U.S. firms substantially less competitive in the global economy.	9**	17**	64
9	Third-party payment results in patients using services whose costs exceed their benefits, and this excess of costs over benefits amounts to at least 5 percent of total health care expenditures.	84**	93**	73*
10	Physicians have the power to influence their patients' utilization of services (i.e., shift the demand curve), and their propensity to induce utilization varies inversely with the level of demand.	68**	77**	67
12	Widespread use of currently available screening and other diagnostic techniques would result in a significant (more than 3%) reduction in health care expenditures (from what they would otherwise be) 5 years from now.	11**	83**	37
13	The primary reason for the increase in the health sector's share of GDP over the past 30 years is technological change in medicine.	81**	37	68*
18	Differential access to medical care across socioeconomic groups is the primary reason for differential health status among these groups.	0**	17**	34*
19	In the long run employers bear the primary burden of their contributions to employees' health insurance.	13**	8**	43
B. *Policy-Value Questions:*				
National health insurance questions:				
3	The U.S. should now enact some plan that covers the entire population.	62	65*	68*
7	The U.S. should seek universal coverage through a broad-based tax with implicit subsidies for the poor and the sick.	54	56	56

(*Continued*)

Table 1.   (*Continued*)

Survey question number[b]	Question	Health economists ($n \leq 46$)	Economic theorists ($n \leq 44$)	Practicing physicians ($n \leq 42$)
14	The U.S. should seek universal coverage through mandates, with explicit subsidies for the poor and the sick.	38	29*	46
15	Given a choice between the Clinton health care plan or no federal health care legislation for at least 5 years, the Clinton plan should be approved.	36	33*	28**
Insurance company underwriting questions:				
8	Insurance companies should be required to cover all applicants regardless of health condition and not allowed to charge sicker individuals higher premiums.	51	29**	69*
17	Health insurance premiums should be higher for smokers than for nonsmokers.	71**	90**	85**
20	Health insurance premiums charged to individuals born with genetic defects (that result in above average use of medical care) should be higher than those charged to individuals without such defects.	14**	20**	13**
All other policy-value questions:				
1	It is inequitable for the government to vary subsidies for health insurance by size of firm.	62	36	86**
2	"Any willing provider" legislation (that requires health plans to include any physician who wants to be included) is desirable for society as a whole.	12**	12**	39
5	National standardized health insurance benefit packages should be established.	42	51	63
6	It is inefficient for the government to vary subsidies for health insurance by size of firm.	66*	42	73*
11	Expenditures on medical R&D are greater than is socially optimal.	27*	29*	16**
16	All health insurance plans should be required to offer "point of service" options (that allow patients to obtain care outside the basic plan at additional cost).	30**	55	83**

[a] Of those who agree or disagree.
[b] Question numbers refer to order of questions in original survey.
*Significantly different from 50 percent at $p < 0.05$.
**Significantly different from 50 percent at $p < 0.01$.

When we turn to the policy-value questions, agreement among the health economists drops sharply. For example, in replies to the four questions dealing with support for national health insurance, the health economists never depart significantly from a 50–50 split. On question 8, which would require insurance companies to cover all applicants regardless of health condition with no premium surcharge for the sick, the health economists are evenly divided: 51 percent agree and 49 percent disagree. Among economic theorists there is slightly more agreement on policy, but not as much as among practicing physicians who, contrary to both groups of economists, show more agreement on policy-value than on positive questions.

The contrasts between the replies by group and type of question are brought more sharply into focus in Table 2, which shows the average absolute difference between the percentage agreeing and the percentage disagreeing. Among health economists the extent of consensus for the positive questions is significantly larger than for the policy-value questions regardless of whether the comparison is between means or medians. Although the sample sizes are very small (7 and 13), the differences by type of question are so large we can reject the null hypothesis with considerable confidence.[aa]

It is also worth noting that the extent of agreement among health economists on the positive questions is much higher than is usually found in surveys of

Table 2.   Average Absolute Difference Between Percentage Agreeing and Percentage Disagreeing By Type of Question.

	Health economists	Economic theorists	Practicing physicians
Mean absolute difference:			
7 positive questions	71.6	64.3	30.9
13 policy-value questions	33.8	36.5	45.0
Difference in means	37.8	27.8	−14.1
Median absolute difference:			
7 positive questions	73.9	66.7	31.7
13 policy-value questions	27.3	33.3	45.0
Difference in medians	46.6	33.3	−13.3
Standard error of the mean:			
7 positive questions	6.8	7.1	3.5
13 policy-value questions	5.9	6.5	6.4
Standard error of the difference in means	9.0	9.6	7.3
Difference in means divided by standard error of the difference	4.2	2.9	−1.9
Chi-square of the difference between type of question	5.5	5.5	2.0

[aa]This was confirmed by Byron Wm. Brown, who examined the data using the bootstrap method.[18]

economists covering a wide variety of fields. For example, in a survey conducted by Alston *et al.* (1992) the authors identify ten questions as "micro-positive" and seven as "micro-normative."[ab] In order to achieve comparability between their survey and mine, I combined their "agree, with provisos" with their "agree," and then calculated the mean absolute difference between percentage agreeing and percentage disagreeing.[ac] This difference (22 percentage points) was much smaller (and less statistically significant) than the difference I found for the health economists.[ad]

Why is there so little agreement among economists regarding policy-value questions when there is so much agreement on the positive questions? One possible explanation is differences in values. Most health policy decisions have significant implications for freedom, efficiency, justice, and security. Health economists (like other Americans) probably desire all these goals, but (again like other Americans) they probably differ in the values they attach to them, or in the way they define them,[ae] and these differences could lead to sharply different views about policy.

Another possible explanation is that there are positive questions embedded in the policy-value questions and that health economists disagree with respect to those positive questions. This is the view taken by Friedman (1953)[af] although he subsequently modified his position in 1966 and 1995.[ag] In order to gain some insights concerning the roles of values and embedded positive issues in policy differences I take a closer look at the policy-value questions bearing on national health insurance (3, 7, 14, 15) and on insurance company underwriting (8, 17, 20).

Consider, for instance, question 3 which calls for some national plan to cover the entire population. The 62–38 percent split among health economists may well reflect differences in values, with those who agree placing a high value on providing all Americans with the right to have access to health care. On the other

---

[ab]The identification is in a longer, unpublished version of their paper.

[ac]I also tried treating "agree, with provisos" as "no opinion"; this reduced the difference between the positive and normative questions with respect to consensus.

[ad]Comparisons based on the entropy index used by Alston *et al.* (1992) are even more striking. The mean entropy (a measure of lack of consensus) was 0.70 for their micro-positive questions, but only 0.52 for the health economists' answers to our positive questions. The mean for their micro-normative questions (0.80) was just about the same as for the health economists' policy-value questions (0.77).

[ae]For a discussion of alternative conceptions of justice, see Sen (1987).

[af]In *Essays in Positive Economics,* Friedman (1953) wrote "Differences about economic policy among disinterested citizens derive predominantly from different predictions about the economic consequences of taking action ... " (p. 5).

[ag]See *Dollars and Deficits* (1966, p. 6); personal communication in 1995.

hand, it is readily apparent that there are many positive questions embedded in this policy-value question. For instance, most economists see a loss in efficiency from requiring everyone to have the same health insurance, but they probably differ in their estimates of the extent of the loss. Some may even believe there is a net gain in efficiency because of imperfections in the private market for health insurance. Strongly held differences about this positive question could produce different answers to question 3 even among respondents with similar values.

Some of the positive questions embedded in question 3 may be beyond the scope of conventional economics. For instance, Professor A may favor national health insurance in part because she believes it will contribute to a more stable and harmonious society.[ah] Professor B may disagree with that prediction, and is therefore less inclined to support national health insurance.

The role of embedded positive questions can also be easily discerned in the three questions (8, 17, 20) dealing with insurance company underwriting. Health economists strongly support charging higher premiums for smokers than for nonsmokers, but are strongly opposed to charging higher premiums to individuals born with genetic defects. On question 8, dealing with requiring insurance companies to insure the sick with no premium surcharge, the health economists are evenly split. One of the positive questions embedded in question 8 is the reason for people's illness. If a respondent thought that most illness was the result of genetic differences, the reply would presumably be consistent with the answer to question 20. On the other hand, if most illness was assumed to be the result of personal behaviors like cigarette smoking, the reply would probably be consistent with the one given to question 17. In as much as leading medical scientists have strongly divergent views about the importance of genetic factors in disease, it is hardly surprising that health economists are unable to reach agreement. The state of knowledge about the links between genes and disease is constantly changing. Thus, if cigarette smoking were found to be determined primarily by genetic factors, the answers to question 17 would probably change even in the absence of any change in values.

Positive economic questions are also embedded in the insurance company underwriting issues. Most economists realize that requiring health insurance

---

[ah] In 1974, I recommended universal comprehensive insurance for several reasons, one of which was the speculation that "a national health insurance plan to which all (or nearly all) Americans belong could have considerable symbolic value as one step in an effort to forge a link between classes, regions, races, and age groups." I also thought it important to add "It will be more likely to serve that function well if not too much is expected of it — if it is not oversold — particularly with respect to its probable impact on health" (Fuchs, 1974a, p. 150).

companies to charge healthy people the same premium as those with a genetic disease will deter healthy individuals from purchasing insurance. But economists may well differ as to how large that effect will be and how large a welfare loss it implies.

It is easy to see that there are positive questions embedded in the policy-value questions, but it is more difficult to believe that disagreement over them, rather than differences in values, explains the low level of consensus among health economists with respect to the policy-value questions. Note that the physicians have a higher level of consensus about the policy-value questions than do the health economists. This probably reflects more homogeneous values among physicians rather than agreement about the embedded positive questions. (Note the low level of agreement among physicians on the explicit positive questions.)

It may be that it is not so much *disagreement* among health economists about the embedded positive questions as it is *uncertainty* about them that make differences in values the driving force in replies to the policy-value questions. Many psychologists and economists have observed that uncertainty about a datum causes most individuals to give it less weight when making choices.[ai]

Uncertainty among health economists concerning the positive questions that are embedded in the policy-value questions is suggested by their use of the "no opinion" option. Unlike the theorists, who chose "no opinion" twice as often for the positive questions as for the policy-value questions (28 percent versus 15 percent), the health economists chose "no opinion" less often for the positive questions than for the policy-value questions (8 percent versus 11 percent).[aj] The role of uncertainty was mentioned by Friedman (1966) as a reason for qualifying his position about the relative importance of scientific judgment and value differences (Friedman, 1966, p. 6).

In order to investigate further the relationship between policy-value and positive questions, I developed two indexes based on the answers to the national health insurance and insurance underwriting questions. The first index measures each respondent's support for national health insurance. It is constructed by assigning a value of 1 to agreement with each of questions 3, 7, 14, and 15, a value of 0 for disagreement with those questions, and a value of 0.5 for no opinion. The sum of the values was divided by 4, giving a range for the index

---

[ai] For a comprehensive review of the role of uncertainty in decision-making see Camerer and Weber (1992).

[aj] The physicians also differed from the health economists, choosing "no opinion" more often for the positive than for the policy-value questions (15 percent versus 9 percent).

Table 3.   Indexes of Support for National Health Insurance[a] and for an Actuarial Model of Private
Insurance Underwriting.[b]

	Health economists	Economic theorists	Practicing physicians	All
National health insurance index:				
Mean	0.48	0.48	0.49	0.48
Standard error of the mean	0.05	0.05	0.05	0.03
Coefficient of variation (percent)	71	70	67	69
Percentage with index = 1	15	9	14	13
Percentage with index = 0	13	18	14	15
Actuarial model index:				
Mean	0.46	0.61	0.44	0.50
Standard error of the mean	0.05	0.04	0.04	0.03
Coefficient of variation (percent)	71	42	64	60
Percentage with index = 1	7	16	7	10
Percentage with index = 0	22	5	14	14
Coefficient of correlation between				
the two indexes	$-0.37^{\dagger}$	$-0.34^{\dagger}$	$-0.37^{\dagger}$	-0.35^{**}

[a]National health insurance index is based on answers to survey questions 3, 7, 14 and 15.
[b]Actuarial model index is based on answers to survey questions 8, 17 and 20.
†Significant at $p < 0.02$.
**Significant at $p < 0.01$.

of 1 (indicating agreement with all four questions) to 0 (indicating disagreement with all four questions). The "actuarial"[ak] model index was based on answers to questions 8, 17, and 20. In the case of question 8, "disagree" was given a value of 1, and for questions 17 and 20 "agree" was given a value of 1. The total score for each individual is divided by 3, again yielding a range for the index from 1 to 0 (indicating complete support or complete rejection of the actuarial approach).

The results are presented in Table 3. We see that with respect to national health insurance the support among the three groups is virtually identical. There is considerable variation around the mean for each group, and the amount of variation is similar across the groups. Thirteen percent of all respondents had an index value of 1, while 15 percent completely rejected the notion of national health insurance with an index value of 0. Not surprisingly, there is a negative correlation between the national health insurance index and the actuarial model index. But there is a significant difference between the groups in the extent of support for

[ak]In actuarially-based insurance it is presumed that premiums will be determined (to the extent feasible) by expected loss. Health insurance did not begin with that assumption; the early Blue Cross/Blue Shield premiums were typically "community rated," with healthy individuals paying the same premiums as those who were ill.

the actuarial model index. The economic theorists have a value of 0.61, compared with 0.46 for the health economists and 0.44 for the practicing physicians. The theorists are as supportive of national health insurance as are the other groups, but if insurance is to be provided through the private market, the theorists are more inclined than the other two groups to have premiums reflect expected loss. One reasonable interpretation of this result is that the theorists give more weight to the efficiency aspects of the actuarial model, whereas the health economists and the practicing physicians give more weight to the distributional aspects.

Is there a close relationship between the respondents' scores on the indexes and their responses to the positive questions? The correlation coefficients presented in Table 4 show that the answer is overwhelmingly in the negative. For the national health insurance index there is only one positive question (10) for one group (the health economists) that reaches statistical significance with $p < 0.05$. For the actuarial model index, only questions 9 and 10 show a significant relationship for the health economists, and questions 10 and 12 for all groups taken together. Whatever it is that is determining the respondents' positions with regard to national health insurance or the actuarial approach, it is not their views on the seven positive questions.

Table 4. Coefficients of Correlation Between the Two Indexes and the Positive Questions and the Other Policy-Value Questions.

Survey question number	National health insurance index				Actuarial model index			
	Health economists	Economic theorists	Practicing physicians	All	Health economists	Economic theorists	Practicing physicians	All
7 positive questions:								
4	0.17	0.00	0.12	0.09	−0.08	0.03	−0.09	−0.09
9	0.10	0.17	0.02	0.09	0.40**	0.01	−0.20	0.11
10	0.31*	0.11	−0.07	0.12	−0.34*	−0.20	−0.10	−0.20*
12	−0.11	0.21	−0.14	−0.03	0.06	0.19	0.14	0.20*
13	−0.27	−0.01	−0.19	−0.14	0.11	0.17	0.20	0.06
18	−0.21	0.04	0.09	0.04	−0.06	0.13	0.15	0.09
19	0.24	0.06	0.10	0.13	−0.02	−0.00	−0.13	−0.11
6 other policy-value questions:[a]								
1	0.11	0.01	0.02	0.06	−0.34*	−0.13	−0.06	−0.27**
2	0.12	0.24	−0.27	0.01	−0.09	−0.29	0.17	−0.06
5	0.62**	0.49**	0.47**	0.52**	−0.54**	−0.17	−0.31*	−0.35**
6	−0.04	−0.16	−0.28	−0.14	−0.06	−0.05	0.12	−0.07
11	0.14	0.05	0.13	0.10	−0.02	0.03	0.26	0.11
16	0.19	0.13	−0.01	0.11	−0.24	−0.13	0.02	−0.14

[a]Policy-value questions not included as part of national health insurance index or actuarial model index.
*Significant at $p < 0.05$.
**Significant at $p < 0.01$.

Correlations between the indexes and the six policy-value questions not utilized in their construction also are typically low, with one striking exception. Respondents agreeing with question 5, which calls for national standardized health insurance benefit packages, also support national health insurance and just as clearly reject the actuarial approach for private insurance underwriting. The actuarial model index is also negatively correlated with agreement with question 1.

The weak relationship between the positive questions and the two indexes is also revealed in Table 5, which presents the results of regressing the indexes on the positive questions.[al] In the national health insurance regression the only

Table 5.   Results of Ordinary Least Squares Regressions of the National Health Insurance Index and the Actuarial Model Index on Seven Positive Questions.

Survey question number	Health economists	Economic theorists	Practicing physicians	All groups	
National health insurance index:					
4	0.206	−0.007	0.048	0.022	0.029
	(0.165)	(0.163)	(0.158)	(0.079)	(0.088)
9	0.053	0.138	0.046	0.056	0.052
	(0.139)	(0.195)	(0.162)	(0.084)	(0.086)
10	0.239*	0.032	−0.104	0.079	0.077
	(0.112)	(0.157)	(0.151)	(0.074)	(0.075)
12	−0.167	0.221	−0.100	−0.053	−0.043
	(0.154)	(0.196)	(0.128)	(0.076)	(0.084)
13	−0.169	0.027	−0.121	−0.088	−0.093
	(0.124)	(0.133)	(0.123)	(0.066)	(0.071)
18	−0.776	−0.031	0.087	0.007	0.012
	(0.699)	(0.162)	(0.133)	(0.093)	(0.094)
19	0.231	0.049	−0.016	0.087	0.089
	(0.141)	(0.198)	(0.145)	(0.080)	(0.083)
ET dummy[a]					−0.026
					(0.086)
PP dummy[a]					−0.024
					(0.089)
Constant	0.402	0.201	0.598	0.438	0.454
	(0.189)	(0.198)	(0.178)	(0.099)	(0.112)
R^2	0.287	0.066	0.080	0.052	0.053
Adjusted R^2	0.156	−0.116	−0.110	−0.001	−0.017
F	2.18	0.36	0.42	0.98	0.76

(*Continued*)

[al]The reliability of the OLS regressions was checked in several ways: values for each respondent were predicted from each regression and found to be always between 0 and 1; regressions run with the

Table 5. (*Continued*)

Survey question number	Health economists	Economic theorists	Practicing physicians	All groups	
Actuarial model index:					
4	−0.102	0.079	−0.029	−0.069	−0.029
	(0.160)	(0.119)	(0.131)	(0.068)	(0.073)
9	0.373**	0.027	−0.102	0.146*	0.142*
	(0.135)	(0.142)	(0.135)	(0.072)	(0.072)
10	−0.224*	−0.211	−0.013	−0.187**	−0.190**
	(0.108)	(0.115)	(0.125)	(0.063)	(0.062)
12	0.026	0.216	0.023	0.146*	0.091
	(0.149)	(0.143)	(0.106)	(0.065)	(0.070)
13	0.094	0.149	0.090	0.041	0.090
	(0.120)	(0.097)	(0.102)	(0.056)	(0.059)
18	0.432	0.068	0.113	0.114	0.109
	(0.678)	(0.118)	(0.111)	(0.079)	(0.079)
19	−0.010	0.080	−0.075	−0.062	−0.028
	(0.137)	(0.145)	(0.120)	(0.068)	(0.070)
ET dummy[a]					0.130
					(0.071)
PP dummy[a]					−0.033
					(0.074)
Constant	0.234	0.491	0.454	0.446	0.391
	(0.184)	(0.144)	(0.148)	(0.085)	(0.093)
R^2	0.279	0.166	0.114	0.145	0.182
Adjusted R^2	0.146	0.004	−0.068	0.096	0.122
F	2.10	1.02	0.63	3.00	3.02*

Notes: Standard error in parentheses.
[a]Health economist is the excluded class (ET = economic theorists and PP = practicing physicians).
*Significant at $p < 0.05$.
**Significant at $p < 0.01$.

statistically significant coefficient is for question 10 for health economists. Other things being equal, those who agree with the induced-demand hypothesis are more supportive of national health insurance than those who disagree, but the effect on the index (0.239) is less than changing one of the four answers from disagree to agree. The actuarial model regressions result in a few additional significant coefficients but, in general, the respondents' replies to the explicit positive questions do not explain their position with respect to such major policy issues as national health insurance or insurance company underwriting changes.

dependent variable transformed to the odds ratio or to a dichotomous variable estimated with a logistic specification that showed even less predictive value than the OLS regressions.

It seems unlikely, then, that their position on these policy issues can be explained by differences in the embedded positive questions.

Although I believe that differences in values lie at the heart of the disagreement about policy-value questions, I recognize that there is scope for work on the embedded positive questions and this work could contribute to a narrowing of policy differences. One indication of where research is needed is the percent of health economists answering "no opinion" on the individual policy-value questions. This option was chosen most frequently (35 percent of the time) for question 11 concerning the optimality of expenditures on medical R&D.[am] Given the importance of technologic change in medicine both from the point of view of health outcomes and of expenditures, this is clearly a high-priority area for research. Two other questions elicited a "no opinion" response from one fifth of the health economists. They are question 1 concerning the subsidies for health insurance by size of firm (a key part of the Clinton plan) and question 20 (about differential premiums for persons born with genetic defects). In the latter case the high percentage responding "no opinion" may reflect uncertainty regarding the magnitudes of the efficiency and distributional implications of eliminating premium differentials. Or, it may reflect a reluctance to choose between conflicting values.

Before leaving the survey it is worth considering what it reveals about the ability of health economists to disseminate their conclusions about the positive questions to a wider audience. Overall, one must conclude that they have not been very successful, as revealed by the political debate of 1993–1994 and the media coverage of policy issues. Consider, for example, question 19 concerning whether in the long run employers bear the primary burden of their contributions to their employees' health insurance. Although 87 percent of the health economists disagreed with that statement, politicians on both sides of the debate assumed, erroneously, that it was correct. Moreover, nearly all of the media made the same error. Most of the politicians and most of the media also showed little understanding of questions 4, 12, 13, and 18.

I am as ready as the next economist to criticize politicians and journalists, but the survey results suggest that their poor understanding of health economics is not entirely their fault. First, the economic theorists and the practicing physicians, two groups with above-average ability and opportunity to absorb the conclusions of the health economists, did not show good command of the positive questions. In my judgment the health economists answered 80 percent correctly, but the average

---

[am] This one question accounted for one fourth of the health economists' "no opinion" replies to the 13 policy-value questions.

theorist answered only 52 percent correctly and the mean score for the physicians was only 53 percent. The differences in the distributions of scores is striking: 45 of the 46 health economists had more correct answers than the average theorist or the average physician.

A second possible reason for the poor understanding of health economics displayed by the politicians and the media in 1993–1994 is the wide disagreement among health economists over the policy-value questions. When health economists interact with politicians and journalists, their discussions probably focus on the policy-value questions; in the absence of a professional consensus on many of these questions, it is not surprising that politicians and journalists fall back on their own values to shape their positions.

Returning to the question posed at the beginning of this section about why economic research failed to result in a more informed and productive health care policy debate, the survey results provide some provisional answers. First, although health economists are in substantial agreement about the positive questions, they have major disagreements about policy-value questions. Second, health economists were not successful in getting their conclusions on positive questions accepted by the politicians or the media, and even had difficulty in communicating their results to economic theorists and practicing physicians. Third, the health economists' disagreements over policy probably reflect differences in values, although it is clear that there are many positive questions embedded in the policy-value questions. In my judgment the problem is not so much that the health economists disagree about the embedded questions as that they are uncertain about them. In the face of such uncertainty, they tend to let their values drive their policy recommendations.

The Future

If values play such an important role in policy disputes, what are the implications for economics and economists? First, we should endeavor to make explicit the differences in values, and seek ways to resolve them. Value differences can take many different forms. Economists are most familiar with the distinction between efficiency and distributional issues, especially greater equality of income versus greater total income.[an] But comprehensive changes in health policy can have other important distributional effects. Even for individuals at the same income level, the costs and the benefits of care could change along many dimensions: rural areas versus central cities, the elderly versus the young, smokers versus nonsmokers,

---

[an] See Okun (1975).

savers versus nonsavers, men versus women, and so on. Health economists who are unanimous in approving gains in efficiency might have very different views regarding the desirability of the distributional changes and might also differ in the weights they give to the changes in efficiency versus the distributional consequences.

Second, greater openness about value differences should force economists to make explicit the positive questions that are embedded in most policy-value questions. This would point the way to productive research. If the embedded questions are identified and studied, it should be possible to reduce the uncertainty about them and thus provide a basis for narrowing differences on policy-value questions.

A third agenda item for economists is to undertake research on the formation of values, especially insofar as they are the consequences of policy. Economists are understandably reluctant to prescribe values or to make normative judgments about them. But when economic policies affect values and preferences, and these in turn affect behavior, it is incumbent on economists to analyze the links between policies and values, and to examine the economic and social consequences of alternative value systems. I believe there is an analogy between the economics of values and the economics of technology. Over the past several decades some economists have begun to treat technology as at least partly endogenous.[ao] Now, a similar effort must be undertaken for values.[1,6,51,56]

Finally, economists must develop more self-awareness of how our values color our judgment about policy, and more candor in making clear to others the respective roles of positive research and of values in our policy recommendations. Alice M. Rivlin, in her AEA presidential address in December 1986, warned economists against letting "their ideological position cloud their judgment about the likely effects of particular policies" (p. 4). She urged us "... to be more careful to sort out, for ourselves and others, what we really know from our ideological biases" (p. 9). In my view, there is a vast difference between a researcher and a reformer, between an analyst and a player in the policy arena. They are all socially valuable occupations, and the same individual may successfully wear different hats at different times. What is not likely to work well, either for economics or for policy, is trying to wear two hats at the same time.

In the remainder of this paper, I present a summary of my policy recommendations for health system reform. The use of the bully pulpit by an AEA president to push personal policy choices has ample precedent, but I also want

---

[ao]For example, Kenneth Arrow, Zvi Griliches, Ed Mansfield, Richard Nelson, Nathan Rosenberg, and Jacob Schmookler.

to use this opportunity to show how those choices are shaped by the interaction between my values and my understanding of health economics. Finally, I identify aspects of my policy recommendations that are problematic and which would clearly benefit from additional research.

My three major recommendations are:

(i)   a broad-based tax earmarked for health care to provide every American with a voucher for participation in a basic plan;

(ii) provision of care through integrated health systems that include hospitals, physician services, and prescription drugs. These systems would be led by physicians, would be reimbursed by capitation plus modest co-payment from patients at the time of use, and would be required to offer a wide variety of point-of-service options to be paid for by patients with after-tax dollars;

(iii) a large private center for technology assessment financed by a small industrywide levy on all health care spending.

My desire to see all Americans insured for a basic health plan is clearly driven in part by values. Although medical care is often not a crucial factor in health outcomes, it is nearly always a source of utility through its caring and validation functions. In my judgment, it fully meets Adam Smith's 1776 definition of a *necessary*: "By necessaries I understand not only the commodities which are indispensably necessary for the support of life but whatever the custom of the country renders it indecent for creditable people, even of the lowest order, to be without" (1776, republished 1937, p. 821). To achieve universal coverage there must be subsidization for those who are too poor or too sick to acquire insurance, and there must be compulsion for the "free riders"[ap] to pay their share.

There are only two ways to achieve systematic universal coverage: a broad-based general tax with implicit subsidies for the poor and the sick, or a system of mandates with explicit subsidies based on income. I prefer the former because the latter are extremely expensive to administer and seriously distort incentives; they result in the near-poor facing marginal tax rates that would be regarded as confiscatory if levied on the affluent.[aq]

[ap] It is true that most of the uninsured currently receive some care, but it is financed through a haphazard hodgepodge of self-pay, cost shifting, government subsidies, and philanthropy.

[aq] The choice of the tax base is primarily a problem of public finance, not health economics. I prefer a value-added tax because it is more efficient than a payroll tax (it does not tax labor while ignoring capital), and I prefer it to an income tax because it encourages saving and discourages consumption (a value judgment). The VAT appeals to my sense of fairness because it is more difficult to escape its impact through tax loopholes or tax evasion, and, when taken in conjunction with the benefit that it provides, is clearly progressive.

Both theory and experience show that integrated health care systems are usually the best way to deliver cost-effective care. The primary reason is the physician's central role in medical decision-making. Under any approach to care, it is the physician who admits patients to hospitals, orders tests and other procedures, and decides when to discharge. It is the physician who prescribes drugs and who refers patients to other physicians for consultation and treatment. Thus physicians' decisions are the major determinant of the cost of care. Only in an integrated system, however, do physicians have the *incentive,* the *information,* and the *infrastructure* needed to make these decisions in a cost-effective way. Integrated systems also have an advantage in avoiding excess capacity of high-cost equipment and personnel.

Given the central importance of physicians to medical care, I believe the integrated systems should be led by them and other health care professionals. At a minimum, health care professionals should have a prominent place in the governance of the systems. One of the greatest errors of health policy-makers today is their assumption that market competition or government regulation are the only instruments available to control health care. There is room for, indeed need for, a revitalization of professional norms as a third instrument of control.[ar] The patient-physician relationship often is highly personal and intimate, similar in many ways to relationships within families or between teachers and pupils or ministers and congregants. This relationship is, in part, what economist[7] called an integrative system, one that depends on mutual recognition and acceptance of rights and responsibilities, enforced by traditional norms as well as market pressures and government regulations. As long as physicians control the use of complex technology in life and death situations, and as long as we expect them to perform priestly functions, they must be endowed with certain privileges and held to certain standards of behavior different from those assumed by models of market competition or government regulation.[as]

Comprehensive government control of medical care has not worked well in any setting. The essence of good care is an informed patient working cooperatively with a health professional who provides personalized attention and concern. The rules, regulations, and bureaucratic controls that almost always accompany governmental activities are inimical to high-quality cost-effective care. It is revealing that countries such as England and Sweden with deep government involvement in the financing of medical care have bent over backwards to leave

---

[ar] See Arrow (1963) for a discussion of professional control in medicine.
[as] The patient-physician relationship presents an extreme case of the principal-agent problem; research by specialists on that topic is badly needed.

physicians with a great deal of professional autonomy — indeed more autonomy than is possessed by many American physicians working in a "private" system.

Market competition also has its problems. It assumes a preoccupation with the bottom line and governance by a corporate mentality that judges the success of each division by its profit growth. Physician-led systems will also have to pay attention to costs, and physicians will also be interested in making a good income, but there is a vast difference between a profit-maximizing corporation and physicians who strive to balance their obligations to patients, the organization, and themselves.[at]

Reimbursement of these integrated systems should be primarily by capitation, adjusted for patient characteristics. In addition, patients should be required to make modest co-payments at the time of use (e.g., $15 for each visit and $5 for each prescription). Such payments will generate some income but, more important, will help to discourage wasteful use of health care. The payments could be waived for patients living below the poverty level, and for essential preventive services such as vaccination.

The earmarked tax would provide every American with a voucher for a basic health care plan. Each integrated system would be required to offer the basic plan, plus a variety of options. These options are not alternative insurance plans; they are services to be paid for at time of use with after-tax dollars.[au] The options could take many forms: a private room in the hospital; a wider choice of physicians and hospitals than is available through the basic plan; or access to new experimental technologies or older technologies not included in the basic plan because they have a low benefit-to-cost ratio.[av]

These options would accommodate the demands of patients with higher incomes or those who choose to spend more of their income on medical care. The options would not constitute establishment of different plans. Everyone would

---

[at] The effects on television network news departments of the subordination of professional norms to the pursuit of profits shows what could happen in medical care.

[au] Readers whose values lead them to prefer a more egalitarian system might consider how individuals now have options to use their income to live in safer neighborhoods, drive safer cars, avoid unhealthy occupations, and make other choices that have larger and more predictable effects on health than the options available in my recommendation for health care.

[av] Many advances in medicine do not spring full-blown from the test tube. They require long periods of development through trial and error and incremental improvements. In my judgment it is desirable to have a system in which technologic opportunities can be explored on a reasonably large scale with the costs borne by those patients who are most willing and able to pay for a chance at unproven benefits. Government- or industry-financed randomized clinical trials with small samples of selected patients treated in selected environments are not always a satisfactory substitute for larger scale efforts to establish the effectiveness, and especially the cost-effectiveness of a medical technology.

be in the same plan and most persons would stick to the basic plan most of the time. An option would be exercised only when the patient desired and was willing to pay for it. This is the quintessential American approach to balancing equality and freedom. On the one hand, this approach avoids the egalitarianism of the English and Canadian systems in which only a small elite have an escape valve. On the other hand, it does not create a separate plan for the poor while the great majority of Americans obtain care from a different system. The experience with Medicaid shows that a separate system limited to the poor is not likely to function well.

Where feasible, the integrated health care system would engage in managed competition.[aw] Having advocated policies similar to such an approach to health care for more than 20 years,[29] I am not unmindful of its virtues. We cannot, however, rely on managed competition alone to contain costs. In most rural areas, population density is too low to support several health care systems. Even in some urban areas, competition is impossible or undesirable because of economies of scale. For instance, only one hospital is needed to serve a population of 100,000 efficiently. Similar constraints apply to competition in physician specialty care, especially if the physicians work full time at their specialties. A population of 1 million would probably not justify enough independent maternity services or open-heart surgery teams to create competitive conditions. Moreover, the public interest is not best served by insisting that health professionals always maintain rigorous arm's-length competition with one another. Patients can benefit from cooperation among physicians and hospitals, both in reduced costs and better service. Managed competition alone will not be enough to contain costs; it must be supplemented by constraints on the supply side, especially with respect to technology and the specialty mix of physicians.

In 1995, Americans spent about $1 trillion for health care, broadly defined. If, during the past 30 years, health care spending had grown at the rate of the rest of the economy, the health care bill in 1995 would have been only a little more than $400 billion. What accounts for this extraordinary excess of almost $600 billion in annual spending? There has been a small increase in physician visits per capita, but use of acute care hospitals has decreased sharply. Patient-days per 1000 population are less than three fifths the level of 30 years ago. By far the most important factor accounting for the increase in health care's share of the GDP is the change in technology.[ax] Physician visits and hospital-days cost more than they

---

[aw] See Refs. 19 and 20.
[ax] For general discussions, see Refs. 63, 69 and 77. For a detailed examination of the role of technology in increasing expenditures on heart attack patients, see Ref. 12.

used to because the content has changed — the technologies used for diagnosis and treatment are more expensive than in the past. Much of this technological change is welcome; it contributes to enhancing the length and quality of life. Some of the change is less desirable because it adds more to cost than to patient benefit. Unfortunately, there is great uncertainty regarding the merits of many technologies. Moreover, even when the advantages and disadvantages are known, there are often significant barriers facing physicians who would like to practice in a cost-effective manner.

To deal with this problem, I propose the creation of a large, private center for technology assessment. Financing for this center would come from a small levy (less than one tenth of 1 percent) on all health care spending. A centralized approach is necessary, because health care is highly fragmented. Individual physicians and health plans lack the incentive and ability to commit the resources needed to assess new technologies. Even the largest insurance companies individually account for only a small percentage of the health care market; they are, therefore, understandably reluctant to pay for large-scale assessments that would benefit all.[ay] Government agencies try to fill the void, but the scale of effort is too small, and a private center would be able to avoid the political interference that often intrudes on government-run agencies.[az] Health care providers would fund and set the agenda for the center, much as the electric power companies do for the Electric Power Research Institute. This institute is financed by a small levy on every public utility bill.

A health care technology assessment center would have two primary functions. First, it would help to develop and disseminate systematic knowledge about the cost-effectiveness of medical technology through support of research and through a comprehensive program of publications and conferences. The center would have some intramural research capability, but most of the research would be conducted extramurally at medical schools, hospitals, and research institutes throughout the country. It would provide health professionals with essential information to evaluate and improve their clinical practices and offer a rational basis for deciding what services should be included in the basic plan.

The second important function would be to provide legitimacy for the cost-effective practice of medicine. Currently, many directors of health plans and many

---

[ay] See Ref. 67.
[az] The federal government's Agency for Health Care Policy and Research has shown that even a modest budget can produce valuable information about medical technologies, but the agency now faces extinction because of the opposition from politically influential medical and surgical specialists who expect to be adversely affected by its findings. See Ref. 55.

individual physicians know they could be practicing in a more cost-effective way, but they are inhibited from doing so because they do not practice in a vacuum. Physicians are influenced by peers who have been trained in settings that emphasized the use of the latest technologies regardless of cost. Patients come with particular sets of expectations based on what they read or hear in the media and what their relatives and friends tell them has been their experience. The threat of malpractice suits lurks in the background. A major function of the center would be to give legitimacy and a stamp of authority to physicians who practice in a more cost-effective way.

My policy recommendations seek to achieve a balance among the diverse values of efficiency, justice, freedom, and security. The link between the earmarked tax and the basic plan would create a healthy tension between the desire to increase benefits and the need to pay for the increase in a responsible and equitable manner. Competition among health care systems in highly populated areas would widen choice and foster cost-effective practice. The private technology assessment center would help to contain costs without the imposition of controls or caps that might stifle innovation and progress.

Are these recommendations politically saleable? In the short run, certainly not. But neither are any other proposals for comprehensive reform. Indeed, for more than 20 years it has been my view that the United States would not enact comprehensive health care reform expect in the wake of a major war, a depression, large-scale civil unrest, or some other event that completely changed the political climate. Why is the United States the only major industrialized nation without national health insurance? Many observers focus on the opposition of "special interests," and that certainly is a factor, but I do not find it a completely satisfactory explanation. After all, special interests are not unknown in Sweden, England, Canada, and other countries that do have national health insurance.

In 1976, I suggested four reasons for its absence in the United States: distrust of government, heterogeneity of the population, a weak sense of noblesse oblige, and strong private voluntary organizations such as nonprofit hospitals and Blue Cross and Blue Shield plans that carry out quasi-governmental functions with respect to the financing and delivery of health care (Fucus, 1976). Upon revisiting this question (Fucus, 1991), I concluded that the first three reasons were stronger than ever, but the fourth had weakened considerably. It is ironic that "the competition revolution" (Fucus, 1988b), which erodes the ability of not-for-profit health care institutions to provide a modicum of social insurance through community rating and cost shifting, may in the long run push the country toward national health insurance.

My plan is certainly not a panacea; it would be difficult to implement and others might seek a different balance of values. Several aspects require additional research. For example, what should be the content of the basic plans? How should the content change over time? How should the plans be reimbursed from the funds raised by the earmarked tax, and especially how should reimbursement be risk adjusted to take account of differences in plan populations? Another problem is how to encourage competition among plans where it is feasible, while recognizing that a competitive approach will not be desirable or possible in areas of low population density. Considerable research is needed on how the out-of-plan options should be priced[ba] and how the providers of such care should be reimbursed. Finally, much thought should be given to how to reinvigorate professional norms as a third instrument of control, along with market competition and government regulation.[bb]

I conclude this tour of health economics — past, present, and future — on a mildly optimistic note. In the past three decades economics has made a positive contribution to health and medical care, and I believe that future contributions will be even greater. Now that the basic ideas of economics are gaining acceptance, it will be more important than ever for economists to master many of the intricacies of health care institutions and technologies. We will also have to consider the problems of dissemination in order to insure that when we agree on research results, these results are understood and accepted by all relevant audiences including the media, politicians, and health professionals. Moreover, we must pay more attention to values than we have in the past. Through skillful analysis of the interactions between values and the conclusions of positive research, we will be able to contribute more effectively to public policy debates. And, if health economists are successful in this demanding assignment, we can lead the way toward progress in areas such as child care and education that face similar problems of reconciling multiple goals and heterogeneity in values. To be useful to our society while deriving pleasure from our work — in the words of the old Gershwin tune, "Who could ask for anything more?"

References

1. Aaron, H. J. (1994). "Distinguished Lecture on Economics in Government: Public Policy, Values, and Consciousness." *Journal of Economic Perspectives* **8**(2): 3–21.
2. Alston, R. M., Kearl, J. R. and Vaughan, M. B. (1992). "Is There a Consensus Among Economists in the 1990's?" *American Economic Review, (Papers and Proceedings)* **82**(2): 203–209.

[ba]For an interesting discussion of the "topper off" problem, see Ref. 23.

[bb]This would undoubtedly require research to uncover the reasons for the erosion of professional control. See, for example Ref. 8.

3. Arrow, K. (1963). "Uncertainty and the Welfare Economics of Medical Care." *American Economic Review* **53**(5): 941–973.
4. Bandura, A. (1991). "Self-Efficacy Mechanism in Physiological Activation and Health-Promoting Behavior." In *Neural Biology of Learning, Emotion, and Affect*, ed. John Madden. Raven Press: New York.
5. Becker, G. S. (1964). *Human Capital: A Theoretical and Empirical Analysis with Special Reference to Education*. National Bureau or Ecdnomic Research and Columbia University Press: New York.
6. Becker, G. S. (1996). *The Making of Preferences and Values*. Harvard University Press: Cambridge, MA.
7. Boulding, K. (1968). *Beyond Economics*. University of Michigan Press: Ann Arbor, MI.
8. Brint, S. (1994). *In an Age of Experts: The Changing Role of Professionals in Politics and Pubic Life*. Princeton University Press: Princeton, NJ.
9. Brook, R. H., Ware, J. E., Jr. Rogers, W. H., Keeler, E. B., Davies, A. R., Donald, C. A., Goldberg, G. A., Lohr, K. N., Masthay, P. C. and Newhouse, J. P. (1983). "Does Free Care Improve Adults' Health? Results from a Randomized Controlled Trial." *New England Journal of Medicine* **309**(23): 1426–1434.
10. Calltorp, J. (1989). "The 'Swedish Model' under Pressure: How to Maintain Equity and Develop Quality?" *Quality Assurance in Health Care* **1**: 13–22.
11. Camerer, C. F. and Weber, M. (1992). "Recent Developments in Modeling Preferences: Uncertainty and Ambiguity." *Journal of Risk and Uncertainty* **5**(4): 325–370.
12. Cutler, D. M. and McClellan, M. (1995). "Technological Change in Medical Care." Unpublished manuscript presented at the National Bureau of Economic Research Conference on the Economics of Aging, Carefree, AZ.
13. Davis, M. M. and Rorem, C. R. (1932). *The Crisis in Hospital Finance*. University of Chicago Press: Chicago.
14. Dranove, D. and Wehner, P. (1994). "Physician Induced Demand for Childbirths." *Journal of Health Economics* **13**(1): 61–73.
15. Eddy, D. M. (1980). *Screening for Cancer: Theory, Analysis, and Design*. Prentice Hall: Englewood, NJ.
16. Eddy, D. M. (1987). "The Frequency of Cervical Cancer Screening: Comparison of a Mathematical Model with Empirical Data." *Cancer* **60**: 1117–1122.
17. Eddy, D. M. (1990). "Screening for Cervical Cancer." *Annals of Internal Medicine* **113**(5): 214–226.
18. Efron, B. (1993). *An Introduction to the Bootstrap*. Chapman and Hall: New York.
19. Enthoven, A. (1986). "Managed Competition in Health Care and the Unfinished Agenda." *Health Care Financing Review Annual Supplement* (annual supplement): 105–119.
20. Enthoven, A. (1988). "Managed Competition: An Agenda for Action." *Health Affairs* **7**(3): 25–47.
21. Farrell, P. and Fuchs, V. R. (1982). "Schooling and Health: The Cigarette Connection." *Journal of Health Economics* **1**(3): 217–230.
22. Feldstein, M. (1967). *Economic Analysis for Health Service Efficiency*. North-Holland: Amsterdam.

23. Frank, R. H. (1996). "Consumption Externalities and the Financing of Social Services." In *Individual and Social Responsibility: Child Care, Education, Medical Care, and Long-term Care in America*, ed. Victor R. Fuchs. University of Chicago Press: Chicago, IL.

24. Friedman, M. (1953). *Essays in Positive Economics.* University of Chicago Press: Chicago, IL.

25. Friedman, M. (1966). *Dollars and Deficits.* Prentice Hall: Englewood Cliffs, NJ.

26. Fuchs, V. R. (1966). "The Contribution of Health Services to the American Economy." *Milbank Memorial Fund Quarterly* **44**(4 Part 2): 65–101.

27. Fuchs, V. R. (1968). *The Service Economy.* National Bureau of Economic Research and Columbia University Press: New York.

28. Fuchs, V. R. ed. (1969). *Production and Productivity in the Service Industries.* National Bureau of Economic Research and Columbia University Press: New York.

29. Fuchs, V. R. (1974a). *Who Shall Live? Health, Economics, and Social Choice.* Basic Books: New York.

30. Fuchs, V. R. (1974b). "Some Economic Aspects of Mortality in Developed Countries." In *The Economics of Health and Medical Care*, ed. Mark Perlman. Macmillan: London, pp. 174–193.

31. Fuchs, V. R. (1976). From Bismarck to Woodcock: The 'Irrational' Pursuit of National Health Insurance." *Journal of Law and Economics* **19**(2): 347–359.

32. Fuchs, V. R. (1979). "Economies, Health, and Post-Industrial Society." Paper presented at the E. S. Woodward Lectures in Economics, University of British Columbia, November 1–2, 1978a; *Milbank Memorial Fund Quarterly/Health and Society* **57**(2): 153–182.

33. Fuchs, V. R. (1978b). "The Supply of Surgeons and the Demand for Operations." *Journal of Human Resources* **13**(Supplement): 35–56.

34. Fuchs, V. R. (1982). "Time Preference and Health: An Exploratory Study." In *Economic Aspects of Health*, ed. V. R. Fuchs. University of Chicago Press: Chicago. pp. 93–120.

35. Fuchs, V. R. (1983). *How We Have.* Harvard University Press: Cambridge, MA.

36. Fuchs, V. R. (1987). "Health Economics," In *The New Palgrave: Social Economics*, eds. J. Eatwell, M. Milgate and P. Newmans. Macmillan: New York, pp. 119–129.

37. Fuchs, V. R. (1988a). *Women's Quest for Economic Equality.* Harvard University Press: Cambridge, MA.

38. Fuchs, V. R. (1988b). "The 'Competition Revolution' in Health Care." *Health Affairs* **7**(3): 5–24.

39. Fuchs, V. R. (1990). "The Health Sector's Share of the Gross National Product." *Science* **247**(4942): 534–538.

40. Fuchs, V. R. (1991). "National Health Insurance Revisited." *Health Affairs* winter, **10**(4): 7–17.

41. Fuchs, V. R. (1993). "Poverty and Health: Asking the Right Questions." In *Medical Care and the Health of the Poor*, eds. D. E. Rogers and E. Ginzberg. Westview Press: Boulder, CO, pp. 9–20.

42. Fuchs, V. R. (1994). "The Clinton Plan: A Researcher Examines Reform." *Health Affairs* **13**(1): 102–114.

43. Fuchs, V. R and Hahn, J. S. (1990). "How Does Canada Do It? A Comparison of Expenditures for Physicians' Services in the United States and Canada." *New England Journal of Medicine* **323**(13): 884–890.

44. Fuchs, V. R. and Kramer, M. (1973). *Determinants of Expenditures for Physicians' Services in the United States 1948–1968,* Occasional Paper 116. National Bureau of Economic Research and Department of Health, Education, and Welfare: New York.

45. Garber, A. M. Fuchs, V. R. and Silverman, J. F. (1984). "Case Mix, Costs, and Outcomes: Differences Between Faculty and Community Services in a University Hospital." *New England Journal of Medicine* **310**(19): 1231–1237.

46. Grossman, M. (1972). *The Demand for Health: A Theoretical and Empirical Investigation.* National Bureau of Economic Research: New York.

47. Grossman, M. (1975). "The Correlation Between Health and Schooling." In *Household Production and Consumption,* ed. N. E. Terleckyj, NBER Studies in Income and Wealth, Vol. 40. National Bureau of Economic Research and Columbia University Press: New york.

48. Gruber, J. and Owings, M. (1996). "Physician Financial Incentives and Cesarean Section Delivery." *Rand Journal of Economics,* Spring **27**(1): 99–123.

49. Haack, S. (1995). "Puzzling Out Science." *Academic Questions* **8**(2): 20–31.

50. Hamilton, W. (1932). "Personal Statement," In *Medical Care for the American People.* University of Chicago Press: Chicago, pp. 189–200.

51. Hirschman, A. O. (1986). "Against Parsimony: Three Easy Ways of Complicating Some Categories of Economic Discourse." In *Rival Views of Market Society and Other Recent Essays,* ed. A. O. Hirschman. Harvard University Press: Cambridge, MA.

52. Huxley, T. H. (1863). "Preface." *Evidence as to Man's Place in Nature* Williams and Norgate: London.

53. Intriligator, M. D. "The Impact of Arrow's Contribution to Economic Analysis." In *Arrow and the Foundations of the Theory of Economic Policy,* ed. G. R. Feiwel. New York University Press: New York, pp. 683–691.

54. Klarman, H. (1965). *The Economics of Health.* Columbia University Press: New York.

55. Lewis, N. A. (1995). "Agency Facing Revolt After Report." *The New York Times,* A8.

56. Lindbeck, A. (1994). "Hazardous Welfare State Dynamics: Endogenous Habits and Norms." Mimeo, Institute for International Economic Studies, University of Stockholm.

57. Lundberg, G. D. and Flanagin, A. (1995). "European Science in JAMA." *Journal of the American Medical Association* **274**(2): 180.

58. Maccoby, N. and Solomon, D. S. (1981). "Health Disease Prevention: Multi-community Studies." In *Public Communication Campaigns,* eds. R. E. Rice and W. J. Paisley. Sage Publications: Beverly Hills, CA.

59. Mark, D. B., Hlatky, M. A., Califf, R. M., Naylor, C., David, L., Kerry, L., Armstrong, P. W., Barbash, G., White, H., Simoons, M. L., Nelson, C. L., Clapp-Channing, N., Knight, J., David, H., Frank, E. Jr., Simes, J. and Topol, E. J. (1995). "Cost-Effectiveness of Thrombolytic Therapy with Tissue Plasminogen Activator as Compared with Streptokinase for Acute Myocardial Infarction." *New England Journal of Medicine* **332**(21): 1418–1424.

60. Mill, J. S. (1987). *Principles of Political Economy with Some of their Applications to Social Philosophy* Little Brown: Boston, 1848; reprinted Augustus M. Kelley: Fairfield, NJ.

61. Mushkin, S. J. (1962). "Health as an Investment." NBER Special Conference 15, *Journal of Political Economy* **70**(5, part 2, Supplement): 129–157.

62. NBER Special Conference 15 (1962). "Investment in Human Beings." *Journal of Political Economy* **70**(5 part 2): 1–157.

63. Newhouse, J. P. (1992). "Medical Care Costs: How Much Welfare Loss?" *Journal of Economic Perspectives* **6**(3): 3–21.

64. Okun, A. (1975). *Equality and Efficiency: The Big Tradeoff.* Brookings Institution: Washington, DC.

65. Redelmeier, D. A. and Fuchs, V. R. (1993). "Hospital Expenditures in the United States and Canada." *New England Journal of Medicine* **328**(11): 772–778.

66. Rivlin, A. M. (1987). "Economics and the Political Process." *American Economic Review* **77**(1): 1–9.

67. Romer, P. M. (1993). "Implementing a National Technology Strategy with Self-Organizing Industry Investment Boards." *Brookings Papers on Economic Activity: Microeconomics* **1993**(2): 345–390, 398–399.

68. Roos, L. L., Fisher, E. S., Sharp, S. M., Newhouse, J. P., Anderson, G. and Buboiz, T. A. (1990). "Postsurgical Mortality in Manitoba and New England." *Journal of the American Medical Association* **263**(18): 2453–2458.

69. Schwartz, W. B. (1987). "The Inevitable Failure of Cost-Containment Strategies: Why They Can Provide Only Temporary Relief." *Journal of the American Medical Association* **257**(2): 220–224.

70. Sen, A. (1987). "Justice." In *The New Palgrave: A Dictionary of Economics*, eds. J. Eatwell, M. Milgate and P. Newman. Stockton Press: New York, pp. 1039–1042.

71. Smith, A. (1937). *An Inquiry Into the Nature and Causes of the Wealth of Nations.* Strahan and Cadell: London, 1776; republished in *The Wealth of Nations*, ed. E. Cannan. Modern Library: New York.

72. Stigler, G. J. (1965). "The Economist and the State." *American Economic Review* **55**(1): 1–18.

73. Thaler, R. A. and Shefrin, H. M. (1981). "An Economic Theory of Self Control." *Journal of Political Economy* **89**(2): 392–406.

74. Townsend, P. and Davidson, N. eds. (1982). *Inequalities in Health: The Black Report.* Hamonds-worth, Penguin Books: England.

75. Weber, M. (1946). "The Social Psychology of the World Religions, 1915." In *From Max Weber: Essays in Sociology*, H. H. Gerth C. Wright Mills. Oxford University Press: New York.

76. Weinberg, S. (1995). "The Methods of Science...and Those by Which We Live." *Academic Questions* Spring, **8**(2): 7–13.

77. Weisbrod, B. A. (1991). "The Health Care Quadrilemma: An Essay on Technological Change, Insurance, Quality of Care, and Cost-Containment." *Journal of Economic Literature* **29**(2): 523–552.

78. Wilkinson, R. G. (1986). "Socioeconomic Differences in Mortality: Interpreting the Data on Their Size and Trends." In *Class and Health: Research and Longitudinal Data*, ed. R. G. Wilkinson. Tavistock: London and New York.

7.3

The Structure of Medical Education — It's Time for a Change

Last spring, in his elegant commencement address to the Harvard Medical School, Dr. Atul Gawande appealed for a dramatic change in the organization and delivery of medical care. His reason, "medicine's complexity has exceeded our individual capabilities as doctors." He accepts the necessity of specialization, but he criticizes a system of care that emphasizes the independence of each specialist. Dr. Gawande is not alone in thinking that scientific, technologic, and economic changes require reorganization of care. Larry Casalino and Steve Shortell have proposed Accountable Care Organizations (ACOs); Fisher, Skinner, Wennberg and colleagues at the Dartmouth Medical School have focused on reforming Medicare, and many others have also called for major changes.

I expressed similar concerns in 1974 in my book *Who Shall Live?*, but at that time I rejected the claim that the problems of medical care had reached crisis proportion. In 2011, however, I agree with those who say the need for comprehensive reform must be marked URGENT. The high and rapidly

Originally the Alan Gregg Lecture was presented at the Annual Meeting of the Association of American Medical Colleges, November 6, 2011; and printed in *More Health Care Reform*, Stanford, CA: SIEPR, 2012.

rising cost of health care threaten the financial credibility of the federal and state governments. The former finances much of its share of health care by borrowing from abroad; the states fund health care by cutting support of education, maintenance of infrastructure, and other essential functions. These are stopgap measures; neither borrowing from abroad nor cutting essential functions are long-run solutions. The private sector is equally distressed. Surging health insurance premiums have captured most of the productivity gains of the past thirty years, leaving most workers with stagnant wages. Not only is there a pressing need for changes in organization and delivery, but Ezekiel Emanuel and I, in our proposal for universal vouchers funded by a dedicated value-added tax, argue that such changes must be accompanied by comprehensive reform of the financing of medical care (Brookings paper).

But that's not what I want to talk to you about today. My subject is the urgent need to change the structure of medical education. It seems to me that such change is necessary, and perhaps inevitable, given the revolution in medicine over the past half century, and given the changes in organization and delivery of care that lie on the horizon.

The Need for Change

Consider the deluge of new medical technologies in recent decades. According to Dr. Gawande, in deciding on interventions for their patients, clinicians now must choose from 6,000 drugs and 4,000 procedures. To be sure, many of the 6,000 are not new chemical entities but rather combination drugs, alternative dosage forms, and other variations. Still, the burden on the clinician to make an appropriate choice is great, especially if, as stated in the Physician Charter, "physicians are required to provide health care that is based on the wise and cost-effective management of limited clinical resources." Economists have been touting cost-effectiveness for years, but it is a harbinger of change to see organizations representing more than half of all active physicians sign a charter committing them to practice cost-effective medicine.

Along with the new technologies, there has been a proliferation of specialties and sub-specialties. Fifty years ago, there were 18 specialty boards and very few sub-specialties. Now there are 36 specialty boards and 116 sub-specialty certifications, for a total of 152. Does such proliferation provide much or any benefit to patients? The United Kingdom has only 97, while, Canada and France have fewer than half as many. Proliferation of specialties and sub-specialties almost certainly adds to the cost of medical education and the cost of care, while its effect on quality of care has not been systematically investigated. The former chair of medicine at a major academic medical center thinks it has an adverse effect on patient care, but other experts disagree. We just don't know the answer. If empirical studies conclude that so many sub-specialities are desirable, the training structure that produces them should and could be made more efficient. Medicine is one of the few fields that requires specialists to have more training than generalists. This may have been rational at one time, but may not be today.

Finally, and closely related to the new technologies and increased specialization, there is the soaring cost of medical care. In 1960 U.S. health expenditures, in 2009 dollars, were $864 per person. In 2009, they were $8085. Along with the cost of medical care, the cost of medical education has increased exponentially.

In the face of such revolutionary changes, how has the structure of medical education adapted? It seems that the answer is hardly at all. Fifty years ago, the basic structure was four years of college, four years of medical school, and three years of post-graduate training. Only after 11 years of post-high school graduation was the physician deemed ready to practice medicine. The same is true today, although a much larger percentage than formerly go beyond 11 years to obtain additional specialized training. And in one medical school I know of fewer than 40 percent graduate in 4 years.

The Goals of Change

A reasonable goal for structural reform might be to reduce that basic period from eleven to nine years. This can be done by cutting time off the front end or the back end of the process or both. About the front end, I note diat there are now 33 medical schools that combine college and medical training in six years. Could there be more such schools? What is known about the quality of care delivered by physicians from these programs compared with the graduates of conventional medical schools? Very little. Most other developed countries combine college and medical school in one program that is typically less than eight years long. Are their physicians inferior to American physicians?

It might be argued that foreign medical schools can admit students directly from high school because the educational achievement of those high school graduates is greater than that of American high school graduates. This is probably true on average, but there are certainly some American high school graduates with educational achievement equal to those who graduate from foreign high schools. Why couldn't American medical schools consider for admission applicants who, through appropriate examinations and interviews, appear to be as well qualified as the college graduates the schools are now admitting, regardless of how many post-high school years the student has completed? I understand that thoughtful leaders in medicine are studying various possibilities for accelerating admission to medical school for qualified candidates. That's great. But I hope they realize that the health care system is entering the "ICU," prompt, decisive action is needed.

In order to reduce time at the back end, schools might consider accelerating choice of specialization. Dr. Gawande notes that there was a time when "doctors could hold all the key information patients needed in their heads and manage everything required themselves." He says that in such a world it made sense for physicians to prize "autonomy, independence, and self-sufficiency." But that time is gone forever. What remains is a structure of medical education based on those outmoded assumptions. For Dr. Gawande, who is as handy with a metaphor as with a scalpel, the bottom line is "we train, hire, and pay doctors to be cowboys. But it's pit crews people need."

A Proposed New Structure

If Dr. Gawande is correct, what does this imply for the structure of medical education? Isn't it time to give up the conventional wisdom that pouring more and more knowledge into each physician about more and more subjects will produce a better system of medical care? Far from rejecting specialization, embrace it sooner. For the purpose of stimulating discussion, I propose the following structure for medical education:

- Two years of medical education taken by all students. This common curriculum would consist of 50 percent basic science with an emphasis on competencies that would be useful to every physician. Subsequent exposure to basic science would depend on its relevance to the student's prospective career.
- One-third of the time would be devoted to an introduction to clinical care of individual patients, making as full use as possible of modern technologies that have been successful in training programs in industry, the armed forces, and other settings.
- One-sixth of the time would be used to cover key aspects of the health of populations and the organization and delivery of care, with emphasis on a team approach to enhance health. It is important for all physicians, regardless of prospective careers, to understand how each element fits into a health care system.

Upon completion of the two years, each student would select a track which launches him or her into the world of specialization. Here is an example of what the tracks might look like:

- Leaders of primary care teams, possibly sub-divided into adult care, pediatric care, and geriatric care.
- Clinical specialists in medicine, hospital based and ambulatory.
- Clinical specialists in surgery and other procedural specialties.
- Possibly another track for those headed for specialities such as radiology and pathology that treat medical and surgical patients.
- A track for students whose major interest is research, possibly similar to current MD-PhD programs but with explicit recognition that the trainees are not preparing to be clinicians.

The content of the training program would differ depending on the track. For example, students training to be leaders of primary care teams would be exposed to more statistics, epidemiology, preventive medicine, and management skills than those in the other tracks. They would learn how to deploy nurse practitioners, physician assistants, and other non-physicians most effectively.

Is it feasible for students to make specialty decisions sooner than they do in the present structure? Before you answer with a resounding "no", let me tell you a "tale of two schools."

A Tale of Two Schools

Just a stone's throw from the Stanford School of Medicine (if you have a good arm) is the Stanford School of Engineering. The latter school accepts students after they have completed two years as undifferentiated Stanford undergraduates. Prospective students of engineering are encouraged to take a wide variety of courses during their first two years at Stanford, but are also advised to make sure they are getting a good start toward engineering through courses in mathematics and science. At the beginning of their junior year the engineering students declare which of 17 fields they plan to specialize in. The fields range (alphabetically) from Aeronautics and Astronautics to Product Design and include such well-known specialties as Chemical, Civil, Electrical, and Mechanical Engineering.

Notice that the choice of specialization is made two years after high school graduation. I may have said that too rapidly. Let me repeat it. Two years after high school, engineering students at Stanford commit themselves to one of 17 specialties. At MIT students must choose their specialty at the end of their freshman year. The heavens do not fall. The SAT scores of the engineering students suggest that they are intellectually about equal to the Stanford medical students. The School of Engineering helps students learn about the various specialties by offering 20 seminars on different subjects with enrollment preference given to freshmen. Examples of seminar subjects are: "Bioengineering Materials to Heal the Body," "Digital Dilemmas," "Water, Public Health and Engineering," and "What Is Nanotechnology?". An additional 12 seminars are offered on other subjects with enrollment preference given to sophomores. Examples of their titles are: "Electric Automobiles and Aircraft," "Environmental Regulation and Policy," "Medical Device Innovation," and "The Flaw of Averages." These seminars provide an opportunity to work closely with faculty. In addition there are many one-unit seminars that provide exposure to key issues and current research in various fields. At the end of four years at Stanford, approximately 80 percent of the engineering students graduate with a bachelor's degree and enter the workforce to practice their specialty. Students who go on for a fifth year typically do so in order to earn a master's degree.

There are of course, many differences between engineering and medicine. Biologic systems are probably more complex than the systems engineers work with, and causal relations are less firmly established. An alleged difference is that physician decisions affect life and death, but the same could be said for many engineers. The men and women responsible for our bridges and tunnels, the design of our airplanes and cars, the safety of our water supply, and many similar functions are surely making decisions that affect life and death. One of the biggest differences is that engineers specialize from the start of their training; they are not expected to know about all aspects of engineering. They typically work in team settings. They are, to use Dr. Gawande's words, "pit crews" not "cowboys". Collectively, they get the job done. Perhaps the biggest difference is that when a medical student chooses a specialty, he or she is usually choosing a life-time occupation. For an engineering student, life-time occupation is not as closely linked to choice of specialty training. One reason for persistence by physicians in a certified specialty is that diminished competition affords the specialist the opportunity to earn a "monopoly rent."

Training Sub-Specialists

As an example of how specialty training in medicine does not have to take as many years as tradition demands, consider Dr. Robert Chase's experience in training plastic surgeons at Stanford. When he began his program, plastic surgery required completion of residency in general surgery followed by another residency program in plastic surgery. The combination took a minimum of seven years and more often eight or nine. Drawing on his experience as chief resident in general surgery at Yale, a two-year fellowship in plastic surgery at the University of Pittsburgh, and active duty in the Valley Forge Army hospital, Dr. Chase was pretty sure he could train plastic surgeons in no more than 6 years and often in four or five. To this end he developed an integrated program that started residents headed for plastic surgery side by side with residents headed for general surgery.

The idea was rejected by the American Board of Plastic Surgery, but he pursued it anyway. Fortunately, the first residents to complete the program did so well at both the written and oral examinations that the Board gave tentative approval to the program. Today there are 27 truly integrated programs similar to Stanford's, and another 62 that combine general and plastic surgery; only 27 of the traditional programs remain. It would be surprising if similar shortening could not be accomplished in other fields of medicine and surgery. What is required is an exceptional clinician-teacher who is willing to confront the established powers and prospective specialists who are willing to commit sooner to their specialty.

Arguments Against and Obstacles to Restructuring

Until now, medical education has proceeded under the premise that "Keeping one's options open" is a free good. It is not; and the costs to the individual and society increase every year. Those who set the rules and requirements must consider the possibility that what their generation had to endure may not be the best path for the future. Many of the existing rules and requirements seem to be based only on "tradition". The same academic physicians who would not prescribe a drug without determining efficacy and safety, have no hesitancy in prescribing the structure of medical education without any studies that examine the appropriateness of that structure relative to alternatives.

Changing the structure of medical education will not be easy, even for those who are enthusiastic about the goal. Opponents will be numerous, and the arguments varied. Many of the most popular ones are not persuasive. Consider the cliché, "If it ain't broke, don't fix it." The existing structure may not be "broke," but it provides the intellectual foundation for a medical care system that is causing the rest of the country to go broke. Some will say that my suggestions are "controversial." I agree. For more than fifty years I have observed and participated in attempts to reform college curricula, and I can tell you that reforms that are not controversial are inconsequential. Some will want to take credit for the gain in life expectancy of 8.4 years over the past half century. But other developed countries with different systems of medical education and medical care have achieved even greater gains and are at a higher level, while their per capita spending on medical care is 35 to 50 percent less.

Two possible objections to changes discussed in this lecture are that they threaten the deeply held (albeit antithetical) visions of the physician as scientist and the physician as humanist. The threats are real, but the visions are increasingly unreal. American medical education is at a cross-road: Shall it continue to strive to produce scientists-humanists or recognize that what society needs most at this time are competent professionals, capable of providing leadership and supervision for the more than 15 million individuals now employed in the delivery of health services. The challenge to the leaders of medical education is to figure out what kind of admission policy and what structure and content of medical education, undergraduate and post-graduate, will produce such professionals at a reasonable cost. It could be correctly argued that the cost of medical education is a relatively small part of the total cost of medical care, so why change medical education? The reason is that a restructured admission policy, earlier specialization, and shorter period of training can contribute to producing a different physician, one better suited for a team approach to remedying the cost, access, and quality problems now evident in American health care.

The obstacles to change will be partly external to the medical education establishment and partly internal. Consider, for example, the dense network of laws and regulations that now govern the practice of medicine. Some are federal, most are state, and often differ from one state to another. Those that are worth preserving should be federalized. These laws and regulations have been passed with the present structure of medical education in mind. Change in that structure will require changes in the existing legal framework. Many of the laws were enacted with the stated purpose of "patient protection", but as is true in so many industries, they often wind up giving providers protection from competition.

Consider also how malpractice attorneys will leap on health outcomes that fall short of ideal and try to tie these lapses to changes in medical education. We badly need a better system of dispute resolution to replace malpractice suits. Consider also, how large insurance companies and hospitals will resist change, not necessarily because the change would harm them in the long run, but because change is usually disruptive and costly in the short run.

Perhaps the biggest obstacle to change will be within the medical education establishment which includes not only the medical schools but also post-graduate training programs and the bodies that control certification for 152 specialities and sub-specialties. Are all these necessary? Restructuring will undoubtedly require some faculty to change what they do and some faculty may be redundant. Many specialty and sub-specialty boards will need to change their criteria, as in the case of plastic surgeons. In some areas it may be difficult at first to find medical educators well-equipped to meet the needs of students in the new structure. For instance, where will medical schools find instructors to train the students who have opted for the track of leaders of primary care teams?

Finally, there is the chicken or the egg problem. There are medical leaders who see the need for significant changes in the financing, organization, and delivery of care. But they feel stymied by the absence of physicians with the preparation and attitudes necessary to be most effective in the new systems of care. There are leaders in medical education who see the need for significant changes in structure and content, but wonder where the graduates of the new programs will find appropriate employment.

All these obstacles suggest that restructuring may be impossible. But I draw some hope from an observation made by Alexis de Toqueville who said, "The United States moves from the impossible to the inevitable without ever stopping at the probable."

This is the end of my jeremiad. If I have offended any in the audience, I apologize. That was not my intent. I have, for many decades, studied the American health care system, focusing on the high cost, the inequalities in access, and the lapses in quality of care. I concluded that these problems will not yield to piecemeal reforms. What is needed is comprehensive change in the financing, organization, and delivery of care.

But I have not paid much attention to medical education. Dr. Gawande's Harvard commencement address made me realize that reform of the health care system must be accompanied by a restructuring of medical education. Hence this lecture. Perhaps my suggestions for restructuring are off the mark. Some in this audience may have better ideas as to how it should proceed. If so, all to the good. If I have convinced you of the urgency of the task and stimulated you to address the problem, my effort will not have been in vain. I greatly appreciate the opportunity you have afforded me, and I thank you for your patience.

I await your questions with interest and a reasonable amount of apprehension.

7.4

Reflections on Economic Research and Public Policy John R. Commons Award Lecture, 2002

An early draft of the bylaws of the American Economic Association states that economists who have attained a certain age are entitled to present papers that begin "Reflections on —." The exact age is unclear because the manuscript is faded, but I have been assured by competent authorities that whatever that age is, I have surpassed it. The purpose of entitling a paper "Reflections on —" is to warn the audience not to expect either a comprehensive or a systematic treatment of the subject. "Reflections" seems preferable to its synonyms, "meditations" or "ruminations." The former is too "new age," while the latter suggests the chewing of cud.

I begin by noting that economists undertake research for a wide variety of reasons. Many wish to pursue a teaching career, but they know some publication is essential if employment is not to be temporary. At one time the median number of publications of economists after the dissertation was zero. By contrast, some

Originally published in *The American Economist*, 46(1): 3–9, Spring 2002. Copyright by Omicron Delta Epsilon.

economists make their living by doing research or supervising the research of others. Approximately one third of the members of the AEA (and a somewhat larger proportion of all professional economists) are not academics; they are employed in government, nonprofit organizations, or private industry. For many of them, the programmatic needs of their employers shape their research agenda.

Another significant motive for research is intellectual curiosity. Most economists like to solve puzzles. This may involve finding solutions to abstract problems or discovering significant patterns in data. Still another motive is the approval of one's peers. Paul Samuelson concluded his Presidential Address to the American Economic Association by saying, "In the long run, the economic scholar works for the only coin worth having — our own applause."[a] Finally, some economists undertake research because they want to influence public policy.

This taxonomy must be immediately qualified in three ways. First, the same economist may have different motives for different pieces of research. Secondly, even a single piece of research may be undertaken for more than one reason. Finally, even research that was not undertaken to influence public policy may have that as a result. With this as background, I come to the principle question of this paper, "Does economic research have a significant influence on public policy?" My answer is "more than you might think — but it's complicated."

To be candid, "more than you might think" is a bit of a fudge. What I really should say is "more than I thought when I started to write this paper." As an economist who has published many outstanding books and papers (so my wife tells me), I have frequently been frustrated by the slow pace at which policymakers embrace my ideas and put them into practice. I suspect that I am not the only economist with this feeling. A simple division of economists into two groups according to whether they think their *own* research has or has not had a significant influence on public policy would probably find the "has nots" in the majority. Frankly, in some cases this shows the good judgement of the policymakers, but that's another story.

One source of complication is the varying time lag between research and its effect on public policy. Some research affects policy almost immediately, while a half century or more may elapse before the influence of other research becomes evident. Also, some research has a direct, almost palpable effect on a particular policy, while other research has an indirect, albeit broader, effect. Additional

---

[a]Paul, Samuelson. "Economists and The History of Ideas." AEA Vol. LII, no. 1, March 1962, pg. 18.

complications arise in determining whether there is a firm causal chain between the research and the policy.

Some Examples from Public Finance

As a prime example of rapid direct effect, consider the paper by John Shoven and David Wise, "The Taxation of Pensions: A Shelter Can Become A Trap." Among other results, Shoven and Wise (1998) showed that the marginal tax rate on income in some sheltered retirement accounts was close to 100 percent.[b] This paper, published in *1998*, is given credit for tax reforms incorporated in the *Taxpayer Relief Act of 1997*. Talk about rapid impact! The explanation lies in the prior dissemination of the Shoven-Wise results in Stanford and NBER Working Papers in the fall of 1996, and the attention given their results by several prominent journalists. Also worth noting is that the Shoven-Wise analysis and its policy implications fit perfectly with Senator Phil Gramm's priors, and he was the major force in pushing the new legislation through Congress.

Another example of research that plausibly had a prompt effect on public policy is the project on taxation of income from capital suggested by Martin Feldstein in 1979 and carried out under the auspices of the NBER (Cambridge, Mass.), the Institute für Wirtschaftsforschung (IFO, Munich), and the Industriens Utrednings Institut (IUI, Stockholm). Teams of researchers in the United Kingdom, Sweden, West Germany, and the United States, in a closely coordinated series of studies, determined the effective rates in each country on 81 types of investment projects that varied by industry, type of asset, source of finance, and ownership category.[c] The authors concluded that within each country effective tax rates varied enormously across projects, and that greater uniformity would contribute to economic efficiency. The tax reforms of the 1980s in the U.S. moved the effective rates in the direction suggested by the research.[d]

For an example of public finance research that influenced public policy only after a long lag, consider the work of Joseph Pechman. In the 1950s, while Pechman was on the staff of the Council of Economic Advisors in the Eisenhower Administration, he calculated that a revenue neutral increase in the income tax base and a decrease in marginal rates could greatly improve economic efficiency.

---

[b]John B. Shoven, and David A. Wise, "The Taxation of Pensions: A Shelter Can Become A Trap," *Frontiers in the Economics of Aging*, ed. David A. Wise, University of Chicago Press, 1998.
[c]*The Taxation of Income From Capital*, Mervyn A. King and Don Fullerton, eds., The University of Chicago Press (an NBER monograph), Chicago, 1984.
[d]Alan Auerbach, "The Tax Reform Act of 1986 and The Cost of Capital," *Journal of Economic Perspectives*, Summer 1987, pp. 73–86.

Pechman convinced a fellow staff member,[19] who later tried to sell the idea to Richard Nixon and, with more success, Ronald Reagan.[e]

In the meantime, Pechman and his colleagues at the Brookings Institution (e.g., Refs. 2 and 16) were developing these ideas further in the 1960s and 1970s.[f] They were finally implemented in the tax reforms of the 1980s. One aspect of Pechman's work that helped make reductions in marginal tax rates more acceptable to political liberals was his finding that the so-called progressivity of the tax schedule was largely illusory. Over a wide range of total income, the sum of all taxes actually paid tended to be proportional to income as a result of tax avoidance by higher income individuals.

Some Giants of Economic Thought

To explore the theme that economic research has had significant influence, but sometimes only with a long lag, let us consider a few of the major figures in the history of economic thought. There is no doubt that the 18th century economist who had the most influence on public policy was Adam Smith — but not right away. *The Wealth of Nations*, published in 1776, was an immediate critical success, but when Smith died in 1790, his influence on public policy was still negligible. Forty years later the ideas of Smith and his successors in classical economics dominated public policy in England, and even made significant inroads on the European continent and in North America. Indeed, his ideas about government's proper role in the economy resonate in the U.S. and many other countries more than two centuries after his research.

Among 19th century economists, no one had as much influence on public policy as Karl Marx. But the time lag between his research and its major application to policy was as long or longer than that of Smith. *Das Kapital* (Vol. I) published in 1867, may have had some influence on political reforms in subsequent decades, but communism did not take hold until well into the 20th century.

Among 20th century economists, two have been particularly influential on policy — John Maynard Keynes and Milton Friedman. Keynes lived for only ten years after the publication of *The General Theory of Employment, Interest, and Money* (1936), just long enough to see his ideas for international finance

---

[e]George Shultz, "Economics in Action: Ideas, Institutions, Policies," *American Economic Review*, Vol. 85, Issue 2, Papers and Proceedings of the Hundred and Seventy Annual Meeting of the American Economic Association, Washington, D.C., Jan. 6–8, 1995 (May 1995) pp. 1–8.

[f]See, for example, Joseph A. Pechman, *Federal Tax Policy*, 1966, and George F. Break and Joseph A. Pechman, *Federal Tax Reform, The Impossible Dream?* 1975.

embodied in plans for the International Monetary Fund, but not long enough to see his theory used to justify the Kennedy tax cut of 1961, Richard Nixon's subsequent announcement that "We are all Keynesians now" would probably have amused him, but the misuse of his ideas by the George W. Bush Administration to justify tax cuts for high income individuals would have invoked sardonic laughter. In 1936, Keynes' recommendation of deficit spending to deal with recession or depression was denounced by most "right thinking" economists and policy analysts, but it eventually became the conventional wisdom of public policy. Policymakers have been much slower to accept the other half of the Keynesian formula, namely that the government should run a budget surplus in prosperous times.

Milton Friedman, despite his great scholarly and popular successes[g] spent many years in the public policy wilderness. His long life, however, has enabled him to see widespread embrace of many of his ideas, such as floating exchange rates. Silk (1976), in a generally critical essay on Friedman wrote, "The collapse of the postwar Bretton Woods international monetary system did not lead to a collapse of the world economy (as had happened in 1931) thanks to the intellectual groundwork that had been laid, in large measure by Friedman, for acceptance of floating rates."[h]

Friedman's research on the importance of money for macroeconomic policy is now the dominant paradigm in the U.S. and other countries. His triumph is not complete, however; few policymakers have followed his recommendation to maintain a steady growth of the money supply and to abolish central banks.

I chose Keynes and Friedman for special mention because this paper focuses on economists whose research has had particularly strong influence on *public policy*. If the focus were on economists whose research had great influence on *economics*, Keynes and Friedman would still qualify, but the work of other 20th century scholars such as Arrow, Fisher, Hicks, Samuelson, Tinbergen and Wicksell would also have to be considered.

I also exclude economists whose ideas have had significant influence on public policy, but the connection between their influence and their research is not obvious. For example, Friedrich Hayek's book, *The Road to Serfdom* (1945), had great influence on policymakers decades later, especially in England during

---

[g]For example, *A Theory of The Consumption Function* (1957), Capitalism and Freedom (1962), *A Monetary History of the United States, 1867–1960* (with Anna Schwartz, 1963), *Free To Choose* (with Rose Friedman, 1980).

[h]Leonard Silk, *The Economists*, New York: Basic Books, 1976, First Discus Printing, January 1978, pp. 76–77.

the period when Margaret Thatcher dominated British politics. But the connection between that book and Hayek's research on the intertemporal structure of capital, monetary theory, or the price system, is weak. Indeed, *The Road to Serfdom* is not even mentioned in a long article on Hayek in the *New Palgrave Dictionary of Economics* (1987). By contrast, an article on Keynes that did not mention *The General Theory*... or one on Friedman that did not mention *A Monetary History*... is inconceivable.

Because this paper is concerned with the influence of economic research on *public* policy, I mention only in passing that some research has had a significant effect on *private* policies. The financial world is rich in examples of private decision makers drawing on the work of economists, including some who are Nobel laureates, e.g., Robert Merton, Myron Scholes, William Sharpe. In the health field, Alain Enthoven's many papers and books on managed competition have influenced private health insurance and health care markets. Research by economists showing negligible marginal benefits from long hospital stays (plus the desire to slow the growth of expenditures) has led to sharp reductions in the average length of stay.

Two Underestimated Contributions of Research to Public Policy

The impact of Smith, Marx, Keynes and Friedman on public policy is relatively easy to see and understand. Their analyses are original and bold, their expositional skills exceptional, and their policy views unequivocal.[i] There are, however, two other kinds of research, often carried out by relatively unknown economists, that also influence public policy. I call them "laying foundations" and "playing defense."

Foundation laying usually depends on teams of researchers patiently building measures of economic activity which, over the long haul, have a large, albeit indirect effect on public policy. Consider, for instance, the role played by the National Income Accounts in the day-to-day and year-to-year decisions about economic policy. The availability of reasonably accurate information on levels and changes in investment, consumption, personal income, and other key indicators of economic activity, creates a framework within which policy makers must maneuver, and helps to shape their ultimate choices.

---

[i]Coincidentally, or maybe not, all four masterpieces were published by authors at age 51, plus or minus a year or two.

These accounts did not come down to us from heaven; they are the result of long, hard work by many economic researchers. The very first project undertaken by the National Bureau of Economic Research was to estimate the national income of the United States.[j] Two teams of researchers worked independently, one trying to measure the value of final output and the other trying to measure the income received by the factors of production. You can imagine how great was their joy when their final results proved to be within shouting distance of one another. Subsequent work by Simon Kuznets in collaboration with colleagues at the National Bureau and the US Department of Commerce helped to refine the methodology and bring the accounts to their present, imperfect but extremely valuable state.

Another example of foundation laying is the business cycle research principally associated with Wesley Mitchell, Arthur Burns, Geoffrey Moore, and their colleagues at the NBER. Their detailed measurement and exposition of patterns of cyclical fluctuations and their approach to dating the peaks and troughs of economic activity continue to shape current policy discussions and actions. Indeed, an NBER committee is the quasi-official "umpire" to decide when a recession begins and when it ends. The committee's "calls" don't determine policy directly, but they do play an important indirect role.

Foundation laying is a long, slow process which has its impact indirectly and often far in the future. "Playing defense" is just the opposite. It must be done quickly, and if successful, affects public policy almost immediately. Ask a random sample of former members of the President's Council of Economic Advisers about major accomplishments during their tenure, and the great majority of them will tell you about the *bad policies they kept from being enacted*, A good example is the killing of a 1960's proposal that the U.S. subsidize the building of a supersonic airplane. England and France went ahead with this project, much to their regret. Just the knowledge that a new dam will have to meet a cost-benefit test or a change in the tax laws will be "scored" by the Congressional Budget Office is often enough to keep many unsound projects from being proposed. Research that either explicitly or implicitly stops bad policy can be just as valuable as research that stimulates good policy.

---

[j]Wesley C. Mitchell, Willford I. King, Frederick R. Macaulay, and Oswald W. Knauth, *Income in the United States: Its Amount and Distribution. 1909–1919*, Vol. 1 Summary, Harcourt, Brace, and Co., 1921.

Disagreement and Agreement Among Economists

If I am correct that economic research can, and sometimes does, have a significant influence on public policy, we might ask why this doesn't happen more often? One possibility is that most economists don't communicate well to other audiences. It may be only a slight exaggeration to say that there are three grades of writing: good, bad, and economics. Probably more important than weakness in exposition, however, is disagreement among economists about policy proposals. Consider the following survey results. Experts in labor economics and public finance at the forty leading American economics departments were asked their opinions regarding thirteen well-defined policy proposals (e.g., increase the federal gasoline excise tax by 25 cents per gallon). Their responses were marked on a continuous scale from zero for "strongly oppose" to 100 for "strongly favor." The median difference between the 25th and the 75th percentile responses was 44, almost half of the entire range of possible responses.[k] Their policy positions were much better explained by their answers to questions about values than by their estimates of relevant parameters (e.g., labor demand and supply elasticities), which tended to vary all over the map. With widespread disagreement among experts regarding parameters, values, and policy recommendations, the failure of much economic research to influence public policy is readily understandable. But President Truman missed the point when he begged for a "one-armed" economist. The problem is not so much that economists are "two-handed" as it is that so many are "lefties" or "righties."

Even when economists agree, however, their conclusions are often ignored by policymakers. Foreign trade policy provides a notorious example. Economists have long been virtually unanimous in their support of free trade but the U.S. pursued protection for many decades. Moreover, the reversal of policy in recent times owes more to a change in how the business community perceives its interests than to any new economic research. U.S. agricultural policy has been an economic disaster for decades. The same is true for water policy in California where urban consumers are urged or forced to conserve water while four-fifths of the available supply is diverted to agriculture at heavily subsidized prices.

Health care is another area where policy makers in both parties routinely ignore the results of economic research. For example, consider the ill-fated efforts of the Clinton Administration at health care reform in 1993–94. According to

---

[k] Victor R. Fuchs, Alan B. Krueger, and James M. Poterba, "Economists' Views About Parameters, Values, and Policies: Survey Results in Labor and Public Economics," *Journal of Economic Literature*, 36:1387–1425m September 1998.

the Clintons, the rapid increase in medical expenditures was largely the result of rising prices, especially drug prices and physician incomes. They ignored the fact that the great majority (80 percent) of the leading health economists in the U.S. believed that *new medical technology* was the primary cause of rising expenditures.[1] The Clintons obviously preferred denouncing rich physicians and greedy drug companies to dealing with the thorny question of technology.

Similarly, the Clintons tried to sell universal coverage on the dubious grounds that this was the best way to improve the health of the population. They ignored a substantial body of economic research that identified cigarette smoking, diet, exercise, and other personal behaviors as the major determinants of health at any given time.[m] Indeed, the Rand Health Insurance Experiment found very few health effects across individuals who had been randomly assigned to different health insurance coverage.

But not all research by health economists has been ignored by policymakers. The Rand Health Insurance Experiment convinced many doubters that the demand was not completely inelastic with respect to price.[n] The conclusion of many economists that the traditional methods of reimbursing hospitals and physicians were inefficient and inequitable helped spark policy innovations such as Medicare's DRG (Diagnosis Related Groups) system for hospitals and the RBRVS (Resource Based Relative Value Scale) system for physician services. The move toward capitation reimbursement in Medicare and Medicaid was also inspired in large part by economic research, as was the repeal of ineffective certificate of need legislation.

The Thorny Question of Causality

My assertion that research by Smith, Marx, Keynes, and Friedman had significant effects on public policy is open to question. How tight was the link between the research of these giants of economic thought and subsequent public policy? Isn't it possible that the policy changes would have emerged anyway as a result of economic, political, demographic, and technologic forces that were mostly independent of economic research? For example, the growing importance of the industrial class in England in the first quarter of the 19th century might have led to

---

[1] Victor R. Fuchs, "Economics, Values, and Health Care Reform," *AEA*, Vol. 86, No. I, March 1996, pp. 1–24.

[m] Victor R. Fuchs, *Who Shall Live? Health, Economics, and Social Choice*, (1974) expanded edition, World Scientific Publishing Co., 1998.

[n] Joseph, P. Newhouse, *Free For All? Lessons From The RAND Health Insurance Experiment*, Cambridge, Mass: Harvard University Press, 1993.

legislation creating relatively free markets for labor, goods, and money even if *The Wealth of Nations* had never been published. Similarly, the abrupt end to Tsarist rule in Russia and the chaos following World War I might have led to soviet-style centralized control of economic and political life even if Marx had not written a single word. Perhaps Keynes was claiming too much when he wrote, "... the ideas of economists and political philosophers, both when they are right and when they are wrong, are more powerful than is commonly understood. Indeed, the world is ruled by little else. Practical men who believe themselves to be quite exempt from any intellectual influences, are usually the slaves of some defunct economist. Madmen in authority, who hear voices in the air, are distilling their frenzy from some academic scribbler of a few years back.[o] Of course, Keynes was himself "an academic scribbler."

For an anti-Keynes perspective on this issue, I turn naturally to the University of Chicago. In the 1960s, George Stigler and his colleagues initiated a significant stream of research on the effects of regulation. They concluded that the stated goals of regulation were usually not achieved and that the legislation frequently protected suppliers, hurt consumers, and contributed to economic inefficiency. Their research was followed by a major deregulation movement that swept through the federal government in the 1970s and 1980s, virtually independent of whether Democrats or Republicans were in power.

Many observers, myself included, believe that Stigler's research deserves considerable credit for the deregulation of airlines, financial institutions, trucking and other industries. It seems, however, that Stigler himself had doubts that this was the case. A recent paper by Claire Friedland (Stigler's long-time assistant and collaborator) notes that in two papers given in the late 1980s, Stigler suggested that changes in public policy can best be understood as responses to changing circumstances, not to ideas or opinions.[p] Drawing on the work of Gregg A. Jarrell,[q] Stigler concluded that deregulation of financial markets resulted from the growing importance of institutional investors and the growth of competition from non-bank banks. According to Friedland, "He [Stigler] found changing economic conditions a sufficient explanation without recourse to 'a revulsion against regulation'."[r]

---

[o] John Maynard Keynes, *The General Theory of Employment, Interest and Money*, Harcourt, Brace and Company, New York, 1936, p. 383.

[p] George, J. Stigler, "The Regularities of Regulation," Presidential Address, David Hume Institute (Edinburgh) May 1, 1986, Hume Occasional Paper No. 3, 1989.

[q] Gregg, A. Jarrell, "A Change At The Exchange: The Causes and Effects of Deregulation," *The Journal of Law and Economics*, XXVII(2) Oct 1984, pp. 273–312.

[r] Claire Friedland, "Stigler and The Theory of Economic Policy: Travels on the Ship of State," *American Journal of Economics and Sociology*, forthcoming 2002.

Still another point of view was provided by Max Weber, the German economist and sociologist whose writings on the connection between religion and economic life have influenced several generations of social scientists. "Not ideas," wrote Weber in 1915, "but material and ideal interests, directly govern men's conduct. Yet very frequently, the 'world images' that have been created by 'ideas' have, like switchmen, determined the tracks along which action has been pushed by the dynamic of interests."[8]

Conclusion

This brief set of reflections leaves me with a few tentative conclusions. First, there is no reason to expect economic research, no matter how well carried out, to always have a quick, direct effect on public policy. Sometimes research works in mysterious ways. It may affect policy only after a long lag. Or it may affect policy indirectly, as when it lays a foundation for subsequent policy or when it keeps unsound policies from being enacted or even proposed.

Secondly, it is unreasonable to expect research to influence policy when the leading experts in the field are in sharp disagreement over the relevant economic parameters as well as the policies themselves. The latter disagreement could result from differences in values, but the former could be resolved with better models, better data, and better analyses.

Finally, with respect to the question of causality, there may be some merit in both the Keynesian and Stiglerian positions but I find Weber's view the most convincing. Research by itself, in the absence of interests, is not likely to carry the day. Like most things in life, there is a "market for messages." For research to have an impact on policy, it is necessary, but not sufficient, that it find someone or some group that has a demand for its message. This is not to say that researchers should tailor their results to the preferences of the moment. Immediate acceptance should not be the goal of serious researchers. Over time, however, high quality research can change the tenor and terms of policy debates, provide new language for discussing policy issues, and yield empirical results that help tip the balance one way or the other.

References

1. Auerbach, A. (1987). "The Tax Reform Act of 1986 and The Cost of Capital." *Journal of Economic Perspectives* **Summer**: 73–86.

---

[8]Max Weber, "The Social Psychology of World Religions (1915)," in *From Max Weber: Essays in Sociology*, edited by H.H. Gerth and C. Wright Mills, Oxford University Press, 1946, p. 280.

2. Break, G. F. and Pechman, J. A. (1975), *Federal Tax Reform, The Impossible Dream?* Brookings Institution: Washington D.C.

3. Friedland, C. (2002). "Stigler and Theory of Economic Policy: Travels on the Ship of State." *American Journal of Economic and Sociology* (forthcoming).

4. Friedman, M. (1957). *A Theory of The Consumption Function.* Princeton Univeristy Press: Princeton, NJ.

5. Friedman, M. (1962). *Capitalism and Freedom.* University of Chicago Press: Chicago, IL.

6. Friedman, M. and Friedman, R. (1980). *Free to Choose.* Harcourt Brace: New York, NY.

7. Friedman, M. and Schwartz, A. (1963). *A Monetary History of the United States, 1967–1960.* Princeton University Press: Princeton, NJ.

8. Fuchs, V. R. (1974). *Who Shall Live? Health Economics, and Social Choice.* Basic Books: New York, NY. Expanded edition: World Scientific Publishing Company: Singapore, 1998.

9. Fuchs, V. R. (1996). "Economics Values, and Health Care Reform." *American Economic Review* **86**(March): 1–24.

10. Fuchs, V. R. Krueger A. B., and Poterba, J. M. (1998). "Economists' Views About Parameters, Values, and Policies: Survey Results in Labor and Public Economics." *Journal of Economic Literature* **36**(September): 387–425.

11. Jarrell, G. A. (1984). "A Change At The Exchange: The Causes and Effects of Deregulation." *The Journal of Law and Economics* **XXVII**(October): 273–312.

12. Keynes, J. M. (1936). *The General Theory of Employment, Interest and Money.* Harcourt, Brace and Company: New York.

13. King, M. A. and Fullerton, D. eds. (1984). *The Taxation of Income From Capital.* University of Chicago Press: Chicago, IL (an NBER monograph).

14. Mitchell, W. C., King, W. I., Macaulay, F. R. and Knauth, O. W. (1921). *Income in the United States: Its Amount and Distribution, 1909–1919*, Vol. 1: Summary. Harcourt, Brace, and Company: New York, NY.

15. Newhouse, J. P. (1993). *Free For All? Lessons From The RAND Health Insurance Experiment.* Harvard University Press: Cambridge, MA.

16. Pechman, J. A. (1966). *Federal Tax Policy.* Brookings Institution: Washington, D.C.

17. Samuelson, P. (1962). "Economists and The History of Ideas." *American Economic Review* **LII**(March): 18.

18. Shoven, J. B. and Wise, D. A. (1998). "The Taxation of Pensions: A Shelter Can Become A Trap." In *Frontiers in the Economics of Aging*, D. A. Wise, ed. University of Chicago Press: Chicago IL.

19. Shultz, G. (1995). "Economics in Action: Ideas, Institutions, Policies." *American Economics Review* **85**(May): 1–8.

20. Silk, L. (1976). *The Economists.* Basic Books: New York (First Discus Printing, 1978), pp. 76–77.

21. Stigler, G. J. (1989). "The Regularities of Regulation." Presidental Address David Hume Institute (Edinburgh), May 1 1986, Hume Occasional Paper No. 3.

22. Weber, M. (1915). "The Social Psychology of World Religions." In *From Max Weber: Essays in Sociology.* H. H. Gerth and C. Wright Mills, eds. Oxford University Press: Oxford.

Op-Ed

Health Reform: Getting The Essentials Right

By addressing the essentials — coverage, cost control, coordinated care, and choice — policymakers can take important first steps toward health system reform, with details to be worked out along the way.

As the ninety-year history and failure of health care reform illustrates, it is easy for policymakers to disagree about the details of any new plan. In this Perspective, the author suggests trying a new approach this time: enacting a plan that encompasses four essential principles and then making midcourse adjustments later to get the details right. He defines the essentials as the Four Cs: coverage, cost control, coordinated care, and choice.

A common phrase states that "the devil is in the details." Many groups claiming to support health reform use this phrase when they wish to conceal opposition to substantive change — or establish their expertise in some small facet of reform. Doubtless, details are important. But as the debate proceeds, Congress and the incoming Obama administration must remember that "God is in the essentials." Without the essentials, no reform plan can succeed. What are the essentials? They are coverage, cost control, coordinated care, and choice — the "Four Cs."

Originally published in *Health Affairs*, 28(2):W180-W183, January 2009. Copyright by Project HOPE, The People-to-People Health Foundation, Inc.

The Four Cs

Coverage. First, truly universal coverage — 100 percent of Americans — is essential. Pressure will intensify to settle for increasing coverage for one group or another. "Cutting the number of uninsured people by half" will be hailed as a great victory for reform. But leaving millions of Americans without coverage is not only unfair, it is also inefficient. The remaining uninsured people will still get some care, albeit haphazard and uncoordinated, and their care will still be paid for by the insured or providers.

Furthermore, Americans left out of the insurance pool are likely to belong to two groups: low-wage workers and healthy people in their twenties. It is unfair to leave out of the social compact Americans who work hard and pay taxes. Young, healthy Americans should not become habituated to being free riders. To demand that insurance companies guarantee issue and not exclude pre-existing conditions requires that everyone be in the insurance pool — including the young and healthy, who are cheap to cover.

Universal coverage can actually result in lower total spending because it can eliminate the high administrative costs that are now necessary to determine who is eligible for coverage and who isn't. Also, universal coverage facilitates the possibility of cost-saving changes in the organization and delivery of care.

Cost control. Politically, cost control is necessary because insured Americans will be more likely to support reform if it moderates the burdensome growth in their premiums and deductibles. It is also necessary because, as the Massachusetts experiment seems to be demonstrating, failure to control costs makes coverage gains unsustainable.

Coordinated care. Coordinated care is essential for both improvement in quality and elimination of unnecessary costs. Coordination requires some reform in how physicians, hospitals, and the entire health care system get paid and deliver care. This is especially true for management of chronic illnesses, which account for 75 percent of all health care spending.[a] Coordination produces wins in two areas: quality and cost. It can curb the excessive use of expensive high-technology interventions that are used inappropriately to produce little or no health improvement. Coordination that improves care for diabetes, congestive heart failure, emphysema, and other chronic conditions also can reduce or eliminate avoidable hospitalizations.

---

[a]Centers for Disease Control and Prevention, "Chronic Disease Prevention and Health Promotion — Chronic Disease Overview," 20 November 2008, http://www.cdc.gov/nccdphp/overview.htm

Choice. Finally, choice is a fundamental American value, and choice of insurance plans as well as networks of physicians and hospitals is essential for successful reform. Perceived restrictions on patient choice were used effectively in the "Harry and Louise" ads of the 1990s to help rally opposition to the Clinton reform proposal. Furthermore, for the many Americans who now have no choice of plans or providers, expanding choice could be an in centive to support reform.

How to Achieve the Goals

When we think of reform, we must think of what Congress can embody in legislation. But laws can't always mandate that these objectives will be achieved. For instance, Congress cannot mandate that physicians coordinate care with hospitals and other providers. Legislation can, however, change the incentives, infrastructure, and information systems to move providers toward greater coordination.

Let's examine how the Four Cs should be dealt with, one by one.

Coverage. There are two reasons why people don't have health insurance: They are unable to acquire it, or they are unwilling to do so. The first group (about three-quarters of all uninsured people) are too poor or too sick to get insurance without financial assistance.[b] The unwilling include young, healthy people who think they can do without coverage and others who "ride free" in the expectation that if they run up large medical bills, the system will take care of them.

The essentials for universal coverage, therefore, are subsidies for those who cannot acquire insurance on their own and requirements for those who are unwilling to do so. There are several methods for achieving these goals. For example, a combination of individual and employer mandates combined with generous subsidies will come close, as the Massachusetts plan is demonstrating. A single-payer "Medicare for All" approach will also do it, as demonstrated by the current Medicare program for those age sixty-five and older. And a universal voucher approach leaving people free to choose among competing health plans will also work, as demonstrated by the current Dutch and Israeli health care systems. Selecting among these methods should be based primarily on their ability to control costs and improve coordination of care.

Cost control. There is no single "magic bullet" for cost control. Multiple forces will have to pull in the same direction to restrain cost increases.

---

[b]P. Fronstin, "Sources of Health Insurance and Characteristics of the Uninsured: Analysis of the March 2008 Current Population Survey," EBRI Issue Brief no. 321, September 2008, http://www.ebri.org/pdf/briefspdf/EBRI_IB_09a-2008.pdf (accessed 6 January 2009).

Entitlements and budgets. One of the essential means is to eliminate open-ended entitlements and create a defined budget for government-funded health programs. Such a budget will provide a strong incentive for insurers and health care providers to focus on high-value interventions and redesign delivery systems to improve efficiency and quality.

Technology/outcomes assessment. According to multiple studies, including most recently those of the Congressional Budget Office, development and diffusion of new technologies drive increases in medical care costs.[c] There is growing agreement that the nation needs some kind of comparative assessment process and increasing likelihood that this will soon be enacted. Such assessments are essential to inform both coverage decisions by health plans and treatment decisions by physicians. Most importantly, these assessments will signal drug and device manufacturers and procedure-oriented providers that interventions will be evaluated for coverage and payment based on effectiveness and cost. Today, pharmaceutical and other companies can charge top dollar for interventions that offer few improvements in quality of life and little additional survival.

Of equal importance is systematic outcomes assessment. Technology assessments typically rely on data from clinical trials with highly selected patients, but they cannot give an accurate picture on how tests and treatments work in "real life," where they are used in combination with other tests and treatments for patients with multiple chronic conditions. A health information superhighway is an essential piece of outcomes assessment, and it seems to be part of President-elect Obama's recovery plan. This infrastructure should be deployed in conjunction with a plan for the systematic collection of data. Combining information from medical records with information on drug usage, laboratory results, and payments can create a "real-time" national database on patient outcomes, the use of services, costs, and the use of technologies in the "real world." This database should be open to all researchers who promise to publicly disseminate their methods and results. The data would facilitate pay-for-performance (P4P) and other methods for holding both insurers and providers accountable for the quality, cost, and efficiency of care.

Payment reform. We know the worst way to pay health care providers: fee-for-service. That is what we mostly do today. We do not know the best

---

[c] See, for example, Congressional Budget Office, "Technological Change and the Growth of Health Care Spending," January 2008, http://www.cbo.gov/ftpdocs/89xx/doc8947/01-31-TechHealth.pdf (accessed 6 January 2009); and Peter Orszag, CBO, "The Long-Term Budget Outlook and Options for Slowing the Growth of Health Care Costs," Testimony before the Senate Finance Committee, 17 June 2008, http://www.cbo.gov/fcpdocs/93xx/doc9385/06-17-LTBO_Testimony.pdf (accessed 6 January 2009).

way to pay. And there probably is not a single best way. Hence, we need experimentation and innovation in payment, whether more P4P with bonuses for good performance, bundled payments, or partial or full capitation. To control costs, it is essential that payers have the freedom to experiment in rewarding value rather than volume.

Competition. If insurers have to provide a standard benefit package with guaranteed issue and no pre-existing disease exclusions, receive risk-adjusted premiums, and have their outcomes monitored, they will have a strong incentive to change their business model from excluding sick patients to actually managing care for efficiency and value. This is how competition can work to control costs.

Sensitivity to cost and value. One way to make the public more sensitive to the cost and value of medical services is for people who want more services of small marginal value to pay with their own after-tax dollars for coverage that is above the standard benefit package. For example, wider selection of physicians or hospitals should require a supplemental fee. A complementary approach is using value-based insurance so that patients face higher copayments for more expensive services when cheaper interventions are just as effective, or when the indications for the tests or treatments are more tenuous.

There is no guarantee that these measures working together will restrain costs, but they have a better chance than any other approach — especially efforts to simply lower unit reimbursement to providers.

Coordinated care. The health care system is a fragmented, nineteenth-century cottage industry in which fee-for-service payment inhibits coordination. Payment reform that rewards coordination and patient outcomes should improve care. Similarly, a national database for outcomes assessment would provide data to rapidly refine guidelines and transform them into physician reminders and templates for ordering tests and treatments. Such a database would also help identify which providers are achieving good patient outcomes and how they are doing it.

Perhaps most important, legal and regulatory reform is essential. There are a myriad of laws that inhibit the financial and administrative relationships among providers that are essential to clinical coordination. For instance, "Stark II" self-referral prohibitions and the federal antikickback laws are meant to ensure that patient care decisions are based on medical need, not providers' financial interest. These rules are overly broad. While prohibiting self-enrichment, they also inhibit using financial incentives to facilitate the collaboration between physicians and other medical providers that improves coordinated care for patients with chronic conditions. They need to be amended, and safe harbors more uniformly defined, to permit closer financial, administrative, and clinical relationships between physicians and hospitals. As suggested by Timothy Jost and Ezekiel Emanuel, establishing a Commission for Innovation in Delivery Systems in the federal government to provide rapid "one-stop" review and authorization of proposals for new payment and delivery system arrangements could facilitate essential innovation.[d] Antitrust and tax laws also need reform to permit combinations that facilitate the coordination of care.

Obviously, there needs to be oversight to ensure that these links improve the quality of care, rather than merely serving as a cover for provider enrichment. Similarly, reform of scope-of-practice laws is essential to permit the more-flexible use of advanced practice nurses and other health care professionals, especially in the primary care setting.

Many providers also want tort reform. Although that would probably not have a significant impact on health care delivery or cost control, it is highly desired by physicians and would be helpful in securing their support for a far broader reform plan.

Choice. Choice is a desirable feature of any reform proposal. The public values choice as a good thing in itself because it confers a sense of power and control. Also, choice is essential to control costs through competition. But too much choice can be counterproductive in health. If the range of choice in insurance is unlimited, insurance companies can manipulate differences in an attempt to cherry-pick. To maintain equity and avoid adverse selection, some limits on choice are necessary. With regard to the organization and delivery of care, some restrictions on choice may be necessary in the interest of quality and cost. For example, "any willing provider" laws can inhibit the formation of efficient medical groups.

Anything that substantially changes 16 percent of U.S. gross domestic product will necessarily be complex. It is easy to disagree about the details of any plan. Failure because of such disagreements is always the easiest course, as the ninety-year history of health reform has demonstrated. But policymakers should keep the focus on the essential objectives and means. They must recognize also that reform of anything as complex as health care will not be perfect the first time. Unintended consequences will occur, and intended consequences will fail.

---

[d]T.S. Jost and E.J. Emanuel, "Legal Reforms Necessary to Promote Delivery System Innovation," *Journal of the American Medical Association* 299, no. 21 (2008): 2561–2563.

Enactment of the essentials with a flexible framework that permits easy midcourse corrections and adjustments can, by successive approximation, get the details right.

The author acknowledges the substantial contribution of Ezekiel Emanuel in writing this Perspective.

Op-Ed

The Transformation of American Physicians

The current transformation of physicians in the United States — from self-employment to salaried employment, from fee-for-service to "bundled" or capitation payment, from providing acute care to providing chronic care, from inpatient to ambulatory settings, and from solo or small group practice to "team care" — complicates the future of the medical profession.

The current transformation was preceded by 2 other major changes for US physicians. An early transformation, usually associated with the 1910 Flexner Report, began around 1900 by the Johns Hopkins School of Medicine and the activities of the American Medical Association.[1] Criteria for admission to medical schools were raised, length of training increased, and standards for faculty were tightened. These innovations, plus stricter licensure laws, resulted in a decline in the number of physicians per 1000 population from 173 in 1900 to 125 in 1930. Hamilton summarized the results of the transformation in 1932, reporting that "An ancient and honorable *craft* had become a *profession*: the profession has lived on into an epoch in which it has had... to respond to the incentives of *business* [emphases added]."[2]

Originally published in *JAMA*, 313(18):1821–1822, May 2015. Copyright by American Medical Association. Written with Mark Cullen, M.D.

Medical practice became more of a business, but not a particularly lucrative one. Thomas[3] wrote that his general practitioner father in Flushing, Long Island, worked long hours for a modest income and noted that his father's black bag "contained nothing but morphine and magic." Doing well by doing good was not a realistic option for most physicians until after World War II.

Preservation of the long-term societal trust of physicians and the special role physicians have in society maybe at stake.

After that war a new transformation, powered by scientific advances, technologic innovations, specialization of practice, health insurance, and a booming postwar economy, created what some have termed a "golden age" of medicine. Between 1950 and 1990 physicians became both more professional and more entrepreneurial. They provided (and sometimes owned) expensive diagnostic and therapeutic technologies. A vast expansion of employer-sponsored health insurance and, after 1965, Medicare and Medicaid, made care seem, to the patient, largely free. Expensive interventions sparked a demand for health insurance to pay for them, and the expansion of insurance fueled the demand for ever more expensive interventions.[4] Health care expenditures per capita, adjusted for inflation, increased at 4.8% per annum between 1950 and 1990.[5] Real gross domestic product (GDP) per capita increased only 2.3% per annum. A gap of this magnitude was not sustainable.

In the early 1990s private and public payers of care responded with managed care. This marked the beginning of the most recent transformation, obscured temporarily by substantial objections later in the decade. However, soaring health care costs induced substantial concern throughout the economy, including their effect on the federal budget deficit; the desire to curb expenditure growth became paramount. Recently, the growth in health care expenditures has slowed, both absolutely and relative to GDP. From 1990 to 2013 the rate of increase of health care expenditures per capita, adjusted for inflation, declined to 3.1% per annum.[5] This is partly explained by the slower growth of real GDP per capita of 1.6% per annum and partly by changes in medical care markets; the Affordable Care Act may have played a role.

The causes of the substantial shifts in medical practice in recent years are reasonably clear, but the consequences for the medical profession less so. Most physicians and many thoughtful nonphysicians wonder whether the change from self-employed practitioners to salaried employees will adversely affect the professionalism of physicians. Preservation of the long-term societal trust of physicians and the special role physicians have in society may be at stake.

Physicians might become less professional, but their professional role could increase as their entrepreneurial role decreases. Several European health care systems (eg, Sweden) function at a high level, with no evidence that salaried physicians are less professional than their counterparts in the United States. Arguably the professionalism of the patient-physician relationship depends on the extent to which, using Boulding's categories, it is an "exchange" system or an "integrative" system. In the former, the physician provides service to the patient in exchange for a fee — an impersonal commercial relationship similar to a stock broker executing an investor's order. An integrative system, according to Boulding, "involves... a whole raft of social institutions which defines roles in such a way that you do things because of what you are and because of what I am."[6] In families and religious communities the integrative system is usually important; it also can be important in the patient-physician relationship absent the entrepreneurial role.

The requisite knowledge for effective practice is also changing. An era in which physicians were trained to "explore every intervention that might help a patient regardless of cost" has given way to one in which published evidence and cost considerations must guide treatment choices. This will demand knowledge and skills (for example, more population health and health economics) different from those conveyed in the typical medical school curriculum.

How well future physicians will serve the public will depend in part on how quickly and how thoughtfully academic medical centers adapt to these new challenges. Will the preclinical curriculum continue to be driven primarily by core principles of biology, or will new content achieve parity? Will rounds reflect the full mix of care providers or continue largely as physician-centric? Most importantly, will postgraduate training continue its traditional focus on acute care in an acute care setting? The record of academic centers in adapting to change is not encouraging. The most experienced observers have continuously lamented the failure of medical education to incorporate changes in medical practice. In 1977, Ebert, dean of the Harvard Medical School, deplored "how little change has taken place in the fundamental organization of medical education over the past half century."[7] Nine years later Rogers, former vice president for medical affairs at Johns Hopkins University, agreed: "in design and organization medical education of the 1930s was not significantly different from that of the 1980s."[8] Much the same could be said today.

In other sectors of the economy, competition from new firms forces established organizations to innovate or lose market share; consider, for example, the effect of Japanese car makers on US automobile firms. Medical schools, by contrast, have rarely faced pressure from new entrants, and when new schools are created, they are pressured to conform to existing structures and practices.

The current transformation of US physicians arises for reasons largely beyond the control of the profession. Change is inevitable. The leaders of the profession, and especially the leaders in academic medical centers, must make the change as constructive as possible. There are some encouraging developments, such as the emergence of academic medical centers of research and training programs to supplement traditional preclinical and clinical experiences. An upsurge in student interest in the primary care specialties coincides with increased emphasis on ambulatory settings for postgraduate education. Most radical of all, the University of Texas at Austin proposes to create a medical school that will include population sciences as well as biological sciences and will train other health professionals alongside physicians. Perhaps the current transformation will have lasting favorable effects on the profession.

References

1. Starr, P. (1982). *The Social Transformation of American Medicine*. Basic Books: New York, pp. 118–121.
2. Hamilton, W. H. (1945). "The Place of the Physician in Modern Society. In *The Practical Cogitator or The Thinker's Anthology*, Curtis, C. P. Jr. and Greenslet, F. eds. Houghton Mifflin: New York, p. 266.
3. Thomas, L. (1983). *The Youngest Science: Notes of a Medicine-Watcher*. Viking Press: New York, p. 6.
4. Weisbrod, B. (1991). "The Health Care Quadrilemma: An Essay on Technological Change, Insurance, Quality of Care, and Cost Containment." *Journal of Economic Literature* **29**(2): 523–552.
5. Hartman, M., Martin, A. B., Lassman, D. and Catlin, A. (2015). "National Health Expenditures Accounts Team. National Health Spending in 2013: Growth Slows, Remains in Step with the Overall Economy." *Health Affairs (Millwood)* **34**(1): 150–160.
6. Boulding, K. (1989). *Three Faces of Power*. SAGE Publications: Newbury Park, CA.
7. Ebert, R. H. (1986). "Medical Education at the Peak of the Era of Experimental Medicine." *Daedalus* **115**(2): 55–81.
8. Rogers, D. E. (1977). "The Challenge of Primary Care." *Daedalus* **106**(1): 81–103.

Part 8

Professional Appreciations

Introduction

Identification of paternity can be controversial, especially in academia where there is no reliable laboratory test for intellectual DNA. I believe, however, that my presence at the scene in the 1960s, when modern health economics was born, and my participation in the field ever since, qualifies me to identify the "founding fathers." In my judgement, Kenneth Arrow, Gary Becker, and Martin Feldstein, each in their own distinct way, deserve recognition for important original contributions, which transformed a field that until the 1960s was primarily descriptive and institutional.

Neither Arrow nor Becker were health economists, and Feldstein stayed in the field only a few years before moving on to other areas of public economics and macroeconomics, but their contributions have had a lasting impact. The most far reaching effect came from a single article published by Arrow in the *American Economic Review* in 1963. With dazzling accuracy and brevity, Arrow's opening paragraph observes that the special economic problems of medical care can be explained by adaptations to *uncertainty* in the incidence of disease and in the efficacy of treatment. Commentators on Arrow's work have sometimes rephrased his insight into the problem of the absence of certain markets or the limitations of insurance markets, but the central point remains the same. In Greek legend, Helen's beauty launched a thousand ships; Arrow's article has launched many more than a thousand papers on uncertainty, health insurance, moral hazard, adverse selection, non-market social institutions, and other subjects. It was and is seminal.

The thousands of citations to Arrow's article testifies to his impact on health economics research, especially that portion that focuses on health insurance and medical care, not on health. Arrow made this distinction at the beginning of his article when he wrote, "the subject is the *medical care industry* not *health*." (italics in original) Arrow was aware that medical care is only one of many causal factors in health and, particularly at low levels of income, nutrition, shelter, clothing, and sanitation may be much more significant.

It is the work of Gary Becker that has provided the most stimulus to research on the economics of *health*. His articles and books on human capital, household production, and the allocation of time have provided the conceptual framework for empirical work on the relations between health and education, income, family, and many other social determinants. Michael Grossman's models of the demand for health and the production of health, which are direct descendants of Becker's work, have in turn stimulated a large amount of empirical research on a host of health affecting behaviors such as alcohol consumption, cigarette smoking, and diet.

Martin Feldstein's contribution was much less theoretical. While at Oxford University as a graduate student in economics, he began a series of interrelated studies of British hospitals. Using a large body of data covering almost all English hospitals, and applying modern econometric tools to his analyses, he published nine papers in appropriate journals while still a graduate student. It was more the stunning example of his work, and its useful applied nature, rather than any significant theoretical or empirical breakthrough that warrants placing Feldstein in the health economist's pantheon. Today, following Feldstein, a great deal of valuable research is produced by health economists that could just as easily be labeled "health services research."

It has been my good fortune to know Arrow, Becker, and Feldstein personally, to have spent considerable time with them, and to have written about each of them. These are the three papers in Part 8. I was the Ford Foundation program officer who invited Arrow to write his *American Economic Review* article. Becker and I were colleagues at the National Bureau of Economic Research for several years in the 1960s, and I sought Feldstein out in Oxford in 1965 when I began health economics because his papers were so superior to anything then being produced in the U.S.

Each of the three papers in Part 8 were written by me in response to requests. In 2003, I was asked to write the preface to a book celebrating the 40th anniversary of Arrow's "Uncertainty and the Welfare Economics of Medical Care." The essay on Becker was invited by the editors of the *Journal of Economic Perspective* on the occasion of his winning the Nobel Prize in Economics in 1992. The third paper is my extended book review of Feldstein's *Economic Analysis for Health Service Efficiency: Econometric Studies of the British National Health Service*, a collection of his papers on British hospitals published in 1967.

In addition to the papers on the three "fathers," I have included in Part 8 my "Appreciation" of the contributions of Michael Grossman and Joseph Newhouse, two of the leading health economists of the current generation who are reaching retirement age. The appreciation of Grossman was written for a symposium, held in January 2003, celebrating the 30th anniversary of the publication of his article, "The Demand for Health." When Newhouse won the ASHE (American Society of Health Economists) Victor R. Fuchs Award for Lifetime Contributions to the Field of Health Economics in 2014, I was asked to present the Award. My remarks on that occasion are included.

8.1

Preface, *Kenneth Arrow and the Changing Economics of Health Care*

This volume celebrates the 40th anniversary of the publication of Kenneth Arrow's classic article, "Uncertainty and the Welfare Economics of Medical Care." By reprinting the article which launched modern health economics, along with more than a score of stimulating new papers by scholars from a half dozen disciplines, Duke University Press performs a valuable service for teachers, students, and researchers in health economics, health services research, health policy, and related fields.

Because I was involved with the article from the start, have been active in the health field for almost four decades, and have had the good fortune to be a colleague and friend of Kenneth Arrow for more than 20 years, I welcome this opportunity to contribute a brief prefatory note. Arrow's accomplishments need no embellishments from me, but I can provide the background and circumstances surrounding the origins of the article, describe its impact, and say a few words about its author.

Kenneth Arrow and the Changing Economics of Health Care 2003, Peter Hammer, Deborah Haas-Wilson, Mark Peterson (eds.), Durham NC: Duke University Press.

In the early 1960s, the Ford Foundation Program in Economic Development and Administration devoted the bulk of its funds to traditional subjects such as economic growth and unemployment. As a Program Associate at the Foundation, it seemed to me there were large areas of the economy such as health, education, and welfare that were relatively neglected. I thought that Ford Foundation sponsorship of a series of monographs and shorter "think pieces" on these subjects would stimulate interest within economics and related fields and prove helpful to those responsible for policy and operating decisions in these areas.

At my request, the Foundation trustees approved a $25,000 project to be administered within the Foundation. The funds were to be used for publication subsidies, distribution of 10,000 copies of each study, and modest honoraria for the authors. My plan was to commission three monographs by economists who were familiar with the institutional and empirical features of their particular field and to find three outstanding economic theorists, each of whom would bring their analytical skills to bear on one of the fields.

For the three applied monographs, I chose Margaret Gordon for welfare, Herbert Klarman for health, and Theodore Schultz for education. Each of them came through splendidly with small books that were published by Columbia University Press. In baseball terms, Gordon delivered a clean hit. She placed U.S. welfare programs in historical context, provided international comparisons, and offered detailed analyses of major U.S. programs such as social security and unemployment compensation, Klarman's book was good for extra bases. It is the definitive description and assessment of the health economics field prior to 1963. In the absence of suitable textbooks in health economics, Klarman's book was assigned to students for many years to provide a grounding for work in this field. With his short essay, *The Economic Value of Education*. Schultz hit a home run. Its impact on the fields of economics, education, and development was tremendous. Although Columbia University Press was certain that the distribution of ten thousand free copies would preclude any further sales, the book went on to sell many times that number, and was translated into several languages. As recently as 2001, the study was cited in six different social science journals.

The results for the economic theory portion of the project were decidedly more mixed. Robert Dorfman, who had the welfare assignment, found that he could not produce the desired kind of article. Carl Kaysen, who was supposed write on education, departed for Washington mid-way through the project to join the Kennedy Administration. Only Arrow remained to bat, and he delivered what can only be described as a home run with the bases loaded in the 9th inning with his team behind by three runs.

According to the dictionary, a classic is "a work generally considered to be of the highest rank or excellence, especially one of enduring significance." Arrow's article fits that description perfectly. It is *the* seminal article of modern health economics. As Mark Pauly puts it in his perceptive and provocative forward to this volume, "Kenneth Arrow's article made research in health economics respectable.... It also made it interesting." In Hollywood, they say that Fred Astaire gave Ginger Rogers class, and she made him sexy. Arrow did both for health economics.

In 1963, there were few courses in health economics offered at any university. Subsequently, the field began to develop, slowly at first, then exponentially. If any of the new courses did not include "Uncertainty.." on its reading list, one can only feel sympathy for the students and outrage at the instructor. In the last two decades, health economics courses and Arrow's article have spread beyond the economics curriculum to schools of business, public health, medicine, law, and public policy. Equally important, health economics has become completely international; approximately 2,000 health economists from all over the world are expected to attend the Fourth International Congress of Health Economics in San Francisco June 2003. For evidence that Arrow's article has had — and continues to have — a large impact on many fields other than economics, the reader need go no further than this book. It is doubtful that any other social science article published in the last half century could elicit so many thoughtful commentaries from so many different perspectives.

One indicator of the continuing influence of Arrow's article is the frequency with which it is cited in social science and related journals. In 2001 alone, there were 24 citations in 19 different journals (excluding the special issue of the *Journal of Health, Politics, Policy and Law*). This almost equals the 28 citations per year pace set in 1991–2000. This is clearly a work of "enduring significance".

What kind of man produced this classic article? There are many who deem this question irrelevant. They believe that the value of a scholarly work is independent of any biographical information regarding its creator. John Meurig Thomas made this point forcefully when he wrote, "Truth is independent of the stimulus that has provoked its discovery, and the conditions that guided its expression."[1] There is something to be said for this view. Consider for example, a proof of a mathematical theorem. The validity of this proof can be judged quite independently of whether the person providing the proof was Mother Teresa or a serial rapist.

There are, however, reasons to think that sometimes biographical background can be helpful. For example, in economic discussions less formal than a mathematical proof, values are nearly always present, either explicitly or implicitly. As Gunnar Myrdal wrote in an earlier volume celebrating Arrow's many theoretical contributions to economic policy, "Prior to answers, there must be questions...in the questions raised and the viewpoints chosen, valuations are implied."[2] For that reason alone, some readers may wish to know more about the author. A related point is that no article can be complete. There are always things that are left out. Biographical information about the author can in some instances help to fill in these unavoidable gaps. Finally, in this particular instance readers should find it inspiring to learn what an extraordinary person Arrow is.

Non-economists may not realize that "Uncertainty..." is not Arrow's only "classic", or even his first. Beginning with his Ph.D. dissertation on social choice and on through other classic contributions to theories of general equilibrium, welfare, uncertainty, information, and much more, Arrow is considered by many to be the premier economic theorist of the last 60 years. When weighed against the totality of the Arrow oeuvre, the article we celebrate in this volume would be judged by most economists as simply another small addition, albeit the most frequently cited of any of his single authored papers.

Intellectually, Arrow is as broad as he is deep. He commands an encyclopedic knowledge of many fields from mathematics to literature. He is interested in and appreciative of music and the arts. He is a prime example of Friedrich Hayek's observation that "nobody can be a great economist who is only an economist."

Politically, Arrow is quite liberal. He has a deep understanding of the efficiency advantages of a market-price system, but distributive issues are also very important to him, and he is willing to accept trade-offs between efficiency and equity. To understand Arrow's values, we need only look at the dedication in his *Collected Papers* where he praises his Columbia mentor Harold Hotelling for setting "the example of human concern combined with analytical rigor that I have always attempted to follow."

Perhaps the most unusual aspect of Arrow is the purely personal side. He is devoted to his family and is a warm and caring friend to many at Stanford and around the world. He cheerfully takes on much more than his fair share of community and professional responsibilities. He is modest, thoughtful, attentive to others. Compared with most who rise to the peak of a difficult field, he is less personally ambitious, less eager to proselytize, less driven by ego.

In short, Arrow is living proof that being a genius does not rule out being an exceptionally nice person. At a luncheon celebrating Arrow's 80th birthday, he was toasted as "supermensch". "Super" because of his extraordinary intellectual powers, and "mensch" because he is an exemplar of the decency and dependability denoted by that Yiddish term. This volume celebrates a great article and a great man.

References

1. Myrdal, G. (1987). "Utilitarianism and Modern Economics." In *Arrow and the Foundations of the Theory of Economic Policy*, G. R. Feiwell, ed. Macmillan Press Ltd: London, pp. 273–278.
2. Thomas, J. M. (1998). "Rumford's Remarkable Creation." *Proceedings of the American Philosophical Society* **142**(4): 597–613.

8.2

Nobel Laureate
Gary S. Becker: Ideas About Facts

In September 1952 *The American Economic Review* published a note on multi-country trade written by an obscure Princeton undergraduate.[1,a] Two months later a paper on monetary theory by the same student and one of his Princeton instructors appeared in *Economica*.[2] Thus was launched the career of one of the most influential social scientists of the second half of the twentieth century, a career that was recognized by the Nobel Prize Committee for Economics in 1992 with its award to Gary S. Becker.

Although the Princeton undergraduate may have been obscure, his talents as an economist were already clearly evident to those who had close contact with him. One of his professors, in recommending him for admission to graduate school, said he was the best student at Princeton in more than a decade. Jacob Viner, a veteran of more than three decades of distinguished scholarship and

---

Originally published in *Journal of Economic Perspectives*, 8(2):183–192, Spring1 994. Copyright by American Economic Association.
[a] As is conventional for this journal, the references to Becker's work are to the numbers of the articles appearing in Table 1. All other citations are by the author (date) system to the reference list at the end of the article.

Table 1.   Work by Gary Becker Cited in this Article.

1	"A Note on Multi-Country Trade," *American Economic Review,* September 1952, *42*:4, 558–68.
2	"The Classical Monetary Theory: The Outcome of the Discussion" (with W. J. Baumol), *Economica,* November 1952, 19:76, 355–76.
3	*The Economics of Discrimination.* Chicago: University of Chicago Press, 1957 (2nd edition, 1971).
4	*Human Capital.* New York: Columbia University Press, 1964 (2nd edition, 1975; 3rd edition, 1993).
5	*Essays in the Economics of Crime and Punishment* (edited with William M. Landes). New York: Columbia University Press for the National Bureau of Economic Research, 1974.
6	*The Allocation of Time and Goods Over the Life Cycle* (with Gilbert Ghez). New York: Columbia University Press for the National Bureau of Economic Research, 1975.
7	"A Theory of Rational Addiction" (with Kevin M. Murphy), *Journal of Political Economy,* August 1988, *96*:4, 675–700.
8	"Rational Addiction and the Effect of Price on Consumption" (with Michael Grossman and Kevin M. Murphy), *AEA Papers and Proceedings,* May 1991, *81*:2, 237–41.
9	"An Economic Analysis of Fertility," *Demographic and Economic Change in Developed Countries,* Conference of the Universities-National Bureau Committee for Economic Research, a Report of the National Bureau of Economic Research. Princeton: Princeton University Press, 1960.
10	"On the Interaction Between the Quantity and Quality of Children" (with H. G. Lewis), *Journal of Political Economy,* March/April 1973, *81*:2, Part 2, S279–S288.
11	"A Theory of Marriage: Part I," *Journal of Political Economy,* July/August 1973, *81*:4, 813–46.
12	"A Theory of Marriage, Part II," *Journal of Political Economy,* March/April 1974, *82*:2, Part 2, S11–S26.
13	"An Economic Analysis of Marital Instability" (with E. M. Landes and R. T. Michael), *Journal of Political Economy,* December 1977, *85*:6, 1153–89.
14	"Crime and Punishment: An Economic Approach," *Journal of Political Economy,* March/April 1968, *76* :2, 169–217.
15	"Human Capital, Effort, and the Sexual Division of Labor," *Journal of Labor Economics,* January 1985, *3*:1, Part 2, S33–S58.
16	*A Treatise on the Family.* Cambridge; Harvard University Press, 1981 (expanded edition, 1991).
17	"Milton Friedman." In Shils, Edward, ed., *Remembering the University of Chicago: Teachers, Scientists, and Scholars.* Chicago: University of Chicago Press, 1991, 138–46.
18	*Economic Theory.* New York: A. Knopf, 1971.
19	"Nobel Lecture: The Economic Way of Looking at Behavior," *Journal of Political Economy,* June 1993, *101*:3, 385–409.
20	*The Economic Approach to Human Behavior.* Chicago: University of Chicago Press, 1976.
21	"Education and the Distribution of Earnings" (with Barry Chiswick), *American Economic Review,* May 1966, *56*:2, 358–69.
22	*Human Capital and the Personal Distribution of Income: An Analytical Approach.* Ann Arbor: University of Michigan Press, 1967.
23	"An Equilibrium Theory of the Distribution of Income and Intergenerational Mobility" (with Nigei Tomes), *Journal of Political Economy,* December 1979, *87*:6, 1153–89.

(*Continued*)

Table 1.   (*Continued*)

24	"Human Capital and the Rise and Fall of Families" (with Nigel Tomes), *Journal of Labor Economics*, July 1986, *4:3*, Part 2, S1–S39.
25	"A Theory of the Allocation of Time," *Economic Journal*, September 1965, 75:299, 493–508.
26	"On the New Theory of Consumer Behavior" (with Robert T. Michael), *The Swedish Journal of Economics*, 1973, *75*, 378–96.
27	"Competition and Democracy," *Journal of Law and Economics*, 1958, *1*, 105–09.
28	"A Theory of Competition Among Pressure Groups for Political Influence," *Quarterly Journal of Economics*, August 1983, *47:3*, 371–400.

teaching, wrote "Becker is the best student I have ever had." It is rumored that this recommendation raised some eyebrows at the University of Chicago, where Viner had been a leading member of the faculty during the period when Milton Friedman and George Stigler were graduate students. An academic diplomat is said to have restored equilibrium by pointing out that Viner probably meant "undergraduate student."

Milton Friedman was quick to add his own favorable assessment. In 1953, when he nominated Becker for an Earhart Foundation graduate fellowship at Chicago, he wrote, "Becker has a brilliant, analytical mind; great originality; knowledge of the history of economic thought and respect for its importance; a real feeling for the interrelationships between economic and political issues; and a profound understanding of both the operation of a price system and its importance as a protection of individual liberty" (Milton Friedman, personal communication, 1993).

From the record it appears that one could say of Becker, as was reportedly said of Joseph Schumpeter, "He was never a beginner." If economics was made for Becker, Becker was clearly made for economics. It is easy to imagine many of the other Nobel Prize winners in economics pursuing successful careers in mathematics, physics, philosophy, or even history. Less so for Becker. He never seriously considered any other field, and although his influence on the other social sciences exceeds that of any economist of his generation, it has been achieved through highly focused, unremitting application of basic economic concepts.

Biographical Notes

Becker's seemingly inevitable journey to Stockholm began in Pottsville, Pennsylvania on December 2, 1930. His parents, born in eastern Europe, had little formal education, but they welcomed their son's intellectual development and encouraged his interest in social problems. His father was a self-employed businessman from the age of 16; his mother cared for their home and children. In 1935 the family, including Gary's older sister, older brother, and younger sister, moved to Brooklyn, where Becker attended public schools, graduating from James Madison High School in 1948. Madison, like many other New York City schools, produced numerous outstanding scholars and professionals, Supreme Court Justice Ruth Bader Ginsberg was just a few years behind Becker at Madison; several years earlier, Nobel Prize-winner Robert Solow had graduated from the same school.

The University of Chicago awarded Becker a Ph.D. in 1955 when he completed his dissertation on the economics of discrimination.[3] In this study Becker revealed the skills and methods that he would use to such great advantage in subsequent research. He identified an important social problem that had been neglected by economists, he showed how the application of relatively simple economic concepts could yield significant results, and he pointed the way for extensions and amplifications, both theoretical and empirical. Jacob Mincer, who was probably the first of Becker's contemporaries to recognize his exceptional potential, notes that three cardinal principles were evident from the beginning: 1) theory should have empirical content; 2) theory should not only minimize assumptions but should maximize explanations of facts; and 3) "changes in taste" is the economist's admission of defeat (Jacob Mincer, personal communication, 1993).

Although Becker's dissertation was extraordinary (the Nobel Prize Committee lauded it as a major contribution to economics), his newly minted Ph.D. degree was not a passport to academic heaven. In the absence of any attractive job offers from other economics departments, Becker remained at Chicago until 1957, when he accepted an appointment as an assistant professor at Columbia University. He taught price theory at Columbia and, with Jacob Mincer, led a workshop which produced many outstanding labor economists. In 1969 he returned to Chicago where he has taught ever since. That university has provided an hospitable environment with many stimulating and supportive colleagues, George Stigler, in particular, was a valued advisor and collaborator until his death in 1991.

One reason why Becker moved from Chicago to New York was to join the staff of the National Bureau of Economic Research. At that time the NBER staff was small and almost entirely resident in the New York area. Despite his youth, Becker quickly became a major intellectual leader at the Bureau and remained so for more than two decades. Indeed, many would say that he was *the* most significant intellectual force as the Bureau shifted from an emphasis on business cycles and national income to a wider set of economic and social issues.

Either directly or indirectly Becker played a large role in the creation of many new Bureau programs, including those in law and economics, education, health, the family, income distribution, and labor economics. Severalof Becker's most important contributions concerning human capital,[4] crime and punishment,[5] and the allocation of time[6] appeared as NBER volumes.[b]

I joined the Bureau staff in 1962 and soon came to appreciate Becker's unusual qualities. Particularly impressive was his seriousness of purpose, his willingness to take chances, and his persistence in the face of criticism and hostility. To be sure, most economists are serious most of the time. In my experience, however, few are as single-minded as Becker in their determination to understand social phenomena and in their hope that this understanding will be used for social good. For Becker, economics has never been a "game," or an opportunity to demonstrate how clever one is, or a vehicle for scoring points at another scholar's expense. Becker has a fine sense of humor, as those who heard his introduction to George Stigler's Nobel Prize luncheon speech at the AEA Meetings in 1983 can testify. His *Business Week* columns show that he also commands a lively, reader-friendly style that can serve as a model for popular writing on economics. But in scholarly publications, his straightforward, almost solemn prose reflects his intense seriousness of purpose.

Becker's willingness to take chances in his choice of research topics is extraordinary, especially since he could easily have reached the front rank of the profession by pursuing a more conventional agenda. Every academic knows how tempting it is to write about what is "hot." Early in our careers we learn that it is much easier to publish the second or third paper on the latest fad than to strike out in new, unexplored territory. But that has never been Becker's way. From his graduate school study of discrimination to his current concerns with addiction and endogenous preferences,[7,8] originality has been the hallmark of his work. Such an approach to research must result in some misses, but over four decades Becker has maintained a high batting average while hitting numerous home runs.

Becker's willingness, indeed eagerness, to open up new areas has come at a price: skepticism, outrage, and scorn have often greeted his efforts to apply economics to allegedly "noneconomic" subjects. Consider the term "human capital." The concept, which dates back at least to Adam Smith, was used to great advantage by Ref. 4, and the term appears explicitly in the titles of papers by Refs. 9 and 13. Nevertheless, when Becker was preparing his treatise[4] he

---

[b]Economists with an interest in inflation should note that the hardcover edition of Becker's *Human Capital*, Ref. 4 distributed by Columbia University Press for the NBER in 1964, was priced at five dollars.

encountered so many negative reactions that he seriously considered choosing a different title for the book.

Hostility to his claim that economics could help increase understanding of fertility,[9,10] marriage and divorce,[11–13] and crime[14] was even more pronounced. Some criticisms have been constructive, but many have been mean-spirited and often contradictory. His ventures into new fields were dismissed by some as trivial applications of elementary price theory, while others said they were misapplications of the theory. His use of an economic model of decision-making to analyze nonmarket choices has been criticized by some as unrealistic, while other critics concede the realism but fault him for making these choices explicit and thereby encouraging such behavior. His attempts to understand sexual division of labor in market and nonmarket production[15] have led to accusations that he is a defender of patriarchal oppression. This charge is particularly ironic because Becker has probably helped more women earn Ph.D.s in economics than has any other Nobel Prize winner. The jokes and criticisms hurt Becker, but he persisted, and for the most part his vision eventually prevailed.

Becker's commitment to a lifetime of scholarship has been accompanied by an equally strong involvement with family. His appreciation of his first wife Doria's encouragement and support is reflected in the dedication of *Human Capital*.[4] After her death in 1971 Becker raised their two daughters as a single parent for many years. In 1979 he married Guity Nashad, a professor of Middle Eastern history. Her contributions to his work and his life are warmly acknowledged in the dedication to *A Treatise on the Family*[16]; their marriage continues to provide mutual intellectual and emotional support.

Despite many opportunities throughout his career, Becker has spent little time in consulting work. He has few hobbies, but he jogs regularly and is a tenacious tennis player, frequently defeating opponents who have more polished strokes. Since 1960 he has summered on Cape Cod, welcoming the isolation and respite from his regular participation in several intense University of Chicago workshops. In recent years he has spent a portion of each winter at the Hoover Institution at Stanford, California, where he is a Senior Fellow.

For 40 years Becker has been a dedicated, effective teacher. His students write and speak of him with admiration and respect, albeit not with the same awe that surrounds the precious few who have been the premier teachers of the discipline.[c] Not surprisingly, Becker's strengths in the classroom have been focus, clarity, and

---

[c]See, for example, Becker's description of how as a student he "looked forward with excitement" to every lecture by Milton Friedman, and how sad he was when the last lecture was finished (Ref. 17, p. 143).

Gary S. Becker

a preference for the concrete over the abstract. Perhaps more surprisingly for those who know Becker only through his writing, his students have always found him to be warm and supportive. One student who took graduate price theory with Becker at Columbia in the late 1950s fondly recalls his "earnest manner and outlandish examples." Because she had minimal undergraduate preparation in economics, she was surprised to receive a grade of A, with the only other A going to an undergraduate. Becker had an easy explanation: "You two had the least to unlearn" (Marina v. N. Whitman, personal communication, 1993).

Becker's text, *Economic Theory*,[18] is solid and serviceable for advanced undergraduates and beginning graduate students, but it has not received the attention or acclaim accorded several of his treatises. Generous in his acknowledgement to his teachers and his university colleagues, Becker does not go to great lengths to reference everyone who has ever written on the subjects that he addresses. No classic review or survey article adorns his bibliography. Some years ago when I lamented the proliferation of new journals in economics, he assured me that it was not difficult to keep up with really significant advances in the discipline.

Becker's Contributions

This essay focuses on the "man," not the "work." The substance of Becker's research has been the subject of numerous reviews (see especially Ref. 12), as well as Becker's own summaries in his Nobel lecture[19] and his introduction to *The Economic Approach to Human Behavior*.[20] I would, however, be remiss if I did not at least remind readers that Becker's influence has been exceptional because it has taken several different forms: an enlargement of our understanding of traditional economic subjects, the opening up of new fields of research, and the transformation of other social sciences.

Within traditional economics Becker's greatest impact has been on labor economics. In the early 1950s, labor economists at most universities focused heavily on the history of the trade union movement, the procedures and the results of collective bargaining, and other descriptive studies of labor institutions. Within a decade, largely as a result of the work of Becker, H. Gregg Lewis, Jacob Mincer, and a few other scholars, research in labor economics became firmly rooted in economic theory, with empirical applications based on modern econometric methods. Traditional questions concerning wage differentials, labor force participation, occupational choice, and job mobility were addressed with new insights, using new data in new ways. As a result, labor economics flourished in the 1960s and 1970s as a major applied field within mainstream economics.

A second traditional field that has been substantially affected by Becker's work is income distribution.[21,22] Not only has Becker enlarged our understanding of cross-sectional differences in income at a point in time, but he has also tackled the more difficult question of intergenerational income distribution effects.[23,24]

The third traditional field that has been substantially affected by Becker is consumer economics. In his view, households are not simply passive consumers of goods and services purchased in the market, but active producers of non-marketable commodities such as health. These commodities are produced by combining market goods and services and the household members' own time, and is affected by the characteristics of the household members.[25,26]

One indication of Becker's influence is his leadership in number of citations in the leading economics journals. For the period 1971–85, there isn't a close second among scholars of his generation (Medoff, 1989). An even more striking dominance is evident in *Social Economics* (Eatwell, Milgate, and Newman, 1989). This subset of articles from *The New Palgrave: A Dictionary of Economics* contains 36 articles on social issues ranging from "aging population" to "women's wages." Becker is mentioned in no fewer than 16 of the articles, with a total of 31 citations. The next most frequently cited economist (also a Nobel Laureate) is mentioned in six articles with a total of nine citations.[d]

Several new fields of economic research owe a great deal to Becker, not only for the intellectual stimulation provided by his books and articles, but also for personal intervention and support. Consider, for instance, the history of law and economics, now a flourishing area with over 400 members in the American Law and Economics Association. William Landes, one of the first economists to work in this area, circulated a draft of a paper on the courts in 1967.[6] At least one leading economist advised Landes to drop this work and get on with subjects that were of interest to most of the profession. In contrast, Becker encouraged Landes, arguing that the work was of high quality and important and would eventually receive the recognition it deserved. Moreover, Becker saw the advantages of bringing a legal scholar into the research and arranged for Richard Posner to become co-director with Landes of the NBER Program in Law and Economics (William M. Landes, personal communication, 1993). Their collaboration has been one of the most fruitful of any involving an economist and a non-economist.[e] Reference 10 provides additional insights about Becker's contribution to the field.

My experience in launching a health economics program at the National Bureau in the mid-1960s was somewhat similar. The president of the Bureau, Arthur Burns, tried to discourage me, pointing out the advantages of working in a more traditional area. Becker, on the other hand, was always supportive of my work in health economics, and one of his students, Michael Grossman, succeeded me as director of the NBER program. Now, throughout the United States and in other countries, there are research programs in law and economics, health, fertility, and the family; they are all, in part, a tribute to Becker's influence.

The third arena in which Becker has had great influence is the other social sciences. Sociology in particular has been changed not only by his publications

---

[d]Readers who are skeptical about the importance of citations might consider a story about Moses from the Babylonian Talmud (Menahot 29b). It seems that Moses was ill at ease and asked God For permission to return to Earth to see how things were going. In an instant he found himself in one of the back rows of a famous academy run by Rabbi Akiba where vigorous discussion was underway among the Rabbi, other scholars, and students. Moses understood the language, but he could not make any sense of their debate about fine points of the Law. He felt even worse than before; as the Talmud says "His strength left him." But at that point one of the students challenged Rabbi Akiba regarding his authority for a particular statement. In reply, Akiba cited Moses. When Moses heard this, he felt comforted and his strength returned.

[e]Emphasis on the roles played by Becker, Landes, and Posner in the development of law and economics is not intended lo deny the significant contributions of Calabresi, Coase, Director, Manne, and other scholars.

but also through his personal involvement. Since 1983 Becker has held a joint appointment in the Sociology Department at the University of Chicago as part of his University Professorship. Becker's contribution (or, as some sociologists would have it, his sin) has been to bring theory to a discipline that has been lost in an atheoretical wilderness for decades (Coleman, forthcoming). Through application of the theory of rational choice to such traditional sociological subjects as discrimination, crime, and the family, Becker has forced sociologists to reexamine their standard views, and in some areas such as fertility research, his approach is becoming dominant.

Becker's efforts to make economic theory the central paradigm of all social science has had an impact on political science[27,28] as well as sociology, albeit major credit (or blame) must be assigned to Downs, Arrow, Buchanan and Tullock, and Becker's Chicago colleagues Stigler and Peltzman. Two other disciplines that have been influenced by Becker are demography and anthropology, the former to a greater extent than the latter.

Does Becker overstate the case for rational choice? Probably so. He concedes that his work "may have sometimes assumed too much rationality".[19] But he sees his writing, in part, as an offset to a vast literature in the social and behavioral sciences that "does not credit people with enough rationality".[19]

Unlike Marc Antony, I have come to praise, not to bury. But candor requires at least a brief look at the other side. It must be acknowledged that some theorists do not think highly of Becker's models. They regard them much as an avant-garde poet would look upon a book by Dr. Seuss. In an era when "mathematics makes the man (or woman)," Becker's theorems and proofs (usually relegated to appendices) would not challenge a graduate student. In econometrics, Becker is not known for any new test or methodological innovation, or for any particularly ingenious use of existing methods. Becker believes strongly in the importance of empirical work, but he has not personally been responsible for the development of new data sets or for the exhaustive mining of those that are available. Finally, it must be noted that Becker has not played any significant role in the policy arena, either as an advisor to political candidates or in a position in government.

What, then, explains Becker's success and his influence? They rest entirely on the importance of his *ideas*. Original ideas, tenaciously held and vigorously exposited, have ultimately proved to be irresistible. Not any ideas, of course, but those that accurately capture important aspects of human behavior. Becker's ideas are the kind that Alfred North Whitehead had in mind when he was asked, "Which are more important, facts or ideas?" The philosopher reflected for a while, then said: "Ideas *about* facts" (Price, 1954; italics in original).

Helpful comments from Jacob Mincer on a preliminary draft are gratefully acknowledged.

References

1. Coleman, J. S. (1993). "The Impact of Gary Becker's Work on Sociology." *Acta Sociologica* **36**(3): 169–178.
2. Eatwell, J., Milgate, M. and Newman, P. eds. (1989). *Social Economics*. Macmillan Press Limited: London.
3. Friedman, M. (1993). Personal Communication.
4. Friedman, M. and Kuznets, S. (1945). *Income from Independent Professional Practice*. National Bureau of Economic Research: New York.
5. Landes, W. M. (1993). Personal Communication.
6. Landes, W. M. (1971). "An Economic Analysis of the Courts." *The Journal of Law & Economics* **14**(1): 61–107.
7. Medoff, M. H. (1989). "The Rankings of Economists." *Journal of Economic Education,* **20**(4): 405–415.
8. Mincer, J. (1993). Personal Communication.
9. Mincer, J. (1958). "Investment in Human Capital and Personal Income Distribution." *Journal of Political Economy* **66**: 281–302.
10. Posner, R. A. (1993). "Gary Becker's Contributions to Law and Economics." *Journal of Legal Studies,* **23**: 211–215.
11. Price, L. (1954). *The Dialogues of Alfred North Whitehead, as recorded by Lucien Price*. Little Brown: Boston.
12. Rosen, S. (1993). "Risks and Rewards: Gary Becker's Contribution to Economics." *Scandinavian Journal of Economics* **95**(1): 25–36.
13. Schultz, T. W. (1961). "Investment in Human Capital." *American Economic Review* **51**: 11–17.
14. Whitman, M. v. N. (1993). Personal Communication.

8.3

A Review of Martin S. Feldstein's
Economic Analysis for Health Service Efficiency

This is the best study of health services ever written by an economist. It is also probably the best book on the British National Health Service to emerge from any discipline. The fact that it was produced by an American in his middle twenties as a Ph.D. thesis (at Oxford) lends additional luster to the achievement.

The study is concerned with identifying and estimating relevant decision-making information and with applying optimizing methods to improve the efficiency of the British National Health Service. It should be of great interest and value to anyone concerned with health service efficiency in any country and will prove particularly rewarding to those engaged in research in this field.

The strengths of the author are his grasp of economic concepts such as production functions and economies of scale, his ability to deploy formal models, and his imaginative use of a variety of statistical techniques including ordinary and two-stage least squares, principal component analysis, and linear programming. Furthermore, in most instances he has not settled for casual illustrations or hypothetical examples (as do many who are skilled in theory and methodology) but

---

Originally published in Health Services Research, Fall 1967.

has provided extensive empirical tests and estimates. All this is served up in a clear narrative style, with technical matters reserved for some 13 appendixes. Each of the eight major chapters has an informative introduction, and most have summaries. In addition there are short nontechnical introductory and summary chapters.

The Hospital as a Producing Unit

The book is divided into two parts. The first deals with the hospital as a producing unit. It consists primarily of a series of related studies of 177 large nonteaching British hospitals. The major purpose of the studies is to investigate the factors affecting hospital costs (defined to exclude outpatient and laboratory services) for the fiscal year ending Mar. 31, 1961. The investigation involves consideration of case mix, productivity, input efficiency, size, occupancy rate, and length of stay. This part concludes with an experimental application of linear programming to selection of cases for hospital treatment.

The adjustment for case mix is based on allocating each case to one of eight exclusive specialty categories — general medicine, pediatrics, general surgery, ear-nose-and-throat, traumatic and orthopedic surgery, other surgery, gynecology, and obstetrics — or to a residual category containing less than 10 percent of the cases. Feldstein finds substantial differences in average cost per case among the nine categories and a significant difference in case mix among hospitals. Case mix differences explain 27.5 percent of the variation in total cost per case among hospitals. Nearly all of this explanatory power, however, is the result of differences in average length of stay among categories. On a cost-per-patient-day basis, only 2.1 percent of the variation in cost is accounted for by case mix.

Feldstein proceeds to define and estimate several measures for each hospital. Output (W) is defined as the weighted number of cases treated, where the weights are the average costs per case for all hospitals for each of the nine categories. These average costs are not directly available; they must be estimated by multiple regression across all hospitals, using the percentage of cases in each category as the regressors.

Costliness (C^*) is defined as total cost (E) divided by output. Productivity (P^*) is defined as output divided by "predicted" output ($\hat{W}$). The latter is based on a production function in which output depends on the hospital's inputs of nurses, doctors, beds, and "other variable inputs." The parameters for the various inputs were estimated by ordinary least-squares regression. Input efficiency (I^*) is defined as predicted output divided by total cost. By definition, $C^* = (P^*I^*)^{-1}$.

The costliness index is said to be a better measure of hospital performance than a simple relative cost index because it allows for differences in case mix. Variation in costliness is found to be due primarily to differences in productivity, that is, to differences in the efficiency with which hospitals use the inputs they have rather than the efficiency with which they divide their budgets among alternative inputs.

In his investigation of the relation between costs and size, Feldstein finds that on balance, size has little effect on cost per case, after adjusting for case mix. Without the adjustment, cost per case would rise by nearly 30 percent between 100-bed and 1000-bed hospitals, because large hospitals tend to have a higher proportion of the more expensive categories of cases. The stability of cost per case for hospitals of different size is said to be the result of two opposing trends, On the one hand, costs per patient day tend to decrease as size increases. On the other hand, the number of cases per bed year tends to decrease as size increases. Feldstein refers to the latter as "case-flow effect." Case flow is proportional to the occupancy rate and inversely proportional to the average length of stay. Later studies show that case flow varies primarily because of differences in length of stay; the variance in occupancy rate across hospitals is small.

Several attempts are made to estimate a production function for hospitals. Output, measured by number of cases adjusted for case mix, is regressed on inputs, usually specified in terms of expenditures for doctors, number of beds, expenditures for nursing, and expenditures for other supplies. The last variable is sometimes disaggregated into drugs and dressings, catering, and other supplies. Feldstein finds very high coefficients for expenditures on medical staff (and drugs and dressings) and very low coefficients for nursing and housekeeping activities. He concludes that "output would increase if a greater proportion of total expenditure were devoted to medical staff and less to nursing and housekeeping activities" (p. 123). A related conclusion is that the value of physicians' time is much more than that implied by their hourly rate of pay. These conclusions are repeated at several points in the book and will be considered in detail below.

An analysis of the relation between costs and the case flow rate produces the not surprising conclusion that cost per case falls as the case flow rate increases. This increase can be obtained either by increasing the occupancy rate while holding average length of stay constant or by shortening stay while holding occupancy rate constant. The hospitals studied by Feldstein apparently have greater variance in length of stay, and this variable is shown to be correlated with hospital size. Feldstein attributes this to a lower level of "managerial," or labor, efficiency in large hospitals (p. 86). Length of stay is also found to be inversely related to waiting-list pressure and, in a different regression, to be inversely related to the physician/bed ratio.

Finally, Feldstein shows that length of stay is inversely related to expenditure per patient day. His suggested explanation is that hospital managers react to tight budgets by increasing the average length of stay and decreasing the number of cases treated. His policy recommendation is to increase hospital budgets where beds are scarce. He also recommends increasing medical staff.

Supply and Demand

The second and shorter part of the book deals with selected aspects of supply and demand, with a view to providing guidelines to planners and "analytic monitoring information" for those operating the system. Current methods of planning hospital bed supply on the basis of manifest demand come in for sharp and deserved criticism from Feldstein. He points out the danger of ignoring "the effect of available bed supply on the demand for hospital admission and on the average duration of stay per case."

Correlations are run across 11 National Health Service administrative regions. (There are 15 such regions in England and Wales, but the four metropolitan London regions are eliminated because of the "many incomparabilities between medical care in urban London and in the rest of the country.") Bed availability explains 42 percent of the variation in admission rates and 70 percent of the variation in bed utilization. Feldstein argues that this is the result of demand adjusting itself to the available supply, rather than the reverse. He points out that (1) most of the supply was created decades ago; (2) the NHS regions are natural catchment areas; and (3) the number of persons in an area is not determined by the demand for or supply of hospital beds. One important finding is that there is no evidence of an upper limit to bed demand: "Within the observed range of supply bed-day demand increases proportionately with availability" (p. 198).

The next study is concerned with the responsiveness of the number of admissions and length of stay to differences in bed supply. The conclusion is rather startling and disturbing. The number of cases treated is about 50 percent *more* responsive than the average stay per case. Feldstein writes that as a potential patient he would be happier if he thought that the relative scarcity of beds in an area affected the length of stay rather than the chance of getting a hospital bed when needed. As explanations for the greater elasticity for admissions than for length of stay, he suggests budget constraints, limitations of medical staff, the physician's preoccupation with "his patients," the desire to "play safe" by conforming to "prevailing practice," patient influence on length of stay, and the possibility that physicians are failing to recognize the choices that they are making between length of stay and unrealized admissions.

Similar analyses by diagnostic category reveal some elasticities that suggest unwise use of limited bed supply. For instance, the elasticity of admissions for tonsillectomies and adenoidectomies is low, although many physicians would consider these to be often elective or even unnecessary procedures. A study of hospital maternity care reveals extremely low elasticity for length of stay and provokes the question, "With a national stay of nearly 10 days and strong pressure of demand for hospital confinement, why do not regions in which beds are relatively scarce reduce stays and thus be able to admit more women?" (p. 233). Feldstein answers his own question by saying that physicians apparently regard the 10-day stay as "appropriate medical practice." They act as if shorter stays would be harmful and as if this harm would not be outweighed by the benefits received by those for whom beds are freed. He is very critical of this behavior.

The criticism is buttressed by an analysis of births and hospital admissions for normal delivery in the area surrounding the city of Oxford in 1962. The study covers approximately 6000 births and 3500 normal deliveries. Regression analysis is used to reveal the factors affecting hospital admissions. These factors are divided into three categories: the patient's medical condition (as inferred from age, parity, and past obstetric history), social characteristics, and availability of services. The regressions are run separately for all hospitals and for teaching hospitals. The dependent variable is simply whether the patient was admitted to hospital or not. The independent variables are all used in dummy form.

One important finding is that, with other variables held constant, patients in the higher social classes are hospitalized for normal delivery more frequently than those in the lower classes, although the opposite might have been expected. Patients in the highest social class are frequently hospitalized in the teaching hospitals. The findings suggest that "the patient's attitude and ability to use the system as reflected by social class are more important determinants of hospitalization than her home conditions" (p. 245). Another interesting finding is that patients living in rural areas have a higher probability of hospital delivery than those in urban areas. Feldstein thinks this is probably due to the greater availability of midwife services in the urban areas. Patients whose general practitioner doesn't provide obstetric care have a high probability of admission to teaching hospitals.

The length of stay of individual patients for normal delivery varies considerably. The mean stay for this population was 8.31 days; the standard deviation was 3.31 days. According to Feldstein, the most important explanatory factor is "the standard practice of the obstetrician in charge" (p. 247). He points out that the hospital does influence the physicians who practice in it, but there is also variation among physicians within a hospital. The consultants (specialist obstetricians) tend to keep their patients in hospital for shorter stays than do the general practitioners. Medical characteristics and social characteristics seem to have little influence on length of stay, except that women in the highest social class have the longest stays. This is again different from what one would expect if length of stay were influenced by home conditions.

The study of maternity care concludes by providing some data and analyses indicating how one could plan to minimize perinatal mortality rates. The optimal conditions for handling this problem as given by Feldstein are: (1) assign women to care groups in a way that minimizes the expected number of perinatal deaths; (2) change the supply of each service so that (subject to the prevailing budget constraint) the risk reduction per dollar of marginal expenditure on each service is equal; and (3) set the overall level of expenditure by comparing the marginal cost of a reduction in risk with the opportunity cost of the funds. Such a system would require that the decision maker be able to state the probabilities of perinatal death for each case conditional upon assignment to different care groups.

By stating the problem in this explicit form, Feldstein poses an issue of crucial importance to health and medical practice. He notes (p. 189) that

> ... the medical profession has not in general been interested in estimating the effects of alternative types of health care on the [probability distributions of] disabilities, impairments and mortality associated with different health conditions. Medical decision-makers are usually only interested in answering an ordinal question: will treatment X improve the health of this patient more than any other available treatment? The cardinal information necessary for comparing costs and benefits has not been sought because doctors have viewed their problems as unconstrained maximizations. With time it may be possible to educate medical authorities to recognize the importance of opportunity costs and therefore to obtain cardinal measures of the efficacy of alternative methods of care.

Amen!

This approach may sound cold-blooded to those brought up in the medical tradition, but it would actually result in more ethical decision making and better health care for any given level of expenditure. Feldstein shows that even with only partial data in hand one can do much better than follow the rules of thumb that have been suggested for the British system (such as hospitalization of all expectant mothers above a certain age or all those above a certain parity).

One of the book's more important conclusions (p. 259) is that

> ... removing financial barriers and incentives does not assure an optimal allocation of care to patients. In a highly decentralized system without a price mechanism, decision-makers may ignore or incorrectly assess opportunity costs. Actual allocations may therefore not be those that medical authorities would choose if fully informed.

Part Two concludes with an aggregate planning model for the health sector. The model uses nine endogenous variables and eleven predetermined ones. Seven structural equations are specified, plus two identities. The parameters of the structural equations are estimated by two-stage least squares. The regressions are run across 60 observations, the observations being essentially counties of England and Wales. The endogenous variables include the local authority health-visiting expenditure, home-nursing expenditure, and midwifery expenditure. Some of the important exogenous and predetermined variables are the ratable value of property in the local authority area, the past availability of general practitioners, and the supply of hospital beds. The work on the model must be viewed as preliminary, but it holds promise for fruitful implementation in the future.

Some Qualifications

The preceding summary does not do full justice to the ambitious scope of the work or to the ingenuity demonstrated in the use of econometric techniques. Good as it is, however, the book has some shortcomings, particularly in the first part.

1. *Absence of behavioral models.* The health service system as analyzed by Feldstein is, for the most part, a lifeless series of events and relationships. Things happen, but the people who presumably make them happen — the physicians, administrators, patients, and planners — are usually shadowy figures on the periphery rather than in the center of the action. Occasionally an observed relationship elicits an ad hoc rationalization in terms of the motivation of a decision maker, but rarely are the hypotheses empirically tested or the behavioral model made explicit. Feldstein frequently expresses the hope that better information will lead to socially more desirable decision making, as when he says (p. 4) that "a knowledge of appropriate marginal cost estimates ... may ... encourage doctors to use facilities more efficiently." Unless we know what motivates physicians, however, it is difficult to predict the effect of additional information on their decisions. Similarly, if one wishes to alter the

behavior of hospital managers, health service administrators, and the like, one needs to know much more about the incentives and constraints under which they operate.

2. *The definition and measurement of hospital output.* In this book the unit of output is a case (even when the outcome is death), and there is no discussion of the possible shortcomings of this measure or of the way the conclusions might be altered if output were defined differently. Equating output with number of cases ignores completely the bed-and-board aspects of longer stay, even if one accepts the notion that the medical portion of output is the same for each case within a speciality category regardless of the length of stay. Some investigators prefer an output measure that combines the medical portion (the treated case) with the bed-and-board portion. Alternatively, it can be argued that a case with a shorter length of stay should be treated as *more* output than one with longer stay, because it frees the patient sooner for other activities.

There is indeed an inconsistency in the treatment of output, even within the framework adopted by Feldstein. In estimating the weights for the nine specialty categories, he includes the cost of nursing and housekeeping, even through he shows that these expenditures do not contribute to medical output. Thus a case in a category with long average stay is treated as more output than a case in a short-stay category. Within specialty categories, however, longer stay is not treated as more output, even though a longer stay clearly requires more nursing services and housekeeping expenditures. To be consistent, the weights for the nine categories should have been determined only by expenditures for medical staff and drugs and dressings. There is no doubt that many of the most important findings are determined by the definition of output. If it had been defined as a patient day, for instance, many of the conclusions would be materially altered.

3. *Neglect of possible biases in results.* Feldstein shows some tendency to take the results of his statistical manipulations too seriously and to neglect possible biases due to errors of measurement and other sources. For instance, he expresses surprise at finding very little correlation ($r = .05$) between productivity (P^*) and input efficiency (I^*), inasmuch as both measures are indexes of a hospital's performance in using its budget to produce treated cases. The low correlation could be explained, however, by regression bias due to errors of measurement. Recall that $P^* = W \div \hat{W}$ and $I^* = \hat{W} \div E$. To the extent that there are errors in $\hat{W}$, the correlation between P^* and I^* is biased downward. Given the method of calculating $\hat{W}$ (regression of W on inputs, where W itself is estimated with the aid of a regression), the errors are likely to be large.

Regression bias might also help explain another result that is left hanging in midair. Feldstein finds that the negative correlation between C^* (costliness) and $P^*(r = -.84)$ is much stronger than between C^* and $I^*(r = -.42)$. The former involves correlating $E \div W$ with $W \div \hat{W}$; the latter correlates $E \div W$ with $\hat{W} \div E$. Errors in measurement of W will bias the first correlation negatively; errors in measurement of E will have the same effect on the second correlation. Because W must be estimated with the aid of average costs derived from a multiple regression, while E is observed directly, it is likely that the errors are greater in W than in E.

Another instance where some attention to possible regression bias would be desirable is in the study of marginal costs. Feldstein finds that these are much lower than average costs and concludes that hospitals should make every effort to increase their case flow rate in order to lower costs per case. If the increase in case flow is achieved by shortening the length of stay, the conclusion is probably warranted, but it is doubtful if there is any hospital administrator who doesn't already know it. To the extent that the increased case flow rate comes about as a result of an increase in the occupancy rate, the gains indicated by Feldstein's regressions are likely to be much larger than those that could be achieved on a long-term basis. Staffing ratios and other inputs are typically based on expected occupancy rates. When one runs a cross-section regression of costs on actual occupancy rates for a single year, a bias will be introduced in a negative direction to the extent that there are deviations between actual and expected occupancy rates. What happens is that in the short run the staff works a little harder or the quality of service falls off, but the hospital doesn't adjust inputs to take account of the higher occupancy rate. In the long run, hospitals tend to adjust inputs in order to maintain the same level of work load and the same quality of care.

4. *Alternative explanations of observed relationships.* The findings throughout the first part of the book are dominated by a few crucial relationships: (1) hospital size is positively correlated with length of stay; (2) length of stay is inversely correlated with productivity and positively correlated with costliness; and (3) length of stay is inversely correlated with the importance of medical staff (and drugs and dressings) relative to other inputs. Feldstein concludes, without qualification, that the longer stays in the large hospitals represent inefficiency. He does not discuss an alternative explanation, namely, that larger hospitals get more difficult cases within specialty categories. This is surely worthy of some consideration because of the finding that with regard to case mix *among* categories, larger hospitals get the costlier types of case. He also concludes that the way to increase efficiency (i.e., shorten stays) everywhere, and especially in large hospitals, is to increase the medical staff input. The process by which additional medical staff reduces stay is never explained. He may be correct in his conclusions, but he does not prove them, and the fact that the relationships appear

in many guises does not "lend support" to the results any more than the finding that A is correlated with B "supports" the finding that B is correlated with A.

Consider his production function. Output (W), measured by number of cases, is said to be a function of the number of beds (B), expenditures for medical staff (M), and other expenditures (O). But the number of cases is equal to 365 times number of beds multiplied by occupancy rate (r), all divided by average length of stay (s) : $(365Br)/s$. Thus the number of beds is on both sides of the equation, and since there is not much variation in occupancy rates, the production function essentially correlates the reciprocal of length of stay with expenditures.

An alternative or complementary interpretation of the results might run something like this: Differences in length of stay among hospitals are the result of several factors other than medical input. In other portions of the book Feldstein provides some evidence indicating what some of these factors might be: hospital size, bed supply, waiting-list pressure, social class of patients, age of patients, and regional differences in prevailing medical practice. Hospitals with short stays require about as much medical input per case as hospitals with long stays, but much less nursing service and housekeeping expenditures per case. The higher ratio of medical staff to other inputs, under this interpretation, is a *consequence* of the shorter stays, not a *cause*. In the absence of specific evidence rejecting this interpretation, Feldstein's conclusions and recommendations should be more tentatively formulated.

Indeed, given the underlying importance of length of stay in all the studies in the first part, it would have been helpful if more explicit attention had been paid to this variable. For instance, what would the elimination of all cases resulting in death in hospital do to the results? Do hospitals with high death rates have short average stays? If so, the inferences about productivity and efficiency might be very different from those actually drawn. Also, some examination of length of stay *distributions* for each hospital might have been enlightening. Do means vary primarily because of a few extreme observations or because of differences in entire distributions? It would have been interesting to know how doctors and administrators explain why their hospitals have particularly long (or short) stays. In short, Feldstein has blazed a trail for researchers in health services, but much work remains to be done.

A Valuable Tool

The book is extremely well organized, and the methods and results are presented with admirable clarity. A good index and an excellent bibliography are included, but one regrettable omission is a statistical appendix to make the calculated measures readily available to other investigators. In addition to its important substantive contributions, the book can serve as a useful supplementary textbook in applied econometrics, explaining and demonstrating the use of several important econometric techniques and discussing the bases for choosing among them. It is a book to be read and reread; economists and other health services researchers will look forward to further output from its impressive young author.

8.4

An Appreciation of Michael Grossman

I am most grateful for this opportunity to add my voice to the many that will honor Mike Grossman on the 30th anniversary of the publication of his seminal monograph, *The Demand for Health: A Theoretical and Empirical Investigation.* As one who was "present at the creation," I have special memories and feelings about Mike and his career, a few of which I would like to share with you in this brief tribute. As Paul Samuelson has written, "The immediacy of experience while it is happening — the contrast with what went before and what will happen later — is something which, if you don't have it there is no way you can get it." (Paul A. Samuelson, "Has Economic Science Improved the System?" in Winthrop Knowlton and Richard Zeckhauser (eds.), *American Society: Public and Private Responsibilities,* Ballinger Publishing Company, Cambridge, MA 1986, p. 300.)

In my judgment, Mike's success was built on two firm foundations. First, there was mentoring Mike received from Gary Becker, whose classic work on human capital and the household production function inspired not only Mike, but many other graduate students at Columbia. Second, there was the nurturing

Remarks prepared for symposium celebrating the 30th anniversary of Michael Grossman's seminal research on the demand for and production of health, 2002.

environment of the NBER, where Mike worked as a research assistant for several years. This environment encouraged and supported young scholars like Mike, Linda Edwards, Gil Ghez, Arlene Leibowitz, Bob Michael, and many others. It provided an intellectual atmosphere that fostered respect for data, attention to detail, honesty, willingness to submit work for review, and acceptance of criticism while maintaining one's own vision. At the Bureau well-trained research assistants helped prepare and scrutinize the tables. (One of them, Carol Breckner, went on from helping Mike to marrying Vernon Smith, who went on to win a Nobel Prize in economics.) Irv Forman drew the charts; Lottie Boschan and others helped with the computing. Last but certainly not least, Jacob Mincer and other senior scholars gave sound advice to and set sterling examples for aspiring young researchers like Mike.

Mike's monograph quickly made a major impression on the field of health economics and has continued to inspire streams of research ever since. The qualities of mind, character, and temperament that Mike brought to, and were enhanced by, Columbia and the Bureau have remained with him throughout his career. And what a career it has been! While continuing to publish many high quality studies, Mike has been the primary mentor to hundreds of graduate students at CUNY. No one else in the U.S. or abroad has produced as many PhD's in health economics as Mike. His intellectual children are making important contributions as researchers and teachers. Although some other universities attracted more highly qualified graduate students than did CUNY, it is doubtful whether the "value added" at the other institutions was any greater than that provided by Mike.

One aspect of Mike's research and teaching that deserves special comment is his emphasis on *health* as distinct from medical economics. No one has done more to add to our knowledge of the relation between health and cigarette smoking, drug addiction, alcohol abuse, and many other non-medical determinants of health than Mike, his students, and his colleagues.

If this were a retirement symposium I would be inclined to also praise Mike Grossman as a wonderful human being. His kindness, his generosity, and his modesty are well known to all who have had the privilege of working with him. But this is surely not a retirement symposium — Mike's productivity in research and mentoring happily continues unabated. I will, therefore, limit myself in closing to hailing Mike for his devotion to his family. He and Ilene have had a wonderful partnership; she has made many contributions to his career, and together they have raised two lovely daughters. On this splendid occasion, it is an honor to join Mike's colleagues and students in expressing appreciation, admiration, and affection for a very special person.

8.5

My Remarks When Awarding the ASHE (American Society of Health Economists) Career Award for Lifetime Contributions to the Field of Health Economics in My Name to Joseph Newhouse (2014)

It is a great privilege and high honor to present the ASHE Award for Lifetime Achievement in Health Economics to Joe Newhouse. Congratulations to Joe, and congratulations to ASHE for recognizing Professor Newhouse's extraordinary contributions to the field.

Elizabeth Barrett Browning's poetic tribute to her husband, Robert, begins "How do I love thee? Let me count the ways." Similarly, we may ask, why do we honor Joe Newhouse? Let me count the ways.

First, early in his career, Joe designed and directed the RAND Health Insurance Experiment. This was, in my judgment, the best executed of all of the country's controlled social experiments. Some 40 years after publication, the RAND results are still cited.

Second, in 1981 Joe founded the *Journal of Health Economics,* and edited it for the next 30 years. He made it the foremost journal in the field and one of the most successful specialized journals in economics.

Third, in 1988 Joe became the John D. MacArthur Professor of Health Policy and Management at Harvard where he serves on four faculties: Arts and Sciences, Medical School, School of Public Health, and the Kennedy School. Over the past quarter century, he has built an outstanding graduate program securing major grants, recruiting faculty, teaching and mentoring. He has served on 70 dissertation committees.

Fourth, Joe's career refutes the old saying, those who can, do, those who can't, teach, and those who can't teach, teach teachers to teach. He has taught with great success including many students who have gone on to their own academic careers. But he certainly can do. In our occupation, a frequent measure of doing is publication. Joe's CV lists 423 papers and other publications. That's right −423. Some are of exceptionally high quality: two won the Kenneth J. Arrow Award for the best article in health economics. Another won the first Zvi Griliches Award for the best empirical article in *Quarterly Journal of Economics.*

Finally, despite his enormous commitment to research, teaching, editing, and administration, Joe has found time for extensive public service to government and the academic community. He has helped many major organizations, including the IOM, the AAMC, the CBO, and the National Research Council. When an important issue involving health care research comes up, Joe is the first one to get called. He has been President of the Association of Health Services Research, the Foundation for Health Services Research, the International Health Economics Association, and he was the first President of ASHE.

I have focused on Joe's contributions and achievements in the belief that an award ceremony is not the time to go all sentimental. Full disclosure, however, requires me to acknowledge that Joe and I have been good friends for a long time. We first met when Joe was a graduate student. Since then, we have interacted frequently at national and international conferences and at visits to Stanford and Harvard. Our wives became good friends, and if Beverly were alive, she would be joining me in sending best wishes to Joe and Meg. Beverly was from Brooklyn which had a baseball team, the Dodgers, managed by Leo "The Lip" Durocher. Leo was a feisty, combative little guy who defended his style by saying, "nice guys always finish last." How wrong he was. Joe Newhouse has shown that sometimes nice guys finish first.

My Philosophy of Life

"Philosophy," wrote, Cavell (1979) is "the education of grownups." This paper recounts my "education" in a broad sense, including the impact of family, religion, schooling, the Army, business, and fellow economists. The reader will discern the effects of this education in my views about economics, research, teaching, and politics.

Family

Family has always been a major influence on my life. My parents, despite the problems of their marriage, gave me great love and attention. Although their families' circumstances made it impossible for either of them to finish high school, they respected learning and were pleased that both their children pursued academic careers. My brother was my closest companion in childhood and has been a loyal friend and critic since then. Our parents' strong social concerns undoubtedly played a role in our choice of fields and our approach to research: the social sciences applied to problems of social policy.

As a child, I was frequently visiting or being visited by my grandparents (immigrants from Austria and Poland), and dozens of aunts, uncles, and cousins

Originally published in *The American Economist*, 37(2): 17–24, 1993. Copyright by Omicron Delta Epsilon.

who would crowd into our apartment in the Bronx to celebrate birthdays, graduations, and holidays. At times these visits conflicted with more urgent matters such as a baseball game or a chance to meet girls, but on balance the many hours spent with different generations contributed much to my development and sense of identity.

For the past forty-five years my wife has been my dearest friend, my most enthusiastic supporter, my most valuable critic. I am constantly amazed at her ability to nurture our family and my career while pursuing her own.

Our children and their spouses have added another dimension of love and understanding and each of them has taught me a great deal. They share with me their knowledge of other fields, they sensitize me to different perspectives, and they provide windows into the next generation. Our grandchildren are a source of inspiration and I hope that they will appreciate my research on the problems of children (1992) and women's quest for economic equality (1989).

To move from the specific to the general, why is family so important? One reason is because it is our first experience with an "integrative system." This has been defined by Boulding (1968) as a system that "involves such things as status, identity, love, hate, benevolence, malevolence, legitimacy — the whole raft of social institutions which defines roles in such a way that you do things because of what you are and because of what I am." Economists in particular need to be aware that the market (exchange) and government (threat) are not the only institutions available to allocate resources and distribute income. Families, religious communities, professions, and other integrative systems are of crucial importance in some societies and can continue to serve vital functions even in our own.

Religion

Boulding believes that religion is necessary for social science and for the social scientist because it is part of the whole experience of life (Silk, 1976, p. 176). I am not sure about the "necessary," but for me it was certainly helpful. Having been born Jewish, I had an early sense of being part of a long historical process, and a feeling of kinship with some of the most extraordinary individuals the world has ever known. I also inherited an ethical code of great power and goodness and a tradition of study with the object of improving both oneself and the world. While still quite young, I was deeply impressed by the injunction "It is not incumbent on you to complete the task, but neither are you free to desist from it" (Mishna, Avot 2:21).

My early exposure to Judaism was unexceptional: a smattering of Hebrew language and an introduction to Jewish history and law; Passover seders; occasional attendance at synagogue; and Bar Mitzvah at age 13. Even this limited involvement, however, left me with an awareness of some fundamental questions about the human enterprise, questions that would not surface in my secular education until much later. For me it is the questions religion asks, more than the answers given, that make it such a valuable part of the human experience.

During adolescence and early adulthood I drifted away from formal connections with Judaism. In my mid-thirties, however, I was introduced to the ideas of Rabbi Mordecal Kaplan (1934) the founder of the Reconstructionist movement, and from then on my engagement with Judaism and my appreciation of religion grew stronger. Kaplan, a professor at the Jewish Theological Seminary, redefined Judaism as an evolving civilization in which religion plays a central but not exclusive role, and he sought to reconcile that religion with democracy and science. He developed a humanistic theology, repudiated the concept of the "chosen people," and pressed for the removal of all gender distinctions in ritual, prayer, and practice. Respect for tradition combined with rejection of dogma ("The past has a vote but not a veto") sounded right to me then and still does thirty-five years later.

Kaplan believed that the principal function of religion is to inculcate faith in the possibility of human improvement. This tempered optimism is congenial to me and much to be preferred over yearning for unrealizable utopias or wallowing in nihilistic pessimism. It does not, however, provide an adequate preparation for the tragic side of life, and in recent years I have become more sensitive to the fact that not all problems have solutions.

Schooling

Perhaps the most noteworthy aspect of my schooling is the fact that it was interrupted three times. When I was 16 I left high school for a semester in order to accompany my father on a business trip to South West Africa (now Namibia); from ages 19 to 22 I was in military service; and after World War II, I spent four years in business before beginning graduate work. In each instance I returned to school with my desire and ability to learn enhanced by the interruption. I do not recommend such breaks for everyone, but neither should they be shunned or deplored.

A favorite subject in school was history, possibly because I had a good memory and that was frequently all that was needed to do well. Also, I have always been curious about what people do and why they do it. Mathematics was another favorite subject, and I regret that I did not pursue it in greater depth. In my elementary school, classes typically consisted of about 40 students with one teacher and no aides. Most of my fellow students were Jewish, while the principal and most of the teachers were Irish. Today large classes and the absence of "role models" are blamed for poor performance, but that can only be part of the story. Our school, backed by strong support from parents, was able to start many of my classmates on paths to professional and academic careers.

In high school I was an indifferent student, perhaps because I entered at age 12 or because the school had 10,000 students (all boys), or for other reasons. I started college (New York University) without any well-defined career goal; business administration seemed moderately interesting and was the path of least resistance. Two professors of economics, Jules Backman and Paul Studenski, made a strong impression on me; indeed, Backman's influence was a major reason why I eventually chose economics as a career. He was a lively, stimulating teacher, and although we often disagreed, I was never bored.

The Army

In January 1943, shortly before my 19th birthday, I enlisted in the Army Air Corps. After a brief period of basic training I was sent to Bowdoin College for a program in pre-meteorology. This meant heavy doses of math and physics, along with excellent courses in history and literature. The humanities were probably added more for the benefit of underemployed humanities professors than for the would-be meteorologists, but these courses have served me well throughout my life. One professor in particular, the poet Robert P. T. Coffin, had a great influence through his detailed critiques of my weekly essays on literary and historical subjects. Coffin gave me confidence in my writing and inspired me to improve.

At the end of my year at Bowdoin the Air Corps announced that it had no need for additional meteorologists; my knowledge of math and physics was to be put to use in a program at Yale University that trained communications officers. At Yale we were given an interesting blend of theoretical work in electrical engineering and practical assignments such as building a radio transmitter and a receiver. These practical tasks taught me two lessons about education: 1) the right incentives can work miracles (I have always been extremely inept in the mechanical arts), and 2) the ability to pass a test is no guarantee that one has learned anything of lasting value (today I have trouble programming my VCR).

After receiving my commission, I was selected for further training in cryptographic security and then sent to the Aleutian Islands to help run an Air Corps message center. My facility with simple statistics led to a promotion and appointment as personnel officer of a communications squadron with over a thousand men located in a dozen detachments throughout Alaska and the Aleutian Islands. At the age of 21, with no previous training or experience in personnel work, I had to deal with a wide range of tasks, including classification and assignment, promotion, training, transfers, and rotation back to the mainland.

The Army experience showed me the potential benefits to young people of immersion in a structured environment and exposure to new settings and new ways of thought and action. I learned that young people are capable of assuming much more responsibility and accomplishing much more than peacetime society normally demands or allows. Given our current domestic problems, why don't we draw on the World War II experience to create new opportunities for work and training for millions of bored, frustrated, and alienated young men and women?

Business

Upon discharge from the Army in 1946 I planned to enroll at Yale as an undergraduate, but a combination of family circumstances resulted in my joining my father in the small but successful firm that he had started many years before. He was an international broker dealing with buyers and sellers of raw furs all over the world. The job required the technical ability to assess the value of fur pelts, as well as a general understanding of business and finance. International exchange rates were in a chaotic state, with blocked sterling accounts selling at great discounts that varied daily. Several business trips abroad taught me much about other cultures, and made me aware of the differences and similarities in human behavior. I also learned the value of reputation by observing how merchants in distant lands who had never met my father trusted him with large amounts of money and valuable shipments of furs.

While employed in the fur business I studied at New York University at night to earn my B.S. in business administration and then continued to take occasional graduate courses. I recall in particular the lectures of Ludwig von Mises, which reinforced my view that a centrally controlled command economy could not function effectively. Another von Mises, Richard, had even more influence on me through his book, *Positivism* [1956]. My attempts to write clearly and succinctly, and my belief that clear writing and clear thinking are closely linked, derive in large measure from that book.

Business was interesting and financially rewarding, but ultimately unsatisfying. It seemed like an exciting game, but something less than a fully adult activity. When my wife graduated from college in 1950, she went to work and I started graduate school at Columbia.

Economics

At that time, Columbia did not have a highly selective admissions policy; this was fortunate for me, given my rather unconventional education. The graduate student body was so large that there were over 100 enrolled in the basic statistics course given by Fred C. Mills. This course had limitations, unknown to me at the time, but his enthusiasm for the practical uses of statistics was stimulating. Ragnar Nurkse's lectures on international economics were notable for their clarity, but his views on exchange rate equilibrium ran counter to my experience in business. Other professors who made a lasting impression included Arthur F. Burns with his incisive critique of Keynesian theory, Karl Polanyi with a sweeping survey of general economic history, Abram Bergson who provided a solid introduction to Soviet economics, and most of all, George Stigler. His erudition, wit, and incisive approach to economic questions continued to inspire me long after my graduate training.

After two years of course work at Columbia without any particular concentration or focus, I began a dissertation on the economics of the fur industry. I was eager to apply some of my newly acquired tools and concepts in an attempt to understand the industry's intense cyclical fluctuations and the implications of its highly atomistic structure.[14] This was a poor choice of subject from the point of view of professional recognition, but I enjoyed the research and was able to complete it expeditiously while holding down a full-time position as an instructor at Columbia.

Curiosity was a key factor for me then and has been ever since. Many graduate students seem to have difficulty finding a dissertation topic because they are insufficiently curious. High intelligence and good work habits are not enough to sustain a lifetime of scholarship in the absence of curiosity.

Economic Research

As an assistant professor I worked on a variety of subjects in industrial organization, including location of industry.[13] After Columbia decided not to give me tenure, I spent two years on the staff of the Ford Foundation's program in Economic Development and Administration. This position provided an opportunity to interact with many of the finest minds in the profession; it gave me a clearer view of what was already being done in economics and a chance to think about what needed to be done.

In order to pursue my own research, I left the Foundation in 1962 to join the staff of the National Bureau of Economic Research (then exclusively in New York City). The time spent at the Bureau was like a late and extended post-doctoral experience. Many Bureau scholars helped me, but by far the greatest influence was that of Gary Becker. His seriousness of purpose, willingness to take chances, and determination to carry on in the face of skepticism provided excellent lessons for this would-be scholar.

The atmosphere at the Bureau reinforced my already revealed predilection for empirical research, but I have great respect for economists who begin their attack on a problem from the side of theory. As Goethe said, "whatever we call a 'fact' is already theory" [quoted by Richard von Mises, 1956, p. 101]. My respect for theorists diminishes, however, if they believe that the solution to real-world problems can be found purely through deduction, or if their models are neither motivated by nor motivate empirical research. For me the best answer to the choice between theory and empiricism was given by Alfred North Whitehead. When asked "Which are more important, facts or ideas?", the philosopher reflected for a while, then replied: "Ideas *about* facts" (ital. in original).[20]

My first major study at the NBER concerned production and productivity in the service industries [1968, 1969]. As a result of this work I became fascinated with the post-industrial society that was evolving in the United States and subsequently in other developed countries. The service industry project aroused my interest in health and medical care [1972, 1974a, 1986a]; this aspect of my career has recently been reviewed by Newhouse (1992). My research on issues of family [1983] and gender [1974b, 1986b] also stemmed from this source.

In 1968, after several years of full-time research, I accepted a joint appointment as Professor of Economics at the CUNY Graduate Center and Professor of Community Medicine at the newly created Mount Sinai School of Medicine. Mount Sinai's president, George James, and Hans Popper, the leading intellectual force at the school, were determined to build a new kind of medical school on three foundations instead of the traditional two of basic sciences and clinical work. The third would emphasize the health of populations and would draw on biostatistics, epidemiology, the behavioral and social sciences, and other disciplines. The effort was only partially successful. The physicians at Mount Sinai were mostly quite capable and some were outstanding. As a group, however, they suffered from a limitation found in many medical school faculties: an excessive parochialism that limited their ability to transcend their specialty in analysis of a problem. Some economists appear to suffer from the same disease.

The faculty at the CUNY Graduate Center included several distinguished scholars, but there was minimal contact across disciplines, and I found that limiting. The students were not the most highly qualified, but what they lacked in their undergraduate preparation they compensated for with hard work and enthusiasm. Many have gone on to highly productive careers as professional economists in academia, government, and business. This experience, plus the earlier one with the large class at Columbia that produced many fine scholars, has left me skeptical about highly selective admissions policies.

A fellowship (1972–73) at the Center for Advanced Study in the Behavioral Sciences at Stanford, California was significant in several respects. During that year I wrote *Who Shall Live? Health, Economics, and Social Choice,* the first of my books addressed to a general audience. Since then much of my writing has been for the general reader, or for specialized audiences (such as physicians) who are not trained in economics. I find this work challenging and rewarding; the need to write clearly and simply forces me to consider and reconsider assumptions and conclusions in economics that might otherwise be accepted too readily. Huxley (1863) once observed "Some experience with popular lecturing has convinced me that the necessity of making things plain to uninstructed people was one of the very best means of clearing up the obscure corners in one's own mind."

My year at the Center for Advanced Study in the Behavioral Sciences also led to my moving to Stanford University, where I have had stimulating colleagues and students and a marvelous opportunity to indulge my interests in multidisciplinary approaches to social problems. The presence of Kenneth Arrow provides a particular strength; his brilliance in economics is matched by the depth and range of his interests in a wide variety of subjects.

I was again a fellow at CASBS in 1978–79, and I also have benefited from two opportunities to be a scholar-in-residence at the Rockefeller Foundation Center at Bellagio, Italy. In explaining to a group from outside academia the value of multidisciplinary centers such as CASBS and the Rockefeller Bellagio center, I drew an analogy with the puzzle of the nine dots. The dots are arranged in a square, made up of three sets of three dots each. The task is to connect all the dots with a single line without retracing any line and without lifting the pencil from the paper. The puzzle can only be solved by going outside the limits of the nine dots and coming back in at an angle. For me, that is what such centers offer — an opportunity to move outside one's customary limits, whether they be the limits of one's discipline, one's environment, or one's mode of thought, and to come back in on an angle in order to solve a problem.

When people ask me what I work on and I mention subjects like health, the family, or gender, they often respond "That doesn't sound like economics." They fail to distinguish between economic *problems* and the economic *perspective*. Unemployment, productivity, and poverty are examples of economic problems. They involve what Polanyi called the "substantive" economy. Economists probably know more about economic problems than anyone else, but many other disciplines, e.g., engineering, law, and psychology, may be needed to deal effectively with them. The economic perspective, by contrast, is unique to economics. It is a way of thinking about problems that can be applied in many areas such as fertility, health, or education, as well as those problems called "economic." It is our mode of thought, not the object of that thought, that most distinguishes economists from other investigators.

In my experience in dealing with physicians, natural scientists, lawyers, and other professionals, the economic perspective provides significant insights to a wide variety of problems. Although we are criticized for our failure to make unemployment or poverty disappear, we should not underestimate the power of our analytical concepts. We can often illuminate problems and identify possible solutions in ways that elude specialists with long experience in their own field.

Critical examination of economics from the margin of the discipline need not be nihilistic or destructive. Indeed, those insights which do stand up and can be made intelligible to non-economists gain strength in the process. The economic perspective alone is rarely sufficient for good policymaking, but it is usually necessary. To neglect it, to assume that resources are unlimited or that human behavior is insensitive to changes in incentives and constraints, is often an invitation to disaster.

This matter of human behavior has been central to my thinking about our subject. For me, economics is essentially a behavioral science, and the principal purpose of our research is to throw light on certain aspects of human behavior from both positive and normative points of view. Moreover, I have never believed in defining those "certain aspects" narrowly, such as limiting them to behavior in formal markets. The behavioral approach does, however, bring to the fore some of the limitations of economists. We are, for instance, inclined to assume that individuals know what they want and that their only problem is to maximize utility through equality at the margin. In fact, one of the most difficult problems facing young (and not so young) people is to know what it is that they really want. The formation of preferences is a major human activity. A bit of folk wisdom says: 'The one thing worse than not getting what you want is getting what you want." This probably means getting what you *thought* you wanted.

Another limitation is our tendency to ignore or decry behavior that does not conform to our view of how people ought to behave. Sometimes we are too quick to assert "irrationality" or "ignorance" when the deficiency may be in our model. I call that the fallacy of misplaced ignorance. If people value symbols, or are concerned about processes as well as final states, we should try to take that into account in our analysis.

Objectivity in Research

I try to be objective in my work, but objectively speaking, complete objectivity is impossible. With respect to economic policy, values *must* enter; purely scientific descriptions of cause and effect cannot tell you whether or not a particular policy is socially desirable. Even the research that lays the basis of the cause and effect statements is not likely to be completely value free. I have some sympathy with Gunnar Myrdal's view that "Valuations are always with us. Disinterested research there has never been, and can never be. Prior to answers there must be questions. There can be no view except from a viewpoint. In the questions raised and the viewpoints chosen, valuations are implied".[18]

But this concern about values can be carried too far. For me it is a warning to be self-conscious about what I am doing and why, and an injunction to try to avoid bias. I reject the view that all research is equally subjective and value-laden, and that all research findings are simply rationalizations for pre-selected conclusions. Perfectly objective research may be impossible, but research can be *more* objective or *less,* and our goal should be to be as objective as possible. Then, when the time comes to discuss economic policy, we should be as forthright as possible about how our policy conclusions are shaped by our values as well as by our analysis.

Directing Research

From 1968 to 1978 I had administrative responsibility for a group of about two dozen NBER researchers gathered under the rubric "Center for Economic Analysis of Human Behavior and Social Institutions." It included programs in the family, income distribution, education, law, and health. With Gary Becker providing the major intellectual stimulus, and with such forceful individuals as James Heckman, Jacob Mincer, Richard Posner, and Finis Welch on the staff, I did precious little "directing." And that's probably the way things should be. Our field does not (yet?) have the deep structure that warrants a massive commitment of research effort to lines laid down by a single individual. The director's main tasks are to help find money to keep the enterprise afloat, to insure the availability of space, computers, support staff, and to create an environment that amplifies the output of the individual researchers. Cooperation is a key element in the success of a research group. If the director has resources to redistribute, he or she will have a good chance of inducing the individual researchers to maximize the output of the group.

Teaching

The longer I teach, the more challenging and complex the task appears. Most of my views are captured in a few aphorisms such as "Less is more," and "There is no teaching; only learning." Most teachers try to present too much. When organizing a course I find it useful to ask myself "What is it that I hope the students will keep from this course five or ten years from now?" I find that the same question needs to be repeated at the beginning of every lecture. Whenever possible, I prefer to combine lectures with discussion. For me, the case method of instruction[23] is particularly effective and rewarding. Student involvement is the key to student learning; the teacher's primary task is to motivate and facilitate that learning.

Education should be a moral as well as an intellectual experience. I believe that teachers should try through example, precept, or mirrors, to help students realize what is best in themselves in terms of honesty, integrity, dependability, and other dimensions of character. The libraries and the computer files are full of substantive knowledge; transmission of information is not the teacher's main job. The teacher who begins and ends each class on time is providing an extra lesson that may last a lifetime. When I teach the course required of majors that emphasizes writing about economic policy, I tell the students that good writing is partly a matter of character: be honest with your readers and respect their needs and abilities.

Politics

Politically I am a Radical Moderate, "Moderate" because I believe in the need for balance, both in the goals that we set and in the institutions that we nourish in order to pursue those goals. "Radical" because I believe that this position should be expressed as vigorously and as forcefully as extremists on the Right and Left push theirs. I value efficiency *and* justice, freedom *and* security, and the economic perspective tells me that we will often have to give up some of one goal in order to insure the partial achievement of others. Both theory and history indicate that the best way to seek multiple goals is through a balance of institutions — market, government, family, and others. Those who stridently advocate reliance only on the market or only on government capture far more attention than their theories deserve. Because moderates see some merit in the arguments presented from both extremes, the moderate position runs the risk of being perceived as weak and indecisive. It need not be that way.

Closing Notes

Nothing comes close to work and family in my priorities, but I do have a few "outside" interests. Sports have always meant a great deal to me. As a boy I played virtually all team sports, including captaining a sandlot football team. Later in life I played tennis, and then switched to racquetball, which I enjoyed the most of all. Sports have taught me the importance of preparation and focus, how to be both a leader and a follower, how to win and how to lose, and, perhaps most importantly, that "It's not over till it's over."

In recent years problems with my back have forced me to forgo all sports except swimming. For diversion, I have turned to writing poetry — an awesome challenge to blend logic and emotion. I have also written and performed stand-up comedy; as an academic and an economist I do not have to look far for material. My interest in history and in trying to write succinctly continues; eventually I hope to summarize the history of the world — past, present, and future — in one word. I am leaning toward "maybe."

References

1. Boulding, K. (1968). "Economic Libertarianism," *Beyond Economics*. University of Michigan Press: Ann Arbor, MI.
2. Cavell, S. (1979). *The Claim of Reason*. Oxford University Press: New York.
3. Fuchs, V. R. and Reklis, D. M. (1992). "America's Children: Economic Perspectives and Policy Options." *Science* **255**: 41–46.
4. Fuchs, V. R. (1989). "Women's Quest for Economic Equality." *Journal of Economic Perspectives* **3**(1): 25–41.
5. Fuchs, V. R. (1986a). *The Health Economy*. Harvard University Press: Cambridge, MA.
6. Fuchs, V. R. (1986b). "Sex Differences in Economic Wellbeing." *Science* **232**: 459–64.
7. Fuchs, V. R. (1983). *How we Live: An Economic Perspective on Americans from Birth to Death*. Harvard University Press: Cambridge, MA.

8. Fuchs, V. R. (1974a). *Who Shall Live? Health, Economics, Social Choice.* Basic Books: New York.
9. Fuchs, V. R. (1974b). "Recent Trends and Long-Run Prospects for Female Earnings." *American Economic Review Proceedings* **64**(May): 236–242.
10. Fuchs, V. R. (1972). *Essays in the Economics of Health and Medical Care.* Columbia University Press: New York, for the National Bureau of Economic Research.
11. Fuchs, V. R. (1969). *Production and Productivity in the Service Industries.* Columbia University Press: New York, for the National Bureau of Economic Research.
12. Fuchs, V. R. (1968). *The Service Economy.* Columbia University Press: New York, for the National Bureau of Economic Research.
13. Fuchs, V. R. (1962). *Changes in the Location of Manufacturing in the United States Since 1929.* Yale University Press: New Haven, CT.
14. Fuchs, V. R. (1957). *The Economics of the Fur Industry.* Columbia University Press: New York.
15. Huxley, T. H. (1863). Preface to *Evidence As to Man's Place in Nature.* Williams & Norgate: London.
16. Kaplan, M. (1934). *Judaism As a Civilization.* Macmillan: New York.
17. Mishna. Avot.
18. Myrdal, G. (1987). "Utilitarianism and Modern Economics." In *Arrow and the Foundations of the Theory of Economic Policy*, G. R. Feiwell, ed. Macmillan Press Ltd: London. (pp. 273–278).
19. Newhouse, J. P. (1992). "Distinguished Fellow: In Honor of Victor Fuchs." *Journal of Economic Perspectives* **6**(3): 179–189.
20. Price, L. (1954). *Dialogues of Alfred North Whitehead,* as recorded by Lucien Price. Little Brown: Boston.
21. Silk, L. (1976). *The Economists.* Basic Books: New York.
22. von Mises, R. (1956). *Positivism.* George Braziller, Inc.: New York.
23. Warner, A. and Fuchs, V. R. (1958). *Concepts and Cases in Economic Analysis.* Harcourt Brace: New York.

Acknowledgements

This book includes papers, articles, speeches, and op-eds written by me (sometimes with co-authors) over a period of fifty years. It also includes my newly written introductions to eight parts and two invited Forewords that were written specifically for this book. My acknowledgements are, therefore, divided into two parts.

First, I acknowledge with gratitude the individuals who made direct contributions to the present volume. Alisha Nguyen, executive editor of World Scientific, started the project by inviting me to prepare a selection of my writings on health, edited the manuscript, and saw it through to its publication. Rossannah Reeves, my assistant for many years, took major responsibility for the volume, including assembling the manuscript, reading proofs, and advising me about many issues. Joseph Newhouse prepared superb comments on drafts of the eight introductions. Sir Angus Deaton and Victor Dzau wrote graceful, thoughtful Forewords from the perspectives of an economist and a physician. Their appreciation of my efforts to bridge the fields of economics and health mean a great deal to me. I thank my co-authors and previous publishers for readily waiving any possible copyright restrictions. The cover was designed by Jimmy Low, and the index was prepared by Jim Farned.

A second set of acknowledgements goes to the individuals and institutions who helped me produce the 40 pieces reprinted in this book. It is not feasible to mention them all here, but most are acknowledged in the introductions and footnotes of the individual contributions. Private foundations have been my principal source of financial support, allowing me to hire research assistants and buy back teaching time in order to prepare articles and books for publication. Two foundations who have played particularly important roles for me are the Commonwealth Fund and the Robert Wood Johnson Foundation. In the mid-1960s, while I was a full-time researcher at the National Bureau of Economic Research, I thought I would follow my study of the service sector with a new program in health economics. The Bureau's leaders were not enthusiastic, pointing out that research in such an obscure field would not enhance my career. Fortunately, I met Quigg Newton, President of the Commonwealth Fund, at a conference and he encouraged me to write to him about my ideas for health economics. When my five page letter to Mr. Newton quickly produced a generous grant from Commonwealth, the Bureau leaders withdrew their opposition and have provided enthusiastic support ever since.

The Robert Wood Johnson Foundation supported me for many years with grants which, even when modest in amount, were particularly valuable because they provided a great deal of flexibility. Thus, I was able to take advantage of unforeseen opportunities such as adding an excellent researcher to a project or acquiring a unique set of data.

I am very grateful to two institutions that have provided me with exceptional intellectual and administrative support: the National Bureau of Economic Research and Stanford University (since 1974). My desire to work a middle ground that combined economics and health was supported by them in many ways, long before the current popularity of "inter-disciplinary research." The Bureau's emphasis on empirical research, policy relevance, and avoidance of partisan polemics provided an excellent fit with my values. I joined the research staff in 1963, served as a vice president 1968–1978, and am still proud to be a member.

Stanford's willingness to appoint me to the regular faculties in the economics department and the school of medicine (subsequently to a university chair) served my priorities exceedingly well. Although I discontinued full time teaching in 1995 at age 71, Stanford's faculty, post-doctoral programs, visitors, and students continue to provide a rich stimulating setting for me as I try to gain a better understanding of health and other social issues. The atmosphere at Stanford is exceptional. It was once described to me by a distinguished colleague who died too young to receive the Nobel Prize for his pioneering research as follows, "At many universities the administrators act as if their job is to keep you from reaching your goal. At Stanford the administrators act as if their job is to help you reach your goal." (Amen.)

List of Co-Authors

M. Kate Bundorf

Mark Cullen, M.D.

Karen N. Eggleston

Ezekiel Emanuel, M.D.

Phillip Farrell

Alan M. Garber, M.D.

James S. Hahn

Edward F. X. Hughes, M.D.

John E. Jacoby, M.D.

Eugene M. Lewit

Donald A. Redelmeier, M.D.

James F. Silverman, M.D.

List of Journals

American Economic Review

American Economist

Annals of Internal Medicine

Health Affairs

JAMA

Journal of Economic Perspectives

Journal of Health Economics

Journal of Human Resources

Journal of Law and Economics

Milbank Memorial Fund Quarterly

New England Journal of Medicine

Proceedings of the American Philosophical Society

Surgery

Author Index

Subject Index